I0138232

THE RANDALL HOUSE BIBLE COMMENTARY

THE RANDALL HOUSE BIBLE COMMENTARY

THE BOOK OF LUKE

by
Dr. Thomas Marberry

FIRST EDITION

RANDALL HOUSE
NASHVILLE, TENNESSEE 37217

RANDALL HOUSE BIBLE COMMENTARY, LUKE

RANDALL HOUSE
NASHVILLE, TN 37217
ISBN: 9780892654116

General Editor:
ROBERT E. PICIRILLI
Professor Emeritus, Welch College
Nashville, Tennessee

Dedication

Affectionately dedicated to Wilma Marberry,
my loving wife and companion in the ministry
for more than thirty-five years.

PREFACE

The Gospel of Luke is one of the treasures of the Christian faith. I consider the opportunity to write this commentary one of the greatest experiences of my ministerial career. It has been my privilege to explore the incredible richness of this book as well as the depth of scholarship, which is currently available on the Gospel of Luke.

The primary goal of this commentary is the correct exposition of the text. Luke's purpose was to present the great truths of the life and ministry of Jesus Christ for his Gentile readers in the second half of the first century. This commentary is designed to help the twenty-first century reader understand and appreciate the riches of this book.

This commentary presumes the inspiration and authority of the Word of God; Luke was written under the leadership and direction of the Holy Spirit. For that reason, it should be treated with the respect that the Bible deserves. At the same time, if the meaning is to be understood correctly, the text must be studied carefully and critically. Since Greek is the original language of Luke, the meanings of Greek words and phrases must be carefully investigated. Where Greek words and phrases can be interpreted in more than one way the reader must be made aware of the various possible interpretations and translations.

This commentary devotes some attention to the sources that lie behind the Gospel of Luke, but that is not my major focus. I am primarily concerned with the Gospel of Luke as a finished product that has influenced the course of Christian history, not the sources that lie behind it. Students of the Gospel of Luke are fortunate that the Greek text is extremely well preserved. There are, however, a few places where there is some doubt concerning the wording of the original Greek text; these have received appropriate attention in the commentary.

In recent years, there has been a great deal of scholarly interest in the Gospel of Luke, resulting in a number of outstanding commentaries and monographs. It is not the purpose of this commentary to survey all of that voluminous literature, but it does call attention to the work of leading scholars where necessary to help explain the meaning of the text. Some attention has been given to the relationship between Luke and the other synoptic gospels, but that has not received major attention. This commentary focuses on explaining the meaning of Luke's Gospel.

I would like to express my personal thanks to those who have assisted me in completing this task. First, I express my thanks to Dr. Ron Hunter and his staff at Randall House Publications for extending to me the invitation to write this commentary. The comments and suggestions of Dr. Spencer Ledbetter and the late Rev. Greg McAllister on the faculty of Randall University have been extremely helpful at every step in the writing process.

Ms. Nancy Draper, the Director of the Learning Resources Center at Randall University, has made a great contribution to this project. She has helped to obtain the many books and articles necessary to complete this commentary.

My wife, Wilma Marberry, has given much assistance. She has proofread every chapter and corrected many errors. I also want to express my thanks to Randall University and the First Free Will Baptist Church of Oklahoma City for their constant help and support.

While the help and assistance of each of these individuals and groups is much appreciated, this commentary reflects the results of my research and study of the Gospel of Luke. I alone am responsible for the conclusions that are presented.

CONTENTS

COMMENTARY ON THE BOOK OF LUKE

INTRODUCTION

The Gospel of Luke contains the longest and most complete account of the life and ministry of Jesus Christ; it is an important and influential Gospel. As Hiebert (*Introduction* 140) notes, it is the most comprehensive of the four Gospels. It includes information about the birth of Christ and the ascension that the other Gospels do not include. It also contains a large amount of material, not found in the other Gospels, between those events. Six of the twenty miracles and nineteen of the thirty-five parables found in Luke are unique to the third Gospel.

Spence (xi) argues that Luke is the most carefully composed of the four Gospels. It is designed to meet the special needs of a cultured and educated man like Theophilus. This Gospel contains the largest number of details concerning Jesus' earthly life. It also presents teachings that would be of great value to His disciples and to future generations of believers.

Author

The third Gospel, like the other Gospels, does not name its author (Plummer xi). The title "Gospel According to Luke" is first found at the end of the earliest surviving copy of the book, a papyrus codex dating from about A.D. 175-200 (Fitzmyer I:35-36). There is considerable difference of opinion concerning the age of the titles attached to Luke and the other Gospels. Fitzmyer (I:36) notes that these titles generally date from the end of the second century. Ellis (40) suggests that Luke's name might have been attached to the Gospel from the very beginning. Although we cannot be certain the name "Luke" was attached to this Gospel from the very beginning, there is no doubt his name was attached to it very early in its history.

The N. T. documents contain only a few references to Luke, and they are found in the writings of Paul. Morgan (9) gives a useful summary of them. Luke is mentioned in Colossians 4:14, "Luke, the beloved physician, and Demas, greet you." His name is also found in Philemon 1:24, "Marcus, Aristarchus, Demas, Lucas, my fellowlabourers." The final reference is found in 2 Timothy 4:11, "Only Luke is with me. . . ." 2 Corinthians 8:18 contains the phrase, "the brother, whose praise *is* in the gospel throughout all the churches" which, since the time of Chrysostom, has been widely accepted as a reference to Luke (Fitzmyer I:36).

Plummer (xviii) suggests that the name *Lucas* is probably a shortened form of the name *Lucanus*, but it is possible that it comes from *Lucilius*, *Lucius*, or *Lucianus*. See also the discussion of Fitzmyer (I:42-43). Plummer also notes that names ending in *as* were often given to slaves; and slaves often worked as physicians, so it is possible that Luke was a freedman. In Colossians 4:11, Luke is separated from "Jesus, which is called Justus" and others who are "of the circumcision." This has led many scholars (but not all) to conclude that Luke was a Gentile and not a convert from Judaism (Plummer xviii-xix).

There is an ancient prologue to the Gospel, generally dated from the end of the second century, which contains the following description of Luke,

Luke was a Syrian of Antioch, by profession a physician, the disciple of the apostles, and later a follower of Paul until his martyrdom. He served the Lord without distraction, without a wife, and without children. He died at the age of eighty-four in Boeotia, full of the Holy Spirit (Fitzmyer I:38).

This ancient prologue also states that Luke wrote the Gospel in the Roman province of Achaia for Gentile converts.

Early Christian writers unanimously attribute the third Gospel to Luke, the companion of Paul. Several scholars provide summaries of the views presented by the early Christian writers. Fitzmyer (I:39-41) explains that Irenaeus was a second-century writer who specifically attributed the Gospel to Luke, the companion of Paul. The Muratorian Canon, generally dated A.D. 170-180, considered Luke to be the author. Tertullian, writing about A.D. 207-208, also recognized the Lucan authorship. In later centuries, other writers such as Origen, Eusebius, and Jerome continued the tradition. Cadbury ("Tradition") gives a summary of how the earliest Christian writers presented the tradition that Luke was the author of both the Gospel and the Book of Acts. He includes extensive quotations from the early church fathers. Ellis (37-42) also provides a useful summary of how the early church viewed this Gospel.

The writings of Luke came to be considered part of the canon of Scripture at an early date. The writings of early Christian fathers contain many quotations from and allusions to the writings of Luke. Ellis (37-42) cites specifically the statements of Tertullian, the anti-Marcionite prologue to Luke, Irenaeus, and others. After examining the evidence, he concludes that the Lucan authorship of the third Gospel was well accepted by the beginning of the third century, and was not seriously questioned for many centuries.

The question of the authorship of Luke was reopened in the nineteenth and twentieth centuries as several scholars began to challenge the traditional view. Kümmel (*Introduction* 147), for example, argues that we simply do not know who wrote the third Gospel. He concludes that the only thing we can know for sure is that he was a Gentile Christian. One traditional argument for Lucan authorship is the use of certain medical terms. According to Kümmel, the use of these terms does not indicate that the author was a medical doctor; the medical terms used are also found in the writings of other Hellenistic authors who have no medical connection. They are the kinds of terms that any literate person would have known. Kümmel (*Introduction* 149) also argues that the third Gospel presents certain theological concepts that differ from those found in the writings of Paul. In his view, this challenges the traditional view that the author was a companion of Paul. Kümmel offers no other possibilities. D. Guthrie (*Introduction* 98-109) summarizes the arguments for and against the Lucan authorship of this Gospel.

The scholars of the Tübingen School challenged many traditional viewpoints concerning the authorship of Luke, Acts, and other books. F. C. Baur and E. Zeller were two of the early defenders of this school; they taught that Luke and Acts were not written until late in the first century or early in the second century. They also challenged the tradition of Lucan authorship of both the Gospel and Acts. Windisch (298-348) provides a useful summary of the arguments presented by those who deny Lucan authorship.

Maddox (6-7) offers another theory that has enjoyed some popularity in recent years. He suggests that the third Gospel was written by a man named Luke, but that he was not necessarily the companion of Paul. Maddox explains that the name was fairly common in the first century, and the author could have been another believer named Luke.

Today there are some scholars who deny that Luke wrote the Gospel; there are also many who defend the traditional view of Lucan authorship. Streeter (218-219, 560-562), for example, suggests that the book was written by Luke the companion of Paul. He also suggests that Luke was with Paul during his two-year imprisonment in Caesarea and he took advantage of that time to collect the information about Christ, which would later be included in his Gospel.

Ellis (40-41) notes that the original text of the third Gospel mentions no author, but he thinks Luke's name may have been attached to the book from the very beginning. It was certainly attached at a very early date. He points out that the tradition of Lucan authorship can be traced as early as the beginning of the third century; there are no competing theories.

Nolland (I:xxxvi-xxxvii) also accepts the tradition of Lucan authorship. He notes that Luke was a colleague of Paul and not his disciple. It is to be expected that there will be some differences between Paul's presentation of the gospel and Luke's, but they are differences in emphasis not differences in substance. Nolland suggests there is not sufficient evidence to reject the longstanding tradition of Lucan authorship.

Caird (15-17) suggests that the evidence presented in the Gospel and in Acts presents a somewhat detailed portrait of its author. He was obviously a well-educated man with a good understanding both of classical Greek and of the style of Greek found in the Septuagint. He reflects a concern for Gentiles and is, likely, a Gentile.

Caird also notes that all of the early church fathers attribute this Gospel to Luke, the companion of Paul. He then gives a list of the most important of these early testimonies. He also explains that in the first century a book intended for publication would likely carry the author's name from the beginning. He argues that Luke was not a prominent person in the early church, and there is no reason his name should have been attached to the Gospel unless he was its author. Caird regards Luke as the author of the third Gospel.

The unanimity of the early church tradition and the absence of any viable alternative theories strongly suggest that

Luke, the companion of Paul, is the author of the book. That is the position taken in this commentary.

Date

Of the four canonical Gospels, Luke is the most difficult to date, and commentators have suggested several possibilities. Scroggie (339) notes that suggested dates for the writing of Luke range from A.D. 58 to 135. The three most widely held dates are A.D. 100, 80, or 60.

According to Liefeld (807-808) there are four factors that must be considered in determining when this Gospel was written. First is the date of the writing of Mark and the relationship between Mark and Luke. Second is the date of Acts and the relationship between Luke and Acts. Third is the relationship between the destruction of Jerusalem, described in chapter 21, and the writing of the Gospel. Fourth is the "theological and ecclesiastical tone of Luke-Acts." In other words, the interpreter must determine the extent to which the style, message, and presentation of Luke help to determine when it was written.

Liefeld (807-809) examines each of these important issues. He concludes that Luke depended on Mark and that Mark could have been written around A.D. 60. The date of Acts is difficult to determine, but it likely was written around A.D. 63 or 64. He concludes that chapter 21 of Luke could have been written either before or after the destruction of Jerusalem in A.D. 70. If his reconstruction is correct, chapter 21 is of little help in determining the date of the Gospel.

The precise theological and ecclesiastical climate in which Luke was written is difficult to determine, and our knowledge of the events of the first century is limited. After considering the available evidence, Liefeld opines that both Luke and Acts were most likely written sometime between A.D. 60 and 70.

Ellis (55-56) presents a somewhat similar approach. He notes that the majority of scholars today date the Gospel between A.D. 60 and 65 or between A.D. 70 and 90. Advocates of the earlier date connect the date of Luke with that of Acts. They point out that Acts mentions no events after A.D. 63. The picture of the Roman state painted by Acts is quite favorable, and it is difficult to imagine such favorable treatment if the book was written after the persecution of Christians by Nero, which began about A.D. 64.

Robertson (*Historian* 37-39) examines the evidence concerning the dating of Luke; he notes that it depends to a considerable extent on the date assigned to Acts. Since he accepts an early date for Acts, Robertson also accepts an early date for Luke. He suggests it was written before the fall of Jerusalem in A.D. 70.

According to Ellis (56), the arguments for an early date are "plausible" but not "compelling." They are arguments from silence, and arguments from silence are inherently weak. Ellis notes that Luke's choice of material was largely governed by his theme and purpose and Acts is not a complete history of everything that transpired. He does view the lack of reference to the destruction of Jerusalem as an important factor that should be considered in dating the book.

Those who defend a date between A.D. 70 and 90 generally present two arguments (Ellis 56): first, that Luke 21:20-24 reflects a knowledge of the destruction of Jerusalem, which could only have been written after the event; second, that both Luke and Acts reflect a "late" theological climate that can be more easily explained after A.D. 70. Ellis analyzes the strengths and weaknesses of each of these two positions and comes to the conclusion that the early date has more in its favor than the later date. His final conclusion is that the book was published during or shortly after the Jewish war for independence, or around A.D. 70 (Ellis 60).

Stein (*Luke* 24-26) examines much of the same evidence and comes to a different conclusion. The earliest possible date for the writing of Luke is the early 60s, shortly after the events described in Acts 28. The latest possible date is around A.D. 170, when early Christian writers began to make use of quotations from Luke in their writings. According to Stein, there are several important pieces of evidence that help the modern reader determine when the Gospel was written. The first is the fact that nowhere does Luke give information about what happened to Paul. The second decisive factor is Luke's use of Mark as a source. Early church tradition closely connected Mark's Gospel with the witness of Peter, and Peter was probably martyred in Rome under Nero about A.D. 65-67. Mark would have written his Gospel after the death of Peter. If Luke used Mark as a source, it is likely that Luke was written after A.D. 70.

Stein (*Luke* 25) notes there are passages in Luke (13:35a, 19:43-44, 21:20, and 23:28-31), which do not demand a date after A.D. 70, but are more easily understood if they were written after the destruction of Jerusalem. He notes that Acts presents a rather favorable view of the Roman government. This suggests the Gospel was written between the persecution by Nero (in the mid-sixties) and the persecution of Domitian (A.D. 95-96). Stein (*Luke* 25-26) argues that Luke omitted information about Paul's trial and execution from the narrative in Acts because they did not fit within his purpose. Luke's purpose was not to write biographies of Peter or Paul, but to show the spread of the gospel among Gentile peoples.

Kümmel (*Introduction* 150-151) suggests a date between 70 and 90 based on two lines of evidence: first, that the "many" writings mentioned in the prologue to the Gospel could not have existed in the decade of the sixties; second, that certain passages such as 19:43+, 21:20, and 21:24 reflect the same understanding of the siege and fall of the city as are found in contemporary descriptions. For him, these factors presume a date after the fall of Jerusalem.

Cullmann (43) takes a similar approach, dating the Gospel about A.D. 80. Barrett (*Luke* 62) suggests that both Luke and John were written in the closing decades of the first century. Maddox (7-8) explains that most scholars today date Luke-Acts in the 80s or 90s. Summers (*Luke* 10) points out that only two dates are seriously considered in modern N. T. scholarship, the early sixties (A.D. 61-63) and after the fall of Jerusalem (about A.D.80). Summers notes that the latter date is preferred by the majority of scholars today, and is the date he defends.

The variety of views presented by scholars testifies to the difficulty in dating Luke. There are no historical references in the book that enable the interpreter to determine with absolute certainty when it was written, but it is clearly a first-century document.

The main point of contention in current scholarship is whether the book was written before or after A.D. 70, and good arguments can be made on both sides. Summers has noted, correctly, that Luke reflects a relatively advanced state of thought. We cannot, however, determine just how early the ideas stressed in Luke actually developed; they might have begun to develop as early as the sixties. All that can be said with certainty is Luke was written shortly before or shortly after the fall of Jerusalem. It is interesting to note that Luke 21:20 includes the phrase "when ye shall see Jerusalem compassed with armies," where Mark has "when you see the abomination of desolation." This change in wording alone is not sufficient evidence by which to determine the date of Luke; the decision must be made based on all the available evidence.

Although dogmatism should be avoided in dating this Gospel, a date in the 60s seems slightly better than a date in the 70s or 80s. The suggestion of Ellis that the book was written shortly before or during the Jewish War of A.D. 66-70 and published shortly thereafter has much to commend it. Marshall (*Gospel* 35) suggests a date around A.D. 70. With the evidence currently available, it is difficult to be more precise than that.

Location

It is virtually impossible to determine where Luke was written. The Gospel itself gives no indication, and there is no wide-spread ancient tradition (Kümmel, *Introduction* 151). The anti-Marcionite Prologue states that Luke was from Antioch and wrote his Gospel in the regions of Achaia (Carson, Moo, and Morris 115). Some late manuscripts mention Rome as the place of composition, but they provide no evidence to support this theory. Scholars have suggested various possible locations, including Caesarea, Achaia, the Decapolis, Asia Minor, and Rome (Kümmel, *Introduction* 151), but none of them have produced a consensus in N. T. scholarship (E. Harrison 202-203). According to Cullmann (43), the text of the book indicates only that it originated in a Christian community that had come out of paganism rather than out of Judaism. The most that can be said with certainty is the Gospel was written outside the land of Palestine.

Sources

In the preface to this Gospel, Luke points out that he was not an eyewitness to any of the events of the life of Christ. His account is based on the information the "eyewitnesses and ministers of the word" have delivered to him and to others of his generation. (See the discussion of Luke 1:1-4 for a more detailed analysis of this important passage.) It is now generally agreed among scholars that Luke is a careful historian who makes good use of the information available to him.

Although there is no doubt Luke uses sources, it is difficult to determine what those sources were and whether they were written or oral. Luke does not specifically identify any source; scholars must depend on a careful analysis of the text of the Gospel and the information that is available concerning the church in the first century. Plummer (xxiii-xxix) offers a good summary of the available evidence. He begins by noting that, according to the traditional interpretation, Luke was a companion of the Apostle Paul and it is highly probable he received information from Paul and those around him. It is also likely that through his work with the Apostle Paul, he came into contact with other apostles and with Mary, the mother of Jesus. It is possible that Luke was with Paul during his imprisonment in Caesarea, and this would have given him the opportunity to gather first-hand information from Mary and others. Plummer posits that some information (such as the genealogy of Jesus) may have already been reduced to writing before Luke began his Gospel.

Scroggie (341-344) provides a useful summary of what the internal evidence reveals concerning Luke's sources. He suggests that Luke made use of six or seven sources. Mark was one of the most important of these; another was the collection of the sayings of Jesus that Matthew and Luke share (commonly called Q). He also suggests that information was provided by Mary, the mother of Jesus, and those around her; and some information might have come from the court of King Herod. Finally, he argues that Luke obtained information about Jesus through his long association with the Apostle Paul. It is impossible to determine which of these sources were written and which were oral; the only one that survives today is Mark.

It is likely that Luke used different sources as he was writing different parts of his Gospel. R. Brown (*Birth* 244-247) outlines several possible sources that might have contributed to chapters one and two of Luke. It is important to note that such reconstructions always involve a considerable amount of conjecture. It is impossible to be dogmatic concerning the number of sources that Luke had access to or how he used them.

Mark is regarded by most scholars as one of the primary sources behind Luke's Gospel (Burkitt 106). Mark and Luke have much material in common; it is likely Mark was written first and Luke had access either to the final version of Mark or to an earlier draft of the Gospel. At times, Luke departs from the order of events given in Mark (such as the whole of Mk. 6:45—8:9, which is absent from Luke), but he later returns to Mark's outline. Stein (*Synoptic Problem* 45-88) presents a useful analysis of the priority of Mark and of Luke's use of Mark. Lenski (16) posits that Mark and Luke had extensive contact with one another, beginning in the forties of the first century; both were close associates of Paul. Mark's Gospel would have come very quickly into Luke's hand, and it is likely that he would have used it as a source. Ramsay (*Physician* 73) also agrees that Luke depended on Mark. For a comprehensive analysis of the relationship between Mark and Luke see Cadbury (*Luke-Acts* 76-97).

It is clear, however, that a considerable amount of Luke's content did not come from Mark. There are approximately 235 verses of material (consisting primarily of the teachings of Jesus), which are common to Matthew and Luke but are absent from Mark. The source or sources behind this material has provoked considerable discussion. There are several possibilities. Luke may have depended on Matthew or Matthew may have made use of Luke. It is possible they both made use of the same oral or written sources.

The letter Q (the first letter of the German word *quelle*, which means "source" or "spring") is often used as an abbreviation for the material in these 235 verses. Some scholars understand Q to be a written source, others an oral source or collection of oral sources. Some use this letter simply as a convenient symbol for this material without affirming that it served as a source for Luke's Gospel.

Many in the early church taught that Matthew was the earliest Gospel and Luke depended on Matthew. Augustine posited that Matthew was written first, then Mark, then Luke, and finally John (Schaff 78). Matthew and John were apostles of the Lord; Mark and Luke were not. Mark and Luke were supported by the other two and became as "sons who were to be embraced, and who in this way were set in the midst between these twain" (Augustine 78). Augustine affirmed that Matthew and Luke have much in common. The obvious implication is that Augustine viewed Matthew as the source of the material these two Gospels have in common.

The view that Matthew was the earliest Gospel—"the priority of Matthew"—was out of favor for many years. By the early twentieth century, the view that Mark was written first came to dominate N. T. scholarship (France 28). Today the priority of Matthew is experiencing something of a revival. France (24-41) provides a useful summary of the current status of that debate.

Most scholars who adhere to the priority of Matthew suggests Mark was written second, and Luke made use of both of them. Farmer (200) provides a slightly different perspective. In his view, Matthew was written first and then Luke. Mark was third, and the material common to Matthew and Luke came from Matthew rather than from Q.

D. Guthrie (*Introduction* 220-236) develops a somewhat different theory concerning the relationship between the Synoptic Gospels. He gives greater weight to the statements of the early Christian writers than do most contemporary scholars; he also finds the Q hypothesis unnecessary.

According to Guthrie, Mark is the earliest Gospel, and it is based largely on the preaching of Peter. Matthew is the second Gospel. The apostle Matthew came into contact with a copy of Mark's Gospel, added information to it, and wrote his Gospel. Luke is the third Gospel. The author was personally acquainted with Mark whose Gospel provides the organizational framework for Luke's Gospel. Luke also did a considerable amount of original research into the information currently available concerning the life and ministry of Christ. Guthrie suggests Luke might have had access to Matthew's Gospel, but he is not certain that he did.

One common theory today is that the material found in both Matthew and Luke, but absent from Mark, comes from the Q source. As noted previously, Q may be a single source or a combination of different sources; it might have been written or oral. For good discussions of the contents of Q see D. Guthrie (*Introduction* 146-150); Hunter (*Work and Words* 131-146), and Stein (*Synoptic Problem* 96-101, 103-108). Hunter (*Work and Words* 131) posits that Q was compiled about A.D. 50, possibly by Matthew, in Aramaic. According to these scholars, it is likely that Q formed a second major source for Luke. Stein (*Synoptic Problem* 109-112) analyzes carefully the strengths and weaknesses of the Q hypothesis. He concludes that this theory has its problems but is still the best explanation for the material common to Matthew and Luke but absent from Mark. Stein recognizes that Q is a hypothetical source, and it is impossible to precisely define its contents. It might have been one source or a combination of sources, some written and some oral. Some form of the Q hypothesis is also accepted by scholars such as Ramsay (*Physician* 73-98) and Creed (lvi-lxx). Creed (lvi) suggests that Luke and Matthew were written about the same time, but that each was written independently. He explains the commonality between these two Gospels by saying that both depended on Mark and Q.

The third Gospel also includes a considerable amount of material found in no other Gospel (such as Luke's account of Jesus' birth). In scholarly circles, this material is commonly abbreviated by the letter "L." It is impossible to determine whether this information comes from a single source or from a combination of sources, written or oral. Plummer (xxvi) notes the Gospel contains a number of Hebraisms, words or expressions borrowed from the Hebrew language. This indicates that some of Luke's sources were likely available to him in Aramaic. Hunter (*Work and Words* 17) suggests this information is largely the result of "Luke's personal enquiry in Palestine round about A.D. 57-59." Creed (lxvi-lxvii) and D. Guthrie (*Introduction* 167-175) provide comprehensive discussions of the material peculiar to Luke.

Cadbury (*Luke-Acts* 110) notes a most interesting fact. He points out that Mark and Q together account for only about one-half of the content of the Gospel. The rest came from other sources. Luke took this large amount of material that he found in different sources, analyzed it, evaluated it, edited it, and adapted it to accomplish his purposes and objectives.

In conclusion, there is no reason to doubt that Luke used a variety of different sources, but it is impossible today to identify these sources with certainty. It is likely some were written and some were oral. Luke carefully investigated the information available to him. He carefully analyzed and organized this information to produce, under the leadership of the Holy Spirit, a reliable account designed specifically to meet the needs of his Gentile readers.

The most common reconstruction found among evangelical scholars today is that Luke used Mark as the basic framework for organizing his Gospel, but he did not always follow Mark's outline. Luke incorporated into Mark's outline material drawn from Q and L in order to produce the Gospel of Luke as it is known today.

The Proto-Lucan Hypothesis

One theory that has gained some popularity in academic circles in recent years is known as the Proto-Lucan Hypothesis. In simple terms, this theory maintains that material drawn from Q (the teachings of Jesus) and L (the material peculiar to Luke) were combined to form the first draft of Luke. At some later time, Mark became available, and Luke incorporated information from Mark into his previously-existing draft. This ultimately resulted in the Gospel of Luke as it exists today. For summaries of this theory see Taylor (23-27) and Streeter (201-222). This fully-developed hypothesis was first presented by Streeter in an article published in the *Hibbert Journal* in October 1921 (volume XX, 103-112); it was later revised and expanded in his book *The Four Gospels*. The most complete presentation of this theory was given by Vincent Taylor in his book *Behind the Third Gospel*, published in 1926.

Streeter and Taylor present several arguments in favor of this theory. One of the strongest is that Luke regularly alternates material drawn from Mark with material drawn from Proto-Luke. For a positive review and analysis of the Proto-Lucan hypothesis see Scott.

One scholar who strongly defends the Proto-Lucan Hypothesis is Caird (23-27). He argues that Luke followed one of two methods of organizing his Gospel; these are the Marcan Hypothesis and the Proto-Lucan Hypothesis. The Marcan Hypothesis holds that the Gospel of Mark forms the basic outline of Luke and the author added other materials to it. The Proto-Lucan Hypothesis is the other possibility. After examining the evidence, Caird (26) concludes that Proto-Luke provides the basic organizational framework for the modern Gospel.

The Proto-Lucan Hypothesis has not been without its critics. Stonehouse, for example, finds it unnecessary. He argues (22) that the Proto-Lucan Hypothesis simply multiplies the number of hypothetical sources behind the Gospel, and he sees that multiplication as a point of weakness.

One of the most strident critics of the Proto-Lucan Hypothesis is Gilmour ("Proto-Luke" 143-152), who disputed two of its basic assumptions. First, he challenged the assumption that the combination of Q and L formed a complete Gospel into which Luke could insert the material from Mark. Second, he questioned the assumption that this combination served as the framework for the final version of Luke's Gospel. After a careful examination of the evidence, Gilmour concluded that Mark, not Proto-Luke, formed the organizational framework into which Luke inserted material coming from several different sources.

Creed is another critic of the hypothesis. He suggests (lviii) that if the Marcan material is removed from Luke, the remainder is not a Gospel at all. It is simply a random collection of discourse and narrative material. For this reason, Creed agrees with other scholars that Mark serves as the basic source behind Luke.

In conclusion, it should be noted that the arguments for and against the Proto-Lukan Hypothesis are technical and beyond the scope of this commentary. The majority of N. T. scholars today do not find the evidence supporting this theory to be convincing. Most regard it simply as an interesting possibility.

Purpose and Readers

It is clear that Luke wrote this Gospel with specific purposes in mind. The difficulty is to determine precisely what those were. Another difficulty is that many scholars consider Luke and Acts to be closely related to each other; some consider them to be two volumes of one book (D. Guthrie, *Introduction* 95). If that is the case, then the purposes of Luke and Acts should be considered together.

In recent years, considerable attention has been paid to the question of Luke's purpose; Maddox (19-23) gives a brief summary of some of the major theories that have been advanced. He also outlines some of the difficulties that students face in trying to determine Luke's purpose or purposes.

Maddox (19) notes that scholars have suggested a variety of possible purposes. Some have suggested an evangelistic purpose, but that is more evident in Acts than in the Gospel. Hendriksen (*Luke* 16) suggests that Luke's immediate purpose was to enlighten those who wanted more information about Christianity and to strengthen the faith of new converts. Another possible purpose is that the Gospel was written to serve as a defense at Paul's trial. This theory is attractive, but it faces two serious problems. The first concerns the issue of dating. Paul was probably executed in the early to mid-sixties during the reign of Emperor Nero. Many scholars believe the book was written too late to serve as a defense brief. Hendriksen (*Luke* 15-16) points out that much of the information in Luke would not have been useful as a trial brief.

A third possibility mentioned by Maddox is that the Gospel was written to defend the Christians before the Roman government. F. Bruce (*Acts* 17-24) develops this concept. According to this view, one of Luke's purposes, both in the Gospel and in Acts, was to show that Christianity was not subversive. It was not a threat to the Roman Empire.

The fourth possibility is that Luke wrote to defend the memory of the Apostle Paul against the attacks of Jewish believers. The fifth possibility listed by Maddox has received considerable attention in recent years: namely, that Luke wrote for primarily theological reasons. The fact that the Second Coming of Christ had not occurred as soon as many expected it caused serious problems within the church. Luke wrote in order to confront this problem of the delayed Parousia. This view has been developed best by Hans Conzelmann.

The sixth possible purpose, as outlined by Maddox (21-22), is that Luke wrote in order to combat the heresy of Gnosticism. The fact that Luke devotes considerable attention to the human birth and the physical life of Jesus may be seen as an argument against Docetism, which was one of the heresies taught by the Gnostics.

The final suggested purpose Maddox (22) discusses is that Luke wrote in order to confirm the gospel that had been preached and taught. His Gospel was designed to encourage Christians whose faith was wavering because of the trials they were suffering.

It is generally accepted by students of Luke's Gospel that it was written for Gentiles. As Nolland (I:xxxii) explains, many students of Luke have long assumed he was a Gentile Christian who wrote this Gospel primarily for the benefit of Gentile believers. It confronts the kinds of issues Gentile churches would have confronted in the second half of the first century. Bock (I:15) suggests that Luke was written to Gentile believers who felt out of place in what had originally been a Jewish movement. Luke writes to these Gentile believers in order to reassure them that the Jewish rejection and God's turning to the Gentiles had been parts of His plan from the beginning.

Nolland (I:xxxii) agrees that Luke was written to and for Gentile Christians, but he suggests the Gospel was written especially for God-fearers. God-fearers were Gentiles who were attracted to Judaism and generally supported the synagogue but who had not become Jewish proselytes. During his missionary journeys, the Apostle Paul often ministered to these God-fearers, and the first Christian converts often came from these groups. Nolland suggests this Gospel was written specifically for this group that was standing at the crossroads between Christianity and Judaism.

There is some truth in Nolland's contention. In the Gospel and Acts, Luke is concerned to explain how the transition from Judaism to Christianity came about and why it was necessary. It is doubtful, however, that a Gospel of this size and magnitude was written only for this group.

Some have argued that the book was written as an apology to Roman officials in order to seek greater toleration from them (Cadbury, *Luke-Acts* 308). This theory is not popular today. Maddox (96-97) argues persuasively that the Gospel was written not to Roman officials, but to Christian believers. He suggests (96) that one purpose Luke had was to remind believers they were not responsible for the execution of Jesus. The blame for this tragic event must be placed on the shoulders of the Jewish and Roman leaders.

Although many accusations had been made against them, both by Jews and by the Roman state, the Christians had always conducted themselves honorably. Luke writes this Gospel to Christians to remind them they have always been subject to unfair accusations. They should willingly accept these false accusations and the persecution that resulted from them. They should seek to be peaceful and good citizens of the empire.

The most widely held view among evangelical scholars is that Luke was written to Gentile Christians who were facing the many trials and difficulties Christians of the first century encountered every day. It is possible the book was written to strengthen Gentile believers in times of persecution, but the Gospel gives no information, which indicates it was written during a specific period of persecution.

The prologue to the Gospel makes a significant contribution to understanding Luke's purpose. It is likely the book was written to Gentile believers of the second and third generations in the Roman Empire in order to strengthen their faith and give them a better understanding of the life and ministry of Jesus.

Major Themes in Luke

The available evidence indicates that Luke was written to Gentile believers living outside the land of Palestine. These were probably believers of the second or third generation. It is likely that Luke intended his Gospel to be read and used in winning Gentiles to Christ and in helping them to grow and mature in their faith. There are certain important themes that Luke develops for the benefit of his Gentile readers.

Virgin Birth. The first of these important themes is the Virgin Birth of Jesus. Both Matthew and Luke emphasize that Jesus was not conceived in the normal manner through human intercourse (Witherington, DJG 70-71). Witherington correctly notes that this event should properly be described as a virginal conception rather than as a virgin birth. As he explains (71), there is nothing in Luke's account which indicates that Mary's pregnancy and delivery were in any way different from what normally occurs when a child is born. The fact that she must later go through the purification ceremony in the Temple also contributes to the conclusion that Mary experienced a normal pregnancy and delivery.

There is one interesting fact that has puzzled interpreters since the earliest days of the church. It is the fact that the N. T. writers make so little use of the virginal conception. They never explain why it was necessary or how it contributes to the Christian faith (Witherington, DJG 72). Once they have concluded their discussions of the birth and infancy of Jesus, neither Matthew nor Luke make further references to it. There are a few passages in the Pauline letters that may indicate Paul was aware of it, but it makes no major contribution to his thought (Witherington, DJG 70). For a worthwhile discussion of how the other N. T. writers make use of the doctrine of the virgin birth see Machen (244-268).

Witherington (DJG 72) presents two important contributions that this doctrine makes to the thought of the N. T. First, it contributes to the humanity of Christ. The virginal conception points out that Jesus is fully human in the sense that He participates in all human activities beginning with His birth and ending with His death. Second, this teaching emphasizes that Jesus is a divine gift sent by God for the salvation of human beings. His birth is not the result of normal human activity; it is a gift that comes from God, through Mary, to a lost world.

Warfield (166) argues that the virgin birth makes an important contribution to the doctrine of redemption. He notes that every member of the human race lives under the curse of Adam's sin. In order for Jesus to be able to serve as man's redeemer, He needed to be outside that circle of condemnation.

From its earliest days, the Christian church has included the doctrine of the virgin birth as an important part of its preaching and teaching. For a useful discussion of the virgin birth in the second century see Machen (2-43).

The doctrine of the virgin birth has not been without its critics. Emil Brunner (*Mediator* 322-327), for example, argues the virgin birth is a theory that obscures the meaning of the incarnation. He asserts that the true humanity of Jesus demands He have a real father. He also suggests that the texts in Matthew and Luke, which affirm the virgin birth, have been altered and do not reflect the original readings.

Karl Barth (172-202) defends the virgin birth and refutes the arguments of Brunner. Barth (184) even makes this surprising statement, "Brunner's denial of the Virgin birth is bad business." Near the end of his discussion, Barth (202) describes the importance of the virgin birth in these words,

The man Jesus of Nazareth is not the true Son of God because He was conceived by the Holy Spirit and born of the Virgin Mary. On the contrary, because He is the true Son of God and because this is an inconceivable mystery intended to be acknowledged as such, therefore He is conceived by the Holy Spirit and born of the Virgin Mary.

For a good summary of the debate concerning the virgin birth see Beckwith (201-214).

People. Throughout this Gospel, Luke manifests a great interest in people. He focuses his attention on individuals and how he can impact their lives (Hiebert, *Introduction* 143). The three famous parables found in chapter fifteen all relate to individuals. They stress how there is rejoicing in Heaven when even one sinner repents. Luke manifests particular interest in individuals who are outcasts. He has time for a man who is demon-possessed and for a rich tax-collector like Zacchaeus. He notices the poor woman who casts her two mites into the temple treasury.

In Luke's account, Jesus manifests a great deal of interest in women and children. Since women and children were often overlooked in the ancient world, this level of interest is significant. Luke's Gospel relates the important contributions of women such as Mary, Elizabeth, the prophetess Anna, and the widow at Nain. Luke notes the important contributions of Mary and Martha of Bethany and the generosity of the women who contribute to the expense of Jesus' ministry.

It is clear that Luke wished to emphasize Jesus' care and concern for people at all levels of society.

Prayer. Hiebert (*Introduction* 145) writes, "The third gospel is the gospel of prayer." While all of the Gospels recognize the importance of prayer, Luke is the Gospel that devotes the most attention to it. D. Guthrie (*Introduction* 92) notes that Luke includes nine prayers of Jesus, and seven of them are not found elsewhere. Jesus prays at major turning points in His ministry, including His baptism, the calling of the twelve, the transfiguration, in Gethsemane, and on the cross. Two of Jesus' parables, the parable of the Importunate Widow and the parable of the Pharisee and the Publican focus specifically on prayer. Jesus emphasized the importance of consistent prayer in His training of His disciples. Luke's Gospel makes a significant contribution to the N. T. teaching on the subject of prayer. The lessons taught in this Gospel are important to Christians of every generation.

Kingdom of God. The Kingdom of God is one of Luke's most important themes. In Luke, Jesus never presents a comprehensive definition of the kingdom. Rather, He allows His teachings and His actions to develop His understanding of the kingdom one step at a time. The kingdom has to do both with God's rule and God's reign over the world. Although the kingdom may not be visible with the physical eye, it exists now and will continue to grow and develop in the future. Bock (DJG 504-505) provides a good overview of Luke's presentation of the kingdom. He notes that the Kingdom of God is a complex theme in Luke, as it is in the other Gospels. It is introduced through divine initiative; the words and deeds of human beings cannot bring in the Kingdom of God. The kingdom is a spiritual entity in that it is not tied to any particular geographical area or to any specific earthly ruler. It is basically the rule of God as He makes it known in the world.

The kingdom has both present and future aspects. The miracles of Jesus are one illustration of the fact that the kingdom is a present reality. In Luke 11:20, Jesus says, "But if I with the finger of God cast out devils, no doubt the kingdom of God is come upon you." During His earthly ministry, Jesus challenged men and women to enter into His kingdom.

The kingdom also has future aspects. The consummation of the Kingdom of God is connected with the Second Coming of Christ, which is discussed in chapters 17 and 21. The kingdom definitely implies that God is in control of the lives and destinies of individuals. One prerequisite for entering the Kingdom of God is a willingness to obey the call of God and seek to do His will.

Sometimes the Kingdom of God demands that people leave their traditional beliefs and practices behind and embark on a new quality of life. For a comprehensive analysis of the Kingdom of God as it is developed in the N. T. see G. R. Beasley-Murray, *Jesus and the Kingdom of God*.

The Death of Christ. Luke devotes chapter 23, entirely, to the crucifixion of Jesus and the events that surround it. Luke's description of these events has much in common with the other Gospels, but Luke's account does emphasize two specific points. First, he emphasizes that Jesus is totally innocent of the charges leveled against Him. Second, Luke emphasizes the widespread responsibility for the great injustice done to an innocent man (Bock II:1806). Luke places most of the blame for Jesus' crucifixion on the Jewish leaders, but he clearly recognizes the culpability of Pilate, who knew that Jesus was an innocent man but condemned Him to execution anyway. Pilate's condemnation of Jesus was clearly motivated by political considerations.

There are some aspects of the story of Jesus' trials and execution that are unique to Luke. For example, the account of Jesus' hearing before Herod is told only in this Gospel. Another unique contribution of Luke is Jesus' discussion with the women as He is walking toward the place of His execution. Only Luke contains the story of the condemned man who says to Jesus, "Remember me when thou comest into thy kingdom." Jesus then assures that man, "To day shalt thou be with me in paradise." One of Luke's many contributions is that this Gospel adds significant information about the trials and death of Jesus, which would otherwise be unknown. For a good discussion of the theological significance of the death of Christ see James Denney.

Eschatology. Maddox points out that eschatology occupies an important place in the theology of Luke. He explains (100-101) that for a number of years many scholars argued one of the main purposes Luke had when he wrote this Gospel was to deal with the crisis in the church created by the delayed Parousia. According to this theory, this Gospel was written late in the first century when many believers had begun to notice that Christ's promise to return to the earth had not yet been fulfilled. The fact that Christ had not yet returned created a crisis of confidence within the church; no longer could the Christian message be regarded as credible. Under these circumstances, Luke felt it necessary to explain the delay in Christ's return.

Maddox explains that this theory was quite popular among scholars but never won universal acceptance. He calls attention to the fact that a number of scholars, including E. Earle Ellis, have never accepted this reconstruction. Ellis (49) notes that both Paul and Luke deal with the expectation of Christ's return. He concedes that Paul and Luke do have somewhat different perspectives; Paul's view is more short-term while Luke reflects a more long-term view.

Luke deals both with individual and corporate eschatology, but more attention is given to the latter. Maddox (103-104) suggests that most of Luke's teaching on the destiny of individuals is found in two passages, 16:19-31 and 23:42-43. Luke 16:19-31 is the famous story of the Rich Man and Lazarus, which most interpreters consider to be a parable. Maddox (103) argues that Jesus has borrowed from a pre-Christian story, which Luke has incorporated into his Gospel. Maddox notes this is not a complete picture of Luke's view of individual eschatology; there is no discussion, for example, of the coming resurrection or of Jesus' involvement in the process. This passage does affirm that the deeds performed here on earth will produce either rewards or punishments in the life to come. Maddox argues that the real point of the story is found in verse 31 which reads, "And he said unto him, If they hear not Moses and the prophets, neither will they be persuaded, though one rose from the dead."

According to Maddox, the other passage in Luke that focuses on the future life of the individual is found in Luke 23:43 where Jesus says to the penitent thief on the cross, "To day shalt thou be with me in paradise." These words of Jesus came in response to the thief's petition, "Lord, remember me when thou comest into thy kingdom." Closely related to this verse is 23:46 where Jesus speaks of His own death in these words, "Father, into thy hands I commend my spirit." Once again, these verses do not present a complete picture of Luke's understanding of the future life. There is, for example, no mention of the Second Coming or of the resurrection of the bodies of believers. These verses do affirm, however, a strong belief both in the justice of God and in the reality of the future life. The Lord promises to the penitent thief that his faith will not go unrewarded. As a result of his personal commitment to Christ, he will be permitted to enter into the fullness of Christ's kingdom when many have been excluded for their lack of faith. In verse 46, Jesus affirms that His death will not be the end of His existence. The implication is that Jesus is commending His spirit (the essence of His life) into the hands of God. He understands that death is not the end of His ministry; He will simply enter into the presence of God for a new dimension in ministry.

Luke devotes more interest to the subject of corporate eschatology, and most of his teaching on this subject occurs in the context of Jesus' instruction to the disciples. Two passages, 17:22-37 and 21:5-33, are especially important. Maddox (125) argues that Luke 17 contains Jesus' most definitive statement on this subject. As this passage explains, the return of Christ will be preceded by a time of trial, persecution, and suffering. Both Jesus and His followers will be called upon to suffer many things before the return of Christ. That day will come suddenly and unexpectedly as people go about their normal affairs of life. There will be no time or opportunity for people to make preparation when Christ returns. It will be a time of separation; as Jesus explains, "one shall be taken and the other left." The time to make spiritual preparation is before Christ returns to earth; when He comes again it will be too late. As Maddox (127) explains, this passage is designed more to warn the unrepentant than it is to assure believers of their final salvation.

The other key passage is 21:5-33 where Jesus instructs His disciples about the future that lies before them. Jesus warns them it will not be an easy time. According to verse 12, "they shall lay their hands on you, and persecute *you*, delivering *you* up to the synagogues, and into prisons, being brought before kings and rulers for my name's sake." They will experience wars and rumors of wars. They will observe "signs in the sun, and in the moon, and in the stars; and upon the earth distress of nations, with perplexity; the sea and the waves roaring" (verse 25). After these events transpire they will see "the Son of man coming in a cloud with power and great glory" (verse 27).

In the conclusion to this section of his discussion, Maddox (128) notes that it is not Luke's purpose to provide "a neat doctrine of eschatology." For Luke, eschatology essentially means judgment; that judgment has already fallen on the Jewish nation. In the future, it will fall on the entire world.

Maddox has correctly noted many of the key ideas developed in Luke's treatment of eschatology, but many scholars would question his late dating of the Gospel. It is clear that Luke manifests a great deal of interest in eschatology. It is also true that he focuses more of his attention on the final destiny of the church as a whole than on the destiny of individual believers. Luke does not deny the destiny of individuals, but that is not the major focus of his eschatology.

Luke also makes a significant contribution to the doctrine of the resurrection. He shares with the other Gospel writers the common conviction that when the earliest witnesses arrived at the tomb on that Sunday morning, they found it to be empty. The only possible conclusion was that Jesus had been resurrected in the pre-dawn hours.

Luke's narrative of the post-resurrection appearances of Jesus is rather unique. Only Luke relates the story of Jesus' conversation with the two disciples on the road to Emmaus. Luke continues to tell about their return to Jerusalem and their discussion with the apostles in Jerusalem. Luke is the only one of the Gospels that relates the story of the Ascension. It is likely the abbreviated account of the Ascension in Luke is intended to prepare the reader for the longer and more detailed discussion presented in Acts. For a useful discussion of the theological significance of the resurrection see Carl F. H. Henry.

LUKE

OUTLINE OF LUKE

I. Literary and Historical Introduction, 1:1-4
II. The Messiah and His Forerunner, 1:5—2:52
  A. Prophecy of the Birth of John the Baptist, 1:5-25
  B. Prophecy of Jesus' Birth, 1:26-38
  C. Mary's Visit to Elizabeth, 1:39-45
  D. Mary's Song of Praise, 1:46-56
  E. Birth of John the Baptist, 1:57-66
  F. Zechariah's Song of Praise, 1:67-79
  G. John's Growth and Development, 1:80
  H. Birth of Jesus, 2:1-20
  I. Jesus' Presentation in the Temple, 2:21-39
  J. Jesus' Growth and Development, 2:40-52
III. The Public Ministry Begins, 3:1—4:13
  A. The Ministry of John the Baptist, 3:1-20
  B. The Baptism of Jesus, 3:21-22
  C. The Genealogy of Jesus, 3:23-38
  D. The Temptations of Jesus, 4:1-13
IV. The Ministry in Galilee, 4:14—9:50
  A. Examples of Jesus' Teaching in Galilee, 4:14-44
  B. The Call of the Disciples, 5:1-39
  C. Conflict Over Sabbath Observance, 6:1-12
  D. Naming the Disciples, 6:13-16
  E. Jesus Challenges His Followers, 6:17-49
  F. Jesus Defines His Messiahship, 7:1-50
  G. Jesus Defines His Kingdom, 8:1-56
  H. Jesus Trains His Disciples, 9:1-50
V. Jesus' Journey to Jerusalem, 9:51—19:44
  A. Commitment to Ministry, 9:51—10:24
  B. Discipleship Lessons, 10:25—11:28
  C. Conflict and Controversy, 11:29-54
  D. Challenges to His Followers, 12:1-53
  E. Understanding the Times, 12:54—13:9
  F. The Power of the Kingdom, 13:10-30
  G. Continued Conflict, 13:31—14:35
  H. The Grace of the Kingdom, 15:1-32
  I. Putting Possessions in Their Place, 16:1-31
  J. Preparation of the Disciples, 17:1—18:17
  K. Sacrificing for Christ, 18:18-34
  L. Blessings and Mercy, 18:35—19:27
  M. Preparations for the End, 19:28-44

VI. Ministry in Jerusalem, 19:45—24:53
   A. Teaching in the Temple, 19:45—21:4
   B. Fall of Jerusalem and the End of the Age, 21:5-38
   C. Betrayal and the Last Supper, 22:1-53
   D. Trials, 22:54—23:23
   E. Crucifixion and Burial, 23:24-56
   F. Resurrection and Ascension, 24:1-53

I. LITERARY AND HISTORICAL INTRODUCTION (1:1-4)

Luke 1:1-4, one long Greek sentence of more than forty words, serves as the historical prologue to this Gospel. As Alexander ("Context" 54) notes, "Luke's preface is simply a short, detachable passage in which the author stands briefly aside from his own narrative to explain who he is, what he is doing, why and for whom." Marshall (*Historian* 278-280, 291) argues that these verses serve not only as the introduction to the Gospel of Luke but also to Acts. In his view, the Gospel and Acts form one organic whole that unites the teaching of Jesus with the life and ministry of the early church. For a good overview of the prologue see Stonehouse, chapter II.

Such historical prologues were common in the Hellenistic literature of that era; Nolland (I:4-5) notes that this passage is similar to other historiographic prologues (Fitzmyer I:288; Geldenhuys 51; and Stein, *Luke* 62). Bock (I:52) points out that similar introductions may be found both in Jewish documents written in Greek and in secular Greek documents. Green (*Luke* 33) notes that in the ancient world the first sentence of a document was important because it prepared the reader to understand and appreciate the material that followed.

This prologue has produced a large amount of scholarly interest. Cadbury notes, "In the study of the earliest Christian history no passage has had more emphasis laid upon it than the brief preface to Luke" ("Preface" 489). In two important works, Alexander has given a most comprehensive analysis of the relationship between Luke's prologue and various forms of prologues found in the Hellenistic world beginning about the fourth century B.C. In one article Alexander ("Context" 60) concludes that Luke's is most similar to prologues found in certain scientific texts and that the scientific tradition provides the necessary background to understand Luke's preface. In a more comprehensive work (*Gospel* 42-46), Alexander defines the term "scientific" to include treatises written by philosophers, medical texts, technical writings done by engineers or mathematicians, and other types of writing.

Other interpreters do not share Alexander's reconstruction. Green (*Luke* 34), for example, finds historical precedent in Greek literature for this type of prologue, but he sets Luke's prologue in a wider context, arguing that such prefaces were commonly found in various kinds of documents including literary, technical, and non-literary. According to Green, all of these prefaces tended to follow, to some degree, the patterns established in ancient rhetoric. Cadbury ("Preface" 490) also finds significant similarities between this prologue and prologues found in other forms of contemporary Hellenistic literature. For more information, see the helpful comments of Marshall (*Gospel* 39-44) and Spence (2-3).

Of the canonical Gospels, Luke is the only writer who includes a prologue summarizing how he plans to approach the task of writing. According to Stein (*Luke* 66), this Gospel not only describes Luke's procedure in writing his Gospel, it also gives a basic outline of how the Gospel traditions were handed down and were ultimately incorporated into the canonical Gospels.

The author has two primary goals in writing this prologue. First, he writes to establish his credibility as a historian and the reliability of the conclusions he presents. He assures his readers that he has carefully researched the available information in order to compile an accurate account of the life and ministry of Christ. He wishes to present that information in an organized and readable way (Nolland I:12). According to Bock (I:66), Luke's primary purpose is to assure Theophilus and other believers that they have received correct information about what the apostles taught concerning Jesus of Nazareth.

Second, the author establishes the reliability of the Gospel traditions his readers have previously received. He has carefully investigated the available sources, both written and oral, in an attempt to reconstruct as accurately as possible, the life and teachings of Christ (Nolland I:12; Bock I:59-61; Ellis 66). It is interesting to note that Luke does not stress his independence from earlier Christian writers. He does exactly the opposite; he emphasizes his dependence upon them. He writes, in part, to confirm the trustworthiness of the Christian message that his Gentile readers had previously received. As S. Brown (62) explains, Luke's purpose is not to present the gospel message for the first time. His goal is to confirm the truthfulness of the message that the followers of Jesus have already received.

Luke's defense of his credibility and of the reliability of his sources may seem strange and unnecessary to the modern reader. This type of defense was not unusual, however, in the ancient world. Liefeld (821) notes that ancient historians, including Josephus, would often justify and defend their work through a preface.

Most early Christian teaching existed in oral form and was passed from one group of believers to the next by word of mouth. This oral system worked well for the first few years of the church, but the rapid spread of the faith and the deaths of the apostles and other eyewitnesses soon made written documents necessary. These early Christians needed reliable writings they could use in their preaching and teaching. Luke saw this need and stepped forward to meet it under the leadership of the Holy Spirit (Geldenhuys 51; Bock I:58).

Several authors have offered helpful analyses of the content of Luke's prologue. Alexander (*Gospel* 102-142) presents a useful commentary on the key terms found in these verses. He points out a number of similarities between Luke's prologue and the prologues found in the Greek scientific texts. The commentaries by Bock (I:51-67), Fitzmyer (I:287-301), and Nolland (I:4-12) provide useful summaries of the main ideas presented in the preface. The commentary that is generally recognized as the most comprehensive is by Cadbury ("Preface" 489-510).

Luke's historical prologue reflects two natural divisions. Verses 1 and 2 describe how the early Christian traditions about Christ were collected and circulated prior to Luke's writing. Verses 3 and 4 outline how Luke carefully researched this previously existing material and incorporated it into his Gospel.

1 Forasmuch as many have taken in hand to set forth in order a declaration of those things which are most surely believed among us,
2 Even as they delivered them unto us, which from the beginning

were eyewitnesses, and ministers of the word;
3 It seemed good to me also, having had perfect understanding of all things from the very first, to write unto thee in order, most excellent Theophilus,
4 That thou mightest know the certainty of those things, wherein thou hast been instructed.

Verse 1 begins with the conjunction *forasmuch* (Greek *epeidēper*); it occurs often in classical Greek but is found only here in the N. T. (Liefeld 821; Cadbury, "Preface" 492). This term is most often used in a causal sense, meaning "because." Occasionally it has concessive force, meaning "although." Here, the idea seems to be concessive; Luke is not saying that the existence of other writings has caused him to write yet another account of the life of Christ. The idea is that the existence of these other works has not prevented him from doing so (Stein, *Luke* 63). Bock (I:54) suggests that it be translated "inasmuch as."

There has been considerable discussion concerning Luke's relationship with his predecessors. The early church historian Eusebius wrote that Luke held a rather low view of those who had written before him; his goal was to correct what they had written (Stonehouse 31). This rather negative view is also found in the writings of Augustine. In Book IV chapter 8 of *The Harmony of the Gospels*, Augustine writes that this passage refers to "those writers who have attained to no authority in the Church, just because they were utterly incompetent to carry out what they took in hand" (Schaff 230).

Most modern scholars do not share this negative opinion. They believe Luke writes not to downplay the contributions of earlier writers but because he has additional information to contribute to the story (Bock I:59; Stonehouse 31). As Marshall explains ("His 'Gospel'" 291), Luke writes because prior accounts are incomplete, not because they are incorrect. Luke has no desire to condemn those who wrote before him or to present a new Gospel; instead, he presents the existing gospel message in a new and systematic way based on a thorough analysis of the available information (Bock I:66). Robertson (*Historian* 45) presents a similar viewpoint. In another work, Bock (*Jesus* 54) suggests that Luke's goal is to present the connection between the ministry of Jesus and that of the early church in a way that no previous writer has done. Cadbury ("Preface" 493) explains that Luke views these earlier writers as precedents and not as failures. See the useful comments of Alexander (*Gospel* 114-116).

"Many" is the most difficult word in verse 1 to interpret, and commentators have understood it in various ways. It is clear that Luke's goal is to identify the Gospel he is writing within the previously-existing Christian tradition. He is not inventing some new information about Christ; he is continuing an already existing stream of tradition about the life and ministry of Christ.

In this context, "many" clearly refers to previous writings that describe the life and ministry of Christ, but it does not suggest any particular number. It may refer to as few as two or three, or perhaps to dozens (Stein, *Luke* 63). Stein suggests the word may say more about the importance of the subject than the number of Luke's predecessors. The idea may be the subject is of such importance that "many" have chosen to write about it. Liefeld (821) correctly notes that when Luke wrote this Gospel there was already much interest in learning about Jesus and His ministry.

Morgan (*Luke* 12-13) suggests that Luke consulted a number of different sources and devoted several years to writing his Gospel. In his view, Luke's sources likely included the earlier Gospels of Mark and Matthew. Morgan also suggests that Luke talked with Jesus' mother Mary and with others who could provide first-hand information. Bock (I:55) posits that Luke's sources included at least Mark and Q.

Bonnet and Schroeder (469-470) suggest a different approach. They argue that the "many" of verse 1 should be distinguished from the "eyewitnesses and ministers of the word" mentioned in verse 2. The word "many" describes those who were not apostles. The "eyewitnesses and ministers of the word" identify those who were apostles. These terms, then, identify two different kinds of sources that Luke used, apostolic sources and non-apostolic sources.

According to Bonnet and Schroeder, the "many" cannot include Matthew because he was an apostle. It may include the Gospel of Mark because Mark was not an apostle, but they doubt the term includes Mark's Gospel. Neither does it include the apocryphal Gospels because they were written later than the canonical Gospels. In their opinion, the "many" includes the writings of unknown Christians who reduced the apostolic traditions to writing. Luke used these writings as some of his sources, but they fell into disuse after the canonical Gospels were accepted and circulated among the churches.

While the theory of Bonnet and Schroeder is attractive, it is built upon a weak foundation. They assume that Luke's intention in this passage is to distinguish between sources written by the "many" of verse 1 and sources written by the "eyewitnesses and ministers of the word" of verse 2. There is, however, no hard evidence that Luke intends to make such a distinction. Instead, he seems to be describing two important steps in the process of collecting and recording the gospel story. During the first stage, the apostolic traditions were collected by "eyewitnesses and ministers of the word" who had first-hand knowledge of what Jesus had done and said. During the second stage, the "many" preserved, collected, and used these apostolic traditions in their writings. Luke's Gospel is stage three in the process. He plans to use these earlier writings as sources for his Gospel, and he wants to assure his readers of their reliability.

Since Luke and Mark have so much material in common, it is quite likely that Mark was one of Luke's principal sources. Luke and Matthew contain about 200 verses of material (mostly the teachings of Jesus) that is not found in Mark. It is possible the teachings of Jesus were collected at an early date in oral or written form and Luke had access to this collection of material. It is also possible that Luke depended on Matthew for a considerable amount of information.

Luke contains approximately 485 verses of material found only in this Gospel. The source or sources of this material cannot be determined with certainty. Some of it could have been provided by Mary, by other members of the family, or by other individuals.

The number of sources (both written and oral) Luke has available to him or the precise content of those sources must be left an open question. Luke's prologue clearly indicates he has located reliable information that enables him to write a comprehensive account of the life of Christ.

The words "have taken in hand" translate a single verb (Greek *epicheireō*), commonly used to describe an author's work in producing some type of document (Stein, *Luke* 63; Bock I:55). Bonnet and Schroeder (469) note that the word occurs only here in the Greek N. T. but that it is often used in classical Greek to note the brevity and difficulty of the task undertaken.

The latter part of verse 1 describes the work these earlier writers had accomplished in producing different accounts of the essential aspects of Christ's ministry. "To set forth in order a declaration" translates two words (Greek *anataxasthai diēgēsin*); the second one describes a historical writing or narration (Bock I:56; Stein, *Luke* 63). The second is a technical term used in the ancient world to describe historical writings or historical accounts preserved in oral form (Bock I:56). The idea is that Luke's predecessors did not simply collect information; they produced real historical accounts of the life of Christ.

The last part of verse 1 could also be translated "concerning those things which have been fulfilled among us," using the tense (Greek perfect) that describes a completed action. The main idea is that the events of Christ's life fulfilled completely the O. T. prophecies concerning the Messiah (see Stein, *Luke* 64). Bonnet and Schroeder (470) suggest this word always carries the idea, "to fulfill completely." Here it suggests the idea of "full persuasion" or "complete certainty." Cadbury ("Preface" 495) explains that this term is used with different meanings and here is best translated "completed."

Marshall ("His 'Gospel'" 278-279) presents a broader interpretation of this phrase. He argues that "the things that have been accomplished among us" must include both the story of Jesus' earthly life and the events that happened during the early period of the history of the church.

Verse 2 completes Luke's analysis of how the "many" went about their work. They not only gathered the information and organized it, they also delivered it to Luke and to other believers of his generation. "Delivered" translates a technical term (Greek *paradidōmi*) that describes the process of handing down an authoritative tradition (Stein, *Luke* 64; Bock I:58-59). The point is that Luke's predecessors did not handle the material casually or carelessly; they treated it with the dignity and respect it deserved. This idea is reinforced by "even as" (Greek *kathōs*); these earlier authors passed the traditions on to Luke and others *just as* they had received them.

"Them" (v. 2) refers to the things fulfilled in verse 1. "Us" refers to the early church, especially those of Luke's generation. The last part of verse 2 outlines stage one in the process of collecting and preserving the information, using two important terms to describe the original recipients of the gospel tradition: "eyewitnesses" and "ministers of the word." Most interpreters see these two terms as describing the same group of people (Stein, *Synoptic Problem*

194, *Luke* 64; Bock I:58; Bonnet and Schroeder 470; Stonehouse 27).

Bonnet and Schroeder (470) suggest that they were eyewitnesses from the baptism and the beginning of Jesus' public ministry and later became ministers of the word. Stein (*Luke* 64) notes the terms "word" and "word of God" are technical terms for the gospel message. They are used over forty times in Luke-Acts with this meaning. Bonnet and Schroeder (471) suggest the term "word" includes both the gospel and the preaching of the gospel.

The phrase "from the beginning" refers primarily to the eyewitnesses and ministers of the word. The idea is that they followed closely the history and development of the Gospel message from its earliest days. Creed (2) suggests that the ministry of John the Baptist was generally considered to be the beginning point of the Christian faith.

In these verses, Luke seems to imply a three-step process. First, the "eyewitnesses and ministers of the word" gathered information through their own personal knowledge and observation or through the knowledge and observation of others.

Second, this information was handed down (probably in oral form) to the "many" who used it to prepare the earliest accounts (probably written) of Jesus' life and ministry. Third, this material was passed on to Luke who used it in compiling his Gospel.

Verses 1 and 2 distinguish Luke from the first generation of believers; he is not an eyewitness to any of the events he describes. He is a member of the second (Ellis 65) or third generation (Fitzmyer I:289). Even so, he does not separate himself from his predecessors; he identifies with them. The Gospel is not the creation of his imagination; it is built on a solid foundation of knowledge passed down within the Christian community (Marshall, *Historian* 19).

The first words of verse 3 are normally translated "it seemed good" (KJV, NIV) or "it seemed fitting" (NASV). Lenski (31) suggests that such a translation is too weak; the idea is rather, "I, too, resolved." In his view, this phrase reflects Luke's determination not simply to repeat what others had previously written. His goal is to prepare an account specifically designed to meet the needs of Theophilus and his other Gentile readers.

The next phrase is "having had perfect understanding of all things from the very first." "Having had perfect understanding" (Greek perfect participle) means "to follow closely," "to pay careful attention to," or "to investigate." Marshall (*Historian* 279) analyzes the various uses of this verb. He concludes that it may be used in two different senses and something of both usages may be implied here. First, it may be used to describe events outside the author's own personal experience. Second, it may also be used to describe participation in current events or keeping oneself informed about them.

Cadbury ("Preface" 501-502) argues that this word (Greek *parakoloutheo*) is used in three different senses in the writings of the Hellenistic era. First, it may mean to follow what is read or spoken. Second, it describes keeping in touch with things that happen or to follow a course of events. Third, it may imply actual presence and participation in the events. The term does not mean "to research" in the modern sense of the term because modern research techniques did not exist in the ancient world.

Cadbury ("Preface" 502) notes that Luke's information did not come to him through academic study but it resulted from information passed down as the events happened. According to Robertson (*Gospel* 6), the key idea is that "Luke got himself ready to write before he began by a full and accurate knowledge of the subject."

"Having had perfect understanding" does not refer to the supernatural inspiration he experienced but to the fact that he has carefully followed the ministry of Christ and the work of the early church. He has made use of all the sources available to him and is able to present an accurate account of the development of the Christian faith from its earliest days (Fitzmyer I:296-297; Lenski 32; Summers, *Luke* 20; Stein, *Luke* 64).

"In order" (v. 3) means "in an orderly manner." Most authorities agree it does not imply that Luke plans to tell the story of Christ in chronological order; it simply means he will present the information in an organized fashion (Lenski 32; Liefeld 822; Cadbury, *Luke-Acts* 345). According to Cadbury ("Preface" 505), it is best translated into English by the words "successively" or "continuously."

As Stonehouse (41) observes, Luke demonstrates comparatively little interest in the precise chronology of events. His Gospel is broadly chronological, but it does not give a day-by-day analysis of Jesus' ministry. The Gospel is partly geographical in that the story moves from one location to another, but the Gospel is also arranged theologically. Luke wishes to show that God's plan to save lost men and women, including Gentiles, has developed. Creed (5) takes a different approach; he suggests that Luke's probable intention is to tell the story of Jesus in chronological order.

Luke's Gospel is addressed to "most excellent Theophilus." Theophilus is a Greek word meaning "lover of God." Here it seems to be used as a proper name (Geldenhuys 53-54; Creed 5). Liefeld (823) suggests that Luke has a specific individual in mind, but "Theophilus" may be a substitute for his real name. He is clearly a believer, or at least an individual who has received some instruction in the Christian faith. Cadbury ("Preface" 507-508) presents an excellent discussion of the background and usage of this name.

Stein (*Luke* 66) argues that "Theophilus" is not a pseudonym but a real name. Theophilus may have been a Roman governor, the official who was to hear Paul's case in Rome, or Luke's literary patron—the individual who paid the cost of writing, duplicating, and distributing the Gospel (Ellis 66). Bonnet and Schroeder (471) explain that early Christian tradition describes Theophilus as a wealthy and powerful man from Antioch.

The word translated "most excellent" is very general in meaning. Lenski (33) suggests it describes a man who enjoys a certain prominence in society because of his wealth or because of the position he holds. Bonnet and Schroeder (471) point out that the word describes one who occupies an elevated social position. Jackson and Lake (178-179) note that this term was never used during the first two centuries to describe a fellow believer. They suggest Theophilus was some type of Roman official.

While most commentators agree Theophilus is a real person (Stein, *Luke* 66), there is considerable disagreement concerning whether he is a believer or an interested unbeliever. Bock (I:64) concludes he was a believer whose faith needed to be strengthened and encouraged. Ellis (66) suggests there is not sufficient information to decide with certainty whether Theophilus is a believer. Bock (I:64) points out that Luke is not writing for Theophilus alone. In the ancient world, books were often dedicated to individuals when the author was writing for the benefit of a wider audience. Cadbury ("Preface" 510) suggests Theophilus is not a believer but an influential non-Christian.

Verse 4 comes to the heart of Luke's two-fold purpose in writing this Gospel. His goal is not to introduce Theophilus and his other Gentile readers to some new doctrine or teaching. Marshall (*Historian* 84) notes that Luke's goal is to present the message of salvation to lead them to faith, or (in the case of Theophilus) to confirm a previously-existing faith. The goal is both to bring Gentiles to faith in Christ and to confirm (and probably amplify) the Christian instruction Theophilus has already received.

"Certainty" (Greek *asphaleian*) is the most important word in this verse; it describes the condition of one who stands firm and is not about to trip or fall (Lenski 34-35). Luke wishes to encourage and strengthen the faith and understanding of Theophilus and his other Gentile readers. Cadbury ("Preface" 509) notes that this word is used in several different ways. In this context, it refers to "the truth" or "the facts" concerning a matter that has been reported. Luke wants to confirm the veracity of the information presented in this Gospel.

"Those things, wherein thou hast been instructed" refer to the teachings about the life and ministry of Jesus Christ that Theophilus had already received. Creed (5) notes that Luke's goal is not to convey new information but to confirm what Theophilus has already learned in a less systematic way. In later years, the term was used to describe the instruction given to new converts before baptism, but that does not seem to be the meaning here (Lenski 35; Stein, *Luke* 66).

There is one aspect of the study of the prologue that has provoked some controversy in academic circles. Cadbury (*Luke-Acts* 346-348) asserts that the preface serves as an introduction not only to the Gospel but to Acts. He also asserts that Luke is more than just a careful compiler of information. He understands the prologue to teach that Luke himself is an eyewitness and participant in at least some of the events described, which would include those in Acts, at least.

Stonehouse takes issue with Cadbury at this point. He argues (35-36) that Luke's language in the preface precludes the type of interpretation that Cadbury has suggested. Luke does not include himself among the "eyewitnesses and ministers of the word"; in fact, he distinguishes himself from them. The preface also looks back to events that happened a number of years in the past. Luke may have been an eyewitness to some of the events narrated in Acts, but the prologue to Luke makes no such affirmation.

Summary (1:1-4)

This brief prologue makes an important contribution to this Gospel. It prepares the reader to understand and appreciate all the important information that follows and outlines the writer's qualifications to write the letter. It also advises the reader about what the author wishes to accomplish in this letter. Luke reminds his readers that this Gospel is not simply his invention or a presentation of his own thoughts and ideas. It is an organized presentation of important information about the life and ministry of Christ that has been a part of the Christian tradition from its earliest days. He has carefully researched all the information available and has presented his conclusions in an organized way.

Luke's primary goal is to strengthen the faith of Theophilus and other Gentiles who may read the Gospel. His plan is to help his readers understand that Jesus is the Son of God and the Savior of all who will trust in Him. Luke's hope is that this Gospel will give his readers a better understanding of the Christian faith and this better understanding will make a difference in their lives and ministries.

Application: Teaching and Preaching the Passage

This passage is the obvious choice for a lesson or sermon that introduces Luke's Gospel to a class or congregation. This introductory lesson or sermon should point out that the Gospel is a distinctively Christian form of literature; the pagan religions of the ancient world had nothing similar to it. It should be noted that the Gospel is not a biography in the modern sense of that term. It is true that Luke reflects some interest in the personal life of Jesus Christ, but that is not his main concern. He is more interested in the theological significance of Jesus' life and ministry; his concern is to demonstrate that Christ is the Son of God and the Savior of both Jews and Gentiles.

There are several major themes in these verses that should be emphasized in preaching or teaching on this passage. One is the meaning and significance of the term "gospel," which literally means "good news." In the context of Luke's Gospel, it is the good news that Jesus Christ has come into the world to save all who have faith in Him, both Jew and Gentile. This gospel message centers on the person and work of Jesus Christ.

For Luke and the other Gospel writers, the good news of Jesus Christ is a powerful thing. It can and will transform lives, but in order to make a difference, this gospel message must be received freely and voluntarily. It must also be communicated to those who have not yet heard it.

Another important theme found here is the power of the written word. Luke expects that the document he is writing will make a difference in the lives of those who read it. It will give them a better understanding of the Christian faith. It will help them know Christ in a more personal way; it will also give them a message they can communicate to those outside the faith.

The historical nature of the Christian faith is also an important theme found in these verses. The preacher or teacher should point out that the teachings of the Christian faith are not simply someone's personal opinion or idea; they are grounded in what God has done in the past. They can be traced back to those who were the eyewitnesses of Jesus' life and ministry. This Gospel is far more than Luke's personal testimony or his private opinion; it is a carefully researched and well-organized message.

The preacher or teacher should also stress the role of the Holy Spirit in the production of the written Gospels. These four verses never mention specifically the role of the Holy Spirit, but the Christian church from its earliest days has maintained that Luke and the other biblical writers did their work under the leadership and direction of the Holy Spirit. That does not mean the Holy Spirit dictated the words Luke wrote; it means the Holy Spirit worked in and through the mind of the human author to produce an inspired and authoritative document.

These verses introduce the important theme of the relationship between divine revelation and human reason. Divine revelation and human reason worked together in the production of the biblical books. The fact that Luke used his God-given ability to reason did not negate the need for divine revelation; neither did divine revelation render human reason unnecessary.

II. THE MESSIAH AND HIS FORERUNNER (1:5—2:52)

A. Prophecy of the Birth of John the Baptist (1:5-25)

Luke begins the gospel story with the announcement of the birth of John the Baptist, the forerunner of the Messiah. This portion of the story is important because John makes a major contribution to the life and ministry of Christ. It is John who baptizes Jesus and first recognizes Him publicly as the Messiah.

Luke's primary purpose in this portion of his Gospel is to show the hand of God at work in every aspect of the life of Christ. Green (*Luke* 47) notes the theological significance of the story of Jesus' birth; it is a testimony to the love of God for all humanity. God's miraculous intervention in the birth of John is a significant part of Luke's story because it underscores the uniqueness of John the Baptist and the importance of his contribution to Christ and His ministry. The birth of John is not a virgin birth, but it is still a miraculous birth. It shows God actively at work in these events and sets the stage for the even more important story of Christ and His birth.

Although Luke's Gospel is written primarily for Gentile readers, the author is careful to establish a strong connection between the O. T. and the life and ministry of Jesus. He understands that his readers cannot interpret correctly the significance of what Jesus said and did unless they understand something of the historical roots of His ministry. Luke points out that both the birth of Jesus and the birth of John the Baptist fulfilled O. T. prophecies. Both Mary's song of praise (1:46-56) and Zechariah's song of praise (1:67-79) are filled with terms and concepts drawn from the O. T. Jesus' presentation at the Temple at the age of eight days demonstrates His family's faithfulness to the Jewish law. As Green (*Luke* 52) notes, this section of Luke does not introduce a new story but continues the story found in the Hebrew Scriptures.

This broad section of the Gospel (chapters 1-3) serves as a bridge between Jesus' O. T. roots and His public ministry. These verses stress several important themes. First, they emphasize the divine origin of the Christ child; the virgin birth serves as a proof of His divine origin. The homage He receives, first from the shepherds and later from Simeon and Anna, also bear witness to His divine origin and power. His discussions with the Jewish leaders in the Temple at age twelve also demonstrate that the hand of God is upon Him in a special way.

Second, this section also stresses Jesus' humanity. Luke is careful to show that He is both fully divine and, with the exception of sin, fully human. Although He is the Son of God, He goes through the process of human growth and development; He does not suddenly appear as an adult ready to begin His public ministry.

Third, this section emphasizes the faithfulness of the men and women who surround the child Jesus. Joseph, Mary, Elizabeth, Zechariah, John the Baptist—and others—are presented as men and women of faith. They are not perfect; they need the forgiveness of God just as all others do. They are, however, committed to doing God's will. They can provide the kind of environment in which the God-man, Jesus Christ, can grow and mature.

Luke 1:1-4 confirms both the reliability and the importance of the Gospel that Luke is writing. Verses 5-25 shift the focus from the written Gospel to the coming Messiah who will remain the central focus for the remainder of the book. These verses announce the birth of John the Baptist who serves as the forerunner of the Messiah and from among whose followers Jesus will call His earliest disciples.

Verses 5-25 are sharply different from the first four verses, both in content and in writing style. Verses 1-4 are one long flowing Greek sentence written in very classical style (Geldenhuys 54-55). Verses 5-25 reflect a very Palestinian form of Greek that is filled with Hebraisms, words and concepts borrowed from Hebrew, and Aramaisms, words and concepts borrowed from the Aramaic language (Nolland I:17-18; Bonnet and Schroeder 472).

This section introduces several important themes that will reoccur throughout Luke's Gospel. First is the fact that God has taken the initiative to send the message of salvation into the world. While there are no artificial limits on those whom God can use in this process, it is not the entire nation of Israel that He uses. He selects those within the nation of Israel that are faithful. The divine activity demonstrated in the birth of John the Baptist does not result in blessing only a narrow circle of Jewish followers; it extends to all who hear and heed God's message of salvation. A second important Lucan theme introduced in these verses is joy. Luke 1:14 points out that future generations will share the joy Zachariah experiences at the birth of his son.

5 There was in the days of Herod, the king of Judaea, a certain priest named Zacharias, of the course of Abia: and his wife *was* of the daughters of Aaron, and her name *was* Elisabeth.

6 And they were both righteous before God, walking in all the commandments and ordinances of the Lord blameless.

These verses identify the parents of John the Baptist and establish the time of his conception and birth. The events take place during the reign of Herod the Great, the son of Antipater, who was given the title "king of Judaea" by the Roman Senate in 40 B.C. (Fitzmyer I:321). Herod actually won control with the help of the Roman legions in 37 B.C. and ruled until his death in 4 B.C.

The birth of John probably occurred near the end of Herod's reign (Bock I:75).

Luke uses the word "Judaea" in different ways (Nolland I:25; Fitzmyer I:322; R. Brown, *Birth* 257). In this context, it refers to the territory over which Herod ruled, which included Judaea proper, Samaria, Galilee, much of Perea, and parts of Syria (Bock I:75; Lenski 37-38). Since Judaea was the most important part of the territory from a religious standpoint, it was common to use the term "Judaea" to describe the entire region.

Several members of the Herod family ruled parts of Palestine at different times. Summers (*Luke* 24) lists them and describes when and where each ruled. In this passage, the reference is clearly to Herod the Great who ruled much of the land of Palestine from 37 to 4 B.C. (Nolland I:25; Bock I:34; Bonnet and Schroeder 472). Herod was not a Jew; he was an Idumean (a descendant of the ancient Edomites) who professed the Jewish religion (Geldenhuys 61). He was never popular among the people he ruled; only the presence of Roman legions in Palestine guaranteed his continued power and control (Green, *Luke* 64).

From an economic standpoint, Herod's rule was very successful; he completed several large building projects including the rebuilding of the Temple in Jerusalem. Religiously and morally, however, his reign was a dismal failure. Herod tolerated the worship of pagan gods; he was also cruel and vindictive, shedding the blood of anyone who might think of opposing him (Geldenhuys 61). He even had several members of his own family put to death. Much to the relief of the Jewish people, he died of natural causes in 4 B.C. For more information about the political, economic, and social conditions in Palestine at this time, see the works of Dana, Matthews, Tenney, and Packer listed in the bibliography.

Zechariah and Elizabeth, the parents of John the Baptist, are introduced in 1:5. Zechariah is a priest of the course of *Abia;* his Hebrew name means "God has remembered again." It was used several times in the O. T. to describe various priests (Fitzmyer I:322).

He is part of a large company of priests who take turns serving in the Temple in Jerusalem. The precise number of priests serving in the Temple in the first century is difficult to determine. The *Letter of Aristeas* gives the number as 18,000 (Bock I:35). Jeremias (*Jerusalem* 204), estimates there were about 7,200 priests and 9,600 Levites actively involved in Temple ministry in the time of Jesus. His discussion includes an analysis of how they were divided and how they did their work.

Edersheim (*Temple* 90) notes that the priests and Levites were divided into 24 groups, or courses, with each course serving for one week every six months from Sabbath to Sabbath. He also gives a comprehensive discussion of the preparation, training, dress, and service of priests in the first century (92-104). A list of the 24 courses may be found in 1 Chronicles 24:7-18. The course of *Abia* (*Abijah* in Hebrew) was the eighth of these twenty-four (1 Chr. 24:10). The rotation system in use at that time seems to have been established after the return from the Babylonian Exile (Fitzmyer I:322). (For further discussion of the Jewish priesthood in the first century see Nolland I:26; Bonnet and Schroeder 472; and Bock I:35.)

Zachariah's wife was named Elizabeth, and Luke notes that she was "of the daughters of Aaron," which probably means she was also of priestly descent. According to O. T. teaching, a priest could marry any pure Israelite woman, but marriage to a woman from a priestly family was to be preferred (Nolland I:27; Green, *Luke* 64). Her name, Elizabeth, has a long history in Judaism; it was the name given to Aaron's wife in Exodus 6:23.

Luke describes them as being "righteous before God" and "walking in all the commandments and ordinances of the Lord blameless." Similar phraseology is used in the O. T. to describe the lives of faithful men and women (Dt. 6:25; Gen. 26:5; 1 Kgs. 3:14; etc.). These words do not imply they were sinless; the idea is they were truly committed to God and faithful in their obligations to serve God in the Temple and elsewhere. They were exemplary in their character and devoted to God. For more analysis of the usage of these words see Bock (*Luke* IVP 35); Fitzmyer (I:322); Nolland (I:23); R. Brown (*Birth* 259).

7 And they had no child, because that Elisabeth was barren, and they both were *now* well stricken in years.

Elizabeth could not bear children. In ancient Israel, childlessness was generally seen as a reproach and, on occasion, as a punishment for sin (Green, *Luke* 65). Leviticus 20:20-21, for example, establishes childlessness as the punishment for committing adultery with one's uncle's wife or one's brother's wife. The fact that Zechariah and Elizabeth were righteous and obedient to God indicates that their barrenness should not be interpreted as a punishment for sin (Bock I:78). It serves, rather, as an opportunity for God to demonstrate His grace and mercy.

Some authorities suggest that in Israel childlessness produced a double sorrow. First, it meant the couple could not be parents. Second, it meant they could not be ancestors of the Messiah (Geldenhuys 62). Since Zechariah and Elizabeth were both advanced in years, there was no human remedy for this situation. God was their only hope of having a child (Green, *Luke* 66). Their sorrow and disappointment had not, however, caused this elderly couple to turn away from God. They accepted this tragic situation, remained faithful to God, and continued to pray that He would bless them with a child.

8 And it came to pass, that while he executed the priest's office before God in the order of his course,
9 According to the custom of the priest's office, his lot was to burn incense when he went into the temple of the Lord.
10 And the whole multitude of the people were praying without at the time of incense.

Priests normally served in the Temple for one week every six months, and they drew lots to determine which priest would perform each specific duty. Offering the incense (at the time of the whole burnt offering) in the Holy Place was the greatest privilege and most awesome responsibility. It was such a great privilege that a priest could ordinarily offer the incense only once during his lifetime (Bock I:78; Nolland I:*28*;

Fitzmyer I:322). On this special day, the lot fell to Zechariah, and he prepared to fulfill this important responsibility.

Whole burnt offerings were normally made twice each day, once at sunrise and again at dusk. Luke does not say whether this important event occurred at the morning or evening sacrifice. Many authorities see the presence of the crowd as an argument for the evening sacrifice (Nolland I:28). Geldenhuys (63) notes that the burning of the incense was a most solemn time. The people gathered for prayer in the Temple court outside the Temple proper. When they saw the smoke ascending, they fell down before the Lord for several minutes of silent prayer.

11 And there appeared unto him an angel of the Lord standing on the right side of the altar of incense.
12 And when Zacharias saw *him*, he was troubled, and fear fell upon him.
13 But the angel said unto him, Fear not, Zacharias: for thy prayer is heard; and thy wife Elisabeth shall bear thee a son, and thou shalt call his name John.
14 And thou shalt have joy and gladness; and many shall rejoice at his birth.
15 For he shall be great in the sight of the Lord, and shall drink neither wine nor strong drink; and he shall be filled with the Holy Ghost, even from his mother's womb.
16 And many of the children of Israel shall he turn to the Lord their God.
17 And he shall go before him in the spirit and power of Elias, to turn the hearts of the fathers to the children, and the disobedient to the wisdom of the just; to make ready a people prepared for the Lord.

At this important time in Zechariah's life, the Lord chooses to speak to him in a very special way. He sees an angel of the Lord standing at the right side of the altar of incense (Stein, *Luke* 74). In the ancient world, the right hand was the place of honor (Green, *Luke* 71). The word "angel" literally means "messenger." It is sometimes used in the Bible to describe a human messenger, but the most common use is to describe a supernatural being that brings a special message from God.

Zechariah responds to this most unusual event with shock and awe. The angel immediately understands and tells him to stop being afraid. (The Greek present imperative, with negative, was often used to forbid an action already in progress.) The angel's message is a positive one, and Zechariah should not respond to it with fear. According to Green (*Luke* 73), these words are a clear echo of Genesis 15:1 where God reminds Abram that he has not been forgotten.

The angel brings the good news that God has heard this elderly couple's prayers for a child. He will take away their reproach and bless them with a son. The angel then gives them very specific instructions to name the child John, which means "Yahweh has been gracious" (Stein, *Luke* 75) or "Yahweh has shown favor" (Fitzmyer I:325). Yahweh is one of the Hebrew names for God in the O. T., generally translated LORD in the KJV. Luke does not take time to explain the meaning of John's Hebrew name, probably because his readers knew well who John was and the important role he played in Jesus' ministry.

Verse 14 states that Zechariah will respond to John's birth with great joy and gladness; he will give praise to God for answering his many prayers for a child. The second half of the verse points out that the rejoicing will not be limited to Zechariah and Elizabeth; many others—at least including family and friends—will join in. In the larger context of this passage, the many may include the followers of Jesus the Messiah for whom John served as forerunner (see Stein, *Luke* 75).

Verses 15-17 describe some of the important characteristics John will manifest when he comes to adulthood. He will not be an ordinary man; he will reflect an unusual degree of dedication to God and will have a profound impact on His people and on the entire world. The most important characteristic is that he will be great in the sight of God. This does not necessarily imply great power and authority, but—more likely—he will rank beside those great men in Israel's history who have accomplished great things in the service of God. According to Green (*Luke* 75), this term indicates the important role John will play in God's redemptive purpose.

He will drink neither wine nor strong drink. The word "wine" normally describes an alcoholic beverage made from grapes. "Strong drink" generally describes alcoholic beverages made from dates, barley, or other fruits and grains. This term is also used to describe beer (Fitzmyer I:326; Bonnet and Schroeder 474).

This prohibition of alcohol may indicate that John was a Nazarite. According to Numbers 6:3 one requirement of the Nazarite vow was abstaining from wine and other fermented beverages. Two important examples of birth announcements somewhat similar to John's were for Nazarites Samson and Samuel (R. Brown, *Birth* 273).

Since other aspects of the Nazarite vow (such as not cutting the hair) are not mentioned here, there is not sufficient evidence to conclude with certainty that John was to be a Nazarite (Liefeld 827). (For more information on the Nazarite vow see Barton.) It is likely that his abstinence from alcohol represented a high level of commitment to God rather than a specific Nazarite vow.

The latter part of v. 15 is significant; it explains that from his mother's womb he would be filled with the Holy Spirit. This phrase serves to connect John with the O. T. prophets who performed their ministries under the leadership of the Spirit of God (Stein, *Luke* 76; Nolland I:30). John was meant to be more than a typical Israelite. He would follow in the footsteps of the prophets who had reflected a high degree of dedication to God and were used by Him in special ways.

Verses 16 and 17 summarize the future ministry of John. He would cause many in Israel to turn to the Lord. The verb "turn" is often used in the N. T. to describe conversion (Acts 9:35, 11:21, 14:15, etc.). In this context, the idea is that John would lead many of his fellow Israelites to turn to Jesus as the Messiah. The "him" in verse 17 refers to Jesus Christ, the Messiah. John would go before Jesus in the spirit and power of Elijah. This is, without doubt, a reference to Malachi 3:1 and 4:5. Malachi 4:5 reads, "Behold, I will send you Elijah the prophet before the coming of the great and dreadful day of the LORD."

Jews of the first century understood this to mean that an appearance by the prophet Elijah would announce the coming of the Messiah (Spence 5). It is difficult to determine if the Jews of that era anticipated a literal return to the earth of Elijah, or if they understood the prophecy to mean that a prophet similar to Elijah would precede the coming of the Messiah.

The meaning that Luke intends is that John would be a prophet similar to Elijah (Liefeld 827). There is nothing in the Gospels or in early Christian tradition that argues for a literal reincarnation of the O. T. prophet Elijah (Childers 438-439). John would minister in the spirit and power of Elijah in the sense that he would have the same energy and commitment to God that Elijah demonstrated. He would have the same spirit within him that Elijah had (Bonnet and Schroeder 475).

It is clear that Luke considers the life and ministry of John the Baptist to be the fulfillment of the prophecies of Malachi. John would work to return the people of Israel to genuine repentance and faith in God just as Elijah did in earlier centuries (Fitzmyer I:327).

The latter part of verse 17 describes the nature of John's ministry. Luke emphasizes that his ministry was to be spiritual and not political in nature. Many in Israel at that time expected the coming of a political Messiah who would free them from Roman domination and restore their country to independence. Jesus did not turn out to be that kind of Messiah, and John did not prepare for that kind of Messiah. In this verse, Luke uses several terms and concepts from the O. T. to explain the nature of John's ministry. First, he will turn the hearts of the fathers to the children. Second, he will turn the disobedient to the wisdom of the just. Third, he will make ready a people prepared for the Lord (for the coming Messiah). These should not be understood as three totally different ministries but as three different aspects of John's preparatory ministry.

The first two aspects of John's ministry are clearly drawn from Malachi 4:6a which reads, "And he shall turn the heart of the fathers to the children, and the heart of the children to their fathers." These words have traditionally been interpreted against the background of the social and political divisions found among the Jews in Palestine during the first century. They were divided into Pharisees, Sadducees, Herodians, Zealots, Essenes, and other groups. According to the traditional interpretation, Elijah would help to heal these divisions and bring the people together (Spence 5).

Many modern interpreters prefer a different interpretation. Spence (5), for example, interprets these words against the background of Isaiah 29:22-23 and 63:16. These verses speak of returning the disobedient children of Israel to the more dedicated lives that their fathers, the patriarchs, had lived. Bonnet and Schroeder (475) advocate a similar approach, as does Morgan (*Luke* 16).

The third aspect of John's ministry, to make ready a people prepared for the Lord, is more difficult to interpret. Many commentaries pay little attention to these words. Perhaps the most natural interpretation is that of Bonnet and Schroeder who view these words not as the fulfillment of any specific O. T. prophecy but as a general summary of John the Baptist's ministry. They write (476), "He can only prepare the people for the Lord to the end that they may be willing to receive Him. Then the Lord himself must do the rest." For Luke, the most important thing is not the specific tasks John will perform. The most important thing is that his life and ministry will fulfill the O. T. prophecies and will prepare the way for Jesus Christ, the Messiah.

18 And Zacharias said unto the angel, Whereby shall I know this? for I am an old man, and my wife well stricken in years.

Zechariah responds to this incredible message from the angel in a most normal and human way. In Hebrew, the verb "know" often expresses the idea of "to experience" or "to know by experience." In effect, Zechariah is asking, "How can I experience this? I am an old man and my wife is of advanced age?" The idea is that both of them are beyond the age of normal childbearing. Abraham uses the same expression in Genesis 15:8 after he is told he will inherit the land of Canaan. He responds, "Lord God, whereby shall I know that I shall inherit it?"

This verse is also similar to Genesis 18:1-12 where God speaks to Abraham in a vision. In the vision three men (apparently messengers from God) come and tell Abraham that his wife, Sarah, will have a son. Sarah responds to this information with a laugh because she is well past the normal age for having children.

Summers (*Luke* 27) offers a somewhat different interpretation of Zechariah's question. He suggests that Zechariah was asking for a sign indicating that this message had, in fact, come from God. The angel responded by giving him a sign; his temporary loss of the ability to speak is the sign of the divine origin of the message. Lenski (52-53) also argues that Zechariah was asking for a sign.

19 And the angel answering said unto him, I am Gabriel, that stand in the presence of God; and am sent to speak unto thee, and to shew thee these glad tidings.
20 And, behold, thou shalt be dumb, and not able to speak, until the day that these things shall be performed, because thou believest not my words, which shall be fulfilled in their season.

Although Zechariah's statement seems very normal in light of the circumstances, it is interpreted by the angel of the Lord as a lack of faith. Zechariah has apparently not learned the lesson of Abraham and Sarah.

Verse 19 establishes that the angel speaking with Zechariah is no ordinary angel. He is Gabriel, the angel who reveals information about the future in Daniel 8-12. *Gabriel* means "Hero of God" or "Mighty One of God." He is one of only two angels mentioned by name in the O. T. (Spence 5). In the Scripture, he is often presented as an angel of mercy (Plummer 16).

In the Jewish literature of the inter-biblical period, Gabriel is one of those important angels who are permitted to stand in the very presence of God (1 Enoch, chapters 9 and 20). In Luke, Gabriel has been sent on a very important mission. He is to inform Zechariah of the important role his son will play in God's plan for the world.

"Glad tidings" refers to the good news that John will be the forerunner of the Messiah. The implication is that

Gabriel, serving as God's spokesman, also has the authority to rebuke Zechariah for his unbelief.

The content of the angel's rebuke is found in verse 20. Zechariah's punishment is that he will lose his ability to speak until the events prophesied by the angel are fulfilled. Luke 1:64 describes how Zechariah will regain the ability to speak at the circumcision of John.

The second half of verse 20 states specifically that the dumbness comes as a result of Zechariah's unbelief. These words should not be interpreted to mean that he has completely lost his faith in God. The idea is that he doubted the angel's specific promise that he and Elizabeth would be the parents of a son at such an advanced age (Summers, *Luke* 27; Lenski 56).

21 And the people waited for Zacharias, and marvelled that he tarried so long in the temple.
22 And when he came out, he could not speak unto them: and they perceived that he had seen a vision in the temple: for he beckoned unto them, and remained speechless.
23 And it came to pass, that, as soon as the days of his ministration were accomplished, he departed to his own house.
24 And after those days his wife Elisabeth conceived, and hid herself five months, saying,
25 Thus hath the Lord dealt with me in the days wherein he looked on *me*, to take away my reproach among men.

Zechariah goes into the Temple to burn frankincense on the golden altar in the Holy Place. This is the high point of his priestly career; it is likely the only time in his life he will have this high privilege (Bock I:79). Later Jewish tradition mentions that four priests would have accompanied Zechariah on this mission, and that after the incense was offered, they would have pronounced a blessing on the waiting crowd (Bock I:94).

The crowd outside the Temple waits for Zechariah to finish the incense offering and come out to bless them. They note that the offering is taking longer than normal. Sprinkling the frankincense on the altar would generally take only a few minutes, and the priest would not stay inside the Holy Place for a long period of time (Lenski 57). Zechariah finally comes out, and when he does he cannot offer the customary blessing; he cannot speak at all.

The crowd wonders what has happened. They keep waiting for him to speak, but he never does. He gestures with his hands until they understand he cannot give them the customary blessing (Lenski 57). Ultimately, they realize he has experienced a vision from the Lord. There is simply no other possible explanation for his sudden loss of speech (Summers, *Luke* 27).

Verse 23 indicates that Zechariah completes the rest of his week of service at the Temple in silence. Luke does not explain how his inability to speak affects his ministry in the Temple; that is simply not important to the story. At the end of the week, Zechariah returns to his home in Hebron (Lenski 58).

Verse 24 explains that God does not wait long to fulfill His promise; Elizabeth becomes pregnant soon after Zechariah returns home. For the first five months of her pregnancy she "hid herself." The most natural interpretation of these words is that she remained in seclusion and did not go out in public during this time. Luke offers no explanation for her decision to remain at home for these five months. There is nothing in Jewish literature to suggest this was a custom among Jewish women of the first century (Fitzmyer I:329). Commentators have offered numerous reasons for Elizabeth's decision to withdraw from society for the first five months of her pregnancy. Bock (I:97) and Marshall (*Gospel* 62) offer excellent summaries of the reasons most commonly suggested today. Summers (*Luke* 28) suggests this is "a time of contemplation on her experience and of rejoicing in her sense of fulfillment." Plummer (19) suggests she does not wish to suffer any more reproaches from neighbors and friends; neither does she wish to debate the issue with them. She decides to wait five months, and, by that time, as Childers (433) argues, her pregnancy would be far enough advanced that people could see that the Lord had taken away her reproach.

R. Brown (*Birth* 282) and Fitzmyer (I:329) both suggest a theological reason. They posit that Luke has included the five months of seclusion to prepare for Luke 1:36 where Elizabeth's cousin, Mary, first learns from an angel, of her pregnancy. According to Fitzmyer (I:329), both Elizabeth's seclusion and Zechariah's dumbness kept the story of her pregnancy from being known until God chose to reveal it. There is not sufficient information to determine with certainty why Elizabeth chose to go into seclusion for five months, but there are several plausible explanations. The suggestion of Brown and Fitzmyer has considerable merit; Luke often emphasizes God's leadership and direction in all aspects of John's life and ministry. This period of silence and seclusion stresses that Elizabeth's pregnancy comes about as a result of divine intervention and is revealed by divine initiative.

Verse 25 explains how Elizabeth responds to what God has done in her life. She seeks no glory and takes no credit for what has happened. She gives all the glory to God and notes how He has blessed her by taking away the reproach of childlessness. She gives all the praise to God just as Sarah did in Genesis 21:6 and Rachel in Genesis 30:23 (Marshall, *Gospel* 62).

B. Prophecy of Jesus' Birth (1:26-38)

This section describes how the birth of Jesus is announced to His mother Mary. It is in some ways similar to the announcement made to Zechariah before the birth of John the Baptist. It is also similar in some ways to birth announcements made in the O. T. concerning Isaac, Sampson, and Samuel (Fitzmyer I:335; Bock I:102). It is also similar to the announcement made to Joseph in Matthew. In both accounts an angel appears, announces that a child will be born to a virgin, and gives instructions to name the child "Jesus." Both Matthew and Luke emphasize that the Holy Spirit will come upon Mary, she will become pregnant, and she will bear a son.

Both accounts also speak of the future ministry the child will have. Neither passage actually uses the Jewish term "Messiah" to describe Jesus, but both authors employ words and phrases with strong messianic connotations. It seems that both Luke and Matthew view this child as the fulfillment of the O. T.

messianic prophecies (Lenski 66-67, 74; Nolland I:52; Liefeld 829; Stein, *Luke* 84).

There are, however, significant differences between Matthew's account and Luke's. Matthew calls the angel "The Angel of the Lord" while Luke names him "Gabriel." In Matthew, the angel speaks with Joseph. In Luke he speaks with Mary. Matthew gives no indication where Joseph is when he receives the angelic vision (although he is probably in Nazareth). Luke states specifically that the vision comes to Mary in Nazareth of Galilee—probably home to both Mary and Joseph.

Matthew's account is written from the perspective of Joseph and answers the natural questions that any thinking man would have in such an extraordinary situation. Luke's account is written from the perspective of Mary and seeks to answer her questions and prepare her for what lies ahead.

The differences between these two accounts should not be viewed as conflicts. Both Matthew and Luke wrote some 30 to 40 years after the death of Christ to meet the needs of particular audiences. Each also had certain specific themes he wished to emphasize. Both selected the information they needed to include about the birth of Christ and organized it in such a way that it would meet the needs of their readers. For more extensive discussions of the relationship between Matthew and Luke see Bock (I:70-73, 106-108); Fitzmyer (I:335-37); R. Brown (*Birth* 33-37).

Luke was not an eyewitness to Gabriel's announcement to Mary; he must depend on the information handed down to him. Nolland (I:43) suggests that his sources were probably written rather than oral. R. Brown (*Birth* 244-245) provides a brief summary of current thinking on the question of Luke's sources.

One likely possibility is that both the information about the announcement and the story of the virgin birth can be traced back ultimately to Mary herself (Bock I:103-104; Marshall, *Gospel* 63). Fitzmyer (I:342) suggests this information comes from an early Christian tradition, but he is unwilling to say it can be traced back to Mary herself. It is difficult to see how this information could have been preserved and later included in Luke's Gospel without the participation of Mary and those around her.

The account of Mary's virginal conception is the most controversial element in the story of Christ's birth. It has long been debated by scholars who suggest there are three possibilities.

First, some scholars suggest the story has no basis in fact. They argue that the early church simply created the story of the virgin birth based on the use of the term "Son of God" to describe Jesus. The early Christians saw Jesus as the Son of God, and, as the Son of God, He would need no human father. James Mackinnon (14) writes that the stories of Jesus' birth "do not belong to the primitive tradition which, in the primitive preaching and in Mark, begins with the baptism by John. They are later additions to counteract Jewish calumny and strengthen the enhanced evaluation of the exalted Christ." In the view of these scholars, the story of Jesus' supernatural conception was not a part of the original Gospel message. It was a later addition designed to meet the needs of the early church.

There are several problems with this theory. One is that the O. T. writers used the term "Son of God" to describe a person whose father is known (2 Sam. 7:14; 1 Chr. 17:13; Ps. 2:7). Another problem is that it is highly unlikely the early church would have created the story of Jesus' supernatural conception simply to meet its own needs.

Second, some scholars suggest the story of the virgin birth was not part of the earliest Christian preaching but was developed later from a Christian interpretation of the Greek text of Isaiah 7:14. The early Christians understood the Greek text of Isaiah 7:14 to mean that the Messiah would be born of a virgin. The early believers, who considered Jesus to be the Messiah, then attributed to Him the prophecy of Isaiah 7:14 and developed the story of the virgin birth. A leading defender of this approach is F. C. Grant (231) who views the virgin birth as "a doctrine derived from a text of the Old Testament and supported by it, a feature of the story of the life of Christ which entered the tradition at a relatively late date."

It is true that the Greek version of Isaiah 7:14 uses "virgin" (Greek *parthenos*). Matthew quotes this Greek version in Matthew 1:23. Luke, however, neither mentions nor quotes from Isaiah 7:14. In fact, there is no evidence to prove that the story of the virgin birth grew out of a Christian interpretation of Isaiah 7:14. Once again, it is highly unlikely that the early Christians would simply invent stories about Jesus to satisfy their theological convictions.

Third, the traditional view is that the story of the virgin birth is based on fact. The early church did not create the story; that Jesus was born to a virgin actually happened and became a part of the Christian tradition at an early date. Luke accepted the virginal conception as fact and included it in his Gospel. Bock (I:104) correctly notes that the early church had no reason to create the story of the virgin birth. According to this view, the story of the virgin birth was known in the early church and was a part of the Christian tradition upon which Luke depended.

Luke 1:26-38 falls into three divisions. Verses 26-27 establish the setting and introduce the major characters in the story of Jesus' birth. Verses 28-37 describe the angel's announcement itself. Verse 38 describes Mary's acceptance of this tremendous message.

26 And in the sixth month the angel Gabriel was sent from God unto a city of Galilee, named Nazareth,
27 To a virgin espoused to a man whose name was Joseph, of the house of David, and the virgin's name *was* Mary.

The angel's announcement comes in the sixth month; this is obviously the sixth month of Elizabeth's pregnancy. The sixth month is also mentioned in 1:36. Luke's reference to the sixth month serves to connect the birth of Jesus with that of His forerunner, John the Baptist. This important announcement is made by Gabriel who also announced the birth of John the Baptist.

Luke emphasizes that Gabriel is not speaking on his own initiative; the message is of divine origin. One of Luke's important goals throughout this narrative is to show that God is behind this miraculous sequence of events.

The message is sent to Nazareth in Galilee, a small village of little importance. It is not mentioned in the O. T., in the writings of Josephus, or in the early rabbinical writings (Fitzmyer I:343).

It is mentioned, however, in a Hebrew inscription found at Caesarea Maritima in 1962 (Fitzmyer I:343). Bock (I:106) suggests that Galilee might have been mentioned because Luke's Gentile readers might not have known the location of Nazareth.

The angel's message comes to a young virgin named Mary. In the original Greek, there were several words Luke could have used to describe a young lady of her age; he chooses one (*parthenos*), which means "virgin," for two reasons. First, he wants to emphasize her sexual purity. Mary confirms her sexual purity in 1:34 where she asks, "How shall this be, seeing I know not a man?" The verb "know" in this context is a Hebrew way of describing sexual intimacy.

Second, Luke wishes to emphasize the supernatural nature of Jesus' conception. Mary's pregnancy is not the result of normal sexual activity. God has intervened in the situation in a very special way and is using this very special event to reveal certain aspects of His work and character. In this passage, Jesus' miraculous conception is a key element in Luke's description of the birth of Christ.

Luke says nothing about Mary's lineage, probably because he is writing to a Gentile audience, and a person's lineage would have been less important to a Gentile audience than to a Jewish one. Bock (I:107-108) notes that she was a relative of Elizabeth and that Elizabeth was a descendant of Aaron (Lk. 1:5), which might indicate that Mary was also of Levitical roots. Several early Christian writers connected her to David.

According to verse 27, Mary is engaged to a man named Joseph who is a descendant of David. Engagement and marriage customs found in ancient Israel were very different from those found in modern western cultures; one key difference is that in those days marriages were generally arranged by the families. In this passage, Luke seems to place Mary at the first stage of a two-stage process. The first stage was an engagement or betrothal that might occur when a girl was as young as age 12. This engagement was formalized in front of witnesses and generally included the payment of a bride price. At this point, the young girl legally became the bride of her husband and she could be described as his wife.

Such an engaged girl would not immediately begin to live with her husband, but would continue to live with her family for about another year. After this year had passed, the actual marriage ceremony, which is the second stage, would take place and the bride would begin to live with her husband (Bock I:107 and Fitzmyer I:344).

28 And the angel came in unto her, and said, Hail, *thou that art* highly favoured, the Lord *is* with thee: blessed *art* thou among women.
29 And when she saw *him*, she was troubled at his saying, and cast in her mind what manner of salutation this should be.
30 And the angel said unto her, Fear not, Mary: for thou hast found favor with God.
31 And, behold, thou shalt conceive in thy womb, and bring forth a son, and shalt call his name JESUS.
32 He shall be great, and shall be called the Son of the Highest: and

the Lord God shall give unto him the throne of his father David:
33 And he shall reign over the house of Jacob for ever; and of his kingdom there shall be no end.

The stage has now been set, and the angel begins to announce the good news to Mary. The announcement begins with two words, in the original, that together form a special greeting. The first, "Hail" (Greek *chaire*), literally means "rejoice," but it was a common greeting among Greek-speaking people at that time. It is difficult to determine how widely this greeting was used in Palestine or what precise meaning it conveyed. Bock (I:109) examines various possible meanings, as does Fitzmyer (I:344-345). After careful consideration, both conclude that the term should be understood as a general greeting (similar to the modern "hello") rather than as a specific call to rejoice.

The second part of the greeting, "highly favored," carries greater theological significance and (as a Greek participle) may simply mean "favored one" (Bock I:109); "thou that art" were added by the translators. It might have meant, more specifically, "favored by God" (Fitzmyer I:345). The idea is that Mary is the recipient of a special outpouring of God's power and grace; she is to be the mother of the coming Messiah. The latter part of verse 28 explains more specifically how Mary is to be blessed. She is blessed among women because God is with her. The idea is not that God is with Mary to the exclusion of other women; the point is that God is with her in a special or unusual way.

In verse 29, Mary responds with perplexity. "Troubled" (Greek *diatarass*) expresses the idea of curiosity and concern. The latter part of the verse implies that Mary continued to ponder for some time (Greek imperfect tense) about what the angel's greeting might mean.

The problem is not that Mary doesn't understand the meaning of the words the angel has used; she knows the words very well. The difficulty is that she doesn't know how to put these incredible words into the context of her life or how to respond to them appropriately. She is simply overwhelmed.

The angel moves immediately to allay her fears, giving the same command he had given Zechariah in verse 13. The idea is "stop fearing" or "stop being afraid." Mary can lay her fears aside because what is happening in her life is God's doing. She has found favor with God; she will conceive and will give birth to a son. Fitzmyer (I:347) notes that the phraseology used in these verses is similar to that found in several O. T. passages.

The angel also tells Mary to name her son *Jesus,* the Greek form of the Hebrew name *Joshua.* Luke says nothing about the origin or derivation of the word "Jesus" but several modern commentators have examined the history and meaning of this important term. Fitzmyer (I:347) notes that it comes ultimately from a Hebrew root that means "to help." Many Jews of the first century connected it with a word meaning "to save."

Verses 32-33 summarize the important ministry Jesus will have. The angel selects a series of terms and concepts from the O. T. to describe Jesus' earthly ministry. He mentions four specific attributes or qualities that Mary's yet unborn son will demonstrate. First, He will be great. The term "great" is used in the

O.T. both to describe God and to describe important people (Bock I:113).

Second, He will be called the "Son of the Highest" or the "Son of the Most High." This is simply another way of saying that Jesus will be the Son of God. The term does not necessarily imply deity; it is used in various ways in Jewish literature, both within the O. T. canon and in writings outside the canon. In 2 Samuel 7:14, God speaks of David as His son; in 1 Chronicle 22:9-10, God speaks of Solomon in the same way.

Bock (I:114) and Evans (45) suggest that the Qumran scrolls use the term "Son of God" to describe the coming Messiah. The idea here is that Jesus will enjoy a filial relationship with God that ordinary men do not have. He will be the perfect reflection of His father's glory.

Third, God will give to Him the throne of His father David. In Hebrew thought, the word "father" was often used in the sense of "ancestor." Jesus will be a descendant of David through Joseph (and perhaps through Mary as well). This prophecy is based directly on the promise God gave to David through the prophet Nathan in 2 Samuel 7:16. That verse reads, "And thine house and thy kingdom shall be established for ever before thee: thy throne shall be established for ever." The angel's point is that the promise God had made to David almost 1,000 years in the past will be fulfilled in the life of Mary's son.

Fourth, He will reign over the house of Jacob forever, and His kingdom will never end. The phrase "house of Jacob" is a common designation for the nation of Israel (Ex. 19:3; Is. 2:5-6; etc.). The promise that David's kingdom will last forever is found in 2 Samuel 7 and in other passages (Bock I:115).

Luke's emphasis is that the life and ministry of Jesus (including His birth) will be the fulfillment of these ancient prophecies. Luke does not delve into the nature of Jesus' eternal reign. He does not explain whether it will be a material reign, a spiritual reign, or some combination of the two. During the years of His earthly ministry, Jesus will explain the nature of His kingdom by His words and His actions.

Verses 32-33 do not contain the word "Messiah" and so do not state specifically that Jesus will be the Jewish Messiah. They do, however, contain terms and concepts that are used in Judaism to describe the coming Messiah. When this passage is examined in light of other passages in this Gospel, it is clear that Luke considers Jesus to be the fulfillment of the O. T. messianic prophecies.

34 Then said Mary unto the angel, How shall this be, seeing I know not a man?
35 And the angel answered and said unto her, The Holy Ghost shall come upon thee, and the power of the Highest shall overshadow thee: therefore also that holy thing which shall be born of thee shall be called the Son of God.
36 And, behold, thy cousin Elisabeth, she hath also conceived a son in her old age: and this is the sixth month with her, who was called barren.
37 For with God nothing shall be impossible.
38 And Mary said, Behold the handmaid of the Lord; be it unto me according to thy word. And the angel departed from her.

In verse 34, Mary responds to this incredible promise with a most logical question, "How shall this be, seeing I know not a man?" As was noted above, the verb "to know" is often used in Hebrew literature to describe sexual intimacy. Mary's question reflects a certain degree of surprise and perplexity, but it should not be interpreted as a lack of faith on her part. In this context, it is a most natural and honest response.

The angel responds in verse 35 with a message of assurance. He explains that the child will not be conceived through the normal process of sexual relations with a husband. The child's conception will be the result of special divine activity. Luke describes this special divine activity in two ways. First, the "Holy Ghost," that is, the Holy Spirit, will come upon her in a special way.

In the O. T. it is the Spirit of God that brings life, and that seems to be the idea here (Bock I:121). The idea is that the Holy Spirit will come upon Mary and work in her life in a special way. There is nothing in the verb itself that suggests any type of sexual relationship (Fitzmyer I:337).

Second, the angel describes God's creative work by saying, "the power of the Highest shall overshadow thee." "The highest" is clearly a reference to God. "Overshadow" (Greek *episkiazō*) is a general word found in a variety of different contexts. In the Greek version of the O. T. (the Septuagint), it is used to describe the Shekinah glory that rested over the tabernacle or God's presence in protecting His people.

These two phrases express the same truth in different words. Luke's message is that Jesus' conception will not be the result of normal human activity. It will be the result of a special work of God's power through the Holy Spirit.

The last portion of verse 35 is important theologically. It explains that His supernatural conception will make Jesus different from other men. The angel specifically calls Jesus "holy" and the "Son of God." The word "holy," used often in both testaments, describes a person or thing set apart for the service of God. In the O. T., for example, the vessels in the Temple are considered "holy" because they are set apart for the service of God and cannot be used for ordinary, secular purposes. People (such as priests) are considered holy because they are set apart in a special way for the service of God. In the N. T., believers are called "holy" in the sense that they dedicate themselves to doing God's will and not to following the dictates of the world.

In this verse, Jesus is also called the "Son of God." The various uses of this phrase have been noted above. These two important terms (*holy* and *Son of God)* stress that Jesus will enjoy a special relationship with God that others do not have. According to Ephesians 1:5, all believers are children of God by adoption based upon the redemptive work of Christ. They enjoy a special relationship with God that unbelievers do not have. Jesus, however, is the Son of God by nature and not by adoption. He shares God's nature and reflects God's attributes in a way that no ordinary human being can. John 3:16 speaks of Jesus as the "only begotten son." He is "only begotten" in the sense that He alone shares God's nature and being.

Bock (I:124) suggests that there is more to the term "Son of God" than a description of Jesus' filial relationship with His heavenly Father. He argues that Luke uses this term to emphasize the fact that Jesus is the Messiah. Fitzmyer (I:340) comes to similar conclusions. Evans (45) notes that the term "Son of God" is used in the Dead Sea Scrolls to describe the coming Messiah.

Verse 38 is Mary's response to Gabriel's announcement. It is much more than a reluctant acceptance of a task; it expresses her willingness to do God's will and to be a part of His plan of redemption. "Handmaid" (Greek feminine form of *doulos*) means "slave" or "servant." The idea is that Mary is not just a woman serving for wages; she is a young lady who is totally dedicated and committed to doing God's will (Lenski 76).

The word translated "be it" (Greek optative) is a modal form used sparingly in the N. T., often expressing strong wishes and prayers. Here Mary asks that the message brought by the angel may become a reality in her young life. The last words in the verse, "And the angel departed from her," serve as a transition. The announcement part of the story is over; the narrative moves on to the actual story of Jesus' birth and the events that led up to it.

C. Mary's Visit to Elizabeth (1:39-45)

39 And Mary arose in those days, and went into the hill country with haste, into a city of Juda;
40 And entered into the house of Zacharias, and saluted Elisabeth.
41 And it came to pass, that, when Elisabeth heard the salutation of Mary, the babe leaped in her womb; and Elisabeth was filled with the Holy Ghost:
42 And she spake out with a loud voice, and said, Blessed *art* thou among women, and blessed *is* the fruit of thy womb.
43 And whence *is* this to me, that the mother of my Lord should come to me?
44 For, lo, as soon as the voice of thy salutation sounded in mine ears, the babe leaped in my womb for joy.
45 And blessed *is* she that believed: for there shall be a performance of those things which were told her from the Lord.

One of Luke's major themes in this section is to establish in different ways that Jesus is the unique Son of God. The praise given by Elizabeth and the fact that the baby, John, leaped in her womb are designed to show that Mary's child is no ordinary child. He is the Son of God. This passage also serves as a precursor to the later relationship that will exist in adulthood between Jesus and John the Baptist. Jesus always occupies the position of supremacy in God's plan while John plays an important but subordinate role.

As was previously noted, Mary and Elizabeth were relatives. Both had conceived children under miraculous circumstances, and both were being used by God in special ways. It is natural that they would want to be together during this important time in their lives. Since Mary was much younger than Elizabeth, she traveled to the home that Elizabeth shared with her husband Zechariah. Mary was probably living in Nazareth at this time and traveled south in haste through the hill country of Judaea. Luke does not name the town where Elizabeth and Zechariah lived because that information is not theologically significant.

The reader is not told if Mary went alone or with others. Since women did not ordinarily travel alone in ancient Palestine, it is likely that others went with her for reasons of safety and security. Bock (I:134) suggests this would have been a journey of three or four days through the hill country south of Jerusalem.

Neither is the reader told why Mary goes in haste. There is nothing in the passage to indicate that Elizabeth is having a difficult pregnancy, although the birth of a child to a woman of her advanced age would certainly have been a matter of concern. It is more likely that Mary's haste does not grow out of any crisis situation but out of a desire to do God's will (Stein, *Luke* 89). God's will is important and should always be done with a sense of urgency.

Verse 41 is the heart of this passage because it emphasizes two ideas that are theologically significant. The first is that Elizabeth's unborn child, John, leaps for joy in her womb when Mary arrives. Leaping for joy is a common O. T. concept (Stein, *Luke* 89). The idea here is that the presence of Jesus the Messiah, though still in the womb, brings joy, and joy is one of Luke's most common and most important theological themes.

The second important idea is that when Mary arrives, Elizabeth is filled with the Holy Spirit. This verse is closely connected with Luke 1:15, which says that John the Baptist will be filled with the Holy Spirit. Luke does not mention any specific outward manifestation of the Holy Spirit in Elizabeth's life. The idea seems to be that she is empowered by the Holy Spirit to play a special role in the life and ministry of the Messiah.

Verses 42-43 are Elizabeth's verbal response not only to Mary's visit but to all the remarkable events that have happened in her life. In the O. T. when a speaker is giving an important and inspired utterance, it is often done in a loud voice (Stein, *Luke* 90). "Blessed" is the key word in these two verses. In verse 42, Elizabeth uses this term to describe Mary. The idea is that God has bestowed special favor upon Mary's life and He is working in her life in a special way. She is to be the mother of the Messiah, and in ancient Israel, the greatness of a mother was often determined by the greatness of the child she bore (Stein, *Luke* 90).

Elizabeth's words to Mary reflect both humility and recognition. Elizabeth is much older than Mary and, in ancient Israel, the younger woman normally recognizes the older. Here the situation is reversed; the older woman honors the younger. Elizabeth understands that she is in the presence of a young woman of great faith and commitment. Mary's faith and commitment are not, however, the most important thing. She is honored because she is the mother of the coming Messiah; to honor Mary is to honor the child she carries.

The phrase "mother of my Lord," is an interesting one. The word "Lord" is a title of respect. In the N. T. it is used to describe God the Father, Jesus Christ, as well as important and powerful people. Many commentators see messianic implications in this use of the word "Lord." The phrase "mother of my Lord" implies that Mary's yet unborn child is both the Jewish Messiah and the Son of God.

Verses 44-45 mark the end of Elizabeth's words and prepare the reader to receive Mary's song of praise that begins in verse 46. As soon as Elizabeth receives word that Mary has arrived, she is filled with joy. The unborn child, John, leaps in her womb. The idea is that John, while still in his mother's womb, announces the arrival of the Messiah by leaping for joy.

Bonnet and Schroeder (482) note that Elizabeth can make such a profound expression of faith only because of the leadership of the Holy Spirit in her life and because of her understanding of the O. T. Scriptures. Childers (438) suggests that Elizabeth's words are directed to Mary and that they serve to encourage Mary's faith in God and in the fulfillment of His promises.

D. Mary's Song of Praise (1:46-56)

This passage is probably the most famous song of praise in the Bible; it is commonly called the Magnificat of Mary. A few later Greek manuscripts of the N. T. and some of the early church fathers attributed this hymn to Elizabeth, but all of the earliest and most reliable Greek manuscripts attribute it to Mary.

The term *Magnificat* comes from the Latin Vulgate, translating the word (Greek *megalunō*), which means "magnifies" (Bock I:148). This song of praise to God reflects a Hebrew poetic structure and uses several terms and concepts from the O. T. It is also similar in some ways to Hannah's song of praise found in 1 Samuel 2:1-10. Bonnet and Schroeder (482) note that the hymn can be easily divided into four stanzas and that it reflects a common type of Hebrew poetry known as "synonymous parallelism." In synonymous parallelism, the same ideas are repeated in different words for emphasis.

Fitzmyer (I:359) suggests that the hymn bears some resemblance to some of the hymns of praise found in the Psalms. It is even more similar, in his opinion, to several hymns of praise to God found in Jewish literature shortly before the time of Christ. He also suggests (I:360) that the hymn falls naturally into three divisions plus a conclusion. Verses 46b-47 serve as the introduction. The body of the hymn is divided into two parts, verses 48-50 and verses 51-53. Verses 54-55 form the conclusion.

46 And Mary said, My soul doth magnify the Lord,
47 And my spirit hath rejoiced in God my Saviour.
48 For he hath regarded the low estate of his handmaiden: for, behold, from henceforth all generations shall call me blessed.
49 For he that is mighty hath done to me great things; and holy *is* his name.
50 And his mercy *is* on them that fear him from generation to generation.
51 He hath shewed strength with his arm; he hath scattered the proud in the imagination of their hearts.
52 He hath put down the mighty from *their* seats, and exalted them of low degree.
53 He hath filled the hungry with good things; and the rich he hath sent empty away.
54 He hath holpen his servant Israel, in remembrance of *his* mercy;

55 As he spake to our fathers, to Abraham, and to his seed for ever.

This hymn does not focus on Mary's goodness or righteousness but on the greatness, power, and majesty of God. This song of praise views the power of God from two different perspectives. Verses 46-49 focus on what God has done for Mary in permitting her to be the mother of the Savior. Verses 50-55 praise God in a more general fashion. They recognize that God shows His mercy on those who fear Him, especially on the nation of Israel. God also brings down those who are mighty and exalts those who are humble.

"My soul" denotes the innermost part of a person's character. It is often used in the Greek versions of the O. T. to mean "I." The phrase "magnify the Lord" means "to glorify God." This implies that Mary recognizes God's greatness and glory; she glorifies God by recognizing His greatness and majesty.

In this context, "my spirit" (v. 47) is a synonym for "my soul" (v. 46). The idea is that Mary gives praise to God from the depths of her being. The last words of verse 47 describe God as "my Saviour." The word "Savior" literally means "deliverer" or "liberator." The idea is that God has liberated Mary from the dominion of sin and has permitted her to serve in His kingdom in a very special way.

Verses 48-49 develop this theme of salvation more completely. The verb "hath regarded" means that God has been mindful of Mary. The words "low estate" may be interpreted in various ways. Some see it as a reference to childlessness; a more likely interpretation is that Mary does not come from a family of wealth or influence. She is one of the common people of the land who are poor but genuinely committed to God (Stein, *Luke* 92; Childers 446).

The last part of verse 48 does not reflect an attitude of arrogance or self-righteousness. It is true that future generations will recognize Mary's importance as the earthly mother of the Savior, but she will be honored in a special way not because of what she has done but because of what God has done through her. There is nothing in the verse to indicate that Mary herself is worthy of worship or veneration.

The words "he that is mighty" is a clear reference to God, expressing the idea that He is omnipotent. He has demonstrated His great power and His desire to save His people through the miraculous conception of the Savior. Mary uses the common Hebrew term "holy" to describe God. God is holy in the sense that He always acts righteously and He is separate and apart from all sin.

Verses 50-55 form the second section of the Magnificat, which is a more general hymn of praise to God. The emphasis is less on what God has done in the life of Mary and more on the great things He has done for all His people. Three ideas dominate these verses, the power of God, His holiness, and His merciful character (Bonnet and Schroeder 482).

In the N. T., mercy is one of God's most important attributes; it refers to His love, kindness, and compassion. God always works in the best interests of His people. He does not give them what they deserve; He bestows His mercy on them in kind and gracious actions. Salvation is the Bible's best and most complete example of God's mercy. Just as God is merciful in His dealings with mankind, He also expects that His children will be merciful in their dealings with others. For a good description of mercy see the article by Towner (NDBT 660-663).

The phrase "them that fear him" refers to those who hold God in reverence and awe, those who show a proper respect for who God is and what He has done. "From generation to generation" implies that God demonstrates His gracious goodness to men and women of all generations.

Verses 51-52 describe the power of God. The basic idea is that God always demonstrates His righteous character in His dealings with mankind. In Hebrew thinking, "the arm of God" is a way of saying that God is powerful and able to do anything He wishes to do. The expression does not mean that God has a body with an arm; in the field of biblical studies, this is called "anthropomorphism," which is the practice of describing God using human terms and characteristics.

One way God demonstrates His righteous character is by humbling those who are proud and arrogant and exalting those who are humble. He also demonstrates His righteousness by helping those who are in need; He provides food to the needy and sends the rich away empty-handed. The word "rich" expresses a rather negative connotation in several places in the N. T. The rich are not condemned simply because they have money or property; the implication is that they have obtained their wealth by taking advantage of the poor. For a brief overview of poverty and wealth in the Bible see the article by Hans Kvalbein (NDBT 687-691).

Verses 54-55 speak specifically of God's help for Israel, His chosen people. Isaiah 41:8-9 and many other O. T. passages speak of the special relationship that exists between God and His chosen people. God remembers His covenant of mercy with His children, especially in their times of need. Verse 55 probably refers to the fact that God has always spoken His word to His people through His servants the prophets; He has never abandoned His people or left them without His message.

56 And Mary abode with her about three months, and returned to her own house.

Verse 56 is a transition verse designed to return the reader's attention to the birth of John the Baptist. According to Luke 1:36, Mary arrived in the sixth month of Elizabeth's pregnancy; she stayed for approximately three months and left shortly before Elizabeth gave birth. Commentators have speculated on why Mary chose to leave then (Bock I:161; Bonnet and Schroeder 484). The text itself gives no indication of why Mary left at this crucial time; it simply states that she left.

Summary (1:5-56)

These verses serve several purposes. They prepare the reader for the events surrounding the birth of Jesus that will be narrated in chapter 2. They also introduce several of the major characters who will play important roles in the life and ministry of Christ. This passage emphasizes their high level of commitment to doing the will of God. Zechariah, Elizabeth, and Mary, in particular, make major contributions to the story. These individuals reflect the humility and commitment necessary to be used by God in a special way; they all willingly accept God's will even though they may not always understand everything that is happening to them. Elizabeth has never lost her prayerful attitude and her devotion to God during the long years of childlessness.

These verses also introduce several themes that are the keys to understanding Luke's purpose; these themes will be developed throughout the Gospel. First and foremost, these verses emphasize the faithfulness of God, which is the major theme of this section and one of the most important themes in Luke's Gospel. All of these events take place in fulfillment of promises that God made to His people in the O. T. God is faithful and will do what He has promised to do. The announcement of the birth of John the Baptist indicates that God not only will send someone to save, He will also send the proper person to prepare the way for the Savior and introduce Him to the nation of Israel.

Another important theme is the purity of God's people. Zechariah, Elizabeth, and Mary all reflect lives that are pure in the sense that they are dedicated to doing the will of God. They are not perfect; they no doubt have their faults and failures. They are, however, committed to doing the will of God and being faithful in their service to Him. They reflect the humility necessary to accept God's will for their lives without bitterness or resentment; they continue being faithful in the face of hostility and rejection.

Application: Teaching and Preaching the Passage

These verses provide rich resources for preaching and teaching. This passage presents several of the actions and attributes of God; it would be an excellent text for a series of sermons and lessons on the greatness and majesty of God. First and foremost is the idea of God's faithfulness. These verses illustrate that God's people can always depend on Him; He will fulfill the promises He has made to them. He will, however, fulfill them in His own time and in His own way. God should never be underestimated; He is and has always been King of Kings and Lord of Lords.

This passage also illustrates the love God has for His people. These verses describe God's first steps in His plan to send a Savior to redeem a world lost in sin. In this passage, love is clearly the motivating factor behind what God does for His people.

These verses point out that God honors those who are poor and humble, provided they are sincere in their commitment to God. The characters in this story all come from the lower classes in Israelite society, but their relatively low status on the social and economic scale does not prevent them from playing an important role in God's plan.

This passage not only addresses the attributes and character of God, it also explains some of the ways the children of God can worship Him. The songs of praise presented by Elizabeth, Zechariah, and Mary serve as examples of how the people of God should rejoice at the privilege of worshiping and serving Him.

Discipleship is another important theme developed in this passage. Zechariah, Elizabeth, and Mary walk with the Lord in the midst of difficult times and trying circumstances. They do not always understand what God is doing, but they continue following the Lord. These three important characters also demonstrate a willingness to be a part of God's work of redemption. They are not content to simply sit on the sidelines and observe; they are quick to participate in what God is doing.

Several verses in this passage would serve well as texts for a series of sermons or lessons on what it means to be a child of God. This passage teaches that purity and a willingness to serve are more important than wealth, position, or natural talent. God can and will use those who are willing to be used.

E. Birth of John the Baptist (1:57-66)

These verses constitute a separate unit of material that will contribute to several important Lucan themes, such as God's miraculous intervention to assist His people. This passage also helps to set the stage for the birth of Christ, which will be presented in chapter two. Both birth accounts will follow a similar pattern. First, the child is born. Then he is circumcised and named (Bock I:163). The hand of God is clearly at work in every step of the process.

57 Now Elisabeth's full time came that she should be delivered; and she brought forth a son.
58 And her neighbours and her cousins heard how the Lord had shewed great mercy upon her; and they rejoiced with her.

Luke describes the birth of John the Baptist in brief and concise terms. The first part of the verse could literally be translated "for Elizabeth the time to give birth was full." That is a Hebrew way of saying that the time had come for the child to be born. Just as the angel had predicted, she gave birth to a son.

Verse 58 describes the joyous reaction to the news of the baby's birth. Luke employs two terms to describe the joy that those around Elizabeth experience. "Neighbors" (Greek *perioikoi*) describes those who live nearby. "Cousins" (Greek *suggenēs*) is a general term that describes one's relatives or fellow countrymen. Elizabeth's neighbors and relatives rejoice with her.

They join in the rejoicing because God has bestowed His blessing on Elizabeth in a special way. He has taken away the stigma of childlessness and has fulfilled His word in her life, although she is beyond the normal child-bearing years. The birth of John the Baptist is a singular demonstration of God's mercy. The mercy of God is a common theme in Luke's Gospel. It means that God is favorably disposed toward one, and He actively intervenes to show His love.

59 And it came to pass, that on the eighth day they came to circumcise the child; and they called him Zacharias, after the name of his father.
60 And his mother answered and said, Not *so*; but he shall be called John.
61 And they said unto her, There is none of thy kindred that is called by this name.
62 And they made signs to his father, how he would have him called.
63 And he asked for a writing table, and wrote, saying, His name is John. And they marvelled all.

These verses relate the story of the circumcision, naming, and presentation of the baby John. The O. T. required that all male children be circumcised (Gen. 17:11-12; Jos. 5:2-9). This was normally done on the eighth day after birth even if that day was the Sabbath (Fitzmyer I:380). In first-century Judaism, circumcision was so important that the command to circumcise outweighed the command to observe the Sabbath. In the Jewish tradition, circumcision served several purposes. It incorporated the child into the family of Israel and assured that he would share in the blessing God would bestow on His people in the future. It also included the obligation to obey the law when the child came of age (Fitzmyer I:376). Luke does not explain where the circumcision took place; the Temple in Jerusalem is the likely location.

Circumcision was a festive occasion; friends and relatives were invited to share in the service. One important part of the service was the official naming of the child. Since it was customary in that culture to name a first-born son after his father or grandfather, those in charge assumed the child would be named Zechariah. Elizabeth suddenly spoke up and said that he was to be named John. This decision seemed strange to those in charge, and they appealed to the father who had the final authority in naming the child (R. Brown, *Birth* 369).

Verse 62 points out that the leaders made signs to Zechariah to indicate what was going on. The reader is not told what kind of signs these were (probably hand signals) or how they would have communicated the information to Zechariah. Luke 1:22 says that Zechariah was unable to speak at this time. This verse indicates either that he could not hear or that the Jewish leaders thought he could not hear.

However the information was communicated, Zechariah understood what was going on and asked for a writing tablet so he could make his wishes known in written form. He wrote that his son was to be named John. The writing tablet was probably a small flat piece of wood covered with wax (Summers, *Luke* 34; Stein, *Luke* 97).

Verse 63 closes by noting that those present (probably the friends and family) marvel. We are not told why they marvel; the most likely reason is that they are surprised because the parents did not name their first-born son after his father. It is doubtful that those present fully understand the significance of this event. For Zechariah and Elizabeth, the naming of their son John is clearly the fulfillment of the Lord's command spoken in Luke 1:13. They understand the will of God and seek to obey it.

64 And his mouth was opened immediately, and his tongue *loosed*, and he spake, and praised God.
65 And fear came on all that dwelt round about them: and all these sayings were noised abroad throughout all the hill country of Judaea.
66 And all they that heard *them* laid *them* up in their hearts, saying, What manner of child shall this be! And the hand of the Lord was with him.

The miraculous events surrounding the circumcision and naming of the infant John provoke a song of praise from his father, Zechariah. This hymn of praise is commonly known as the *Benedictus*, a title derived from the first word of the Latin translation of the hymn. The term *Benedictus* means "blessed."

The hymn naturally falls into two divisions. Verses 67-75 are a general hymn of praise to God, which celebrates the coming of the Messiah. Verses 76-79 focus more specifically on the role that John the Baptist was to play in the coming of the Messiah. Verse 80 is a transition verse that draws the discussion of John the Baptist to a close and prepares the reader to return to the story of Jesus.

F. Zechariah's Song of Praise (1:67-79)

67 And his father Zecharias was filled with the Holy Ghost, and prophesied, saying,
68 Blessed *be* the Lord God of Israel; for he hath visited and redeemed his people,
69 And hath raised up an horn of salvation for us in the house of his servant David;
70 As he spake by the mouth of his holy prophets, which have been since the world began:
71 That we should be saved from our enemies, and from the hand of all that hate us;
72 To perform the mercy *promised* to our fathers, and to remember his holy covenant;
73 The oath which he sware to our father Abraham,
74 That he would grant unto us, that we being delivered out of the hand of our enemies might serve him without fear,
75 In holiness and righteousness before him, all the days of our life.

The Holy Spirit, who has filled both Mary and Elizabeth earlier in the story, now moves in the heart of Zechariah. The role of the Holy Spirit in the life and ministry of Christ is a major theme of Luke's Gospel; the author is concerned to show that Jesus is the Messiah and that every aspect of His life and ministry happens under the direction and control of the Holy Spirit. In these verses, Zechariah praises God both for sending the Messiah and for bringing to pass a series of O. T. events that prepare the way for the coming Messiah.

The fact that Zechariah's utterance is given under the specific direction of the Holy Spirit adds a sense of urgency and importance to what is being spoken. Spence (11) notes that this hymn occupies a prominent place in Christian worship. It is likely that it was first used in public worship as early as the sixth century.

In the original Greek, verses 68-75 form one long flowing sentence that emphasizes who God is and what He has done for His people. These verses are a general summary of how God has delivered Israel in the past. They are designed to prepare the reader for the specific deliverance that God will accomplish in the birth of the Messiah.

According to this passage, God is worthy of worship for several reasons. First, He has visited His people. He has come to them in their hour of need; He has not left them to shift for themselves.

Second, God has redeemed His people and raised up a horn of salvation for them. Throughout its history, God has delivered Israel from many different dangers. In the future, He will deliver them in a much greater and more dynamic way through the birth of the Messiah. The "horn of salvation" is an idiomatic expression drawn from the fact that an animal's strength is found in its horn. The idea is that God has demonstrated His great power in the past as He has delivered His people in times of danger. Stein (*Luke* 99) suggests that the "horn of salvation" in this verse refers not to John the Baptist, but to the Messiah for whom John is preparing the way.

Third, God has spoken to His people repeatedly through the O. T. prophets. Once again, God has not left His people alone; He has communicated His will to them and strengthened them through His word.

Fourth, God has delivered His people from their enemies. For most of its history, Israel was a small and relatively weak nation in the midst of larger and more powerful countries. It is only by the power of God that she was able to survive.

Fifth, God has kept His covenant with His people. A covenant is a pact or agreement, similar in some ways to a modern contract. God has entered into a special relationship with the nation of Israel. He has never forgotten them and has bestowed His mercy upon them even when they didn't deserve it. God has always been faithful to the covenant He made centuries ago with Abraham.

Verses 74-75 outline the key element of this covenant, the idea that God will deliver them from the hand of their enemies and bring them into a land where they could serve Him in holiness and truth.

76 And thou, child, shalt be called the prophet of the Highest: for thou shalt go before the face of the Lord to prepare his ways;

77 To give knowledge of salvation unto his people by the remission of their sins,
78 Through the tender mercy of our God; whereby the dayspring from on high hath visited us,
79 To give light to them that sit in darkness and *in* the shadow of death, to guide our feet into the way of peace.

These verses contain several terms and concepts drawn from the O. T. They continue the theme of God's faithfulness to His people, which was developed in the previous section, but they also move the discussion in a different direction. They focus specifically on how John will contribute to God's plan to bring His Messiah to the earth.

John will contribute in two important ways. First, he will serve as a prophet; he will communicate God's message to His people. In this context, the idea is that he will help the people of God to know that Jesus is the Messiah and assist them in understanding His ministry. Second, he will serve as the forerunner. He will go before the Messiah with a message of repentance in order to prepare the people to receive the larger, more comprehensive message Jesus will proclaim.

Verse 77 is theologically important. In the first century, many Jews looked for a political Messiah. They looked forward to the day when God would send them a great military leader who would free them from Roman domination and restore them to independence and greatness. John will help to correct this misguided interpretation. He will show the people that the focus of the Messiah's ministry will be on the forgiveness of sins and not on winning military victories. This passage is in some ways similar to Gabriel's announcement to Zechariah. It may also be an allusion to Malachi 4:5-6.

The Messiah will bring the light of God's mercy and grace to the people who sit in the darkness of sin—perhaps an allusion to Isaiah 9:2. He will liberate them from the tyranny of death and guide them not in the paths of war but in the ways of peace. In other words, John will help the people understand and appreciate the kind of Messiah that Jesus will be. The priority of His mission will be the forgiveness of sins and not the end of Roman rule in Palestine.

G. John's Growth and Development (1:80)

80 And the child grew, and waxed strong in spirit, and was in the deserts till the day of his shewing unto Israel.

Verse 80 is a transition verse that briefly summarizes John's childhood and prepares the reader for the next element in the story, the birth of Jesus. Luke's emphasis is that John went through a process of growth and development in preparation for his role as the forerunner of the Messiah. The desert or wilderness is the sparsely-populated area south of Jerusalem, which receives very little rainfall; the idea seems to be that John spent his formative years away from the corrupting influences of the city. It was there God prepared him for the important ministry that would later be his.

During this time John developed physically, mentally, and emotionally. A similar statement is made about Jesus' childhood in Luke 2:52. Some authorities have tried to connect John the Baptist with the Essenes who were a radical Jewish group that considered the Temple establishment in Jerusalem to be corrupt. They lived in isolated communities in the wilderness and followed strict codes of conduct. One such group, the Qumran community, lived near the Dead Sea and left some very important documents that have come to be known as the Dead Sea Scrolls.

While there are certain similarities between John and the Essenes, there are also significant differences. It is certainly possible that John was influenced by Essene thought, but there is not sufficient evidence to conclude that he was actually a member of this movement. For discussions of the relationship between John and the Essenes see Stein (*Luke* 102), Fitzmyer (I:389), and Bock (I:198).

Summary (1:57-80)

These verses describe the events surrounding the birth of John the Baptist, the forerunner of Jesus. Throughout the passage, however, the emphasis is not on John but on the One whom he will serve. The child is given the name "John" rather than following the tradition of naming a son after his father or grandfather. This is done in response to the Lord's instructions given in Luke 1:13. The result that his naming produced is also surprising. Normally, the naming of a child would attract little attention outside the immediate family, but the naming of this child stirs up a great deal of interest in the entire area. The people recognize that the hand of God is at work, but they don't understand what it all means.

The most beautiful part of this passage is the prophecy of Zechariah. The term "prophecy" is used in several ways in the Scriptures. It may refer to a prediction of some future event, a message from God proclaimed, or to a song of praise and adoration. The prophecy of Zechariah reflects something of all three elements. Zechariah is filled with the Holy Spirit; he recognizes that God will raise up a "horn of salvation" for the people. He also recognizes that his son, John, will have the honor of preparing the way for the Messiah. The ultimate goal of this entire process, according to verse 74, is that the people would serve the Lord without fear.

The last verse of the passage calls attention to the fact that John would grow up in the deserts of the land of Israel away from the corrupting influences of the city. It is important that the purity of his life and commitment to the Lord be maintained.

Application: Teaching and Preaching the Passage

The primary lesson that can be learned from the passage is the importance of being obedient to the call of God. The parents seek to follow closely the instructions that have been given to them by the angel. They name the child *John*. They also have him circumcised as provided in the O. T. The parents consistently reflect the kind of humility and respect for God that make true obedience possible.

Spiritual sensitivity is another important theme for preaching and teaching. Both Elizabeth and Zechariah are sensitive to the leadership and direction of the Lord in all of the events surrounding the birth of their son. In his prophecy, Zechariah reflects great spiritual sensitivity. He seems to understand what the Lord is doing and how his son, John, will be able to share in it. Spiritual sensitivity and obedience go together. It is important that believers be sensitive to the leadership of the Lord, but they must also be willing to follow that leadership.

Verse 74 establishes a very important principle. For Zechariah, the primary goal is that God's people might serve Him without fear. He does not desire fame, or power, or personal advancement. He simply wants to serve the Lord in holiness and righteousness; for the people of God that should be enough.

A spirit of thankfulness pervades this entire section. Both Elizabeth and Zechariah realize they are highly privileged, and they always express their thanks to God for all that He has done for them and for permitting them to be the parents of John.

H. Birth of Jesus (2:1-20)

Matthew and Luke are the only Gospels that describe Jesus' birth, and their accounts present that important event from somewhat different perspectives. Matthew tells the story from the viewpoint of Joseph, while Luke interprets the events from the perspective of Mary. Witherington (DJG 61-66) presents an insightful comparison of these two passages and the themes that each develops.

Luke was not an eyewitness to the birth of Christ; he wrote this account several years later primarily for the benefit of Gentile readers. Although he was not an eyewitness, Luke carefully investigated what happened and used reliable sources. It is possible that Mary herself served as a source for much of the information found in this passage (Bock I:199-200; Marshall, *Gospel* 97).

The story of Jesus' birth emphasizes that Jesus was not born in a rich and powerful family but into a humble family that was committed to serving God. This passage emphasizes both the divine origin of Christ and His universal mission. The birth of Christ is no ordinary birth. God has taken the initiative to send His Son to the world as the Messiah; the birth of Jesus is good news "to all people."

The adoration of the angels shows that this child is the Son of God, deserving of all glory and honor. The visit of the shepherds shows that Christ intends to bring the message of salvation to people at all levels of society.

In recent Lucan studies, there has been a tendency to interpret the story of Christ's birth as a separate unit of material that bears little relationship to the doctrinal development of the Gospel (R. Brown, *Birth* 239-243). More traditional scholars see the birth and infancy narrative as an integral part of the Gospel that serves to introduce many of the theological themes (such as the idea that salvation is for all the world) that Luke will later develop. For an insightful analysis (by a rather liberal scholar) of how this chapter contributes to the overall message of Luke, see the article by Minear.

2:1 And it came to pass in those days, that there went out a decree from Caesar Augustus, that all the world should be taxed.
2 (*And* this taxing was first made when Cyrenius was governor of Syria)

These two verses place the birth of Jesus in its historical context; they illustrate how God makes use of political and historical forces to accomplish His will. They also present one of the most perplexing problems in the interpretation of this Gospel, the dating of the census mentioned in verse 2.

The words "in those days" connect this chapter with the birth of John the Baptist in the previous chapter. Luke sees John the Baptist as the forerunner of Jesus; he connects the birth of Jesus with that of John the Baptist in order to show that God is working among His people through a series of related events.

"Caesar Augustus" is a title rather than a proper name (Childers 444). The reference is to the Roman Emperor Octavian, the great-nephew of Julius Caesar. After eliminating several rivals to become sole ruler in 31 B.C., he ruled the empire with considerable peace, stability, and prosperity until his death in A.D. 14. He was followed on the imperial throne by his designated successor, his stepson Tiberius. According to Luke 3:1, Jesus began His public ministry in the fifteenth year of Tiberius (about A.D. 29 or 30). Luke clearly intends to show that God has used the secular power of Rome to accomplish His will; not even the most powerful empire in the world is outside His power and control.

"All the world" literally means "all the inhabited earth." In the first century, this term was normally used to describe the Roman Empire (Summers, *Luke* 36; Childers 444). The words "should be taxed" may also be translated "should be registered" or "should be enrolled" (Green, *Luke* 124; Stein, *Luke* 104-105; Liefeld 843). This passage describes the taking of a census in preparation for future taxation rather than to the actual taxation itself. Census taking was often done over a period of several years in different parts of the Empire. Those who were not Roman citizens would be included in a census for two reasons. The first was for the collection of taxes; the second was for military service. Since Jews were exempt from Roman military service, a census in Palestine would be for purposes of taxation. R. Brown (*Birth* 547-555) gives a good summary of Roman census and taxing procedures.

Luke 2:1-2 helps to determine the year when Jesus was born. They speak of Jesus' birth as taking place during a census taken under the leadership of Cyrenius, preferably spelled "Quirinius." Publius Sulpicius Quirinius was an important Roman official in this time period. He was a capable soldier and administrator who became a proconsul in 12 B.C. and led the Roman armies to victory over the Homonodensians in south Galatia. He served as governor of Syria-Palestine from A.D. 6-9 and then returned to Rome where he died in A.D. 21. William Ramsay (*Bethlehem* 227-248; *Trustworthiness* 275-295) summarizes what is known about his life and career.

In the first century, Syria and Palestine were considered one province for administrative purposes. Historical evidence from Roman sources indicates that Quirinius served as governor of Syria-Palestine between A.D. 6 and 9; it is quite possible that he took a census while serving in that position. Acts 5:37 briefly mentions a census that apparently provoked considerable conflict in Palestine; that census could have been taken during the governorship of Quirinius.

There is, however, strong biblical evidence that Jesus was born several years before Quirinius served officially as governor of Syria-Palestine. According to Matthew 2:1-11, Jesus was born while Herod the Great ruled Palestine. Luke 1:5 places both the birth of John the Baptist and the birth of Jesus within the context of Herod's reign. While the date of Herod's death cannot be determined with absolute certainty, the preferred view is that he died in March or April of 4 B.C. (R. Brown, *Birth* 166). Larson (*Star)*, however, dates the death of Herod in 1 B.C. If this is the correct interpretation of these passages in Matthew and Luke, Jesus was born not later than 4 or 5 B.C. (perhaps as early as 6 B.C.). Luke 3:23 speaks of Jesus as being about 30 years of age during the fifteenth year of Tiberius. All of these passages indicate that Jesus was born before Quirinius served as the official governor of that area.

How, then, is Luke 2:2 to be interpreted in light of these other passages? Has Luke confused the census of Acts 5:37 with a census taken several years earlier? Has he dated incorrectly the time when Quirinius served as governor? Various answers to these questions have been suggested.

Critics of the Gospel of Luke assert that the author, writing a number of years after Christ's birth, was simply mistaken. They argue that Luke either depended on incorrect sources or that he wrongly interpreted his sources. If this view is correct, Luke wrongly dated the birth of Christ during the governorship of Quirinius. This is the position taken by Emil Schürer.

Schürer (407-422) finds several errors in Luke's description of the birth of Christ. He posits that there is no historical evidence for any empire-wide census during this time. He cites as evidence the Roman historian Josephus who knew nothing of any Roman census during the time of Herod. Another error, in his opinion, is Mary's participation in the journey to Bethlehem. Under Roman census-taking procedures, Joseph could have registered for the entire family.

His final argument is that a census under the administration of Quirinius could not have taken place in Herod's lifetime because Quirinius never served as governor while Herod was alive. In conclusion, Schürer (426) writes, "There is in fact no alternative but to recognize that the evangelist based his statement on uncertain historical information." He also argues (427) that Luke committed other historical errors in his writings.

Stauffer (21) presents a brief summary of the arguments that are often made against the historicity of this passage. Creed (28) suggests that Luke chapter 1 is probably correct, but chapter 2 dates the census under Quirinius some ten or eleven years before it actually took place.

R. Brown (*Birth* 554) also posits that Luke's dating of the birth of Christ is in error. His arguments are similar to those presented by Schürer. He concludes that Luke chapter one dates the birth of Christ during the reign of Herod, but chapter two dates the birth after Herod's death.

Conservative scholars have challenged these arguments in different ways. One of the first to deal with the issue in a comprehensive way was Ramsay who carefully examined the available information about how censuses were taken in the Roman provinces, and in Palestine in particular.

Ramsay analyzes the Greek terms used in Luke 2:2 in light of their use by Luke and other writers of the Hellenistic era. He notes (*Bethlehem* 229) that the term translated "governor" might be applied to any Roman official holding an important position in the province of Syria-Palestine. He suggests (*Bethlehem* 236, 244) that Quirinius occupied positions of leadership in Syria-Palestine on at least two different occasions. The first of these took place not later than 5-3 B.C. when Quirinius was administering Syria's external affairs.

Ramsay (*Bethlehem* 244, *Trustworthiness* 238-254) concludes that the first census mentioned in Luke 2:2 occurred during this period of the life and career of Quirinius. This census was made in Palestine during the late summer or fall of 6 B.C., while Quirinius was commanding the armies and directing the foreign affairs. It was in this capacity that Quirinius directed the taking of the census; several years later he would return as governor of the province and order the census mentioned in Acts 5:37.

Witherington examined many of the same issues and came to similar conclusions.

He points out (DJG 67-68) that the Greek text of Luke 2:2 can be interpreted in different ways. For example, the word translated "first" (Greek *prōtos*) may also be translated "former," "prior to," or "before." Luke may be saying that Jesus was born during a census that was earlier than the more famous census undertaken during the governorship of Quirinius. Arndt and Gingrich (732-734) analyze the various uses of this term in the N. T. It may indicate an earlier time, but it may also express the idea of "most important" or "most prominent." After a careful analysis of the available evidence, Witherington concludes that the attacks against Luke's credibility as a historian are unfounded. He argues that Luke's account of the census does not suggest a date for Jesus' birth different from that intended by Matthew.

Other scholars such as Hoehner (DJG 118), Stauffer (22), Ellis (80-81), and Summers (*Luke* 136) have taken similar positions. Lenski (117-118) carefully analyzes the usage of the various Greek terms in the passage. He also critically examines statements made by Josephus and by early Christian writers such as Tertullian. After his examination, he arrives at conclusions very similar to those of Witherington and Summers.

Marshall (*Historian* 69) concludes there are some problems involved in reconstructing the precise order of events but that Luke is a very reliable ancient historian. For that reason, his testimony should not be quickly discounted.

Several points should be considered before reaching any conclusion concerning the relationship between Luke 2:2 and the other passages that deal with the time of Christ's birth. Luke's account is a brief one; he is not trying to fill in all the details. His primary interest is not chronology; he is more concerned with what happened than when it happened. It should also be noted that our knowledge of census-taking procedures in the Roman Empire of the first century is incomplete (Green, *Luke* 126).

While the precise date of Jesus' birth cannot be determined with certainty, the evidence given by Matthew and Luke points toward a date around 6 B.C. Both Summers (*Luke* 36) and Ramsay (*Bethlehem* 198) argue that 6 B.C. is the most likely possibility. Hoehner (DJG 118) suggests that Jesus was born in December of 5 B.C. or January of 4 B.C.

It is quite possible that two censuses would have been taken, the first about 6 B.C. while Quirinius was serving as a high-ranking official in Syria-Palestine. That is the one mentioned in Luke 2:2. The second census, then, would have been taken about A.D. 6-9 while Quirinius was serving as governor. That is likely the census mentioned in Acts 5:37.

In conclusion, there is not sufficient evidence to conclude that Luke 2:2 presents a date for the birth of Christ that is different from what is presented in other N. T. passages. Luke often demonstrates himself to be a reliable ancient historian, and he should be so regarded here. Marshall (*Historian* 69) concludes that readers should not be quick to conclude that Luke is in error, but he recognizes that only the discovery of additional historical evidence will fully solve this problem.

3 And all went to be taxed, every one into his own city.

4 And Joseph also went up from Galilee, out of the city of Nazareth, into Judaea, unto the city of David, which is called Bethlehem; (because he was of the house and lineage of David.)

5 To be taxed with Mary his espoused wife, being great with child.

6 And so it was, that, while they were there, the days were accom-

plished that she should be delivered.
7 And she brought forth her firstborn son, and wrapped him in swaddling clothes, and laid him in a manger; because there was no room for them in the inn.

Verses 3-5 describe Joseph and Mary as traveling from their home in Nazareth of Galilee to Bethlehem. Jews would normally bypass Samaria while traveling from Galilee to Judaea, thus making a trip of about ninety miles; such a journey normally took three days (Bock, *Luke* IVP 54). The text does not indicate how they traveled, but it is most likely that they walked or rode donkeys; some of the road was rather mountainous and difficult to travel. Luke does not mention any other travelers, but people generally traveled in groups because traveling alone in the ancient world was dangerous.

Mary was pregnant with the baby Jesus during the trip and gave birth after their arrival. The text does not say that she gave birth immediately upon their arrival; it says only that she had the child while they were in Bethlehem.

These verses raise several important issues. The first concerns the need to travel to Bethlehem for the census. Romans and provincials normally registered for a census where they lived, not in their ancestral homes (Marshall, *Gospel* 101). Deissmann (271), however, cites one example of a census document from Egypt that requires people to return to their original homes to register. He also notes that the practices of the Roman government in Egypt are often similar to practices found in Palestine. Blaiklock (25) quotes from the first paragraph of this document. It reads, "Gaius Vibius, chief prefect of Egypt. Because of the approaching census it is necessary for all those residing for any cause away from their own districts to prepare to return at once to their own governments, in order that they may complete the family administration of the enrollment."

Ramsay (*Bethlehem* 133) notes that Roman officials often made concessions to allow conquered peoples to maintain their traditions. Since the Jewish custom was to return to one's ancestral home to register, it is reasonable to assume that the Roman authorities permitted the Jewish leaders in Palestine to determine the details of the administration of the census (Bock, *Luke* IVP 54; Childers 444). Bethlehem was not Joseph's home; Luke 1:39 speaks of Nazareth as the family home; Joseph had probably never lived in Bethlehem. Although it is possible he owned property there, there is nothing in the narrative to indicate that he did (Marshall, *Gospel* 101). He was, however, a descendant of David, and for that reason, Bethlehem can be considered his ancestral home. According to the Jewish custom, it was the logical place for him to register.

The traditional view is that Mary did not have to go to fulfill the Roman legal requirements because Joseph could have registered for the entire family (Childers 445). Marshall (*Gospel* 102) suggests a different explanation; he notes that women in Syria had to pay a poll tax. It is possible that she went along for this reason. Edersheim (*Life* I:183) offers another possible explanation; he suggests that Mary went because they planned to leave Nazareth and establish a new home in Bethlehem. It is also possible that Mary went with Joseph because she could not safely remain alone in the small village of Nazareth.

The most important reason for Mary's presence was not legal but theological. She made the long, arduous journey so her son, the Messiah, would be born in Bethlehem. Both Mary and Joseph would have been well aware that the O. T. speaks of Bethlehem as the place where the Messiah will be born (Mt. 2:5-6). They made the journey under the leadership of the Holy Spirit (Childers 445).

The words "his espoused wife" translate one Greek word that means "betrothed" or "promised to marry" (Bock I:205). This word has provoked considerable discussion because it was unlikely in the culture of ancient Palestine that an unmarried couple would travel together. Bock offers a likely and culturally sensitive explanation. He suggests that a marriage ceremony may have taken place before they left Nazareth, but that the marriage had not been consummated. Luke has chosen his words carefully to emphasize that Mary was still a virgin at the time Jesus was born. Stein (*Luke* 107) suggests a similar interpretation.

"Great with child" simply means "pregnant." The word itself gives no indication how late in the pregnancy the trip to Bethlehem occurred. Summers (*Luke* 37) writes that later verses in the passage indicate the trip occurred near the end of her pregnancy.

While Joseph and Mary were staying in Bethlehem, Jesus was born. No doubt the birth was a difficult time for this couple in many ways. They were away from home. It was Mary's first child, and she did not have the help of her mother and other female relatives who would normally assist in a birth. While Luke emphasizes that the birth took place in humble circumstances, he presents the story of the birth in a factual manner with little attention to how it must have impacted Joseph and Mary.

The term "firstborn" (v. 7) has provoked some discussion among scholars. Most scholars conclude that it does not mean "only" (Stein, *Luke* 107). In their view, the term allows for the birth of other children later, but it does not demand that other children be born. It is likely that Luke chose this word rather than "only" because he knew other children would be born later (Lk. 8:19-21).

Spence (38) suggests a different interpretation. He argues that this term does not allow for the birth of other children at a later time. In his view, Jesus' brothers and sisters are either cousins or Joseph's children from a former marriage. There was much debate on this issue in the early church, beginning about the fourth century; for a good summary of this discussion see Lightfoot (252-291). Modern Protestants generally view the brothers and sisters mentioned in the N. T. as the natural children of Joseph and Mary. Roman Catholics, on the other hand, argue for the perpetual virginity of Mary.

Luke gives no indication of the time of year when Jesus was born (Marshall, *Luke* NBC-1970 893). Beginning in the fourth century, the churches of the Roman Empire began to celebrate Christmas. While there was some dispute on the appropriate time to celebrate Jesus' birth, many of them began to celebrate it on December 25. We are not totally sure why (Geldenhuys 102) they chose this date. Edersheim (*Life* I:187) defends the traditional date, but there is no hard evidence to indicate that

Jesus was actually born on December 25.

Verse 7 also explains that Mary laid the baby Jesus in a manger because there was no room in the inn (Greek *kataluma*). The Septuagint uses this word for a public shelter where a group of people might gather for the night (Bock I:208). Luke uses the same word in 22:11 of his Gospel to describe the guest room in a private house. R. Brown (*Birth* 400) notes that three interpretations of the word are commonly suggested: (1) a private house; (2) a room in a private house or other unspecified location; (3) a public inn such as the well-known traveler's inn near Bethlehem.

Bonnet and Schroeder (492) regard the word as a general term, rather like the words *posada* in Spanish or *lodging* in English. Plummer (54) explains that the word is used in the Septuagint to translate no less than five Hebrew words and can be used in several different ways. Ellis (81) notes that when the animals were out in the pasture, an innkeeper would often improvise lodging places for poor people in the area normally occupied by the animals. He also points out that in the early Christian tradition the place of Jesus' birth is described as a cave or a courtyard. Barclay (21) notes that eastern inns often consisted of a series of stalls around an open courtyard; he suggests that the birth took place in this open courtyard.

Summers (*Luke* 37-38) writes that the birth took place in a rude shelter used by caravans. Such a shelter would have included a small inn surrounded by open areas for the animals. Whatever the precise location might have been, it is clear that Mary gave birth to the Savior in humble circumstances, though not necessarily circumstances of abject poverty.

There is an early Christian tradition going back to the time of Justin and Origen that connects the birth of Jesus with a cave near Bethlehem (Bonnet and Schroeder 492; Stauffer 21). The mother of Constantine later ordered that a church be built on that site (Bonnet and Schroeder 492); the present Church of the Nativity currently rests on that traditional site (Bock I:208). This tradition is quite early and widespread; it probably reflects a common belief of many early Christians.

The Gospel of Luke does not say specifically where in Bethlehem Jesus was born. One possibility is that Mary gave birth in the home of a friend or relative, perhaps in the area where the animals were normally kept. The guest quarters of the house ("upper room" in 22:12) would have been limited and were already filled with people who had come to register for the census. If the birth occurred in an area normally used for keeping livestock, the animals might have been taken to another location so Mary could have a little space and privacy. Luke makes no mention of animals actually being present where Jesus was born.

"Manger" is commonly used for a stall where animals are kept or a trough in which animals are fed (Ellis 81; Summers, *Luke* 38). Creed (34) explains that while the term may be used to describe a stall, the most likely interpretation is that it describes a moveable feeding pan or trough that was placed on the ground. The use of this term may suggest that Jesus was born in a stable, but it is by no means absolute proof. In ancient Palestine, animals were often kept inside the family home (usually in a separate part of the house) or in an enclosure beside the family home.

"Swaddling clothes" refers to the practice of wrapping a baby in strips of cloth to keep the limbs straight (Stein, *Luke* 107). Barclay (21) gives a description of swaddling clothes which seem to have been the normal method of dressing a newborn infant at that time.

8 And there were in the same country shepherds abiding in the field, keeping watch over their flock by night.
9 And, lo, the angel of the Lord came upon them, and the glory of the Lord shone round about them: and they were sore afraid.
10 And the angel said unto them, Fear not: for, behold, I bring you good tidings of great joy, which shall be to all people.
11 For unto you is born this day in the city of David a Saviour, which is Christ the Lord.
12 And this *shall be* a sign unto you; Ye shall find the babe wrapped in swaddling clothes, lying in a manger.

These verses provide one of the most beautiful and familiar parts of the Christmas story. Countless children and adults have portrayed the shepherds coming to Bethlehem in plays and dramas presented in local churches. Luke has a definite purpose for including the shepherds in the story; his goal is to show God's desire to communicate the message of the birth of Christ to men and women at all levels of society. It is also important that "an angel of the Lord" came and spoke to the shepherds. God was not silent; He was actively involved in communicating the message of the birth of Christ.

Sheep-raising was widespread in ancient Palestine; it served as an important part of the economy. Madeliene and Lane Miller (121-188) give a good summary of the daily life of both shepherds and farmers in first-century Palestine. Stewart (1174) presents a good summary of the term *sheep* and summarizes the various ways in which the term is used in Scripture. Johnson (DJG 751-754) provides a comprehensive analysis of both the O. T. background and the N. T. usage of "sheep" and "shepherd."

In the mild climate of the Near East, sheep would often be left out in open pastures at night; Bonnet and Schroeder (492) point out that this custom persists even today. Childers (447) explains that there are several theories concerning when the sheep would be left at night in an open field. One possibility is they were kept outside from the spring until early October; another possibility is they were kept outside at any time of year when the weather permitted.

Edersheim (*Life* I:186-187) suggests, based on the Jewish Mishnah, that the sheep mentioned in this passage were not ordinary sheep but were special flocks from which the animals sacrificed in the Temple were taken; these sheep were kept out in the pasture during the entire year.

Since the sheep had to be protected from wild animals at all times, the shepherds stayed in tents near where the sheep were grazing and took turns guarding them during the nighttime hours. The word translated "country" carries the connotation of "open country" or land that is not under cultivation but is used for grazing (R. Brown, *Birth*

401). Luke does not say exactly where these shepherds were grazing their flocks or how far away they were from Bethlehem. The traditional site of the "Shepherd's Fields" is about two miles from the city (R. Brown, *Birth* 401). It is possible that many of the sheep grazing near Bethlehem were destined for use in the temple in Jerusalem, but that is not certain (Bock I:213).

Later Jewish writings portray shepherds in a rather negative fashion; they are considered untrustworthy and outcasts from society who do not observe the Jewish laws (see Bock I:213-214; Liefeld 845). Stein (*Luke* 108), like Liefield, assume that such descriptions fit the shepherds of Bethlehem and notes that shepherds were generally regarded as dishonest and unclean; in this passage they seem to represent just the type of sinners that Jesus came to save.

All commentators do not, however, accept such a negative description of the shepherds of Bethlehem. They point out that such negative statements come from Jewish writings of the fifth century A.D., and it is difficult to determine if such negative conceptions should be applied to the first century. Bock (I:213) writes that the N. T. writers tend to view shepherds in favorable terms.

Beyreuther (NIDNTT 564-567) notes that after the Babylonian Exile shepherds came to enjoy a reputation as thieves; they were regarded as outcasts and were much despised. He also notes that such negative attitudes do not extend to the N. T. The shepherds described in the N. T. are portrayed favorably; they are hard-working and protect their flocks.

There is nothing in this passage to indicate that Luke has a negative impression of shepherds; they are no better and no worse than other members of society. They are, however, part of the common people of the land in that they have neither wealth nor political power nor social position. It is no accident that the good news of Jesus' birth came first to a group of poor, hard-working shepherds.

A single angel appears in verse 9; a multitude of angels arrive in verse 13. The shepherds understand immediately that God is at work in this situation in a very special way. At first, the shepherds are filled with fear because they have never seen or heard anything like this. Later, they come to understand that the message God has for them is one of goodness and grace. After receiving the good news that the Messiah has been born in the nearby village of Bethlehem, they go with haste and anticipation to see the child that has been born.

There are several words in verse 9 that deserve special attention. The verb "came upon them" is often used both in the Bible and in secular Greek to describe the appearance of visions, heavenly beings, etc. (Plummer 55). The word "angel" (Greek *angelos*) also means "messenger." It is used to describe both an earthly messenger and a heavenly representative. An angel has no authority of his own; he does not speak on his own behalf. His authority is derived from the one who sent him; his message is that which has been entrusted to him. In this verse, the shepherds understand immediately that the angel speaking to them brings a message from God. For a useful analysis of the word "angel" see Bietenhard (NIDNTT 101-103). It should be noted that the earliest manuscripts do not contain the article before the word "angel" in verse 9; the best translation is probably "an angel from the Lord."

The word "glory" is significant. In the Greek O. T. and N. T. it is used to express the idea of God's self-revelation in all His greatness, power, and majesty (NIDNTT 44-48). In this passage, the main idea is that God has chosen to communicate with the shepherds in a special and personal way by sending an angel to speak to them. They understand the angel has come from God, and they know the entire scene is filled with the power and glory of God. The words "sore afraid" express the idea of being overcome with fear. The shepherds come into the presence of God suddenly and unexpectedly; their reaction is natural and understandable.

In 2:10, the angel speaks a message of encouragement to the shepherds: "fear not," used in the same way as in 1:13, 30 (Greek negative present imperative), suggesting, as often, that the shepherds should "stop fearing" or "stop being afraid" (Lenski 129).

The clause "I bring you good tidings" means "I announce good news." The context has to determine both the content and the origin of the good news (Lenski 129). The same word will be used later in the N. T. to describe preaching the gospel, the good news of salvation through Jesus Christ. The English word "gospel" comes from this family of Greek words (Bock I:84; Stein, *Luke* 108).

The words "of great joy" are added for emphasis. All good news brings joy; the specific idea here is that the birth of Christ will produce outstanding joy, joy that will ultimately spread throughout the world. Lenski (130) points out that the birth of Christ will produce great joy rather than great fear.

The words "to all people" have provoked considerable discussion. The word is normally used to describe the Jewish people (Lenski 130; Stein, *Luke* 108). Stein argues that in this specific context, however, the term includes Gentiles. He notes, quite correctly, that Luke's Gospel is for all people.

Verse 11 outlines the content of the good news. The good news is that the Savior, Christ the Lord, has been born in Bethlehem, the city of David. The verb "is born" (Greek aorist) is a simple past tense; the baby was born before the shepherds received the angel's message. God's work was already an accomplished fact.

The titles the angel uses in this verse to describe the infant Jesus are most significant. The first is "saviour." This term describes someone who delivers from some danger. It is used in many different contexts, both secular and religious. In classical Greek it is used to describe rulers, military leaders, doctors, and other important people (Bock I:217). In the O. T., the term is most often used in contexts of divine deliverance. God is the one who saves or delivers His people in their time of need (see Dt. 20:4; Ps. 25:5). The word translated "salvation" also comes from this family of words; see Ellis (81).

The idea is that Jesus will be the great Deliverer of His people; He will continue the work of deliverance His Father began in the O. T. The emphasis here is not on a physical deliverance from the power of Rome; the idea is that Christ will deliver His people from the power and dominion of sin.

Two additional terms are used to describe this newborn child. He is also called "Christ" and "Lord." Bock (I:216) calls attention to the fact that this is the only passage in the N. T. where all three terms "Saviour," "Christ," and "Lord" are used together to describe Jesus of Nazareth. "Christ" is the N. T. term used to render the O. T. word for *Messiah*. The idea is that this child is the fulfillment of all the messianic prophecies of the O. T. He is no ordinary child (Wilcock 46-47).

"Lord" is used in several ways in Scripture. It is commonly used in both the O. T. and the N. T. to describe God, and that seems to be the idea here. The Child in Bethlehem's manger is not only the promised Messiah; He is also God in human form. See Bock (I:216-218) and Ellis (82) for more detailed analyses of these important terms.

It is doubtful that the shepherds understood the full significance of the angel's words, and Luke does not take time to explain them. His goal in this verse is to prepare his readers for the portrait of Christ, which he will later develop in this Gospel and in Acts.

"Sign" (Greek *sēmeion*, v. 12) is used in several ways in the N. T. (see Arndt and Gingrich 755). Here it expresses the idea of a distinguishing mark or identification; the fact that this baby is lying in a manger serves to distinguish Him from other babies in the village of Bethlehem. As Bonnet and Schroeder (493) point out, the fact that this child is found in a manger would be sufficient to identify this particular child in a small village like Bethlehem. They also suggest this sign is not meant only for the shepherds. For modern believers, the fact that a baby is born indicates His humanity. The fact that He sleeps in a manger indicates His poverty and humility. Plummer (57) prefers a somewhat different interpretation of the sign. He argues that it is not meant to help the shepherds identify this particular child, but it is designed to convince them that the message they have received is true.

13 And suddenly there was with
the angel a multitude of the heav-
enly host praising God, and saying,
14 Glory to God in the highest,
and on earth peace, good will
toward men.
15 And it came to pass, as the
angels were gone away from them
into heaven, the shepherds said
one to another, Let us now go even
unto Bethlehem, and see this thing
which is come to pass, which the
Lord hath made known unto us.
16 And they came with haste, and
found Mary, and Joseph, and the
babe lying in a manger.
17 And when they had seen *it*,
they made known abroad the say-
ing which was told them concern-
ing this child.
18 And all they that heard *it* won-
dered at those things which were
told them by the shepherds,
19 But Mary kept all these things,
and pondered *them* in her heart.
20 And the shepherds returned,
glorifying and praising God for all
the things that they had heard and
seen, as it was told unto them.

Verses 13 and 14 are designed to convey an important message not only to the shepherds who first received this vision but to all those who will read about it in the future. It is a message that gives praise to God for the miraculous events that have transpired. The first angel is joined by a multitude of heavenly beings (probably other angels) who break out in a song of praise to God. "Host" can mean an earthly army or a company of angelic beings. In this passage, it clearly refers to a multitude of angels. This angelic choir praises God for what He will do in and through the life of this newborn child.

Verse 14 gives praise to God both in Heaven and on earth. The phrase "in the highest" refers to the highest or most exalted place, Heaven. The latter part of the verse gives praise to God on earth. The "peace" of which this verse speaks is much more than the absence of war (Larson 50-51). It refers to the kind of peace that only Christ can bring (Liefeld 846); the emphasis is clearly on peace with God rather than on the absence of earthly conflict. Stein (*Luke* 109) suggests that this peace is the fullness of God's blessing and is equivalent to salvation. Ellis (82) explains that this peace can heal the estrangement that exists between sinful humanity and a holy God.

Because of differences in the early manuscripts, English translations will translate the latter part of verse 14 in different ways. The reading found in the earliest manuscripts can be translated "peace among men on whom His favor rests." The text found in later manuscripts is translated "peace, good will toward men." The main idea is that God's blessings will come upon men because of the child born in Bethlehem and what He will do in the world. Spence (39) gives an insightful treatment of this passage.

The story continues in verse 15 with the response of the shepherds; they overcome enough of their fear to travel to Bethlehem and find the baby. The term "angels" probably includes both the angel who had delivered God's message and those who had participated in the heavenly chorus (Nolland I:109). The last phrase of verse 15, "which the Lord hath made known unto us," makes no mention of the angel who had actually delivered God's message. Luke wishes to emphasize that the angel functions only as God's spokesman; the words are the Lord's (Stein, *Luke* 109).

Verse 16 notes that the shepherds came with haste. They understood that what was happening was very important, and they wanted to see what God had done in their midst. The text gives no indication of how far the shepherds had to travel, but it was probably not a great distance. Neither does the text explain how the shepherds located the child (Nolland I:109); Luke often omits such details in order to focus on the key elements of the story.

When the shepherds arrive at the stable, they first notice Mary, then Joseph, and finally the baby lying in the manger. There is probably no theological significance to the order in which the shepherds notice the various members of the family. The important thing is that the shepherds find the baby in the manger just as the angel had predicted (Stein, *Luke* 110).

The text does not indicate how long the shepherds stayed with the family. That information would be interesting to know, but it has no theological significance. The important thing is they do not keep silent about what they have seen and heard; they begin to share this good news with those nearby.

Spence (39) points out that the shepherds, who are at the low end of the social scale, are the first to have the opportunity to share the good news of Christ's birth. Luke does not say with whom they shared this good news. Since a large crowd had come to Bethlehem for the census, they probably had many opportunities to share their story (Nolland I:109; Bock I:222).

Verses 18 and 19 make a significant contribution to the developing story of Jesus' birth. Those who heard the story simply do not know what to make of it. They do not understand what it means for them. Neither do they know how to apply it to their lives; they can only wonder. As is often the case, when God's work is made known in a new and different way, those who hear about it are amazed (Bock I:222-223).

Mary's situation is somewhat different. She has received more information than the people around her; she has, for example, heard the words of the angel Gabriel (Lenski 138). "Kept" (Greek imperfect tense) can mean "was guarding" or "continued guarding." The idea is that Mary does not share her thoughts with others; she continues to ponder within herself the significance of the important event that has just transpired in her life. As Green (*Luke* 138) notes, Mary needs more time for reflection in order to come to a correct interpretation of these events. According to Ellis (82), Luke may be hinting that Mary stored up this information so she might later reveal it to the church.

The word "heart" is often used as a psychological term in the N. T. It is the center of thought and intention, the proper place for serious reflection (Bock I:223; TDNT III:612; NIDNTT II:180-184). The idea here is that Mary has been deeply affected by everything that has happened to her, and she is carefully considering the implications of these events.

Verse 20 forms a fitting conclusion to this section of the narrative; it focuses on the response of the shepherds. They do not respond with inward reflection as Mary does; they continue to glorify and praise God for all the things they have seen and heard. "Glorifying" and "praising" (Greek present participles) imply continuous or on-going action. The idea is that they continue to praise and glorify God (Lenski 139).

On several occasions in this Gospel, different characters respond with praise to singular manifestations of God's power (5:25-26, 7:16, 13:13, 17:15, 18:43, 23:47, etc.). Luke does not explain how they glorify and praise God; it probably involves giving oral testimony to those they encounter. The shepherds are glad to share the miraculous events they have seen and heard.

The last words of verse 20, "as it was told unto them," are often overlooked by commentators, but they are theologically significant. The shepherds had heard the voice of the angel and had gone to Bethlehem where they had found the Christ child, but they were not eyewitnesses of the birth of Christ or of any of the events leading up to it. They had heard and seen only a part of the story. Probably they talked with Joseph and Mary, who shared additional details with them. Like modern believers (and like Luke himself) the shepherds are dependent on the testimony of those who have gone before them.

Summary (2:1-20)

These simple but profound verses tell the story of the birth of the Son of God; Jesus Christ had always existed as the second person of the Trinity. This passage relates how He was born in humble circumstances and became incarnate for us and for our salvation. Jesus did not simply have the appearance of a man, as a number of early heretics suggested; He became a real human being. The key idea in this passage is that God took the initiative to send His Son in the form of a person so He might make salvation possible for human beings lost in sin and transgression. The incarnation is the avenue that God chose to make His mercy known and to make possible reconciliation between a holy God and a sinful humanity.

Luke begins the story by setting this important event in its historical context. It happened at a specific place in the Roman Empire and at a specific time God had determined. This passage gives us some information about Joseph and Mary, the poor couple from Nazareth, who believe God's incredible promises and are committed to doing His will. The story of the child's birth is told with a minimum of words; it takes place in humble circumstances in the village of Bethlehem. All of these events take place in fulfillment of the O. T.

The angels rejoice at the good news of Jesus' birth; they also carry the message to a group of nearby shepherds who are guarding their flocks by night. These shepherds soon conquer their fear and make the short trip to Bethlehem to see the newborn baby. After spending some time with Mary, Joseph, and the baby Jesus, the shepherds begin to share the news of these events with those in the village. They then return to their flocks, still glorifying and praising God for what they had seen and heard. Mary, however, remains silent and ponders the significance of what God has done in her life.

Application: Teaching and Preaching the Passage

These verses have been used as the text for countless Christmas sermons, and that is a most appropriate use of this beautiful passage. It is, after all, the story of the first Christmas. Preachers and teachers should emphasize the key ideas that are presented in the passage. One of these key ideas is clearly the grace and mercy of God. God has not left men and women alone to find Him as best they can. He has sent His Son to earth as a human being to be the Good Shepherd who brings the lost men and women of this world into the presence of their heavenly Father. Sermons and lessons on this passage should emphasize the grace, mercy, love, and power of God.

This passage also presents the theme of revelation. God has revealed Himself to mankind in various ways, but He has generally chosen to reveal Himself to human beings through other human beings. That is certainly the case in this passage as God reveals Himself first and foremost through the birth of the Lord Jesus. God also uses other human beings—Joseph, Mary, and the shepherds—to reveal His love and goodness.

Mary, Joseph, and the shepherds all contribute to the story in significant ways, and they deserve special attention in preaching and teaching. They serve as good role models for modern believers. They come from humble backgrounds; they are part of the common people of the land. This reminds us that God can and does use people who come from all levels of society, even the poor. Their poverty, however, is not the most important aspect of their lives; God does not choose them because they are poor.

They are faithful to God; they are committed to doing His will and following His leadership. Poverty is no excuse for not doing what God calls us to do.

Praise and rejoicing provide another major theme developed in these verses. When the angels appear to the shepherds, they sing praises and bring glory to God. After they have seen the Christ child, the shepherds also praise and glorify God. Praise and rejoicing can be done in different ways, and these verses do not demand any particular way of doing it. The important thing is that we who are people of God always praise and worship Him with our songs, with our attitudes, and with our lives.

I. Jesus' Presentation in the Temple (2:21-39)

21 And when eight days were accomplished for the circumcising of the child, his name was called JESUS, which was so named of the angel before he was conceived in the womb.
22 And when the days of her purification according to the law of Moses were accomplished, they brought him to Jerusalem, to present *him* to the Lord;
23 (As it is written in the law of the Lord, Every male that openeth the womb shall be called holy to the Lord;)
24 And to offer a sacrifice according to that which is said in the law of the Lord, A pair of turtledoves, or two young pigeons.

Luke's goal, here, is to demonstrate that Joseph and Mary are faithful Jews who are committed to following the commandments of God. The prophecies of Simeon and Anna are a clear indication that God is at work in this situation in a special way; they are obviously led by the Holy Spirit and function as God's spokesmen. The themes of faithful obedience to the law of God and direct leadership from God are closely connected in this passage, and both will continue throughout the earthly life of Christ.

Verses 21-24 develop four important themes: the naming of the child, His circumcision, His redemption, and the purification of Mary. These themes are intertwined and sometimes difficult to separate. Luke begins with the circumcision of Jesus because that is the most important part of the story theologically. Verse 21 does not specifically state that Jesus was circumcised, but that is the clear implication of the passage (Lenski 139). Circumcision officially set the child apart as a member of the nation of Israel.

The command to circumcise is one of the most important of the O. T. commandments. Genesis 17:11-12 says, "And ye shall circumcise the flesh of your foreskin; and it shall be a token of the covenant betwixt me and you. And he that is eight days old shall be circumcised among you, every man child in your generations, he that is born in the house, or bought with money of any stranger, which *is* not of thy seed." The command to circumcise was so important that failure to circumcise a male child would automatically exclude him from the nation of Israel. Genesis 17:14 says, "And the uncircumcised man child whose flesh of his foreskin is not circumcised, that soul shall be cut off from his people; he hath broken my covenant." Hahn (NIDNTT I:307-312) gives a useful summary of the importance of circumcision in ancient Israel. According to Vila and Escuain (582), Jesus was circumcised on the eighth day and given the name "Jesus" as the angel had earlier commanded in Luke 1:31. There was no legal requirement that the name be given on the eighth day, but the official naming of the child would have been appropriate on this important occasion.

The birth of a child rendered a woman ritually unclean, which meant she could not participate in public worship until the uncleanness was removed. According to Leviticus 12:2-8, a woman was unclean for seven days after giving birth to a male child. On the eighth day, the male child is circumcised, but the mother then remains unclean for an additional period of thirty-three days. During this interval of time "she shall touch no hallowed thing, nor come into the sanctuary." At the end of this period, the woman must make a sacrifice to God. Ordinarily this sacrifice was a young lamb, but in the case of a poor family, she might offer two domestic birds (such as turtledoves or pigeons). One of these birds served as a burnt offering the other as a sin offering. The fact that Mary offered two young birds indicates that the family was of modest means (Liefeld 849).

In the first century, such offerings were normally made at the Nicanor Gate in the Court of Women (Stein, *Luke* 113). Edersheim (*Life* II:195-198) describes how the rites of purification were observed in the Court of Women. Vila and Escuain (582) suggest that Mary and Joseph went again to the Temple forty days after the birth of Jesus and that Mary made the purification offering the law demanded during the later visit (see Lev. 12).

Doves and pigeons come from the same family of birds. According to the O. T., they were the only species of birds that could be offered in sacrifice to God (R. Brown, *Birth* 437). Vila and Escuain (582) posit that during this second visit, forty days after the birth of Jesus, Joseph and Mary also fulfilled the requirements of Numbers 18:15-16, which specify that firstborn sons must be redeemed by the payment of five shekels.

The words of Luke 2:23—"...Every male that openeth the womb shall be called holy to the Lord"—are drawn from Exodus 13:2, 12, and 15. The context of Exodus 13 is not circumcision but the redemption of the first born. Exodus 13:12 says, "That thou shalt set apart unto the LORD all that openeth the matrix, and every firstling that cometh of a beast which thou hast; the males *shall be* the LORD's." This probably meant that the first-born male animal would be offered to God in sacrifice. Exodus 13:13 contains a special provision that a lamb might be substituted for the young male donkey, but there is no specific explanation in this passage of how first-born sons are to be redeemed.

The last words of verse 24 describe the offering of "a pair of turtledoves, or two young pigeons." It is difficult to determine whether this humble offering should be connected with the purification of Mary or with the redemption of the baby Jesus. Lenski 142) writes that Luke has now left the discussion of Jesus' redemption and returned to Mary's purification.

It is clear that Luke's description of events in verses 21-24 is compressed and many details are omitted. For this reason, it is difficult to determine the precise order of events or the intervals of time between them. Luke's goal is to make clear to his Gentile readers that Joseph and Mary are faithful to observe all the requirements of the law.

25 And, behold, there was a man in Jerusalem, whose name *was* Simeon; and the same man *was* just and devout, waiting for the consolation of Israel: and the Holy Ghost was upon him.
26 And it was revealed unto him by the Holy Ghost, that he should not see death, before he had seen the Lord's Christ.
27 And he came by the Spirit into the temple: and when the parents brought in the child Jesus, to do for him after the custom of the law,
28 Then took he him up in his arms, and blessed God, and said,
29 Lord, now lettest thou thy servant depart in peace, according to thy word:
30 For mine eyes have seen thy salvation,
31 Which thou hast prepared before the face of all people;
32 A light to lighten the Gentiles, and the glory of thy people Israel.
33 And Joseph and his mother marvelled at those things which were spoken of him.
34 And Simeon blessed them, and said unto Mary his mother, Behold, this *child* is set for the fall and rising again of many in Israel; and for a sign which shall be spoken against;
35 (Yea, a sword shall pierce through thy own soul also,) that the thoughts of many hearts may be revealed.

When Joseph and Mary arrive at the Temple for the redemption of Jesus, they meet Simeon and Anna; both make significant contributions to Luke's story. They indicate that this infant's future ministry will be of great significance. Both Simeon and Anna interpret the ministry of Jesus as the fulfillment of O. T. messianic prophecies.

"Simeon" was a common Jewish name of the first century (Marshall, *Gospel* 118). Nothing is known of this Simeon other than what is revealed here; his personal history is not important to Luke's account. What is important is his testimony concerning the infant Jesus (Stein, *Luke* 114). Verse 25 makes three significant statements about Simeon: (1) he is just and devout; (2) he is waiting for the consolation of Israel: (3) the Holy Spirit is upon him. The terms "just" and "devout" go together. In this passage, they indicate he is a faithful Jew who observes carefully the requirements of the Jewish law (Marshall, *Gospel* 118).

The phrase "consolation of Israel" refers to the deliverance the coming Messiah will bring to the nation of Israel (Marshall, *Gospel* 118; Stein, *Luke* 114; Summers, *Luke* 41). This phrase probably refers to Isaiah 40:1-2 where it likely describes the time when God will bring Israel's suffering and humiliation to an end through the coming of the Messiah (Liefeld 850). The reader is not told how this information was communicated to Simeon, but in some way God had let him know that this child would fulfill the Jewish messianic expectations. Stein (*Luke* 115) notes that in the first century Jewish messianic hopes included different elements, some of them political, others religious. See also the comments of Lieu (17). Simeon is a faithful Jew who is eagerly awaiting the coming of the Messiah, but here he clearly emphasizes the salvation the Messiah will bring rather than the reestablishment of David's throne.

In the final words of verse 25, Luke emphasizes that when Simeon gives this prophecy he is under the special direction of the Holy Spirit. Luke's goal is to show that every aspect of the birth of Christ reflects the leadership of God's Spirit (Lieu 18; Ellis 83). According to verse 27, Simeon comes into the Temple under the leadership of the Spirit so he can be there at the proper time (Marshall, *Gospel* 119).

In some way, the Spirit of God had revealed to Simeon that he would not die until he had seen the arrival of the Messiah. Nothing is told about Simeon's age at the time these events took place, but this promise may indicate he was an older rabbi. Ellis (83) notes there was a Jewish tradition that parents would bring their infants to the Temple to be blessed by an aged rabbi.

Simeon takes the child in his arms and begins to bless God by pronouncing a brief song of praise. This song is often called *Nunc Dimittis*—"Now Dismiss"—drawn from the opening phrase of the Latin version (Summers, *Luke* 41; Liefeld 849). The song is presented as a prayer to God in the form of three poetic couplets. Verse 29 indicates that Simeon is now ready to die because the Lord's promise to him has been fulfilled. His goal in life was to see the promised Messiah, and that has now come to pass. The phrase "according to thy word" does not necessarily imply a written word. In this context, it probably refers to the Lord's promise that Simeon would live to see the coming Messiah.

The word "salvation" in verse 30 literally means "deliverance." Here the term refers to the deliverance from the power and dominion of sin that will be accomplished through the life and ministry of the child whom Simeon held in his arms. Verse 31 is drawn from the Greek text of Isaiah 52:10; it further develops the idea of salvation introduced in the previous verse. God's plan to bring salvation through the birth of this child is not new; it has been a part of God's purpose for His people from the beginning.

The phrase "all people" at the end of verse 31 has provoked considerable discussion. Does it refer only to Jews or does it include Gentiles as well? Most commentators are of the opinion that Luke's desire is to include both Jews and Gentiles in this promised salvation (Stein, *Luke* 116; Marshall, *Gospel* 120-121; Liefeld 849; Wilcock 48). This interpretation is certainly correct in light of Luke's mention of both Jews and Gentiles in verse 32.

Verse 33 gives the reaction of Joseph and Mary to these events. Some manuscripts of this verse read "Joseph" while others read "his father" (Ellis 84; Marshall, *Gospel* 121). This should not be understood as a denial of the Virgin Birth; Luke has already affirmed that Jesus had no human father. Although he is not the physical father of Jesus, Joseph functions as His legal father (Morris, *Luke* 88).

Joseph and Mary find Simeon's words astonishing. They go beyond anything that the shepherds had spoken; they speak for the first time about Jesus' ministry among the Gentiles. Joseph and Mary no doubt wonder how Simeon came to know this information and how his words should be understood (Morris, *Luke* 88-89).

In verses 34-35, Simeon outlines in general terms certain aspects of the future ministry of this child. He makes four specific statements that are directed to Mary: (1) this child will bring about the rise and fall of many in Israel; (2) He will engender opposition; (3) His mother Mary will suffer on account of His ministry; (4) He will reveal the thoughts of many. These statements are negative in tone and stand in sharp contrast to the optimistic tone of Simeon's earlier words (R. Brown, *Birth* 460). Simeon, like an O. T. prophet, sees both the greatness of what God will do in the future and the difficulties that will be faced in accomplishing it.

The first statement, "the fall and rising again of many in Israel," speaks of two different groups. Those who fall are punished for their disobedience to Jesus' message; those who rise are rewarded for their obedience. There is some difference of opinion concerning the identities of these two groups. R. Brown (*Birth* 460) sees them as two different groups of Jews. Some Jews will accept Jesus and His message; others will reject Him. Stein (*Luke* 117) sees this passage as a contrast between the poor and humble who accept Jesus' message and the proud and haughty who reject it. Morris (*Luke* 89) offers a similar interpretation, noting that in order to be exalted by Jesus, men must lose their spiritual pride and confidence in their own ability to achieve salvation.

The second statement, "a sign which shall be spoken against," refers to Jesus. Jesus becomes a sign of God's grace and His desire to save. Men should welcome this message, but many reject it. They set themselves in opposition to what God is doing through His Son, Jesus (Marshall, *Gospel* 122).

The third phrase, "a sword shall pierce through thy own soul also," takes the discussion in a slightly different direction. It focuses on the negative aspects of Jesus' ministry and how they will affect His mother. This passage clearly refers to the pain Mary will suffer when her son is rejected and ultimately crucified (Marshall, *Gospel* 123l Stein, *Luke* 117).

The final statement, "that the thoughts of many hearts may be revealed," briefly summarizes the ministry of Jesus. One result of Jesus' ministry will be division; men cannot remain neutral (Morris, *Luke* 89). They will be for Him or they will be against Him; the life and ministry of Christ will reveal who men truly are.

36 And there was one Anna, a prophetess, the daughter of Phanuel, of the tribe of Aser: she was of a great age, and had lived with an husband seven years from her virginity;
37 And she *was* a widow of about fourscore and four years, which departed not from the temple, but served *God* with fastings and prayers night and day.
38 And she coming in that instant gave thanks likewise unto the Lord, and spake of him to all them that looked for redemption in Jerusalem.
39 And when they had performed all things according to the law of the Lord, they returned into Galilee, to their own city Nazareth.
40 And the child grew, and waxed strong in spirit, filled with wisdom:

and the grace of God was upon him.

At this point, a new character, Anna, enters the story. Morris (*Luke* 89) points out that both Simeon and Anna make significant contributions to the story. Their endorsement of Jesus shows that not all the Jewish leaders were hostile to Him; at least some of those leaders recognized that He was truly sent from God. Nothing more is known about Anna than what is told here, but these verses reveal several things.

First, she is a prophetess, and prophetesses are mentioned in several places in the Bible (Acts 2:19; 1 Cor. 11:5; Ex. 15:20; Jg. 4:4; 2 Kgs. 22:14; etc). The O. T. prophets served as spokesmen for God, and Anna clearly occupies that role here (Larson 57). Since the Jews only officially recognized seven prophetesses (Morris, *Luke* 89), this was a great honor. Her status as a prophetess gives her an insight into and an understanding of the things of God beyond what a typical Israelite would have (Marshall, *Gospel* 123). It is also important to note that Anna comes from a family that had long been a part of the nation of Israel. Asher was one of the ten tribes when the kingdom was divided after the death of Solomon; nothing is known about her father Phanuel.

Second, this passage speaks of her long life of devotion to God. She was of great age in a time when advanced age was seen as a singular blessing from God. She was married as a young woman, but her husband died after seven years of marriage. She did not remarry; she lived the rest of her life as a widow. Verse 37 mentions that she was a widow of about 84 years. It is not clear whether the 84 years refer to her age at the time this event happened or whether she had been a widow for 84 years when this event happened (Morris, *Luke* 90; Stein, *Luke* 118; Green, *Luke* 151). Either interpretation is possible.

One of the most significant things about Anna is how she spent the long years of her widowhood. She spent them in the temple in Jerusalem faithfully serving God. The passage says she "departed not from the temple" and she served God "day and night." These phrases have been interpreted in various ways. One possible interpretation is that she had living quarters within the temple area (Morris, *Luke* 90; Spence 41). The fact that women were not normally allowed to remain in the temple area overnight (Stein, *Luke* 118) renders such an interpretation doubtful. The more common interpretation is that she was in the temple on a daily basis actively serving God (Morris, *Luke* 90; Green, *Luke* 151).

Anna served God with prayer and fasting, which often go together in Jewish literature (NIDNTT I:612). There is an ancient tradition that called for all Jews to pray twice a day, at sunrise and at sunset. There is also a tradition calling for prayer at the sixth hour, which would be at mid-day.

When Jews fasted, it was normally from morning until evening (Jg. 20:26; 1 Sam. 14:24; 2 Sam. 1:12). The Jewish law originally called for fasting only on the Day of Atonement (Lev. 16:29-31, 23:27-32; Num. 29:7), but additional fast days were added after the destruction of Jerusalem (Zech. 7:3-5, 19). Rothenberg (NIDNTT I:611-613) and Banks (DJG 233-234) provide excellent summaries of fasting as it was practiced in the time of Jesus.

The meaning of verses 36 and 37 is clear. Anna is no ordinary woman; she has demonstrated her faithfulness to God over a period of many years. She is just the kind of person God will use to make His will known. While Luke does not record her precise words, verse 38 explains what happened when Joseph and Mary arrived with the infant. Not accidentally, Anna came into the Court of Women while Joseph, Mary, and the baby Jesus were there. Her arrival at that specific time was part of God's providence (Lenski 157). Anna immediately begins to give thanks to God for what He had done. The tense of the verb used (Greek imperfect) generally describes action that is repeated or continuous; the idea may be that Anna continued to give thanks even after the family had returned to Nazareth (Lenski 157).

The last words of verse 38 explain that Anna did not just give thanks to God; she also began to spread the good news of Jesus' birth among "those that looked for redemption in Jerusalem." In this context, these words refer to those who were faithful to God (Bock, *Luke* NIV 94). Stein (*Luke* 118) suggests that the phrase "redemption in Jerusalem" is a synonym for the phrases "consolation of Israel" found in 2:25 and "salvation" found in 2:30. According to Morris (*Luke* 90), the phrase "redemption in Jerusalem" refers to the future deliverance the Messiah will bring to Israel. Marshall (*Gospel* 124) gives a similar interpretation.

J. Jesus' Growth and Development (2:40-52)

40 And the child grew, and waxed strong in spirit, filled with wisdom: and the grace of God was upon him.

Verses 39-40 are transition verses designed to bridge the gap between Jesus' presentation in the Temple as an infant and His visit to the Temple as a young boy. When they had completed all the requirements of the Jewish law, the family returned to their traditional home in Nazareth of Galilee. Luke uses four significant phrases to summarize Jesus' childhood in Nazareth: He (1) grew, (2) waxed strong in spirit, (3) was filled with wisdom, and (4) experienced the grace of God. As Green (*Luke* 154) correctly notes, Luke often uses brief summary statements to advance the story. Most of Luke will be devoted to describing Jesus' ministry as an adult; this passage demonstrates that even as a child Jesus began to manifest those qualities that would characterize His later ministry.

It is interesting to note how different commentators interpret verse 40. Some (like Liefeld 850) believe that it presents Jesus' childhood as a normal one. Others such as Geldenhuys (122) see the childhood of Jesus as extraordinary. The best interpretation lies somewhere between these two extremes; in some respects, Jesus' growth and development were quite normal. In other respects, they were extraordinary.

The first phrase, "and the child grew," refers to physical growth. Similar statements are made in the O. T. concerning Isaac and other characters (R. Brown, *Birth* 469). Nothing in the text indicates Jesus' physical growth and development were different from those experienced by other young men of His age in Israel. That is not true, however, of the second and third phrases. The fact that Luke calls attention to growth in spirit and in wisdom indicates that His childhood was somewhat unusual; the growth Jesus experienced in these areas was not typical. Morris (*Luke* 90) and other commentators understand the phrase "waxed strong in spirit" to refer to mental or intellectual growth. Green interprets the third and fourth phrases together. He asserts (*Luke* 154) that even as a child Jesus began to demonstrate the wisdom and divine favor that would become even more important in His later life.

Luke's description of Jesus' infancy ends with the family's return to Nazareth. There is no doubt that other events happened, but he omits any mention of them. While the later apocryphal gospels contain many fanciful stories about Jesus' words and deeds as a child, all four of the canonical Gospels remain silent. With the exception of His visit to the temple at age twelve, which is told only in Luke, the Gospel writers include no other information about Jesus' childhood. This silence does not mean that the Gospel writers regarded these years as unimportant; they were simply not germane to the story. All of the Gospels focus on the redemptive work of Jesus as an adult.

It is important to note that Luke makes no mention of the journey to Egypt or of Herod's murder of the innocent children of Bethlehem, both of which figure prominently in Matthew's account (Mt. 2:13-23). Summers (*Luke* 42) suggests two possible reasons for this omission. First, it is possible that the sources Luke was using did not contain this information. Second, if Luke's sources contained this information, he chose not to include it because it was not important for his purpose. Geldenhuys (121) notes that it was not Luke's purpose to record everything that happened.

41 Now his parents went to Jerusalem every year at the feast of the passover.
42 And when he was twelve years old, they went up to Jerusalem after the custom of the feast.
43 And when they had filled the days, as they returned, the child Jesus tarried behind in Jerusalem; and Joseph and his mother knew not *of it*.
44 But they, supposing him to have been in the company, went a day's journey; and they sought him among *their* kinsfolk and acquaintance.
45 And when they found him not, they turned back again to Jerusalem, seeking him.
46 And it came to pass, that after three days they found him in the temple, sitting in the midst of the doctors, both hearing them, and asking them questions.
47 And all that heard him were astonished at his understanding and answers.
48 And when they saw him, they were amazed: and his mother said unto him, Son, why hast thou thus dealt with us? behold, thy father and I have sought thee sorrowing.
49 And he said unto them, How is it that ye sought me? wist ye not that I must be about my Father's business?
50 And they understood not the saying he spake unto them.
51 And he went down with them, and came to Nazareth, and was

subject unto them: but his mother kept all these sayings in her heart. 52 And Jesus increased in wisdom and stature, and in favour with God and man.

This interesting story is the only incident from Jesus' childhood presented in the Gospels, and it is found only in Luke. This visit to the Temple continues to portray Jesus and His family as faithful Jews who are careful to fulfill the requirements of the law. Jewish tradition required that all Jewish males who were able to travel should go to Jerusalem for important feasts such as the Passover (Lieu 19). Geldenhuys (126) explains that in the first century it was the custom for Jews living outside Jerusalem to attend only the Passover. Marshall (*Gospel* 127) points out that the two feasts of Passover and Unleavened Bread lasted a total of seven days, and that pilgrims were required to remain at least two days. Luke does not explain how long Joseph and his family stayed in Jerusalem. Marshall (*Luke* NBC-1970 894) also notes that as many as 100,000 people would travel to Jerusalem in large caravans for the Passover.

Since the boy Jesus was soon to enter into the responsibilities of adulthood, it was appropriate that He should make the trip with Joseph and Mary (Lieu 19; Marshall, *Gospel* 126). Luke does not explain how long they stayed in Jerusalem or precisely what they did while they were there.

At the end of the seven festival days (Geldenhuys 126), Joseph and Mary begin the trip home in the company of friends and relatives from Nazareth. The women normally walked first with the younger children while the men followed after. The older boys might walk either with the mother or with the father (Geldenhuys 126). Joseph and Mary did not notice Jesus' absence until time came to camp for the first night; they probably thought He was walking with some of His friends in the group. At the end of the day, they looked for the twelve-year old boy, but He was not to be found.

There was little that Joseph and Mary could do that evening; they were tired and it was dangerous to travel alone at night. They waited until morning when they retraced their steps to Jerusalem where they found Jesus sitting in the Temple, talking with the doctors of the law. He was listening to them and asking them questions. All those who heard Him were amazed at His level of understanding; it was certainly not normal for a child of twelve to sit and have an adult discussion in the Temple with the doctors of the law.

Luke notes that they found the child "after three days." The most common interpretation is that the first day is the day they traveled from Jerusalem toward Nazareth. The second day is the day they returned to Jerusalem in search of Jesus. They found the boy in the temple sometime on the third day (Geldenhuys 127; Marshall, *Gospel* 127; Stein, *Luke* 122). A typical day's journey would have been twenty to twenty-five miles.

Mary and Joseph are surprised to find Jesus in the temple having a religious discussion with the teachers of Israel. Mary responds to this situation with the kind of question a mother would ask. She asks her son, "Why have you done this to us? We were worried about you." The answer given by her twelve-year-old son constitutes the first recorded words of Jesus; Marshall

(*Gospel* 128) correctly notes that this response will set the tone for Jesus' later public ministry. Jesus responds with two questions. The first is, "How is it that ye sought me?" or, in other words, "why have you been searching for me?" Summers (*Luke* 43) suggests that the idea behind the question is "Why were you looking for me elsewhere?" The implication is that His parents should have known to look for Him in the Temple.

The second question is more significant theologically. It is, "Wist ye not that I must be about my Father's business?" This phrase may be interpreted in two different ways. It may mean, "Did you not know that I had to be about my Father's business?" It may also mean, "Did you not know that I had to be in my Father's house?" See the comments of Stein (*Luke* 122) and Green (*Luke* 157) for a discussion of the correct translation and interpretation of this phrase. One fact comes through clearly in Jesus' response. Even at the young age of twelve, He is committed to doing the will of His heavenly Father. Jesus is already conscious that He has a special relationship with God, and He is determined to do His heavenly Father's will (Summers, *Luke* 43-44).

"They" (v. 50) probably means Joseph and Mary. Although they understood the words Jesus spoke, they did not fully understand the significance of what He said (Summers, *Luke* 44). After this conversation, Jesus returned to Nazareth with Joseph and Mary and lived as a child under their control (Morris, *Luke* 92). Mary did not fully understand what had transpired; she kept "all these sayings" in her heart and continued to meditate on their significance. This is Luke's last mention of Joseph; it is generally assumed that he died before Jesus' public ministry began some eighteen years later (Morris, *Luke* 92; Geldenhuys 129).

Verse 52 is a summary of the theological significance of Jesus' childhood and youth. Although no specific events are recorded in the Gospels, these years should be regarded as a time of growth, development, and preparation for His future public ministry. Jesus grew in "wisdom" and in "stature." In other words, He grew and developed both spiritually and physically (Geldenhuys 129). Green (*Luke* 157) interprets these words to mean that Jesus grew both in His understanding of the Scriptures and in His understanding of God's purpose in His life. The last words in the verse indicate that Jesus also developed "in favour with God and man." Throughout the first two chapters of Luke, Jesus has met with a favorable reaction from all those who have had contact with Him. It seems that God has placed His hand on this young man in a very special way (Green, *Luke* 157-158).

Jesus' visit to the Temple at age twelve sets the stage for His later public ministry. It reflects an understanding of and commitment to the will of God far beyond what a normal twelve-year-old would be expected to have. It is clear that God is leading and directing in His life in a special way; God is preparing Him for what He will accomplish in the future.

Summary (2:21-52)

Luke 2:21-52 serves as a bridge between the birth of Christ and His public ministry, which will begin in the next chapter. This passage continues the development of several important themes (such as the grace and mercy of God), which figure prominently in the theological message of Luke's gospel. This section begins with the story of Jesus' birth in humble circumstances in Bethlehem of Judaea. The fact that all these events took place among the common people of first-century Palestine foreshadows Jesus' public ministry to all levels of society including those who have little in the way of economic or political power. It is also significant to note that all of these events fulfill the O. T. By sending His Son to be born in Bethlehem, God is continuing to develop His plan for saving lost and fallen mankind.

The second section of this passage outlines Jesus' first visit to the Temple in Jerusalem at the age of eight days. Luke writes this passage primarily for a Gentile audience that may not understand the details of Jewish laws and customs. He compresses the story and eliminates unnecessary details. The theme of O. T. fulfillment is important, however, even to Gentile believers. They are part of the family of God, and they need to understand their spiritual roots.

The purification of the mother Mary after the birth of her son is based on Leviticus 12; the presentation of the firstborn son to God is drawn from Exodus 13 and Numbers 18; the dedication of the firstborn to the service of God is based on 1 Samuel 1 and 2 and other passages. Mary and Joseph are faithful to obey the teachings of God; from His earliest days, the child Jesus grows up in an atmosphere of commitment to obedience.

Simeon and Anna make major contributions to the story; they are pious Jews who have served the Lord for many years. They not only give thanks to God for what He is doing for His people, they also give insight into the kind of messianic ministry Jesus will have when He comes to adulthood.

This section concludes with the story of the family's return to Nazareth and the second visit to the Temple at age twelve. During this visit, Jesus demonstrates that He is already developing an extraordinary awareness of the special relationship He enjoys with His heavenly Father. The main contribution of these verses is to prepare the reader of this gospel for the public ministry of Jesus. They emphasize that Jesus will begin His public ministry with the proper spiritual, mental, and physical preparation to serve as the Messiah.

Application: Teaching and Preaching the Passage

These verses present many important themes that should be developed in teaching and preaching. First and foremost is the grace and mercy of God. These verses remind us once again that it is God who has taken the initiative to send His Son into the world to serve as mankind's redeemer. The Holy Spirit is the unseen hand working behind the events narrated in these verses. In these verses, God brings His will to pass through the lives of ordinary men and women such as Mary and Joseph, Simeon and Anna. These men and women have one thing in common. As different as they are, they are all committed to listening to the call of God and obeying His instructions. That is exactly the kind of spirit men and women must have today. We must allow God to lead us and direct us; we must also be dedicated to doing His will.

A second important theme found in these verses is the need for spiritual discernment. This is clearly evident in the lives of Simeon and Anna. They have been involved in the Lord's work for a long time. During these years they have moved away from the influences of the world; instead, they have developed a close and loving relationship with their heavenly Father. They recognize that God is doing something special and they want to take part in it. If we want to be used in the work of the Lord, we must be spiritually aware; we must be sensitive to who God is and what He is doing in our world. We must be willing to separate ourselves from the world in order to hear the voice of God more clearly.

A third important theme for preaching and teaching is patience. Sometimes things happen rapidly in the Lord's work, but many times they do not. Active involvement in the service of the Lord may require years of preparation and experience. When the infant Jesus was brought to the Temple for His dedication, Anna and Simeon had already been involved in the worship and service of God for many years. They were, in fact, in the final years of their lives; they brought a level of spiritual maturity and judgment, which was very important. Even Jesus needed a considerable amount of training and preparation before beginning His public ministry. He visited the Temple as a young man of twelve years, but He had to wait until He was around thirty years of age to begin His public ministry. God works according to His own timetable, and His followers must be faithful and patient.

A fourth important lesson from this passage is the uniqueness of Jesus. Many in the modern world present Jesus as one important religious leader among many. Luke's account refutes all such claims. The visit to the Temple at age twelve validates the uniqueness of Jesus; all are astounded that a young man of only twelve years could demonstrate such a high level of spiritual understanding. He is rapidly becoming aware of the special ministry that His Father has for Him. After the visit to the Temple, Jesus' relationship with the other members of His family receives little attention in this Gospel. Luke only notes that Jesus returned to Nazareth and was subject to Mary and Joseph. Jesus' relationship with the Father has clearly become the central focus both of His life and of Luke's account.

III. THE PUBLIC MINISTRY BEGINS (3:1—4:13)

This passage serves as the introduction to Jesus' public ministry; it focuses on His qualifications and preparation for that ministry. It also introduces several themes that will be developed as the ministry of Christ unfolds. Luke begins this section with a historical introduction that determines the time of Jesus' ministry and places His public ministry in the larger context of world events. He then continues the development of the relationship between Jesus and John the Baptist, who serves as a transition figure between the O. T. and the N. T. This section emphasizes that the ministries of both Jesus and John the Baptist serve to complete God's plan by fulfilling the O. T. prophecies.

Luke then continues with Jesus' baptism, which serves as the official inauguration of His messianic ministry. The genealogy serves to place Jesus in the context of Jewish history and demonstrates His legitimacy as God's Son; it also establishes that Jesus is the Savior of all mankind. The concluding verses of this section describe the forty days of temptation Jesus endured during the early part of His earthly ministry. These verses stress the difficulties Jesus faced in His messianic ministry; the temptations He faced were real and in some ways similar to the temptations faced by His followers today.

A. The Ministry of John the Baptist (3:1-20)

1 Now in the fifteenth year of the reign of Tiberius Caesar, Pontius Pilate being governor of Judaea, and Herod being tetrarch of Galilee, and his brother Philip tetrarch of Ituraea and of the region of Trachonitis, and Lysanias the tetrarch of Abilene,
2 Annas and Caiaphas being the high priests, the word of God came unto John the son of Zacharias in the wilderness.
3 And he came into all the country about Jordan, preaching the baptism of repentance for the remission of sins;
4 As it is written in the book of the words of Esaias the prophet, saying, The voice of one crying in the wilderness, Prepare ye the way of the Lord, make his paths straight.
5 Every valley shall be filled, and every mountain and hill shall be brought low; and the crooked shall be made straight, and the rough ways *shall be* made smooth;
6 And all flesh shall see the salvation of God.

The first two verses of this chapter set the events of Jesus' public ministry in the larger context of Jewish and world history. Luke mentions seven specific rulers, and seems to move from the more important to the less important (Bock I:281-282). According to Luke 3:1, the preaching of John the Baptist and the public ministry of Jesus began in the fifteenth year of the reign of Tiberius Caesar. In the ancient world, there was no uniform calendar; events were often dated in relationship to the reigns of important kings or governors. As Bock (*Luke*, IVP 64) explains, the chronology of this passage is difficult because several different calendars were in use at this time. It is possible that Luke is using either the Roman calendar or the Jewish calendar. Sometimes they would consider the year a king assumed the throne to be the first year of his reign; sometimes they would begin counting with the first year after he assumed the throne.

Marshall (*Gospel* 133) points out another difficulty in the interpretation of this passage. It is widely accepted that Augustus died on August 19, A.D. 14 (Morris, *Luke* 93); his stepson Tiberius served as co-regent with him beginning about 11 or 12. It is difficult to determine whether Luke begins counting with the year Tiberius became co-regent or with the year when he became sole ruler. If he begins with the date when Tiberius became co-regent, the ministry of John began about 26 or 27. Most modern authorities suggest that Luke uses the Roman calendar and begins counting when Tiberius becomes sole ruler. If that is the correct interpretation, the fifteenth year would be about 28 or 29. Marshall posits a date about 28 for these events. Morris (*Luke* 93) suggests a date between 27 and 29. For a good discussion of the date of the beginning of John's ministry, see Robertson (*Historian* 166-168). For more information about the dating of events in N. T. times, see Finegan and Hoehner (*Life*).

Green (*Luke* 167) points out that Luke is not so concerned to establish a precise chronology as he is to outline the social and political context in which the ministries of John and Jesus take place. Wilcock (53-54) calls attention to the fact that the most important element in the story is not the preaching ministry of John or the baptism of Jesus but the fact that God speaks in a very special and powerful way in the fifteenth year of Tiberius.

During the first century, the entire eastern end of the Mediterranean was under the control of the Roman Empire and the different territories were ruled by governors appointed either by the Emperor or by the Roman Senate. The highest ranking of these were known as *legates*, who were military men in charge of the Roman army units stationed in a particular territory. *Procurators* (or *prefects*) occupied a lower rank; they were administrative officials who collected taxes and performed other duties (Bock I:282). Pontius Pilate was prefect of Judaea from A.D. 26 to 36 or 37 (Green, *Luke* 168; Nolland I:139). Luke uses a common term, translated *governor*, to describe him. He was known as a cruel and arbitrary ruler who had little respect for the Jewish people whom he ruled. He often had people executed for little or no reason (Green, *Luke* 168).

The Herod mentioned in 3:1 is Herod Antipas, the son of Herod the Great, who ruled Galilee and Perea from 4 B.C. to A.D. 39 (Liefeld 854). His half-brother, Herod Philip, ruled an area northeast of Palestine, including Iturea and Traconitis, from 4 B.C. to A.D. 33 or 34 (Liefeld 854; Fitzmyer I:457). Abilene was a territory northwest of Damascus. There are some vague references in Josephus and some early inscriptions that refer to Lysanias, but little is known about him (Fitzmyer I:457).

Verse 2a sets the ministries of John the Baptist and Jesus within the context of Jewish history. The first words of this verse could be literally translated "in the high priesthood of Annas and Caiaphas" (Fitzmyer I:458). Morris (*Luke* 94) explains the meaning of this rather enigmatic phrase. Annas was high priest A.D. 6-15, when he was deposed by the Roman governor Gratus. In the succeeding years, five of his sons held the office of high priest. Caiaphas was a son-in-law who served in this important position A.D. 18-36. Caiaphas was the official high priest during the years of Jesus' public ministry, but Annas exercised a great deal of influence.

In verse 2b, Luke notes that "the word of God came unto John the son of Zacharias in the wilderness." These words establish a connection between John the Baptist and the O. T. prophets; his ministry is, in some sense, a continuation of theirs. The passage says the "word of God" came to John in the wilderness. The specific content of the "word of God" is not given; it is probably the message he was to proclaim. The term "wilderness" is usually used to describe the desert area south of the city of Jerusalem. Summers (*Luke* 46) suggests it describes the largely uninhabited area north of the Dead Sea.

Verses 3-6 are Luke's summary of the preaching ministry of John the Baptist. God gives him the message in the wilderness; he is commissioned to proclaim it in the Jordan River Valley. Luke explains that John preaches "the baptism of repentance for the remission of sins." The term "repentance" implies both a change in one's mind and a change in one's conduct (Summers, *Luke* 46-47); without genuine repentance no forgiveness is possible. The people to whom John is to proclaim this message are not specifically identified, but the location would indicate that they are primarily Jews. The idea is that Jews are sinners in the eyes of God; they need to repent of their sins and accept God's forgiveness. This must have been a difficult message for many to accept. Verses 4-6 establish the connection between the preaching of John and a key O. T. passage, Isaiah 40:3-5. All of the Gospel writers quote from Isaiah 4:3 to explain why John the Baptist is in the desert (Mt. 3:3; Mk. 1:3; Jn. 1:23). He is there to prepare for the coming of the Messiah. Luke alone cites Isaiah 40:4-5, which explains that John is preparing the way for the coming of the Messiah so all may see the salvation of God. Luke quotes primarily from the Greek version of the O. T. (the Septuagint), the version with which his Gentile readers would have been familiar (Morris, *Luke* 95; Summers, *Luke* 47). The fact that salvation is available to all through Christ will become a favorite theme of Luke's Gospel.

John is not the message; he is the one who has the privilege of preparing the way for the coming of the Messiah. In verse 5, the coming of the Messiah is described in terms of the arrival of an oriental king. Before the king arrives every effort will be made to make the roads he will travel as smooth and level as possible. The Messiah is certainly worthy of all this preparation because He will bring the message of salvation to all the people. Luke's goal in this passage is to make clear to his readers that these important events are the direct result of divine intervention.

7 Then said he to the multitude that came forth to be baptized of him, O generation of vipers, who hath warned you to flee from the wrath to come?
8 Bring forth therefore fruits worthy of repentance, and begin not to say within yourselves, We have Abraham to *our* father: for I say unto you, That God is able of these stones to raise up children unto Abraham.
9 And now also the axe is laid unto the root of the trees: every tree therefore which bringeth not forth good fruit is hewn down, and cast into the fire.
10 And the people asked him, saying, What shall we do then?
11 He answered and saith unto them, He that hath two coats, let him impart to him that hath none; and he that hath meat, let him do likewise.
12 Then came also publicans to be baptized, and said unto him, Master, what shall we do?
13 And he said unto them, Exact no more than that which is appointed to you.
14 And the soldiers likewise demanded of him, saying, And what shall we do? And he said unto

them, Do violence to no man, neither accuse *any* falsely; and be content with your wages.
15 And as the people were in expectation, and all men mused in their hearts of John, whether he were the Christ, or not.

These verses summarize John's preaching to the crowds who came to be baptized and how he responded to their questions. They also outline the specific instructions that John gave to those who came to be baptized. The verb "said" (Greek imperfect tense) suggests that John was saying or that he used to say. Luke does not specifically identify the "multitude" that come to be baptized, but there is little doubt that they are Jews, probably Jews in positions of influence. Later verses in the passage single out publicans and soldiers for special attention. It is likely that the multitude included a mixture of different people, including both Pharisees and Sadducees (Lenski 185).

The words John uses to address them are strong and harsh; he calls them a "generation of vipers." This strong language indicates that John has a very low regard for them, probably because they have used their power and influence to take advantage of others. They have come to be baptized out of a desire to "flee from the wrath to come." The wrath of God is a concept that occurs throughout the N. T.; it describes God's rejection of and hostility toward all that is evil. For an excellent discussion of the wrath of God in the N. T. see Morris (*Preaching* 179-184). The people understand they have done wrong and that the judgment of God will fall upon them at some point in the future. Luke does not explain why John uses such harsh language. Probably the reason is that he wishes to eliminate those who are not truly repentant and who are not willing to make the necessary changes in their conduct. Those who have not laid aside their pride and arrogance will not tolerate such language; they will leave without being baptized. Perhaps some thought John's baptism might serve as a substitute for genuine repentance (Plummer 88).

The first words of verse 8, "Bring forth therefore fruits worthy of repentance," illustrate an important truth. The word "repentance," as used in the N. T., implies much more than a change in one's mind or opinion; it demands a change in the direction of one's life. If those who have come to be baptized by John are sincere, they will make the necessary changes in how they treat other people. They can no longer rely upon the Jewish tradition that the physical descendants of Abraham are safe from God's wrath. They must begin to rely on God in the same way Abraham did and demonstrate their faith in God by meaningful actions as their forefather did.

The last words of verse 8 are significant. Many Jews of the first century thought the mere fact that they were the descendants of Abraham guaranteed them a special relationship with God. John denies that such a special relationship exists. He points out that if He desired to do so, God could raise up children to Abraham from the stones of the earth. The idea is that John's hearers must live as Abraham lived if they wish to be his descendants; physical descent does not guarantee them a special place in God's kingdom. Neither does it exempt them from God's righteous judgment.

Verse 9 is an illustration of God's judgment drawn from the agricultural practices of ancient Palestine. If an olive tree or a fig tree did not bear fruit within a certain number of years, it was cut down and replaced by another tree. The idea here is that if John's hearers do not bring forth fruits as evidence of their repentance, they will be judged by God.

Those who heard John's preaching were deeply affected by it; they asked in desperation, "What shall we do?" John then outlines what would be an appropriate response to his preaching. First, they must agree to be baptized by him, but baptism alone will not be sufficient. Second, they must also change the direction of their lives. John begins by giving some general instructions that everyone in the crowd could understand and obey. Those who have two coats should share with those who are lacking. The "coat," as the word was commonly used, was an undergarment worn to help keep the body warm; if necessary Jews might wear more than one (Plummer 90-91). The word translated "meat" is a general word describing various types of food. The idea is that if the person is genuinely repentant, a spirit of generosity will replace a spirit of selfishness.

John then gives two specific illustrations of the type of change that God demands. The first concerns the "publicans." The Roman government did not use its own employees to collect taxes; wealthy individuals purchased the right to collect taxes in certain provinces of the Empire. They then hired others to do the actual collection for them; this created a system that was ripe for graft and corruption. The term "publican" was used to describe Jews who were hired to collect taxes from their fellow Jews. They took advantage of their position to collect additional money for their own pockets. Because of the way they mistreated their fellow Jews, they were widely hated. Here John tells them that if they are sincere in their repentance, they must collect no more than they are supposed to collect. They must quit robbing the people.

The second specific illustration concerns soldiers. Luke does not specify whether these are Roman imperial soldiers or Jewish soldiers in the service of Herod—probably the latter (Lieu 24). These soldiers often took advantage of their privileged position to extort money or property from the people or to make false charges against them (Lenski 195-196). John instructs them to be content with the salary that they receive and quit robbing the people.

These verses teach one important lesson; true repentance is more than just an intellectual exercise. It implies more than simply changing one's opinion; it demands a change in one's manner of living. Such a change involves, among other things, one's relationship with other people.

Verse 15 is a transition verse that serves to prepare the reader for the next section. It explains that the preaching and teaching of John caused people to stop and think. The teachings of John also produced a certain amount of perplexity as the people were struggling to understand what the teachings meant. Some were even thinking that John might be the promised Messiah; later verses will explain that he is not the Messiah but the one who prepares the way.

16 John answered, saying unto *them* all, I indeed baptize you with

water; but one mightier than I cometh, the latchet of whose shoes I am not worthy to unloose: he shall baptize you with the Holy Ghost and with fire:
17 Whose fan *is* in his hand, and he will throughly purge his floor, and will gather the wheat into his garner; but the chaff he will burn with fire unquenchable.
18 And many other things in his exhortation preached he unto the people.
19 But Herod the tetrarch, being reproved by him for Herodias his brother Philip's wife, and for all the evils which Herod had done,
20 Added yet this above all, that he shut up John in prison.

Verses 16-18 are directed to those who have come to be baptized by John. The first thing John does is to recognize the limitations of his ministry; he can baptize with water as an outward sign of their repentance and cleansing from sin. He cannot, however, baptize them with the Holy Spirit because that ministry is reserved for the Messiah. The "one mightier than I" is the Messiah, who is greater than John in every way. He is the Son of God, and John is not. He has the power to forgive sins and give eternal life while John can do neither of these. John is important, but his task is to prepare the way for the One who is even greater.

In ancient Palestine, most people wore some type of sandals rather than modern shoes that cover the entire foot. The term "latchet" describes the thong or strap that held the sandal on the foot. In a first-century household, it was the responsibility of the lowest-ranking slave to remove and clean the sandals of the master and of guests that might be visiting the home (Lenski 198-199). Morris (*Luke* 97) suggests this task was so lowly that it was restricted only to slaves; a disciple was forbidden to remove and clean the sandals of his teacher. By saying that he was unworthy to remove even the strap of the Messiah's sandal, John was not humiliating himself. On the contrary, he was recognizing the greatness, power, and majesty of the One who would come to be baptized by him.

John next explains to the crowd that the coming Messiah will perform a baptism that is much greater and more important than the water baptism he offers. The Messiah will baptize "with the Holy Ghost and with fire." These words should not be understood to mean that the Holy Spirit did not minister before this time. The idea is that the Messiah will pour out the Holy Spirit upon His followers in an unusual and powerful way. They will be empowered to do things that they have never been able to do before. This prophecy was fulfilled on the Day of Pentecost described in Acts 2.

The phrase "and with fire" is interpreted in different ways. Fire is used in the Bible to symbolize both destruction and purification. Summers (*Luke* 48) connects the baptism by fire with the judgment described in verse 17. In his view, the coming of the Holy Spirit will mean salvation for those who are baptized with the Holy Spirit and judgment for those baptized with fire. Creed (54) suggests the fire symbolizes both testing as well as destruction.

Most interpreters, however, understand the baptism with the Holy Spirit and with fire to describe one baptism and not two. The fire does not serve to destroy the unbeliever but to purify the believer and prepare him for service (Plummer 95; Lenski 201-202). According to this view, the baptism of the Holy Spirit and the baptism by fire work together. The followers of Christ will receive the power that can come only from the baptism by the Holy Spirit; they will also be purified for effective service.

The next verse presents a sharply different picture; it is a message of judgment for those who refuse to hear and heed the Messiah's message. Since the N. T. writers connect eternal judgment with Christ's Second Coming rather than with His first coming, these words should be understood against the background of the Second Coming. As Lenski (202) notes, John the Baptist (like the O. T. prophets) speaks of both comings of Christ without calling attention to the interval of time between them.

Verse 17 describes God's judgment, using the illustration of a farmer who harvests grain. The wheat is carried to the threshing floor where the stalks are separated from the heads, and the stalks are discarded. The heads of grain are then walked over to separate the kernels of grain from the husks, leaving a mixture of the two on the threshing floor. The farmer throws this mixture into the air with a large wooden shovel. The wind blows the chaff to the side while the heavier grain lands on the threshing floor. The chaff is then burned while the grain is gathered into bags to be ground into flour. At the end of the season, the farmer will cleanse his threshing floor of any remaining grain; the term "fan" is probably a reference to the broom that the farmer will use to clean his floor and prepare it for the next harvest.

The chaff in verse 17 clearly symbolizes those who reject the Messiah's message. They will be burned with a fire that never goes out. The idea is not that they will be totally destroyed or annihilated but they will be eternally punished in the most severe fashion.

Verses 18-20 serve to conclude Luke's description of the ministry of John the Baptist; from this point on his emphasis will be on the ministry of Jesus. Verse 18 explains that the words given here do not constitute the entirety of John's preaching; he had many other important things to say to the people. Verse 19 summarizes John's condemnation of the sins committed by Herod Antipas; fuller accounts are given in Matthew 14:1-12 and Mark 6:14-29. Herodias was the daughter of Aristobulus, a half-brother to Herod Antipas; she was married to another half-brother. Herod Antipas persuaded her to divorce her husband and marry him, even though he had to divorce his own wife to do so. John the Baptist bitterly condemned this incestuous marriage between Herodias and Herod Antipas. For his condemnation of this immoral relationship, John was imprisoned and ultimately executed (Morris, *Luke 98).* In verse 20, Luke points out that the worst of Herod Antipas' many crimes was the imprisonment of John the Baptist. With these words Luke concludes his discussion of the ministry of John the Baptist.

B. The Baptism of Jesus (3:21-22)

21 Now when all the people were baptized, it came to pass, that Jesus also being baptized, and praying, the heaven was opened,

22 And the Holy Ghost descended in a bodily shape like a dove upon him, and a voice came from heaven, which said, Thou art my beloved Son; in thee I am well pleased.

With these brief and simple words Luke relates the story of Jesus' baptism. Jesus came with a group of people who desired to be baptized. He came in an attitude of prayer; Luke gives special emphasis to prayer in the life and ministry of Jesus. Heaven was opened and the Holy Spirit came down like a dove and descended upon Jesus. Then the voice of God sounded from Heaven and said, "Thou art my beloved Son; in thee I am well pleased."

That "the heaven was opened" is theologically significant. Ellis (92) suggests the event should be understood as a vision. Marshall (*Gospel* 152) opines that the opening of heaven indicates that a divine revelation was about to take place. These words underscore the importance of the baptism of Jesus.

Luke notes that the Holy Spirit came down in bodily form as a dove. These words imply the Holy Spirit made Himself visible on that specific occasion so there could be no doubt about the reality of the Holy Spirit in Jesus' life. Luke does not explain who among those present was able to see this appearance of the Spirit. The fact that the Holy Spirit comes upon Jesus at this special time does not imply the Spirit had not been at work in His life on earlier occasions. The idea is that the Holy Spirit comes upon the Son of God in a special way, at the beginning of His public ministry, to prepare Him and empower Him for His future ministry (Lenski 211).

The word "dove" is used to describe several small birds of the pigeon family. The dove was a popular bird; it was widely raised domestically. It could be offered in sacrifice to God by poor families. In Jewish symbolism, the dove often stood as a symbol for Israel (Plummer 99). Commentators have speculated concerning the precise significance of the dove in this passage (Marshall, *Gospel* 153-154; Lenski 211). It has been suggested that the dove symbolizes friendliness, purity, innocence, or graciousness. The landing of a dove may indicate the gentleness with which the Spirit came upon Jesus. For an analysis of the significance of the dove in Jewish literature see Barrett (*Holy Spirit* 37-39).

The phrase "Thou art my beloved Son; in thee I am well pleased" seems to be drawn from two O. T. passages, Psalm 2:7 and Isaiah 42:1. These passages were understood (by some Jews at least) to be messianic. Lieu (27) explains that Jesus did not become the Son of God by virtue of His baptism. He had always been the Son of God. The idea is that God is fully satisfied with the life and ministry of His Son. As early as His visit to the Temple at age twelve, Jesus had demonstrated a growing understanding of His mission and of His relationship with His heavenly Father. That relationship has now come to maturity and will be fully manifested in Jesus' earthly ministry.

As Barrett (*Holy Spirit* 34) explains, the question of why Jesus submitted to baptism at the hands of John has been discussed in the church from its earliest days. In the case of Jesus, it is not a baptism of repentance because Jesus has no sin for which repentance is necessary. Barrett (*Holy Spirit* 35) suggests that it served to identify Jesus with the "same circle of prophetic and eschatological concepts as the Baptist." It indicated a break with the past and looked forward to the New Age to come. The baptism of Jesus placed God's official stamp of approval upon Him and upon His ministry. It affirmed that He is more than just the Messiah predicted in the O. T.; He is the very Son of God who has come to earth to do His Father's will.

Summary (3:1-22)

This important section makes a significant contribution to the theological development of Luke's Gospel. It is designed to help the reader understand the nature of Jesus' messiahship and to prepare him to receive the information that will be presented in the Gospel. The early verses of chapter 3 set the ministry of Jesus in its historical context. They serve to assure the reader that the events of Jesus' public ministry were real events that took place in a specific historical context. They must be interpreted from within that context.

In Luke's Gospel, John the Baptist serves as a transition figure. He is the last of the O. T. prophets; he serves to prepare the way for the larger and more comprehensive ministry that Jesus will exercise. Jesus is baptized by John the Baptist, but His baptism is different from that experienced by others. Jesus' baptism has nothing to do with the forgiveness of sins because He is the perfect Son of God and has no sins to be forgiven. His baptism provides an opportunity for a powerful and direct testimony by God. The Holy Spirit descends upon Jesus like a dove, and God places His stamp of approval on Jesus and His ministry.

Information about John the Baptist figures prominently in all three of the Synoptic Gospels, but Luke's use of it is rather unique. In Matthew and Mark the material about John is presented in different places in the Gospel. Luke, however, presents most of the information in these verses; only in 7:18-22 does John again enter the story. Luke wishes to complete his discussion of the life and ministry of John so from this point on he can concentrate his attention on Jesus. Luke's goal in this passage is that his Gentile readers understand the events that led up to the public ministry of Jesus.

These verses begin by placing the ministry of Jesus within the context of Judaism as Luke gives a brief description of the political context within which Jesus will minister. The preaching and teaching of John the Baptist help to outline the religious context of Jesus' ministry. The fact that John has to preach such a stern message of repentance gives some indication of the difficult religious conditions that existed at that time; it is inevitable that Jesus will face conflict with such an entrenched religious and political system.

John proclaims a message of repentance that is drawn from key O. T. passages. He summons his hearers to make a radical break with the past and establish an entirely new direction in their lives. This serves to prepare Luke's Gentile readers to receive the message of Jesus who will present teachings which are, in some ways, similar to John's preaching.

In the latter verses of this passage, John clarifies his own relationship with Jesus. He stresses that he is not the Messiah; his task is to prepare the way. He proclaims a baptism of repentance while Jesus will in the future proclaim a baptism by the Holy Spirit and fire. One thing that should be noted in this passage is John's consistent condemnation of sin wherever he finds it. He describes the people coming to be baptized as a "brood of vipers;" he even condemns the governor, Herod Antipas, for his incestuous marriage with his brother's wife. John plays no favorites; he condemns sin at all levels of society.

The final verses in this section describe the baptism of Jesus. Jesus is baptized by John, but Luke does not specifically state that. Nor does he explain *why* Jesus is baptized; as the perfect Son of God, Jesus needs no repentance. The most likely explanation is that Jesus is baptized in order to place His stamp of approval on the ministry of John; He also wants to identify publicly with those who are repenting of their sins and beginning a new direction in their lives. The baptism also serves as a fitting inauguration of His public ministry.

Application: Teaching and Preaching the Passage

A character study of John the Baptist would be a most profitable series of sermons or lessons. He demonstrates a sincere commitment to serve the Lord Jesus and displays an attitude of humility. He does not demand a high rank or status; he is content to be the forerunner. His life is characterized by righteousness in that he takes the commands of God seriously; he lives a consecrated life and he also wants others to live that kind of life. John understands the evils of the society around him, and he calls the people to repentance. He challenges them to change the direction of their lives and make their lives conform to their confessions. They can never expect to be right with God if they continue as they are.

Repentance is another key theme in this passage that deserves to be preached and taught. This passage clearly points out that repentance, in its true Christian sense, is more than just a mental or intellectual change. It is a reorientation of the believer's character as one's goals and priorities are changed. There is a new emphasis on serving God and living according to His instructions. Repentance is both necessary and possible. Those whom John baptizes in this passage are giving an outward testimony to the inward change that has taken place in their lives. No one is excluded from the necessity of repentance.

God's judgment is another theme that figures prominently in this passage. Those who refuse to repent and who choose to continue in their sinful ways will face the judgment of God. God is patient and longsuffering, but He will only tolerate sin so long. Throughout these verses, John warns of the tragic consequences that sin produces. No one is exempt from God's judgment; it even reaches to the palace of the governor.

C. The Genealogy of Jesus (3:23-38)

23 And Jesus himself began to be about thirty years of age, being (as was supposed) the son of Joseph, which was *the son* of Heli,
24 Which was *the son* of Matthat, which was *the son* of Levi, which was *the son* of Melchi, which was *the son* of Janna, which was *the son* of Joseph,

25 Which was *the son* of
Mattathias, which was *the son* of
Amos, which was *the son* of Naum,
which was *the son* of Esli, which
was *the son* of Nagge,
26 Which was *the son* of Maath,
which was *the son* of Mattathias,
which was *the son* of Semei, which
was *the son* of Joseph, which was
the son of Juda,
27 Which was *the son* of Joanna,
which was *the son* of Rhesa, which
was *the son* of Zorobabel, which
was *the son* of Salathiel, which
was *the son* of Neri,
28 Which was *the son* of Melchi,
which was *the son* of Addi, which
was *the son* of Cosam, which was
the son of Elmodam, which was
the son of Er,
29 Which was *the son* of Jose,
which was *the son* of Eliezer,
which was *the son* of Jorim, which
was *the son* of Matthat, which was
the son of Levi,
30 Which was *the son* of Simeon,
which was *the son* of Juda, which
was *the son* of Joseph, which was
the son of Jonan, which was *the
son* of Eliakim,
31 Which was *the son* of Melea,
which was *the son* of Menan,
which was *the son* of Mattatha,
which was *the son* of Nathan,
which was *the son* of David,
32 Which was *the son* of Jesse,
which was *the son* of Obed, which
was *the son* of Booz, which was
the son of Salmon, which was *the
son* of Naasson,
33 Which was *the son* of
Aminadab, which was *the son* of
Aram, which was *the son* of Esrom,
which was *the son* of Phares,
which was *the son* of Juda,
34 Which was *the son* of Jacob,
which was *the son* of Isaac, which
was *the son* of Abraham, which
was *the son* of Thara, which was
the son of Nachor,
35 Which was *the son* of Saruch,
which was *the son* of Ragau, which
was *the son* of Phalec, which was
the son of Heber, which was *the
son* of Sala,
36 Which was *the son* of Cainan,
which was *the son* of Arphaxad,
which was *the son* of Sem, which
was *the son* of Noe, which was *the
son* of Lamech,
37 Which was *the son* of
Mathusala, which was *the son* of
Enoch, which was *the son* of Jared,
which was *the son* of Maleleel,
which was *the son* of Cainan,
38 Which was *the son* of Enos,
which was *the son* of Seth, which
was *the son* of Adam, which was
the son of God.

Luke begins, now, to focus on the person of Jesus Christ. He wants to ensure that his Gentile readers understand who Jesus is and what qualifies Him for the important ministry He is about to begin. It is interesting to note that Luke alone among the Gospel writers notes that Jesus' public ministry began when He was about thirty years old (Geldenhuys 150). This was the approximate age when a Jewish priest began his active service (Liefeld 861); it may also indicate that Jesus was of sufficient age and maturity to undertake such an important ministry (Nolland I:171). Barclay (39-40) suggests Joseph may have died at a relatively young age and Jesus accepted the responsibility of supporting the family until His younger siblings could take over the family business. One thing is certain, those years in Nazareth gave Jesus the opportunity to learn first-hand what it meant to be a Palestinian Jew. He learned what life was like and how to put His own teachings into practice. Liefeld (861) explains that the number "thirty" is a round number; he posits that Jesus was probably in His mid-thirties when His public ministry began.

Genealogies were important in ancient Israel because they helped to establish one's identity and to trace one's ancestral history (Jeremias, *Jerusalem* 297). Since Joseph and Mary were descendants of David, the line from which the Messiah would come, it is possible they paid special attention to preserving their genealogies (Geldenhuys 151). Nolland (I:169) notes that genealogies served several purposes in Israel and that we cannot today determine with absolute certainty what all of those purposes were. They established individual identity, social status, and helped determine an individual's fitness for office. Genealogies of priests were kept as matters of public record, and in the times of Ezra and Nehemiah priests lost their positions because they could not produce a genealogy (Barclay 40).

Both Matthew and Luke understand the importance of determining the genealogy of Jesus (Liefeld 861), but there are several important differences between these two genealogies. Matthew begins his Gospel with the genealogy; Luke places his at the beginning of Jesus' public ministry. Matthew follows the traditional order by beginning with Abraham (Nolland I:167-168); this emphasizes Jesus' Jewish heritage. Luke reverses the normal order (Nolland I:167; Fitzmyer I:491); he begins with Jesus and traces His heritage all the way back to Adam. In the opinion of many commentators, this indicates that Jesus is the Savior of all of humanity (Liefeld 861; Geldenhuys 152; Morris, *Luke* 101).

In the various manuscripts of the N. T. there are some differences in the number of names found in this genealogy, but most scholars agree that Luke's genealogy consists of 78 names (including both *Jesus* and *God*) implying 77 generations. The names in Jewish genealogies were often given in groups of seven or ten as an aid to memorization, and that seems to be the pattern here. Several of the individuals mentioned in this list are found in the O. T., but thirty-six of them are otherwise unknown (Fitzmyer I:490-491).

A detailed analysis of the differences between Luke's genealogy and Matthew's is beyond the scope of this commentary. Fitzmyer (I:492-496), Nolland (I:167-170), and Bock (I:348-362) provide useful summaries of this important issue. The existence of these differences has been recognized since the earliest days of the church, and several different explanations have been offered. One popular explanation is that Matthew gives Joseph's genealogy while Luke gives Mary's (Bock, *Luke* IVP 80). This view is ably defended by Geldenhuys (150-155) and Lenski (218-221), but it has never won the support of a majority of scholars. The major disadvantage of this view is that there is in Judaism no history of tracing a female line of descent (Bock, *Luke* IVP 81; Fitzmyer I:497). Also, in his genealogy Luke never mentions Mary; instead, he specifically mentions Joseph and refers to him as "the son of Heli."

Edersheim (*Life* I:149) notes that almost all interpreters view both as genealogies of Joseph, but many interpreters posit that Matthew and Luke trace Jesus' line of descent in two different ways. For example, Matthew may present the natural line while Luke presents the royal line (Bock, *Luke* IVP 81). These explanations often involve the use of the Jewish custom of levirate marriage described in Deuteronomy 25:5-10.

The father of Joseph is the one person mentioned in both genealogies who has received the most attention from ancient and modern commentators. Luke 2:23 refers to Joseph as the son of Heli while Matthew 1:16 describes him as the son of Jacob. The third century writer Africanus explained this difference as the result of a levirate marriage. He suggested that Heli died childless; his widow married a man named Jacob. Jacob was the physical father of Joseph, but Heli was regarded as the legal father under the Jewish laws of levirate marriage. According to Africanus, both Matthew and Luke give genealogies of Joseph, but Matthew lists the physical father while Luke names the legal father (Morris, *Luke* 100). A similar explanation is offered by Machen (204-205). It seems that Luke is concerned to show that Jesus was a descendant both of Judah and of Levi; that would make Him both king and priest.

Nolland (I:173-174) suggests that Mary was an heiress who had no brothers. When she married Joseph, Joseph was adopted by Mary's father whose genealogy is found in Luke. Nolland explains that Jesus was not the natural son of Joseph, but His genealogy properly is that of Joseph because under Jewish law he has the status of a son and heir.

The comparison of the genealogies in Matthew and Luke is a difficult and complex issue. Marshall (*Gospel* 158) gives an excellent summary of the solutions, which are most commonly offered today. He notes that we do not have sufficient information to resolve all the differences between them. Machen (209) also recognizes the difficulties faced in the study of these two genealogies, but he concludes that the differences are not irreconcilable. In his view, both are genealogies of Joseph. Matthew gives the legal descendants of David, the list of those who would have occupied the throne if the Davidic line had continued. Luke, on the other hand, gives the particular line of David's descendants to which Joseph belonged (Machen 204).

The most important issues in Luke's genealogy are theological. The author's purpose is to show that Jesus is a true son of David who satisfies the legal requirements to serve as the Messiah. As Bock (*Luke* IVP 81) affirms, Jesus can claim David's royal throne because of His Davidic heritage; He is also related to all humanity through His descent from Adam. In another work, Bock (I:350) suggests this genealogy is designed to show that Jesus meets all the requisite qualifications to be the promised Messiah. He is in David's royal line, He is connected to the Jewish patriarch Abraham, and His descent from Adam connects Him to all of humanity. The most important thing, however, is that He is the Son of God. He is the unique Son whom the Father has sent to accomplish this important ministry. Morris (*Luke* 101) suggests that Luke uses the genealogy to show Jesus' true humanity. Geldenhuys (155) posits that Luke's main purpose is to show that from the standpoint of human descent, Jesus is one with all of humanity.

Summary (3:23-38)

Genealogies were important in ancient Israel for several reasons, and this genealogy serves an important historical and theological purpose. It traces Jesus' lineage back to God and to the creation of Adam in the Garden of Eden. It connects Jesus with all of humanity and not just with the nation of Israel. The idea is that Jesus is the universal Son of God who came to make salvation available to all mankind.

Application: Teaching and Preaching the Passage

This genealogy should be used in conjunction with other passages that deal with the heritage of Jesus. It is designed to confirm for Luke's Gentile readers that Jesus is both the Son of God and the Son of Man; He is the perfect representative of the Father. He is also the perfect human being who can offer the perfect sacrifice for sins that God demands. He is the universal Savior, and the forgiveness of sins is available through Him for all the peoples of the world. This genealogy is one of the proofs offered by Luke that Jesus fully satisfies all of the requirements to be the Messiah.

D. The Temptations of Jesus (4:1-13)

Jesus' temptation in the wilderness is, according to Spence (84), "perhaps, the most mysterious and least understood of any of the scenes of the public ministry related by the evangelists." The biblical texts offer no reason why this testing is necessary (*Stein, Messiah* 103); they simply assume that it is. This testing of Jesus in the desert is the final episode in His preparation for the public ministry; Fitzmyer (I:506) notes that it is closely connected both to the baptism and to the genealogy. This entire series of events serves to demonstrate that Jesus is indeed the Son of God and possesses all the qualifications necessary to begin His public ministry. He has overcome severe trials and is now ready to assume the ministry His Father has for Him.

Summers (*Luke* 55) explains that scholars tend to interpret these temptations in one of two ways. Some see them as a representative summary of all the temptations Jesus faced during His earthly ministry. Others see them as a singular experience that Jesus endured after His baptism and before the beginning of His public ministry. The second of these is the traditional interpretation, which Summers prefers.

According to Barclay (42) and Stein (*Messiah* 103), these temptations demonstrate what kind of Messiah Jesus would be and how He would perform His ministry. Jesus will reject a messiahship based on earthly power and glory in favor of one built upon service and suffering. His goal is not to draw attention to Himself but to do the will of His heavenly Father; He will not use His divine power to serve Himself but to minister to others (Bock I:363). Barrett (*Holy Spirit* 48) explains that this is a messianic temptation in the sense that only the Messiah "could be tempted to establish himself over against God as an independent divine being."

The story of the temptations is told in all three Synoptic Gospels. Mark's account is very brief; it simply mentions the fact that Jesus was tempted and notes that after His temptations were completed the angels came and ministered to Him. Matthew and Luke both give more detailed accounts of the temptations, and there is much agreement in their accounts. In fact, the only significant difference between them lies in the order of the temptations. The temptation for Jesus to cast Himself down from a pinnacle of the Temple is the second temptation in Matthew; it is the third in Luke.

Many commentators have examined the relationship between these two accounts and tried to explain this difference in order. While some argue that Luke's order is the original one, the consensus of scholars today is that Matthew's order came first. Because of his special interest in the Temple and in the city of Jerusalem, Luke has reversed the second and third temptations in order to bring the temptations to a climax in Jerusalem (Twelftree, DJG 823). It should be noted that chronology was not as important in the ancient world as it is today; books were often arranged topically rather than chronologically (Bock I:366). The most important thing is not the precise order in which the temptations took place, but the message that Jesus is victorious over the temptations.

4:1 And Jesus being full of the Holy Ghost returned from Jordan, and was led by the Spirit into the wilderness,

The phrases "full of the Holy Ghost" and "led by the Spirit" imply that Jesus was under the complete control of the Holy Spirit; this does not mean He was not under the control of the Holy Spirit at other times in His ministry. Luke's purpose is to show that at this crucial time there were no ulterior motives; His life and ministry were totally under the Spirit's direction. The coming temptations were not contrary to the Holy Spirit's plan for His life; they were part of it.

The phrase "returned from Jordan" connects the temptations with the baptism of Jesus, which was described in the previous chapter. "Returned" (Greek *hupostrephō)* can be interpreted in two different ways. It may mean that Jesus left the Jordan River and returned to His home in Galilee. Or it may simply mean that He withdrew from the Jordan River Valley and went into the wilderness. In light of the context, the second of these two interpretations is to be preferred.

The term "wilderness" describes the large desert area that occupies the southern part of the land of Palestine (Lenski 223). Early Christian tradition suggests that the temptations took place in a hilly area on the road between Jericho and Jerusalem (Spence 86); but the text itself mentions no specific location. Bock (I:369) notes that the wilderness is often presented as an area of demonic activity, but in this passage it seems that He went there to commune with His heavenly Father.

2 Being forty days tempted of the devil. And in those days he did eat nothing: and when they were ended, he afterward hungered.

The key word here is the verb "tempted" (Greek *peirazō*), with the root idea "to try, test, or prove" (Lenski 225; Marshall, *Gospel* 169; Barrett, *Holy Spirit* 51). The word occurs often in the

Greek O. T. where it is used in several ways. It is used to describe God's testing of human beings to determine the strength and vitality of their faith. It is also used to describe how men put God to the test, often in times of doubt and unbelief (Marshall, *Gospel* 169). During the period of the wilderness wanderings, God often tested the faithfulness and commitment of His people (Ex. 16:4, 20:20; Dt. 8:2, 13:2-5). The word may also, in certain contexts, include the negative idea of "to tempt"—to entice to sin—which is the case here (Lenski 225).

In this passage, Jesus is put to the test and tempted; He must demonstrate His sincerity and His commitment to the ministry entrusted to Him by His heavenly Father. He must show by His words and His actions what kind of Messiah He will be (Morris, *Luke* 102). In this passage, Jesus is not tempted by any human being or by His own desire (as in James 1:14); He is tempted by the Devil. The implication of the passage is that such testing is a necessary and appropriate prerequisite to beginning His public ministry; the testing is done with God's permission.

In his brief account of the temptation, Mark uses the proper name "Satan" to describe the tempter. "Satan" is a Hebrew word that means "adversary." Matthew and Luke use the term "devil" to describe the tempter. This word is an adjective meaning "the slanderer" or "the adversary," used here for Satan. The period of temptation lasts forty days; whether Jesus was tempted continuously or intermittently during this time, Luke does not explain. The number *forty* has a long and interesting history in the O. T. Israel wandered in the wilderness for forty years; forty lashes was the most a person could receive; forty days was the period of a woman's uncleanness after birth. Forty days was the length of Moses' fasts described in Exodus 34:28 and Deuteronomy 9:9. These O. T. events lasting forty days marked very important events in the history of Israel. In a similar way, the temptations constitute an event of singular importance in the beginning of Jesus' public ministry. Luke's purpose is to demonstrate that Jesus' temptations are important, and He more than met every test that confronted Him.

The second half of verse 2 introduces the element of fasting into the story. Although he does not specifically use the term "fasting," it is clear that Luke has fasting in mind. Many commentators (such as Lenski) simply assume that the phrase "in those days" means Jesus went without food for the entire period of forty days. Luke does not, however, make that specific—although Matthew may. Technically, Luke may mean that Jesus fasted during the entire forty days or that He fasted at times during the forty day period.

Fasting was an important religious and social custom both for Jews and for early Christians, but it is difficult to determine whether or not Jesus' temptations reflect the normal practices of the Jews. There is no evidence that indicates Jesus fasted on a regular basis, but He did on certain occasions (Jn. 4:31-34) go without food and drink (DJG 234). When Jesus did fast, it was often in the context of prayer, evangelism, or other spiritual struggles.

H. Guthrie (242-243) points out that there are comparatively few references to fasting among the Jews prior to the Babylonian Exile. During the Exile, fasts generally grew out of the needs of a specific situation; after the Exile, they became more common and better organized among the Jews. The annual Day of Atonement became a regular time for fasting. Matthew 9:14, Mark 2:18, and Luke 5:33 indicate that in the time of Jesus, the Pharisees and the disciples of John fasted regularly while the disciples of Jesus were criticized for not observing these fasts. Lewis (ISBE 1099) explains that the Jews fasted in different ways. A fast could be total or partial; those fasting might, for example, avoid certain foods but not all foods. They might avoid solid food but drink liquids; fasting could be practiced for an extended period of time or for a brief time.

"And in those days He did eat nothing" indicates that Jesus' fast was a total one. Probably the best interpretation is that Jesus was so focused on His ministry as the Son of God that He did not eat during this time. No doubt His physical body was in a weakened condition at the end of His fast, but God gave Him the spiritual strength necessary to endure the temptations.

3 And the devil said unto him, If thou be the Son of God, command this stone that it be made bread.
4 And Jesus answered him, saying, It is written, That man shall not live by bread alone, but by every word of God.

This is the first of three temptations; it deals with how Jesus would use the power given to Him. After a period of fasting, Jesus' physical body was hungry. Bread was the staple food of ancient Israel, and it was normally baked in small flat loaves that were similar in appearance to the stones at Jesus' feet. The devil tempts Jesus to use His divine power in a selfish manner to satisfy His physical hunger. There is nothing inherently wrong with making bread from stones; Jesus will perform various miracles during His public ministry. To change stones into bread to satisfy His own hunger, however, would be a selfish use of divine power and would reflect a lack of trust in His Father's provision (Marshall, *Gospel* 170-171, Bock I:372-373; Lenski 229).

Jesus responds by quoting a portion of Deuteronomy 8:3, "man shall not live by bread alone but by every word of God." Moses was giving his people instructions about what they were to do after entering the land of Canaan. He reminded Israel how God had protected them and provided for them during the wilderness wanderings. Jesus can reject this temptation because He is confident that God will provide food for Him just as God had provided manna for the people of Israel during their wilderness sojourn. Even in a time of fasting, Jesus is more concerned with doing the will of God than He is with satisfying His physical hunger.

The phrase "if thou be the Son of God" (v. 3) has produced considerable discussion among the commentators. This grammatical construction (Greek first class condition) assumes that the condition stated in the "if" clause will be fulfilled or is very likely to be fulfilled: thus, "since you are the Son of God." Satan is not challenging the fact that Jesus is the Son of God; such a temptation would be too obvious. His temptation is more subtle, tempting Jesus to use His power and authority in an improper fashion. Satan may be suggesting that Jesus, because He is the Son of God, has the power to do anything. Jesus refuses to fall into his trap and remains faithful to the ministry God has entrusted to Him.

5 And the devil, taking him up into an high mountain, shewed unto him all the kingdoms of the world in a moment of time.
6 And the devil said unto him, All this power will I give thee, and the glory of them: for that is delivered unto me; and to whomsoever I will I give it.
7 If thou therefore wilt worship me, all shall be thine.
8 And Jesus answered and said to him, Get thee behind me, Satan: for it is written, Thou shalt worship the Lord thy God, and him only shalt thou serve.

The second temptation also deals with the nature of Jesus' messiahship. As Lenski (234) notes, this temptation appeals to Jesus' human nature. It is designed to offer Him the opportunity to exercise great power and authority without the suffering and death that His ministry would demand. It is clear that Jesus views all the inhabited earth and is offered the opportunity to exercise all earthly power (Bock I:375). If He will but prostrate Himself before the devil, Jesus can achieve the crown quickly and easily and without paying such a high price for it (Lenski 234).

Satan's offer is a mixture of truth and error (Bock I:376); there is no doubt he has great power and authority in the world. His authority is, however, neither legitimate nor unlimited; Satan is the great usurper and the father of lies. He often promises more than he can deliver. Yet, his temptations are real; countless men and women have fallen victim to them. Jesus does not yield to the devil's temptation to give to him the worship and service that rightfully belong to God alone (Marshall, *Gospel* 172). Once again, Jesus responds with words selected from the O. T. He answers with a summary of Deuteronomy 6:13, "Thou shalt worship the Lord thy God, and him only shalt thou serve." Jesus understands that to offer to Satan the worship and obedience he demands would destroy His relationship with God, and that He refuses to do.

This second temptation has produced considerable discussion among conservative commentators for different reasons. Many manuscripts of Luke do not include the words "into a high mountain." According to these manuscripts the devil "takes him up and shows him all the kingdoms of the world" (Lenski 232). The other issue is the nature of this experience. Some interpret it to mean that the body of Jesus is physically transported to a high place from which He can see "all the kingdoms of the world." Lenski (232-233) defends this position; he writes that we cannot explain how this event happened, but he views it as a physical experience.

Other conservative commentators, like Spence (85), argue that there is no mountain or high place from which one can see the world. He notes that such spiritual experiences are found in the lives of the O. T. prophets. His conclusion: "The whole transaction lay in the spiritual region of the life of Christ, but on that account it was not the less real and true." Twelftree (DJG 822) posits that this was a spiritual experience similar to other encounters that Jesus had with Satan in Luke 10:18 and 22:31-32. Whether the temptation involves a physical transportation or a spiritual journey, the basic lesson is that Jesus must accomplish His mission in the proper way.

Stein (*Messiah* 104) suggests that Jesus' temptations contain a mixture of physical and spiritual elements. The temptations take place at a definite time and place; they are real events. They should not be viewed as totally visionary or spiritual in nature. On the other hand, the temptations also contain visionary or spiritual elements. There is no physical place from which all the kingdoms of the earth can be seen. That particular experience, then, must be viewed as spiritual or visionary.

9 And he brought him to Jerusalem, and set him on a pinnacle of the temple, and said unto him, If thou be the son of God, cast thyself down from hence:
10 For it is written, He shall give his angels charge over thee, to keep thee:
11 And in *their* hands they shall bear thee up, lest at any time thou dash thy foot against a stone.
12 And Jesus answering said unto him, It is said, Thou shalt not tempt the Lord thy God.
13 And when the devil had ended all the temptation, he departed from him for a season.

In Luke's third temptation, Jesus is taken to a pinnacle of the Temple in Jerusalem, which has been interpreted in various ways. Barclay (44) understands it to mean the high point of the Temple in Jerusalem where Solomon's Porch and the Royal Porch met. From this point there was a drop of 450 feet to the floor of the Kidron Valley. Bock (*Luke* IVP 84) argues that the precise location cannot be determined with certainty; it could be the high temple gate. More likely it refers to the Royal Porch. Nolland (I:181) agrees that the location cannot be determined with certainty. He suggests the "royal colonnade" mentioned by Josephus as a possibility.

Satan's challenge begins in the same way as the preceding one, with a condition assumed true (Greek first class condition), which could accurately be translated, "since you are the son of God cast thyself down from hence." Once again, Jesus is being tempted to use His power as the Son of God in an improper manner. Satan follows this challenge with two quotations from Psalm 91:11-12 in the Greek O. T. In their original context, these verses emphasized God's care for His people. Satan misapplies this teaching and uses it to encourage Jesus to begin His public ministry by performing a miracle rather than by being obedient to His heavenly Father. Once again, Jesus does not fall into Satan's trap; He chooses to be obedient to God rather than amaze the crowds. He will not put His heavenly Father to the test; He understands that to put God to the test is not an act of faith but an act of unbelief (Bock, *Luke* IVP 85).

Jesus responds to the temptation by quoting the first words of Deuteronomy 6:16, "Thou shalt not tempt the Lord thy God." The full text of Deuteronomy 6:16 reads, "Ye shall not tempt the LORD your God, as ye tempted *him* in Massah." According to Exodus 17:1-7, Massah was the location where the people tempted God by doubting His provision for them during the wilderness wanderings. There was a shortage of water, and the people accused both God and Moses of bringing them into the wilderness only to let them die of thirst. Had Jesus yielded to Satan's temptation, He would have doubted the provision and protection of God just as the people of Israel had done during the wilderness wandering. Nolland (I:181) notes that "the faithful man does not seek to dictate to God how He must express His covenant loyalty and fulfill His promises."

Should this third temptation be interpreted to mean that Jesus was physically transported from the wilderness to Jerusalem? Does it mean that Satan appeared and spoke with Jesus in a physical sense? Conservative commentators are divided on these issues. Lenski (237) argues that Jesus was physically transferred to the Temple in Jerusalem. Most interpreters, however, do not go that far. Bock (I:364), for example, sees all three temptations as actual historical events; not dreams or hallucinations; but he accepts that the temptations might have included inward or spiritual experiences.

Shepard (77) expresses no definite opinion on the issue. He writes that the temptation was just as real whether Jesus was transported physically or mentally. When the passage quotes what the Devil said, does that necessarily mean the Devil appeared there physically? Most commentators would say "no," because the Bible uniformly presents Satan as a spiritual being. Spence (85) argues that the devil did not appear physically or bodily, but that Jesus met him and defeated him in the spiritual realm.

Luke concludes the discussion of the temptations by saying that when the devil had ended the temptation, "he departed from Him for a season." This specific period of temptation had ended, but Satan's efforts to hinder the work of Christ would continue. In Luke 22:3, Satan will enter into Judas Iscariot and lead him to betray Christ. There are in Luke other examples of conflict between Christ and Satan and his demons (Lk. 4:33-36, 8:12, 9:38-42, 10:18, 11:14-20).

Summary (4:1-13)

Jesus' temptations contribute to the structure and development of Luke's Gospel in important ways. They serve as a bridge between His baptism and the beginning of His public ministry. Both Jesus' baptism and His temptations are important parts of a series of events demonstrating that Jesus is indeed the Messiah. They also help define the kind of Messiah that Jesus will be and how He will accomplish the ministry God has given Him. In His baptism, Jesus closely identifies with His followers.

The temptations could only have come to one who had great power and who was conscious of His ability to use that power (Barclay 42-43). No ordinary man can be tempted to turn stones into bread. He knows his limitations; he simply does not have the ability to work such a miracle. For Jesus, however, the temptations are very real. They come directly to the heart of His ministry; they help to establish the kind of Messiah He intends to be. It is important to note that Jesus establishes His Messiahship as much by what He *does not* do as by what He *does*. He refuses to allow Satan to determine His agenda. There is no doubt that Jesus is able to work miracles, but He is under no obligation to do so. He alone determines when a miracle is needed and appropriate. As A. Bruce notes, temptation does not weaken spiritual power; rather it strengthens it (EGT I:488).

Marshall (*Luke* NBC-1994 987) explains that the temptations were not so much a challenge to Jesus' messiahship as they were a challenge to His relationship with His heavenly Father. Had Jesus succumbed to these temptations, His relationship with God would have been seriously affected. It is important to note that Jesus responds to each of the temptations by quoting from the Scripture. He understands the power that lies behind God's Word and how the Word will enable Him to resist even the most difficult temptation.

Application: Teaching and Preaching the Passage

Jesus is the Son of God. While He was here on earth He could be tempted to perform miracles that no ordinary human being could be tempted to do. No ordinary human being will, for example, be tempted to turn stones into bread. There are, however, certain similarities between the kind of temptations Jesus faced in this passage and the temptations and trials His followers face every day. Preaching and teaching on this passage should focus on the importance of resisting temptation and how it can be successfully resisted. It is not the will of God that His children fall victim to the wiles of the Devil.

Temptations and trials are not the same, but they are closely related. God may test our faith in order to strengthen us, but He will never tempt His children to sin. The events described in these verses should be understood, from Satan's perspective, as temptations rather than as trials or tests. They are not initiated by God; they are initiated by Satan. They are not designed to strengthen Jesus' relationship with His heavenly Father but to weaken or destroy that relationship.

Jesus is tempted to do good things for the wrong reasons. There is nothing inherently wrong with changing stones to bread, for example; during His earthly ministry Jesus performed a number of miracles that were equally supernatural. When Jesus performed miracles, He always did them to glorify God and for the benefit of mankind. He never performed miracles for selfish reasons. In this passage, Jesus is tempted to use His divine power for selfish reasons. He refuses to use the power that has been entrusted to Him to glorify Himself or to satisfy His own desires.

Jesus understood the reality of temptation; He also understood that it came not from God but from Satan. Christians today must have that same understanding. They will face many different types of temptations; they may be tempted by material goods, physical pleasures, selfish desires, position, prestige, and many other things. Recognizing temptation is not always easy. Believers must develop the capacity to recognize what temptation is and understand that it comes from Satan. They must be able to distinguish between desires that may be good and temptations that are harmful.

Believers may be tempted to do good things but in a manner that is not pleasing to God and is ultimately harmful to the Christian life. Temptation involves both what we do and how we do it. Those who preach and teach on this passage have an obligation to assist their hearers in recognizing the variety of temptations they will face in life. Temptation is not, in and of itself, sin; but it can lead to sinful conduct.

Although He was the Son of God, Jesus did not depend on His own resources to resist temptation. He turned to the Word of God where He found the knowledge and the strength necessary to defeat Satan's attacks. This illustrates an important principle for the follower of Christ. Believers do not have within themselves the resources to defeat temptation, but the resources are available in God's Word. It is important that the believer be prepared to resist temptation, which will surely come. A good understanding of Scripture can do much to help the Christian stand against the temptations he will face.

Temptations may be subtle and hard to recognize, but the followers of Christ do not have to yield to them. The Word of God and the leadership of the Holy Spirit are powerful weapons to use against Satan and his devices.

IV. THE MINISTRY IN GALILEE (4:14—9:50)

This large section of Luke's Gospel presents an overview of the early part of the ministry of Jesus, beginning at His home town of Nazareth and continuing as His ministry spreads into other areas. These chapters focus on Jesus' teaching and the working of miracles. These teachings and miracles together serve not only to establish that Jesus is the Messiah, but also to help define the type of messianic ministry He will have. Jesus will focus His attention on liberating the people from the power of sin and darkness; He will not undertake to establish any type of political or military kingdom. The goal of His ministry will be the transformation of individuals into His own likeness, and His appeal will be to the common but pious people of the land rather than to the rich and powerful.

A. Examples of Jesus' Teaching in Galilee (4:14-44)

These verses provide a brief summary of Jesus' ministry in Galilee; in this passage He combines teaching (4:16-30) with miracles (4:31-44). They also serve to introduce several themes that will be developed throughout the Galilean ministry. The sermon in the synagogue at Nazareth, for example, illustrates how Jesus will take the teachings of the O. T. and apply them to Himself. The negative reaction of the congregation illustrates how difficult it will be for the people to understand His ministry. His teaching and preaching will often lead to rejection and ridicule. The miracles in Capernaum emphasize that Jesus will continually struggle with the evil forces that seek to destroy His ministry. The passage concludes with a description of how Jesus withdraws from the crowds for a time of reflection on the nature of the ministry God has entrusted to Him. Jesus comes out of that time of reflection with an even greater determination to preach the Kingdom of God.

14 And Jesus returned in the power of the Spirit into Galilee: and there went out a fame of him through all the region round about. 15 And he taught in their synagogues, being glorified of all.

These verses are similar to other summary statements given by Luke (Acts 6:7, 12:24-25, 16:4-5). They serve both as an introduction to and a summary of the early part of Jesus' public ministry in Galilee (Bock I:390). Lieu

(31) suggests these verses serve as an introduction to Jesus' sermon in Nazareth. These transition verses serve several purposes. First, they move the reader from the temptations to the early portion of Jesus' public ministry in Galilee. Second, they give a brief summary of Jesus' activities and explain how He came to be well known in that region. Teaching in the synagogues was not all that Jesus did, but it is a key element in His public ministry from its beginning. Third, they indicate that the ministry takes place under the leadership of the Holy Spirit. Luke does not explain in detail how the Spirit works in the life of Jesus; his goal is to show that Jesus' public ministry is more than a mere human effort. Finally, these verses indicate that during the early part of His ministry Jesus' teachings and miracles are generally well received by those who hear Him. The attacks and opposition will come later.

After the temptations that take place in Judaea, Jesus turns north and returns to Galilee where He had grown up (Lk. 2:51). Galilee was the northern part of the land of Palestine. After the conquest under Joshua, this territory was given to the tribe of Naphtali who never fully expelled the Gentiles from it (Jg. 1:33). In later years, this territory was expanded to include the land given to Zebulun and Issachar. In the time of Jesus, it extended as far south as the valley of Esdraelon. Some Jews settled in this region after the Babylonian Exile, but it was not brought under Jewish control until the time of John Hyrcanus about 135-105 B.C. (Dana 40). In Jesus' day this land was controlled by the Jews, but the form of Judaism practiced there was less strict than in Judaea. Many Gentiles also lived in this territory (Dana 40-41); because of the large number of Gentiles living there, the more strict Jews regarded Galilee as a corrupt area.

Luke calls attention to the fact that Jesus returns to Galilee "in the power of the Spirit." The idea is that the power of the Holy Spirit is upon Jesus in a special way. The Spirit's primary role is to lead and guide Jesus in His ministry of teaching (Bock I:391). The leadership of the Spirit is not limited to the working of miracles; it extends to teaching and to other aspects of Jesus' public ministry (Fitzmyer I:523). A. Bruce (EGT I:488) points out that the temptations had not weakened the Spirit's power in the life of Jesus; in fact, they strengthened it.

During the first century, the Temple and the Synagogue existed side by side; they were the two most important institutions in Jewish society. There was only one Temple, located in Jerusalem. There animals were offered in sacrifice to God; there Jesus had been dedicated during His infancy. The Temple that was standing in Jesus' day is commonly known as the Second Temple or Herod's Temple. The first temple, constructed by Solomon, was destroyed during the Babylonians conquest of Judah. It was rebuilt on a much smaller scale after the Jewish people returned from exile. During the time of Herod, it was expanded and improved; that renovation and expansion was still going on during Jesus' ministry. For more information about the Temple as it existed in the first century, consult M. Wise ("Temple" in DJG) and NIDNTT (I:135-137; III:785-793, 1055-1068).

"Synagogue" (Greek *sunagogē*) means "a gathering together." In the time of Jesus, the synagogue was still a relatively new institution, never mentioned in the O. T. Its origins are somewhat shrouded in mystery. The most commonly accepted theory is that it originated during the Babylonian Exile when the Jewish people were separated from their homeland and their Temple (Fitzmyer I:523-524; Bock I:392). In order to preserve their religious life, the Jews began to meet together for worship, prayer, the reading of the O. T., as well as instruction in Hebrew language and other aspects of the Jewish faith. It became common to invite a rabbi to give a homily or a teaching based on the Scripture passages that were read on a given Sabbath. By the time of Jesus, there were Jewish synagogues both in the land of Palestine and in other areas of the world where Jewish people lived.

The term "synagogue" was originally used to describe the congregation of people gathered for worship, but in later years it was also used to describe the building in which they met. For more information about the use of the term "synagogue" in the first century see Coenen (NIDNTT I:305).

Verse 14 notes that "there went out a fame of Him through all the region round about." "Fame" (Greek *phēmē*) carries the idea of news or a report; the word had apparently spread that Jesus was returning to Galilee. It is impossible to determine the precise content of these reports, and Luke offers no explanation. Probably Jesus had already engaged in some public ministry in Judaea that Luke has chosen not to include (Stein, *Messiah* 113; Summers, *Luke* 56; Geldenhuys 166). These reports likely included information about what Jesus has previously done and said in Judaea.

Luke explains (v. 15) that teaching in the synagogues was the focus of Jesus' early ministry in Galilee. "Taught" (Greek imperfect tense) describes action in past time that was continuous, habitual, or repeated. Jesus was teaching continually or habitually in the synagogues (Lenski 244). A. Bruce (EGT I:488) interprets this verb as a summary statement of Jesus' preaching ministry in Galilee. The last phrase of verse 15, "being glorified of all" probably refers to those who heard Jesus' teaching. The most common interpretation of this phrase is that the teaching of Jesus provoked a large response and that He was, at this early stage in His public ministry (and especially in Galilee and the surrounding area), held in high esteem by the people (Geldenhuys 166). A. Bruce (EGT I:489) understands it to be a summary statement indicating general admiration.

Lenski (244) explains that the leaders of a synagogue might permit any rabbi to speak to the assembled people. Since no active opposition to Jesus' ministry had yet arisen in Galilee, it is likely that Jesus had several opportunities to speak in the synagogues and that the people responded favorably to His preaching.

16 And he came to Nazareth, where he had been brought up: and, as his custom was, he went into the synagogue on the sabbath day, and stood up for to read.
17 And there was delivered unto him the book of the prophet Esaias. And when he had opened the book, he found the place where it was written,
18 The Spirit of the Lord *is* upon me, because he hath anointed me to preach the gospel to the poor; he hath sent me to heal the brokenhearted, to preach deliverance to the captives, and recovering of

sight to the blind, to set at liberty them that are bruised,
19 To preach the acceptable year of the Lord.

In this paragraph, Luke moves from a general introduction to Jesus' ministry in Galilee to a specific incident: His first visit to His home in Nazareth after beginning His public ministry. It is difficult to determine the precise chronology of this period in Jesus' public ministry, and Luke is more concerned with what happened than with when it happened. John 1:35—4:44 mentions some ministry in Judaea, which was likely completed prior to this visit to Nazareth. Luke 4:23 refers to some prior ministry in Capernaum of Galilee. Both Matthew (13:53-58) and Mark (6:1-6) describe a visit to Nazareth, which is in some ways similar to the visit described here. Neither Matthew nor Mark include the sermon, but both call attention to the fact that Jesus marveled at the unbelief of the people. Mark points out that because of unbelief Jesus could do no mighty work there; He only "laid his hands upon a few sick folks, and healed them."

The problem is that both Matthew and Mark locate their visit to Nazareth at a later point in Jesus' ministry. Scholars are divided about whether Jesus made one or two visits to Nazareth during His public ministry. Earle (*According to Luke* 232-233) presents a good summary of this debate. A. Bruce (EGT I:489) suggests there was only one visit and Luke describes the visit at this early point because it serves as a fitting introduction to his presentation of Jesus' Galilean ministry. For Luke, the theological message he wishes to present is often more important than maintaining a precise chronology.

Lenski (245) suggests this visit took place approximately one year after the beginning of Jesus' public ministry. There is little doubt that the people in Nazareth had heard reports about what Jesus had done in other places; some of them might have actually seen the miracles He did in Capernaum, which was about 20 miles away (Wilcock 61).

Bock (*Luke* IVP 88) gives a brief summary of how a service was conducted in a first-century synagogue. In order to have a service, at least ten adult males had to be present. The *Shema* (Dt. 6:4-6) was recited, and certain prayers were spoken. The Scriptures were read, first a passage from the *Torah* (Law) and then a passage from the Prophets. A time of instruction followed, when the speaker delivered a homily based on the passages read that day; he might also make reference to other passages in the homily. If one were available, a visiting rabbi was often invited to give the homily. After this time of instruction, the service would close with a benediction. The fact that Jesus is invited to deliver the homily indicates that He has already gained something of a following, and the people are anxious to hear what He has to say.

Geldenhuys (167) explains that during the synagogue service the passage from the *Torah* was read in Hebrew and then translated into Aramaic by the official interpreter. After the reading from the *Torah*, the reading from the prophets was given. This is the point in the service when Jesus stands and begins to read from the prophets. He probably reads the passage in Hebrew with an Aramaic translation. His reading includes several phrases from Isaiah 61:1-2 and one phrase, "to preach deliverance to the captives," which is not found in Isaiah 61. It probably comes from Isaiah 58:3 (Bock I:409). As noted above, it was not unusual for several passages to be combined in one service (Bock I:404).

It had been Jesus' custom since childhood to go to the local synagogue to worship every Sabbath (Geldenhuys 167), and this is probably the synagogue in which He had grown up. Now things are different; He is an adult, fully conscious of the special ministry God had given Him. He is no longer sitting at the rabbi's feet and learning; it is time for Him to share the wisdom His heavenly Father has given Him.

20 And he closed the book, and he gave *it* again to the minister, and sat down. And the eyes of all them that were in the synagogue were fastened on him.
21 And he began to say unto them, This day is this scripture fulfilled in your ears.
22 And all bare him witness, and wondered at the gracious words which proceeded out of his mouth. And they said, Is not this Joseph's son?

Bock (I:394) notes that Jesus' sermon emphasizes three main themes. First, it points out that Jesus fulfills the promise of the O. T. Scriptures. Second, it describes the rejection of Jesus by His home community. Third, it explains that the miracles God performs may be limited because God bestows His power and mercy when and where He chooses and upon whom He chooses.

Following the custom of the day, Jesus stands to read the Scripture, and then sits down to teach. The "book" (v. 20) is literally a "scroll." Jesus rolls up the scroll and hands it to the attendant. "Minister" literally means "servant"; the word reflects the Hebrew word that describes an assistant who performs various tasks in the synagogue.

The sermon begins in verse 21. Luke's wording should not be understood as a verbatim transcript of everything that Jesus said; it is probably a summary of the main points of the message (Geldenhuys 168; Lenski 253, Bock I:405).

Jesus begins His sermon in a striking fashion. By the statement "This day is this scripture fulfilled in your ears" Jesus affirms that He is the fulfillment of the words Isaiah had spoken centuries earlier. While these words may not constitute a specific claim to be the Jewish Messiah, they can certainly be understood that way. Barrett (*Luke* 64-65) asserts these words are a specific claim by Jesus to be the fulfillment of the O. T. prophetic passages. These words are, no doubt, both surprising and perplexing to the congregation; they are not sure how to interpret them. They have known Jesus since childhood; they think of Him as Joseph's son who grew up in the carpenter shop. How can He make such claims for Himself?

The initial reaction of the congregation is favorable (Barrett, *Luke* 65). The phrase "all bear him witness" can be used as an expression of praise (Marshall, *Gospel* 185). According to verse 22, the people marvel at the gracious words Jesus has spoken.

23 And he said unto them, Ye will surely say unto me this proverb, Physician, heal thyself: whatsoever

we have heard done in Capernaum, do also here in thy country.
24 And he said, Verily I say unto you, No prophet is accepted in his own country.

Jesus notes that the response of the congregation is not entirely positive. Many in the congregation are unsympathetic and somewhat skeptical of His words (Geldenhuys 168). Jesus anticipates how they will respond to the striking statement He has just made. They will respond, first, with the traditional proverbial saying, "Physician, heal thyself." Second, they will respond by asking Jesus to authenticate His striking claim by performing the same kinds of miracles in Nazareth that He has performed in the nearby town of Capernaum. In other words, the people will respond by demanding that Jesus provide proof to substantiate His claim to be the Messiah.

Jesus offers them no miracle or other sign to indicate He is the promised Messiah. Instead, He responds to their doubts with another traditional proverb, that "no prophet is accepted in his own country." He views their reaction as unbelief because they refuse to accept what God is doing in their midst. It is interesting to note that in their accounts of the visit to Nazareth, both Matthew and Mark also emphasize the unbelief of the people.

"Verily" (v. 24) is the same word (Greek *amēn*) that is often translated "amen." Marshall (*Gospel* 187) points out that this expression occurs only six times in Luke (4:24; 12:37; 18:17, 29; 21:32; 23:43). This word was borrowed from Hebrew, where it signifies truth or verity (Lenski 255). In Luke the term is used to add a note of authority and importance to a particular statement made by Jesus.

25 But I tell you of truth, many widows were in Israel in the days of Elias, when the heaven was shut up three years and six months, when great famine was throughout all the land;
26 But unto none of them was Elias sent, save unto Sarepta, a *city* of Sidon, unto a woman *that was* a widow.
27 And many lepers were in Israel in the time of Eliseus the prophet; and none of them was cleansed, saving Naaman the Syrian.

Jesus turns His attention to the demand that the congregation has made for signs to prove the truthfulness of the claim that He has made. He uses two illustrations from the O. T. to establish that God gives signs only on rare occasions and only when He chooses. God is under no obligation to accede to their demand for signs; Jesus does not need to prove to anyone the truthfulness of His words. The veracity of His teaching is self-evident.

The first illustration comes from 1 Kings 17:8-16 where in a time of famine God sent the prophet Elijah to the house of a poor widow in Zarephath (*Sarepta* is the Greek spelling). In the house of this humble widow, God multiplied the grain in the barrel to sustain both the prophet and the widow and her family. The second illustration comes from 2 Kings 5:1-14 where God, through the prophet Elisha, commanded Naaman, an important Syrian commander, to dip himself seven times in the Jordan River. After making initial objections, Naaman obeyed God's instructions and was cured of his leprosy.

Jesus' point is that while there were many hungry widows in Israel during this time of famine, God worked a miracle in only one household. There were, no doubt, many men suffering from leprosy in the time of Elisha, but God healed only one. God performs miracles when and where He chooses. As Lenski (258) notes, God bestows His grace and mercy freely, but not arbitrarily or in response to human demands. The congregation in the synagogue in Nazareth has no right to demand that Jesus perform any type of sign or miracle to confirm His claims.

28 And all they in the synagogue, when they heard these things, were filled with wrath,
29 And rose up, and thrust him out of the city, and led him unto the brow of the hill whereon their city was built, that they might cast him down headlong.
30 But he passing through the midst of them went his way,
31 And came down to Capernaum, a city of Galilee, and taught them on the sabbath days.
32 And they were astonished at his doctrine: for his word was with power.

The congregation responds to this series of events with a mixture of anger and unbelief. Jesus has claimed to be the fulfillment of certain O. T. messianic passages, but He has also refused to perform any miracles to substantiate that claim. The congregation probably considers His words and actions to be blasphemy. Bock (*Luke* IVP 92) and Marshall (*Gospel* 178) suggest the stories Jesus told about the widow of Zarephath and Naaman the Syrian might imply God would bestow His blessings on the Gentiles. This implication the Jews of Nazareth simply will not accept.

The village of Nazareth is located in a hollow in the hills (Geldenhuys 169). After the service, Jesus is taken to a nearby high place from which He can be thrown down the mountainside. "Rose up" (Greek *anistēmi)* is used elsewhere in the New Testament to describe hostile actions (Marshall, *Gospel* 190). The idea is that Jesus is taken by force to the brow of the hill in order to kill Him; this is clearly an example of mob violence. Luke's description of Jesus' response to this physical attack is brief; he gives no details, noting simply that Jesus walks through the crowd and goes away. While Luke does not describe this as a miraculous event, the implication is clear that the power of God is at work to protect the life of Jesus in this dangerous situation. As Geldenhuys (169) points out, it is not yet the time for Jesus to lay down His life.

Verse 31 explains that the rejection in Nazareth did not mean the end of Jesus' ministry in Galilee. He went down to the larger and more important city of Capernaum where He continued His teaching ministry. The grammatical construction used here (Greek imperfect tense) implies that Jesus' teaching ministry continued for several Sabbaths. His ministry received a much more favorable response in Capernaum than it had received in Nazareth; the people were "astonished." This is a strong word (Greek *ekplēsomai*) that suggests being dumbfounded (Lenski 261). Jesus' teaching had such an impact because it was so different from the teaching they generally received in the synagogue. In the first century, Jewish rabbis were reluctant to give their own opinion; instead they would quote from the sayings of past generations of rabbis (Morris, *Luke* 109). Jesus did not follow this customary pattern. He taught with freshness, power, and authority. As John 7:46 notes, no one had ever spoken as Jesus spoke.

33 And in the synagogue there was a man, which had a spirit of an unclean devil, and cried out with a loud voice,
34 Saying, Let *us* alone; what have we to do with thee, *thou* Jesus of Nazareth? art thou come to destroy us? I know thee who thou art; the Holy One of God.
35 And Jesus rebuked him, saying, Hold thy peace, and come out of him. And when the devil had thrown him in the midst, he came out of him, and hurt him not.
36 And they were all amazed, and spake among themselves, saying, What a word *is* this! for with authority and power he commandeth the unclean spirits, and they come out.

As Summers (*Luke* 59) notes, these verses describe the first miracle presented in Luke's Gospel. A miracle is an extraordinary event in which God acts in an unusual way that transcends the normal order of things. During His earthly ministry, Jesus used miracles in two important ways: to alleviate human suffering and meet human need; and to substantiate His claims to be the Messiah and to stimulate faith in Him and His work.

This healing is absent from Matthew, but it is found in Mark 1:21-28. It is important to note that in this section of the Gospel, Luke incorporates several stories of healing miracles into His preaching mission in Galilee. It is clear that Jesus saw no conflict between preaching the gospel and performing deeds of mercy. When Jesus came to the synagogue in Capernaum, He found a man who was under the control of an evil spirit. In the ancient world, many kinds of evil and suffering were attributed to the work of evil spirits (Morris, *Luke* 109). The last words of verse 33 indicate that the man (or possibly the demon within him) cried out with a loud voice. This loud cry indicates the demon understood that the coming of Jesus placed him at risk. Geldenhuys (173) understands it as a cry of terror.

The first part of verse 34 can be literally translated, "What is that to you and to us, Jesus of Nazareth? Did you come to destroy us?" It is clear that the demon immediately recognizes who Jesus is. The demon then continues, "I know thee, who thou art, the Holy One of God." The phrase "Holy One of God" is a rather unusual title for Jesus. According to Morris (*Luke* 109), it stresses Jesus' commitment to the service of God.

One key aspect of Jesus' ministry in Galilee is to defeat the work of the Devil and of the demons that do his bidding. In verse 35 He rebukes the demon, instructs it to keep quiet, and orders it to come out of the man. The demon obeys Jesus' instructions and leaves the man without doing him harm. Before coming out of the man, the demon makes one last attempt to do him harm. Luke writes, "And when the devil had thrown him in the midst." Marshall (*Gospel* 193) understands this to mean that the demon threw him into the middle of the room. Geldenhuys (173) understands it to mean that the demon threw him down in an attempt to harm him. The parallel passage (Mk. 1:26) says the unclean spirit "had torn him." This event may involve some type of seizure. By the power and grace of God, the man is delivered from the power of the demon without further injury.

This miracle of exorcism profoundly affects those who witness it. As Geldenhuys (173) explains, they have never before seen this kind of deliverance. Immediately they begin to discuss among themselves what this event might mean (Bock I:435). The phrase "What a word is this!" explains something of their perplexity. "Word" (Greek *logos*) is used in the N. T. with several different meanings. Marshall (*Gospel* 193) understands it as a reference, here, to the *command* that Jesus has given to the demon. Bock (I:435) sees it as a reference to the entire set of circumstances the crowd has just witnessed.

The last words of verse 36 explain the cause of the spectators' amazement. Jesus has spoken with such power and authority that even the evil spirits are forced to obey Him. He ordered them to come out of the man and they obeyed. In this way, Jesus demonstrates His power over the forces of evil (Bock I:435).

Word of this miracle in Capernaum on the Sabbath soon spread over all the region of Galilee. Jesus had not made use of any of the incantations, spells, or magical roots to which exorcists often resorted in the ancient world (Barclay 50-51). He simply spoke a word, and the forces of evil were defeated. There is little doubt that some who heard the story questioned whether or not it was lawful to perform such a miracle on the Sabbath, but that issue is not raised here. That is a controversy that will arise later.

37 And the fame of him went out into every place of the country round about.

In this summary verse, Luke explains that the reports about Jesus begin to circulate widely throughout the region. Based on Luke 4:31, there is little doubt that Galilee is the region Luke has in mind. The fact that Jesus is able to defeat the power of the demons has greatly affected those who hear these reports.

38 And he arose out of the synagogue, and entered into Simon's house. And Simon's wife's mother was taken with a great fever; and they besought him for her.
39 And he stood over her, and rebuked the fever; and it left her: and immediately she arose and ministered unto them.

These verses include Luke's first reference to Simon Peter. According to John 1:44, Peter's traditional home was Bethsaida which was near Capernaum (Bock I:436). The reader is not told whether Capernaum had become Peter's permanent residence or if this was a temporary situation. The most likely explanation is that Peter had moved to the larger city of Capernaum sometime prior to the beginning of Jesus' Galilean ministry. Mark 1:29 mentions that this is the house of Peter and Andrew and that James and John are also present. Luke does not explain why they have gone to Simon Peter's house.

Since several people are in the group, it is likely that Jesus and His companions have gone there in order to share a meal and rest (Lenski 269). When they arrive at the house, they find that Simon Peter's mother-in-law is ill. Barclay (52) notes that Luke uses a series of medical terms to describe her illness. She is literally "in the grip of a severe fever." The phrase "and they besought him for her" indicates that Peter and the others ask Jesus to do something about her illness (Bock I:436). Jesus stands over her and rebukes the illness; the fever leaves her and she immediately begins to minister to those who have come to the home. As Lenski (270) explains, Jesus' word is an expression of His will. It is also an expression of His power; when He speaks even the winds and the waves obey Him.

The healing of Peter's mother-in-law is important to Jesus' ministry because illness was regarded as an outward manifestation of the forces of evil that operate in the world (Lieu 35). The casting out of demons and the healing of illness not only demonstrated His power; they also helped establish the nature of His messiahship. The fact that she rose up immediately and began to serve her guests serves as an eloquent testimony to the power of Jesus even over a serious illness.

40 Now when the sun was setting, all they that had any sick with divers diseases brought them unto him; and he laid his hands on every one of them, and healed them.
41 And devils also came out of many, crying out, and saying, Thou art Christ the Son of God. And he rebuking *them* suffered them not to speak: for they knew that he was Christ.
42 And when it was day, he departed and went into a desert place: and the people sought him, and came unto him, and stayed him, that he should not depart from them.
43 And he said unto them, I must preach the kingdom of God in other cities also: for therefore am I sent.
44 And he preached in the synagogues of Galilee.

These verses summarize the early portion of Jesus' ministry in Galilee; they also introduce several important themes that will be developed in later sections of this Gospel. According to Wilcock (64), this section of Luke is dominated by two concerns: to introduce the man Jesus, and to introduce the message that He will share during His earthly ministry. Both of these themes are illustrated in these verses.

Jesus is presented as the Son of God, the one who has God's power dwelling within Him. In His healings, Jesus makes known His determination to use that power for the good of mankind. The message He will preach centers on the proclamation of the Kingdom of God. In other words, God's reign has become a reality on the earth. By His teachings and by His actions, Jesus demonstrates that the Kingdom of God has been introduced. As the story moves forward, the nature of that kingdom will become clearer.

"When the sun was setting" and "when it was day" indicate that the events narrated in verses 40-41 take place during one night. The first indicates these healings took place after the Sabbath ended at about 6:00 p.m. (Lieu 35). Verse 40 points out that people from the local area came bringing those who were ill with different diseases; Jesus laid His hands on them and healed them.

In verse 41, Jesus demonstrates His power by casting demons out of several individuals; this serves as a powerful evidence that the Kingdom of God has in fact come to the earth. Interestingly, as He casts the demons out He does not allow them to speak. The fact that He has control over the demons is further evidence of His divine power; it also reflects His desire to control the message He shares with the people. "Christ" in the N. T. means the (Jewish) Messiah. The demons understand that Jesus is this Messiah and, for some reason, wish to proclaim that fact. Jesus forbids them to speak, and Luke does not explain why.

Ellis (101) suggests two possible reasons for this command. The first is that the speech of demons is considered unclean. The second, a more likely possibility, is that Jesus does not want to be publicly identified as the Messiah at this early stage in His ministry. Many Jews of the first century expected the Messiah to come with military power and free the land of Israel from Roman control. That is not the type of Messiah Jesus is to be. It is likely that Jesus forbids the demons to speak because He wants to define His Messiahship in His own time and on His own terms.

The next morning Jesus goes away into a desert place. "Desert" is used in several ways in the N. T. Sometimes it refers to the arid area south of Jerusalem, but probably not here; this area would have been too far away from the city of Capernaum where Jesus was staying. The word is also used at times, more generically, to describe a solitary place (Bock I:439; Lenski 273). In the context here, it probably describes some solitary place outside the city of Capernaum. Luke does not explain why Jesus goes to this area, but Mark 1:35 notes that He goes out to pray. He is probably seeking some time away from the crowds for rest, reflection, and prayer.

The crowds continue to follow Him; they come to Jesus and entreat Him not to leave their city. The phrase "stayed him" indicates the people try to keep Jesus from leaving Capernaum. They are not successful in this effort; Jesus explains that He must go and preach the Kingdom of God in other cities also. The idea seems to be Jesus goes about preaching that in His person the Kingdom of God has come to earth. Geldenhuys (179) presents a brief explanation of the meaning of the phrase "Kingdom of God." He understands it to include both God's kingly rule over the earth and the field within which this rule is exercised. The Kingdom of God will be fully realized in the end time. The proclamation of the Kingdom of God is at the very heart of Jesus' preaching ministry.

In the summary in verse 44, Jesus' preaching (Greek imperfect tense) in the synagogues of Galilee should be understood as continuing for some time. Luke does not define the precise content of Jesus' preaching. He is probably proclaiming that the Kingdom of God has come to earth; He is also beginning to explain the nature of that kingdom.

Summary (4:14-44)

Luke does not purpose, in this passage, to give a detailed account of everything Jesus said and did in Galilee. His goal is to present an accurate overview of this part of Jesus' earthly ministry so his readers may better understand the nature of Jesus' messiahship. During the Galilean ministry, Jesus defines His ministry through a combination of teaching and the working of miracles. As Lenski (266) explains, Jesus does not specifically claim to be either the Messiah or the Son of God. Instead, He allows His teachings and His actions to speak for themselves. By His words and His actions, He outlines the kind of Messiah that He intends to be. He also challenges the people to accept Him as the Son of God. His teachings and His miracles produce various reactions. Some accept Him; others rejected Him.

In these verses Jesus clearly demonstrates His love for people; He has a genuine concern for their welfare. He does not heal people simply to gain praise and adoration from the crowds. His two goals are to meet the needs of suffering people and to illustrate the true nature of the Kingdom of God. God has no desire to build a kingdom that is based on military force; it will be built on love and mercy. It is significant that Jesus refuses to perform some type of miracle when requested to do so by the people in His home town of Nazareth. He will not be manipulated or controlled by others; He has come to do the will of God.

The rejection He experienced in Nazareth is a foretaste of coming events. As His earthly ministry develops, many will reject both the Messiah and His message. The fact He could walk through a hostile crowd without suffering any injury served to indicate that the grace and power of God were upon Him in a special way.

Application: Teaching and Preaching the Passage

Many important themes can be stressed when teaching and preaching on this chapter. One important lesson is that culture may give people an incorrect understanding of who Jesus is and what He came to earth to accomplish. The people of Nazareth knew Jesus as the boy who had grown up in their village, and they had difficulty accepting Him as the Messiah sent from God. Modern cultures that emphasize earthly success, monetary gain, independence, and self-sufficiency make it difficult for people to understand their spiritual needs. They may have difficulty moving beyond the picture of Jesus given by their culture, to a true understanding of Him based on Scripture.

These verses also emphasize the independence and authority of Jesus. He is under no obligation to respond to their calls for miracles to provide supporting evidence for His claims. God has worked miracles in the past, and Jesus will work additional miracles in the future. He will not, however, perform miracles to satisfy the whims of the crowd. He will perform miracles, when and where He chooses, in order to accomplish His goals and objectives. Too many people today try to bargain with God, or they develop the attitude that God is obligated to reward them for their faithfulness and obedience. In reality, God is King of Kings and Lord of Lords. He loves His people and He intervenes on their behalf, but they have no right to make demands on Him. He will reward His people in His own time and in His own way.

Preachers and teachers should note the sharp contrast between the responses of the people in Nazareth and of those in Capernaum. The people in the synagogue in Nazareth, where He had grown up, were impressed with Jesus and His teaching. They could not, however, accept Him as God's anointed Messiah. In the end, many in the village became so upset they even tried to kill Him. The people in Capernaum were much more open to Jesus and to the message He brought. They were amazed at the remarkable authority with which He taught, but they accepted Him. There was no attempt to reject Him or His teaching. People today may be like those in Nazareth or those in Capernaum; they may accept His message or they may reject it. Jesus always challenged His hearers to make a decision, but He never took away their freedom to accept or reject Him.

Throughout His earthly ministry, Jesus demonstrates His compassion. He heals those who are suffering and casts demons out of those who are being destroyed by them. His love and compassion are clearly demonstrated in His healing of the mother-in-law of Simon Peter. Preachers and teachers must never forget that Jesus is a compassionate and loving Savior.

It is significant to note that Jesus, at this important time in His ministry, takes time to leave the city of Capernaum and spend some time alone with His heavenly Father. He understands He cannot fulfill the important ministry God has given Him without spending time with God in prayer. That was important in the life of Jesus, and it is equally important in the lives of Christians today.

B. The Call of the Disciples (5:1-39)

This chapter develops two major themes, carefully interwoven. The first concerns Jesus' demonstration of His power and authority as the Son of God. Three significant miracles—the miraculous catch of fish, the healing of a leper, and the healing of a man with palsy—demonstrate that He is more than just a capable teacher; He is the Son of God. These miracles also provide the background for Jesus' call of the disciples. They not only serve to impress upon His future disciples the messiahship of Jesus; they also illustrate something of the nature of the kingdom in which they will serve. These events open the door for Jesus to reveal more about Himself and the nature of His ministry.

The second major theme is the uniqueness of Jesus' ministry. He calls disciples not from among the leaders of Jewish society but from among those who are often scorned. In this chapter, Jesus ministers to those, like the leper, who are regarded as outcast. He shares a banquet with tax-collectors, the most hated members of Jewish society; He personally violates the most sacred of the Jewish customs and encourages His disciples to do likewise. In this chapter, Jesus has the first of many disputes with the scribes and Pharisees. Luke concludes this chapter with a rather enigmatic passage, which emphasizes the difference between Jesus' teachings and the teachings of those who have gone before Him.

This chapter divides itself into five major divisions: the call of the first four disciples, verses 1-11; the healing of a man with leprosy, verses 12-16; the healing of a man with palsy, verses 17-26; the call of Levi to discipleship, verses 27-32; and teaching concerning fasting, verses 33-39. This chapter reveals that Jesus is truly the Son of God with power, authority, and wisdom that the world has never seen before.

1 And it came to pass, that, as the people pressed upon him to hear the word of God, he stood by the lake of Gennesaret,
2 And saw two ships standing by the lake: but the fishermen were gone out of them, and were washing *their* nets.
3 And he entered into one of the ships, which was Simon's, and prayed him that he would thrust out a little from the land. And he sat down, and taught the people out of the ship.
4 Now when he had left speaking, he said unto Simon, Launch out into the deep, and let down your nets for a draught.
5 And Simon answering said unto him, Master, we have toiled all the night, and have taken nothing: nevertheless at thy word I will let down the net.
6 And when they had this done, they inclosed a great multitude of fishes: and their net brake.
7 And they beckoned unto *their* partners, which were in the other ship, that they should come and help them. And they came, and filled both the ships, so that they began to sink.
8 When Simon Peter saw *it*, he fell down at Jesus' knees, saying, Depart from me; for I am a sinful man, O Lord.
9 For he was astonished, and all that were with him, at the draught of fishes which they had taken:
10 And so *was* also James, and John, the sons of Zebedee, which were partners with Simon. And Jesus said unto Simon, Fear not; from henceforth thou shalt catch men.
11 And when they had brought their ships to land, they forsook all, and followed him.

The call of the disciples is such an important event during the early part of Jesus' ministry that it is mentioned in all of the Gospels (Mt. 4:18-22; Mk. 1:16-20; Lk. 5:1-11); all locate the call of the disciples on the shores of the Sea of Galilee. Luke 5:27-28 describes the call of Levi; the geographical location is not mentioned but is likely Galilee. John 1:35-51 also describes the call of the disciples, but this passage locates the call in Judaea immediately after the baptism of Jesus. Several commentators have noted the difficulty in reconciling John's account with those given in the Synoptic Gospels (A. Richardson, *John* 50-51; Barrett, *John* 149-150). Whitacre (70) suggests that the initial call of the disciples took place in Galilee and is described in the Synoptic Gospels. The call described in John 1 took place later and was specifically directed to the disciples of John the Baptist. Bernard (57), instead, suggests that the call described in John 1 is an earlier call while the call described in the Synoptic Gospels is a later call to apostleship.

The first four men Jesus calls to be His disciples are two sets of brothers: Andrew and Simon, James and John. The call in Luke is probably not Jesus' first contact with Andrew and Simon Peter. John 1:35-42 describes a meeting that took place in Judaea shortly after Jesus' baptism. That passage describes Andrew as a disciple of John the Baptist. After hearing Jesus, Andrew leaves John the Baptist and becomes a disciple of Jesus. He also finds his brother, Simon Peter, and brings him to Jesus. Apparently, these two brothers are fishermen from Galilee; they follow Jesus back to Galilee where they resume their fishing business. For a discussion of the relationship between Luke 5 and key passages in the other Gospels, see the comments of Summers (*Luke* 62), Bock (I:448-449), and Ellis (101).

In Luke, Jesus calls His first four disciples on the shores of the lake of Gennesaret. This was a large fresh water lake, about thirteen miles long and eight miles wide, on the Jordan River. It was also known as the Sea of Galilee or the Sea of Tiberias. In the O. T., it is identified in Numbers 34:11 as the Sea of Chinnereth. During the first century, this lake was a center of the fishing industry; some nine communities were located on its shores (Barclay 56).

By this time, Jesus had already gained considerable notoriety among the people of Galilee, and a large crowd of people came out to the shore of the lake to hear Him teach. The phrase "the word of God" is used both in Luke and Acts. In Acts, it is the gospel message as proclaimed by the apostles; in Luke's Gospel it often means the words of Jesus Himself (Fitzmyer I:565). "Of God" probably indicates source or origin. Luke's goal is to affirm that the message Jesus proclaims is of divine origin.

Apparently the crowd was quite large, and Jesus saw that it would be easier for all to see and hear Him if He could move into the shallow water near the edge of the lake. He saw two fishing boats nearby—probably open boats, some twenty to thirty feet long (Ellis 102). Apparently, the fishermen had left the boats on the shore while they washed their nets after a night of fishing.

Jesus steps into the boat that belongs to Simon Peter and asks Peter to move away from the shore a short distance. Peter does as Jesus requests; Jesus then sits down to teach, as was the custom among the rabbis (Fitzmyer I:566). Luke does not indicate how long Jesus speaks or what He says; the focus of this passage is on the call of the disciples not on the specific content of Jesus' teaching. After He finishes His teaching, Jesus asks Peter to launch out into the deeper water and let down their nets in an effort to catch fish. Peter responds to this request by saying, "We have toiled all night and have taken nothing: nevertheless at thy word I will let down the net." Peter is an experienced fisherman who knows the Sea of Galilee well; he understands that the best time to fish is at night. Because of his respect for Jesus, he obeys this most unusual request. Peter's response may indicate that he has had some prior contact with Jesus in Galilee or in Judaea.

The nets were soon filled with a large catch of fish; it was so big their nets began to break (Summers, *Luke* 567). That the net "brake" means it began to break (Greek ingressive aorist; Bock I:457). They soon found that one boat was not large enough to hold all the fish.

They brought in a second boat, and soon both boats were filled to the point of sinking. This was clearly a miracle designed to show the power and authority of Jesus.

Peter's response is immediate. It is doubtful that at this early point in the ministry Peter fully understands who Jesus is, but he knows that something profound is happening in his life. He is astonished; he realizes that only God can perform the miracle he has just witnessed. Peter falls to his knees before Jesus and responds with the words, "Depart from me; for I am a sinful man, O Lord." At first, Peter's response seems rather strange; his immediate reaction is to ask Jesus to depart. This miracle has produced a sense of unworthiness in Peter; he realizes that he is in the presence of God and that, as a sinful human being, he has no right to be there (Bock I:458). These words are not so much a confession of Peter's personal sin as they are a recognition of human unworthiness to stand in the presence of God.

This astonishment is not limited to Peter. It extends to those who witnessed the miracle along with him. Luke specifically mentions James and John, the sons of Zebedee who are partners with Peter in the fishing business.

The last words of verses 10-11 carry special significance. Jesus responds to Peter's astonishment with both a command and a prediction. The command is "fear not," which is apparently "stop being afraid" (Greek negative present imperative). The second portion of Jesus' response is a prediction of Peter's future ministry. His career will no longer be focused on catching fish; in the future, he will catch men for the Kingdom of God. Although Jesus speaks directly to Peter, His words are intended for the others as well. Their response to Jesus' prediction is immediate; they land their boats, give up the fishing business, and follow Jesus. Fitzmyer (I:569) notes that the verb "to follow," in first-century Judaism, was used to describe a disciple who follows after a rabbi. In the N. T. it carries the connotation of self-commitment; it describes one who forsakes other commitments to become a disciple of Jesus in an exclusive way.

12 And it came to pass, when he was in a certain city, behold a man full of leprosy: who seeing Jesus fell on *his* face, and besought him, saying, Lord, if thou wilt, thou canst make me clean.
13 And he put forth *his* hand, and touched him, saying, I will: be thou clean. And immediately the leprosy departed from him.
14 And he charged him to tell no man: but go, and shew thyself to the priest, and offer for thy cleansing, according as Moses commanded, for a testimony unto them.
15 But so much the more went there a fame abroad of him: and great multitudes came together to hear, and to be healed by him of their infirmities.
16 And he withdrew himself into the wilderness, and prayed.

The connection between this healing and the call of the disciples is neither chronological nor geographical; it is theological. Luke makes no attempt to identify where or when this event happened (Geldenhuys 185). Jesus' goal in the early part of His ministry is to define and explain the nature of His kingdom. One of the major characteristics of His kingdom will be deeds of mercy as illustrated by the healing of this leprous man.

In ancient Israel, leprosy was a much-feared disease. It not only produced serious consequences for the patient, it also made the person an outcast from society. One of the most complete discussions of leprosy in the O. T. is found in Leviticus 13—14, which outline both the symptoms of the disease and how the person who recovers from leprosy can be restored to society. Modern authorities understand that a variety of different skin diseases can produce the symptoms described in Leviticus (Bock I:472-473; Marshall, *Gospel* 208; Lieu 38). Suffering from one of these diseases rendered a person ritually unclean in that he could not return to society until the priest had certified he had been cleansed of the disease. Leprosy is also regarded in the Bible as a symbol for sin (Geldenhuys 186). For a good discussion of the term "leprosy" in the N. T., see R. Harrison (NIDNTT II:463-466): after a careful analysis of the evidence, he concludes that the term may describe several different skin diseases including what is known today as leprosy or Hanson's Disease.

Luke does not explain how the leprous man had heard of Jesus. Regardless, the man understands the medical science of his day can offer him no hope of recovery; Jesus is his only hope. He falls on his face before Jesus with the words, "if thou wilt, thou canst make me clean." Jesus then violates the ceremonial law by touching the leprous man (Geldenhuys 186). Jesus tells him, "I will: be thou clean." He is then immediately healed of his illness. This is a most notable miracle because the man is healed instantaneously; ordinarily no one recovers instantaneously from such a disease. Recovery from this type of illness, when it occurs, is a long process. Jesus continues the conversation by telling the man not to tell anyone about his healing. Instead, he is to go to the priest and show that he has been cleansed; he is also told to offer the proper sacrifice as outlined in the Law of Moses.

This miracle serves to illustrate several important aspects of Jesus' kingdom. It illustrates that deeds of love and mercy are at the heart of Jesus' ministry. It also illustrates that, for Jesus, meeting the needs of people is more important than observing the ceremonial law. Luke offers no explanation why Jesus tells the man to keep the news of his healing secret. Probably it is because Jesus does not want the crowds to become overly excited about His healing power (Geldenhuys 186); He does not want them to understand His messiahship solely in terms of physical healing. As His ministry develops, Jesus will reveal the true nature of His messiahship through a series of events and teachings.

Verses 15-16 provide a summary of this early stage of Jesus' ministry; they also serve as a transition into the next section of the story. In spite of Jesus' instructions to keep this miracle story secret, word gets out. People come from all over the area to hear His preaching and to be healed of their diseases. The healing of the leprous man is not an isolated incident; healings will become characteristic of Jesus' ministry. They provide one proof that the Kingdom of God has come to earth. After this miracle of healing, Jesus withdraws to a quiet place to get away from the crowds and to commune with His Father in prayer. Luke is well aware of

Jesus' humanity, and throughout the Gospel, he is careful to note that Jesus seeks His Father's guidance at every point in His ministry.

17 And it came to pass on a certain day, as he was teaching, that there were Pharisees and doctors of the law sitting by, which were come out of every town in Galilee, and Judaea, and Jerusalem: and the power of the Lord was *present* to heal them.
18 And, behold, men brought in a bed a man which was taken with a palsy: and they sought *means* to bring him in, and to lay *him* before him.
19 And when they could not find by what *way* they might bring him in because of the multitude, they went upon the housetop, and let him down through the tiling with *his* couch into the midst before Jesus.
20 And when he saw their faith, he said unto him, Man, thy sins are forgiven thee.
21 And the scribes and the Pharisees began to reason, saying, Who is this which speaketh blasphemies? Who can forgive sins, but God alone?
22 But when Jesus perceived their thoughts, he answering said unto them, What reason ye in your hearts?
23 Whether is easier, to say, Thy sins be forgiven thee; or to say, Rise up and walk?
24 But that ye may know that the Son of man hath power upon earth to forgive sins, (he said unto the sick of the palsy,) I say unto thee, Arise, and take up thy couch, and go into thine house.
25 And immediately he rose up before them, and took up that whereon he lay, and departed to his own house, glorifying God.
26 And they were all amazed, and they glorified God, and were filled with fear, saying, We have seen strange things to day.

These verses follow what will become a common pattern in Luke. First, Jesus performs an unusual action, such as some type of miracle. Second, there arises a protest against what Jesus has done. Third, Jesus silences His critics. Fourth, Jesus uses the event as an opportunity for greater teaching about the nature of His kingdom (Ellis 103).

Luke makes no attempt to identify where or when the healing of the palsied man takes place; the miracle itself is the important thing. Jesus is teaching, apparently in someone's home, in the company of a crowd that includes dignitaries. Luke notes that Jewish leaders (Pharisees and doctors of the law) from Galilee, Judaea, and even Jerusalem are present. It is difficult to distinguish precisely between Pharisees and doctors of the law. Ellis (104) notes that the doctors of the law are those who are authorized to give official interpretations of the Scriptures. They may be a sub-group within the Pharisees.

The last words of verse 17, "and the power of the Lord was *present* to heal them" are unusual. The idea seems to be that the power of God is present on this occasion in a special way so all who come to be healed may find the healing they desire. Jesus uses this occasion to demonstrate His deity in the presence of important Jewish leaders (Ellis 104; Lieu 39).

Friends bring to Jesus a man who is paralyzed; they carry him on some type of pallet or mat. The streets are narrow and crowded with people; they can find no way to get the man into the house where Jesus is teaching. They take him up to the roof of the house, open a hole in the tiles, and let him down before Jesus. Marshall (*Gospel* 213) notes that different types of roofing materials were used in Palestine and that tile roofs were in use by this time. There is no doubt that tearing up the roof created quite a scene.

Jesus views such an extraordinary action as an indication of great faith, on the part of both the man who is carried and the men who carry him. Jesus rewards their faith in two ways. First, He announces that the man's sins are forgiven. Second, He heals the man and instructs him to walk out of the house carrying his pallet. The idea is the man's sins have been forgiven by God (Greek perfect tense) and Jesus is authorized to announce that forgiveness on God's behalf.

Jesus' pronouncement that the man's sin has been forgiven provokes a controversy with the Jewish leaders. They understand, correctly enough, that only God has the power to forgive sins. God may have given to individuals the power to heal, but He has not given them the power to forgive sins. For this reason, they consider what Jesus has said to be blasphemy. What they do not understand (and are not willing to admit) is that Jesus is divine; He is the Son of God. As the Son of God, He has the same power to forgive sins that the Father has.

Jesus understands their reasoning, and He challenges them with a question (v. 23). He asks them whether it is easier to say, "Your sins are forgiven" or to say "Take up your bed and walk." They don't respond to His question, and Jesus doesn't expect they will. Jesus considers both the forgiveness of sins and healing to be examples of God's power and mercy. He instructs the paralyzed man to get up, pick up his pallet, and walk out of the house. Immediately the man does as Jesus directs; he walks out of the house rejoicing and praising God. The fact of his healing testifies to the forgiveness of his sins.

Verse 26 concludes the story. All who have witnessed the miracle are astonished; they glorify God and are filled with fear. Their summary statement is, "We have seen strange things today." The word translated "strange" expresses the idea of something unexpected or unanticipated (Marshall, *Gospel* 217). As Lenski (266) explains, in this passage Jesus does not call Himself the Messiah or the Son of God, but He allows people to come to that conclusion based on His words and His deeds.

This incident serves to introduce two groups of people, the Pharisees and the doctors of the law, who will figure prominently in Luke. The Pharisees are described in different ways, and it is difficult to get a complete picture of who they were and what they believed (Lieu 41). There is no doubt they formed a political-religious group that exercised great influence in the time of Jesus. They preserved traditional interpretations of the Law of Moses and were committed to applying those laws directly to the daily lives of the people of Israel. Over the years, they had developed a detailed code of how the Law of Moses was to be applied in different situations (Bock I:479). They seem to have been very concerned to maintain the purity of the Temple (Lieu 41). They are often portrayed in the Gospels as the enemies of Jesus (Marshall, *Gospel* 212).

The "doctors of the law" mentioned in verse 17 is the group often called "scribes" elsewhere in the Gospels. They are closely linked with the Pharisees; their goal is to maintain the established traditions and to apply the Law of Moses to many different situations in life (Bock I:479). It is difficult to determine how much popularity or influence the Pharisees enjoyed in first-century Palestine. Bock (I:479) suggests they were not popular among the people but they did have considerable power and influence within the government.

In verse 24, Luke uses the term "Son of man" for the first time; it was apparently Jesus' favorite term to describe Himself, one that has provoked considerable discussion. "Son of man" is of O. T. origin, where it is used in three different ways. In Psalm 8:4, it is used in parallel fashion with the term "man" to describe a human being. In Ezekiel 2 the term is used to describe Ezekiel as he fulfills the office of God's prophet or spokesman. In Daniel 7:13 the term is used to describe the shadowy (perhaps Messianic) figure who comes to the earth with the Ancient of Days. It is difficult to determine specifically what Jesus meant by the term and how His hearers would have interpreted it (Lieu 42-43). The available evidence does not indicate that "Son of man" was a common title for the Messiah in the first century (Bock I:924). Ellis (105) suggests Jesus might have chosen the term because it was ambiguous, and He could give to it the meaning He wished. It is also likely that Jesus chose this term to avoid the political implications of the term "Messiah." For excellent presentations of current thinking on the meaning of *Son of man* see Bock (I:924-930) and Michel (TDNTT III:613-634).

27 And after these things he went forth, and saw a publican, named Levi, sitting at the receipt of custom: and he said unto him, Follow me.
28 And he left all, rose up, and followed him.
29 And Levi made him a great feast in his own house: and there was a great company of publicans and of others that sat down with them.
30 But their scribes and Pharisees murmured against his disciples saying, Why do ye eat and drink with publicans and sinners?
31 And Jesus answering said unto them, They that are whole need not a physician; but they that are sick.
32 I came not to call the righteous, but sinners to repentance.

Once again, for Luke the event is the significant thing, not when or where it transpired, because it illustrates other important aspects of the Kingdom of God that Jesus is inaugurating. This new kingdom includes those who are outcasts from society. In the previous section, Jesus has included those who are excluded because of illness; He now includes those who are social outcasts. Jesus comes into contact with a minor customs official named Levi (or Matthew, as he is often known), whose job is to collect excise taxes for the government. He is probably a subordinate official working for Herod Antipas who is the Roman governor of the province (Lieu 44; Marshall, *Gospel* 219). These excise taxes are levied on those who are moving goods through Palestine. His office is probably little more than a table beside the road, but he might have had a tent to shade him from the sun. These tax collectors—*publicans*—are Jews who accept employment with the hated Roman government. They not only collect the taxes Rome requires; they also take advantage of their fellow Jews by collecting additional amounts for their own use. Many are little more than thieves (Green, *Luke* 246).

Jesus comes to him and says, "Follow me." There might have been some previous contact between Jesus and Levi, but if so Luke makes no mention of it. Levi responds by rising up from the customs table and following Jesus. The implication is that he is giving up his profession as a tax collector in order to become a disciple of Jesus (Bock, *Luke* NIV 159). Levi's first activity as a disciple is to host a large banquet for his fellow tax collectors and their associates. Ellis (107) suggests this dinner may serve two purposes. First, it is a way to introduce this crowd to Jesus. Second, it serves as a farewell dinner for Levi among his colleagues.

It is doubtful the scribes and Pharisees attend this banquet, but they, no doubt, hear about it. It is also possible that Jesus and His disciples have attended similar feasts on other occasions. The scribes and Pharisees are not pleased that a Jew like Jesus is so openly violating the Jewish laws and traditions, and they address their complaints to His disciples. A summary of their complaints is that Jesus and His disciples are sharing table fellowship with tax collectors and other sinners. In the ancient world, eating together implies a certain level of acceptance (Bock, *Luke* NIV 159). The Pharisees, with their emphasis on strict separation, cannot condone this type of activity. As His ministry develops, they will often condemn Jesus and His followers for eating and drinking with outcasts. According to the Pharisees, the term "sinner" includes all those who do not strictly adhere to the rules and regulations laid down by the rabbis (Ellis 107).

Jesus responds to this accusation in two ways. First, He notes that those who are well do not need a physician but those who are ill do. Jesus considers tax collectors and other social outcasts to be people who are suffering and in need of spiritual help. They need redemption, not condemnation. Second, Jesus explains that He has not come to call the righteous but sinners to repentance. Jesus' use of the terms "righteous" and "sinners" in this context is important. He uses the term "righteous" in a rather Jewish sense; it describes those who obtain their righteousness by observing the regulations laid down by the Jewish rabbis. The term "sinner" is understood in different ways. According to Ellis (107), in this context it describes those who do not observe the ceremonial rules and regulations as outlined by the rabbis. Fitzmyer (I:591) understands the term to include both Jews who do not keep the requirements of the Mosaic Law and Gentiles who have no hope of salvation.

Even at this early stage in the ministry of Jesus, the contrast between His approach and the approach of the Pharisees is becoming clear. One of the main goals of the Pharisees is to maintain their purity through a strict separation from those who do not observe the Jewish law. Jesus' goal is not separation but transformation. He recognizes that sinners are away from God, but He has no desire to leave them in this condition. His goal is to transform them from sinners to disciples; the strict separation advocated by the Pharisees can never accomplish that.

33 And they said unto him, Why do the disciples of John fast often, and make prayers, and likewise [the disciples] of the Pharisees; but thine eat and drink?
34 And he said unto them, Can ye make the children of the bridechamber fast, while the bridegroom is with them?
35 But the days will come, when the bridegroom shall be taken away from them, and then shall they fast in those days.

Luke does not identify those who challenge the teachings and practices of Jesus; Fitzmyer (I:597) suggests they are the scribes and Pharisees who were mentioned in verse 30. Once again, the key issue is not the identity of the opponents but the nature of the new kingdom that Jesus is inaugurating. The preaching and teaching of Jesus differ in significant ways from the Judaism practiced by the Pharisees; one of those differences concerns prayers and fasting.

Jesus' opponents have noted, quite correctly, that His disciples do not adhere to the schedule of prayer and fasting the most zealous Jews observed. Fitzmyer (I:596) notes that first-century Jews fasted for different reasons. They would fast on the Day of Atonement to make expiation for sins. They would also fast as an expression of penitence and in times of mourning. For a brief summary of fasting as it was practiced by first-century Jews see Marshall (*Gospel* 221). Geldenhuys (198) notes that during the Babylonian Exile the Jews developed the belief that fasting was a meritorious work God would reward. In the time of Jesus, it was the habit of the Pharisees to fast twice a week, and this fasting often included a great deal of outward display. Jesus fasted at times, and He permits it as a voluntary form of spiritual discipline. He totally rejects, however, the meritorious aspect that was common in His day.

Jesus responds to this challenge with the analogy of a wedding; He points out that fasting would be totally inappropriate during a wedding celebration. A wedding is a time for joy and feasting. The phrase "children of the bridechamber" refers to the friends of the groom who participate in the wedding activities. During the wedding activities they want to share in the joy of the bridegroom; they have no interest in fasting. The meaning of this passage is clear. The coming of Jesus is like a wedding; it is a time for joy, not fasting.

Verse 35 is interesting because Jesus becomes the bridegroom in the analogy. While He does not give a detailed prediction of future events, Jesus points out that the atmosphere of joy that surrounds His earthly ministry will not last forever. In the future, He will be taken from His disciples, and fasting will then be appropriate. Lenski (317) suggests that this passage may refer either to the dark days between Jesus' death and resurrection or to future periods of distress and persecution. Luke does not explain how the disciples responded to this startling statement, but it likely produced considerable thought and discussion.

36 And he spake also a parable unto them; No man putteth a piece of a new garment upon an old; if otherwise, then both the new maketh a rent, and the piece that was *taken* out of the new agreeth not with the old.
37 And no man putteth new wine into old bottles; else the new wine will burst the bottles, and be spilled, and the bottles shall perish.
38 But new wine must be put into new bottles; and both are preserved.
39 No man also having drunk old *wine* straightway desireth new: for he saith, The old is better.

Jesus continues the discussion with a story that illustrates the difference between the existing Jewish religion and the Kingdom of God He is proclaiming. The word translated "parable" (Greek *parabolē*) is broader than our English word. It can be used to describe proverbs, riddles, similitudes, or other figurative expressions that involve some type of comparison (Fitzmyer I:600). Jesus explains that no person would use a piece of new un-shrunken cloth to patch an old garment that has been washed several times; the patch would be incompatible with the original cloth. The first time the garment is washed, the tear would become worse (Fitzmyer I:600-601; Lenski 317).

Neither would a person take newly-made wine and put it into an old, brittle wineskin. "Bottle" (Greek *askōs*) does not describe a glass bottle but a container made from the skin of an animal, usually a goat (Fitzmyer I:601; Lenski 318). The new wine is still fermenting; it will put pressure on the skin that an old brittle wineskin cannot stand (Lenski 318). The old wineskin will tear, and both the wine and wineskin will be lost.

The message is that Jesus has not come simply to repair or improve the existing Jewish system. He has come to introduce a new conception of the Kingdom of God. Jesus understands that many will find it difficult to accept the new system He is proclaiming.

Verse 39 has provoked considerable discussion (Lenski 319-320; Fitzmyer I:601-602; Marshall, *Gospel* 228). Most commentators find a note of irony and sarcasm in it. Jesus explains that men will naturally prefer the old wine to the new; it has had time to age and develop a better flavor. The point is that the disciples of Jesus must be willing to forego that which is accepted and familiar in order to follow Him. Jesus understands that change is difficult because people are generally content to continue with what is known and familiar. The people of Galilee need to give this new conception of the Kingdom of God a fair trial, but many are not willing to do so. They are determined to continue in the familiar ways of Judaism even though a better alternative is available. The followers of Jesus must not be so tied to the past they are unable to accept the changes He is bringing about.

Summary (5:1-39)

This chapter introduces several themes that will become even more important as the ministry of Jesus develops. Luke focuses attention on the radical changes in life that Jesus brings about. First, Jesus calls Peter to be His disciple and later calls Levi. It would be difficult to imagine two more different people than Peter and Levi; one is a professional fisherman while the other is a tax collector. Yet Jesus has a place for both of them in the Kingdom of God.

Two miracles of healing figure prominently. The first is the healing of a leprous man; the second is the healing of a paralyzed man brought to Jesus by some of his friends. Both of these miracles serve several purposes, first to demonstrate the divine power Jesus exercises; this power is used to authenticate His ministry of healing. If Jesus has the divine power necessary to heal a lame man, He must also have the authority to forgive sins. These healings serve to illustrate the kind of kingdom Jesus has come to inaugurate: a kingdom based on love and mercy, one that seeks the best for all mankind.

The miracles also help attract the attention of the people of Galilee so they might hear the teachings Jesus has for them.

The final verses present the first conflict between Jesus and the Jewish leaders in this Gospel. The Jewish leaders challenge the disciples of Jesus because they do not participate in the fasts which both the disciples of John the Baptist and the Pharisees observe. Jesus responds by telling them that His coming has brought a time of joy like a wedding feast. In such an atmosphere, fasting is both unnecessary and inappropriate. In the new kingdom He is inaugurating, fasting and other ritual observances will not be necessary. In this context Jesus also makes one of His first predictive statements. In the future, when He is taken away from them, it will then be appropriate for His disciples to fast.

Luke relates two brief parables of Jesus. The first deals with the repair of an old garment, the second with putting new wine into old wineskins. No one would use a piece of new un-shrunken cloth to patch an old garment because when the garment is washed the damage will be made worse. In the same way, no one would put new wine into old wineskins. The new wine, as it continues to ferment, will destroy an old, brittle wineskin. These parables explain that the new kingdom Jesus is establishing is different from the Jewish system of worship they have known.

The idea is that Jesus has not come to earth just to improve the existing Jewish system; He has come to introduce something new. This does not mean, however, that the O. T. no longer has any role in the kingdom. The ministry of Jesus should be thought of as fulfillment and not as replacement; see Matthew 5:17 and the insightful comments of Whitacre (61).

Application: Teaching and Preaching the Passage

Those who preach and teach from this passage should keep in mind the major themes Luke wishes to stress. He emphasizes the power and authority of Jesus as the Son of God. The three important miracles presented in this chapter point out that Jesus is much more than a great teacher. He is the Son of God who manifests all of the power and authority of His heavenly Father. The call of the disciples occupies an important place in this chapter. While there are certainly differences between the call of the disciples and

Jesus' call to men and women today, there are also many similarities. Those who wish to become followers of Christ today must demonstrate a high level of commitment just as the first disciples did.

The chapter also focuses attention on the uniqueness of Jesus' ministry. He demonstrates a genuine care and concern for those whom society rejects. He even accepts tax-collectors into His spiritual family. Although in this passage Jesus does not specifically claim to be the Messiah, He allows His words and actions to explain the kind of Messiah He will be. He manifests no desire to come as a conquering hero. Rather, He comes in humility and service, as the Good Shepherd of His flock.

Faith is another theme developed in this passage. Both Peter and Levi demonstrate an extraordinary degree of faith when they give up long-established careers to become His disciples. Levi goes so far as to host a farewell banquet for his friends and fellow tax-collectors. While Jesus does not call all of His disciples to leave their homes and occupations, He does call the twelve to do so; for them He has a special ministry. The man who asks to be healed of his leprosy reflects a rather hesitant faith, but it is faith, nonetheless. Another example of exemplary faith in this passage is found in the men who come to Jesus bringing a paralytic. These verses reflect both their faith in Jesus and their love and concern for the helpless man whom they let down through the roof.

It is no accident that every example of faith in this passage produced action. Peter and Levi did not just proclaim orally their faith in Jesus; they acted upon that faith. The men who brought the lame man went so far as to dig up the roof tiles and let him down through a hole in the roof. Christian faith is more than just intellectual assent; it calls the followers of Jesus to do things they would never have done without it.

Those who preach and teach from this chapter should take note of the themes of love, mercy, and forgiveness that are presented here. Jesus truly loves the people of Galilee and seeks the best for them. He loves the disciples, and they also love Him. Their willingness to leave their homes and families in order to become Jesus' disciples is a response to His love for them. The miracles of healing demonstrate the love of Jesus in action. Those un-named men who brought the paralytic to Jesus did so because of their love and concern for the helpless man. Modern believers do not have the power to perform miracles or forgive sins as Jesus did, but they can demonstrate a genuine love and concern for the world in which they are called to serve.

In the last verses of the chapter, Jesus encounters opposition from the Jewish leaders; He also begins the task of outlining the differences between the existing Jewish system of worship and the new kingdom He has brought to earth. There are several lessons that can be learned from these verses. During His earthly ministry, Jesus often encountered opposition from the established system of worship. His disciples today will also encounter opposition from an increasingly secular world. The closing verses remind us that Jesus did not come simply to repair or improve the existing system. He came to introduce something radically new and different; at the heart of this new system is a relationship with God that is built on grace and faith rather than on the observance of ritualistic practices like fasting.

C. Conflict Over Sabbath Observance (6:1-12)

1 And it came to pass on the second sabbath after the first, that he went through the corn fields; and his disciples plucked the ears of corn, and did eat, rubbing *them* in *their* hands.
2 And certain of the Pharisees said unto them, Why do ye that which is not lawful to do on the sabbath days?
3 And Jesus answering them said, Have ye not read so much as this, what David did, when himself was an hungered, and they which were with him;
4 How he went into the house of God, and did take and eat the shewbread, and gave also to them that were with him; which it is not lawful to eat but for the priests alone?
5 And he said unto them, That the Son of man is Lord also of the sabbath.

Jesus continues to develop His new understanding of the Kingdom of God. Rather than giving abstract teachings, He gives concrete examples of what it means to participate in this new relationship with God. He points out that this new concept of the kingdom includes a new understanding of the Sabbath and how it should be observed. He also gives His disciples a new understanding of what it means to do the will of God.

Sabbath observance was an important issue among the Pharisees of Jesus' day (Geldenhuys 199). The O. T. describes the Sabbath as a day of rest when regular work activities are forbidden, but the O. T. documents contain no definition of the term "work." Over the years, the Pharisees had developed an extensive list of what activities were considered work and, therefore, could not be done on the Sabbath. Some of these rules were very minute. For example, a woman could not look in a mirror on the Sabbath day because if she saw a gray hair and pulled it out, that would be work. For a useful discussion of Sabbath observance see Stott (NIDNTT III:405-415).

Jesus and His disciples were walking through the grain fields on the Sabbath. In the Bible "corn" refers to wheat, barley, and other grains. (What we know as "corn" was unknown in first-century Palestine.) The disciples were hungry; they plucked some of the ears of grain, rubbed them together in their hands to remove the chaff, and ate the grains. According to Deuteronomy 23:25, it was lawful for the disciples to pick enough grain to satisfy their own hunger when they passed through a field of ripe grain. The O. T. passage does not explicitly state that such picking could be done on the Sabbath.

Some of the Pharisee heard about what the disciples had done and complained to Jesus that His disciples had violated their laws concerning the Sabbath. Jesus responded by citing an example from the O. T. In 1 Samuel 21:3-6, David and his men entered the Temple and ate the Bread of Presence ("Shewbread"), which was prepared in a special way for use only in the Temple. It was to be eaten only by the priests.

What David and his men did was obviously a violation of the law, but, according to Jesus, their need for food was of greater importance than the technicalities of the law. In the same way, the hunger of the disciples justified their harvesting and eating a small amount of grain on the Sabbath.

Jesus' response to the Pharisees raises two important issues. First is the issue of human need. For Jesus, people are the priority, and meeting their legitimate needs is of greater value than the technicalities of the law. Second is the issue of authority. David was doing God's work, and he had the authority to do what was necessary to accomplish God's will (Marshall, *Gospel* 228). In Luke 6:5, Jesus says, "the Son of man is Lord also of the Sabbath." The full implications of this statement will become more apparent as the thought of this Gospel develops, but the basic idea is clear. Jesus is the Son of God; in that capacity, He has the authority to determine the proper observance of the Sabbath. His teaching carries greater weight than the interpretations of the Pharisees.

6 And it came to pass also on another sabbath, that he entered into the synagogue and taught: and there was a man whose right hand was withered.
7 And the scribes and Pharisees watched him, whether he would heal on the sabbath day; that they might find an accusation against him.
8 But he knew their thoughts, and said to the man which had the withered hand, Rise up, and stand forth in the midst. And he arose and stood forth.
9 Then said Jesus unto them, I will ask you one thing; Is it lawful on the sabbath days to do good, or to do evil? to save life, or to destroy *it*?
10 And looking round about upon them all, he said unto the man, Stretch forth thy hand. And he did so: and his hand was restored whole as the other.
11 And they were filled with madness; and communed one with another what they might do to Jesus.

Luke introduces the story of a man with a withered hand who comes to the synagogue to worship on the Sabbath day. The animosity of the scribes and Pharisees is growing (Summers, *Luke* 71); they are watching Jesus closely to see if He will heal this man on the Sabbath day. The laws of the Pharisees prohibited the practice of medicine or surgery (except for circumcision) on the Sabbath day (Summers, *Luke* 71). They permitted work of an emergency nature on the Sabbath, but this was no emergency. The man had suffered from this malady for some time, and he was in no immediate danger of death. Jesus could easily have waited until the Sabbath had ended to heal him. Jesus deliberately chose to heal him publicly on the Sabbath day. It is significant to note that Jesus asks the man to step forward so all may observe the healing; He wants there to be no doubt about the miracle He is about to perform.

Jesus knows what the Pharisees are thinking. He takes the initiative and asks them a probing question, which He phrases in two ways: "Is it lawful on the Sabbath days to do good or evil?" and "Is it lawful to save life or to destroy *it*?"

Jesus gives the scribes and Pharisees an opportunity to answer, but they refuse to do so. They understand that He has them in a corner. If they answer the question according to their traditional teaching, they will be discredited in front of the people. Their hardness of heart will be apparent for all to see.

In reality, the answer is obvious; it is lawful to do good on the Sabbath day. As Morris (*Luke* 123) notes, Jesus sets up two alternatives. One is to do good; the other is to do evil. The implication is that a failure to do good is, in fact, to do evil. The scribes and Pharisees would have Jesus do nothing for this unfortunate man because it is the Sabbath; in Jesus' view, to do nothing would be to do the man even further harm. Jesus chooses to do good. He restores the withered hand to its normal state, and He does so instantaneously (Geldenhuys 203).

The reaction of the scribes and Pharisees is predictable. They reflect no care and concern for this man who now has two normal hands, probably for the first time in his life. They are incensed because Jesus has broken their law, and He has done so in a way that increases His popularity among the people (A. Bruce, EGT I:502). The Jewish leaders begin to discuss among themselves how they might act against Jesus. As the thought of this Gospel develops, their plans will become reality.

In this encounter, Jesus is calling for a re-evaluation of how the Sabbath is to be understood and observed. It was originally intended to be a day of rest for hard-working men and women. After the development of the synagogue, it became a day devoted to worship and the study of the law (Sampey, ISBE IV:2631). It also included refraining from any secular employment. During the inter-biblical period, many elaborate rules and regulations for the proper observance of the Sabbath were developed; two entire treatises in the Jewish Mishnah are devoted to the details concerning the proper observance of the Sabbath (Sampey, ISBE IV:2631). Jesus took a sharply different position on Sabbath observance. He taught that it was never God's plan to encumber it with a multitude of rules and regulations. Jesus held the Sabbath in high esteem, but He saw it as an institution designed to serve human needs. The Sabbath was intended to be a time of active involvement in the service of God. Deeds of mercy and kindness are always appropriate, even on the Sabbath (Geldenhuys 203).

12 And it came to pass in those days, that he went out into a mountain to pray, and continued all night in prayer to God.

This is a transition verse, which serves both as a conclusion to this section of chapter six and as an introduction to the next section. The time reference is deliberately vague; it is not Luke's goal to give a precise chronology of events (Morris, *Luke* 124). The focus is on Jesus' relationship with His heavenly Father. Jesus went away to a mountain (probably near the city of Capernaum) where He could experience some solitude and be alone with God (A. Bruce, EGT I:503). This verse illustrates two important themes that Luke will develop throughout the Gospel. The first is prayer; it is no accident that Jesus prays at crucial times in His ministry. Prayer is an important part of His relationship with God. Luke does not explain why prayer is so important to Jesus, but the most likely explanation is that His humanity produced the same need for prayer that other human beings experience. The fact that the prayer continues all night stresses the importance and solemnity of the occasion (Marshall, *Gospel* 238). The second important theme is Jesus' total and absolute dependence on the leadership of His heavenly Father (Geldenhuys 205). Jesus is the Son of God, but He never acts independently. His goal is always to seek His Father's will and then to do it.

D. Naming the Disciples (6:13-16)

13 And when it was day, he called *unto him* his disciples: and of them he chose twelve, whom also he named apostles;
14 Simon, (whom he also named Peter), and Andrew his brother, James and John, Philip and Bartholomew,
15 Matthew and Thomas, James the *son* of Alphaeus, and Simon called Zelotes,
16 And Judas *the brother* of James, and Judas Iscariot, which also was the traitor.

The list of the disciples' names is found in several places in the N. T. (Mt. 10:2-4; Mk. 3:16-19; Lk. 6:14-16; Acts 1:13). Luke's list of names follows most closely the list given in Mark (Marshall, *Gospel* 237). In every account, the names are arranged in groups of four; Simon Peter is the leader of the first group; Philip is the leader of the second group; James the son of Alphaeus is the leader of the third (Summers, *Luke* 72).

In all of the lists Peter is named first; this probably indicates his leadership within the apostolic band (Geldenhuys 206). John 1:45 mentions Nathanael; the other lists have "Bartholomew" instead of "Nathanael." Geldenhuys (206) suggests that the word "Bartholomew" is not a proper name but a term meaning "the son of Tholomai." In other words, this apostle is Nathanael, the son of Tholomai. Matthew is sometimes called Levi; Judas, the son of James, is also known as Thaddeus (Marshall, *Gospel* 240).

Luke includes Simon called "Zelotes" (the Zealot) in his list. In Mark 3:18, he is known as "Simon the Canaanite." The word translated "Canaanite" is an Aramaic word which means "zealot" (Marshall, *Gospel* 240). Luke uses the equivalent Greek term.

"Zealot" may be interpreted in two different ways. First, the term was used in a generic sense to describe a person who was zealous and firmly committed to his beliefs. Second, it was used later as a technical term to describe a member of a Jewish nationalist sect that fought bitterly against Roman rule during the Jewish war for independence, A.D. 66-70 (Marshall, *Gospel* 240). It is difficult to determine whether this sect officially existed in the time of Jesus. It is possible that Simon was an early follower of a radical sect of zealots, but that has not been conclusively proven.

All of the lists conclude with Judas Iscariot; according to most commentators the term "Iscariot" means "man of Kerioth" (Morris, *Luke* 125). Marshall (*Gospel* 240) suggests another possibility. The term may be derived from the Aramaic word *seqar,* which means "falsehood." All of the lists also include the fact that Judas was a traitor or he became a traitor. Luke states that he became a traitor, thus leaving open the possibility that he was at first a faithful follower of Christ.

The two most important terms in this passage, "disciple" and "apostle," are found in verse 13. Jesus began by calling together a group of His disciples. A *disciple* (Greek *mathētēs*) is both a student and a follower. Morris (*Luke* 124) explains that a student in the first century did not just study a subject; he also studied a teacher. He would travel with his teacher and interact with him on a daily basis; there was an element of personal attachment, which is generally lost today. For a discussion of this term see Müller (NIDNTT I:480-494).

Out of this group of disciples, Jesus selected twelve to whom He gives the title *apostle* (Greek *apostolos*), from a verb meaning "to send." It implies an official messenger or representative who has authority to speak on behalf of another (Marshall, *Gospel* 238-239; Geldenhuys 206). According to many commentators, this word grows out of an Aramaic term, which describes a fully accredited representative. (See NIDNTT I:135-137.)

The number twelve is significant; in the history of Israel, there are twelve tribes and twelve patriarchs. In Revelation, the number 144,000, which serves as a symbol for completeness, is a multiple of the number twelve (Lenski 337-338). While the apostles' precise role is yet to be determined, it is clear they will play a key role in establishing Jesus' new conception of the Kingdom of God. They will also become leaders in the church that will continue the ministry after Jesus' death.

E. Jesus Challenges His Followers (6:17-49)

17 And he came down with them, and stood in the plain, and the company of his disciples, and a great multitude of people out of all Judaea and Jerusalem, and from the sea coast of Tyre and Sidon, which came to hear him, and to be healed of their diseases.
18 And they that were vexed with unclean spirits: and they were healed.
19 And the whole multitude sought to touch him: for there went virtue out of him, and healed *them* all.

This is a summary statement describing the general nature of Jesus' ministry and how it affects the people of Palestine (Fitzmyer I:622). Jesus makes certain ethical demands of His disciples, and this passage outlines the most important of them (Bock, *Luke* NIV 186).

Jesus comes down from the mountain where He has called the twelve apostles; He is accompanied by the disciples that had gone up the mountain with Him. He comes to a level place where He begins to speak to the crowd. The latter portion of verse 17 indicates the widespread appeal of Jesus' ministry; He is probably still in Galilee when these events occur. Luke explains that a large crowd of people is present from Judaea and Jerusalem, which lay some distance to the south. Others are present from Tyre and Sidon, two ancient pagan cities, which lay to the north in the territory of Phoenicia (Fitzmyer I:622-624). In other words, people have come from considerable distances to hear Jesus' teachings and to experience His healing. This indicates something of

His growing popularity and importance. It may also indicate something of Jesus' desire that the gospel be shared with all, even with those from pagan cities.

Luke makes a distinction between those who are suffering from diseases (v. 17) and those who are suffering from demons or other unclean spirits (v. 18). Both groups stand in need of healing, which only Jesus can provide, and He gives them the healing they desire. Verse 19 explains how this important event concludes. The people have a natural desire to touch Jesus; they want to have real contact with Him (Fitzmyer I:624). "Virtue" (Greek *dunamis*) is "power." These healings are not accomplished through some form of magical art or incantation, they are the result of power going forth from the Son of God. The last words of verse 19 indicate the extent of Jesus' ministry. He does not heal only the select few; He bestows His divine power upon all who are willing to receive it.

20 And he lifted up his eyes on his disciples, and said, Blessed *be ye* poor: for yours is the kingdom of God.
21 Blessed *are ye* that hunger now: for ye shall be filled. Blessed *are ye* that weep now: for ye shall laugh.
22 Blessed are ye, when men shall hate you, and when they shall separate you *from their company*, and shall reproach *you*, and cast out your name as evil, for the Son of man's sake.
23 Rejoice ye in that day, and leap for joy: for, behold, your reward *is* great in heaven: for in the like manner did their fathers unto the prophets.

With these words, Luke begins the important passage that is commonly known as the Sermon on the Plain, a passage clearly intended for the instruction of His disciples (Lenski 342). Here "disciples" probably indicates the larger body of Jesus' followers; it is not limited to the twelve apostles (Lieu 50). These verses emphasize the blessedness of those who enter into the Kingdom of God (Lenski 343).

Luke's Sermon on the Plain is often compared to the Sermon on the Mount found in Matthew 5–7. Some commentators argue that they are two different sermons, but most conservative interpreters view them as two different versions of the same sermon (Lenski 342; Bock I:931-944). The relationship between these two passages is interesting; they have much material in common. The passage in Matthew contains approximately 111 verses; Luke contains 29 verses. That means that only about one-fourth of the content of Matthew's sermon is found in Luke. Additional material from Matthew's sermon is found in different places in Luke (Summers, *Luke* 73). It is beyond the scope of this commentary to examine all the possible ways of understanding the relationship between the two passages. Probably the best explanation is that both Matthew and Luke, under the leadership of the Holy Spirit, selected and arranged the material in such a way as to best accomplish each Gospel writer's goals and objectives. It is possible that Matthew reflects the original form of the sermon, and Luke has rearranged the material to suit his own purposes. It is also likely that Jesus gave these teachings in various forms and on different occasions during His public ministry. It should not simply be assumed that a particular teaching was given on only one occasion.

Verse 20 is the first of four beatitudes that Luke includes; it includes two key terms, "blessed" and "poor." The English word "blessed" (Greek *makarios*), in secular Greek, describes a person's inner happiness (Fitzmyer I:632). In this context, it denotes neither a wish for a future blessing nor a description of the person's present condition. It is, in reality, a judgment (Lenski 344). The idea is that those who belong to the Kingdom of God are considered by God to be blessed even though the world may not see the blessing. The blessings are spiritual, not material. In the Greek version of the O. T. this term expresses the idea of God's favor resting upon a person (Fitzmyer I:633). The person who is blessed experiences joy as a result of God's favor (Bock I:572).

"Poor" (Greek *ptōchos*) has its roots in the O. T. and the pronouncement probably reflects Isaiah 61:1; in Luke, it describes those to whom Jesus proclaims the good news. The term implies more than economic poverty; it describes those who are not only poor but also pious and dependent on God for their daily needs (Bock I:573; Green, *Luke* 267). In this context, the term refers to the disciples who have sacrificed economic security in order to become followers of Christ.

In these beatitudes, Jesus reverses the way people normally interpret the events of daily life. In the first century, wealth was considered a sign of God's blessing (Green, *Luke* 265). It was also seen as God's reward for faithful service. In this passage, that traditional interpretation is rejected; wealth is not an indication of one's faithfulness to God. According to Luke, wealth may actually detract from a person's relationship to God; it may lead to an arrogant self-security (Green, *Luke* 267).

The verse concludes with the words "for yours is the kingdom of God." This passage implies more than a future promise. The idea is that the disciples have already entered into a special relationship with God; they are blessed in a way that others are not (Green, *Luke* 265-266). There is an element of paradox here. The disciples have sacrificed material blessings on earth to obtain entrance into God's kingdom; they have suffered material loss to obtain spiritual gain. The world may not understand what they have done, but their commitment has brought the blessings of God upon them.

In the second and third beatitudes (v. 21), Jesus promises a special blessing upon those who hunger and those who weep. Those who hunger and mourn are the poor from the previous verse. Luke does not explain the cause of their weeping; it probably has something to do with the daily sufferings they encounter. They live on the margins of society and have to depend totally on God, but in the future all of their needs will be met. The idea that God will bestow future blessings upon those who suffer on earth is a common O. T. theme. Isaiah 32, for example, points to the time when the judgment of God will fall on the unrighteous who live in luxury, but the people of God "shall dwell in a peaceable habitation, and in sure dwellings, and in quiet resting places."

The fourth beatitude (v. 22) speaks of those who are rejected by men because of their allegiance to God. Because they become followers of Jesus and embrace His new understanding of the Kingdom of God, they are rejected by a traditional society.

"For the Son of man's sake" (v. 22) limits the application. People may be rejected by society for a variety of different reasons; sometimes their words and actions justify this reaction. God's blessings are promised only to those who are rejected because of their identification with Jesus and His ministry. They may be rejected on earth, but in heaven they will leap for joy because they have received God's favor. In this passage and others, Jesus makes no attempt to conceal from His disciples the price they will have to pay because they are His followers (Lenski 352).

Jesus points out that this type of rejection is nothing new (v. 23). The nation of Israel has often turned its back on those most faithful; true prophets of God have often been rejected while false prophets have been exalted (Green, *Luke* 268; Lenski 353). This injustice may never be remedied here on earth, but those faithful to God will experience great reward in Heaven.

24 But woe unto you that are rich! for ye have received your consolation.
25 Woe unto you that are full! for ye shall hunger. Woe unto you that laugh now! for ye shall mourn and weep.
26 Woe unto you, when all men shall speak well of you! for so did their fathers to the false prophets.

These three verses contain a series of woes, which are the opposite of the beatitudes presented in the earlier verses. In the previous section, Jesus has bestowed a blessing upon those who are normally outcasts; here He pronounces a curse on those whom society would normally recognize and commend (Barclay 76-77). The phrase "you that are rich" implies more than the possession of wealth; it is the opposite of "poor." In verse 20, the poor are those who have been marginalized. They are faithful to God, but they have no wealth, influence, or political power. Here the "rich" are the opposite. They have wealth and political power, but they have little or no consideration for the poor (Green, *Luke* 267). Jesus reverses the traditional thinking that riches are God's reward for righteousness. The rich often trust in their worldly possessions rather than in God. They have already received their reward on earth; no further blessings are to be expected.

"You that are full" and "you that laugh now" describe this same group of people. Hunger was always a serious problem in ancient Israel, but it presented no difficulties for the rich. They had the resources to buy all the food they wanted. It was easy for them to laugh because of the abundance of their possessions. Verse 26 corrects the traditional theology, that wealth is a blessing from God, often a reward for being righteous. In that kind of theological climate, it is natural to speak well of the rich. Once again, Jesus challenges the traditional theology. He identifies the rich with the false prophets of Israel who preached what the people wanted to hear (Jer. 5:12-13, 6:13-15). The adoration of the crowds is not a sign of God's endorsement. As Lenski (357-358) points out, a disciple not only needs the right kind of friends; he needs the right kind of enemies. If he has made no enemies, he is probably not a faithful disciple.

27 But I say unto you which hear, Love your enemies, do good to them which hate you,
28 Bless them that curse you, and pray for them which despitefully use you.
29 And unto him that smiteth thee on the *one* cheek offer also the other; and him that taketh away thy cloke forbid not *to take thy* coat also.
30 Give to every man that asketh of thee; and of him that taketh away thy goods ask *them* not again.
31 And as ye would that men should do to you, do ye also to them likewise.

Jesus outlines the basic attitudes that should guide the disciple in his or her personal relations. As Lenski (362) explains, in these verses Jesus expounds the law of love, which is to guide the believer. God has placed punishment and retribution in the hands of the state; He has placed the law of love in the hearts of His disciples. They are to suffer wrong in order to overcome evil with good. This kind of love is not normal; it is the kind of love that God produces in the lives of those who have been truly transformed (Ellis 114). Jesus is advocating more than a passive response to evil; He is calling for an active response of love.

Geldenhuys (212-213) emphasizes that these verses must be understood in light of the total context of Jesus' ministry; they must not be viewed in isolation. The goal of the disciple is to seek the best interest of the one who sins. This excludes ideas of revenge and retaliation, which serve no redemptive purpose. They do not forbid strong action when necessary, but the ultimate goal is not to defend one's self-interest. It is to bring the guilty to repentance. In order to accomplish this goal, the disciple must be willing to subordinate his own interest to the advancement of the Kingdom of God. This passage does not forbid self-defense in case of a physical attack (Ellis 115).

Wilcock (75) sees these verses as a part of Jesus' developing conflict with the Pharisees who have come to view Him as a dangerous revolutionary. Jesus' goal is to demonstrate how different His system of thought is from that of the Jewish leaders. The traditional Jewish teaching is "Love your neighbor and hate your enemy" (Summers, *Luke* 76). Jesus instructs His followers to expand the meaning of love to include one's enemies.

In the words "but I say unto you," both strong authority and sharp contrast appear. "But" (Greek *alla*) implies a definite contrast with that which has gone before. Jesus is establishing a significant difference between His teaching and the traditional teachings of Judaism. He is also asserting His authority as the Son of God. The implication is that He has the necessary authority from God to change long-established teachings. Love is the principal theme of these verses, but it is not the kind of love people ordinarily feel for one another (Bock I:586). It is love to an extraordinary degree, which extends to those who are not the ordinary objects of human love. It is the kind of love that can be shown only by one who has experienced God's forgiveness (Bock I:588).

"Enemy" (v. 27, Greek *echthros*) has a long history both in secular Greek and in the Septuagint. It is used to describe personal enemies, military opponents, and adversaries in courts of law (NIDNTT I:553-555). Here it suggests one who bitterly opposes Jesus and His ministry. It is inevitable that His disciples will also share in the animosity demonstrated toward Jesus.

After giving general instruction on loving one's enemies, Jesus gives six concrete examples of how this teaching can be implemented in the daily lives of His followers. Several of these examples reflect the social structure of first-century Palestine.

First, He instructs His disciples to "do good to them which hate you," meaning those who are hostile to Jesus and His ministry. Although Jesus does not enumerate any specific actions, it is clear He is demanding more than pious expressions of one's love for his enemies. He is commanding that love be put into practice by performing deeds of love and mercy that benefit one's enemies (Marshall, *Gospel* 259).

Second, Jesus tells His followers to "bless them that curse you." "Bless" (Greek *eulogeo)* and "curse" (*Greek kataraomai*) both have strong religious connotations. The second term may describe the curse pronounced upon a person who was expelled from the synagogue (Marshall, *Gospel* 259). The key idea is that rather than praying for God's judgment upon their enemies, disciples should pray for God's blessings upon them.

Third, Jesus instructs His followers to "pray for them which despitefully use you." "Despitefully use" (Greek *epēreazo*) means to insult or to mistreat.

Fourth, Jesus instructs His followers that when someone strikes them on one cheek, they are to offer the other also. "Smite" (Greek *tuptō*) generally means to strike a blow with the hand or fist. In the eastern cultures, striking a person on the cheek was a great insult (Marshall, *Gospel* 260). Manson (*Sayings* 51) explains that this passage may refer to a slap with the back of the hand, which was especially insulting. Summers (*Luke* 76-77) suggests Jesus is offering an alternative to the law of retaliation, which is expressed in such O. T. passages as Exodus 21:23-24; Leviticus 24:19-20; and Deuteronomy 19:21. The point is that the followers of Jesus should control the natural desire to retaliate in the face of such a personal insult; it is more important to maintain a positive testimony to the power of God.

Fifth, Jesus tells His followers that when someone takes their cloak, they should also allow that person to take their coat. "Cloke" (Greek *himation*) often means an outer garment that was also used as a blanket at night. The "coat" (Greek *chitōna*) is the inner garment. Apparently, Luke has in mind a common thief who steals one's garments. In this passage, Jesus is not giving a regulation to be legalistically observed; rather, He is exhorting His followers to focus on the spiritual things of life rather than on the material.

For His sixth concrete example (v. 30) Jesus says, "Give to every man that asketh of thee; and of him that taketh away thy goods ask *them* not again." The first half of the verse relates to those who are needy and lacking in the basic necessities of life. Jesus always encourages His followers to be generous with those in need. The second half of the verse may be interpreted in two different ways. One possibility is it teaches that one is not to demand the return of something that is taken by theft or by stealth (Fitzmyer I:639). The other possibility is that one is not to continually demand the return of something that has been borrowed (Manson, *Sayings* 51-52).

The general teaching of this passage is quite clear; the disciple of Jesus Christ must show a genuine love to all, even those who are his enemies. The proper application of these six concrete examples in a modern society is more difficult. They are stated in absolute terms without considering the circumstances or the condition of the person who is mistreating the disciple. Summers (*Luke* 77) suggests they should not be understood as absolute commands but are designed to teach that the Christian life is a life of giving and not a life of grasping. Lieu (51) argues that the purpose of these examples is not to teach that the disciples should become passive but they should by their own actions seek to break the cycle of violence and retaliation. It is clear these examples deal with personal insults and not with violent attacks; there is nothing in this passage that forbids a believer to defend himself in the case of an assault.

The closing verse of this passage is commonly known as the Golden Rule: "And as ye would that men should do to you, do ye also to them likewise." Lieu (51) notes this saying is found in various places in ancient literature, in both positive and negative forms. Ellis (115) points out that this teaching is presented in a negative form by the famous Jewish rabbi Hillel. Even so, it provides a profound summary of the teachings of Jesus. He has taught His disciples to love God and to love their neighbors; this verse gives specific instruction to the disciples on how they are to carry out the instruction to love their neighbors. They are to take the initiative and show the love of God in a positive manner, whether or not the other person loves in return. To love in situations where love is the normal reaction is to do what is right; to love in situations where love is not normally expected is the kind of love that Jesus enjoins (Marshall, *Gospel* 262).

32 For if ye love them which love you, what thank have ye? for sinners also love those that love them.
33 And if ye do good to them which do good to you, what thank have ye? for sinners also do even the same.
34 And if ye lend *to them* of whom ye hope to receive, what thank have ye? for sinners also lend to sinners, to receive as much again.
35 But love ye your enemies, and do good, and lend, hoping for nothing again; and your reward shall be great, and ye shall be the children of the Highest: for he is kind unto the unthankful and *to* the evil.
36 Be ye therefore merciful, as your Father also is merciful.

These verses continue the general theme of true discipleship that Jesus began developing in verse 27. In verse 31, Jesus told His disciples to do unto others as they would like for others to do to them. In these verses, He further develops that theme and provides several examples of how they can demonstrate their discipleship in practical ways.

Verse 32 explains that it would be nothing special for the disciples to love those who love them; even sinners do that. "Thank" (Greek *charis*) is often translated "grace." In the Greek O. T., it is used to describe approval or approbation given by one's superior or by God (Manson, *Sayings* 54). The word is used in several different ways in the N. T.; here, it seems to express the idea of merit. If the disciples only love those who love them, they are doing nothing worthy of commendation. Verse 33 makes the same point. If the disciples do good only to those who do good to them, they are doing nothing special. They are not demonstrating any real discipleship.

Verse 34 illustrates the same point from a different perspective. If they lend only to those who can repay the loan on time and with interest, they are doing nothing special. If they lend to the poor who often have trouble repaying, they are showing themselves to be real disciples.

Verses 35-36 summarize the teachings of the passage. The disciples are to love their enemies, do good to all, and lend to the poor who cannot repay. The O. T. writers often describe God as merciful (Ex. 34:6; Dt. 4:31; Jl. 2:13; Jon. 4:2). The disciples of Jesus are to demonstrate the same kind of mercy that God has shown. If they do this, their reward will be great in Heaven. The greatest commendation is they will be regarded as true children of the Highest (God), because they will be imitating the character of God. He is kind to those who are unthankful and evil; the disciples should be as well.

37 Judge not, and ye shall not be judged: condemn not, and ye shall not be condemned: forgive, and ye shall be forgiven:
38 Give, and it shall be given unto you; good measure, pressed down, and shaken together, and running over, shall men give into your bosom. For with the same measure that ye mete withal it shall be measured to you again.

In verse 36, Jesus instructed His disciples to be merciful. In these verses, He illustrates that instruction with two negative commands, two positive commands, and a final comment. "Judge" (Greek *krinō*) can mean "to come to a correct decision," "to rule," or "to condemn" (Marshall, *Gospel* 265). Here the idea is "condemn." "Condemn" (Greek *katadikazō*) has a similar meaning but is stronger.

It is doubtful that Jesus is prohibiting all judgment; sometimes fair and impartial judgment is appropriate and necessary. For example, in 1 Timothy 3:1-10 Paul lists certain qualifications for those who wish to serve as ministers. Prior to ordination, someone must evaluate the life and character of the ministerial candidate in light of these qualifications and then make a judgment. What Jesus is prohibiting here is the development of a critical and censorious spirit that condemns others unnecessarily. Bock (*Luke* NIV 192) understands this passage to mean that the disciple should be slow to judge.

"Forgive" (Greek *apoluō*) may mean "to release," "to acquit," or "to forgive" (Manson, *Sayings* 56). It is often used in connection with the forgiveness of debts; in this passage, it is used with reference to the forgiveness of sins or personal insults committed against a follower of Christ. Disciples simply cannot fulfill their responsibilities when they are dominated by a spirit of bitterness or a desire for revenge.

Verse 37 adds an important idea. Disciples should expect to receive from

God what they extend to others. In order to escape condemnation, they must refrain from condemning. In order to receive forgiveness, they must forgive. Jesus is reminding His disciples that their earthly actions have eternal consequences.

Verse 38 tells the disciples that they must have a spirit of generosity. They are told to give, but Jesus does not spell out any details. How to give in an appropriate and helpful way generally depends on the people involved and on the circumstances. In order to illustrate the kind of giving that He desires, Jesus talks about a merchant who sells grain in the marketplace. An honest merchant will deliver to the customer the full amount of grain for which he is paying, and perhaps a little more. The disciples have freely received God's mercy and forgiveness; they must freely share what they have received. The last part of this verse continues the thought of verse 37; the disciples may expect to receive from God the same kind of mercy and grace they demonstrate to others.

39 And he spake a parable unto them, Can the blind lead the blind? shall they not both fall into the ditch?
40 The disciple is not above his master: but every one that is perfect shall be as his master.
41 And why beholdest thou the mote that is in thy brother's eye, but perceivest not the beam that is in thine own eye?
42 Either how canst thou say to thy brother, Brother, let me pull out the mote that is in thine eye, when thou thyself beholdest not the beam that is in thine own eye? Thou hypocrite, cast out first the beam out of thine own eye, and then shalt thou see clearly to pull out the mote that is in thy brother's eye.

Jesus has explained the kind of conduct He wishes to see in the lives of His disciples. In the final verses of chapter six, Jesus deals with the inner life and character of a disciple. He points out those attitudes that will produce the kind of lifestyle a disciple should manifest (Marshall, *Gospel* 267).

"Parable" (Greek *parabolē*) is broad enough to include several types of wise sayings. In some contexts, it is translated "proverb." For a good discussion of the various ways in which this word is used see Manson (*Teachings* 57-81). Jesus begins with two rhetorical questions. The first demands an answer of "no." There is simply no way one blind man can guide another blind man down the right path. The second demands an answer of "yes." If one blind man seeks to guide another, they will both fall into the ditch.

Jesus continues the teaching by declaring that the disciple is not above his teacher. "One that is perfect" (Greek substantival perfect participle) uses a verb form meaning "to correct," "to put in order," "to perfect," or "to complete." In this context, it means one who is mature or well instructed. A disciple who is mature and who has absorbed the teachings of his master will manifest the same attitudes and actions as his master.

In verses 41-42, Jesus employs a humorous illustration. The word translated "mote" refers to a small speck or sliver of wood; the term "beam" refers to a larger piece of wood such as a log. It is obvious that a person with a log in his own eye cannot see how to remove the speck of wood from his neighbor's eye. He must first remove the log from his own eye.

What lesson is Jesus teaching in these verses? He is condemning the sins of arrogance and self-assurance; He is also contrasting the attitudes He wants to see in His disciples with those found in the Pharisees (Ellis 116). The Pharisees were quick to condemn the sins of others while they were totally oblivious to their own arrogance and self-righteousness. The disciples must not follow in their path. Jesus recognizes there is a natural tendency to condemn the sins of others while we overlook our own sins, but such an attitude is unacceptable in the life of a disciple. The disciple must learn to demonstrate the same types of actions and attitudes Jesus demonstrated. Jesus does condemn the sins of others (especially those of the scribes and Pharisees), but He does so with an attitude of humility. The disciples simply cannot condemn the sins of others while at the same time overlooking their own sins. They must bear evidence of a life transformed by the power of Christ (Manson, *Sayings* 58).

43 For a good tree bringeth not forth corrupt fruit; neither doth a corrupt tree bring forth good fruit.
44 For every tree is known by his own fruit. For of thorns men do not gather figs, nor of a bramble bush gather they grapes.
45 A good man out of the good treasure of his heart bringeth forth that which is good; and an evil man out of the evil treasure of his heart bringeth forth that which is evil: for of the abundance of the heart his mouth speaketh.

Jesus continues the themes of honesty, sincerity, and transformation that He has presented in the previous verses. The word translated "corrupt" is often used in the sense of "rotten," "putrid," or "rancid" (Manson, *Sayings* 59). Here the meaning seems to be "useless" or "worthless." It describes fruit that has such a bad flavor it cannot be eaten. Verse 44 points out the obvious truth that some trees or bushes bear fruit that is eatable and others do not. No one would try to find figs on a thorn bush or grapes on a bramble bush; the type of tree or bush determines the character of the fruit that is produced.

In verse 45, Jesus explains and applies His teaching. In ancient Israel, the heart was considered to be the center of thought and intention, the essence of a person's character (Lieu 53). It determines what a person will be and what he or she will do. The mouth is the vehicle that expresses the internal nature of the person. The lesson for the disciples is clear. If they wish to be true followers of Jesus, they must first experience the radical transformation of character that only He can bring about. Rituals and outward conformity are not enough; there must be a radical change beginning at the deepest point of a person's character.

46 And why call ye me, Lord, Lord, and do not the things which I say?
47 Whosoever cometh to me, and heareth my sayings, and doeth them, I will shew you to whom he is like:

48 He is like a man which built an house, and digged deep, and laid the foundation on a rock: and when the flood arose, the stream beat vehemently upon that house, and could not shake it; for it was founded upon a rock.
49 But he that heareth, and doeth not, is like a man that without a foundation built an house upon the earth; against which the stream did beat vehemently, and immediately it fell; and the ruin of that house was great.

Jesus concludes the "sermon" by stressing the importance of both hearing and heeding His teachings. The passage does not specify whether Jesus is speaking only to the twelve or to a larger group of His disciples. The implication that some have paid little attention to Jesus' teaching may indicate a larger audience. In this passage, Jesus speaks of Himself as "Lord" (Greek *kurios*), which implies a higher level of power and authority than the term "Son of man," which Jesus often uses to describe Himself, or "Rabbi," which others often use to describe Him. The terms "master" or "ruler" render the idea well.

The disciple who both hears and heeds Jesus' instructions is compared to a man who builds his house on a solid foundation. In the land of Palestine, there are many areas where a layer of soil lies on top of a layer of solid rock. Although it requires more labor to remove the layer of soil, the wise builder goes to that extra effort. When the spring rains bring local flooding, the house will stand because it is built on a solid foundation.

The disciple who hears the teachings of Jesus but who does not abide by them is compared to a foolish builder. He does not go to the extra time and effort to remove the layer of soil; he simply builds on top of it. Everything goes well until the spring rains undermine the foundation of the house and it collapses.

Jesus understands that His disciples will go through times of trial and difficulty. It is not easy to be a disciple. Manson (*Sayings* 61-62) suggests two possible interpretations of these trials. They may be the struggles that the followers of Jesus will encounter from time to time. Another possibility is that this may refer to the final judgment when the disciples will be called upon to give an account of their stewardship before God. The lesson is that faithful discipleship requires more than a simple acknowledgement that Jesus is Lord; it requires a personal acquaintance with Him (Wilcock 86).

Summary (6:1-49)

This chapter is designed primarily for the instruction of the disciples. While Luke does not define the term "disciple," in the context of this chapter it apparently includes a larger circle of Jesus' followers, not just the twelve. Jesus' goal is to help His new and inexperienced disciples understand what it means to be His followers and leaders in the new kingdom He is establishing. One basic lesson they must learn is that Jesus' way is a new way. Jesus is the one who has ultimate authority; He is the Son of God. He is pointing them in a new direction, and they must allow Him to do that. While they owe much to Judaism, and the teachings of the O. T. are very important to them, Christ has introduced them to a new way of life.

Changes are both necessary and appropriate.

The chapter begins with the issue of Sabbath observance. The disciples are accused of violating the law by harvesting and eating a small amount of grain on the Sabbath day; that is a violation of the law as outlined by the Pharisees. Then Jesus cures a man with a withered hand on the Sabbath day; that is also a violation of the law as understood by the Pharisees. Jesus rejects their criticism; He offers a new interpretation of how the Sabbath should be observed.

This passage reflects the clear difference that exists between what the O. T. itself teaches and how the Pharisees of Jesus' day interpreted and applied those teachings. The law of Sabbath observance was originally intended to give human beings a day of rest from the arduous agricultural labor that life in the ancient world required. By their multitude of rules and regulations, the Pharisees had turned a benefit into a burden. It had become impossible to carry on normal activities or to perform deeds of goodness and mercy. Jesus was determined to correct that.

In one sense, Jesus is introducing a new concept of Sabbath observance in which meeting human needs outweighs the observance of legalistic rules and regulations. In another sense, Jesus is not introducing a new concept; He is simply returning to the correct interpretation and application of the O. T. teachings. It is crucial that the disciples understand they are living in a new era. Their loyalty must be, first and foremost, to Jesus and His teachings.

In the latter portions of this chapter, Jesus continues to present Himself as having the authority of the Son of God. He heals a number of people who are afflicted with different diseases; these healings demonstrate Jesus' mercy and power. Luke follows these healings with a series of teachings commonly known as the Sermon on the Plain. These teachings present some of the basic principles and ideas that govern the new kingdom Jesus is proclaiming. These teachings differ sharply from the traditional view of life to which the Jews of Palestine were accustomed. Wealth is no longer a sign of God's blessing; in fact, it may become an obstacle to serving God. Jesus proclaims God's blessings upon the poor and those who are regarded as outcasts by society.

In this sermon, Jesus challenges His followers to adopt new standards in attitude and conduct. Rather than emphasizing revenge and retaliation, they should manifest love, patience, and understanding. They should be willing to suffer personal insult to advance the Kingdom of God. Jesus also encourages His disciples to focus more of their attention on the future and less on the present. Their rewards for serving Christ will not come on earth but in Heaven.

Judging is another major theme of this chapter. It should be noted that Jesus does not prohibit all judgment; sometimes a fair and impartial judgment is both appropriate and necessary. What He is prohibiting is the harsh, legalistic, and unfair type of judging that is often manifested by the Pharisees. The disciples must be vigilant to carefully examine their own lives and testimonies. What they are on the outside is a reflection of what they are on the inside. They cannot hope to lead people in the right direction when their own lives are contrary to Jesus' teachings. They must lead by example; in the Kingdom of God, humility and service are essential.

In the closing verses of the chapter, Jesus gives a direct and personal challenge to His followers. They must not only believe His words; they must also put His teachings into practice in their everyday lives. They must be like the man who puts forth extra effort to remove the soil and build his house upon the rock. Only a life built on the rock will stand when the storms blow upon it.

Application: Teaching and Preaching the Passage

This chapter is rich in material for preaching and teaching because it outlines the kind of attitudes the follower of Jesus Christ should manifest in different situations. In order to preach and teach correctly from this passage, one should focus on the correct interpretation and the correct application. *Interpretation* deals with the original meaning, which the author intended to convey. Interpretation seeks to answer the question, "What did this passage mean to those who first received it?" *Application* deals with how the preacher or teacher can correctly apply the lessons taught in the passage to contemporary situations. Life in the modern era is very different from life in the ancient world, and people living today face situations unlike the ones faced by those who lived in the first century. Modern believers not only need help in interpreting this passage correctly, they also need help in applying the teachings of the passage in a modern context.

The first issue faced in chapter six concerns the proper observance of the Sabbath. As was noted in the commentary, the Jews of Jesus' day had more than the O. T. teachings concerning the Sabbath; they also had literally hundreds of rules and regulations that had been developed over the centuries. Jesus not only broke these rules, He went out of His way to break them. He healed people on the Sabbath when He easily could have waited until the next day. Did Jesus break the O. T. commandments concerning the Sabbath, or did He break only the Jewish interpretations of them? Scholars have disagreed on this, but most are of the opinion that Jesus did not break the O. T. commandments. He did, however, break the Jewish interpretations and applications because He considered them to be an unnecessary burden on the people. They frustrated God's original intent, which was to give a day of rest to those who labored.

It is clear that Jesus considered the advancement of the Kingdom of God to be of greater value than observing the law. He cited, with approval, the example of David and his men who ate the consecrated bread when the O. T. law forbade them to do so. Jesus then healed the man with the withered hand on the Sabbath. What lessons can be learned from these teachings? How should they be applied to the lives of modern believers? These are not easy questions to answer, but they are questions that must be faced by preachers and teachers today.

The question of the relationship between Saturday as the Jewish Sabbath and Sunday as the Lord's Day has been much debated throughout Christian history. Some have seen the Lord's Day as a continuation of the Jewish Sabbath; others have interpreted it as an entirely new observance designed to commemorate the resurrection of Christ. The question of how modern Christians should regard the Lord's Day is an important issue. For a careful analysis of the issue of Sabbath observance see *From Sabbath to Lord's Day* edited by D. A. Carson.

The closing verses of chapter six call for careful application on the part of the teacher or preacher. Beginning in verse 27, Jesus gives instruction on some of the most important subjects He addresses in His ministry. In these verses, He outlines something of the attitudes and conduct a child of God should manifest in the world. He tells His followers to love their enemies and do good to them. He teaches His followers to turn the other cheek rather than retaliate. He even goes so far as to say, "Give to every man that asketh of thee." All interpreters recognize that these are broad statements designed to illustrate how the Kingdom of God is different from the world.

Difficulties arise when modern Christians try to apply these general teachings to the specific situations they face in everyday life. In what ways should the believer do good to his or her enemies? What happens if the enemy refuses to accept the good the believer wishes to do? Does the command to turn the other cheek forbid self-defense, or does it forbid only retaliation and revenge? Does this command apply only to personal insults, or does it also apply to physical attacks?

When Jesus told His disciples to give to those who asked, it was clear He was encouraging His followers to be generous with those in need. How can modern Christians who have limited resources put this commandment into practice? Can this passage be understood to teach that the Christian should help those who are in need in reasonable and appropriate ways? Christian people need the help of faithful pastors and teachers as they work through these difficult and sometimes controversial issues.

Verse 37 calls for special attention. It says, "Judge not, and ye shall not be judged." Does this passage prohibit all judgment or does it prohibit only judgment that is unfair and hypocritical? Does it mean the church must tolerate false teaching or immoral conduct among its members? Most interpreters are of the opinion that Jesus is prohibiting only the kind of unfair judgment and condemnation that was practiced by the Pharisees.

These passages are not easy to interpret or apply correctly. Before preaching or teaching on these verses, one should give thoughtful and prayerful study to these issues. There is too much at stake for hasty and thoughtless words.

These verses have much to say on the subject of hypocrisy. "Can the blind lead the blind?" Obviously, they cannot. Can one see to remove a small sliver of wood from his neighbor's eye when he has a log in his own eye? Obviously, he cannot. The point here is that believers should be honest and truthful with themselves and others. They should not attempt to tell others how to live when their own lives reflect little real commitment to Christ. The preacher or teacher needs to help the people of God recognize hypocrisy and respond to it in appropriate ways.

This passage also speaks to the issue of integrity. It stresses that what the believer is, on the outside, is a result of what he or she is on the inside. Real change in the character of a person must come from within. The Lord must be allowed to come in and make the necessary changes in the heart. Closely related to integrity is the idea of obedience. It is not enough to hear the words of Jesus; one must also act upon what he has heard. He must build his house on the rock and not on the sand. The preacher or teacher must stand ready to give guidance to those who are struggling with issues of integrity and obedience.

F. Jesus Defines His Messiahship (7:1-50)

Jesus returns to Capernaum, His Galilean headquarters, where He performs two miracles and gives several teachings relating to the nature of His kingdom. At first glance, the teachings and incidents narrated here seem rather disconnected, but they are not. Jesus is revealing, little by little, how His kingdom is new and different from what most people in that day expected (Wilcock 89-90). According to Marshall (*Gospel* 276), the overall theme that binds this chapter together is compassion. Compassion for the lost, and for those who suffer, lies at the very heart of Jesus' understanding of the Kingdom of God. There is, however, a second theme that permeates this chapter: power and authority. Jesus demonstrates His power over sickness, sin, and death. He uses His divine authority to bring people who would otherwise be unacceptable, into the Kingdom of God. He reserves the right to define His messiahship on His own terms and not allow others to define it for Him (Larson 130-136).

1 Now when he had ended all his sayings in the audience of the people, he entered into Capernaum.
2 And a certain centurion's servant, who was dear unto him, was sick, and ready to die.
3 And when he heard of Jesus, he sent unto him the elders of the Jews, beseeching him that he would come and heal his servant.
4 And when they came to Jesus, they besought him instantly, saying, That he was worthy for whom he should do this:
5 For he loveth our nation, and he hath built us a synagogue.
6 Then Jesus went with them. And when he was now not far from the house, the centurion sent friends to him, saying unto him, Lord, trouble not thyself: for I am not worthy that thou shouldest enter under my roof:
7 Wherefore neither thought I myself worthy to come unto thee: but say in a word, and my servant shall be healed.
8 For I also am a man set under authority, having under me soldiers, and I say unto one, Go, and he goeth; and to another, Come, and he cometh; and to my servant, Do this, and he doeth *it*.
9 When Jesus heard these things, he marvelled at him, and turned him about, and said unto the people that followed him, I say unto you, I have not found so great faith, no, not in Israel.
10 And they that were sent, returning to the house, found the servant whole that had been sick.

Sometime after Jesus returns to Capernaum, He encounters a group of local Jewish leaders bearing sad news. Bock (*Luke* NIV 202) and Bonnet and Schroeder (537) suggest they are not the leaders of the synagogue but local civic leaders. Summers (*Luke* 82) offers the contrary opinion that they were leaders of the synagogue.

A friend of these Jewish leaders, a Roman centurion, has a slave who is desperately ill and at the point of death. The centurion cares a great deal about this slave, and he has sent the Jewish leaders to intercede with Jesus and ask Him to come and heal him. There are several interesting facets to this story. For one thing, it indicates that Jesus has gained a reputation as a healer; in an age when medical science can offer little hope to the victims of illness or accident, Jesus demonstrates both the power and the compassion necessary to do what others cannot do.

This story also reveals a great deal about the character of this centurion. He is an officer who commands about one hundred soldiers. He is probably a mercenary, serving in Herod's army, although there is some possibility he serves in a Roman unit (Bock, *Luke* IVP 132; Fitzmyer I:651). It is likely he is Roman, but Luke does not mention his nationality. The Lucan narrative distinguishes him from the Jews, thus indicating he is one of many Gentile residents in Galilee. Green (*Luke* 285) suggests he is both a Gentile and a Roman citizen.

The centurion has not accepted Judaism but is favorably disposed toward the Jewish religion; his situation is somewhat similar to that of Cornelius in Acts 10. The Jewish leaders explain to Jesus that "he loveth our nation, and he hath built us a synagogue." This may mean he had constructed the synagogue at his own expense (Manson, *Sayings 64),* or it may mean he contributed significantly to its construction (Marshall, *Gospel* 280). Green (*Luke* 286) suggests he had born the cost of constructing the synagogue in order to garner the favor of the Jewish leaders. Summers (*Luke* 82) opines that the centurion did not bear the expense personally, but through his leadership the synagogue was constructed at Roman expense.

Jesus consents to go with the Jewish leaders. As they are drawing near to the house a messenger arrives with a rather unusual message; the centurion has sent word that he does not consider himself worthy for Jesus to enter his house; neither does he consider himself worthy to address Jesus personally. He understands that Jewish tradition would forbid Jesus to enter the home of a Gentile. He says simply, "speak the word and my slave will be healed." The centurion then uses himself as an illustration of what he wants Jesus to do. He is a military officer; he gives orders and those orders are obeyed whether he is physically present or not. He believes Jesus has the power to heal his slave without being physically present. Jesus recognizes the greatness of the centurion's confession of faith, and He responds to it with these words, "I have not found so great faith, no, not in Israel." The last phrase probably means "not even in Israel" (Summers, *Luke* 83). Jesus has certainly found examples of faith among the people of Israel, but none are greater than the faith expressed by this Gentile centurion.

The story concludes by saying that when the messengers sent by the centurion return to the house, they find that the slave has been healed. This centurion's attitude and conduct illustrate what it means to be a part of the Kingdom of God. Jesus not only has the power to heal, He uses that power both to meet human needs and to overcome the social and religious barriers that often separate people (Green, *Luke* 288). As Lieu (54) and Twelftree (*Jesus* 153) note, the key element in the story is not the healing of a sick slave, but the faith demonstrated by the centurion and Jesus' response to that faith.

Matthew presents a somewhat different version of this story (Mt. 8:5-13). The main difference is that in Matthew the centurion speaks directly to Jesus while in Luke the centurion sends Jewish representatives to speak on his behalf. Both Matthew and Luke have presented the story in such a way as to accomplish their own goals and objectives. Geldenhuys (220) seeks to combine the two stories by suggesting that the centurion first sends representatives, and then later decides to go himself.

11 And it came to pass the day after, that he went into a city called Nain; and many of his disciples went with him, and much people.
12 Now when he came nigh to the gate of the city, behold, there was a dead man carried out, the only son of his mother, and she was a widow: and much people of the city was with her.
13 And when the Lord saw her, he had compassion on her, and said unto her, Weep not.
14 And he came and touched the bier: and they that bare *him* stood still. And he said, Young man, I say unto thee, Arise.
15 And he that was dead sat up, and began to speak. And he delivered him to his mother.
16 And there came a fear on all: and they glorified God, saying, That a great prophet is risen up among us; and, That God hath visited his people.
17 And this rumour of him went forth throughout all Judaea, and throughout all the region round about.

This passage further develops two important themes: the compassionate nature of Jesus' ministry and His miraculous power (Morris, *Luke* 139). Jesus performs a miracle of healing that restores an only son to his grieving mother, a widow. In other words, she is left with no male protector; she has neither a husband nor a son. In a world where women have few legal protections, she is left in a very vulnerable position (Morris, *Luke* 139; Bock I:649; Malina and Neyrey 63). This is the only reference to the village of Nain in the Scriptures; it is often identified with the modern community of Nein, which is located approximately six miles southeast of Nazareth (Morris, *Luke* 139; Summers, *Luke* 84; Marshall, *Gospel* 284).

The Gospel writers mention three specific occasions when Jesus restored to life someone who has died. The raising of the widow's son is found only here. The story of the raising of the daughter of Jairus is found in Matthew, Mark, and Luke; the raising of Lazarus is told only in John (Summers, *Luke* 83). This story has similarities to miracles performed by Elijah and Elisha, especially the resuscitation of the son of the widow at Zarephath found in 1 Kings 17:8-24 (Nolland I:321).

Luke notes that Jesus is not alone when He performs this miracle; He is accompanied both by the disciples and by a large crowd of people. His goal is to use this event to help His followers develop a more complete and mature understanding of the nature of His ministry.

"Gate" (Greek *pul)* is used in different ways. It may describe a gate in a city wall or in a general sense to describe an opening or entrance (NIDNTT 29). Here it probably refers to the entrance to the city; there is no archaeological evidence indicating that the city was walled at this time (Summers, *Luke* 84; Nolland I:322). Bock (I:649) suggests the gate is for decorative rather than for defensive purposes. As they draw near to the city, Jesus and His followers encounter a funeral procession. Following the Jewish custom, the mother is walking ahead of her son's bier. Burials take place in cemeteries located outside the city, and funerals generally occur on the day of death (Bock I:649).

"Carried out" (Greek *ekkomizō)* is a technical term used to describe carrying a corpse to its burial (Marshall, *Gospel*, 284). When Jesus sees this woman, He is moved with compassion. He encourages her to stop crying; "Weep not" (Greek negative present imperative) means to cease an action already in progress (Bock I:650).

Jesus next draws near to the corpse and touches the "bier" (Greek *soros*), a word with different meanings. Sometimes it denotes a coffin, sometimes a stretcher or platform of wood used to carry the corpse. Since the Hebrews did not normally bury in coffins, this term probably refers to the piece of wood on which the corpse, wrapped in cloth, is carried (Bock I:652). Note the comments of Green (*Luke* 291) and Marshall (*Gospel* 286).

It should be noted that touching the bier of a dead person would render Jesus ritually unclean (Marshall, *Gospel* 286), but to Him ministry is more important than ritual cleanliness. Jesus speaks directly to the corpse and commands the dead son to rise up; "young man" can be used of a person between 24 and 40 years of age (Reiling and Swellengrebel 300).

Jesus tells the young man to "arise." He responds by sitting up and beginning to speak. Jesus then turns him over to the care of his mother; this is a reminder of Jesus' concern for the widow (Marshall, *Gospel* 286). Geldenhuys (223) notes that Jesus does not invite the young man to become His disciple; because of His concern for the mother, Jesus returns him to her.

This great miracle produces dramatic results; fear immediately falls upon all those who witnessed the resuscitation of the young man. "Fear" (Greek *phobos*) is used in several different ways in the N. T. (NIDNTT I:621-624). It may express the idea of panic or fright; in this context, it expresses the idea of reverence or awe (Fitzmyer I:659). The eyewitnesses recognize that God is ultimately responsible for what has taken place. They give glory to God by saying that "a great prophet is risen up among us." "Glorified" (Greek imperfect tense) represents an ongoing action; they continue to glorify God. They compare Jesus to the great prophets of the O. T., Elijah and Elisha, who also performed notable miracles. Reiling and Swellengrebel (302) note that the appearance of a great prophet is a sign that the messianic age has arrived. They also glorify God by saying "God hath visited his people." They understand that God by this miracle is doing something very special among His people; the implication is that the Kingdom of God has come upon them in great power and glory.

The news of such a great and notable miracle cannot be kept quiet. The event actually takes place in Galilee, but Luke explains that the news of it spreads throughout Judaea and "all the region round about." The term "Judaea" is used in different ways. Most commentators suggest that in this context it includes both Judaea and Galilee (Bock I:654; Geldenhuys 224; Ellis 101, 118). The idea is that the news of Jesus' great power is spreading into a larger area. More and more people within the Jewish community are hearing reports of Jesus' miracles.

18 And the disciples of John shewed him all these things.
19 And John calling *unto him* two of his disciples sent *them* to Jesus, saying, Art thou he that should come? or look we for another?
20 When the men were come unto him, they said, John Baptist hath sent us unto thee, saying, Art thou he that should come? or look we for another?
21 And in that same hour he cured many of *their* infirmities and plagues, and of evil spirits; and unto many *that were* blind he gave sight.
22 Then Jesus answering said unto them, Go your way, and tell John what things ye have seen and heard; how that the blind see, the lame walk, the lepers are cleansed, the deaf hear, the dead are raised, to the poor the gospel is preached.
23 And blessed is *he*, whosoever shall not be offended in me.

Luke has told the stories of two notable miracles that Jesus performed; now he moves to a series of three incidents involving John the Baptist. Twelftree (*Jesus* 154) suggests that the two miracle stories served to heighten the power of Jesus in preparation for the questions that would come from the disciples of John the Baptist.

The first of these three incidents is Jesus' response to a series of questions sent by John (7:18-23); the second is Jesus' testimony to the importance of John the Baptist (7:24-30); the third is Jesus' condemnation of those who reject both His preaching and that of John the Baptist (7:31-35). All these incidents contribute, in some way, to the development of a better and more mature understanding of the Kingdom of God.

As we have seen in Luke 3, Jesus was baptized by John the Baptist. In that passage, John expressed great faith in Jesus; it is clear that John viewed Him as the expected Messiah. In John 1:29-34, John the Baptist specifically identified Jesus as the coming Messiah. In Luke 3, John was imprisoned because of his consistent attacks upon Herod for his immorality and abuse of power.

Apparently, John the Baptist is still in prison when he sends the two messengers in Luke 7:19. The phrase "he that should come" has its roots in the O. T. where it is used in several different ways. One of these uses is to describe the coming Messiah, which seems to be how the term is used here (Summers, *Luke* 85; Stein, *Luke* 227; Bock I:665).

It seems rather strange that John the Baptist now expresses doubt concerning whether or not Jesus is the Messiah after having previously affirmed Jesus' messiahship. Luke offers no explanation of why, but there is little doubt that the conditions of his imprisonment have affected his thinking (Barclay 89). While it is possible that John takes this step for the benefit of his disciples, the most likely explanation is that John is perplexed because Jesus' messianic reign is not developing as he expected it to. Jesus is not living up to the common Jewish expectations of the Messiah (Bock I:665; Stein, *Luke* 226). He is making no attempt to establish an earthly kingdom, lead a revolt against Roman rule, or restore the nation of Israel to a position of power and influence in the world (Summers, *Luke* 86). Jesus is making no attempt to condemn the wicked; He is, in fact, seeking their restoration (Manson, *Sayings* 67). He is doing nothing to obtain John's release from prison. How can He be the Messiah?

Verse 21 is a parenthetical statement (Bock I:666) that Luke uses to establish the context within which Jesus' reply is given. He notes that Jesus cures many people of their illnesses, restores sight to the blind, and casts out evil spirits. Luke's readers understand that these miracles all reflect the power of God. It is possible that this verse is the explanation of the phrase "all these things" found in Luke 7:18 (Stein, *Luke* 227).

In verse 22, Jesus instructs the messengers to return to John. The message He gives to them is not a direct answer but an invitation to examine the good deeds He is doing. Jesus is restoring sight to the blind, giving the lame the ability to walk, healing the lepers, giving hearing to the deaf, raising the dead, and preaching the gospel to the poor. One of the things the Jews of Jesus' day expected the Messiah to do was to perform miracles (Bock I:668). In effect, Jesus is communicating to John the Baptist the message "I may not live up to the common expectations, but I am the Messiah nonetheless" (Manson, *Sayings* 67). Jesus expects John to understand His words and actions.

Jesus concludes His discussion with the messengers in verse 23 by saying, "And blessed is *he*, whosoever shall not be offended in me." This statement presents a challenge to John the Baptist and his followers because Jesus understands that it may be difficult for John and others to see Him as the Messiah. At times, even Jesus' own disciples have trouble understanding that He is truly the Messiah. Jesus confounds many, including His own followers, when He makes no effort to free Israel from Roman domination or set up an earthly kingdom. In this passage, Jesus is in the process of defining the true nature of His messianic kingdom, and He will define it in His own terms. He will not be bound by the traditional expectations of Jewish society. The kingdom Jesus is introducing is something entirely new (Lieu 57). Stein (*Luke* 227) notes that this insight will not only be of value to John the Baptist and his followers; it will also be meaningful to the later generations of believers who read of this Gospel.

24 And when the messengers of John were departed, he began to speak unto the people concerning John, What went ye out into the wilderness for to see? A reed shaken with the wind?
25 But what went ye out for to see? A man clothed in soft raiment? Behold, they which are gorgeously apparelled, and live delicately, are in king's courts.
26 But what went ye out for to see? A prophet? Yea, I say unto you, and much more than a prophet.

27 This is *he*, of whom it is written, Behold, I send my messenger before thy face, which shall prepare thy way before thee.
28 For I say unto you, Among those that are born of women there is not a greater prophet than John the Baptist: but he that is least in the kingdom of God is greater than he.
29 And all the people that heard *him*, and the publicans, justified God, being baptized with the baptism of John.
30 But the Pharisees and lawyers rejected the counsel of God against themselves, being not baptized of him.

At this point in the narrative, Luke does not identify the people to whom Jesus is speaking. Probably they are followers of John the Baptist (Nolland I:339). Some of Jesus' own followers may also be included. The audience is not, however, the most important factor; the content of the message is the key element. In these verses, Jesus provides more information about the important ministry of John the Baptist and how he contributes to the Kingdom of God that Jesus is inaugurating. Jesus wants His followers to understand that His previous comments should not be understood as a rebuke of John the Baptist.

The word "desert" is often used for the semi-arid region south and west of the city of Jerusalem. It is also used metaphorically in Isaiah 40:3 to describe the place from which the announcement of the coming of the Messiah is made.

In this passage, Jesus employs a series of rhetorical questions designed to help His hearers understand the true nature of John's ministry. In the first of these, Jesus asks whether they had made the long and arduous journey to the wilderness only to see a reed shaken by the wind, a common sight in that region. The implication is that they have not made the journey to see a man who is weak and wavering. In the second rhetorical question, Jesus asks if they have gone into the wilderness to see a man dressed in fine apparel. He then gives the obvious answer, "No." People who dress in fine apparel do not live in the desert; they live in the homes of the wealthy.

Jesus comes to the heart of the matter in the third question. He asks if the crowd has come to the wilderness to see a prophet. This time the answer is a definite "Yes." They have made this long journey to see, in John, a man who is not only a prophet but who is more than a prophet. "Prophet" is used in various ways in Scripture. At times, the O. T. prophets do predict the future, but prediction is not their primary ministry. The prophets are first and foremost God's spokesmen; they proclaim His message in the midst of an often hostile world.

When Jesus describes John the Baptist as "much more than a prophet" He is emphasizing the importance of his ministry. John is no ordinary prophet; he is given the special privilege of announcing the coming of Jesus, the Messiah. In order to explain the true nature of John's ministry, Jesus quotes from two important O. T. passages. "Behold, I send my messenger before thy face" comes from the Greek version of Exodus 23:20. "Which shall prepare thy way before thee," comes from Malachi 3:1 where it agrees more closely with the Hebrew version than with the

Greek (Marshall, *Gospel* 295). In this context, "thee" clearly refers to Jesus. John's testimony to Jesus is important because it is the fulfillment of these important O. T. passages.

In verse 28, Jesus gives additional information about the importance of John's ministry. "For I say unto you" underscores the importance of the statement that Jesus is about to make. "Those that are born of women" means human beings. Jesus points out that no human being, not even one of the great O. T. prophets, is more important in preparing the way for the ministry of Christ than John the Baptist.

"He that is least in the kingdom of God" is difficult. The most widely accepted interpretation is that the phrase refers to those who are followers of Jesus, those who have already entered into the new kingdom that He is inaugurating. The clause "is greater than he" understands John to occupy a subordinate position to them. He is the last of the O. T. prophets. He is also the forerunner of the Messiah, but he has not yet entered into the kingdom. The purpose of this passage is not to downplay the importance of John the Baptist and his ministry, but to stress the importance of Jesus as the Messiah and of the new ministry He is introducing. Jesus' goal is to show that the message is more important than the messenger. For good discussions of this difficult passage see Barclay (90); Bock (*Luke* IVP 138-139); Marshall (*Gospel* 296); Nolland (I:337-338); and Spence (174).

Verses 29-30 serve as Luke's summary and transition. They serve both to conclude the previous section and to prepare the reader for the upcoming section. Verse 29 outlines the positive response of the people to the preaching and teaching of John the Baptist. "All the people who heard him" refers to the audience that heard Jesus' tribute to John the Baptist. The "publicans" were Jews who were ostracized by their fellow Jews for accepting employment as tax collectors who often robbed their own people. The idea is that the crowd that heard the teaching of Jesus even includes those who were social outcasts but who were open to the message He had for them.

"Justified," in this context, means "to declare righteous or just." Nolland (I:342) suggests that it expresses the idea of "glorified" here. The meaning is that those who heard and accepted the message of John the Baptist publicly declared God's righteousness and justice by accepting baptism at John's hands (Marshall, *Gospel* 298-299). Ellis (120) suggests the phrase "And all the people that heard him...justified God" means they accepted God's judgments as true and correct.

Verse 30 presents the negative response of the Jewish leaders to the ministry of John the Baptist. Although some individual Pharisees express interest in the ministry of Jesus, this group is generally hostile to Him. The lawyers are experts in the Jewish law; they are generally understood to be a subgroup within the Pharisaic party. These groups refuse the baptism of John, probably because they are not willing to repent and confess their sinfulness. Luke describes their rejection in these terms, "the Pharisees and lawyers rejected the counsel of God against themselves." They turn a deaf ear to God's plan and purpose for them; He has opened the door of salvation to them, and they have refused to enter.

31 And the Lord said, Whereunto then shall I liken the men of this generation? and to what are they like?
32 They are like unto children sitting in the marketplace, and calling one to another, and saying, We have piped unto you, and ye have not danced; we have mourned to you, and ye have not wept.
33 For John the Baptist came neither eating bread nor drinking wine; and ye say, He hath a devil.
34 The Son of man is come eating and drinking; and ye say, Behold a gluttonous man, and a winebibber, a friend of publicans and sinners!
35 But wisdom is justified of all her children.

Verse 31 serves as the introduction to this brief story. Jesus asks the rhetorical question, "how can I describe this present generation?" or "to whom may I compare them?" This question does not seem to be directed to any particular group or individual. As Blomberg (*Gospels* 89) explains, this type of expression was often used to introduce a parable. "Men of this generation" refers to the Jewish leaders who have seen the ministries of John the Baptist and Jesus and who have chosen to reject both of them (Lenski 417; Fitzmyer I:677). Stein (*Luke* 232) suggests that this term describes those who oppose Jesus and His gospel.

Verse 32 is a brief parable that Jesus uses to illustrate the impossibility of satisfying those who oppose His ministry. The parable is drawn from the common experience of seeing children at play in the marketplaces and other open spaces in the cities. As children often do, in their play they imitate the actions of adults. Apparently, there are two groups of children, and the first group wants the second group to join in their play. The first group of children invites the second group to join in a wedding celebration; the second group refuses the invitation. There is no explanation why they refuse; the fact that they refuse is the important thing.

The first group then tries a second type of play. They imitate a funeral with the loud dirges the professional mourners provided. Although the game is different, the result is the same. The second group of children once again refuses to join in the play.

In verse 33, Jesus draws His conclusion from this brief parable. He compares the two groups of children with His own ministry and that of John the Baptist. John came living a simple, ascetic lifestyle; he came neither "eating bread" nor "drinking wine," which probably means he did not eat the foods that were normally consumed in the cities. Instead, he ate the products of the desert. Jesus came "eating and drinking," which means He shared in the foods and drinks that were generally consumed. At that time, bread made from wheat or barley and wine made from grapes were staples in the Palestinian diet.

John's message is rejected with the words, "He hath a devil," which probably means they regard him as crazy (Fitzmyer I:681). Jesus' message is rejected with the words, "Behold a gluttonous man and a winebibber, a friend of publicans and sinners!" A "winebibber" is a drunkard (Morris, *Luke* 145). Jesus' opponents do not stop there; they also accuse Him of associating with tax collectors and sinners, people who are social outcasts. The tax collectors work for the hated Roman government; they are often dishonest and steal from their own people. The word "sinner" is used in various ways in the N. T. In this verse, it refers to Jews who were unable or unwilling to observe all the laws as interpreted by the Pharisees (Stein, *Luke* 182).

The point is this: both John the Baptist and Jesus have come preaching the message God has given them. Although there are significant differences in the manner of their presentations and in the lifestyle each maintains, the message is basically the same. The Jewish leaders refuse to accept God's message no matter how it is presented. They not only treat God's messengers with contempt, they reject His message as well.

Verse 35 provides a fitting and challenging conclusion to this section. "Justify" in this context carries the connotation of accepting something as right or demonstrating that something is right or correct (Stein, *Luke* 233; Morris, *Luke* 145). The "children" of wisdom are those who are willing to follow its teachings. The point of this important passage is those who are truly wise (the children of wisdom) will see that Jesus and John are teaching the truth and will be willing to follow them (Morris, *Luke* 145). Those who are unwise will follow the Jewish leaders in their rejection of the truth.

36 And one of the Pharisees desired him that he would eat with him. And he went into the Pharisee's house, and sat down to meat.
37 And, behold, a woman in the city, which was a sinner, when she knew that *Jesus* sat at meat in the Pharisee's house, brought an alabaster box of ointment,
38 And stood at his feet behind *him* weeping, and began to wash his feet with tears, and did wipe *them* with the hairs of her head, and kissed his feet, and anointed *them* with the ointment.

Luke begins a new section in verse 36; Fitzmyer (I:684) suggests there is little connection with the preceding material. Other interpreters, however, see a connection. For example, Bock (I:689) sees this passage as a further development of Luke 7:34 where Jesus spoke openly about associating with sinners. This passage continues the theme that Jesus has come to seek and to save that which was lost.

Stein (*Luke* 234) suggests several possible reasons for Luke's including this section. It is most likely that his goal is to help Theophilus understand who Jesus is. Morris (*Luke* 146) notes that all four of the Gospels contain stories of Jesus being anointed by a woman (Mt. 26:6-13; Mk. 14:3-9; Jn. 12:1-8), but this account is different from the others. The other Gospels set this incident near the end of Jesus' ministry; Luke presents it at a much earlier point in His ministry. Ellis (121) suggests there are too many differences between Luke's account and the others for them to be descriptions of the same incident. He also points out that this type of anointing might have happened on more than one occasion. Dodd (*Tradition* 162-173) takes a different position. He suggests that all four accounts are derived from one original, which was likely oral.

Jesus accepted invitations to eat and talk with a variety of different people. Here He accepts an invitation from a

Pharisee named Simon. Luke does not explain why the invitation is issued; neither does he explain any details about the meal. Barclay (94-95) suggests three possible reasons the invitation was issued: (1) the Pharisee may be an admirer of Jesus and wants to learn more about Him; (2) the Pharisee hopes that Jesus will say or do something that can be used against Him; (3) the Pharisee simply wants to meet Jesus because of His growing fame and notoriety. According to Barclay, the third is the most likely.

This meal is apparently a special occasion where the guests recline on couches at a low table with their feet away from the table. The guests would have removed their sandals before eating (Fitzmyer I:688; Morris, *Luke* 146-147). Edersheim (*Life* I:564-566) offers a summary of the social customs surrounding such a meal.

Barclay (94) and Bock (*Luke* NIV 218) suggest that when a rabbi or other important person was invited to a meal other people would be permitted to listen in on what he had to say. B. Smith (212) writes that such an occasion as this would have been a semi-public event. The doors would have been open and people of the city would have been able to crowd around and hear what was said.

The entrance of a woman into such a formal meal is a surprising and unexpected event, as women were not generally invited to such events. Edersheim (*Life* I:564) confesses that we simply do not know how she was admitted. Perhaps she had such a strong desire to see Jesus that she hid among the servants and entered without permission. Bonnet and Schroeder (543) suggest this was probably not her first encounter with Jesus and she was attracted to His compassionate teaching and was willing to suffer the rejection she would inevitably experience in the Pharisee's house.

The woman is described as a "sinner," which is commonly understood to mean a prostitute (Summers, *Luke* 89; B. Smith 212). Lenski (424) does not accept this understanding; in his view the term implies only that she has done wrong at some time in the past and that her failure has become known. Stein (*Luke* 236) suggests that her sin involved some type of moral failure. Ellis (122) explains that the term may also describe the wife of a person who is not religious. For a good discussion of the role of women in situations like this see Malina and Neyrey (63). Bonnet and Schroeder (543) note that some in the early church identified her with Mary Magdalene, but there is no biblical evidence in support of such a theory.

Apparently, she enters without any invitation and brings with her an expensive perfume. The "alabaster box" denotes a round container used to carry perfume (Morris, *Luke* 146; Lenski 424). It may be made of alabaster or of some other material; the perfume is a costly liquid. "Kissed" (Greek *kataphile*) is a strong verb meaning, literally, "to cover with kisses" (Lenski 426) or to "kiss with fervor" (Summers, *Luke* 89). This action denotes the depth of the woman's devotion to Jesus.

This "woman of the city" begins to anoint Jesus' feet with this expensive perfume. She also begins to cry and to wipe away the tears with her long hair. This kind of action would have been highly unusual in the Palestinian culture of the first century; for a woman to untie her hair in the presence of strangers would have been totally unacceptable

(Lenski 425; Stein, *Luke* 236). These actions should be considered extraordinary acts of devotion and gratitude. The fact that Jesus is able to produce such an extraordinary level of devotion testifies both to His compassion and to His authority.

39 Now when the Pharisee which had bidden him saw *it*, he spake within himself, saying, This man, if he were a prophet, would have known who and what manner of woman *this is* that toucheth him: for she is a sinner.

The Pharisee, who will soon be identified as Simon, begins to reflect on what is going on, and he does not like what he sees. He has, no doubt, heard stories about Jesus performing miraculous deeds and enjoying a special relationship with God. He immediately concludes that such stories must be false. If Jesus were a true prophet of God, He would not allow Himself to be touched by this kind of woman (Stein, *Luke* 236).

40 And Jesus answering said unto him, Simon, I have something to say unto thee. And he saith, Master, say on.
41 There was a certain creditor which had two debtors: the one owed five hundred pence, and the other fifty.
42 And when they had nothing to pay, he frankly forgave them both. Tell me therefore, which of them will love him most?
43 Simon answered and said, I suppose that *he*, to whom he forgave most. And he said unto him, Thou hast rightly judged.
44 And he turned to the woman, and said unto Simon, Seest thou this woman? I entered into thine house, thou gavest me no water for my feet: but she hath washed my feet with tears, and wiped *them* with the hairs of her head.
45 Thou gavest me no kiss: but this woman since the time I came in hath not ceased to kiss my feet.
46 My head with oil thou didst not anoint: but this woman hath anointed my feet with ointment.
47 Wherefore I say unto thee, Her sins, which are many, are forgiven; for she loved much: but to whom little is forgiven, *the same* loveth little.
48 And he said unto her, Thy sins are forgiven.
49 And they that sat at meat with him began to say within themselves, Who is this that forgiveth sins also?
50 And he said to the woman, Thy faith hath saved thee; go in peace.

Jesus responds to the accusation that He is not a prophet by telling a parable, which is one of His most commonly-used teaching devices. It is important to note the term that Simon uses in addressing Jesus: "teacher" (Greek *didaskalos*) generally translated "teacher" or "master." The word is commonly used as a title of respect, and it is possible that Simon uses the word in this way (Fitzmyer I:690). Stein (*Luke* 236) notes this is the first time this word is used in Luke to describe Jesus. It is also possible the term is used in this context with a note of sarcasm. Bock (I:698) maintains that Simon's address to Jesus is cordial, but there is clearly tension in the air. If some insult is intended, Jesus does not respond to it. He moves directly to the parable.

The parable reflects the harsh economic realities of life in first-century Palestine, where good people often fall into a pattern of debt they cannot repay (Lieu 59). Two men have borrowed money from a money-lender, and neither of them can repay the debt. The first owes five hundred denarii and the second fifty. A denarius was a small Roman silver coin that represents a day's wage for a working man (Ellis 197). The man whose debt is 500 denarii owes approximately one and a half year's wages; the second owes about fifty days wages (Stein, *Luke* 237). When he sees that neither man has the ability to settle the debt, the money-lender forgives both of them.

In the latter part of verse 42, Jesus asks Simon a significant question, "Which of them will love him most?" In other words, which of the two will have greater gratitude for the man who forgave him (Marshall, *Gospel* 311). Simon responds, "I suppose that *he*, to whom he forgave most." Jesus states that Simon has answered correctly; it is logical to assume that the one who has been forgiven the larger debt will have greater appreciation.

Jesus then launches into an immediate application of the parable by contrasting the reception He received from Simon with the actions of the sinful woman. He points out that Simon has failed to provide the most common courtesies that would normally be extended to a guest. He has provided no water for Jesus to use in washing the dust off His feet; Simon has not welcomed Him with the customary oriental kiss of greeting. Neither has Simon instructed a servant to anoint Jesus' head with olive oil. In that culture, the failure to extend these basic courtesies would be regarded as a great insult.

Jesus contrasts the rude conduct of Simon with the loving conduct of the woman. She has gone far beyond the requirements of courtesy; she bathed His feet with her tears and dried them with her hair. She has anointed His feet with costly perfume. These actions demonstrate that she has a great love for Jesus, and He responds to that love by forgiving her many sins. Kelley (121) suggests this was not the first time she had encountered the grace of Christ. She already believed in Christ, and her faith brought her to Him. During this conversation she learns that her faith has not only brought her to Christ, it has saved her as well.

In the last part of verse 47, Jesus turns His attention back to Simon with these words, "to whom little is forgiven, *the same* loveth little." The idea is that Simon's actions and attitude have demonstrated little or no love for Jesus; the result is that Simon has not received the forgiveness that Jesus offers. The implication is that he is a much greater sinner than the woman. He has rejected Jesus' forgiveness while she has accepted it. Jesus then tells the woman directly and forthrightly that her sins are forgiven. In verse 50, Jesus tells her to go in peace; her faith in Christ has saved her.

The reaction of the other guests in verse 49 is significant. They begin to ask themselves, "Who is this that forgiveth sins also?" In other words, they are asking by what authority Jesus claims this power. As faithful Jews, they understand that only God can forgive the sins of human beings. When Jesus claims to have the power to forgive sins, He is making a statement they can neither understand nor accept. As far as they are concerned, such a statement is blasphemy. Luke gives no answer to this question because the answer will become obvious as the narrative develops. By His words and His actions, Jesus will show Himself to be the true Son of God with power to forgive sins.

Summary (7:1-50)

Chapter seven includes a collection of miracles and teachings that seem, on the surface, to bear little or no relationship to each other. There is, however, one factor that ties them together. Each miracle or teaching helps the reader understand more about the developing nature of Jesus' messiahship. They help explain what type of Messiah He will be and what kind of kingdom He is developing.

This chapter clearly illustrates Luke's desire to present Jesus as maintaining a balanced ministry. As Twelftree (*Jesus* 179) has noted, the chapter illustrates the proper balance between Jesus' teachings and His miracles. Both contribute toward the development of a mature understanding of the Kingdom of God. Luke makes no attempt to connect these teachings and miracles either chronologically or geographically. There is no reason to believe they are presented in chronological order or that they occur without any interval of time between them. Their importance lies in how each teaching or miracle contributes to the message Jesus wishes to convey.

The passage begins with the healing of the centurion's servant, which illustrates Jesus' power and compassion. He does not need to be present to heal. Although He has ministered previously to the lower classes in Jewish society, here Jesus demonstrates a willingness to minister to a Gentile who possesses a certain amount of wealth. Jesus is beginning the process of expanding His kingdom beyond the limits of Judaism.

Luke then turns his attention to the raising of the widow's son at Nain. This powerful story stresses both Jesus' compassion for suffering people and His divine power. Death has always been the greatest enemy of mankind, and this passage demonstrates that Jesus is the Son of God with power even over man's most formidable enemies.

The chapter continues with additional information about John the Baptist, who was previously discussed in chapter three. In this passage, John sends representatives to ask Jesus whether He is the promised Messiah, or whether they should look for someone else. Jesus gives them no direct answer, but He points to the deeds of mercy and kindness that He is doing. Jesus answers their questions not with words but with actions; He notes that He is already doing the kind of things the Messiah will do.

After John's representatives leave, Jesus compliments him in the highest terms in the presence of the crowd. He makes two important points. First, He explains that even the most sincere follower of Jesus may go through times of discouragement and doubt. Second, He reserves the right to define His messiahship in His own way and in His own terms. He will not be bound by the expectations of society.

Jesus then describes the current generation with a brief parable about some children who are playing. Some of the children want to imitate a wedding, but some refuse to participate. Then the children propose to imitate a funeral, but once again some refuse to participate. Just as some of the children will reject all invitations to participate in the game, some of the Jews will refuse to hear and heed either John the Baptist or Jesus.

The last section of chapter seven describes events that take place when Jesus is invited to dine in the home of a prominent Pharisee. Jesus accepts the invitation, and sometime during the meal a most unusual event occurs. A woman who has a bad reputation enters the room and begins to anoint Jesus' feet with an expensive perfume. She also publicly weeps and dries the tears with her long hair. The Pharisee who is hosting the meal becomes angry because her actions are socially unacceptable. Also, he is offended because Jesus has allowed a woman of ill-repute to touch Him.

This event provokes a discussion between the Pharisee and Jesus. Jesus tells the parable of two debtors, which illustrates the contrast between the humble heart of the woman and the proud, arrogant attitude of the Pharisees. Jesus concludes the story by telling the woman that her sins have been forgiven; her faith has saved her. She can now depart in peace. Jesus' forgiveness of the woman's sin causes those who are present to ponder, "Who is this that forgiveth sins also?"

Application: Teaching and Preaching the Passage

This chapter makes a significant contribution to Jesus' definition of who He is and what He has come to earth to accomplish. Through a series of teachings and actions, Jesus informs His followers about the type of Messiah He intends to be and what kind of kingdom He has come to establish. This chapter emphasizes two themes that should be the focus of preaching and teaching: Jesus' compassion and His divine power. The late Rev. Greg McAllister, of the Randall University faculty, outlined how this chapter presents the power and authority of Jesus: (1) Jesus' authority over illness, verses 1-10; (2) Jesus' authority over death, verses 11-17; (3) Jesus' authority over His messiahship, verses 18-30; (4) Jesus' authority over His message, verses 31-35; (5) Jesus' authority over sin, verses 36-50.

In every section of the chapter, these two themes are interwoven as Jesus reveals His love and concern for suffering humanity. He is concerned about a widow who has lost her only son. He heals the slave of a Gentile who has been kind to the Jews in Palestine. He accepts the repentance of a sinful woman who intrudes into a banquet and anoints Him with expensive perfume. Instead of condemning John the Baptist for a lack of faith, Jesus commends him and expresses compassion for him and his disciples. The only ones upon whom Jesus does not bestow compassion are the proud Pharisee and his companions who trust in their own righteousness and refuse to accept Him as the promised Messiah. Those who preach and teach from this chapter should devote considerable attention to the various ways Jesus demonstrates His compassion.

They should also emphasize how Jesus uses His power and authority. He is the one who has the power to heal the sick and raise the dead. He preaches and teaches with authority, and He expects His followers to recognize that authority. Jesus has the power both to forgive the sins of a repentant woman and to condemn the attitude of an arrogant Pharisee. As this chapter clearly demonstrates, Jesus is indeed the King of Kings and Lord of Lords. His power is unlimited, but He always uses it for the benefit of human beings and for the advancement of His kingdom.

G. Jesus Defines His Kingdom (8:1-56)

In chapter eight, Jesus, in Luke's account, continues to develop two major themes that have been His focus almost from the beginning of the Gospel. The first is the nature of the Kingdom of God, which He is establishing; the second is the nature of His authority as the Messiah. Jesus gives no comprehensive definition of the kingdom (Fitzmyer I:155), but He outlines the nature of His kingdom by presenting a series of teachings and miracles such as those found in this chapter. In the early chapters of Luke, Jesus is always on the move; He goes from place to place in Galilee teaching and performing miracles. Ellis (123) suggests that Jesus' travels in chapter eight are designed to prepare the reader for the mission of the disciples, which will follow in the next chapter. In this chapter, the grace of God moves into active service; it also emphasizes that those who have experienced the grace of God are transformed by that experience (Kelly 123). The content of this chapter alternates between teaching and performing miracles (Bock I:711).

This chapter makes a significant contribution to the authority of Jesus. He demonstrates His power over the winds and waves as well as His control of demons and other forces opposed to the work of God. Luke includes this material on Jesus' authority because it makes a major contribution to his developing doctrine of Christology.

1 And it came to pass afterward, that he went throughout every city and village, preaching and shewing the glad tidings of the kingdom of God: and the twelve *were* with him,
2 And certain women, which had been healed of evil spirits and infirmities, Mary called Magdalene, out of whom went seven devils,
3 And Joanna the wife of Chuza Herod's steward, and Susanna, and many others, which ministered unto him of their substance.

These verses summarize Jesus' Galilean ministry and are similar to 4:40-44. The phrase "he went throughout every city and village" expresses the idea that Jesus was going through Galilee in a systematic manner, town by town and village by village (Lenski 439). He has an important message to share, and He is determined to share it.

Jesus and His disciples are accompanied by a group of women who provide financial support for the ministry. As Bock (I:713) notes, an itinerant ministry was common for Jewish rabbis; it was also common for women to provide financial support for a rabbi. It was not normal, however, for women to travel with a rabbi and his disciples. Jewish rabbis often refused to teach women and generally gave them an inferior status (Morris, *Luke* 148). Marshall (*Gospel* 317) notes that giving women such a prominent place in the ministry would have been very unusual in first-century

Palestine. Green (*Luke* 318) points out that this level of participation by women would have been unusual even in the Greco-Roman culture. This involvement is no accident; one of the characteristics of Luke's Gospel is that it pays greater attention to the contributions of women than the other Gospels do (Stein, *Luke* 240; D. Guthrie, *Introduction* 91). For a good discussion of the role of women in the N. T. see NIDNTT (III:1055-1068).

Lieu (61) takes a somewhat different approach to this passage. She argues that women in the first century were accorded a larger role in society than commentators have generally recognized. If she is correct, this action by Jesus is less revolutionary than is commonly thought.

Verses 2-3 provide additional information about these women; three are mentioned by name. The first is "Mary called Magdalene, out of whom went seven devils." "Magdalene" identifies her as a native of Magdala, a town about three miles from Tiberias on the west side of the Sea of Galilee (Marshall, *Gospel* 316; Green, *Luke* 320). Some commentators in the past have connected her with the unnamed woman of Luke 7:36-50 or with Mary, the sister of Lazarus, but such interpretations are not widely held today (Kelly 123; Stein, *Luke* 240).

Perhaps Mary is selected for this important mission because she had already experienced the healing power of Jesus. The words "out of whom went seven devils" are interpreted in various ways. Most commentators connect the demon possession with some type of illness or infirmity. It may mean that she has been cured of seven maladies at one time or at different times. Since the number seven is often used in Jewish literature as a symbol for completeness, it is also possible that these words indicate the severity of her infirmity (Summers, *Luke* 91; Marshall, *Gospel* 316; Stein, *Luke* 241) and the magnitude of Jesus' healing.

The second woman named in the story is Joanna, the wife of Chuza (a servant of King Herod). Little is known about her; she is also mentioned in Luke 24:10, where she goes to the tomb with other women and returns to tell the apostles of the miraculous events that have transpired. The fact that her husband is a servant of King Herod indicates that the message of Jesus is beginning to penetrate into the higher levels of society.

The last is Susanna, who is mentioned only here in the N. T. Spence (200) points out that her name means "lily" and that Jews were fond of giving the names of flowers and trees to their daughters. Nothing further is known about the extent of her involvement in the ministry of Jesus. Stein (*Luke* 241) suggests that no further identification of these women is necessary because the original readers of this Gospel already knew about them and their contributions to the ministry.

Luke notes that these three are part of a larger group of women who "ministered unto him of their substance." "Ministered" (Greek imperfect tense) indicates an action that continues over a period of time, not just a one-time event. The fact they can provide continuing financial support for the ministry of Jesus indicates they are women of some wealth and position in society.

Beginning in verse 4, Luke gives an overview of Jesus' major teachings and of the important events that occur during His tour of Galilee. This passage should not be understood as a summary of everything that happens; it serves rather to illustrate the kind of teachings and events that characterize the early part of Jesus' public ministry. Luke begins this section with one of Jesus' most famous parables, known as the "Parable of the Sower" or the "Parable of the Sowed Seed" (Fitzmyer I:699-700). It is also known as the "Parable of the Soils" (Stein, *Luke* 241; Buttrick 41).

The parable was a common and effective teaching device in ancient Israel; it was often used by the Jewish rabbis. It is not surprising that Jesus adopted it and used it on many occasions. A "parable" (Greek *parabolē*) involves some type of comparison. It may describe a proverb, a riddle, a comparison or contrast, a simple story, or a more developed story (DJG 593). Jesus uses the parable to teach important lessons about the Kingdom of God by comparing it to situations with which people could easily identify. They often serve as effective illustrations of spiritual principles. Since the planting of wheat and barley were common occurrences in first-century Palestine, Jesus' hearers would have easily identified with this parable.

4 And when much people were gathered together, and were come to him out of every city, he spake by a parable:
5 A sower went out to sow his seed: and as he sowed, some fell by the way side; and it was trodden down, and the fowls of the air devoured it.
6 And some fell upon a rock; and as soon as it was sprung up, it withered away, because it lacked moisture.
7 And some fell among thorns; and the thorns sprang up with it, and choked it.
8a And other fell on good ground, and sprang up, and bare fruit an hundredfold.

Jesus has previously used other forms of comparison, such as similes and metaphors (as in Lk. 6:29, 48), but this is the first of Jesus' parables that Luke has included. Spence (201) suggests this seems to be the first parable Jesus spoke and it came to be of singular importance in the lives of the disciples. Buttrick (42) recognizes its importance, but he argues that it is not the first of Jesus' parables. This is one of four major parables found in all three Synoptic Gospels (Lk. 13:18-19, 20:9-17, and 21:29-31) (Stein, *Luke* 242). Each Gospel writer presents this parable in his own unique way, which is designed to meet the needs of his own particular audience (Kistemaker 18-19). Luke's is the shortest and most concise account; he uses it to illustrate how different people accept or reject the gospel (Kistemaker 20). It remains even today among the best-known and most loved of Jesus' parables. For a good summary of current evangelical thought concerning the interpretation and use of parables in the first century see Craig Blomberg (*Parables*).

In the opinion of many commentators, this is a difficult passage to interpret (Stein, *Luke* 242; Spence 201-202). According to verse 4, Jesus spoke the parable to a crowd of people who had gathered from the surrounding towns and villages to hear Him. There is, however, no further mention of the crowd in the passage. Almost immediately, the focus shifts to the disciples; it is clear that Jesus' message is designed to meet the needs of His closest followers.

Wheat and barley were normally sown in the fall of the year during the month of October (Kistemaker 16). There was no mechanization; all field work was done by hand with the help of oxen and donkeys. According to most authorities, the seed was spread first and then the ground was plowed with rough wooden plows to cover the seed (Jeremias, *Rediscovering* 9; Kistemaker 17). A minority of scholars have concluded that plowing preceded the sowing; see Fitzmyer (I:703) and Lieu (62). It is possible that both patterns were followed by Palestinian farmers.

The farmer begins to sow the seed; this is ordinarily done by dropping the seeds in rows. It is inevitable that some of the seed will fall on the path where the soil has been packed down over many years by the feet of oxen, donkeys, and agricultural workers. This seed has no chance to grow and is soon eaten by the birds. Some of the seed falls on the rocky ground. This does not mean fertile soil with rocks in it; it implies a narrow layer of soil on top of a bed of limestone (Kistemaker 17; Fitzmyer I:704). This seed may sprout and grow as long as the topsoil is moist, but the plant will not survive when the hot and dry weather arrives.

Some of the seed falls in that part of the field where thorn bushes and other weeds have grown. The weeds and bushes may not be growing at the time the wheat is planted, but their seeds are there and they will soon begin to grow (Buttrick 46). The wheat or barley seeds may sprout, but they are soon choked out by the hardier weeds and bushes.

Some of the seed falls on fertile soil where it can grow and develop. At the time of harvest, these seeds produce an abundant crop. In Mark's version of this parable (4:8), these seeds brings forth "some thirty, and some sixty, and some an hundred." In the interest of brevity, Luke mentions only that the seed on the good ground brings forth a hundredfold, which would have been a truly miraculous harvest at that time.

8b And when he had said these things, he cried, He that hath ears to hear, let him hear.
9 And his disciples asked him, saying, What might this parable be?
10 And he said, Unto you it is given to know the mysteries of the kingdom of God: but to others in parables; that seeing they might not see, and hearing they might not understand.

In the last part of verse 8, Jesus exhorts His followers by saying, "He that hath ears to hear, let him hear." These words have traditionally been understood to underscore the importance of responding to the Gospel message in the proper way (Stein, *Luke* 245; Fitzmyer I:702). In verse 9, the disciples reveal their perplexity. Up to this point in His ministry, Jesus has not taught through parables. The disciples are not accustomed to this type of teaching, and they need Jesus' help in understanding the meaning of the parable and how it applies to them and their ministry.

Verse 10 contrasts the status of the disciples with that of other, more casual, followers of Jesus. The idea is that Jesus speaks openly to the disciples because they can handle the difficult lessons He is presenting. The term "mystery" is generally used to describe an idea that cannot be discovered through human wisdom alone; it is a truth that God makes known in some way. Liefeld (906) suggests it refers specifically to "the purpose and plan of God, which He works out phase by phase in human history and through the church." Stein (*Luke* 245) notes that in this context the Greek word should be translated "secret" rather than "mystery."

Jesus speaks to the disciples openly, but to the "others" He speaks in parables. Jesus does not define "others," but He apparently means those who are outside the circle of His immediate followers. Ellis (125) suggests the parable is something of an enigma. It reveals the true nature of the kingdom to Jesus' disciples while for the "others" the meaning is concealed. Stein (*Luke* 245) suggests the phrase "in parables" expresses the idea of "enigmatically" or "in riddles." The point seems to be that Jesus speaks openly to His closest disciples who have the necessary spiritual maturity to understand His teachings. He speaks to the crowds with sayings like parables that require interpretation or explanation.

The last part of verse 10 is drawn from Isaiah 6:9-10, where the prophet is called to go and speak the word of God to the people of Judah. Isaiah is warned not to expect great results; the people will hear the words but will not understand and apply the message he has for them. As the opposition to His ministry grows, Jesus will make greater use of parables in teaching. His disciples will understand the true meaning of His teaching, but others, including His enemies, will fail to grasp the meaning of the parables. Their hardness of heart will prevent them from understanding the message Jesus has for them. See the comments of Fitzmyer (I:707) and Bock (I:729).

11 Now the parable is this: The seed is the word of God.
12 Those by the way side are they that hear; then cometh the devil, and taketh away the word out of their hearts, lest they should believe and be saved.
13 They on the rock *are they*, which, when they hear, receive the word with joy; and these have no root, which for a while believe, and in time of temptation fall away.
14 And that which fell among thorns are they, which, when they have heard, go forth, and are choked with cares and riches and pleasures of *this* life, and bring no fruit to perfection.
15 But that on the good ground are they, which in an honest and good heart, having heard the word, keep *it*, and bring forth fruit with patience.

Jesus explains the parable to His disciples. This interpretation has produced a great deal of controversy among N. T. interpreters. Critical scholars, almost without exception, attribute these explanations or interpretations not to Jesus but to the early church. They reject the interpretations because they explain the parables in an allegorical fashion; they believe that allegorical interpretations could not have come from Jesus (NTE 255). Jeremias (*Parables* 77) writes, "I have long held out against the conclusion that this interpretation must be ascribed to the primitive Church; but on linguistic grounds alone it is unavoidable." Jeremias then explains the reasons he considers this interpretation to be a later addition to the text. Dodd (*Parables* 145) comes to similar conclusions. He argues that these verses are "a striking example of the way in which the early Church re-interpreted sayings and parables of Jesus to suit its changing needs."

Not all scholars accept this radical approach. They point out that allegory was often used in ancient literature and the modern distinction between an allegory and a parable did not apply in the ancient world (NTE 256-257). Bock (I:730-731) and Marshall (*Gospel*, 323-324) argue that the interpretation is authentic. Buttrick (44) also defends its authenticity. It is likely that the parable itself was spoken to the crowd while the interpretation was given to the disciples only.

Beginning in verse 11, Jesus applies the teachings of the parable to His disciples. These verses should be understood in light of the missionary journey upon which the disciples will embark in chapter nine of Luke. Buttrick (41) sees this parable as somewhat autobiographical in that it describes Jesus' own ministry of sowing the seed. Some accept His preaching and others do not.

The seed sown is the Word of God, the good news of salvation through Christ. It is proclaimed both by Jesus and His followers. The seed that falls on the pathway describes those who hear the Word of God but they are under the control of Satan and do not give the good news any lodging in their hearts.

The seed that falls in the shallow soil on top of the rock represents those who hear the Word and receive it gladly. They do not, however, have the necessary depth to continue in the faith during times of trial. They do very well for a while, but they fall away in difficult times.

The seed that falls among the thorns represents those who begin well, but their spiritual lives are sooner or later choked out by the cares, riches, and pleasures of this life. "Perfection" expresses the idea of maturity or completeness; they never develop a mature and stable Christian life.

The seed that falls on the good ground stands for those who hear the Word and accept it. They then grow and develop into mature disciples; they receive the word honestly and truly and then continue in it. They hold on to the Word they have received and they bring forth fruit. "Patience" has the idea of perseverance; these believers keep going even in times of trial and adversity. As Kistemaker (29) correctly notes, "The faithful proclamation of the gospel will never fail to bring forth fruit."

What lesson, then, is Jesus teaching in this the most famous of His parables? There are two interpretations that have been widely held in Christian history (Hunter, *Interpreting* 47). The first is an ancient interpretation dating back to the time of the early church. According to this view, Jesus is addressing the multitudes and His main point of the parable is "take heed how you hear." The seed is good; it is the gospel. It is sown correctly according to the agricultural practices of the day. The difference comes in the types of soil; in some soil conditions the seed grows. In others it does not. Those who hear the gospel must take care to respond to it with "an honest and good heart." Buttrick (41-48) gives an effective presentation of the traditional interpretation.

The second interpretation is preferred by most modern scholars; it stresses the abundant harvest. In ancient Palestine a harvest of ten times as much grain as the farmer had planted was considered a good harvest (Hunter, *Interpreting* 47). According to the parable, the seed sown in the good ground brought forth "an hundredfold" (Lk. 8:8). According to this interpretation, the parable is meant to encourage Jesus' disciples. The message is that the gospel will grow and develop in spite of the many obstacles that may come (Hunter, *Interpreting* 101). According to Barclay (100) and Hunter (*Interpreting* 101-102), something of both ideas may be involved in the parable.

C. Smith (64-65) offers a rather unique interpretation of this parable; he sees it primarily as a parable of persistence. The farmer understands from the beginning that some of the seed will be wasted; it will produce no harvest. He also understands that part of the seed will bear fruit and perhaps produce an abundant crop. Therefore, he continues to plant year after year in hope of making a good crop. Smith argues that this parable illustrates the persistence of God who continues to raise up prophets and leaders in hope of producing an abundant spiritual harvest.

One important issue in the interpretation of this and other parables concerns the number of lessons Jesus presents in a given parable. Jeremias (*Rediscovering* 89; *Parables* 77-79, 149-151) and Dodd (*Parables of Jesus* 7, 145) are typical of many modern scholars who teach that the parables, as originally presented by Jesus, were designed to teach one principal lesson and any allegorical interpretations were added by the church in later centuries.

Bock (I:731) and Blomberg (*Parables* 20-21) challenge this view; they argue there is no evidence that limits a parable to teaching only one point or lesson. Blomberg asserts that each major character in a parable may present a particular teaching; he suggests this parable teaches three major lessons (*Parables* 228). The first is that God sends His word to many different kinds of people around the world. The second is that many will not respond to the message with saving faith. The third is that "the only legitimate response to God's word is the obedience and perseverance which demonstrate true regeneration."

Although all will not agree with it, the analysis of Blomberg moves in the right direction. In this beautiful parable, Jesus challenges both His followers and the crowds to respond to the gospel in the proper fashion. He also encourages His disciples by reminding them that the preaching of the Gospel will produce an abundant harvest even if all people are not willing to receive it.

16 No man, when he hath lighted a candle, covereth it with a vessel, or putteth *it* under a bed; but setteth *it* on a candlestick, that they which enter in may see the light.
17 For nothing is secret, that shall not be made manifest; neither *any thing* hid, that shall not be known and come abroad.
18 Take heed therefore how ye hear: for whosoever hath, to him shall be given; and whosoever hath not, from him shall be taken even that which he seemeth to have.

The first words of verse 18 form the connecting link between these verses and the teachings Jesus has given earlier in this chapter. The idea is that the words of Jesus are the words of God, and the disciples must pay close attention to them. They cannot be the kind of disciples they need to be unless they correctly understand and obey the teachings Jesus has given them.

Verses 16-18 are directed to the disciples; they emphasize the truth that men must correctly hear, accept, and respond to the Word of God. Some scholars consider these verses to be a parable (Marshall, *Gospel* 327; Geldenhuys 247), while others consider them to be more of a traditional proverb (Bock I:742). Fitzmyer (I:716) suggests this is not one parable, but a series of three independent sayings of Jesus, which have been brought together. Liefeld (909) notes that all three of these sayings are also found in Matthew and Mark, but that Matthew places two of them in different contexts. It is very possible these three sayings were repeated several times in different situations. The message is the same whether these verses form a brief parable, a traditional proverb, or a collection of independent sayings.

In verse 16, the teachings of Jesus are compared to a lamp that gives light in an otherwise dark house. "Candle" (Greek *luchnos*) can be used in different ways; here it probably refers to a small lamp that burns olive oil; there is a related word (Greek *luchnia*) used to describe the stand upon which such a lamp is placed (Fitzmyer I:719). Typical Palestine houses were generally very dark; they were small with no windows and only one door. In these circumstances the small amount of light produced by a lamp of this type would be extremely important. No one would be so foolish as to light a lamp and cover it with some type of vessel or put it under a bed; that would defeat the very purpose of lighting the lamp. The householder will put the lamp on a lampstand where it can give light to the room.

Verse 17 continues to describe the teachings of Jesus as light. This verse explains how the teachings of Jesus will bring to light human thoughts that would otherwise remain hidden. The verse does not explain specifically what secrets are to be revealed. It is possible the verse teaches that God's truth is made known and vindicated (Fitzmyer I:718-719); it is also possible the verse refers to the exposure of man's evil thoughts and desires by the light of the gospel (Bock I:745-746). The general idea is the gospel brings things to light that would otherwise be hidden. Liefeld (909) opines that God's truth, which is partially hidden from those who do not receive it, will in the future be publicly vindicated.

Verse 18 is a rather enigmatic statement that Jesus could have spoken in a variety of circumstances. Most commentators (Geldenhuys 247-248; Liefeld 909-910; Marshall, *Gospel*, 327-328; Spence 205) view it as a warning to the disciples and others who undertake to teach the Word of God. If they are humble and willing to learn, their responsibility will be increased. If they develop an attitude of arrogance or self-righteousness, this important ministry will be taken from them.

19 Then came to him *his* mother and his brethren, and could not come at him for the press.
20 And it was told him *by certain* which said, Thy mother and thy brethren stand without, desiring to see thee.

21 And he answered and said unto them, My mother and my brethren are these which hear the word of God, and do it.

This story is told in all of the Synoptic Gospels, but Matthew and Mark place it in a different context (Mk. 3:31-35; Mt. 12:46-50). Jesus' mother and brothers appear on the scene; Luke does not explain why. Perhaps they are concerned about Jesus' welfare; perhaps they wish to see Him perform a miracle (Ellis 127). In order to maintain the perpetual virginity of Mary, the Roman Catholic Church understands the word "brothers" to mean "step-brothers" or "cousins," but such translations go beyond the normal meaning of the word. According to Protestant interpreters, those referred to here are probably Jesus' younger brothers, the natural children of Joseph and Mary (Liefeld 910; Geldenhuys 250).

The message presented in this story is clear. The physical family of the Messiah enjoys no priority in the Kingdom of God; they must come to Him by faith as others do. They must follow His teachings. Liefeld (910) suggests the phrase "God's Word" may be another way of saying "God's will." In this passage, Jesus also provides an example for His followers who will have to renounce family for the sake of the Kingdom of God (Ellis 127). If Jesus' mother and brothers wish to be part of the spiritual family of God, they must respond to the Gospel just as others do.

22 Now it came to pass on a certain day, that he went into a ship with his disciples: and he said unto them, Let us go over unto the other side of the lake. And they launched forth.
23 But as they sailed he fell asleep: and there came down a storm of wind on the lake; and they were filled *with water*, and were in jeopardy.
24 And they came to him, and awoke him, saying, Master, master, we perish. Then he arose, and rebuked the wind and the raging of the water: and they ceased, and there was a calm.
25 And he said unto them, Where is your faith? And they being afraid wondered, saying one to another, What manner of man is this! for he commandeth even the winds and water, and they obey him.

Jesus begins a series of mighty works designed to teach the disciples important lessons about His power, authority, and grace. By His actions, Jesus will explain in greater detail what it means to be the Son of God; He will also share more information about the nature of the kingdom He is establishing. Jesus goes down to the shore of the lake with His disciples; together they climb into a boat and begin to sail across the lake. This body of water is a large fresh-water lake on the Jordan River, commonly known as the Sea of Galilee; it is sometimes called the Lake of Tiberias. Here Luke simply calls it "the lake." Luke does not give the size of the boat (the same Greek word means both "boat" and "ship"). A typical fishing boat used on the lake would have been 15 to 17 feet long. Luke does not explain why they want to sail across the lake or where they plan to land; such details are not necessary for the narrative.

Jesus is tired after a heavy schedule of preaching and teaching; He falls asleep probably on a pillow in the stern of the boat (Spence 206). While He is asleep, a sudden storm blows up and threatens to sink the boat. The Sea of Galilee is normally peaceful and quiet, but it is subject to sudden storms (Geldenhuys 251). Spence (206) explains that strong winds could suddenly and unexpectedly sweep down from the area around Mount Herman and churn up the water. The phrase "were filled *with water*" (Greek imperfect tense) means the boat is being swamped. The disciples are, no doubt, experienced in sailing on the Sea of Galilee, but this storm is more than they can handle. They wake Jesus and cry out in desperation, "Master, master" (Greek" *epistatēs*) implies a sense of urgency in this context (Marshall, *Gospel* 334). The disciples are filled with fear and believe they are about to perish in the storm.

Jesus stands up in the boat and rebukes the wind and the waves. The storm ceases, and the lake returns to its normal state of calm. Jesus asks the disciples, "Where is your faith?" This question does not imply the disciples have lost all faith in Jesus. The idea is they do not yet have a sufficient degree of faith to accept the full extent of His power; they do not yet fully understand who Jesus is and what He can do in the world. This event produces a spirit of wonder, awe, and fear in the disciples; they do not know how to understand what has just happened to them. The disciples reflect their confusion and inner turmoil with the exclamation, "What manner of man is this!" Prior to this event, they understood that Jesus had great power, but they did not realize His power extended even to the natural world. What God did in the O. T. when He parted the waters, Jesus has now done in their presence. This experience will challenge them, but it will also help them understand more fully the greatness and power of the One whom they are following.

26 And they arrived at the country of the Gadarenes, which is over against Galilee.
27 And when he went forth to land, there met him out of the city a certain man, which had devils long time, and ware no clothes, neither abode in *any* house, but in the tombs.
28 When he saw Jesus, he cried out, and fell down before him, and with a loud voice said, What have I to do with thee, Jesus, *thou* Son of God most high? I beseech thee, torment me not.
29 (For he had commanded the unclean spirit to come out of the man. For oftentimes it had caught him: and he was kept bound with chains and in fetters; and he brake the bands, and was driven of the devil into the wilderness.)
30 And Jesus asked him, saying, What is thy name? And he said, Legion: because many devils were entered into him.
31 And they besought him that he would not command them to go out into the deep.
32 And there was there an herd of many swine feeding on the mountain: and they besought him that he would suffer them to enter into them. And he suffered them.
33 Then went the devils out of the man, and entered into the swine:

and the herd ran violently down a steep place into the lake, and were choked.
34 When they that fed *them* saw what was done, they fled, and went and told *it* in the city and in the country.
35 Then they went out to see what was done; and came to Jesus, and found the man, out of whom the devils were departed, sitting at the feet of Jesus, clothed, and in his right mind: and they were afraid.
36 They also which saw *it* told them by what means he that was possessed of the devils was healed.

Jesus demonstrated His power over the forces of nature; now He demonstrates His control over the demonic entities that make life miserable for mankind and oppose the work of God. "They" (v. 26) apparently refers to Jesus and His disciples. The disciples play no part in Luke's account, but they are likely witnesses to what transpires. They arrive by boat at a certain place on the eastern shore of the lake, opposite the land of Galilee (Ellis 128). Green (*Luke* 335) suggests that the phrase "over against Galilee "or "opposite Galilee" indicates they have entered into a predominantly Gentile territory. The Greek manuscripts of verse 26 contain different spellings of the name of the place where they landed (Marshall, *Gospel*, 336-337; Liefeld 914). Many commentators, taking "country of the Gerasenes" to be the original word, identify this with the modern town of Kersa (Ellis 128; Geldenhuys 255). There is a steep bank nearby and the remains of several tombs.

When Jesus arrives at the shore, He is met by an unidentified man whose life has been destroyed by the demons that have long controlled him. The demons have obviously produced severe mental illness; he does not wear proper clothing, and he lives among the tombs rather than in a house. According to Liefeld (913), these verses provide a classic description of a case of demon possession. Liefeld also notes that tombs were often located in caves, which would provide at least some level of protection from the elements.

The man recognizes Jesus immediately; he addresses Him as "*thou* Son of God most high." "Most High God" is found in several places in the O. T. (Gen. 14:18-21; Num. 24:16; Is. 14:14; Dan. 3:26, 4:2), where it emphasizes the power and majesty of God. The man's petition is simple: "Torment me not." "Torment" (Greek *basaniz*) often carries the connotation of physical or mental torture (Liefeld 913). Apparently the man has suffered greatly at the hands of the demons, and he is afraid that Jesus will inflict even more pain on him.

In verse 29, Luke provides some background material that is designed to set the stage for the miracle and to give the reader a better understanding of what is about to transpire. Jesus is not content to allow the man to continue to suffer; He orders the evil spirit to leave him alone. Apparently, this man has fallen under the control of evil spirits on several occasions in the past. These episodes were so bad, he had to be bound both hand and foot. The "chains" are placed on the wrists; the "fetters" bind the feet (Marshall, *Gospel* 338). This was certainly cruel treatment, but in the ancient world there was simply no other treatment for this type of behavior.

The man was very strong, and even these restraints could not hold him. The situation was so desperate that the devil caused him to leave the city and flee into the deserts—probably the relatively uninhabited areas away from the lake. In this verse, Luke paints a very sad picture of a man whose world can offer him no hope; Jesus is the only one who can remedy this situation.

Jesus' conversation with the man resumes in verse 30, when Jesus asks his name. He responds with the word "Legion," a term that is not really a proper name. "Legion" describes a unit in the Roman army normally having thousands of soldiers (Liefeld 913); Barclay (108) suggests that a Roman legion contained approximately 6,000 soldiers. The man is under the control of a large number of demons.

Verse 31 is somewhat difficult. "They" clearly refers to the demons, who plead with Jesus not to send them into "the deep" (Greek *abussos*), which may be translated "the abyss," "the depth," or "the underworld." This term is used in the N. T. to describe the place where the evil powers are held (Marshall, *Gospel* 339). Bock (*Luke* NIV 241) notes that the term refers both to the place of the dead and to a place of judgment. The idea seems to be that the demons are begging Jesus not to destroy them. Instead, the demons ask Jesus to permit them to enter into a nearby herd of pigs. Luke does not explain why they would make such a strange request. Spence (207) suggests the demons ask to go into the pigs because any fate would be better than going to the abyss. Since pigs were unclean animals, faithful Jews would have nothing to do with them. They were, however, raised in Gentile areas.

Jesus grants their request; the demons leave the man and enter into the herd of swine. The result is disastrous; the pigs immediately run down the steep slope and into the lake where they are drowned. The herders who watched over the swine then go into the surrounding areas to tell what has happened. They are no doubt quite perturbed because they have lost a valuable herd of swine.

Many questions have been raised concerning this passage. Scholars have questioned the ethics of sending the demons into innocent swine, which are then drowned in the lake (Barclay 108; Geldenhuys 256). Nolland (I:410) suggests the fact that pigs are unclean animals makes them an appropriate place to send the demons. He notes that sending demons into animals is common in Hellenistic demonology.

Jesus never condones cruelty to animals, but He offers no explanation of why He permitted this to happen. Nolland (I:411) explains that the time has not yet come for the final destruction of the demons; sending them into the swine is a method of getting them out of the way. Barclay (108) suggests the man had such a strong belief in demons that nothing less than the visible departure of them would have convinced the man he had been healed. Stein (*Luke* 257) writes that the evangelist's two primary concerns are the healing of the demon-possessed man and the judgment of the demons; all other considerations are secondary. The emphasis of the account is clearly on the power of Jesus and the healing of the demon-possessed man rather than on the fate of the swine. Although there are many unanswered questions about this passage, the loss of a herd of swine is, in reality, a small price to pay for the deliverance of a man who had suffered for many years.

Verses 35-36 form an appropriate conclusion to the account. Luke does not identify the individuals referred to as "they" in verse 35. They could be the disciples; more likely, they are a group of the people who lived in the area. Their curiosity has been aroused, and they come out to see what has happened. They find the one they had known is no longer like he was before; he has been radically transformed. The man who had formerly lived among the tombs and wore no clothes is now fully clothed, in his right mind, and sitting at Jesus' feet. It is clear he has been freed from the domination of the demons. The crowd responds to this important event with fear. They have never seen anything like this, and they do not know what to make of it. Verse 36 notes that those who had witnessed the event (probably those who herded the pigs and others) explained to the crowd how the demon-possessed man had been healed. They no doubt told how Jesus had suddenly and miraculously liberated him. "Healed" (Greek *sōzō*) is the same word that is often used in the N. T. to mean "saved." Stein (*Luke* 258) asserts that the term means more than just deliverance from the demons. It means that all obstacles to a relationship with Jesus have been removed, and the man is now a disciple of Jesus.

37 Then the whole multitude of the country of the Gadarenes round about besought him to depart from them; for they were taken with great fear: and he went up into the ship, and returned back again.

38 Now the man out of whom the devils were departed besought him that he might be with him: but Jesus sent him away, saying,
39 Return to thine own house, and shew how great things God hath done unto thee. And he went his way, and published throughout the whole city how great things Jesus had done unto him.

The healing of the demon-possessed man produces a significant change in the attitude of those who live in the surrounding country. Rather than rejoicing at the healing of this unfortunate man, they ask Jesus to leave. Luke mentions they have great fear; it is likely that fear has led them to ask Jesus to leave. Morris (*Luke* 157) posits that their reaction might have been a superstitious reaction to the supernatural power they had just witnessed. It is also possible they focused their attention on the material loss of the herd of swine.

It is clear they have never seen any man perform the kind of miracle Jesus has performed. Morris (*Luke* 157) also suggests they might have viewed Jesus as a person who disturbed the normal nature of things and who was more interested in saving the unfortunate man than in material prosperity. Barclay (109) notes two possible factors that might have contributed to the people's negative reaction. First, Jesus had made a significant change in their community, and people often find it difficult to accept change. Second, the people placed greater value on the pigs that had been lost than upon the soul of a human being that had been saved.

The man who has been healed responds in a totally different way; he begs Jesus to allow him to accompany them on their journey. "Besought" (Greek imperfect tense) implies a continuing action; the man continued to beg Jesus. Bock (I:779-780) mentions two factors that might have contributed to his desire to go with Jesus. First, he might have wanted Jesus to protect him. Second, he wished to learn from Jesus. Another possibility is that he wished to follow Jesus out of a sense of gratitude for the miracle he had received. Luke does not explain the reason or reasons that might have contributed to his strong desire to be with Jesus, but it is likely that his desire was to learn more from the one who has given him new life.

The man is certainly to be commended for his desire to be with Jesus, but the Lord has other plans for him. He instructs the man to return to his home and tell others what God has done for him. The people who live in this predominantly Gentile area need to know who Jesus is and what He can do in their lives. The man obeys Jesus' instructions and shares what he has experienced with his friends and neighbors. Fitzmyer (I:735) calls attention to the fact that this man was probably a pagan. Both Fitzmyer and Nolland (I:413) suggest this incident serves to prepare the way for Jesus' future ministry to the Gentiles.

40 And it came to pass, that, when Jesus was returned, the people gladly received him: for they were all waiting for him.
41 And, behold, there came a man named Jairus, and he was a ruler of the synagogue: and he fell down at Jesus' feet, and besought him that he would come into his house:
42 For he had one only daughter, about twelve years of age, and she lay a dying. But as he went the people thronged him.
43 And a woman having an issue of blood twelve years, which had spent all her living upon physicians, neither could be healed of any,
44 Came behind *him*, and touched the border of his garment: and immediately her issue of blood stanched.
45 And Jesus said, Who touched me? When all denied, Peter and they that were with him said, Master, the multitude throng thee and press *thee*, and sayest thou, Who touched me?
46 And Jesus said, Somebody hath touched me: for I perceive that virtue is gone out of me.
47 And when the woman saw that she was not hid, she came trembling, and falling down before him, she declared unto him before all the people for what cause she had touched him, and how she was healed immediately.
48 And he said unto her, Daughter, be of good comfort: thy faith hath made thee whole; go in peace.

Luke presents two intertwined miracles. Mark 5:21 states that these miracles took place at the eastern shore of the Sea of Galilee. For Luke the time and location are not central to the story. The miracles are significant in and of themselves; they are designed to demonstrate the power of Jesus (Fitzmyer I:742). In the first miracle, Jesus is confronted with a girl of about twelve years of age who is ill and at the point of death; the nature of her illness is not given. The second miracle presents a woman who has been losing blood, probably through some type of wound or hemorrhage, for twelve years. She has spent a great deal of money on physicians, but none have been able to heal her.

As Jesus is passing along on the way to the girl's home, the woman comes up behind Him and touches the hem or tassel of His garment. Jewish men often wore a long robe with tassels at the bottom. "Border" (Greek *kraspedon*) may describe either the tassel or the hem of a garment (Lenski 484; Marshall, *Gospel* 344)—in this context, probably the tassel. She is probably afraid to approach Jesus in a direct manner, and she may share the common misconception that she must be touched by Jesus to experience His healing power. Lenski (484) suggests she approaches Jesus from behind in order to keep her ailment a secret.

Jesus responds in a rather surprising manner, asking, "Who touched me?" Lenski (485) posits that Jesus knew very well the answer to His question. In fact, He knew all about this woman and her condition. Jesus asked the question for her benefit and for the benefit of those around her; He wanted her to understand who had healed her and how it had been done.

Apparently, Jesus had not directed His question to anyone in particular. Peter, as the spokesman for the apostolic band, feels compelled to answer. His response indicates that so many people are so close to Jesus it is impossible to determine who touched Him. Jesus responds that this was no casual touch; Jesus realizes power had gone out from Him. The woman then steps forward with a sense of fear and trembling. Bock (I:797) suggests several possible reasons for her fear. He concludes the most likely explanation is that she is afraid of what Jesus would do; she is unsure of how He will handle the situation.

She then falls down before Jesus and explains, within the hearing of the crowd, how she had touched the Lord and how she had immediately been healed. Jesus seems satisfied with her response. He addresses her as "daughter," which implies a loving family relationship. He tells her that she has not been healed through some magical incantation; her faith brought her to this point.

The term "faith" is used in several different ways in the N. T. Here the idea is that she had trust and confidence in Jesus and His divine power; Ellis (130) defines it as "the *trust* in expectation that produces an *act* in expectation" (italics his). Spence (209) points out that faith in Christ is a broad, inclusive term; see the comments of Marshall (*Gospel*, 342), Fitzmyer (I:744), and Bock (I:798).

Jesus' statement "thy faith hath made thee whole" can be interpreted in more than one way. "Made whole" (Greek *sōzō*) is often used in the N. T. with the meaning "to save." As Hunter (*Theology* 91) explains, the term "salvation" often refers to a state of wholeness, which is both physical and spiritual. Many commentators (Bock, Fitzmyer, and Marshall, for example) see more in this passage than physical healing; they argue that she is also saved from her sins. Other interpreters see this as a reference to physical healing only; Spence (209-210) and Liefeld (916-917), for example, make no mention of spiritual healing.

Jesus says to the woman, "Go in peace," and peace is one of the key terms in Luke's Gospel. In Luke 10:5-6, the one who welcomes the disciple with the gospel message into his home is called a "son of peace." The term implies much more than an inner feeling; it implies the state of hostility that previously existed between the woman and God has been replaced by a state of love and acceptance (Bock I:799). Fitzmyer (I:747) explains that this phrase is the normal Hebrew dismissal.

49 While he yet spake, there cometh one from the ruler of the synagogue's *house*, saying to him, Thy daughter is dead; trouble not the Master.
50 But when Jesus heard *it*, he answered him, saying, Fear not: believe only, and she shall be made whole.
51 And when he came into the house, he suffered no man to go in, save Peter, and James, and John, and the father and the mother of the maiden.
52 And all wept, and bewailed her: but he said, Weep not; she is not dead, but sleepeth.
53 And they laughed him to scorn, knowing that she was dead.
54 And he put them all out, and took her by the hand, and called, saying, Maid, arise.
55 And her spirit came again, and she arose straightway: and he commanded to give her meat.
56 And her parents were astonished: but he charged them that they should tell no man what was done.

In these verses, Luke finishes the account of the healing of Jairus' daughter, which began in verse 41. Jesus' encounter with the woman with the issue of blood has delayed His trip to the house of Jairus. A servant arrives with the news that the young girl has died. Therefore, there is no need to trouble Jesus further; the assumption is that if the child is already dead, there is nothing Jesus can do about the situation. "Master" (Greek *didaskalos*) is often used to describe Jesus, usually translated "teacher." It is clearly a title of respect.

Jesus hears the report of the servant, and immediately begins to correct the assumption that there is nothing He can do; His power to heal is not limited to the living. He tells them "Fear not"—in other words, "stop being afraid" (Greek negative present imperative to forbid an action that is already in progress). He tells them to have faith and the girl will be made whole.

Luke does not explain how long it takes to travel to the house. When they arrive, Jesus takes the initiative. He goes into the room where she lies, and He allows only Peter, James, John, and the girl's parents to go into the room with Him. All those present were weeping, and Jesus tells them to stop (again using the negative present imperative in Greek with this meaning).

Then Jesus makes a most unusual statement: "She is not dead, but sleepeth." Many commentators (Marshall, *Gospel* 348; Spence 210; Ellis 130; Liefeld 916) believe the girl has really died. This is supported by the words "her spirit returned" or "came again" found in verse 55. It was commonly believed that the spirit departed from the body at death (Marshall, *Gospel* 348). The fact that her spirit returned to her body indicates she was really dead and Jesus had restored her to life. Why, then, did Jesus use the term "asleep" to describe her condition? He probably used it to indicate that her condition was only temporary because His messianic power extended even to those who were already dead (Fitzmyer I:749; Lieu 68).

In verse 53, Luke makes no attempt to identify those who ridiculed Jesus because He had described her condition as sleep. Many commentators overlook this verse completely (such as Lieu 68; Liefeld 917; Fitzmyer I:749). Spence (210) and Bock (I:801-802) suggest that they were the hired mourners who played a role in Jewish funerals during that time period. This seems to be the most likely possibility, but the mockers cannot be identified with certainty. In one sense, the scoffers were correct. The girl was, in fact, dead; what they did not recognize was Jesus' power to restore her to life.

Verses 54-55 describe how Jesus brings her back to life. First, He asks all who are present to leave. He then takes her by the hand and tells her to get up; the phrase can be literally translated, "Child, wake up" (Fitzmyer I:749). "Spirit" (Greek *pneuma*) can mean "breath," "wind," or "spirit." The return of breath to the lifeless body indicates that her physical life has been restored. Marshall (*Gospel* 348) suggests there is a parallel here between the actions of Jesus and those of the O. T. prophet Elijah. The young lady immediately gets up from her bed, and Jesus asks that she be given something to eat; "meat" in this context is an old English word meaning "food." The fact that she is able to get up and eat are additional proofs of her resuscitation.

Verse 56 concludes Luke's account of this miracle by describing how her parents and Jesus respond to these miraculous events. The parents are astonished. They are, no doubt, overjoyed to see their daughter alive, but they are unable to understand or explain what has happened. Jesus instructs them not to tell what has happened to others. Luke does not explain why Jesus makes this request, but many commentators suggest Jesus does so because He is not yet ready to reveal Himself publicly as the Messiah. See the discussions of Fitzmyer (I:749-750), Lieu (68), and Bock (I:805). Spence (211) suggests that the crowds around Jesus are growing and becoming more enthusiastic, and Jesus does not wish to increase this enthusiasm.

Summary (8:1-56)

The series of miracles narrated in Luke eight develops progressively the comprehensive nature of Jesus' lordship. He is Lord over the forces of nature, over the power of demons, and finally over sickness and death. Faith is important in all of these miracle stories, but it is more evident in some of them than in others. In some situations in His ministry, Jesus performs a miracle because someone has demonstrated faith in Him. In other situations, Jesus performs a miracle to produce faith or to strengthen an already-existing faith. Faith is obvious in the healings of the seriously-ill girl and the woman with the issue of blood. In both cases, there is a certain level of faith in Jesus, but it is undeveloped. In this chapter, "faith" does not necessarily imply saving faith; it reflects confidence in Jesus and His power to heal. As Bock (I:785) explains, "Essentially, faith is relying on Jesus to care for His disciples."

The healing of the demon-possessed man is very different. He is likely a pagan who has some knowledge of

Jesus; he falls down before Jesus and addresses Him as "thou Son of God most high." There is no indication at the beginning of the story that the man has any personal faith in Jesus. The miracle is clearly designed to produce faith in this unfortunate man. It is also likely that the miracle is designed to introduce Jesus to the Gentile people who live in that area.

The teachings found in this chapter are primarily designed to give to the disciples and others a more in-depth understanding of the Kingdom of God that Jesus is bringing to earth. The gospel must be heard and received; when it is, it will produce a miraculous harvest of souls. The gospel is like a lamp that gives light to the house. It must not be hidden where others cannot see it. It must be lived in the presence of the community.

The visit of Jesus' mother and brothers shows that being blood relatives of Jesus does not entitle them to special privileges. They must enter into His kingdom in the same way others do. In fact, Jesus makes clear to them that He has come to regard those who hear and do the will of God as His true spiritual family. That must have been difficult for Mary and the brothers to accept, but that was the reality of Jesus' earthly ministry.

Application: Teaching and Preaching the Passage

There are a number of important themes for preaching and teaching that grow out of this passage. One is the exclusiveness of the Kingdom of God. The relationship that exists between Jesus and His earthly family does not guarantee them entrance into the kingdom. They must enter it in the same way all others do, by personal faith in Jesus. The kingdom demands serious commitment. The women who provide financial support for the ministry of Jesus and His disciples illustrate this demand.

This chapter provides excellent texts for sermons or lessons on discipleship and commitment to Christ. God calls all of His followers to serve Him. Some will follow Jesus in their home communities; others will go into the far country. Faithful service, wherever it occurs, is the key.

Another important theme is Jesus' commitment to people. He responds in appropriate ways to their physical, emotional, and spiritual needs. He liberates a man who has long been under the control of demons who have destroyed his life. He intervenes to restore a young girl to life and heals a woman who has suffered for many years with an issue of blood. Jesus responds to people's real needs in a variety of different ways. In a world where so many people feel so alone, they need to hear that Jesus cares for them.

This chapter would serve well for sermons or lessons on the gospel message. The good news of Jesus Christ brings light into a dark world. It must not be hidden; it must be allowed to do its work. The Parable of the Sower is a very important passage dealing with the growth of the gospel message. There will be opposition; all the seed that is sown will not grow to maturity. Some will grow to maturity and will produce a great harvest. The Kingdom of God demands persistence.

The parables of Jesus are challenging. They are extremely valuable for preaching and teaching, but they have often been abused. As a general rule, the preacher or teacher should avoid trying to allegorize all the details of a parable. A better route is to look for the lesson or lessons that Jesus is presenting in a given parable and then seek to explain and apply those lessons for the benefit of our congregations today.

H. Jesus Trains His Disciples (9:1-50)

Luke 9:1-50 brings this portion of Jesus' ministry in Galilee to a close; He will return to Galilee for additional ministry in the future. The primary focus of this passage is on the training of the disciples. Jesus' goal is to prepare them for the difficult ministry that lies ahead for them. This passage may be divided into five sections: the disciples' preaching mission, the feeding of the 5,000, the Transfiguration, the healing of a demon-possessed boy, and two predictions of Jesus' passion (Plummer 238). Each of these sections will contribute in a significant way to the training of the disciples.

1 Then he called his twelve disciples together, and gave them power and authority over all devils, and to cure diseases.
2 And he sent them to preach the kingdom of God, and to heal the sick.
3 And he said unto them, Take nothing for *your* journey, neither staves, nor scrip, neither bread, neither money; neither have two coats apiece.
4 And whatsoever house ye enter into, there abide, and thence depart.
5 And whosoever will not receive you, when ye go out of that city, shake off the very dust from your feet for a testimony against them.
6 And they departed, and went through the towns, preaching the gospel, and healing every where.
7 Now Herod the tetrarch heard of all that was done by him: and he was perplexed, because that it was said of some, that John was risen from the dead;
8 And of some, that Elias had appeared; and of others, that one of the old prophets was risen again.
9 And Herod said, John have I beheaded: but who is this, of whom I hear such things? And he desired to see him.

This preaching and healing mission serves an important purpose in Luke's account of the life and ministry of Christ. Because Jesus is the Son of God, He not only has power to perform miracles; He can bestow that power on His apostles (Geldenhuys 264). This tour of Galilee gives the disciples their first real experience of ministry on their own without Jesus being physically present to guide and direct them. Stein (*Luke* 266) notes another important contribution of this missionary journey. It gave the disciples an opportunity to discuss and debate both among themselves and with others the things Jesus had said and done. As a result of this debate and discussion, the oral traditions about Jesus became fixed in their minds; these oral traditions would later be incorporated into the written Gospels. Fitzmyer (I:752) notes that this commission to preach and heal foreshadows the greater commission the disciples will later be given in Luke 24:46-47.

In verse 1, Jesus gives His apostles power and authority in two specific areas: first, to drive out demons, and second, to cure diseases. Summers (*Luke* 104) explains that the word "diseases" is a general term that may describe various illnesses. Since it is mentioned in connection with the devils, Summers also suggests it refers specifically to diseases that may be attributed to the presence of demons in a person. Stein (*Luke* 267) offers a different interpretation, that Luke is distinguishing between illness and demon possession.

In verse 2, Jesus gives them more specific instructions. They are, first, to preach the Kingdom of God and, second, to heal the sick. The specific content of the preaching is not spelled out. Lieu (69) suggests they are not to teach about the kingdom or announce its imminence. Rather, they are to stress the hope the Kingdom of God gives and the demands it makes on those who receive it. The healing of diseases and authority over the demons should be understood to indicate that the inauguration of the Kingdom of God on earth has begun. Jesus' dominion over disease and demons should be viewed as the fulfillment of messianic prophecies. The apostles are to proclaim that the Kingdom of God has come to earth in the person of Jesus Christ. Those who hear the message should respond to it with repentance and faith; they should accept the kingship and rule of God over their lives. For useful analyses of the Kingdom of God in the O. T. and the N. T. see Liefeld (155-156) and Fitzmyer (I:154-156).

Beginning in verse 3, Jesus gives them specific directions concerning how they should undertake this ministry. He instructs them to leave behind many of the things a traveler would normally carry on a journey; He tells them to take "nothing for *your* journey." Geldenhuys (266) understands this to mean they are to carry no extra provisions. Plummer (238) understands it to mean they are not to make any special provisions; they are to go as they are. The term "staff" refers to a walking stick such as traveling teachers often carried; Geldenhuys (266) suggests that in this context it may refer to an extra walking stick. "Scrip" (Greek *pēra*) may refer to a bag for carrying provisions or to a beggar's bag (Summers, *Luke* 105). The disciples are not to take bread or money. The "coat" refers to an inner garment or tunic worn beneath an outer robe (Summers, *Luke* 105). They are not to carry two tunics. In verse 4, they are told to enter into the first house that is willing to receive them and remain there as long as they are in the area. They should not waste their valuable time going from house to house, looking for more comfortable accommodations (Geldenhuys 265; Lieu 69).

In verses 5-6, Jesus tells His disciples that when a village refuses to listen to them, they are to shake the dust off their feet and leave. As they leave the village they are to stop and stomp their feet so they remove the dust that has accumulated (Summers, *Luke* 105). They are to do this "as a testimony against them." This means the apostles will break all ties to this village. The villagers have rejected the message, and the apostles have no more obligation toward them (Geldenhuys 265; Stein, *Luke* 268; Plummer 240). Fitzmyer (I:754) explains that shaking the dust off one's feet was a symbolic way of severing all association with a town or village. Jews returning to Palestine from pagan territories were expected to perform this ritual.

The instructions given here apply only to this specific journey. Different instructions will be given for later and longer journeys. In this passage, the main point is that the apostles need to learn to depend upon God and upon the hospitality of God's people (Stein, *Luke* 268).

Verse 6 reports, in summary, that the apostles do as they were instructed; they go throughout the villages in that part of Galilee preaching the Kingdom of God and healing. This demonstrates that the power and authority Jesus has given them is sufficient for the task (Geldenhuys 265).

Verses 7-9 interrupt briefly the story of the mission of the twelve; they describe the reaction the ministry of Jesus produced among the governing authorities. These verses may refer to Herod's reaction to the totality of Jesus' ministry (preaching, teaching, miracles, etc.) rather than just to this specific missionary tour (Plummer 240). By this time in His ministry, Jesus has attracted a large enough following to gain the attention of those in positions of power (Morris, *Luke* 165). Green (*Luke* 361) argues that the specific focus of these verses is on Jesus' ministry through His disciples. These verses pose the question, "Who is this Jesus?" In the following sections, Luke will answer this important question in different ways.

The Herod mentioned in this passage is Herod Antipas, the son of Herod the Great, who ruled Galilee and Perea from 4 B.C. to A.D. 39. Luke uses the correct technical term "tetrarch" to describe the position he holds (Bock I:822). "Tetrarch" was used in the Roman provincial administration for a ruler of lower rank and lesser authority than a king (Arndt and Gingrich 821). In Mark 6:14, Herod Antipas is described using the more popular term "king." Herod has heard several different explanations of Jesus' identity; Luke presents three of them in verses 7-8. First, he has heard that Jesus is John the Baptist whom he has already put to death. This may mean Jesus has the spirit of John the Baptist or He is a reincarnation of John the Baptist (Bock I:822). The second possibility is that Jesus is Elias (Elijah), the famous prophet of the O. T. The third possibility is that an un-named prophet from the O. T. has reappeared. Marshall (*Gospel* 356-357) explains that such beliefs were popular expectations rather than the fulfillment of O. T. prophecies. It was widely believed, for example, that Elijah would return to earth in the end times. Lenski (502) suggests that all three of these opinions require belief in a bodily resurrection. Other scholars would not agree with Lenski on this because Elijah was translated, and it is doubtful that the reappearance of one translation would require belief in a bodily resurrection.

Herod responds only to the first of these three opinions. Verse 9 reflects that he has heard different stories, but he does not seem to be convinced by any of them. He is particularly critical of the popular opinion that Jesus is some type of reappearance of John the Baptist because he has already had John the Baptist executed. In the latter part of the verse, Herod asks the important question, "Who is this?" He expresses a desire to meet Jesus in order to answer the question. Marshall (*Gospel* 357) explains that this desire is the result of curiosity and not of faith. At this point in the story, Luke does not mention that Herod will later meet Jesus, although not in the way he expects. Herod will later be associated with the Pharisees' opposition to Jesus in Luke 13:31 and with Jesus' trial before Pilate in Luke 23:7-12. That he "desired" (Greek imperfect tense) means he demonstrated a continuing desire to see Jesus (Plummer 242).

10 And the apostles, when they were returned, told him all that they had done. And he took them, and went aside privately into a desert place belonging to the city called Bethsaida.
11 And the people, when they knew *it*, followed him: and he received them, and spake unto them of the kingdom of God, and healed them that had need of healing.
12 And when the day began to wear away, then came the twelve, and said unto him, Send the multitude away, that they may go into the towns and country round about, and lodge, and get victuals: for we are here in a desert place.

In verse 10, Luke returns to the story of the mission of the twelve. He does not give the details of the disciples' report to Jesus; he simply notes that they share with Jesus what has transpired. Probably they focus on the great things God has done in the lives of the people they encountered. After hearing their report, Jesus takes the disciples to a solitary place near the town of Bethsaida, located on the north end of the Sea of Galilee and east of the Jordan River. This area lies outside the jurisdiction of Herod (Morris, *Luke* 166). Marshall (*Gospel* 358) explains that Bethsaida was a relatively new town, having been built on orders from Herod Philip. Luke probably mentions it because it is the town nearest to the remote area where Jesus takes His apostles. He offers no explanation why they go to this solitary place; perhaps it is to escape the crowds for a time and allow the apostles an opportunity to relax and rest. Lenski (504) suggests Jesus wants to confer privately with the apostles. Green (*Luke* 362) posits that they withdraw in order to pray. Summers (*Luke* 106) suggests this withdrawal may have been a time for rest or for further instruction.

Whatever their reasons for going to this solitary place, they are soon interrupted by the arrival of a crowd of people. Their arrival indicates there is much interest in Jesus and His ministry. John 6:2 mentions that the crowds were more interested in Jesus' miracles than in His teachings. Jesus does not try to send this crowd away; He receives them and teaches them about the Kingdom of God, although the content of Jesus' teaching is not given. He also heals those who have need of healing.

Apparently, the teaching and healing continue for several hours; Geldenhuys (270) suggests the phrase "when the day began to wear away" describes a time period shortly after midday. As the afternoon progresses, the disciples are afraid that some of the weaker members of the crowd may begin to suffer from heat and fatigue. The apostles make the obvious suggestion that Jesus should dismiss the crowd so they will have time to go to the surrounding towns and villages to find food and lodging before dark. Since some of the people might have been from the local area, they would have time to return to their homes where they might find food and lodging (Bock I:830). Sunset was the normal time for the evening meal (Marshall, *Gospel* 360).

13 But he said unto them, Give ye them to eat. And they said, We have no more but five loaves and two fishes; except we should go and buy meat for all this people.
14 For they were about five thousand men. And he said to his disciples, Make them sit down by fifties in a company.
15 And they did so, and made them all sit down.
16 Then he took the five loaves and the two fishes, and looking up to heaven, he blessed them, and brake, and gave to the disciples to set before the multitude.
17 And they did eat, and were all filled: and there was taken up of fragments that remained to them twelve baskets.

Jesus does not accept the suggestion made by the apostles that He dismiss the crowd. Instead, He gives His disciples instructions to do something that is physically impossible; they are told to provide food for this crowd of approximately 5,000 men. "Men" (Greek *anēr*) normally means adult males as distinct from women and children (Plummer 244). Matthew 14:21 notes that the crowd included "about five thousand men, beside women and children." Luke makes no specific mention of the presence of women or children. Morris (*Luke* 167) and Plummer (244) posit that such a crowd would have included only a small number of women and children.

The apostles recognize immediately the impossibility of the situation. They have neither sufficient food for such a large crowd nor the money to buy such a quantity—if it were available in the local area. They explain to Jesus that they have only five loaves of bread and two fish. Summers (*Luke* 107) explains that bread was normally baked in small round loaves about the size of a small hamburger bun. No indication is given about the size of the two fish—probably dried—or what kind of fish they were. Luke offers no explanation for the source of the loaves and fish; John 6:9 notes that a lad provided the five barley loaves and two small fish. This small amount of food would have been enough to sustain a young boy for a day, but it was not at all sufficient to feed a multitude.

Jesus then gave the disciples additional instructions. They were to have the crowd be seated on the ground in groups of fifty. After this was done, Jesus took the loaves and the fish, lifted His eyes toward Heaven, and blessed them. As Morris (*Luke* 167) explains, Jesus said a prayer of thanksgiving for the food God had provided. Ellis (139) gives an example of the kind of prayer that would be prayed on such an occasion. Jesus then began to break the loaves and the fish; the disciples distributed the food to the people. The people ate all they wanted, and the disciples gathered up twelve baskets of fragments after the meal was completed.

"Basket" (Greek *kophinos*) was the food sack or basket carried by a Jew so he would not have to buy food from Gentiles (Plummer 245; Geldenhuys 271). Ellis (139) suggests that each apostle gathered up one basket, but there is no evidence in the text to support such a conjecture.

Barclay (117) posits that there are two possible interpretations of this miracle. The first is that Jesus multiplied the bread and fish to provide sufficient food for such a large company. The second is that the people had brought food with them, but they were selfish and unwilling to share what they had with others. Jesus, by the example of His generosity, motivated the crowd to share their food so all were fed. The traditional interpretation is that Jesus in some miraculous way multiplied the bread and the fish to feed the multitude. There is nothing in the text to indicate the people had brought food with them or that they were unwilling to share it. Such an interpretation is pure conjecture.

This miracle is commonly known as the Feeding of the Five Thousand. The fact that it is narrated in all four Gospels (Mt. 14:13-21; Mk. 6:32-44; Jn. 6:1-15) indicates that it must have made a significant impact on the early church (Bock, *Luke* NIV 164). The context provides the key to a correct understanding of the meaning of this miracle. Through a series of teaching and events, including this miracle, Jesus gives His disciples a more complete understanding of the nature of His kingdom.

Marshall (*Gospel* 357) suggests that this miracle was designed to communicate a message more to the disciples than to the crowd. Jesus was consciously imitating certain miracles from the O. T., especially when Moses and Elijah multiplied the food to feed hungry people (Ex. 16; Num. 11; 2 Kgs. 4:42-44).

This miracle is the climax of Jesus' Galilean mission. At this stage in His ministry, Jesus is concerned to prepare the apostles for the difficult days that lie ahead. He wants them to understand, as fully as possible, who He is and what He came to do. He also wants them to understand that He can and will provide for the material and spiritual needs of His followers. Bock (*Luke* NIV 164) suggests this passage serves two purposes. First, it helps to identify Jesus. Second, it teaches the disciples that they can trust Jesus to supply their needs. According to Bock, the fact that Luke includes no reaction from the crowd indicates the teaching is for the apostles.

Lieu (70-71) closely connects this passage with Jesus' proclamation of His coming kingdom. The fact that twelve baskets full of scraps are gathered indicates that all Israel will be entitled to participate in the coming salvation. Marshall (*Gospel* 362) draws a comparison between the Lord's Supper and this miracle. He asserts that the Lord's Supper testifies to Jesus' ability to meet the spiritual needs of His followers, while this miracle establishes His ability to meet their physical needs. It is clear that this miracle teaches a lesson intended primarily for the disciples; they need a more complete understanding of who Jesus is and how He can provide for their needs (Bock, *Luke* NIV 165). There is no doubt that this miracle made a deep impression on them.

18 And it came to pass, as he was alone praying, his disciples were with him: and he asked them, saying, Whom say the people that I am?

19 They answering said, John the Baptist; but some *say*, Elias; and others *say*, that one of the old prophets is risen again.

20 He said unto them, But whom say ye that I am? Peter answering said, The Christ of God.
21 And he straitly charged them, and commanded *them* to tell no man that thing;
22 Saying, The Son of man must suffer many things, and be rejected of the elders and chief priests and scribes, and be slain, and be raised the third day.

This passage is another important part of the Lord's training program for His disciples. It is commonly known as Peter's Confession at Caesarea Philippi; it is found in all the Synoptic Gospels (Mt. 16:13-20; Mk. 8:27-30). Matthew and Mark locate this important confession in the area of Caesarea Philippi, a Greco-Roman city located in a Gentile area north of the Sea of Galilee. The population of this area was mostly pagan; in fact this was a center of the worship of pagan gods (Wilkins 557).

Again, Luke makes no attempt to explain where or when Peter's confession takes place. Ellis (139) suggests that Luke omits the information found in Matthew and Mark because he wished to connect this event directly with the feeding of the 5,000. Geldenhuys (273) posits that Luke omitted this material because he has only a limited amount of space on a roll of papyrus, and he records only the information that is necessary for his story. For Luke, the most important thing is how this account contributes to the training and development of the disciples. Luke places this event in the context of prayer. As Ellis (110) explains, Luke gives more emphasis to the role of prayer in the life and ministry of the Lord than any of the other evangelists.

The first part of verse 18 is somewhat difficult. Geldenhuys (275) suggests "alone," here, means "apart from," that Jesus was away from the multitude. Probably the idea is that Jesus was praying by Himself, away from the crowd, but His disciples were not far away. After He had finished His time of prayer, Jesus began a conversation with His disciples. At the beginning of this conversation, Jesus asked them for a summary of the people's opinion of Him. The disciples responded that the people held different views. Some thought He was John the Baptist—which is understandable in light of the fact that Jesus was a preacher of righteousness and repentance just as John was (Summers, *Luke* 108). Some suggested He was Elijah (or a reincarnation of Elijah). This view is also understandable; Jesus was a worker of miracles just as Elijah had been (Summers, *Luke* 108). A third suggestion was that one of the prophets from the O. T. had come back to life. Matthew 16:14 includes Jeremiah in the list. This is also understandable because Jesus, like Jeremiah, was known for His compassion. Lenski (510) notes that Jesus did not ask this question because He needed to know; He already understood perfectly the various opinions held by the people. He asked the question so these incorrect and incomplete views might be contrasted with the correct view that would be presented shortly.

In verse 20, Jesus asks the really important question, "But whom say ye that I am?" Peter answers, "The Christ of God." Matthew and Mark give slightly different renditions of Peter's answer: in Matthew 16:16, "Thou art the Christ, the Son of the living God"; in Mark 8:29, "Thou art the Christ." There is no serious difference between these responses; Luke's answer is brief and understandable to his Gentile readers. It is not clear whether Peter is speaking only for himself or for the disciples as a group. It is likely they had already discussed this question among themselves and Peter is presenting the shared view of the apostles.

Ellis (139) argues that up to this point in His ministry, Jesus had made no specific claim to be the Messiah. Based on His teachings and the miracles He had performed, His apostles had come to the conclusion that He must be the Jewish Messiah. Jesus does not condemn the apostles for this answer; His acquiescence implies they had come to a correct, but probably incomplete, understanding of who He was. In verse 21, Jesus orders the disciples not to share with others their conclusion that He is, in fact, the Messiah. Jesus offers no explanation for this order, but it is probably because a public proclamation of His messiahship would give a wrong impression. Many Jews of Jesus' day had a very political understanding of the Messiah. They considered him to be a figure who would free the Jews from Roman rule and restore Israel to a position of greatness. Jesus did not wish to encourage this type of thinking because that was not the type of Messiah He intended to be (Geldenhuys 274). At the proper time, Jesus would reveal Himself as the Messiah, but that hour had not yet arrived.

In verse 22, Jesus explains that His messiahship includes suffering, rejection, and death. He is to be killed and will arise on the third day. The elders, chief priests, and scribes were the leaders of the Jewish community in Palestine. They were the ones who had the power and authority; the mention of these three groups may indicate that Jesus had more support among the common people of the land than He had among the leaders. Since the leaders held the power in their hands, they were in a position to do harm to Jesus and His ministry.

Apparently, this information concerning Jesus' suffering and death is new and surprising to the disciples; they have, no doubt, been influenced by the popular political and military conceptions of the Messiah. In this verse, Jesus explains that the disciples' view of Him is not incorrect, but it is incomplete. Jesus is the Messiah, but He is not the type of Messiah the people envision. He will not accomplish His mission through military force or political action; He is a Messiah who accomplishes His mission through suffering and death (Bock, *Luke* NIV 167). The disciples need to understand they also will be involved in these sad events.

23 And he said to *them* all, If any *man* will come after me, let him deny himself, and take up his cross daily, and follow me.
24 For whosoever will save his life shall lose it: but whosoever will lose his life for my sake, the same shall save it.
25 For what is a man advantaged, if he gain the whole world, and lose himself, or be cast away?
26 For whosoever shall be ashamed of me and of my words, of him shall the Son of man be ashamed, when he shall come in his own glory, and *in his* Father's, and of the holy angels.
27 But I tell you of a truth, there be some standing here, which shall

not taste of death, till they see the kingdom of God.

These words provide a powerful lesson in discipleship; the apostles need to understand that to be a follower of Jesus requires a total commitment. As Green (*Luke* 372) explains, these words are not meant just for the twelve. They are meant for all of Jesus' disciples. Luke includes these words immediately after Peter's great confession, but there is no indication they were spoken right after that great event. Luke has placed them here because they are an important part of the training program for the disciples.

The words "if any man will come after me" imply much more than a casual commitment to follow Jesus when it is convenient to do so. They imply a commitment that is both deep and long lasting. Lenski (517) suggests it means to follow Christ, knowing He is going to His death. The words "deny himself" teach the disciple must lay aside anything that stands in the way of following Christ. This includes personal desires and ambitions, whether good or bad; self must take second place.

In the Roman Empire, the cross was an instrument of death; it was used to execute the most heinous offenders such as terrorists and slaves who killed their masters. The phrase "to take up the cross" does not refer to illness, financial reverses, family troubles, or other disasters that may occur in one's life (Geldenhuys 276). It refers specifically to doing the will of God even though it may lead to death (Summers, *Luke* 111; Marshall, *Gospel* 371-373; Morris, *Luke* 170). Jeremias (*Theology* 242) gives an insightful explanation of how this phrase would have been understood in the first century. The condemned criminal was required to carry the crosspiece (Latin *patibulum*) to the place of execution. As he went out from the judgment hall into the narrow streets of the city he would face a hostile, howling mob. He would be "an outcast, the helpless object of contempt and mockery." The question for the disciples is, "Are you willing to bear the hatred of men in order to serve Christ?"

Verse 24 presents a general statement about discipleship that applies to all of those who want to follow Jesus. The truth is presented in the form of a paradox. "To save one's life" means to hold on to it, preserve it, and to reserve it for one's own use. It means *not* to sacrifice one's life in the service of Christ. In this context, "to lose one's life" means to give up control of one's own destiny and dedicate oneself fully to the service of Christ. It means to place one's life in a position of total surrender to doing the will of God. The last words of verse 24 express the idea that only by placing one's life totally in the hands of God can one find real meaning and purpose in life. Only then can life become what it is intended by God to be. Jesus has confronted His disciples with a choice that they must make. They can follow Christ, or they can follow their own desires and inclinations. They cannot do both.

Verse 25 continues the thought of the previous verse with a rhetorical question designed to stimulate the disciples to think about the decision they are being called to make. "World" (Greek *kosmos*) is used in different ways in the Scripture. In this verse, it describes the things the world can provide for a human being; it may include material possessions, food, home, family, prestige, earthly satisfaction, etc. The phrase "lose himself or be cast away" also refers back to the previous verse. The underlying assumption is that real meaning and purpose in life are found in serving Christ. No one is going to gain "the whole world;" that is an impossible goal. But even if a person could gain the whole world, and miss the real meaning and purpose of life, what has he or she gained? In fact, such a person has not gained but lost. The disciple of Jesus must make a decision; he or she needs to make the right decision.

The two previous verses have described discipleship in general terms; in verses 26-27, Jesus applies these general teachings specifically to the disciples of His generation. He recognizes that the disciples may be "ashamed" of Him in the sense they are reluctant to identify publicly with a man who will be rejected, scorned, and ultimately crucified. This is a temptation the disciples must resist. The validity of Jesus' ministry and teachings is not determined by earthly popularity; it is determined by God, who has already placed His stamp of approval on His Son's ministry. They must resist this temptation because if they are ashamed of Jesus and His ministry while on earth, then Jesus will be "ashamed" of them at the time of His Second Coming. In other words, they need to confess Christ publicly while they are on earth for Jesus to confess they are His true disciples on the Day of Judgment. They will be held accountable for what they have said and done concerning the Son of God.

Verse 27 has provoked much discussion. Jesus tells His disciples that some standing there at that time will not taste death until they see the Kingdom of God come. There is little doubt that the phrase "taste of death" refers to physical death (Morris, *Luke* 171). The difficulty is to determine the correct meaning of the phrase "till they see the kingdom of God." Morris notes the Kingdom of God may come in different ways. Geldenhuys (277) explains Jesus is referring to a specific event, which will occur within the life time of that generation. Plummer (249-50) lists seven possible events that may satisfy this requirement, including the Transfiguration, the Resurrection and Ascension, the Day of Pentecost, the spread of Christianity, the destruction of Jerusalem, and the Second Coming of Christ. He concludes that the destruction of Jerusalem is the most likely of these events to fulfill this prediction of Jesus. Geldenhuys (277) agrees.

Morris (*Luke* 171) suggests another option. He argues that it may well refer to the complex of events surrounding Jesus' death, burial, resurrection, and the coming of the Spirit. There is much to commend this view; these events marked an important step in the inauguration of the Kingdom of God on earth. This is a difficult passage, and it is impossible to determine exactly what event (or events) Jesus had in mind. One thing, however, is clear. The disciples will experience the inauguration of the Kingdom of God within their lifetime, and they must be prepared for it.

28 And it came to pass about an eight days after these sayings, he took Peter and John and James, and went up into a mountain to pray.
29 And as he prayed, the fashion of his countenance was altered, and his raiment *was* white *and* glistering.

30 And, behold, there talked with him two men, which were Moses and Elias:
31 Who appeared in glory, and spake of his decease which he should accomplish at Jerusalem.
32 But Peter and they that were with him were heavy with sleep: and when they were awake, they saw his glory, and the two men that stood with him.
33 And it came to pass, as they departed from him, Peter said unto Jesus, Master, it is good for us to be here: and let us make three tabernacles; one for thee, and one for Moses, and one for Elias: not knowing what he said.
34 While he thus spake, there came a cloud, and overshadowed them: and they feared as they entered into the cloud.
35 And there came a voice out of the cloud, saying, This is my beloved Son: hear him.
36 And when the voice was past, Jesus was found alone. And they kept *it* close, and told no man in those days any of those things which they had seen.

This famous passage is Luke's account of the Transfiguration; it is also found in Matthew 17:1-13 and Mark 9:2-13. The term "transfiguration" is not found in Luke's account; it is based on Matthew 17:2, which says Jesus "was transfigured before them." "Transfigure" (Greek *metamorphoō*) means "to be changed in form" or "to be transformed." Luke explains this in greater detail; Jesus' countenance was changed and His clothing appeared radiant and glistening. This passage is similar to the description of Moses' glory in Exodus 34:29-35. Marshall (*Gospel* 383) suggests that Jesus has been transformed while in prayer and has come to reflect the glory of the divine nature. Plummer (251) and Bock (I:867) suggest Luke avoids the verb "transfigured" because his Gentile readers might associate it with the metamorphosis of the pagan gods. It is clear that a radical change in Jesus' outward appearance took place, and the disciples correctly attributed this change to Christ's special relationship with His Father.

Luke's goal in this passage is to instill in the minds of three of Jesus' closest disciples a better understanding of His deity. Since Jesus had come to earth as a human being, it is likely the disciples recognized the fullness of His humanity. They understood Him to be a full and complete human being, but it is doubtful they recognized the full extent of His deity. In this passage, God takes the initiative to assure Jesus' followers that He is more than a great human being. He is, at the same time, the Son of God and the embodiment of deity.

According to Luke's account, this historic event took place approximately eight days (which would be about a week) after Peter's confession or after Jesus' instruction on the meaning of discipleship. Matthew and Mark say the event took place after six days. Jesus went up into a mountain with three of His closest disciples, Peter, James, and John, but the mountain is not specifically identified. Three places are commonly suggested: Mt. Herman (near Caesarea Philippi), Mt. Tabor (about six miles from Nazareth), and Mt. Meron (northwest of the Sea of Galilee). For a discussion of the identity of the mountain see Bock (I:866) and Marshall (*Gospel* 382-383).

The presence of Moses and Elijah at the Transfiguration has led to much debate about the role they play. Moses was clearly one of the most important characters in the O. T. He led the people out of Egypt and to the border of the Promised Land; he was responsible for writing down the laws God gave His people. Elijah was one of the most important of the prophets; one who performed a number of miracles. That they appear in this important event and pay homage to Jesus is an indication of His superiority over them.

These two men appear in glory and speak of Jesus' "decease which he should accomplish in Jerusalem." "Decease" (in Greek) is, literally "exodus." The idea is that Jesus, by His death in Jerusalem, will accomplish an even greater exodus than Moses was able to accomplish in the O. T. Plummer (251) suggests that "decease" has reference to Jesus' death, resurrection, and ascension. For more detailed discussions of the role played by Moses and Elijah see Bock (I:868-870); Marshall (*Gospel* 383-384); and Morris (*Luke* 172).

Peter, James, and John enter the story in verse 32. The fact they are tired and asleep when the Transfiguration begins may indicate that this event occurs during the night. They wake up, see Christ's glory and Moses and Elijah with Him. Lieu (75) points out that the word "glory," in the O. T., is "the expression of the inexpressible presence of God." It is doubtful these three apostles comprehend fully the significance of the Transfiguration, but this important event serves to increase their understanding of Jesus and His mission.

As Moses and Elijah enter into the cloud, Peter makes a comment and then offers a suggestion. His comment, "it is good for us to be here," often receives little attention from commentators. Lenski (533) suggests the word "good" (Greek *kalos*) be translated "excellent" here. Morgan (*Luke* 127) and Lenski (533) explain that it is good for the disciples to see Christ in this way; it is good for them to see Him in His glory.

Peter then offers a suggestion; he wants to build three tabernacles, one for Jesus, one for Moses, and one for Elijah. That he did not know what he said probably means that Peter did not really understand the implications of his proposal. The word "tabernacle" comes from the O. T., where it is used for the tent or tabernacle in which the Jews worshiped prior to the construction of the Temple, and also for a hut or other temporary shelter such as the tabernacles used during the Feast of Tabernacles (Morris, *Luke* 172; Marshall, *Gospel* 387). Luke does not explain why Peter wishes to build these tabernacles, but it is likely that his goal is to prolong the experience (Geldenhuys 282; Lenski 533). Bock (I:870-871) suggests another reason: that Peter's goal is to celebrate the Feast of Tabernacles on the mountain. The Feast of Tabernacles was an important celebration in first-century Judaism. It reminded the people of God's provision during the Exodus; it also looked forward to God's provision in the future.

While Peter was speaking, a cloud overshadowed them. The precise significance of the cloud is debated; Liefeld (927-928) gives a good discussion of the various possibilities. One thing is clear; it symbolized the presence of God as in Exodus 19:16. Out of the cloud came a voice which said, "This is my beloved Son: hear him." The speaker, though not identified, is clearly God (Marshall,

Gospel 387). Marshall notes that this passage is similar to words spoken by God at the baptism of Jesus in Luke 3:22. There is, however, one important difference. At the baptism, God speaks *to* Jesus; at the Transfiguration, God speaks to the disciples *about* Jesus. The voice of God clearly affirms for the disciples the ministry of suffering, which lies ahead for Jesus. This is God's confirmation of the rectitude of Jesus' mission as a suffering Messiah. Lieu (76) suggests that the command "hear him" may be related to the command given in Deuteronomy 18:15, "The LORD thy God will raise up unto thee a Prophet from the midst of thee, of thy brethren, like unto me; unto him ye shall hearken."

Verse 36 concludes the story of Jesus' Transfiguration. Moses and Elijah are gone; the voice of God ceases to speak. Jesus is left alone with His three closest disciples. The clause "and they kept it close" probably means the disciples kept the story of the Transfiguration to themselves. During the earthly ministry of Jesus, they told no one what they had seen and experienced. According to Matthew 17:9, Jesus instructed Peter, James, and John to tell no one the story until after His resurrection. Neither Luke nor Matthew give a reason for this. Bock (I:875) posits that even the disciples did not have, at that time, a complete understanding of the nature of Jesus' ministry. The premature dissemination of this information might lead to misunderstandings and might even encourage the kind of political and military views of the Messiah that were common in first-century Palestine.

37 And it came to pass, that on
the next day, when they were come
down from the hill, much people
met him.
38 And, behold, a man of the com-
pany cried out, saying, Master, I
beseech thee, look upon my son:
for he is mine only child.
39 And, lo, a spirit taketh him,
and he suddenly crieth out; and it
teareth him that he foameth again,
and bruising him hardly departeth
from him.
40 And I besought thy disciples to
cast him out; and they could not.
41 And Jesus answering said, O
faithless and perverse generation,
how long shall I be with you, and
suffer you? Bring thy son hither.
42 And as he was yet a coming,
the devil threw him down, and tare
***him*. And Jesus rebuked the**
unclean spirit, and healed the
child, and delivered him again to
his father.

After Jesus has come down from the Transfiguration, a man who is deeply troubled because his only son is demon-possessed, cries out to Him from the crowd. Bock (*Luke* IVP 175) explains that in ancient cultures sons were highly prized, and only sons especially so. The words "look upon" mean "to look upon with pity"; this is an invitation to Jesus to bring healing to this deeply-troubled boy. The symptoms are described in verses 39 and 42; the evil spirit suddenly comes upon the boy and causes him to cry out. These attacks bring convulsions and cause him to foam at the mouth. Verse 42 adds the additional detail that these attacks threw him to the ground. These details paint a picture of a serious condition the boy has experienced for several years. The symptoms are very similar to the disease known today as epilepsy. Lenski (540) suggests it is not an ordinary case of epilepsy, but an especially severe case brought on by demonic activity.

At some time in the past, the father has taken his son to Jesus' disciples, but they could do nothing for him. His hope is that Jesus will do what His disciples could not do, restore his only son to health. In verse 42, Jesus does exactly that; He heals the boy and returns him to his father.

In verse 41, Jesus responds to this sad situation by crying out, "O faithless and perverse generation, how long shall I be with you, and suffer you?" Luke does not say to whom these words are addressed; both the crowd and the disciples of Jesus are present. According to Marshall (*Gospel* 391), Jesus' rebuke is directed to the entire group: the father, the crowd, and the disciples. Green (*Luke* 388) notes that the disciples have previously been given power over demons (Lk. 9:1). For that reason, he believes the rebuke is directed primarily at the disciples, although the crowd is not entirely innocent. They are unbelieving as well.

43 And they were all amazed at the mighty power of God. But while they wondered every one at all things which Jesus did, he said unto his disciples,
44 Let these sayings sink down into your ears: for the Son of man shall be delivered into the hands of men.
45 But they understood not this saying, and it was hid from them, that they perceived it not: and they feared to ask him of that saying.

The crowd is amazed by what they have seen and heard; they have seen the mighty power of God at work. While the crowd continues to ponder these events, Jesus takes advantage of this situation to speak with His disciples. Luke does not explain whether Jesus talks with His disciples in the presence of the crowd or whether He takes them aside for a private conversation. Luke focuses his attention on what is said.

"These sayings" are the things the disciples had seen and heard; Luke does not specify which particular sayings Jesus has in mind. Probably Jesus has specifically in mind those sayings that deal with His suffering and betrayal into the hands of men. The disciples had seen Jesus transfigured; they had also seen Him heal a demon-possessed boy. These are powerful testimonies to the power and position of Jesus; they demonstrate that He is indeed the Son of God and His Father has bestowed divine power upon Him.

The second part of the verse is the other side of the coin. Jesus has spoken to them about what He must suffer and what they will suffer for being His disciples. Jesus is the Messiah, but His messianic ministry will be accomplished by suffering, death, and resurrection. Green (*Luke* 390) reminds us of these two realities, Jesus' exaltation and humiliation, are often presented together. Although He is the Son of God, He will suffer rejection at the hands of human beings.

Verse 45 reveals the disciples' lack of a true understanding of the significance of these teachings. They cannot understand how Jesus can be the Messiah and, at the same time, suffer shame and humiliation. As Green (*Luke* 390-391) explains, the honor and shame culture in which they have lived all their lives makes it difficult for them to understand how Christ's exalted nature and His humiliation can be reconciled. Lenski (541) notes that the disciples must not allow their admiration for the miracles He has performed to obscure their understanding of the suffering that lies ahead. The phrase "it was hid from them" may mean that God had prevented them from fully comprehending Jesus' sayings about suffering and death. Or it may mean that Satan or their own limitations stood in the way (Bock, *Luke* NIV 277). At this point in the ministry, they are reluctant to ask Jesus for more explanation. They are probably somewhat confused and embarrassed by their lack of understanding.

46 Then there arose a reasoning among them, which of them should be greatest.
47 And Jesus, perceiving the thought of their heart, took a child, and set him by him,
48 And said unto them, Whosoever shall receive this child in my name receiveth me: and whosoever shall receive me receiveth him that sent me: for he that is least among you all, the same shall be great.

The connection between these verses and the previous ones is thematic rather than chronological. As often, Luke does not indicate when or where this event happens. It is placed here because it continues to develop the theme of the disciples' lack of understanding. Mark 9:33 explains that this event happened in Capernaum, which was the headquarters for Jesus' Galilean ministry. "Reasoning" (Greek *dialogismos*) can have several different meanings; here it conveys the sense of a debate or an argument. Probably, the disciples are debating which of them will occupy the places of honor (those nearest to Jesus) in the Kingdom of God. It includes issues of position, prestige, and rank (Marshall, *Gospel* 395). This type of rivalry is not surprising since it reflects the natural desire of human beings. Jesus had, after all, given special privileges to Peter, James, and John.

Because He is the Son of God, Jesus understands fully the thoughts of His disciples. In the ancient world, the "heart" is often the center of thought and intention; that is the way it is used here. Jesus responds to this conflict with an illustration. He brings a small child and has the child stand beside Him. He then tells His disciples that to receive the child in His name is to receive Him, and to receive Him is to receive the Father who sent Him. Children were not highly regarded in the ancient world; they were viewed as powerless and unable to contribute to society in a meaningful way (Bock, *Luke* NIV 278; Morris, *Luke* 176; Green, *Luke* 391). For an extensive analysis of the status of children in the ancient world see Oepke (TDNT V:639-654).

The phrase "in my name" has provoked considerable discussion. It normally carries the connotation of "by my power" or "on my authority." That doesn't seem to be the meaning here. Summers (*Luke* 120) suggests that in this context the meaning is "in one's place" or "as one's representative." The idea is that the disciples are to act as Jesus' representatives; they are to receive this little child as Jesus would receive him. Accepting a child in this way would be an act of humble service, and that is precisely the point Jesus wishes to make. The disciples should be concerned with humbly serving in the Kingdom of God; issues of position and influence are of no importance. Those who are truly great among the apostolic band are those who humbly serve.

49 And John answered and said, Master, we saw one casting out devils in thy name; and we forbad him, because he followeth not with us.
50 And Jesus said unto him, Forbid *him* not: for he that is not against us is for us.

One of the important themes in this portion of Luke is the spiritual immaturity of the disciples. Even though they have been with Jesus for some time, they still have a great deal to learn. John has observed an unnamed individual casting out demons in the name of Jesus. Luke does not explain where or when this happened; once again, the event is more important than the circumstances. Apparently, this person was doing what the disciples were commissioned to do in Luke 9:1 but were unable to do in Luke 9:40. John and his fellow apostles forbade the person to cast out demons, probably because they were jealous of their position with Jesus. Neither did they want to see the ministry of Jesus compromised by unworthy persons. The phrase "in thy name" means this individual was doing the exorcisms by the authority of Jesus. "Followeth not with us" means this individual was not one of the official followers of Jesus who traveled with Him and learned from Him.

Jesus gives an unexpected reply. "Forbid him not" is a construction (Greek *mē* with present imperative) that often forbids an action already in progress. It could be translated "stop forbidding him." Jesus then lays down an important general principle. If the person is doing the same thing that Jesus and His disciples are doing, he is not working against them but with them. The disciples need to learn that the power of God is not limited to a select few official representatives. They will soon find out that Jesus has a multitude of disciples from many different places.

Summary (9:1-50)

This section of Luke marks a significant turning point in the ministry of Jesus. He begins to focus His attention on preparing His disciples for His future suffering and death (Bock, *Luke* IVP 166). This focus on the training and equipping of the disciples will continue throughout the remainder of Jesus' earthly ministry. Coleman (38-43) provides a useful overview of the time Jesus spent with them; he notes that during the Passion Week, Jesus hardly let the disciples out of His sight.

In His preaching and teaching, Jesus discards the traditional models of messiahship with their political and military overtones. His concept of messiahship is based on humility, service, and suffering. Jesus' earthly ministry will not end in physical triumph but in death. This death will not, however, be the final word. On the third day He will be raised from the dead, and His concept of messiahship will gain the final victory.

This section also reflects a significant stage in the developing concept of the Kingdom of God, as Jesus imparts to His disciples the true meaning of being a member. The Kingdom of God is not like earthly kingdoms that depend on conquest and military might for their continued existence. It is a kingdom based on humility and service; the key element is that those who are members of this kingdom do the will of God.

This passage also reflects a significant development in the concept of discipleship. Jesus confronts His disciples with the bitter reality that a difficult road lies ahead for them and for all true followers of Jesus. He demands a high degree of commitment and sacrifice; their commitment to Him may even cost them their lives. In this passage, Jesus answers this important question, "What is greatness in the Kingdom of God?"

The chapter begins with the mission of the twelve closest followers of Jesus. They are sent out on their own for the first time. They will no longer observe as Jesus carries on the ministry; they themselves are now responsible to put into practice what they have been learning from Him. In Luke 9:2, they are sent out to preach the Kingdom of God; in Luke 9:6, they go from village to village preaching the gospel. The similarity between these two expressions indicates there is little difference between preaching the gospel and preaching the Kingdom of God. The good news that the Messiah has come is the very heart of the proclamation of the kingdom.

Jesus gives His disciples some rather unusual instructions. Rather than following the pattern set by many religious teachers of that era, they are not to go from house to house asking for money. They are to "travel light" and accept such hospitality as is offered to them. If a certain village does not welcome them, they are to shake the dust off their feet and go to another.

This preaching mission met with a considerable degree of success; the disciples were able to preach and heal the sick. This successful mission and the things that Jesus had done were enough to raise concern among those who were in positions of power and authority. Even Herod the tetrarch was perplexed and did not know what to think.

After the return of the disciples, Jesus takes them on a retreat to the town of Bethsaida, but they are not able to escape the crowds for long. Jesus does not tell the crowds to go away; He begins to teach them. The hour is growing late and the people are hungry. Instead of sending them away to their homes or to find lodging in nearby areas, Jesus orders the disciples to feed them. He multiplies the five loaves and two fish and feeds a hungry multitude; everyone's hunger is fully satisfied and there is food to spare. This miracle must have made a great impact on both the disciples and the crowd.

The next section of chapter nine is devoted to Peter's confession. Peter serves as the spokesman for the apostolic band, and Jesus asks him two questions: "Who do the people say that I am?" and "Who do you say that I am?"—which is the really important one. Peter responds that Jesus is the Christ of God. In other words, the disciples believe and confess that Jesus is the Messiah sent from God. Jesus instructs them not to tell this to anyone. Probably the idea is that they are not to share this information now. In the future, there will be time and opportunity to publicly proclaim that Jesus of Nazareth is indeed the Messiah.

After Peter's confession, Jesus gives the first prediction of His coming passion. This is the first prediction of His suffering and death to be given in Luke; it may be the first time Jesus has taught the disciples about the difficult days that lie ahead. It is crucial that the disciples understand what lies ahead; it will not be easy to be a faithful follower of Jesus.

The prediction of the passion is followed by several verses that emphasize the high level of commitment and dedication that Jesus' disciples must demonstrate. Those who wish to save their lives for themselves will lose them. Only those who willingly lose their lives in the service of Christ will find the true meaning of life. This is the great paradox of discipleship.

The Transfiguration is one of the truly great events narrated in the Gospels; it serves to confirm Jesus' deity. The disciples may now go forth into an uncertain future with the confidence that God has confirmed the divine power and authority of Christ.

Following the Transfiguration, Jesus performs another miracle of healing, delivering a young boy that is convulsed by an evil spirit. This miracle serves to convince all who witness it of the greatness of Jesus. This miracle is immediately followed by the second prediction of the passion. Jesus tells His disciples that He will be betrayed into the hands of evil men. This prediction produces consternation among the disciples; they are afraid, at this point, to ask Jesus for further clarification.

This section of Luke concludes with two lessons for His disciples. They are arguing over which of them is the greatest, precisely the kind of thing that worldly men do. In response to this sad conflict, Jesus takes a child, the symbol of innocence and dependence, and has the child stand beside Him. Then He tells the disciples that in order to be great in His kingdom, they must become like this young child. The second lesson concerns an unnamed individual who, although not a member of the apostolic band, is casting out demons in Jesus' name. The disciples had tried to stop the man, but they were unable to do so. Apparently, John thinks Jesus will stop this man from casting out demons in His name, but Jesus gives an unexpected reply. He tells the disciples to cease trying to stop the man. If he is not against the work Jesus is doing, he is for it. The work of the kingdom cannot be limited just to the circle of Jesus' immediate followers. Both of these teachings speak of the kind of humility and service true disciples render. It is doubtful the disciples understood the full impact of these teachings at that time, but the principles taught here have become an important part of God's work in the world.

Application: Teaching and Preaching the Passage

This portion of chapter nine is dominated by two closely-related questions. The first is, "Who is Jesus?" The second is "What kind of Messiah is He?" Much of the information in these verses is intended for the disciples. It is important that all men understand who Jesus is, but the disciples must learn that lesson first. It is from them the men and women of the Roman Empire will hear the message. Jesus does not give quick and simple answers to either of these important questions. Instead, through a series of words and deeds, He outlines for the disciples the kind of Messiah He will be and the kind of kingdom He has come to earth to create.

First, this passage affirms that Jesus is a merciful Savior. In the early portion of the chapter, Jesus sends the disciples out to heal the sick and preach the gospel. Later, He multiplies the fish and the loaves of bread to feed 5,000 hungry people who have listened to His teaching. Then Jesus heals the only son of a desperate father. Our teaching and preaching should stress that Jesus is a Savior who really cares about people and intervenes on their behalf. We should never be guilty of rigidly separating between the preaching of the gospel and helping to meet human needs in appropriate ways. Jesus did not make such a separation.

Second, these verses affirm that Jesus is a powerful Savior. He has the power to heal the sick and cast out demons. He not only has that power Himself, He also is able to bestow that power on His disciples. He has the power to multiply five loaves and two fish, satisfy the hunger of a large group of people, and have food left over. He also has power to heal a boy who is suffering greatly. It should be noted, however, that Jesus never uses His power in a selfish way. He uses it only for good and for the advancement of His kingdom.

Third, this passage emphasizes that Jesus is a divine Savior. The people of Jesus' day wondered about who He was and what He had come to earth to do. It is clear that even His disciples had difficulty understanding Him. The Transfiguration experience helps to clarify the situation. It establishes that Jesus is much more than a prophet or a great teacher sent by God. He is the very Son of God who possesses all the divine attributes. Modern Christians live in a very pluralistic world that wants to place Jesus on an equal footing with other great religious teachers of the past. We must always resist that temptation. We must show by our lives and by our testimonies that we regard Jesus as the unique Son of God and the world's only Savior.

Discipleship is another important theme developed in these verses. Jesus takes His teaching in a new direction. He begins by outlining the kind of suffering He must endure, the death He will die, and the resurrection He will experience. There is no doubt the disciples found that kind of message a bitter pill to swallow.

For the first time in Luke, Jesus speaks of the suffering and sacrifice the disciples will encounter because of their commitment to Him. Those who wish to follow Him must deny themselves, take up the cross, and follow Him on a daily basis. The road will not be easy; it may well end in their deaths. These themes are important in our preaching and teaching. We should present the joys and blessings that come from following Jesus, but we should never be afraid to share the hardships and sacrifices as well. We should never teach or preach that following Jesus will be an easy path to follow.

Finally, the disciples reflect a considerable amount of spiritual immaturity. They argue about which of them is the greatest; they also try to hinder someone from outside their group who is casting out demons in the name of Jesus. These two incidents point out an important lesson. Disciples can be immature; they may say and do things they should not. We should certainly do everything we can to help one another grow and mature as disciples. We also need to realize that the work of the Kingdom of God goes on in spite of our spiritual immaturity.

V. JESUS' JOURNEY TO JERUSALEM (9:51—19:44)

A. Commitment to Ministry (9:51—10:24)

This section of Luke is known by various names. Ellis (146) and Hendriksen (*Luke* 529) call it "the central section." Fitzmyer (I:823) entitles it "the so-called travel account," but it is most commonly known as "The Travel Narrative." This title comes from the fact that these chapters contain several references to Jesus' journey to Jerusalem (9:51, 53, 56; 13:22; 17:11; 18:31; 19:28). Marshall (*Historian* 149) correctly notes that not all of the segments of this section include a travel motif.

This passage—long a source of difficulty for students—raises two questions. The first concerns the number of trips Luke is describing: one or more than one? The second question concerns the relationship between Luke and John. Interpreters generally agree that John mentions three visits to Jerusalem (chapters 7, 11, 12). Robertson (*Harmony* 278) argues that Luke also mentions three visits to Jerusalem in this section (9:51; 13:22; 17:11).

Hendriksen (*Luke* 542-543) summarizes the three main positions taken by scholars on this issue. He notes, first, that some follow Robertson in arguing for three visits to Jerusalem, but this view has never developed a widespread following. Second, there are scholars who assert that we simply do not know how many visits Jesus made to Jerusalem because Luke does not give us sufficient information to come to a definite conclusion.

Third, the most popular view is that this entire passage describes one final visit to Jerusalem that begins in Capernaum and ends with Jesus' death, burial, and resurrection in Jerusalem. A. Bruce (EGT I:567) and Green (*Luke* 394-399) analyze this trip.

There is general agreement that a natural division of Luke begins at 9:51. There is, however, no general agreement on where this section ends. Lieu (80) concludes it at 11:13. For Lenski (552), the next division falls at 18:3. According to Shepard (376), the natural ending to this passage comes at 18:14. For Bonnet and Schroeder (556) the end falls at 18:15 where Luke rejoins the discussion as presented by Matthew and Mark. Kümmel (*Introduction* 125) finds the end at 19:27. Bock (*Luke* IVP 179) and Geldenhuys (291) continue the passage through 19:44. In another work, Bock (II:957) outlines the viewpoints of leading scholars on this issue; their endings for this important passage range from 18:14 through 19:48. For purposes of this commentary, the section will end at 19:44.

Marshall (*Historian* 149-153) gives an overview of the major themes presented in this important passage and a summary of how the Travel Narrative is interpreted by leading scholars. He notes that the motif of travel is a common one in Luke. Beginning in 4:42, Jesus is often on the move as He begins His public ministry. The Travel Narrative takes up approximately 390 verses or about one-third of the Gospel's entire contents. This passage contains several different kinds of material and departs significantly from the outline of Mark that Luke has followed previously. Lieu (80) notes that much of the material found in this section is not found in Mark; some of the material is found in Matthew. Miracles play only a small role in these chapters; they are dominated by two concerns: discipleship and the growing conflict between Jesus and the Jewish authorities.

Bonnet and Schroeder (566) note the important contribution these chapters make to the overall structure of this Gospel. They point out that Luke's presentation is neither strictly geographical nor strictly chronological. Jesus leaves His evangelistic mission long enough to make a trip to Jerusalem for the Feast of Dedication. After this visit, He resumes His work in Galilee and Perea. These chapters serve to fill in a large gap left in the narratives of Matthew and Mark who give little attention to events taking place between the Transfiguration and Jesus' arrival in Jerusalem for the Passover. This portion of Luke serves to fill in the story and contributes much to Jesus' teaching.

As mentioned above, Ellis (146) does not describe these chapters as the "Travel Narrative"; he prefers "central division." He argues, in fact, that it is improper to refer to this material as "The Travel Narrative," suggesting that—beginning at Luke 4:42—Jesus is presented as having no home, always on the move, always on a mission. Luke assumes the freedom to include incidents taken from various times in Jesus' ministry without regard to a rigid chronological order. In Luke 10:38-42, Jesus seems to be on the outskirts of Jerusalem, while in 13:31 and following He is again in Galilee or Perea.

Summers (*Luke* 122) points out that Jesus begins His journey to Jerusalem in 9:51, but does not arrive until 19:28. Luke first describes incidents that occur in Samaria; then Jesus returns to Galilee; Luke next cites events in Perea on the way to Jerusalem. Luke follows this with material relating to the border between Samaria and Galilee. The section concludes with material located in Judea. It is clear that Luke's controlling purpose in this section is neither geographical nor chronological, but theological. As Summers (*Luke* 122) explains, "There was one thing which loomed above everything else and took precedence over everything else—the journey to Jerusalem where death awaited Him."

Hoehner (*Antipas* 216) notes that the material in this portion of Luke is arranged thematically rather than chronologically. He believes it is virtually impossible to determine the precise chronological order in which the events occurred. Luke's goal in this section is to present Jesus as a teacher rather than as a traveler.

D. Guthrie (*Introduction* 98) offers a somewhat different analysis and suggests that "the journey motive may never really have been in Luke's mind." He argues that Luke has collected a group of materials relating to the final period in Jesus' earthly ministry and has fitted them in between the Galilean and Judean ministries.

Most commentators recognize that the preparation and training of the disciples is a major motif of the Travel Narrative. As Jesus moves toward Jerusalem where He will face the ultimate crisis of His earthly ministry, it is imperative that the disciples be as prepared as possible for what lies ahead of them. Discipleship is the theme that provides the key to unlocking this complex and somewhat difficult section. In the Travel Narrative, Luke outlines several different elements he views as integral to the training of the disciples. In particular, he presents discipleship as prayer, commitment, wisdom, and understanding.

The second major theme developed in the Travel Narrative is the escalating conflict between Jesus and His opponents. This information will be of great value to the disciples and to later generations of believers because they will live and work in a world where they will encounter much hostility (Ellis 146-147).

Geldenhuys (291) explains that this section may be the most important part of Luke's Gospel because it preserves a large amount of material that is not found in the other Gospels. It also records some parables, which are found only in Luke, such as the Good Samaritan, the Prodigal Son, the Lost Sheep, and the Lost Coin.

51 And it came to pass, when the time was come that he should be received up, he stedfastly set his face to go to Jerusalem,
52 And sent messengers before his face: and they went, and entered into a village of the Samaritans, to make ready for him.
53 And they did not receive him, because his face was as though he would go to Jerusalem.
54 And when his disciples James and John saw *this*, they said, Lord, wilt thou that we command fire to come down from heaven, and consume them, even as Elias did?
55 But he turned, and rebuked them, and said, Ye know not what manner of spirit ye are of.
56 For the Son of man is not come to destroy men's lives, but to save *them*. And they went to another village.

As they are making their way toward Jerusalem, Jesus sends messengers—probably some of His disciples—into an un-named Samaritan village to make preparations for His arrival. It is likely they have gone ahead to prepare overnight accommodations for the group (Summers, *Luke* 122). Luke's account is brief; he gives few details because he is most concerned with the event itself. Luke does not explain, for example, whether the group includes only the Twelve or a larger group of Jesus' followers. The messengers are not well received; the people of the village refuse to provide the requested hospitality. Luke explains that they refused "because his face was as though he would go to Jerusalem."

Their refusal to assist Jesus and His followers is probably due to the long history of hostility between the Jews and the Samaritans. For a good overview of the development of this hostility see Jeremias (*Jerusalem* 352-358). Geldenhuys (293) explains that this hostility can be traced to the early period of the history of Israel, perhaps to the time of the judges and the early monarchy. It became more pronounced in the time of Ezra and Nehemiah when the Samaritans were not permitted to help in the rebuilding of the Temple in Jerusalem. The Samaritans responded by building their own temple and establishing their own system of worship on Mt. Gerizim.

The conflict between these two groups was especially bitter in the time of Jesus. Jeremias (*Jerusalem* 353) notes that during the reign of Procurator Coponius (about A.D. 6-9) several Samaritans entered the Temple in Jerusalem, in the middle of the night, during the Passover and defiled it by scattering human bones.

This passage raises questions about why Jesus chose to go through Samaria and why the inhabitants there chose to reject Him. Lieu (81) suggests that most Jewish pilgrims crossed the Jordan River and traveled south through Transjordan to avoid this area. Marshall (*Gospel* 406) disagrees; he argues that Jewish pilgrims normally traveled through Samaria on their way to Jerusalem. He notes, however, that relationships between the two groups were strained, and that even friendly overtures might be rejected. Manson (*Sayings* 256) concurs that Jewish pilgrims often traveled through Samaria.

Ellis (151) suggests Jesus was no ordinary pilgrim and that the rejection by the Samaritans had a special meaning for Luke. Jesus had previously been rejected by the Jews in Nazareth (4:28-29) and by the Gentiles in Gerasa (8:37). The rejection in Samaria continues this pattern of rejection. Ellis implies that Jesus traveled through Samaria for the specific purpose of continuing this tradition of rejection. Fitzmyer (I:827) takes a similar approach.

Lenski (554) offers a different explanation. He asserts that even large groups of Jews going to and from the festivals in Jerusalem often found hospitality among the Samaritans. On this occasion, the Samaritans object because Jesus is with them. They have heard of His miracles; He is now going to Jerusalem to display His power and authority. He is passing through their land and does not even recognize their sanctuary on Mt. Gerizim. In short, the Samaritans do not reject Him because He is the Jewish Messiah, but because in their eyes He has insulted them and their system of worship.

James and John respond to this situation with a high level of zeal and a low level of spiritual maturity. They offer to command that fire come down from heaven and destroy the village as Elijah had done in 2 Kings 1:9-12. Jesus rebukes them soundly for their hasty and ill-advised offer. This is certainly not the type of attitude Jesus wants His followers to demonstrate (Morris, *Luke* 179). His goal is not to destroy but to redeem. The passage concludes with the simple statement that they went on to another village; Luke does not explain whether the other village was located in Samaria or Galilee (or possibly Perea).

The clause "when the time was come that he should be received up" has provoked some discussion. Geldenhuys (291) suggests the lifting up of Jesus refers to the time after His crucifixion and resurrection when He ascends to the Father. Marshall (*Gospel* 405) posits the primary reference is to the crucifixion but it may also include the ascension. The phrase "he set his face" implies a strong commitment to fulfill God's plan, which He knows will end with His death, burial, and resurrection in Jerusalem.

The last words of verse 55 and the first words of verse 56 are not found in the oldest manuscripts of Luke. Many scholars consider them to be a later addition to the text. For a good analysis of this issue see Marshall (*Gospel* 407-408), Liefeld (934), and Morris (*Luke* 179).

57 And it came to pass, that, as they went in the way, a certain *man* said unto him, Lord, I will follow thee whithersoever thou goest. 58 And Jesus said unto him, Foxes have holes, and birds of the air

have **nests; but the Son of man**
hath not where to lay *his* head.
59 And he said unto another,
Follow me. But he said, Lord, suf-
fer me first to go and bury my
father.
60 Jesus said unto him, Let the
dead bury their dead: but go thou
and preach the kingdom of God.
61 And another also said, Lord, I
will follow thee; but let me first go
bid them farewell, which are at
home at my house.
62 And Jesus said unto him, No
man, having put his hand to the
plough, and looking back, is fit for
the kingdom of God.

Luke returns to the theme of discipleship; the key word is "follow." Jesus' goal is to help the disciples understand the nature of the commitment they have made and the sacrifice their commitment will entail. The story is a simple one. Jesus encounters three men who pledge to become His disciples; they affirm they will follow Jesus wherever He may lead them. As usual, Luke focuses on the essential elements of the story. He does not identify the men; neither does he explain where or when these events happened. It is possible Luke is combining incidents that took place at different times. As was common in ancient storytelling, there are three main characters who interact with Jesus.

These three individuals have two things in common. First, they all profess a willingness to become Jesus' disciples. Second, they all offer excuses that on the surface seem to be plausible but in reality reflect a shallow commitment to Christ and His work. It is evident that all three fail to realize the radical nature of the commitment that Jesus demands of His followers.

In response to the first individual, Jesus remarks that even the animals have a home where they can seek refuge. Foxes have their holes; birds have their nests. Jesus, however, has no permanent home. He must depend on the generosity of strangers and of His followers to provide Him with food and lodging. In His response to this man, there is the implied question, "Are you willing to follow me if it means giving up your home and your security?" Jesus is challenging him to count the cost before making such an important commitment. Either the man makes no response, or Luke has not included it.

The second man affirms that he wishes to become a disciple, but he first must bury his father. This passage must be understood in light of the funeral and burial customs of ancient Palestine. To provide a proper burial for one's father was both a religious and a social obligation (Liefeld 935; Stein, *Luke* 301). The passage does not say anything about the father's condition; he could have been living or dead. He could have been sick or well. Since burial ordinarily took place within 24 hours of death, it is unlikely that the man would have had this conversation with Jesus during that brief interval. It is more likely to assume that the father was still living, but he might have been in poor health.

Jesus' response is rather striking and involves a word play. The first occurrence of the word "dead" refers to those who are spiritually dead; those who are not followers of Christ. Those who are physically dead are unable to bury anyone. The second occurrence of the word refers to those who are physically dead. Jesus' message to the man is that he should leave the burial of the father to other members of the family. His priority is to go and proclaim that the Kingdom of God has come to earth in the person of the Lord Jesus Christ. Jesus regarded the work of the kingdom as being so important that it even took precedence over one's sacred obligation to bury the dead (F. Bruce, *Hard Sayings* 162).

The third person also wishes to become a disciple, but before following Christ, he wants to go home and bid farewell to his friends and relatives. This passage is in some ways similar to 1 Kings 19:19-21 where Elijah grants Elisha permission to go home and say goodbye to his family. Jesus' response is different from Elijah's in that He does not grant the permission. Instead, He responds with a common agricultural metaphor. The plowman guides the plow with his left hand while he goads the oxen with a stick in his right hand. He must keep his eyes on the field before him if he wishes to plow a straight furrow (Liefeld 935-936).

The meaning of this passage is clear. Jesus is teaching His disciples that even the most important of family obligations must not stand in the way of their commitment to follow Jesus. Jesus demands of those who wish to become His disciples a truly radical kind of discipleship.

One of the key elements in the Travel Narrative is Jesus' own commitment to the ministry to which His Father has called Him. Another is the training and preparation of the disciples for the important roles they will play in the proclamation of the gospel. In the early portion of this chapter, Jesus broadens the circle of disciples to include a larger group than the original twelve apostles. He seeks to prepare them both by teaching and by practical experience on the field of service.

10:1 After these things the Lord appointed other seventy also, and sent them two and two before his face into every city and place, whither he himself would come.
2 Therefore said he unto them, The harvest truly *is* great, but the labourers *are* few: pray ye therefore the Lord of the harvest, that he would send forth labourers into his harvest.
3 Go your ways: behold, I send you forth as lambs among wolves.
4 Carry neither purse, nor scrip, nor shoes: and salute no man by the way.
5 And into whatsoever house ye enter, first say, Peace *be* to this house.
6 And if the son of peace be there, your peace shall rest upon it: if not, it shall turn to you again.
7 And in the same house remain, eating and drinking such things as they give: for the labourer is worthy of his hire. Go not from house to house.
8 And into whatsoever city ye enter, and they receive you, eat such things as are set before you:
9 And heal the sick that are therein, and say unto them, The kingdom of God is come nigh unto you.
10 But into whatsoever city ye enter, and they receive you not, go your ways out into the streets of the same, and say,
11 Even the very dust of your city, which cleaveth on us, we do wipe off against you: notwithstanding

be ye sure of this, that the kingdom of God is come nigh unto you.
12 But I say unto you, that it shall be more tolerable in that day for Sodom, than for that city.
13 Woe unto thee, Chorazin! woe unto thee, Bethsaida! for if the mighty works had been done in Tyre and Sidon, which have been done in you, they had a great while ago repented, sitting in sackcloth and ashes.
14 But it shall be more tolerable for Tyre and Sidon at the judgment, than for you.
15 And thou, Capernaum, which art exalted to heaven, shalt be thrust down to hell.
16 He that heareth you heareth me; and he that despiseth you despiseth me; and he that despiseth me despiseth him that sent me.

The instructions given to this larger group are somewhat similar to those that had been given to the twelve in Luke 9:1-6. Jesus' goal in this passage is to involve a greater number of workers in the proclamation of the Kingdom of God; He understands the task is great and the twelve will not be able to carry the entire load alone. It should be noted that some of the early manuscripts of Luke give the number sent out as 70 while other manuscripts give the number at 72; the evidence is about equally divided (Stein, *Luke* 304; Ellis 155). Summers (*Luke* 126) suggests the original number was probably 70 because an early copyist would have been more likely to raise the number than to lower it.

A number of commentators (Stein, *Luke* 304; Marshall, *Gospel* 415; Creed 144) suggest that when He sent out these disciples, Jesus might have had in mind Genesis 10. The Hebrew text lists 70 nations that existed after the flood while the Greek Septuagint lists 72 (Creed 144).

In verse 2, Jesus employs a common agricultural metaphor, the harvest. When harvest time came, many workers would be required to harvest the wheat or barley. Jesus, of course, is speaking of a spiritual harvest; He is speaking of a great opportunity to bring men and women into the Kingdom of God. They are open to the gospel now, but they may not always be. The spiritual harvest must be gathered while it is ripe. How is this need for workers to be met? First and foremost, it must be through prayer. Only the Lord can change the human heart and produce disciples where none existed before.

Beginning in verse 3, Jesus gives the disciples their instructions; He begins with a word of warning. He tells them He is sending them out as lambs in the midst of wolves. In the ancient world, the lamb was a symbol of helplessness; it really has no natural defense against any predator (Ellis 156). It is likely this warning is designed to accomplish two objectives. First, it alerts these new disciples to the reality of the situation. They need to understand the difficult task that lies before them. Second, the lesson may be that they will have no human defense against the attacks of the enemies of Christ. They may have to give their lives in the service of their Lord. Their only hope is the Lord will protect them.

In verse 4 and following, Jesus orders the disciples not to make any of the customary preparations that one would make before beginning a journey. They are to depend on God and on those whom God sends their way. Plummer (273) explains that according to the Jewish Talmud, no one was to go up to the Temple Mount carrying a staff, shoes, or money in a purse. In their missionary journey, the disciples are not to be distracted by material things.

"Purse" describes a small bag for carrying coins; "scrip" describes a larger bag for carrying food or other items. The phrase "nor shoes" refers to the sandals that were commonly worn in Palestine. These words are interpreted in different ways; they may mean that the disciples are not to wear sandals. More likely, the meaning is they are not to carry extra pairs of sandals. The main idea is they are not to be burdened down by the things they carry. They are to trust in God and in those whom God uses to meet their needs.

The phrase "salute no man by the way" must be understood in light of the social customs of first-century Palestine. Formal greetings, while traveling, would involve considerable time, which the disciples did not have (Marshall, *Gospel* 418). Jesus is not encouraging His disciples to be rude, but He is imparting to them a sense of urgency. They must not be distracted by things that are unnecessary; 2 Kings 4:29 has a similar instruction.

In verse 5, Jesus instructs His disciples to offer the traditional Hebrew greeting, "Peace to this house," to those who offer hospitality. In Judges 6:23, the Lord offered a similar greeting to Gideon. In Judges 19:20, an unnamed man offers the same greeting to a Levite passing by on his way to Jerusalem. "Peace" in this context implies more than the absence of earthly conflict; it is the inner peace that results from a proper relationship with God. Something of a similar idea is found in verse 6. A "son of peace" is a person who is oriented toward peace (Plummer 273). In this context, it may describe a person who is in a right relationship with God and thus open to Christ and His ministry.

This kind of peace is available only to those who are open to the life and ministry of Jesus. If those in that house are not willing to receive Jesus, the peace will return to the disciples. Although the text does not state this, the implication is the disciple will then leave the house that has rejected him in order to seek accommodations elsewhere.

When they find a household willing to accept them, the disciples are told to abide in that house and eat and drink what is set before them. They are not to go from house to house seeking better food or more luxurious accommodations. They are laborers in the Kingdom of God, and as such they are worthy to receive the sustenance of the people of God. In the minds of some commentators, the Jewish laws concerning food may enter into the picture. Creed (145), for example, is of the opinion that observance of the Jewish food laws is not an issue in this passage. It will become an issue later in the ministry of Jesus.

Other commentators, however, take the position that the urgency of the mission demands the disciples eat the food that is offered to them whether it is "kosher" or not (Summers, *Luke* 128; Geldenhuys 300). Plummer (274) offers a rather interesting interpretation, arguing that the issue is not food but the hospitality extended to the disciples. Their food and shelter are to be regarded as compensation for their services rather than as a gift or an alms. The disciples should regard themselves as members of the family and not as guests.

In verse 9, the disciples are told to do the same kind of things Jesus did when He visited in a village. They are to heal the sick and tell the residents the Kingdom of God has come upon them. This does not mean the kingdom has come upon them in its fullness; the idea is that the kingdom has come to earth in the person and work of Christ. The establishment of the Kingdom of God has begun, and they are to have the privilege of being a part of it.

The next three verses recognize that all families and all villages will not be open to the ministry of Jesus. In that case, the disciples are not obligated to continue the ministry in that location. They are to go into the streets and announce publicly they are wiping the dust of that city off their feet and sandals. This is a very public demonstration both of the villagers' rejection of the disciples and of the rejection of the villagers by the disciples. The villagers have been given the opportunity to accept the Messiah, and they have refused. Therefore, the judgment of God will come upon them, and that judgment will be a very severe one. They will suffer an even worse judgment than the terrible city of Sodom suffered in Genesis 19:24-28. In the O. T., the judgment of Sodom becomes proverbial for a very severe judgment (Is. 1:9-10).

Verses 13-15 provide a severe rebuke of those communities who refuse to accept the Lord's disciples. Nothing more is known about Chorazin (sometimes spelled Korazim) than what is given here; apparently it was a town Jesus had visited or with which He was personally familiar (Creed 146). Bethsaida was an important community; the feeding of the five thousand (Lk. 9:10-17) had taken place near it. Those who lived there had seen firsthand the miraculous power of Jesus, but they still refused to accept Him as the Messiah. Tyre and Sidon were two well-known pagan cities located to the North in Syria; they are often mentioned as representative of the heathen world (Creed 146; Marshall, *Gospel* 424). In this passage, they are compared with those cities within the land of Palestine who refused to accept Jesus. The idea here is that Tyre and Sidon, even though they were thoroughly pagan, would have repented had they seen the miracles Jesus performed in Israel. Sackcloth is a rough cloth made from goat's hair, worn in times of mourning. Ashes were sat on or placed on the head; sackcloth and ashes were signs of repentance or deep mourning (Marshall, *Gospel* 424-425). For other references to sackcloth and ashes see Jonah 3:6, Isaiah 58:5, and Daniel 9:3.

Verses 14-15 provide a bold statement that expresses the seriousness with which Jesus regards the sin of rejecting His messengers. The pagan cities of Tyre and Sidon will receive a less severe judgment than will the Palestinian cities that rejected Jesus. According to these verses, rejecting Jesus and His messengers merits a more severe judgment than the open paganism of these two important cities.

Capernaum was the city in which Jesus performed some of His first miracles; it became something of the headquarters of His Galilean ministry (Lk. 4:23; 7:1-10). If any of the cities in Palestine should have accepted the teachings of Jesus, it was Capernaum. Those living in that city had witnessed, with their own eyes, the good works

Jesus did. It is doubtful Jesus intended to say that every single individual in Capernaum rejected Him; the idea is that the city as a whole was not open to the message Jesus and His disciples presented.

Two clauses—"which art exalted to heaven" and "thrust down to hell"—call for special comment. The first probably indicates that Capernaum expected to be exalted above other cities because of the miracles Jesus had performed there. According to Plummer (277), the phrase refers to the height of glory, while "thrust down to hell" implies depth of shame. "Hell" (Greek *hadēs*) is used in several different ways in the Scriptures. It is often used to translate the Hebrew word (*sheol*) for the abode of the dead. Sometimes it means simply the land of the dead, without making any distinction between the righteous and the wicked. In other places, it is used to describe the place (or state) where the wicked dead are punished. Summers (*Life Beyond* 27-28) offers a useful summary of the N. T. uses of this term. In this passage, the idea is that this city, which could have enjoyed a special relationship with Jesus, has forfeited that opportunity. It is singled out for special condemnation because of its unbelief.

Verse 16 explains why Jesus regards the rejection of His disciples as such a serious sin; to reject the message of the disciples is the same as rejecting Jesus. To reject Jesus is the same as rejecting God the Father, and such a sin will not be taken lightly.

17 And the seventy returned again with joy, saying, Lord, even the devils are subject unto us through thy name.

18 And he said unto them, I beheld Satan as lightning fall from heaven.

19 Behold, I give unto you power to tread on serpents and scorpions, and over all the power of the enemy: and nothing shall by any means hurt you.

20 Notwithstanding in this rejoice not, that the spirits are subject unto you; but rather rejoice, because your names are written in heaven.

21 In that hour Jesus rejoiced in spirit, and said, I thank thee, O Father, Lord of heaven and earth, that thou hast hid these things from the wise and prudent, and hast revealed them unto babes: even so, Father; for so it seemed good in thy sight.

22 All things are delivered to me of my Father: and no man knoweth who the Son is, but the Father; and who the Father is, but the Son, and *he* to whom the Son will reveal *him*.

23 And he turned him unto *his* disciples, and said privately, Blessed *are* the eyes which see the things that ye see:

24 For I tell you, that many prophets and kings have desired to see those things which ye see, and have not seen *them*; and to hear those things which ye hear, and have not heard *them*.

This passage is apocalyptic in nature. In His response to the successful ministry of His disciples, Jesus moves beyond the great victory the disciples have won as they visited the various towns and villages in preparation for His ministry in those areas. These verses anticipate the great victory that will be won over all evil at the Second Coming (Caird 143-144; Marshall, *Gospel* 428-429).

After this most memorable experience, the disciples returned, filled with joy because of the victories they had won in the Lord's name. This was probably the greatest joy that many of them had ever experienced. They mentioned two specific aspects of the victory they had won. First, the devils were subject to them through the name of the Lord. The devils are Satan's servants; their defeat means God is triumphing over the forces of evil. This victory at the hands of the disciples is a foretaste of the even greater victories that Jesus will win in the future. The fact that many people in the ancient world lived in mortal fear of demons makes this victory all the more significant (A. Richardson, *Stories* 68-69).

The second reason for their rejoicing was that Christ had seen Satan falling like lightning from the sky. It is difficult to determine what Christ intended by this statement. Perhaps the idea is that Christ had seen Satan fall in the same way lightning falls from the sky during a thunderstorm ("sky" and "heaven" are the same word in Greek). Barclay (135) suggests two possible meanings. First, it may mean the forces of evil and darkness are being defeated, and the Kingdom of God is on its way. Satan's final defeat has not yet arrived, but it has begun. Second it may be a warning against pride and overconfidence. His pride led Satan to rebel against God, and this rebellion has brought about his downfall. The disciples must take care they do not fall into a similar trap.

Bock (*Luke* NIV 292-293), following a meaning similar to Barclay's first, suggests that the imagery is drawn from Isaiah 14:12 where the fall of Lucifer is connected with the coming of the Messiah. The success of the disciples' ministry is evidence that the fall of Satan has begun. The authority of Jesus is not yet fully manifest, but the victories the disciples have won over death and the devils indicate that the process is beginning. Creed (147) and Plummer (278) present similar interpretations.

F. Bruce (*Hard Sayings* 134-135) presents a different view. He argues that Jesus is not referring to some past event but to the events taking place during His own earthly ministry. The demons had been defeated during the mission of the seventy. Many of the rabbis believed that at the end of time the Messiah would overthrow Satan. The victories the disciples had experienced during their mission provide proof that the kingdom of Satan is already being defeated by the Kingdom of God.

Verse 19 further develops the ideas presented in the previous verses. "Power to tread on serpents and scorpions" can be interpreted literally or figuratively (Morris, *Luke* 185). According to Summers (*Luke* 132), the phrase should be understood symbolically. The scorpions and serpents, which desert travelers feared, are symbols for the devil and his agents. Lieu (84) offers a similar interpretation, noting that serpents and scorpions threatened the people of Israel during the wilderness wandering. That "nothing shall by any means hurt you" is a message of assurance given in poetic form. The idea is that the power of God will be with the disciples as they fulfill the commission Jesus has given them.

Verse 20 is not designed to dampen the joy and enthusiasm of the disciples but to instruct them that their joy must be channeled in the right direction. They should rejoice, first and foremost, because they are members of the family of God. That is the meaning of "Your names are written in heaven" (Creed 147). Any rejoicing because the evil spirits have been subject to their control must clearly occupy second place. They must be careful to glorify God and not themselves.

Luke consistently emphasizes the prayer life of Jesus, and that emphasis is clear in verses 21-22. This passage also sheds light on the relationship between Jesus and His heavenly Father (Geldenhuys 306). Jesus rejoices in the Holy Spirit because God has chosen to reveal Himself not to the wise or to the powerful but to the common people of the land who are like babes in their understanding of the things of God. Those "wise" and "prudent" are the religious leaders who should have had a more mature understanding of God and His ways in the world than they did (Lieu 85).

Nolland (II:572) summarizes the various uses of "babe" in Jewish literature. It is sometimes used to refer to the poor and the simple who are the special recipients of God's grace. It may describe the simple people of the land who have not had the formal religious training of the leaders, but they have experienced God at work in their own lives. For that reason, they are better able than their leaders to appreciate and accept the ministry of Jesus. In some contexts, it may refer to those who are lacking in understanding but who are willing to grow and develop. Childers (500) understands it as a reference to the 70 disciples Jesus had sent out. Caird (145) presents a similar view.

Jesus does not explain specifically what He means by "these things." In this context, He is probably referring to a proper understanding of Him and His ministry. This proper understanding has been hidden from the religious leaders, but revealed to the ordinary people of the land. The future of the Kingdom of God rests with them and not with the religious leadership of Israel.

In verse 22, Jesus says that all things have been delivered to Him by His Father, but He doesn't define "all things." Perhaps He means His power and authority; more likely, He refers to the content of the teaching He has delivered to the disciples and to the crowds (Creed 148; Plummer 282-283). The lessons He has taught and continues to teach do not reflect a human origin; they reveal the mind of God.

The latter part of verse 22 has the idea that no man can fully know or understand the mind of God; only the Son enjoys the intimate relationship that makes a full understanding possible. Likewise, no human being can fully understand the Lord Jesus; the Father is the only being who possesses such knowledge. Human beings can have some understanding of God only because the Son has revealed Him. The disciples can be confident that the lessons Jesus is teaching them are true because they come from God. This passage also reminds them that Jesus presents a true and authentic picture of God the Father.

In verses 23-24, Jesus finishes His discussion with the 70 by reminding them they have enjoyed great privileges that few will ever enjoy (Lenski 594). They have had the privilege of seeing Jesus at work through them. They have seen the ill restored to health and the devils defeated. Jesus reminds them they have seen and heard things the prophets and kings of the O. T. would have liked to witness, but they were unable to do so. Being a disciple of Jesus involved a high degree of sacrifice and commitment, but it also involved indescribable blessings. The prophecies of the O. T. are finding their fulfillment in the deeds Jesus is doing and in the words He is speaking, and they are witnesses (Creed 150).

Summary (9:51—10:24)

In Luke 9:51-56, Jesus sent some of His disciples ahead to prepare for His trip through Samaria. The Samaritans refused to receive Him. James and John then asked if they should call down fire from Heaven to destroy those who refused to receive Jesus. Jesus rebuked them by saying He had not come to destroy men's lives but to save them. This incident of rejection helps to illustrate the nature of Christ's kingdom.

The closing verses of chapter 9 relate the story of several men who came to Jesus wanting to become His disciples. It is clear that none of them realized the depth of commitment necessary to become true followers of Jesus. A true disciple must demonstrate a high degree of commitment and perseverance.

In chapter 10, Jesus is concerned both with His own commitment to ministry and to the preparation of His disciples for the important ministry that lies ahead of them. The chapter begins with the mission of the seventy disciples who are sent into the towns and villages (probably in Galilee) to prepare for Jesus' upcoming visit. It is important to note that this mission is not limited to the twelve; it includes a larger group of disciples who have had less experience in ministry. Jesus warns them of the dangers involved in this itinerate ministry, but they willingly accept the challenge. There is a sense of urgency about their mission; they are not to be burdened down with the things a traveler would normally carry. They are to learn they can depend on the Lord and on His followers. Their task is to heal the sick and to announce that the Kingdom of God has arrived in the person of Jesus Christ.

Jesus warns them in advance that not everyone will be open to their ministry. If they are rejected in a particular town or village, they are not to end their mission. Rather, they are to shake the dust off their feet and go on to other communities that will be more open. Jesus then pronounces a word of judgment against those who would reject the ministry of His disciples.

The ministry of the seventy is successful; they return rejoicing because of all the great things God has done. It is clear that the fall of Satan has begun. The passage concludes with a reminder from Jesus that the disciples must give all the glory and honor to God. They are privileged to be used by God in such a special way, but they must remember that the work is God's and not theirs. Many O. T. saints had desired to see the things in which these disciples had participated, but they had not been able to do so. The disciples are truly blessed.

Application: Teaching and Preaching the Passage

The closing verses of chapter 9 are an important part of Jesus' training program for His disciples. There are many lessons modern believers can learn from this passage. Two of Jesus' most faithful followers wanted to bring down God's judgment upon those Samaritan villages that refused to receive Jesus. Jesus rebuked His disciples; He had not come to destroy men's lives but to save them. In this passage, Jesus also tells the story of several individuals who wanted to become His disciples without understanding the depth of commitment that discipleship would require. These are important lessons for preachers and teachers today. We must stay true to the purpose for which Jesus came to earth. We must also reflect a high level of commitment.

There are also many lessons that can be learned from the sending of the seventy disciples to minister in advance of Jesus' visits to the towns and villages of Galilee. The first is the need for personal involvement; there is simply no substitute for human contact between those who have received the good news and those who have not. Jesus understands that the mission is too large to be carried on by the twelve disciples alone. In every generation there is a need for active involvement in the cause of Christ. We must pray to God that He will supply that need. God is sovereign; He alone can call forth workers. All do not need to become pastors or missionaries, but all need to be involved.

There is much we can learn from the commission Jesus gives to these disciples. He tells them to heal the sick and tell the people that the Kingdom of God has come near to them. In other words, they are to do what they can to relieve human need, and they are to give God the glory for all that is accomplished. The seventy are also to call for a decision. The Kingdom of God is drawing near, and they are to challenge the people to accept it and enter it.

Another lesson is the importance of the message they carry. The consequences of rejecting the Kingdom of God are serious. If the people in these towns and villages reject God's message, then He will also reject them. It will be more tolerable for the pagan cities of Tyre and Sidon on the Day of Judgment than for the rebellious cities of Galilee. The disciples must make good use of the limited time they have. If a town or village rejects the message, they are to shake the dust off their feet and go on to those who are more responsive.

It is interesting to note that the Lord sends them out two by two. It is not Jesus' intention to say this is the only way that evangelism can be done, but in this situation this type of arrangement has advantages. Two disciples can provide help, encouragement, and accountability to each other on the journey. It is certainly advantageous to have another person available to help in times of danger. This passage reminds us that the work of evangelism is a shared ministry; it is not designed for lone rangers.

B. Discipleship Lessons (10:25—11:28)

25 And, behold, a certain lawyer stood up, and tempted him, saying, Master, what shall I do to inherit eternal life?
26 He said unto him, What is written in the law? how readest thou?
27 And he answering said, Thou shalt love the Lord thy God with all thy heart, and with all thy soul, and with all thy strength, and with all thy mind; and thy neighbour as thyself.

28 And he said unto him, Thou hast answered right: this do, and thou shalt live.
29 But he, willing to justify himself, said unto Jesus, And who is my neighbour?

These words form the introduction to one of Jesus' most well-known parables, the Parable of the Good Samaritan. "Lawyer" (Greek *nomikos)* does not describe a modern attorney who practices civil or criminal law. Instead, this term identifies an expert in the Jewish law, both written and oral. Creed (152) suggests that Luke uses "lawyer" because he is writing to a Gentile audience, while Matthew prefers the Jewish term "scribe" (Greek *grammateus*). There doesn't seem to be much difference in meaning between the two terms, but "lawyer" would have been more readily understandable to a Gentile audience. Lenski (595) opines that the lawyers were a subgroup within the larger community of scribes, but he makes no effort to distinguish between the two groups. Ellis (160, 171) identifies this lawyer as a theologian. Ellis sees little or no difference between "lawyer," "scribe," and "doctor of the law." Spence (274) notes that these men occupied important positions in Jewish society of the first century. They were not just scribes or secretaries. They were professional teachers and interpreters of the Mosaic Law and the hundreds of applications that had been appended to it.

Luke does not give any information about the circumstances in which Jesus told this parable, and it is certainly possible it was told on more than one occasion. Probably He was teaching in a house or an open courtyard with a group of people seated around Him. Apparently, the lawyer stood up to gain Jesus' attention and asked his question.

The question the lawyer asked, "What shall I do to inherit eternal life?" was a commonly-asked question that probably came up several times during Jesus' earthly ministry (Ellis 159). The term "eternal life" was something of a technical term referring to the blessings the righteous would inherit after the resurrection (Bock II:1023; Ellis 160). It is significant that the lawyer does not ask how he may obtain eternal life, but what he must *do* to obtain it. The idea that one's future salvation could only be obtained by doing good works was a basic presupposition of society. It was a society based on the observance of law codes, and debates over this and other similar questions were common.

Commentators have raised questions about the sincerity of the lawyer's motives. "Tempted" (Greek *ekpeirazō*) may be used to express both the idea "to test" and the idea "to tempt." In other words, it is possible the lawyer's question was a sincere one; he genuinely wanted to hear Jesus' opinion on this important question. It is also possible the lawyer was there as a representative of the Jewish leaders who were already becoming hostile to Jesus and His message. If that is the case, the lawyer's goal was to test Jesus and see if He would say something contrary to the traditional view. Spence (274) argues that it is likely the lawyer was trying to get Jesus to make some unorthodox statement that would serve to discredit Him in the eyes of the people. Bock (II:1023) and Lenski (597) also challenge the sincerity of the lawyer's motives. Summers (*Luke* 134) presents a similar position.

Plummer (284), on the other hand, sees no sinister motive in the lawyer's question. His goal is simply to "test His ability as a teacher." Jeremias (*Parables* 202) argues that the lawyer is asking the question sincerely. The preaching of Jesus has disturbed his conscience, and he wants to know more about His message. Geldenhuys (311) suggests the lawyer's motives are probably mixed.

Jesus responds to his question with a question for the lawyer: "What is written in the law? how readest thou?" In this context, Jesus' response is understandable. The lawyer is an expert in the Jewish law; he should already have formed an opinion on this important issue. Jesus is a layman; He has not had the privilege of the theological training the lawyer has received. Jesus expects him to know what the Law says about how to obtain eternal life.

The lawyer reflects a good knowledge of the O.T. He quotes from Deuteronomy 6:4-5 and Leviticus 19:18. These two verses stress the need to love the Lord with all aspects of one's character and being—heart, soul, strength, and mind. Stein (*Luke* 316) connects "heart" with the emotions, "soul" with consciousness, "mind" with intelligence, and "strength" with motivation. The idea is that a person is to love God with every aspect of his being. He is also to love his neighbor. According to the traditional Jewish understanding, the neighbor was one's fellow Jew. That term would not have included Samaritans or Gentiles (Geldenhuys 311; Stein, *Luke* 316; Hultgren 94; Jeremias, *Parables* 202).

Jesus tells the lawyer that he has answered correctly and adds, "This do, and thou shalt live." The implication is that the lawyer must do more than repeat the correct words. In order to gain eternal life, he must actually put them into practice in his own life. The lawyer is probably somewhat surprised by Jesus' response, which he may view as something of a rebuke. It is likely that he understands the response to be a rebuke for not putting these important teachings into practice in his own life. In the face of this rebuke, the lawyer feels he must defend or justify himself (Hultgren 94). He does so by asking Jesus the question, "Who is my neighbour?" He may be hoping Jesus will compromise Himself by giving an incorrect definition of the word "neighbour." Rather than giving a direct answer to the lawyer's question, Jesus tells the famous parable of the Good Samaritan.

30 And Jesus answering said, A certain *man* went down from Jerusalem to Jericho, and fell among thieves, which stripped him of his raiment, and wounded *him*, and departed, leaving *him* half dead.
31 And by chance there came down a certain priest that way: and when he saw him, he passed by on the other side.
32 And likewise a Levite, when he was at the place, came and looked on *him*, and passed by on the other side.
33 But a certain Samaritan, as he journeyed, came where he was: and when he saw him, he had compassion *on him*,
34 And went to *him*, and bound up his wounds, pouring in oil and wine, and set him on his own beast, and brought him to an inn, and took care of him.

35 And on the morrow when he departed, he took out two pence, and gave *them* to the host, and said unto him, Take care of him; and whatsoever thou spendest more, when I come again, I will repay thee.
36 Which now of these three, thinkest thou, was neighbour unto him that fell among the thieves?
37 And he said, He that shewed mercy on him. Then said Jesus unto him, Go, and do thou likewise.

This and similar parables are often entitled "Parables of Exemplary Behavior" (Hultgren 92); B. Smith (180) includes this one among the "Parables for Pharisee and Sinner." The parables in this group are designed to provide examples of human conduct for the disciples to follow. In this parable, Jesus moves beyond the simple definition of the term "neighbor." He challenges His followers to truly follow the example of love Jesus has given them. Rather than limit the term "neighbour," as the lawyer and other Jews would do, Jesus amplifies the term. The idea is that anyone can be a neighbor by providing help to those in need. Issues of race, ethnicity, or national origin do not prevent one from being a neighbor. C. Smith (17-24) argues that Jesus often used the parables as weapons in His ongoing struggle with the Jewish leaders. Jesus was frequently under attack for His teachings, and He often used parables as ways of taking the offensive. On some occasions, He even used parables as a way of attacking the traditional morality of the day.

The social and cultural situation in Palestine, during the first century, provides the background for understanding this parable. Israel was an occupied country; Roman soldiers were everywhere. Jews in Judea were separated from those in Galilee by the presence of the Samaritans. There was an influx of non-Jews into the country at this time (Kistemaker 167). The long history of conflict between Jews and Samaritans is well known (Hultgren 98). This hostility had been intensified a few years earlier when some Samaritans had defiled the Temple by scattering human bones during a Passover (Bailey, *Eyes* 48). Jeremias (*Parables* 203), Plummer (285), and Kistemaker (167) opine that this parable grows out of an actual incident, but most scholars are content to say it reflects a true to life situation (Green, *Luke* 429).

There are three principal, active characters in the parable: a priest, a Levite, and a Samaritan. The wounded man is not identified; he is simply a traveler going from Jerusalem to Jericho. This was a journey of approximately seventeen miles over a steep, rough, and mountainous path (Buttrick 150; Kistemaker 167) where attacks and robberies occurred frequently. It is assumed that the traveler is a Jew, but his nationality is not stated. No reason is given for making the trip. As C. Smith (150) notes, in a parable such details are generally omitted. The wounded man never speaks or makes any contribution to the story; he is simply part of the scene. He is described, after the attack on him, as "half dead" (Greek *hēmithanē*), found only here in the N. T. It may mean that the man could be taken for dead or that he was unconscious and looked like a corpse.

The priests were descendants of Aaron who had the responsibility for maintaining the sacrificial system at the Temple in Jerusalem. Jericho was a city with a high concentration of priests (Kistemaker 168), and it would not have been an unusual sight to see a priest traveling to or from Jerusalem. The Levite was a descendant of Levi who could not offer sacrifices but regularly assisted the priests. For an old, but still valuable, discussion of priests and Levites in the first century, see the article by Baudissin.

Commentators disagree on the level of obligation these two fictional characters had to render aid to a fellow Jew. Hultgren (97) examines the issue and comes to the conclusion the priest was under obligation to help. If the priest saw the man was still alive, he should have aided him. Some commentators suggest that if the priest was on his way to Jerusalem to minister in the Temple, he might have stayed away from the man to avoid ceremonial defilement (Childers 503; Morris, *Luke* 189). For a good discussion of this complex issue see Jeremias (*Parables* 203-204). For whatever reason, both the priest and the Levite in the story pass by on the other side of the path to avoid contact with the wounded man. Jesus' point is to contrast the failure of the religious leaders to minister to a man in need with the generous spirit of a hated Samaritan (Creed 151).

Since such stories generally involved three characters, it is likely the hearers expected the arrival of a third character who would remedy this terrible situation. Jewish society was divided into priests, Levites, and other Israelites; it is likely the hearers anticipated the arrival of an Israelite layman who would fill that role (Hultgren 98; Morris, *Luke* 189). They were in for a big surprise. The hero of the story arrives, but he is not a Jew; he is a hated Samaritan.

The Samaritan applies the accepted form of first aid for a wound; he washes it with wine and olive oil. He places the wounded man on his donkey—which probably implies the Samaritan walks alongside—and takes him to a nearby inn where he continues to care for the stranger. Before he leaves the next day, he gives the innkeeper "two pence" and asks him to continue caring for the stranger. Most commentators are agreed that the "two pence" are two Roman denarii, which would have been an amount large enough to care for the man for a number of days (Morris, *Luke* 190). If the two pence are not sufficient, the Samaritan promises to pay any additional charge when he returns in the future. In this story, the Samaritan is not only helpful; he is generous. He goes above and beyond the call of duty.

The history of the interpretation of this parable is long and complicated; it is also beyond the scope of this commentary. For more information see Bailey, Guerra, and Marberry.

After telling the parable, Jesus' question to the lawyer in verse 36 is short and to the point. The lawyer has no option but to say the neighbor was the one who rendered aid in the hour of need. Jesus concludes the interview by saying, "Go, and do thou likewise." Stein (*Luke* 318) suggests the lawyer deliberately avoids using the term "Samaritan" in his reply.

In his original question, the lawyer had asked for Jesus' understanding of the term "neighbour." He was seeking to determine who should be the proper object of one's kindness and benevolence (Creed 151). It is quite possible he was seeking to limit the circle of people to whom he was obligated to render assistance. In the parable, Jesus answers the question in a totally different and unexpected way. He does not define "neighbour" from the standpoint of one who is entitled to receive the benefit of acts of mercy. He defines it, instead, in terms of one who renders aid in the time of need. The neighbor is the one who gives rather than the one who receives. Anyone can be a neighbor; in this parable, it is a hated Samaritan. In another situation, it could be someone else. The race or ethnicity of the wounded man is never identified because it is not important to the story. It is enough that he is a human being in need, and the Samaritan has the means and the willingness to render aid.

Manson (*Sayings* 261-262) suggests that no simple definition of neighbor is even possible. He writes, "For love does not begin by defining its objects: it discovers them." If the lawyer truly has love in his heart, he will soon discover who the neighbor is.

38 Now it came to pass, as they went, that he entered into a certain village: and a certain woman named Martha received him into her house.
39 And she had a sister called Mary, which also sat at Jesus' feet, and heard his word.
40 But Martha was cumbered about much serving, and came to him, and said, Lord, dost thou not care that my sister hath left me to serve alone? bid her therefore that she help me.
41 And Jesus answered and said unto her, Martha, Martha, thou art careful and troubled about many things:
42 But one thing is needful: and Mary hath chosen that good part, which shall not be taken away from her.

Most Jewish teachers in the first century were unwilling to accept women as disciples (Liefeld 944). That was clearly not the case with Jesus, who welcomed the participation of women in His movement. In Luke 8:1-3, Jesus had accepted the financial support of a group of women including Mary Magdalene, Joanna, and Susanna. That passage does not tell us these women traveled with the disciples, but they became an important part of the support network for Jesus and His disciples. In this passage, two more women, Mary and Martha, become part of that group of women. Luke does not mention where they lived, but these two sisters are probably the same Mary and Martha who lived in Bethany, near Jerusalem, according to John 11:1.

Verse 38 speaks of the house as the home of Martha; the name "Martha" means "lady" or "mistress" (Fitzmyer II:893). Since there is no mention of a husband, it is likely she is a widow (Marshall, *Gospel* 452). Mary is probably a younger sister living in Martha's home. Summers (*Luke* 137) notes that in verse 38, there is a shift from the third person plural to the third person singular. The verse says, that "as they went," "he entered into a certain village." This change may indicate that Jesus stopped in the home of Martha while His disciples went on into Jerusalem.

Martha is anxious to make her guest (or guests) welcome and entertain them well. According to verse 40, Martha is concerned about the serving. "Was cumbered" (Greek imperfect tense, generally used to describe continuous or repeated action) suggests she feels burdened by all the work that has to be done, especially the preparation of a meal for her family and guests. The tyranny of the urgent has overwhelmed her. Prior to the development of modern conveniences, preparing a good meal for the group would have involved considerable time and effort.

Martha's sister, Mary, is not helping with any of the work that needs to be done. She is sitting at Jesus' feet and listening to His teaching; she is already a disciple or is interested in becoming one.

In verse 40, Martha asks Jesus to speak with Mary and encourage her to help with the work. In a most courteous way, Jesus declines her request; His repetition of her name indicates His love and concern for her (Plummer 291). The Master understands Martha's concern; in verse 41, He says "thou art careful and troubled about many things." The word "careful," in this context, is an old English word that means "full of care."

He explains that Mary is not neglecting her work. In fact, she has chosen the "good part." The idea is that Martha is doing an important work in preparing the meal, but Mary is doing an even more important work by sitting at Jesus' feet and learning from Him. A willingness to learn from Jesus and put His teachings into practice are the marks of a true disciple. Jesus and His disciples are willing to settle for a lesser meal in return for giving Mary the opportunity to learn from Jesus.

The Greek manuscripts of verses 41-42 contain several different variant readings. Marshall (*Gospel* 452-454) and Manson (*Sayings* 264) give good analyses of these variants, but none of them would change the basic meaning of the passage.

There is some discussion among commentators concerning the meaning of the phrase "one thing that is needful." Marshall (*Gospel* 454) sees it as a reference either to the teachings of Jesus or to the blessings of the Kingdom of God. Liefeld (945) understands it to mean that Mary has established the right priority. She has given first place in her life to the Lord and His word, even over and above loving service. Bock (*Luke NIV* 304) understands it to mean that Mary has chosen to sit and spend time with Jesus, which is an essential part of discipleship. It is certainly not Jesus' desire to condemn Martha for her loving service, but it is His desire to recognize the importance of spending time with Him and learning from Him.

In this context, "good" means "better," or perhaps even "best" (Stein, *Luke* 321). (In Greek usage of the time, a simple adjective could be used as a comparative or even superlative.) Mary has not only made a good choice; she has made the best choice. She has chosen the Kingdom of God (Manson, *Sayings* 264). For the disciple, hearing the Word of God must take priority over other concerns (Fitzmyer II:892).

11:1 And it came to pass, that, as he was praying in a certain place, when he ceased, one of his disciples said unto him, Lord, teach us to pray, as John also taught his disciples.

2 And he said unto them, When ye pray, say, Our Father which art in heaven, Hallowed be thy name.

Thy kingdom come. They will be done, as in heaven, so in earth.
3 Give us day by day our daily bread.
4 And forgive us our sins; for we also forgive every one that is indebted to us. And lead us not into temptation; but deliver us from evil.

Luke devotes more attention to prayer than the other Gospels do; it is one of his major themes. The first thirteen verses of this chapter present three of Jesus' most important teachings on prayer. The first is Luke's version of the Lord's Prayer. Second is the parable of the Friend at Midnight, which stresses the importance of persistence in prayer. Third is Jesus' general instruction on the attitudes the disciples should manifest when they pray. This passage forms an excellent summary of Jesus' teachings on prayer; it is an important part of His training program for the disciples.

The Lord's Prayer follows closely on the heels of Jesus' prayer of thanksgiving found in Luke 10:21. It focuses on the disciples' need to trust in God and rely upon Him even in the difficult times in life. The prayer deals with three specific subjects, the establishment of God's kingdom, the daily needs of the disciples, and forgiveness. Luke gives no indication whether the term "disciples" is limited to the original twelve or whether it includes the larger group of disciples who became involved in the previous chapter.

Matthew's version of this prayer (Mt. 6:9-13) is a part of the Sermon on the Mount and is considerably longer than Luke's version. An even longer version of the prayer is found in an early Christian writing known as the Didache (8:2). The unknown author of the Didache concludes the prayer by writing, "You should pray in this way three times a day."

The differences between Matthew's version and Luke's have provoked considerable discussion (Morris, *Luke* 192; Lenski 620-621). Some scholars think Jesus delivered the prayer only once and that Luke and Matthew have included different versions of the same prayer. If that is true, it is possible that Luke has included only those sections of the prayer that would be most relevant to his Gentile readers. Others think it likely that Jesus gave different forms of the prayer at different times in His ministry.

Plummer (293) suggests Jesus might have given the prayer on one occasion to a larger group of His disciples and then later to a smaller group who were not present when the prayer was initially given. While neither Matthew nor Luke indicates how many times the prayer was spoken, there is nothing that would forbid Jesus from using this prayer in different ways at different times (Morris, *Luke* 192). R. Brown (NTE 266) offers a slightly different explanation of the differences. He suggests the different ordering of the material in these two Gospels presents no real problem. The Gospels are designed to be used in preaching and teaching, and the materials are arranged to meet the needs of preaching and teaching.

Luke does not explain whether Jesus intended this very prayer should be repeated by the disciples or if it should serve as an example of how they should pray. Liefeld (946) suggests these instructions imply that the disciples should regularly repeat this prayer. Summers (*Luke* 138) takes a somewhat different view. He argues that the prayer was originally intended to serve as a model or example of how the disciples should pray.

The early manuscripts of Luke's prayer contain some differences. Some of the early manuscripts, for example, say only "Father" while others have "Our Father which art in heaven." The earliest manuscripts omit the words "Thy will be done, as in heaven, so in earth." A number of the early manuscripts omit the words "but deliver us from evil." Marshall (*Gospel* 454-455) suggests that from the earliest days this prayer existed in two forms, the longer version found in Matthew and the shorter version found in Luke.

As often, Luke does not provide details; he simply notes that Jesus was praying in a certain place. When He had finished, one of His disciples came and asked Him to give them instruction on how to pray just as John the Baptist had given instruction on prayer to his disciples. The N. T. does not record any specific teaching on prayer given by John the Baptist, but it was common in the first century for outstanding Jewish rabbis to compose prayers for their disciples (Creed 155). Since some of the followers of John the Baptist had become disciples of Jesus, it was natural that they should want their new leader to teach them about prayer.

"Father" is probably a translation of the word *abba* (Aramaic), which was used within the family circle (Creed 156). It expresses the idea of "dear father." It implies both the respect that a child would have for his father and the endearment that grows out of a loving and caring relationship. Jesus begins this prayer by teaching His disciples to address God as one deserving of their respect and admiration but also as one who loves and cares for them. He is not some far-off pagan god whose love must be earned. Although He dwells in Heaven, He loves and cares about His earthly children.

In Luke's version of the prayer, there are five major petitions. The first two relate to God and the establishment of the Kingdom of God. The last three refer to the human needs of the disciples, which only God can supply. For useful discussions of these petitions see R. Brown (NTE 228-253) and Summers (*Luke* 139-141).

"Hallowed be thy name" expresses the first of these five petitions. It serves to introduce the prayer. In ancient Jewish thought, the name stood for the person. To hallow the name of God is another way of saying to recognize God as a holy being. "Hallow" means "to recognize as holy," "to treat as holy," or "to venerate" (Plummer 295; Summers, *Luke* 138). The disciples are to reverence the Lord; they are to recognize the exalted position He occupies as Lord of the universe.

The second of these petitions is "Thy kingdom come," which indicates the disciples should pray that God's reign or rule should be evident not only in Heaven, but also upon the earth. These words have to do with God's power, authority, and dominion over the created order. There is no doubt that God's power and authority in Heaven are absolute, where His will is always done. That is not always true on the earth where God's will is often ignored, and Satan is often in control of events. Jesus teaches His disciples to pray that God's control will become just as effective on earth as it already is in Heaven. That rule begins first within the heart of man and ultimately will spread to all the earth.

"Thy will be done, as in heaven, so in earth" serves to further explain the meaning of the words "thy kingdom come." When God's kingdom comes, when it becomes a reality in the lives of His people, then they will do His will rather than their own. The first thing for which the disciple of Jesus should pray is that God's will be done in the hearts and lives of His followers.

The third petition is "Give us day by day our daily bread." Bread made from wheat or barley was a staple of the diet in ancient Palestine; many of the poorer people survived on a diet of bread and cheese made from goat's milk. They ate meat only on special occasions. In that culture, bread was absolutely necessary to sustain life. In this context, "bread" probably stands for necessary food (Marshall, *Gospel* 458). The disciples are instructed to pray that the merciful hand of God will supply the physical needs of His people.

"Give" (Greek present imperative) expresses the idea of continuing action. The disciples are to pray to God that He would continue to provide them with the necessities of life. "Daily" (Greek *epiousion*) is a rare word, occurring in the N. T. only here and in Matthew 6:11; it is also found in a few places in early Christian writings outside the N. T. Marshall (*Gospel* 459) suggests several possible meanings. It may refer to something that is necessary for existence; it may also mean "for the current day" or "for the coming day" (R. Brown, NTE 239-240; Creed 157). The phrase "day by day" should probably be understood as explanatory. Although the precise meaning of the word translated "daily" is difficult to determine, the general idea is clear. The disciples must depend on God for their daily subsistence, and they should not be afraid to pray about their needs. God cares about the physical, spiritual, and emotional needs of His people.

The fourth petition is "Forgive us our sins." The parallel passage, Matthew 6:12, uses the word "debts," which would have been readily understandable to a Jewish audience. It was common in Judaism to view sin as a debt owed to God. In this passage, Luke uses the word "sins," which would have been more easily understood by his Gentile audience (R. Brown, NTE 244). (Both "debts" and "sins" probably translate the same Aramaic original.) This petition recognizes that although the disciples have dedicated their lives to God, they are not perfect. At times, they will sin, and they will need God's forgiveness. The disciple must have the humility necessary to recognize his own sinfulness and his utter dependence on the grace and mercy of God.

"For we also forgive every one that is indebted to us" makes clear that the disciples must not only be willing to receive forgiveness, they must also be willing to extend it to others. The teaching of Scripture is that sin is universal; there is no one who can live a truly sinless life. Repentance and forgiveness are necessary to maintain a proper relationship with God. They are also necessary to maintain proper relationships within the family of God. The Christian must always be willing both to seek the forgiveness of others and to extend it to them because forgiveness is a two-way street.

The last petition is "Lead us not into temptation." This petition has troubled many interpreters because it seems to conflict with James 1:13, which teaches that God doesn't tempt any man.

Perhaps the key to understanding these two passages is found in the word "temptation" (Greek *peirasmos*), which expresses both the ideas of testing and temptation. James 1:13 refers to temptation as an enticement to engage in sinful conduct, and God will never lead His children into sin. The idea in Luke is that the disciple will face many times of trial and difficulty, and he may not have sufficient spiritual strength to resist them. These words are a prayer to God that He will protect His followers and not lead them into times of trial, which they may not be able to handle.

Morris (*Luke* 194) suggests that in this prayer the meaning is "temptation." The idea is not that God leads His followers into temptation; that would be contrary to the teaching of James. According to Morris, this passage deals with the attitude the disciple should demonstrate. He understands his weakness and vulnerability, and he prays God will lead him away from temptation rather than into it.

F. Bruce (*Hard Sayings* 83) offers a different interpretation. He argues that temptation is not entirely bad; if the faith of the believer is never tested it will not grow and mature as it should. Some tests, however, are so severe the faith of the believer cannot endure them. Under such severe temptation, faith will fail. The prayer is that the believer will be protected from the level of trials and temptations that would cause his faith to be destroyed.

"But deliver us from evil" is found in Matthew's version of the prayer, but not in the earliest manuscripts of Luke. It should be understood as an explanatory phrase. The prayer of the disciple should be that the Lord would lead him not into times of testing and temptation but away from them. God understands the weaknesses of His disciples, and He can be trusted to lead His people in the right direction.

5 And he said unto them, Which of you shall have a friend, and shall go unto him at midnight, and say unto him, Friend, lend me three loaves;
6 For a friend of mine in his journey is come to me, and I have nothing to set before him?
7 And he from within shall answer and say, Trouble me not: the door is now shut, and my children are with me in bed; I cannot rise and give thee.
8 I say unto you, Though he will not rise and give him, because he is his friend, yet because of his importunity he will rise and give him as many as he needeth.

Jesus must have had a sharp sense of humor, and no passage better illustrates that fact than this familiar parable. It is commonly known as the Parable of the Friend at Midnight or as the Parable of the Importunate Friend (B. Smith 146). Jesus' parables are works of fiction, but they reflect the real-life situations of the common people of Palestine. Most people in ancient Palestine made their living in agriculture. They lived in small villages for mutual assistance and protection; they would walk every morning from their houses to till their nearby fields. These villagers could readily imagine the situation of someone who was awakened in the middle of the night by a neighbor beating on his door.

In ancient Palestine, people often traveled at night to avoid the oppressive heat of the day. This parable relates the simple story of unexpected guests who arrive late at night at the humble home of a villager. The hospitality of the day requires that the villager offer his guests something to eat after their long journey, but he has nothing to offer them. Bread is usually baked in the morning, and when the travelers arrive late at night there is none left.

The villager knocks on the door of his neighbor hoping to borrow some bread. The neighbor does not wish to be bothered at such a late hour. He responds, "My children are with me in bed; I cannot rise and give thee." The situation of the neighbor is understandable; homes of the poorer people were generally only one room and the entire family slept there. Some commentators suggest that the members of the family slept on a raised platform in the back of the room while the goats and sheep occupied the front part (C. Smith 223). Other commentators suggest that the entire family slept lined up on the floor with the mother at one end and the father at the other (B. Smith 147). Given the crowded conditions and the lateness of the hour, it is understandable that the neighbor is reluctant to get up and search for bread.

The villager is desperate; he sees no other way to obtain bread to serve his newly-arrived guests. He continues to knock and implore his neighbor to get up and give him the bread. Verse 8 explains that the neighbor will not get up and give him the bread out of a desire to be neighborly, but he finally does so because of his importunity. The word "importunity" literally means "shamelessness" (Morris, *Luke* 195). According to Bock (*Luke* NIV 311), this Greek term includes both the ideas of shamelessness and boldness. The idea of persistence is not specifically stated, but it is implied. The villager is so intent on obtaining the bread that he continues to knock even though his continued knocking will wake up the entire village and bring embarrassment to him.

The point of the parable is not expressly stated, but it is clearly implied. If one's neighbor, with all his human limitations, can, by persistent knocking, be persuaded to get up and provide bread, how much more will a kind and gracious heavenly Father grant the petitions of His children (Manson, *Sayings* 268)? Morris (*Luke* 195) opines that if a believer does not want a particular petition enough to continue praying for it, then he doesn't really want it. The lesson of this beautiful parable is the disciple should pray regularly, earnestly, and persistently that God would supply his needs.

9 And I say unto you, Ask, and it shall be given you; seek, and ye shall find; knock, and it shall be opened unto you.
10 For every one that asketh receiveth; and he that seeketh findeth; and to him that knocketh it shall be opened.
11 If a son shall ask bread of any of you that is a father, will he give him a stone? or if *he ask* a fish, will he for a fish give him a serpent?
12 Or if he shall ask an egg, will he offer him a scorpion?
13 If ye then, being evil, know how to give good gifts unto your children: how much more shall *your* heavenly Father give the Holy Spirit to them that ask him?

Jesus concludes this parable on prayer with some general instructions that apply not only to the disciples of that generation but to all of His followers. Verses 9-10 have an almost poetic structure about them. The three verbs, ask, seek, and knock (Greek present imperatives) express the idea of continuous or ongoing action (Summers, *Luke* 140). The disciples are to continue to ask, seek, and knock. These words do not mean the disciples are to pray all the time; the idea is they are to pray regularly. Consistent prayer should be a part of the life of the believer. The three verbs in verse 9 are followed by three future tense verbs that express God's promise to respond to the prayers of His disciples. If they ask, it will be given to them. If they seek, they will find. If they knock, the door will be opened.

The three future tense verbs are followed in verse 10 by three restatements of the promise to (literally) the one asking, the one seeking, and the one knocking. These (Greek present tense participles) also express the idea of continuous action. The disciples are to continue asking, seeking, and knocking.

This passage must be interpreted in the light of other N. T. teachings on prayer. Jesus is not making an unconditional commitment to grant all petitions whether or not they are in accord with God's will. The Scripture is very clear that God responds to the prayers of His people in His own time and His own way. He is certainly not obligated to grant a prayer that is contrary to His will. For example, 1 John 5:14 says, "And this is the confidence that we have in him, that, if we ask any thing according to his will, he heareth us." The most important lesson for the disciples is they should pray regularly and consistently with the confidence that God will hear their prayers and respond to them in the most appropriate way. If they do not seek the will of God in prayer, it is certain they will not find it.

Beginning in verse 11, Jesus uses some ridiculous comparisons to illustrate how God will respond to the prayers of His children. He uses the analogy of an earthly father who provides for his son. If his son asks for something good—like bread, a fish, or an egg—the father will not give him something that will do him no good and perhaps even harm him—like a stone, a serpent, or a scorpion. The father loves his son and gives him only what he intends for his good; he does not give that which is evil.

Verse 13 begins with "If ye then, being evil." "Evil" (Greek *pon ros*) basically means "grasping" (Summers, *Luke* 141), but in this context, "evil" is probably the best translation. Ellis (166) suggests the idea here is that a human father is imperfect by nature; Luke and other N. T. writers accept the idea that human sinfulness is universal. The father in the story is not a bad father; he is simply a sinful human being. He possesses the same sinful nature all human beings possess. "How much more" is really the heart of the story. If a human father, with all of his inherent limitations, knows how to give good gifts to his children, how much more does the perfect God give to His spiritual children exactly what they need?

There is one significant difference between this passage and the parallel passage in Matthew 7:11, which says, "How much more shall your Father which is in heaven give good things to them that ask him?" while Luke 11:13 says, "How much more shall *your* heavenly Father give the Holy Spirit to them that ask him?" Ellis (166) suggests that the term "good things," which is used in Matthew, is something of a technical term used to describe the blessings of the messianic age. Luke gives great emphasis to the Holy Spirit in his writings, and it is possible that the term "Holy Spirit" would have had greater meaning for his Gentile audience than the term "Spirit of God," which was normally used by the Jews. Lenski (631) opines that the Holy Spirit is the highest and greatest spiritual gift, which includes all the lesser spiritual gifts. Marshall (*Gospel* 470) notes there are several ways of explaining this difference between Matthew and Luke, and he does not see a great deal of difference between them.

The basic teaching of these verses is that the disciples can and should pray with total confidence God will hear and answer their prayers according to His infinite will. God may be trusted to supply all their needs (Manson, *Sayings* 81-82).

14 And he was casting out a devil, and it was dumb. And it came to pass, when the devil was gone out, the dumb spake; and the people wondered.
15 But some of them said, He casteth out devils through Beelzebub the chief of the devils.
16 And others, tempting *him*, sought of him a sign from heaven.
17 But he, knowing their thoughts, said unto them, Every kingdom divided against itself is brought to desolation; and a house *divided* against a house falleth.
18 If Satan also be divided against himself, how shall his kingdom stand? because ye say that I cast out devils through Beelzebub.
19 And if I by Beelzebub cast out devils, by whom do your sons cast *them* out? therefore shall they be your judges.
20 But if I with the finger of God cast out devils, no doubt the kingdom of God is come upon you.
21 When a strong man armed keepeth his palace, his goods are in peace:
22 But when a stronger than he shall come upon him, and overcome him, he taketh from him all his armour wherein he trusted, and divideth his spoils.
23 He that is not with me is against me: and he that gathereth not with me scattereth.
24 When the unclean spirit is gone out of a man, he walketh through dry places, seeking rest; and finding none, he saith, I will return unto my house whence I came out.
25 And when he cometh, he findeth *it* swept and garnished.
26 Then goeth he, and taketh *to him* seven other spirits more wicked than himself; and they enter in, and dwell there: and the last *state* of that man is worse than the first.

These verses begin a new section in Jesus' training program for His disciples. Luke makes no connection with the previous verses; nor does he identify when or where the teaching takes place. As often in this Gospel, the teaching is more important than the circumstances. There are two important themes developed in these verses. The first is the growing opposition between Jesus and the Jewish authorities. The charges that are made against Him in verse 14 probably have their origin in the Jewish leadership. The second important theme is the power and authority of Jesus, who explains to the disciples, both by His words and by His actions, what it means to be the Son of God. The fact that Jesus has power over the spirit world is a strong evidence of His divinity.

In verse 14, Jesus casts out a demon or an "evil spirit," a Jewish expression describing a devil (Liefeld 952). That this spirit was dumb means the demon had rendered the man unable to speak. When Jesus cast the devil out of the man, his ability to speak returned. The people who witnessed this event wondered how Jesus had been able to perform such a notable miracle.

In verse 15, Jesus is accused of casting the demon out of the man not by the power of God but by the power of Beelzebub. Luke identifies Beelzebub as "the chief of the devils." Luke does not specifically identify the person or persons who make the charge, but in a similar passage in Matthew 9:34, it is the Pharisees who make the accusation. This accusation against Jesus probably has its origin in the Jewish leadership. This charge is a serious one because if Jesus is indeed casting out demons by the power of Beelzebub, then His claims to be the Son of God are false.

The origin and derivation of the term "Beelzebub" (most Greek manuscripts spell it "Beelzeboul") have produced considerable discussion (Liefeld 952; Marshall, *Gospel* 472-473). Verse 18 implies it is another name for Satan. Lenski (632) suggests that Beelzebul is the original name of the Philistine god Baal; in later years, it was used to describe Satan.

Jesus responds by showing that this accusation is ridiculous on its face. The devils are Satan's emissaries. How much sense would it make for Jesus to use the power of Satan to cast out Satan's own emissaries? That would mean that Satan's kingdom is hopelessly divided; it would be engaging in self-destruction (Kelly 194).

In verse 19, Jesus calls attention to the fact the Jewish leaders also have those who cast out demons. Through whom are they casting out demons? If Jesus is casting out demons through the power of Satan, could not the same charge be made against these Jewish exorcists? If the Jewish exorcists cast demons out through the power of God, what is to prevent Jesus from doing the same thing? The actions of the Jewish leaders themselves demonstrate the absurdity of the charge against Jesus.

In verse 20, Jesus looks at the other side of the coin. If He is really casting out demons by the power of God, the Kingdom of God has come upon them. If He casts out demons by the finger of God, then Jesus must be the Son of God who has inaugurated the new kingdom that God is establishing. "By the finger of God" is based on Exodus 8:19, where Aaron smote the dust of the earth with his rod and it became lice. When the magicians of Egypt could not duplicate this miracle, they told Pharaoh the finger of God was responsible. Jesus' casting out the evil spirits was another great miracle that demonstrated the power of God. Manson (*Teachings* 83) explains that Jesus is performing a miracle the demons cannot reasonably be expected to duplicate. It must, therefore, be the work of God.

The parallel passage in Matthew 12:28 reads, "But if I cast out devils by the Spirit of God, then the kingdom of God is come upon you." Morgan (*Luke*

144) suggests there is no contradiction between Luke and Matthew because the terms "finger of God" and "spirit of God" are synonymous. Marshall (*Gospel* 475) asserts that the two expressions are very similar in meaning. Barrett (*Luke* 63) states there is no real difference between the two terms; both are metaphors for the mighty power of God.

The establishment of the Kingdom of God is one of Luke's major themes. At this point in Jesus' ministry, the Kingdom of God has not yet been fully revealed, but its revelation has begun in the mighty deeds He performs. Verses 21-22 allude to Jesus' victory over the forces of Satan (Liefeld 951). Satan is the "strong man" who has been successfully defending his kingdom. Now the situation has changed; Jesus has come and is in the process of defeating the forces of Satan. No longer does Satan enjoy the same level of power and influence he has enjoyed.

Verse 23 is directed specifically to the crowd mentioned previously in verse 14. This powerful demonstration of Jesus' power has put them in a position where they must make a choice. They must choose between Jesus and Satan; they can no longer straddle the fence. If they do not choose to follow Jesus, they will automatically become followers of Satan (Summers, *Luke* 143).

Verses 24-26 present an interesting little story about the relationship between demons and human beings. It illustrates the fallacy of trying to remove evil from one's life without replacing it with God's control and direction. Demons or evil spirits desire to live within human beings. In verse 24, the evil spirit decides to leave the human being within whom it has been living. The implication is that the evil spirit is looking for a human host that will be more congenial, but, in the end, it finds no one better and decides to return to its previous host.

When the evil spirit returns home, it finds that the house is all swept and garnished. The idea is that the human host has cleaned up his life. The evil influence resulting from the demon's previous habitation, has been removed. He is now ready for better things.

Then the demon returns and brings with him seven demons even more wicked than he. The end result is that the man is worse off than he was before the demon left. The teaching of this story is that the follower of Jesus cannot be content to simply remove evil from his or her life. The disciple must replace that evil with something good; the Spirit of God must be allowed to come in and direct the disciple's life. Christianity is more than just the absence of evil; it is the presence of God. As Kelly (192) explains, "But the mere absence of outward evil will never bring a soul to God. God Himself must be known, and Jesus Himself received, not merely the unclean spirit be gone out."

Lenski (642-643) applies the teachings of this passage to the Jews of Jesus' day. They had heard the message of the gospel, but they refused to believe it. That refusal left them worse off than they would have been otherwise.

27 And it came to pass, as he spake these things, a certain woman of the company lifted up her voice, and said unto him, Blessed *is* the womb that bare thee, and the paps which thou hast sucked.

28 But he said, Yea rather, blessed *are* they that hear the word of God, and keep it.

These two verses are unique to this Gospel, probably included because of Luke's special interest in women. Luke establishes a very loose connection between them and the material which has gone before; he notes that this event happened as Jesus "spake these things." Otherwise, Luke gives no specific information about when or where this happened; the event itself is the important thing.

Plummer (306) suggests that the arrival of Jesus' mother might have provoked the unnamed woman to express these kind words about Him. According to this woman, the mother of Jesus is blessed to have Him as her son; she can be very proud of Him because of all the good things He is doing. Manson (*Sayings* 88) explains that this kind of language would have been used when one wished to be especially complimentary of Jesus.

Jesus responds to these kind words by saying that those who hear and obey the Word of God are even more blessed than His earthly mother. "Yea rather" (Greek *menoun*) is used in several different ways in the N. T. Stein (*Luke* 333) explains that it is sometimes used in an adversative sense of "on the contrary" or "no, but rather." Sometimes it is used to affirm a statement in the sense of "indeed." In other places, it is used in a corrective sense expressing the idea of "yes, but rather."

The corrective use best fits the context here. Jesus would agree that His mother is blessed because she has given birth to the Son of God, but those who hear and obey the Word of God are even more blessed. They are members of Jesus' spiritual family, and, for Jesus, the spiritual family is always more important than the natural family (Lenski 644). True blessedness comes from being in a right relationship with God through Jesus Christ. Liefeld (952) correctly notes that Jesus' response in verse 28 should not be interpreted as a negative statement concerning His mother Mary.

Jesus' use of "word of God" in this context is significant, apparently referring to the teachings He has given. The idea is that the disciples need to understand He is the Son of God and His words are also the Word of God (Lieu 94). Since they are the Word of God, Jesus' teachings should not only be heard, they should also be obeyed.

Summary (10:25—11:28)

Luke 10:25 begins the Parable of the Good Samaritan, told in response to the question "Who is my neighbor?" which is asked by an expert in the Jewish law. Jesus does not answer the question directly; instead, He tells the story of an unidentified traveler who is going down from Jerusalem to Jericho. This traveler is attacked, robbed, beaten, stripped of his clothing, and left for dead. Two religious professionals, a priest and a Levite, walk around this unfortunate man and continue with their journey. Then a third character enters the story, a hated Samaritan. In contrast to the unconcern of the priest and the Levite, the Samaritan goes out of his way to render aid. He binds the man's wounds, places him on his own donkey, and takes him to a nearby inn. There he continues to care for this unfortunate traveler and even leaves money with the innkeeper to provide additional care after his departure.

After concluding the parable, Jesus asks the legal expert a pointed question, "Which now of these three, thinkest thou, was neighbour unto him that fell among the thieves?" The lawyer does not use the word "Samaritan" in his response; he replies "He that shewed mercy on him." Jesus has changed the direction of His discussion with the lawyer. He does not define the term "neighbour" from the standpoint of one who is entitled to receive assistance; He defines it from the standpoint of one who renders aid in a time of need. Nor is "neighbour" to be understood in terms of any racial or ethnic considerations. Anyone, even a hated Samaritan, can be a neighbor.

Chapter 10 concludes with a brief account of a visit by Jesus and some of His disciples to the home of Mary and Martha. Luke does not mention where the home is located, but it is probably Bethany, a village near Jerusalem (Jn. 11:1). Martha is an excellent hostess; she is busily preparing to provide the best hospitality possible for Jesus and His disciples. Mary, on the other hand, is doing nothing to help prepare the meal. She is sitting at the feet of Jesus and learning from Him. Martha asks Jesus to encourage Mary to get up and help with the necessary preparations. Jesus politely declines her request. What Martha is doing is certainly important, but to sit at Jesus' feet and learn from Him is even more important. That is the essence of discipleship.

Chapter 11 begins with an object lesson on prayer. One of His disciples (who perhaps had previously been a disciple of John the Baptist) comes to him with an important petition, asking that Jesus give the disciples instruction on how they should pray. "Them" is plural; this lesson is designed for all of the disciples.

Luke's version of the prayer focuses on three main themes, the establishment of God's kingdom, the daily needs of the disciples, and forgiveness. Jesus teaches His disciples to pray "Thy kingdom come. Thy will be done, as in heaven, so in earth." He wants His followers to understand that God's work on earth is larger than a small band of disciples in an obscure Roman province. They are called to honor the name of God and to pray that God's will may be done on earth. The implication is they must make their contribution to the will of God being done on earth.

Jesus encourages the disciples to pray that their daily needs will be supplied. He is not encouraging them to be idle while they wait on God to send them what they need. The idea is that as they faithfully serve Him, God will see that their needs are supplied.

The final subject is forgiveness. The disciples need to know that forgiveness is essential in the Kingdom of God. They must be willing both to forgive others and to accept God's forgiveness.

Luke follows this teaching on prayer with a humorous parable that points out prayer must be consistent. In ancient Palestine, hospitality to visitors was extremely important. This parable tells the story of a villager caught in a difficult situation. His guests arrive in the middle of the night, and he has no bread to offer them.

He begins to pound on his neighbor's door and ask for bread. He understands that making such a noise in the middle of the night will awaken the entire village, but he does it anyway. The neighbor is unwilling to get up and give him the leftover bread, but the man is persistent. Finally, the neighbor is so frustrated that he gets up and gives the man what he wants. His persistence has enabled the villager to accomplish his goal. If the disciples are to have the kind of relationship with God they need to have, a consistent prayer life is a must.

Luke follows this humorous parable with some general instruction on prayer. The disciples are not to be afraid to pray to God about their needs, whether material or spiritual. God is a kind and generous Father who loves and cares for His children. They can depend on Him.

Verse 14 begins a new section in Jesus' training program for the disciples. It is possible Luke has brought together teachings that Jesus gave on different occasions. Verses 14-26 develop two important themes, the growing opposition of the Jewish leaders to Jesus and His ministry, and the power and authority of Jesus. Jesus is accused of casting out demons by the power of Beelzebub, the leader of the demons. Jesus responds that such a charge is ridiculous. The fact that He is able to cast out demons is an evidence of Jesus' divine authority.

Beginning in verse 21, Jesus confronts His disciples with the necessity of making a choice. The people have, in reality, only two options. They can trust in Christ, or they can trust in themselves. He tells the story of an unclean spirit driven out of a house. He goes around seeking a better place; he finds none and decides to return to his former home. He finds everything swept and garnished; he goes and finds seven other spirits more wicked than he. Together they occupy the house, and "the last state of that man is worse than the first." The point is that the disciples must continue to trust in Jesus and follow Him. They cannot make it on their own. Eliminating the evil in their lives is not enough; they must have the presence of the Lord in their lives.

This passage concludes with a brief story about a woman who voices a blessing on the mother of Jesus. Jesus does not rebuke her for pronouncing this blessing. He responds by telling her that those who hear and keep the word of God are even more blessed than His physical mother. For Jesus, His spiritual family is more important than His natural family.

Application: Teaching and Preaching the Passage

The Parable of the Good Samaritan is an extremely rich passage for teaching and preaching purposes. It gives concrete expression to the biblical injunction that the Lord's followers should love one another as they love God. The parable is not, however, easy to interpret and apply. In the early church, this parable and others were commonly interpreted by the allegorical method, which sought some spiritual meaning in every detail. While this method of interpretation may be attractive, it is dangerous because it divorces the parable from its original context in the teachings of Jesus. In doing that, the interpreter determines the meaning of each point in the parable. When this method is followed, the parable is interpreted according to the whim of the interpreter, and its original meaning is often lost.

In the nineteenth and twentieth centuries, the interpretation of the parables turned in a totally different direction.

Such scholars as Jeremias and Dodd taught that each parable makes one point and only one. The truth lies somewhere between these two extreme positions. A parable may teach more than one lesson, but every detail should not be allegorized. The preacher or teacher should seek to understand the parable in its original context. He or she should seek to answer such questions as these: How did Jesus originally use this parable? What did it mean to those who first received it? How can I apply this teaching to our situation today?

One important lesson we can learn from this parable is that situations do matter. When circumstances change, one's traditional enemy may suddenly become a neighbor. It is always appropriate to respond to human need; barriers of race, religion, ethnicity, or culture should never be allowed to hinder that response. Another important lesson is that power or position is no substitute for true neighborliness. The priest and the Levite could have made an effort to help, but they did not. Apparently, they used their religious positions to avoid being of service to one in need. This passage also teaches some important lessons about discipleship. Anyone can be a disciple, even a hated Samaritan. Being a disciple requires more than saying the right words; it involves doing the right thing at the right time and in the right way. For an excellent discussion of the proper application of this parable see Blomberg (*Parables* 232-233).

The final section of chapter ten tells the story of a visit that Jesus and some of His disciples made to the house of Martha and Mary. The story is not about the role of women in the Lord's work; it is about discipleship. In order to be effective, a disciple must spend time at the feet of Jesus and learn from Him. The disciple must always be a dependent person in the sense that he or she must always depend on Jesus for leadership, guidance, and direction. The disciple must also establish proper priorities in life. In the modern world, people have so many demands on their time and energy they simply cannot fulfill all of them. Choices must be made and proper priorities established. Discipleship requires self-discipline, time, and effort.

Luke 11:1-13 have much to say about the subject of prayer. These verses emphasize that a consistent life of prayer and devotion is a key to effective discipleship. In the first part of this passage, Jesus gives His disciples a list of some of the things for which they should pray regularly. First, they are to pray for the glory of God and the advancement of His kingdom. Second, they are to pray that their daily needs will be met. Third, they are to pray for forgiveness of their sins. As a condition for receiving forgiveness, they must be willing to forgive others. These are the kind of petitions Christians of every generation should present before the throne of God. They are the core of a positive and meaningful relationship with God.

The brief parable about the friend who comes at midnight also teaches an important lesson about prayer. Our prayers must be frank, open, and persistent. God welcomes our deepest needs and our greatest desires. Prayer must also be a consistent activity; it should be made on a regular basis. Prayer changes things; it changes both the one who prays and the one for whom prayer is given.

This passage also tells us a great deal about the character of the God to whom we are praying. He does not give His children a scorpion when they ask for a fish. He loves all of His children and wants what is best for them. He is truly King of Kings and Lord of Lords. That means we must be ready to accept and trust His decisions.

This passage would be a good text for sermons or lessons on the authority of God. The Jewish leaders accused Jesus of casting out demons by Beelzebub, but His ability to free people from the control of demons came from God and not from Beelzebub. Any limits on the power of God are strictly self-imposed; He can accomplish anything He wishes to accomplish. He is stronger than Satan and all of his demons. Therefore, we can rely upon God in the hour of trial and difficulty.

The last two sections of this passage bring out points that should be part of Christian teaching. It is good to remove sin from one's life, but doing that is not enough. The evil must be replaced by the presence of God. All the demons were removed from the house, but the demon later returned with seven demons more evil than himself. As a result, the man was worse off than he had been before. God must be allowed to come in and fill that vacuum in our lives.

The final two verses of this passage were probably part of a larger teaching, which Luke did not choose to include. A well-meaning woman wishes to give praise to the mother of Jesus. Bock (*Luke* IVP 324) notes in that culture it was common to honor a mother for her sons' accomplishments. Jesus accepts this high compliment, but He notes that those who hear and heed the word God has for them will be even more blessed. For Jesus, the members of His spiritual family are the most important.

C. Conflict and Controversy (11:29-54)

29 And when the people were gathered thick together, he began to say, This is an evil generation: they seek a sign; and there shall no sign be given it, but the sign of Jonas the prophet.

30 For as Jonas was a sign unto the Ninevites, so shall also the Son of man be to this generation.

31 The queen of the south shall rise up in the judgment with the men of this generation, and condemn them: for she came from the utmost parts of the earth to hear the wisdom of Solomon; and, behold, a greater than Solomon *is* here.

32 The men of Nineve shall rise up in the judgment with this generation, and shall condemn it: for they repented at the preaching of Jonas; and, behold, a greater than Jonas *is* here.

33 No man when he hath lighted a candle, putteth *it* in a secret place, neither under a bushel, but on a candlestick, that they which come in may see the light.

34 The light of the body is the eye: therefore when thine eye is single, thy whole body also is full of light; but when *thine eye* is evil, thy body also *is* full of darkness.

35 Take heed therefore that the light which is in thee be not darkness.

36 If thy whole body therefore *be* full of light, having no part dark, the whole shall be full of light, as when the bright shining of a candle doth give thee light.

This passage contains several of Jesus' teachings, which Luke has brought together for the benefit of his Gentile readers. In some of these teachings, Jesus is responding to attacks that had been brought against Him. Luke 11:16 has already called attention to the fact people were seeking a sign from Heaven, and that discussion continues in this passage. It is likely some in the crowd were asking Jesus to perform some miracle in order to authenticate His claims to be the Son of God and His power to forgive sins. While Jesus did perform miracles on a number of different occasions, He refused to make Himself subject to the whims of the crowd. He alone determined when and where miracles were performed.

In verse 29, Jesus labels the crowd an "evil generation" because they are requesting miraculous signs. He tells them the only sign they will receive is the sign of the O. T. prophet Jonas—that is, Jonah. Geldenhuys (334) takes this to mean the only sign they will receive is like that given by Jonah. Jonah appeared as one sent by God after having been delivered from the great fish. In the same way, Jesus will demonstrate that He is the Messiah by His resurrection from the dead. Lenski (647) presents a similar viewpoint.

Another interpretation is that the sign of Jonah has already been given and no new signs are necessary. Rather than demanding new signs, the crowd should heed the sign that God has already given. At the command of God, Jonah went and preached to the wicked city of Nineveh. Those in the city listened to His message and repented. As a result of their repentance life in the city was radically changed (Jonah 3).

Jonah did not need to perform miraculous signs to amaze the crowds or to obtain a hearing. The message he preached and the power he demonstrated were enough. In a similar vein, Jesus does not need to perform miraculous signs to demonstrate His credibility. The message Jesus preaches and the changes His preaching produces are enough to establish the credibility of His ministry (Ellis 167; Lieu 94).

The point is that the crowd following Jesus should not seek after miraculous signs because His message is self-authenticating. They should repent at the preaching of Jesus just as the people of Nineveh repented at the preaching of Jonah. God has spoken to them through His Son, Jesus Christ, and they should be content with that. Ellis (168) notes there is nothing inherently evil about signs. When they are given, they should be received. The problem is that this crowd is seeking signs to satisfy curiosity or to entrap Jesus. They are demanding something they have no right to expect.

Verse 31 states the "queen of the south" will rise up to judge the men of that generation. Although "queen of the south" is not specifically defined, the description fits the Queen of Sheba mentioned in 1 Kings 10:1-13 and 2 Chronicles 9:1-12 (Geldenhuys 335; Lenski 648). She had heard of the wisdom of Solomon and traveled a great distance to hear his words. She not only heard his words; she took them to heart. The Jewish leaders have refused to do the same with the teachings of Jesus even though Jesus is much greater than Solomon. For this reason, they deserve the judgment they will receive.

In verse 32, the story of Jonah resumes. The city of Nineveh was a pagan city, but its people were willing to repent at the words of Jonah. The people of Israel were not willing to repent at the words of Jesus who is much greater than Jonah, and they will be judged for their refusal. F. Bruce (*Hard Sayings* 97-98) understands the words "a greater than Jonah" to mean "something greater than Jonah," referring to the Kingdom of God that Jesus proclaimed. As Bruce notes, the people of Nineveh will be viewed more favorably on the Day of Judgment than will the Galileans who rejected Jesus' message.

Verses 33-36 deal with the subject of light. The idea is that Jesus, in His preaching and teaching, has brought to mankind the spiritual light they need to receive. They are not, however, willing to receive this spiritual light. Jesus uses the analogy of physical light to illustrate the tragic mistake they are making and the consequences they will suffer. These verses are probably directed to the Jewish leaders who are hostile toward Jesus and His ministry.

The homes of the common people of Palestine were small, with only one door and perhaps one window. In such a house, a small amount of light can make a big difference. "Candle" refers to a small clay lamp that burned olive oil. No normal person would light such a lamp and then hide it in an out-of-the-way place (Greek *kruptēn*, literally a cellar) or cover it with a basket. The small amount of light produced by the lamp would then be hidden; it would be of no value. A normal person would light the lamp and then set it on a lampstand so it would give light to those in the house.

Jesus then applies this analogy to the human body. The lamp of the body is the eye. If it is functioning as it should, the person will be able to see clearly; it will be like the lamp on the lampstand. If something is wrong with the eye, the person will be unable to see properly; it will be like the lamp hidden under a basket.

Verses 35-36 contain both words of warning and words of instruction. Jesus warns His followers they must not allow the light they have received to become darkness. In other words, they must not allow the things of this world to hinder them from receiving the true spiritual light Jesus has brought to them. They need to open their hearts and minds to the teachings of Jesus. If the true spiritual light Christ has brought is allowed to enter every part of the body, there will be no darkness. The person's entire being will be filled with spiritual light, just like the lamp that brings physical light to the entire room.

37 And as he spake, a certain Pharisee besought him to dine with him: and he went in, and sat down to meat.

38 And when the Pharisee saw *it*, he marveled that he had not first washed before dinner.

39 And the Lord said unto him, Now do ye Pharisees make clean the outside of the cup and the platter; but your inward part is full of ravening and wickedness.

40 *Ye* fools, did not he that made that which is without make that which is within also?

41 But rather give alms of such things as ye have; and, behold, all things are clean unto you.

42 But woe unto you, Pharisees! for ye tithe mint and rue and all manner of herbs, and pass over judgment and the love of God: these ought ye to have done, and not to leave the other undone.

43 Woe unto you, Pharisees! for ye love the uppermost seats in the synagogues, and greetings in the markets.
44 Woe unto you, scribes and Pharisees, hypocrites! for ye are as graves which appear not, and the men that walk over *them* are not aware *of them*.

These verses continue the development of Jesus' conflict with the Jewish leaders, which is a major theme of the Travel Narrative. This incident occurs in the home of a Pharisee who has invited Jesus to share table fellowship with him. As is his custom, Luke does not specify the time or place; he doesn't even give the name of the Pharisee who extends the invitation. The event itself is designed to convey the teaching. Similar teachings are found in Matthew 15:1-20 and 23:1-33.

Luke does not identify the specific meal to which Jesus is invited, but most authorities consider it to be a morning or mid-day meal rather than a supper (Plummer 309; Edersheim, *Life* II:205), which would have been a more formal occasion. The washing mentioned in verse 38 refers to the custom of ceremoniously washing one's hands before eating. This was not done for hygienic purposes; at that time, little was known of sanitation. The washing was done for religious reasons. We are not totally sure about how this washing was done in Jesus' day, but Edersheim (*Life* II:205-207) gives a detailed explanation of how it was done a few years later. Edersheim also notes that this event might have occurred on the Sabbath. This washing was not commanded by the O. T. but was a part of the tradition of the Pharisee that had developed over the years (Mk. 7:1-5). Barclay (155) also gives a rather detailed description of how this ritual washing was done.

The Pharisees were an influential group of laymen within the Jewish community of the first century. Their origins are somewhat difficult to determine, but the most widely-accepted view is they developed during the intertestamental period. During this period, Seleucid overlords tried to force the Jewish people to accept the Greek religion, and they had some success in doing so. Those who refused to compromise their Jewish faith (often at the cost of their lives) came to be known as *Hasidim*, which means "the saints" or "the godly" (Manson, *Sayings* 97). They later received the nickname *Perushim* or "separatists" because they insisted on a strict separation from anything considered to be ungodly.

The Pharisees of Jesus' day are thought to be their spiritual descendants. In the time of Jesus, they were dedicated to a strict interpretation of the Jewish law, both the written law of the O. T. and the oral law, which is often called "the tradition of the elders." Their goal was to make the law applicable to the daily lives of the people. The scribes were a group of professional scholars; they were experts in interpreting and applying the law, both written and oral. Most of them were Pharisees, and they provided the intellectual leadership to the Pharisaic party.

Liefeld (956) notes that by the time of Jesus the religion of the Pharisees had lost much of its vitality. It had degenerated into a ritualistic observance of a multitude of rules and regulations. In this passage, Jesus condemns them, not for their religious beliefs but for their practices. In particular, He criticizes their lack of concern for the poor and outcasts in society. Jesus also challenges their heavy reliance on the Jewish traditions reflected in the oral law. He considers these to be unnecessary additions to the teachings of the O. T. and a heavy burden upon the shoulders of the people. In one sense, Jesus is seeking a return to the simpler teachings of the O. T. documents themselves. He recognizes that obedience to a multitude of rules and regulations will not produce true spirituality (Geldenhuys 341; Marshall, *Gospel* 490-491).

In verse 39, Luke uses the term "Lord" to describe Jesus, thus clearly recognizing His equality with the Father. Jesus uses the analogy of a cup and platter to illustrate the spiritual condition of the Pharisees. Goppelt (TDNT VI:149) notes that the command to wash the inside of the cup was based on the teachings of the O. T. in Leviticus 11:33 and 15:12. The command to wash the outside of the cup was added by the Pharisees. The implication is that the Pharisees' lives are clean on the outside but full of spiritual impurity on the inside. They are like a cup that has only been washed on the outside while the inside remains filthy. Their inner being is "full of ravening and wickedness." These words may be interpreted in different ways, but the idea is that the Pharisees are wicked in the sense that they are obsessed with a desire for power and control. They are taking advantage of the people; they are dominated by a wicked desire to impose their religious conceptions on others. Summers (*Luke* 146) suggests these words reflect "greed, injustice, and a lack of compassion." "Ravening" expresses the idea of pillage, or of taking things from other people. "Wickedness" (Greek *ponēria*) is a general term for all kinds of evil.

In verse 40, Jesus speaks of the Pharisees as "fools" (Greek *aphrōn*), meaning one lacking in sense. In the O. T., "fool" describes one who is unwilling to accept God's leadership and direction in his life (Bock II:1113). The last part of verse 40 is a rhetorical question that can be translated, "The one who made the outside also made the inside, didn't he?" Both the inside of the cup and the outside are made by the same potter, and they are both important. If the outside is washed, the inside should also be washed.

The spiritual lesson is that the ritual washings of the Pharisees affected only the exterior part of man. They did nothing to change the heart, the interior part of a human being. They left the heart, mind, and conscience of the human being under the dominion of sin and Satan.

Verse 41 is difficult. Rather than simply condemning the Pharisees, Jesus offers them one thing they can do to begin to correct this situation. The giving of alms should not be viewed as a complete solution to their hypocrisy but as a step in the right direction. According to Luke, the Pharisees are told to give alms, to give money or food to the poor to relieve their destitute condition (Bock II:1114). The parallel passage, Matthew 23:26, instructs them to "cleanse first that *which is* within the cup and platter."

"Such things as ye have" (v. 40; Greek *enonta*) literally means "that which is inside." Lenski (659) suggests that "such things as ye have" is the best possible translation of the phrase. Ellis (171) opines that it refers to those things the Pharisees have taken from the people. Lieu (97) takes the phrase to refer to what is within the means of the Pharisees to give. They can restore what they have taken by unjust means. Geldenhuys (341-342) takes a slightly different approach. He suggests that the phrase refers specifically to the contents of the cups and platters. In a wider context, however, it refers to the totality of a man's possessions, which should be placed at God's disposal and used in the service of one's fellow men.

The Pharisees are placing too much emphasis on externals. They should instead be giving gifts that are internal (from the heart). Instead of taking advantage of the poor, they should give alms in order to relieve the misery of others. Summers (*Luke* 146) interprets this verse to mean the Pharisees should offer their inner selves to God rather than just offering external washings. Only by doing this can they be truly clean, both within and without.

The words "and, behold, all things are clean unto you" (v. 41) imply that only by changing the direction of their lives can the Pharisees have lives that are pure and acceptable to God. The way they are going will lead them only to destruction; their lives must be changed inwardly and outwardly.

Beginning in verse 42, Jesus pronounces six woes or announcements of condemnation. The first three are directed against the Pharisees; the second three are against the lawyers (or scribes). "Woe" (Greek *ouai*), in English, normally conveys the idea of a curse or a wish that something bad may happen to someone. Manson (*Sayings* 25) suggests the word does not express the idea of a curse, here, but is a statement of fact and suggests translating it "alas." According to Bock (I:583), the word conveys the idea of pity for the pain that one will experience. Ellis (171) explains it refers to the grief that accompanies giving someone up to judgment. In this passage, the idea is not so much that Jesus wishes or prays that the Pharisees will be condemned; instead, He is warning that their condemnation is a sad fact; they will be judged for the evils they have committed.

The first woe (v. 42) warns that the Pharisees stand condemned because they have not obeyed the laws as God intended they should be obeyed. They have carried the law of tithing to such an extreme they even tithe on the small amount of herbs that were grown in the garden to flavor their food. As Bornkamm (TDNT IV:66) explains, the O. T. does not require that the tithe be paid on these garden plants. Marshall (*Gospel* 497) presents a slightly different opinion. He notes that some garden plants were subject to the tithe while others were not. In essence, the tradition of the Pharisees demands that their followers go beyond what the law requires. At the same time, they are totally overlooking the more important matters such as judgment (or justice) and the love of God. The first term refers to the practice of judging the people of God fairly and righteously (Lenski 660). The second term refers to the all-encompassing love of God that will lead the people to a full devotion to Him. The exaggerated emphasis on relatively minor matters will hinder the people from loving God as they ought.

In verse 42, Jesus is not teaching that it is acceptable to ignore the teachings of the law. The laws given by God should be obeyed, but the teachings of God must be correctly understood and applied. There is certainly nothing wrong with tithing on garden herbs, but that is not more important than dealing justly with others and loving God sincerely. The followers of Jesus need to maintain a proper sense of perspective and proportion. Religion should never become simply a matter of proper conduct (Geldenhuys 342).

The second woe (v. 43) relates both to the attitude and to the conduct of the Pharisees. They are devoting too much time and attention to seeking the recognition of men; this has clearly become an issue of arrogance and pride. As Nolland (II:671) observes, the synagogue and the market place were the two primary locations for social interaction in Jesus' day. For an excellent discussion of synagogue worship as it existed in the first century see Edersheim (*Life* I:430-450). The "uppermost seats" were probably a row of seats located in the front part of the synagogue near the rabbis; these seats faced the congregation (Barclay 156). The greetings in the market place were much more than a simple "hello." They were rather long and elaborate greetings intended to convey respect (Bock II:1117). The Pharisees were spending too much time and effort seeking the recognition of men rather than the favor of God.

The third woe (v. 44) compares both the Pharisees and the scribes to unmarked graves that may inadvertently cause people to become ritually impure. According to Numbers 19:16 a person who touched a grave would be ritually unclean for seven days and unable to participate in worship during that period of time. Lenski (662) explains that tombs were often whitewashed during Passover so people might avoid them. The scribes and Pharisees resembled these unmarked graves in the sense that their influence was not positive but negative. They were an important part of the religious leadership of the land of Palestine, but in reality they were not leading people toward God but away from Him. Outwardly they seemed to be righteous, but inwardly they were doing spiritual harm.

Barclay (156-157) summarizes the failures of the Pharisees under two headings. First, they focus on externals rather than on the things that are most important. Second, they concentrate on the details of one's religion rather than on the essentials of one's relationship with God. They need to give more attention to the truly important things like love, kindness, justice, and generosity.

45 Then answered one of the lawyers, and said unto him, Master, thus saying thou reproachest us also.
46 And he said, Woe unto you also, *ye* lawyers! for ye lade men with burdens grievous to be borne, and ye yourselves touch not the burdens with one of your fingers.
47 Woe unto you! for ye build the sepulchres of the prophets, and your fathers killed them.
48 Truly ye bear witness that ye allow the deeds of your fathers: for they indeed killed them, and ye build their sepulchres.
49 Therefore also said the wisdom of God, I will send them prophets and apostles, and *some* of them they shall slay and persecute:
50 That the blood of all the prophets, which was shed from the foundation of the world, may be required of this generation;

51 From the blood of Abel unto the blood of Zacharias, which perished between the altar and the temple: verily I say unto you, It shall be required of this generation.
52 Woe unto you, lawyers! for ye have taken away the key of knowledge: ye entered not in yourselves, and them that were entering in ye hindered.
53 And as he said these things unto them, the scribes and the Pharisees began to urge *him* vehemently, and to provoke him to speak of many things:
54 Laying wait for him, and seeking to catch something out of his mouth, that they might accuse him.

Verse 45 is a transition verse that introduces the lawyers into the story. As was noted in the comments on Luke 10:25, "lawyer" in the N. T. is an expert in the laws of the Jews, both the written law of the O. T. and the oral laws developed by the rabbis. This is probably the same group of people often described by the term "scribes." On some occasions Luke uses "scribe," but he prefers "lawyer" because his Gentile audience would think of a scribe as some type of clerk or secretary rather than as an expert in the law. In this verse, the lawyer correctly notes that Jesus has included them in His condemnation.

The first of three denunciations of the lawyers is in verse 46; they are accused of placing heavy burdens on the people and then doing nothing to help them to bear those burdens. Luke is probably referring to the common people of Israel who would find it most difficult to observe all the multitude of rules and regulations the lawyers taught. Plummer (312) suggests this verse refers not to the requirements outlined in the O. T., but to the multitude of applications that had been developed over the years by the rabbis. According to Marshall (*Gospel* 500), the teaching is that the lawyers placed heavy requirements upon the people, which they themselves made no effort to obey. Summers (*Luke* 149) suggests a different interpretation. He argues that the lawyers set down these rules and regulations and gave no thought to the impossible requirements they placed upon the people. The scribes would not even give advice on how the requirements could be met.

Lenski (664) offers yet another interpretation: namely, that this verse refers to the way in which the scribes treated the O. T. They took the O. T. message of salvation and turned it into a list of laws, which they demanded the people obey.

While we should not be dogmatic, the key idea is not that the lawyers imposed laws on others that they did not impose on themselves; the scribes and Pharisees were required to observe the laws as well. The key idea is the lack of care and concern for the people of the land of Palestine who found it difficult, if not impossible, to observe this multitude of rules and regulations. They had to work to support their families, and obedience to all of those laws was virtually a full-time job.

In the second woe directed against the lawyers (v. 47), Jesus accuses them of constructing sepulchers in honor of the prophets of previous generations which their ancestors had slain. "Ye allow the deeds of your fathers" (v. 48) means that the Pharisees approved of what their fathers had done to the prophets. (Matthew 23:29-31 presents a somewhat different version of this same condemnation.) Geldenhuys (345-46) correctly notes that Jesus does not condemn the building of monuments to honor prophets from the past. It is, however, hypocritical for that generation to build monuments honoring prophets who were murdered while, at the same time, rejecting the prophets God sends to them.

As Summers (*Luke* 149-150) explains, there are few documented instances in the O. T. where prophets were actually slain. There were, however, many instances when the true prophets of God encountered severe opposition from the leaders of Israel (Jeremiah 26, for example). The tradition that the prophets were slain developed during the inter-biblical period and was quite widespread in the time of Jesus.

There is a sense of irony in these verses. In the past, the leaders of Israel refused to hear the voice of God when He spoke to them through the prophets. But now, they erect monuments in honor of those prophets. The Jewish leaders of Jesus' day are fully willing to honor those prophets who are dead, but they refuse to listen to the true prophet, Jesus, who is now living among them. The lawyers have such a commitment to the past that they refuse to pay heed to what God is doing in the present.

"Therefore also said the wisdom of God" (v. 49) sounds a little strange and interpreters offer different explanations (Stein, *Luke* 342; Marshall, *Gospel* 502-503). The most widely-accepted interpretation is to take them to mean "God, in his wisdom, said." The verse continues with God's promise to send prophets and apostles, some of whom will be persecuted and killed. While the verse does not specify a time frame for these events, many commentators see this verse as a prophecy of what God intends to do in and through the church (Stein, *Luke* 343; Marshall, *Gospel* 504).

Verses 50-51 state because of their rejection of God's Son, that generation of lawyers will be held accountable for the blood of all the prophets who have been slain since the creation of the world. The idea seems to be that the generation then living was no more willing to repent than past generations had been. They were therefore responsible before God for Israel's failure to worship and honor Him. "Prophet" is used in a broad sense to include all of those who have been faithful servants of God.

The reference to Abel is based upon Genesis 4:8-10, where he was slain by his jealous brother, Cain. That is the first murder recorded in Scripture. There is some difference of opinion concerning the identity of the Zechariah mentioned in verse 51. Liefeld (957) and Marshall (*Gospel* 506) summarize the various possibilities. The traditional view is that this verse refers to Zechariah the son of Jehoiada whose murder is described in 2 Chronicles 24:20-22. Since 2 Chronicles is the last book in the Hebrew O. T., Abel would be the first person killed for his faithfulness to God and Zechariah would be the last. The words "which perished between the altar and the temple" indicate he was slain in that part of the Temple, before the Holy Place where the priests served (Creed 168). The O. T. passage notes that Zechariah was killed "in the court of the house of the Lord." Since the lawyers of Jesus' day continued in the same state of rebellion against God as those who killed the prophets, they were guilty before God. The blood of these righteous men will be required at their hands.

Summers (*Luke* 150) explains that this passage does not mean that generation will be punished for what their fathers did hundreds of years in the past. The idea is that the current generation is guilty because it continues the rebellion against God, which past generations have practiced. Just as past generations have rejected the prophets and killed them, the current generation rejects Jesus as the Son of God and is seeking to kill Him.

Verse 52 is the third and final woe directed against the lawyers or scribes. According to Summers (*Luke* 150) the "key" refers to the "responsibility to interpret God's way." The parallel passage (Mt. 23:13) says, "Ye shut up the kingdom of heaven against men." The idea is that the lawyers have not only refused to understand and apply God's Word correctly for themselves, they have also prevented other people from understanding it as well. Their rigorous application of the traditions of the rabbis have not brought the people closer to God. They have, in fact, kept people from understanding correctly the will of God.

Verses 53-54 form Luke's conclusion to this passage; he outlines something of the increasing hostility between Jesus and the Jewish leaders. Interestingly, Luke uses "scribes" rather than "lawyers" here. "Urge him vehemently" translates two words (Greek *deinōs enexein*) that emphasize having a grudge against someone or being hostile to someone. "Provoke" (Greek *apostomatizō*) refers to mouthing certain questions to which certain "correct" answers were expected. Combined, the words mean they were hostilely besieging him with questions (Liefeld 958). Verse 54 explains that the scribes and Pharisees were not asking Jesus these questions because they wanted to learn from Him. They were trying to trap Him; the same expression is used in Acts 23:21 where a group of forty men was waiting to trap the Apostle Paul. The goal of the scribes pressing questions on Jesus in hostility is to provoke Him to say something contrary to the Jewish law, which they can use to accuse Him. Luke's portrayal of this group of Jewish leaders is very negative; they are totally unwilling to give heed to the truths that Jesus has come to earth to present. In these last two verses, Luke is probably anticipating Jesus' upcoming trials and death in Jerusalem.

Summary (11:29-54)

One important theme in Luke's Gospel is the increasing conflict between Jesus and the Jewish leaders. This conflict will continue to grow and develop through the remainder of the book. In verse 29, Jesus' remarks are directed to "the people." This group probably consists of those who are under the influence and control of the Pharisees or other leaders. Jesus accuses them of being an "evil generation" because they continue to seek after signs. The implication is that they are not content with Jesus' teachings and the miracles He has performed in their midst. They continue to demand additional proofs that He is, in fact, sent from God. Jesus will not perform miracles to satisfy the whim of the crowds; He will not be manipulated. He alone determines when and where miracles will be performed.

Jesus argues that instead of demanding additional signs, the people should accept the signs God has already given in the O. T. The prophet Jonah has already come; the city of Nineveh repented at his preaching. The Queen of Sheba has already come; she willingly received the wise sayings of Solomon. Jesus' point is that the people of Israel should listen to His message just as the people of Nineveh paid heed to the preaching of Jonah. He has come to bring light into their dark world, but they refuse to receive it. For this refusal, they will be judged.

Beginning in verse 33, Jesus uses the image of light to describe His mission in the world. He has come to bring spiritual light into a world that is spiritually dark. He gives two illustrations. First, He explains that no man would light a lamp and then hide it. He would put it on a lampstand where it could shed light into the house. The second illustration is the human eye. If the eye is functioning normally, the light of the world enters into the body. The individual can see what he or she is doing. Jesus came to bring spiritual light into the world, but the people refuse to receive it. They are like the man who lights a lamp and then hides it; they are like the eye that does not see. The implication is that Jesus has done what He can; the burden now rests on the shoulders of the people who must accept His teachings.

In the last two sections of this passage, Jesus condemns a group of Pharisees and lawyers. The Pharisees, an influential party within Jewish society, have developed hundreds of rules and regulations to interpret the law written in the O. T. and make it applicable to the daily lives of the people. Jesus accuses them of giving so much emphasis to these rules and regulations that they overlook entirely what God was trying to accomplish when He gave the law. In addition to that, Jesus accuses the Pharisees of practicing hypocrisy. They act in a pious manner in order to gain the adoration of the people, but in reality they are more interested in themselves than in serving God.

The group called "lawyers" in this passage is probably the same group known as "scribes" in this and other passages. They are experts in the Jewish law, both the written law given in the O. T. and the oral law which had been developed by the rabbis over a process of several centuries. Jesus accuses them of hypocrisy and misleading the people. They erect tombs to honor the prophets of past centuries, but they refuse to heed the teachings of an even greater prophet who stands in their midst. They lay heavy burdens upon the common people of the land, and they do nothing to help them bear those burdens. In short, they are not an asset to the work of God; they are a hindrance to it.

By the end of this chapter, the contention between Jesus and the Jewish leaders has become so severe that the scribes and Pharisees are hostile and trying to trap Him. They are trying to provoke Jesus into saying something they can use to bring charges against Him before the Roman authorities.

Application: Teaching and Preaching the Passage

There are few passages in Luke that present the consequences of sin and rebellion against God more clearly than this passage. Conflict is the dominant theme in this portion of Luke. Jesus came to earth to bring a message of life, light, and hope to the people of Israel. This was also a message that challenged the established power structure, and that structure responded with vigor. The scribes and Pharisees were determined to do everything they could to destroy Jesus and His ministry because they understood clearly that His message and ministry threatened their power and control.

This is not an easy passage from which to teach and preach, but it is a passage that is timely and important. There are several important themes that Christian people need to hear and heed. The first of these is the simple fact that there is a difference between truth and error. The modern world is relativistic in the sense that many people no longer recognize any absolutes. The line between right and wrong is very fuzzy—if it exists at all. In this passage, Jesus defends the truth and condemns error. He challenges the Pharisees and the scribes for their false teachings and for their hypocrisy. God is at work among them, and they refuse to recognize it. They make demands on Jesus they have no right to make. They misinterpret what God has done in the past, and they refuse to recognize what He is doing in the present.

Jesus did not simply look the other way when He witnessed this kind of error and hypocrisy. He confronted it. Christians today need to be bold enough and strong enough to confront the false teachings found in our world today. There is such a thing as heresy in the world; all teachings are not correct and should not be endorsed.

Doctrine is important. In this passage, Jesus challenges the people to adopt a correct view of who He is and what He came to earth to do. We live in a time when little emphasis is given to correct doctrine, and that is a serious matter. Whether our world wants to recognize it or not, there is still a difference between truth and error. We have the responsibility to teach and preach the truth even when opposition arises.

This passage also outlines the importance of establishing proper priorities in life. Jesus accuses the Pharisees of tithing on garden herbs while they pass over justice and the love of God. In other words, they have established incorrect priorities. They are emphasizing things that are relatively unimportant while they ignore those aspects of God's message, which are truly important. This is a danger against which Christians must guard. In the church, there is always the temptation to get hung up on minor matters and overlook the things that are truly important.

Another important theme in this passage is concern for people. Jesus accuses the Pharisees of leading the people into error. He accuses the lawyers of laying heavy burdens on the common people and doing nothing to help them bear those burdens. In the ministry of Jesus, all people are important. He came to bring light to them. It is important to note that Jesus seldom focused His attention on the people who were rich and politically powerful. On many occasions, He came into conflict with them. He spent time with all classes of people, from those high up on the social scale to those who were outcasts. Buildings, budgets, and programs are certainly important, but the church must never forget that it is here to minister to people.

D. Challenges to His Followers (12:1-53)

1 In the mean time, when there were gathered together an innumerable multitude of people, insomuch that they trode one upon another, he began to say unto His disciples first of all, Beware ye of the leaven of the Pharisees, which is hypocrisy.

Verse 1 is a transition verse, serving both as the conclusion to Jesus' condemnation of the scribes and Pharisees found in the previous chapter and as the introduction to the instruction Jesus gives to His disciples in this chapter. This instruction will continue through 13:21. Creed (168) and Stein (*Luke* 344) suggest this passage is a collection of Jesus' teachings that have been brought together by the author of this Gospel. Geldenhuys (350) holds, instead, that the parts of this teaching fit logically together, and it is likely they were all given at one time. Geldenhuys does recognize, however, that Jesus may have given the same or similar teaching at different times in His ministry. Stonehouse (103) also calls attention to the fact that Jesus' teaching probably involved much repetition.

The first part of verse 1, indicates that the teaching of Jesus had attracted a large following. Apparently, by this time Jesus had left the house of the Pharisee and was teaching in a more open area, perhaps in the street in front of the house. Plummer (317) suggests the crowd was divided, with some supporting Jesus and others identifying with the Pharisees. As usual, Luke gives no indication as to where this took place. "Innumerable" (Greek *muriadōn*) describes the crowd as large without indicating a specific number. The multitude was, however, large enough that the people began stepping on one another in their attempt to get close enough to hear what Jesus was saying.

"First" (Greek *prōtos*) probably means "in the first place" or "above all." According to Plummer (317), the idea is that Jesus' words were primarily directed to His disciples, but the crowd was permitted to listen as well.

The large size of the crowd indicates Jesus has become a popular figure, especially among the common people of the land. This popularity makes it difficult for the Pharisees to sustain any effective action against Him. They would like to eliminate Him entirely, but they can find no practical way to do that.

Jesus tells His disciples to beware of and watch out for the "leaven of the Pharisees." "Leaven" refers to the yeast that made the dough rise so it could be baked into bread. Here it serves as a symbol for the evil influence of the Pharisees. The Pharisees were held in high esteem by many because of their strictness and their commitment to the oral as well as the written law. Jesus points out that this outward appearance is deceiving. In reality, their influence is so evil and corrupt He uses the term "hypocrisy" to describe it. This word was originally used to describe an actor playing a role on a stage; it later came to describe something done without sincerity or in pretense.

2 For there is nothing covered, that shall not be revealed; neither hid, that shall not be known.
3 Therefore whatsoever ye have spoken in darkness shall be heard in the light; and that which ye have

spoken in the ear in closets shall be proclaimed upon the housetops.
4 And I say unto you my friends, Be not afraid of them that kill the body, and after that have no more that they can do.
5 But I will forewarn you whom ye shall fear: Fear him, which after he hath killed hath power to cast into hell; yea, I say unto you, Fear him.
6 Are not five sparrows sold for two farthings, and not one of them is forgotten before God?
7 But even the very hairs of your head are all numbered. Fear not therefore: ye are of more value than many sparrows.
8 Also I say unto you, Whosoever shall confess me before men, him shall the Son of man also confess before the angels of God:
9 But he that denieth me before men shall be denied before the angels of God.
10 And whosoever shall speak a word against the Son of man, it shall be forgiven him: but unto him that blasphemeth against the Holy Ghost it shall not be forgiven.
11 And when they bring you unto the synagogues, and *unto* magistrates, and powers, take ye no thought how or what thing ye shall answer, or what ye shall say:
12 For the Holy Ghost shall teach you in the same hour what ye ought to say.

Verses 2-3 are in direct response to the Pharisees, whom Jesus has just accused of hypocrisy; their hypocrisy will ultimately become apparent. The disciples are not to imitate the Pharisees; they are to be honest and sincere both in word and in deed. What they have spoken in the darkness will ultimately be expressed in the light. What they have spoken in "closets"—secret places—will finally be proclaimed from the flat roofs of the houses. The truth will eventually come out, but Jesus does not explain in the passage whether it will come out here on earth or in the end times. Creed (170) understands this passage to be an exhortation to the disciples to proclaim in public what they have learned from Jesus in private. The gospel message will be of little value as long as it is confined to a few; the disciples must be prepared for the day when they will be called upon to preach the good news to the entire world.

In verse 4, Jesus addresses His disciples as "my friends." This is the only place in the Synoptic Gospels where Jesus speaks of His disciples as friends (Creed 171). There is, however, an important passage in John 15:14-15 where Jesus emphasizes that His relationship with the disciples is based on friendship. Here in Luke, Jesus stresses the personal relationship He has with His disciples because He is about to challenge them with a very difficult teaching.

Jesus tells His disciples they are not to fear those who can only kill the body, such as their Jewish and Roman persecutors. They are to fear God because He alone has the power both to kill the body and to cast the soul into hell. When Jesus tells His disciples to fear God, He does not imply the idea of terror or earthly fear. The idea is that they should recognize God for who He is; they should hold Him in respect and awe.

Those who persecute and kill are able to do great damage, but there is a limit to what they can do. They can kill the body, the material part of a human being, but they are powerless to destroy the immortal soul. Only God can do that. "Hell" (v. 5) (Greek *gehenna*) was originally used to describe the Valley of the Sons of Hinnom just outside the walls of the city of Jerusalem. At certain times during the O. T. era, children were sacrificed in this valley to the pagan god Molech. According to 2 Kings 23:10, King Josiah put a stop to this pagan practice. In later years, this valley was used as a trash dump for all kinds of refuse (Jer. 7:32). For a detailed discussion of Gehenna see Jeremias (TDNT I:657-658). In the N. T., this term is used to describe the final destiny of the wicked (Mt. 5:29, 30; 10:28; and 23:15, 33).

In verses 5-7, Jesus explains to His disciples that their relationship with God must include both fear and trust. The disciples should fear God because He alone has the power to cast the soul into hell; they should render to Him the awe and respect He is due. They can trust in God because He knows them intimately and provides for them.

Jesus uses two illustrations that describe the Lord's care and concern for even the smallest of things. The word "sparrows" can refer to any of several species of small birds that were captured and used for food (Marshall, *Gospel* 514). This was the cheapest meat available and was often eaten by the poor. A "farthing" (Greek *assarion*) was a small copper coin worth about 1/16 of a denarius. In the second illustration, Jesus tells the disciples that even the hairs on their heads are numbered. In the ancient world, there was no way of counting the number of the hairs on the head, but God knows exactly how many there are. The point of these two illustrations is given in verse 7. If God cares about small things such as the sparrows or the number of hairs on a person's head, how much more does He care about the disciples who are of infinitely greater value.

In verses 8-12, Jesus develops a basic prerequisite for discipleship; the disciple must be one who confesses Christ in the presence of other men. He must bear faithful witness even in times of trial and difficulty. "Confess" (Greek *homologe*) means to acknowledge publicly or to declare allegiance to. The point is that the disciples cannot remain silent; they must be willing to declare publicly that they are followers of Christ. This public acknowledgment will not always be easy. If they confess their allegiance before others, then the Son of Man will respond by confessing their relationship with Him before the angels in Heaven. The "angels of God" are those angels who serve God on the Day of Judgment. Matthew 13:37-50 describes the important role angels will play in God's judgment of mankind. The idea is that if His disciples confess their relationship with Him before men while on earth, Jesus will confess His relationship with them before the Father in Heaven. Verse 9 presents the other side of the coin. If the disciples deny their relationship with Christ, then He will deny any relationship with them on the Day of Judgment.

Verses 10-11 are two of the most difficult and controversial verses in Luke's Gospel. Jesus understands that all of His future disciples will not remain faithful to Him; some will fail to publicly confess their relationship with Him. In these verses, Jesus distinguishes between saying a word against the Son of Man and blaspheming the Holy Spirit, but He does not clearly define that distinction. Matthew 12:31-32 and Mark 3:28-29 also refer to the blasphemy of the Holy Spirit, but they place it in the context of Jesus' defense against the accusations of the scribes and Pharisees. They had accused Jesus of casting out demons in the name of Beelzebub. Luke places this teaching in the context of Jesus' instruction that the disciples must not deny Him even in times of trial and persecution.

To speak "a word against the Son of Man" probably refers back to what Jesus has said in verse 9. To deny one's relationship with Jesus before men is a serious charge, but it is one that can be forgiven. There are many examples in the N. T. of those who initially rejected Jesus and later turned to Him (Summers, *Luke* 154). Barrett (*Holy Spirit* 106) analyzes how this sin was understood in the early church. He explains that many in the early church considered this to be a sin committed by unbelievers who might yet be won to the faith. This was a sin committed before baptism, and it was likely that even many of Jesus' followers had spoken blasphemous words against Him prior to their conversion. It was a serious sin, but one that could be forgiven.

The phrase "him that blasphemeth against the Holy Ghost" is more difficult to define; it seems Jesus expected His followers to understand the meaning. As a general rule, the verb "blaspheme" means to speak ill of someone or to speak in an abusive manner (Green, *Luke* 484). There is considerable difference of opinion concerning the precise meaning of the word in the Synoptic Gospels. For a good discussion see Twelftree (DJG 75-76), who argues that in this context it refers specifically to denying the ability of the Holy Spirit to provide support for the disciples in times of persecution.

Since all three of the Synoptic Gospels state that the blasphemy of the Holy Spirit cannot be forgiven (Mt. 12:31-32; Mk. 3:28-29; Lk. 12:10), it is often referred to as the "unpardonable sin." Since this expression is not fully explained in the Gospels, there is considerable debate concerning the nature of the unpardonable sin and who can commit it. A comprehensive discussion of this issue is beyond the scope of this commentary, but some attention needs to be given to it. Bock (II:1140-1143) and Fitzmyer (II:963-966) give extensive discussions of the most commonly-held interpretations.

Bock (II:1141-1143) concludes that the blasphemy of the Holy Spirit is not a one-time rejection of the work of the Holy Spirit, but that it is the persistent refusal to accept the Spirit's leadership and direction concerning the person and work of Christ. In fact, this is how Bock distinguishes between saying a word against the Son of Man and the blasphemy of the Holy Spirit. Saying a word against Jesus is a single act of rejection while the blasphemy of the Holy Spirit is a permanent rejection. Plummer (321) and Stein (*Luke* 348) present similar viewpoints. Plummer argues that constant opposition to the work of the Spirit renders true repentance impossible. Stein notes that blasphemy is more than just speaking against the work of the Holy Spirit; it is "unrelenting opposition to what he is doing." Barclay understands the unforgiveable sin to be the repeated refusal to listen to God's Word and a persistent determination to go in one's own way rather than God's way. This sin is unforgiveable because the person's heart has become so hard he cannot respond to God in the proper way. Barclay (162) writes, "God has not shut him out; by his repeated refusals he has shut himself out."

According to Creed (172), the unpardonable sin is "to be untrue to the testimony which the Holy Spirit will put into the mouth of the disciples." Lenski (680-681) explains it is the Holy Spirit that brings about repentance, and blasphemy against Him renders the work of repentance impossible.

Picirilli (106) argues that the blasphemy of the Holy Spirit consists of attributing the obvious work of the Holy Spirit to Satan. He writes, "This is blasphemous, indeed, representing a settled and perverted rejection of, a willful slander of, the work of God." Picirilli goes on to explain that this blasphemy represents a "*knowing* (italics his) or willful accusation against the Spirit of God." Geldenhuys (350) and Summers (*Luke* 154) also understand the unpardonable sin to consist of attributing the work of the Spirit of God to Satan.

Manson (*Sayings* 110) presents a somewhat similar position. He suggests the unpardonable sin is an extreme form of opposition to God. It describes one who has so completely come to identify with the forces of evil that the work of the Holy Spirit seems to him to be madness. According to these interpretations, the unpardonable sin can only be committed by an unbeliever, one who stands outside the Christian faith.

There are other possible interpretations of the blasphemy of the Holy Spirit. For example, a number of modern interpreters adhere to an interpretation often found in the early church. They understand the unpardonable sin to be apostasy (Ellis 176). Green (*Luke* 484) defines the blasphemy of the Holy Spirit as "committing apostasy in the face of persecution." A. Richardson (*Introduction* 108) argues that "to reject the demonstration of the reign of God, in the power of the Spirit, as it is experienced in the life of the Church, is to put oneself outside the sphere of forgiveness altogether." He then specifically identifies the blasphemy of the Spirit with the sin of apostasy as described in Hebrews 6:4-6, 10:26-31, and 12:14-17.

The context of Luke 12 is an argument in favor of this interpretation. In verse 9, Jesus warns His disciples against the danger of denying Him before men; that denial could constitute apostasy. A similar interpretation is presented by F. Bruce (*Hard Sayings* 91-93) who also connects this passage with the warnings given in Hebrews. According to this interpretation, the unpardonable sin can be committed only by a believer, one who stands within the Christian faith.

Barrett (*Holy Spirit* 106-107) also understands the blasphemy of the Holy Spirit to be the sin of apostasy. He notes that many in the early church identified this sin with sins committed after baptism, which could not be forgiven. Barrett writes, "Blasphemy against the Holy Spirit seems, then, to be a sin committed within the Church, which, because it denies the root and spring of the Church's life, cannot rediscover the forgiveness by which the sinner first entered the community of the forgiven" (107). Barrett identifies the blasphemy of the Holy Spirit in the Gospels both with the sin of apostasy in Hebrews and with the sin unto death mentioned in 1 John.

The multitude of interpretations that have been offered through the centuries bears witness to the difficulty in defining precisely the nature of the unpardonable sin. In the context of Luke's Gospel, the best interpretation is to identify it with apostasy. The danger is that the disciples may be tempted to abandon their faith in Christ in the face of severe persecution.

Lenski (681) sounds a note of warning that all believers should heed. They should not be quick to judge who has committed apostasy and who has not; that is a judgment only God is qualified to make. The sin of apostasy cannot be committed "inadvertently or unconsciously."

Verses 11-12 are specifically designed to help prepare the disciples for the persecution they will inevitably face in the future. Jesus assumes they will be brought before Jewish or Roman authorities where they will be compelled either to defend their faith in Christ or abandon it. If they remain faithful to Christ, their end may be physical suffering and death. The emphasis of the passage is that they will not be left alone in such a difficult hour; the Holy Spirit will guide them. Plummer (321) connects this passage directly with the warning against the blasphemy of the Holy Spirit, which was given in the previous verses. He writes that the disciples will have no fear of committing the unpardonable sin before such a tribunal because the Holy Spirit will guide their words. Summers (*Luke* 154) explains the phrase "take no thought" expresses the idea of not being anxious or distracted. The disciples are not to panic in such a situation; they are to retain their faith in God and trust the Holy Spirit to guide them.

Bock (*Luke* NIV 339) sees no conflict between these instructions and 1 Peter 3:15, which teaches that the believer should always be prepared to "give an answer to every man that asketh you a reason of the hope that is in you with meekness and fear." The believer should be prepared to defend his faith; this preparation does not, however, eliminate the need to depend on the leadership of the Holy Spirit in the hour of trial and persecution.

13 And one of the company said unto him, Master, speak to my brother, that he divide the inheritance with me.
14 And he said unto him, Man, who made me a judge or a divider over you?
15 And he said unto them, Take heed, and beware of covetousness: for a man's life consisteth not in the abundance of the things which he possesseth.
16 And he spake a parable unto them, saying, The ground of a certain rich man brought forth plentifully:
17 And he thought within himself, saying, What shall I do, because I have no room where to bestow my fruits?
18 And he said, This will I do: I will pull down my barns, and build greater; and there will I bestow all my fruits and my goods.
19 And I will say to my soul, Soul, thou hast much goods laid up for many years; take thine ease, eat, drink, *and* be merry.
20 But God said unto him, *Thou* fool, this night thy soul shall be required of thee: then whose shall those things be, which thou hast provided?

21 So *is* he that layeth up treasure for himself, and is not rich toward God.

Jesus warns His disciples not to be overly concerned with material security and the accumulation of things. He also explains that He has not come to serve as an arbiter in earthly disputes. Luke does not explain whether the claim against the brother is a just claim or an unjust claim. For Jesus, that is not the important point. He uses this simple story to impress upon the disciples the truth that their priority must be on the things of God and not on material possessions. The last words of verse 15 emphasize that the essence of one's life is not found in material possessions but in one's relationship with God.

Beginning in verse 16, Jesus reinforces this truth with the well-known parable of the rich fool. It is a simple story about the foolishness of basing one's hopes for happiness on the accumulation of material possessions (B. Smith 142). Material wealth was something that few people in ancient Palestine had experienced, but for which many people had dreamed and hoped. In this parable, the land owned by the rich man produced abundant crops; he had so much produce, he did not have sufficient room to store it. He decided to solve his problem not by selling it or by giving it to those in need. He resolved to tear down his barns and build larger ones so he would have room to store the abundance. Then he would not have to worry about producing future crops; he would have sufficient grain stored up to live in luxury for many years. He could take his ease and "eat, drink, *and* be merry."

The parable takes a sharp turn in verse 20. God enters the story, and He calls the rich man a fool. Plummer (554) notes that four different Greek words can be translated "fool." The one used here (Greek *aphrōn*) is a strong word that literally means "without reason" (Vine 113; Lenski 689). It describes one who lacks a common-sense understanding of either physical or spiritual reality. This word is also found in Luke 11:40 and 24:25.

Then God says, "this night thy soul shall be required of thee." The idea is that the rich man will die suddenly. His earthly life will end, and he cannot take his produce with him. All of the earthly possessions that are so important to him will be left for someone else to enjoy.

The lesson for the disciples is obvious. The things of this world are transitory; they will be left behind when men are called to stand before God in judgment. In this context, the fool is the person who lays up treasure for himself and is not rich toward God. "Is not rich toward God" describes a person who places little or no value on a relationship with God, for whom earthly treasures are the most important things in life. Jesus is not teaching that His disciples must always live in absolute poverty. The idea is that for the disciple the focus of his or her life must always be on the things of God and not on the accumulation of material possessions (Barclay 165).

22 And he said unto his disciples, Therefore I say unto you, Take no thought for your life, what ye shall eat; neither for the body, what ye shall put on.
23 The life is more than meat, and the body *is more* than raiment.

24 Consider the ravens: for they neither sow nor reap; which neither have storehouse nor barn; and God feedeth them: how much more are ye better than fowls?
25 And which of you with taking thought can add to his stature one cubit?
26 If ye then be not able to do that thing which is least, why take ye thought for the rest?
27 Consider the lilies how they grow: they toil not, they spin not; and yet I say unto you, that Solomon in all his glory was not arrayed like one of these.
28 If then God so clothe the grass, which is to day in the field, and to morrow is cast into the oven; how much more *will he clothe* you, O ye of little faith?
29 And seek not ye what ye shall eat, or what ye shall drink, neither be ye of doubtful mind.
30 For all these things do the nations of the world seek after: and your Father knoweth that ye have need of these things.
31 But rather seek ye the kingdom of God; and all these things shall be added unto you.

"Take no thought for" does not mean the disciples are to make no plans or provision for the future; neither does it justify laziness or a lack of effort. These words prohibit worry and anxiety. As Caird (163) notes, Jesus prohibits worry or anxiety because it is pointless and pagan. It can distract the disciples from their mission, which is to follow Jesus. In one sense it is pointless to worry because death may come unexpectedly, and no amount of worry can prevent it from happening. God is the giver of life. If He has given life to a person He will also provide the smaller things, like food and clothing, which are necessary to sustain that life. Rather than worrying about food and clothing, they should leave such things in the hands of God.

"Meat" (v. 23) is an old English word for "food." "Raiment" is an archaic word for clothing. Jesus knows His disciples will need food and clothing as they serve Him, but they should not be anxious about such things. They should trust in God to provide their necessities because He cares for them. Beginning in verse 24, Jesus gives a series of illustrations that explain how God provides for His creatures. A "raven" (Greek *korakos*) belongs to a family of birds including crows, rooks, and jackdaws (Plummer 326). They were unclean birds; the Jews were forbidden to eat them (Fitzmyer II:978). They were rather useless birds; they did not sow or reap. They did not build barns or storehouses, but God cared for them anyway.

The second illustration comes from the human realm. "Stature" (Greek *hēlikia*) is used in different ways in the N. T., sometimes to mean height and at other times to mean "age" or "span of life" (Plummer 326). "Cubit" was a unit of distance, about 18 inches. Nolland (II:692) suggests that in this context it means "a small amount."

Manson (*Sayings* 113) explains that two interpretations are possible: (1) "Which of you by worry can increase your height?" (2) "Which of you by worry can lengthen your life?" The commentators are divided on this issue, but the main idea of the verse is clear. Worry or anxiety is of no value to the believer because it can't change anything. Here the idea seems to be that no one can by worry add even a small amount of time to his or her lifespan.

If the disciples are unable to add even one hour to the length of life, why should they worry about much larger matters that concern the Kingdom of God? Jesus is not teaching that these things are unimportant; the point is they are beyond human control. There is no reason His disciples should waste their time and energy worrying about things beyond their control. They should have enough faith to leave such matters in the hands of God (Liefeld 963; Marshall, *Gospel* 528).

Beginning in verse 27, Luke adds two more illustrations of how God cares for all of His creatures; if He cares for the plants and animals He has created, then He will also care for His disciples. "Lilies" (Greek *krina*) occurs only here in the N. T., but it is fairly common outside the N. T. It is a generic term that describes brightly-colored flowers. They do not do any of the kinds of work that human beings do, such as spinning, but they present an even more beautiful appearance than King Solomon, the richest of Israelite kings. "Grass" (Greek *kortos*) is a general word describing various types of vegetation. In 1 Corinthians 3:12, it is translated "hay." Since wood was in short supply in Palestine, grass and other types of vegetation were often used as fuel (Plummer 327). "Oven" (Greek *klibanos*) is a portable oven rather than an oven in a fixed or permanent location. In the O. T., this word is often used to indicate great heat (Hos. 7:4-7).

The meaning of the passage comes out clearly in the last words of verse 28. If God takes care of the flowers and the grass, which show their beauty only for a short time, how much more will He take care of those who have committed their lives to His service. The disciples are described as "ye of little faith." These words are not meant to disparage the faith and commitment the disciples have already demonstrated. The point is they are still in the process of developing their level of faith and trust in God. Their faith is not yet where it needs to be if they are to successfully face the trials that lie ahead.

In verse 29, "seek ye not" (Greek present imperative) implies an action that continues. The idea is that the disciples are not to spend their lives seeking after food and drink. "Neither be ye of doubtful mind" expresses the idea of worry or anxiety. They are not to allow their ministries to be hindered by constant worry and anxiety. Instead, they should continually trust in the one who has called them into His service.

The point of verse 30 is that the disciples should not spend their lives imitating the world. The world, in this context, means people who are dominated by worldly concerns, who spend their lives trying to obtain food, material possessions, money, security, power, prestige, etc. Since they have no trust in God, they must rely on their own efforts to obtain and retain these things. "The nations" is often used to describe the heathen or the Gentiles; that may be the meaning here. The disciples do not have to live lives dominated by these earthly concerns because they trust in God. God knows they need certain necessities in order to live, and He can be trusted to provide for them. We should, however, not over-interpret what Jesus says here. He is not promising to His disciples an abundance of material possessions; neither is He promising a life free from work and toil. The idea is that God can be trusted to provide for His children.

Verse 31 gives the disciples positive instruction in the way they should direct their lives. Rather than seeking material possessions, they should seek to be the best disciples they can be. To "seek the kingdom of God" may mean several things (Marshall, *Gospel* 530). In this context, the idea is that the disciples should seek the spiritual blessings that come from serving God rather than the material blessings the world can offer. It also includes the idea they should submit freely to doing the will of God. "Seek" (Greek present imperative) implies continuous action. The point is they should always seek to advance the Kingdom of God. "All these things" describes the things necessary for the disciples to carry on an effective ministry. Jesus is not promising them a life of luxury, but that God will be with them and supply their needs.

32 Fear not, little flock; for it is your Father's good pleasure to give you the kingdom.
33 Sell that ye have, and give alms; provide yourselves bags which wax not old, a treasure in the heavens that faileth not, where no thief approacheth, neither moth corrupteth.
34 For where your treasure is, there will your heart be also.
35 Let your loins be girded about, and *your* lights burning;
36 And ye yourselves like unto men that wait for their lord, when he will return from the wedding; that when he cometh and knocketh, they may open unto him immediately.
37 Blessed *are* those servants, whom the lord when he cometh shall find watching: verily I say unto you, that he shall gird himself, and make them to sit down to meat, and will come forth and serve them.
38 And if he shall come in the second watch, or come in the third watch, and find *them* so, blessed are those servants.
39 And this know, that if the goodman of the house had known what hour the thief would come, he would have watched, and not have suffered his house to be broken through.
40 Be ye therefore ready also: for the Son of man cometh at an hour when ye think not.

Jesus is preparing His followers for times of difficulty and crisis they will face in the future, but it is difficult to determine precisely which crisis He has in mind. Without doubt, He expected He and His followers would encounter a great deal of opposition when they entered Jerusalem. There are, however, several verses in this passage (such as v. 40), which move beyond the situation they will face upon their arrival. Perhaps the best interpretation is to take a long-term view of this passage. Jesus is preparing His disciples for whatever types of crises they will face in the future. It may be the immediate crisis they will face in Jerusalem or the ultimate crisis of Christ's Second Coming and the final judgment (Summers, *Luke* 159-160).

"Fear not" (v. 32) is a construction (Greek present imperative) that may mean either "stop fearing" or "don't have the habit of fearing." Either meaning is possible in this context. The idea is that the lives of the disciples should not be dominated by fear but by trust in God. Luke does not define the term "little flock," but in this context it probably refers to the disciples to whom Jesus has been speaking (Plummer 329). The most likely meaning of Jesus' promise that the Kingdom of God will be given to the disciples is that their heavenly Father will give to His disciples the privilege of being members of this kingdom. This great blessing cannot be earned or merited; it can only be received as a free gift given by God. The fact they are disciples of Jesus does not guarantee them positions of wealth, power, or influence in the world. Membership in God's kingdom means both privileges and responsibilities. The disciples have committed their lives to the service of Christ; one result of that commitment is a special place in the family of God.

Verse 33 does not imply the disciples are obligated to give up all of their possessions. Jesus' goal is not to reduce His disciples to absolute poverty but to defeat the enemy that is covetousness. As Plummer (329) explains, the giving of alms benefits both the person who receives the gift and the person who gives it. The benefit to the receiver is obvious. The benefit to the giver is that he is freed from the need to preserve and protect what he has gained. The disciples cannot be effective leaders in the Kingdom of God if they are preoccupied with obtaining and maintaining material possessions.

The things of this world can be easily lost or destroyed. Instead of concentrating their efforts on material things, the disciples need to focus their attention on laying up spiritual treasures in Heaven where they can neither be lost nor destroyed. Grammatically, the word for "heaven" is plural (in Greek) because the Jews thought of multiple heavens. The first heaven, for example, is the atmosphere in which human beings live and work. The second heaven is the abode of the sun, the stars, the moon, and other heavenly bodies. The third Heaven is the abode of God.

Verse 34 is very similar to Matthew 6:21; it reflects a common and very important biblical idea. The "heart," in Hebrew thinking, describes the center of thought and intention, the place where the most important decisions are made. If the disciples have their treasures here on earth, they will make their decisions from an earthly perspective. If their treasure is in Heaven, they will make decisions from the perspective of the Kingdom of God. If the disciple of Jesus is to serve as he should, he or she must focus on the things of God and not on the things this world can provide. This verse expresses both a timeless truth and a great challenge to the followers of Jesus.

The first words of verse 35 refer to the long robes that men in the East ordinarily wore. In order to perform any strenuous activity, it was necessary to tie the lower parts of the robe to the body (Creed 175-176). The last words of the verse refer back to Matthew 25:1, where the Kingdom of Heaven is compared to ten virgins who took their lamps and went out to meet the bridegroom. In verse 36, the disciples are told they must be like a group of faithful servants who remain on duty as they await the return of their master. They want to be ready to welcome him and meet his needs immediately upon his return. The word translated "wedding" can be used in different ways, sometimes for a wedding feast in particular, and at other times for another kind of festival or banquet. Plummer (330) suggests that in this context it probably refers to a wedding feast.

Verse 37 describes a scene where the master is so pleased with the conduct of his servants that he tells them to sit down and eat while he serves them. This would have been most unusual conduct for the master of a household. Lieu (104) explains that such a reversal of roles would never have occurred in an ancient near-eastern household, but it regularly occurs in Jesus' presentations of the kingdom. Several commentators (Creed 176; Plummer 330) opine that this verse may not refer to a typical eastern householder but to Jesus Himself. The idea is that Jesus will reward His disciples in the future. This is somewhat similar to the service Jesus rendered when He washed the feet of the disciples in John 13.

In verse 38, the thought returns to a Palestinian master and his servants. If the servants are faithful, they will remain awake and ready to receive their master throughout the night. The Jews normally divided the night into three watches, while the Romans divided it into four (Creed 176). According to the Jewish system, the second watch would have included roughly the hours between 10:00 p.m. and 2:00 a.m. The third watch would have lasted from about 2:00 a.m. to 6:00 a.m. Blessed are the servants who would remain awake and have food ready to serve to the master regardless when he arrived. The lesson for the disciples is, if they are to be the kind of disciples they need to be, they must be faithful at all times and in all circumstances. They must be like the faithful servants in this story who await the return of their earthly master.

The "goodman of the house" (v. 39) probably refers to a faithful slave who has been entrusted with the responsibility of supervising the day-to-day operation of the household (Lieu 104). This is probably the same position described in other passages by the terms "steward" or "chief steward." The idea of a thief coming in the night was a common metaphor for something that occurs unexpectedly (Plummer 331). The phrase "broken through" refers to the common practice of gaining entrance to a house by digging through a wall made of sun-dried bricks. The point here is that the disciples must always be prepared and ready to serve the Lord Jesus (Lieu 104).

Verse 40 applies the teachings of this passage not only to the immediate circle of Jesus' disciples, but to all the followers of Jesus of all ages. Clearly, Jesus had spoken to His disciples concerning His Second Coming. He had taught them that this important event could occur at any time, and He wanted them to base their service as disciples on this reality. They are not serving just for the moment; they are serving in light of Christ's future return. It is likely, however, that the disciples do not fully appreciate the importance of this instruction until after His death, burial, and resurrection.

Luke is writing this Gospel not only for the first generation of believers, but also for the second and third generations. He uses the teachings of Jesus to explain to later generations of believers concerning what they should expect in the future. Jesus will return; His coming will be, in some ways, like the return of the master who arrives at home late after attending a wedding feast for a friend or relative. It is impossible to predict the time of Christ's return. It may occur during the second or third watch of the night. In other words, there may be a delay of indefinite length. The disciples must always remain faithful and ready for service. "At an hour when ye think not" means no one can predict the time of the Second Coming. Throughout Christian history different individuals and groups have tried to determine when Christ will return, and their predictions have always failed. The Second Coming will occur at a time unknown to man but known to God.

41 Then Peter said unto him, Lord, speakest thou this parable unto us, or even to all?
42 And the Lord said, Who then is that faithful and wise steward, whom *his* lord shall make ruler over his household, to give *them their* portion of meat in due season?
43 Blessed *is* that servant, whom his lord when he cometh shall find so doing.
44 Of a truth I say unto you, that he will make him ruler over all that he hath.
45 But and if that servant say in his heart, My lord delayeth his coming; and shall begin to beat the menservants and maidens, and to eat and drink, and to be drunken;
46 The lord of that servant will come in a day when he looketh not for *him*, and at an hour when he is not aware, and will cut him in sunder, and will appoint him his portion with the unbelievers.
47 And that servant, which knew his lord's will, and prepared not *himself*, neither did according to his will, shall be beaten with many *stripes*.
48 But he that knew not, and did commit things worthy of stripes, shall be beaten with few *stripes*. For unto whomsoever much is given, of him shall much be required: and to whom men have committed much, of him they will ask the more.

"Parable" (v. 41; Greek *parabol* , reflecting the Hebrew *mashal*) is used to describe different types of wise sayings including parables, metaphors, riddles, allegories, etc. (Stein, *Parables* 16-21). Here it refers to one or both of the parables Jesus has just spoken: the parable of the householder (vv. 36-38) and the parable of the thief (vv. 39-40). The passage does not clearly indicate which of these Peter has in mind. Peter is asking whether the message of the parable is intended specifically for the disciples then present or for the larger circle of Jesus' followers. Jesus does not give a direct answer. Instead, He tells another parable, which forces the disciples to think carefully about the situation and come to their own conclusion.

The setting of this parable is the household of a man who is wealthy enough to have a number of servants. One of them is the "steward," the slave who has been given the responsibility of supervising the other slaves in the household (Childers 529). If he is faithful and fulfills the master's instructions, the steward will be rewarded with even greater privilege and responsibility. If he thinks the master will delay his return and begins to indulge himself and abuse the servants under his control, he will be punished by the master upon his return.

Verse 46 notes that the master will return unexpectedly; the point is that the return of Christ will also be unexpected. The last words of verse 46 are strong. To "cut him in sunder" means "to cut him in pieces." "Appoint him his portion with the unbelievers" indicates this unfaithful steward will share the destiny of the religious leaders who have opposed the ministry of Jesus (Liefeld 966-967). Both statements reflect the seriousness of what he has done. Jesus is probably using these words to indicate the final destiny of those who oppose the Gospel.

Some commentators are of the opinion "that servant" (v. 45) means a servant who is different from the faithful servant discussed in the previous verses. If this interpretation is correct, the parable implies there are two different servants, one who is faithful and one who is unfaithful. Other commentators are of the opinion the parable envisions only one servant, who is initially faithful and then becomes unfaithful when the master leaves. According to these interpreters, the term "that servant" means the unfaithful servant who is introduced in verse 45 is the same as the faithful servant discussed in verses 42-44. Marshall, for example (*Gospel* 542) takes "that servant" to be the same as the faithful steward mentioned in the previous verses. The steward who was at one time faithful to safeguard the master's interests has now become unfaithful. He takes advantage of the master's absence to abuse the other slaves and to make improper use of the master's property that has been entrusted to his care. Hendriksen (*Luke* 680) presents essentially the same interpretation.

Summers (*Luke* 162), by contrast, understands this passage to mean that the servants divide themselves into two groups. On one hand, there are the faithful servants who carefully perform their assigned tasks. On the other hand, there are the unfaithful servants who abuse the trust the master has placed in them. Bock (II:1180-1181) presents a similar interpretation. He argues that this passage reflects four classes of servants. The first class includes the faithful servants, while the other three classes indicate unfaithful servants.

Either interpretation stresses the importance of being faithful disciples. In the future, Jesus will no longer be on earth with His disciples. They must be faithful and prepared to assume significant responsibilities in His kingdom. If the second interpretation is correct, the parable emphasizes the additional idea of perseverance. Not only must a servant of Jesus Christ be a faithful steward of the responsibilities entrusted to him, he must also remain faithful. He must not fall prey to the temptations that will surround him.

Verse 47 refers to the kind of punishment an unfaithful servant could expect; he would be beaten. Verse 48 moves beyond the punishment of an unfaithful steward and outlines a general principle that is followed in the Kingdom of God. The general idea is that those men and women who have entered the kingdom have undertaken a serious responsibility, and along with responsibility goes accountability. If they serve faithfully, they will be rewarded. If they are not faithful, they will be punished, but the punishment will be fair and in proportion to the degree of unfaithfulness. Men and women must be faithful to their responsibilities on earth; the same principle applies in the spiritual realm.

49 I am come to send fire on the earth; and what will I, if it be already kindled?
50 But I have a baptism to be baptized with; and how am I straitened till it be accomplished!
51 Suppose ye that I am come to give peace on the earth? I tell you, Nay; but rather division.
52 For from henceforth there shall be five in one house divided, three against two, and two against three.
53 The father shall be divided against the son, and the son against the father; the mother against the daughter, and the daughter against the mother; the mother in law against her daughter in law, and the daughter in law against her mother in law.

In these verses, Jesus is preparing His disciples of all generations for the harsh realities that accompany membership in His spiritual family. Allegiance to Jesus and obedience to His commands have always produced conflict, division, and strife. In the original language of verse 49, "fire" is the first word in the sentence for emphasis. Jesus has come to cast a fire upon the earth rather than something else.

This fire has been interpreted in different ways. Ellis (182) suggests it may refer to God's judgment, but a more likely view is it refers to the outpouring of the Holy Spirit. The Holy Spirit will serve both to cleanse and to judge. Lenski (712-713) connects the fire with the baptism mentioned in the next verse; he understands both terms to refer to the passion and death of Jesus. Fitzmyer (II:996) writes that the term is used figuratively; in the O. T. the symbol of fire is a means of judgment, purification, or discernment.

The last words of verse 49 are difficult, both to translate and to interpret (Plummer 334; Creed 178). Many commentators interpret them as a wish expressing the idea "I wish it were already ablaze." It is doubtful this passage refers to a physical fire. The idea is probably that after His death and resurrection, the spread of the gospel will be like a fire. It will certainly introduce division and strife, but it will also inaugurate a new era of salvation through the blood of Christ. Jesus does not look forward to His time of trial and suffering, but He realizes His suffering and death will introduce His disciples into a new and better relationship with God.

The term "baptism" in verse 50 is easier to interpret. The word (Greek *baptizō*) means "dip" or "immerse." It is used metaphorically to describe a person who is overwhelmed by a difficult situation (Barclay 169; Creed 178). In this context, it is a clear reference to Jesus' upcoming death (F. Bruce, *Hard Sayings* 125). "How I am straitened" (v. 50) expresses the idea of being hard pressed or in a difficult situation (Fitzmyer II:997). The point is that Jesus anticipates the remainder of His earthly life will be filled with trials and difficulties. His sufferings on earth will only be ended by His death.

F. Bruce (*Hard Sayings* 128-129) offers another interpretation of "how am I straitened till it be accomplished!" He connects these words with John 7:39, which mentions that the Spirit had not yet been given because Jesus had not yet been glorified. In his view, Jesus' ministry was limited or constrained in the sense that the fullness of the Holy Spirit's power had not yet come upon the disciples. Jesus' death would bring about the outpouring of the Holy Spirit and His ministry would become much greater and much more expansive. In the view of Ladd (30), this passage not only indicates that Jesus is aware of His upcoming death; it also indicates that His death is the goal of His earthly mission.

Verses 51-53 refer to Jesus' first coming; they explain that His coming does not mean peace and unity for the world. On the contrary, it means conflict and division. The common belief of the Jews was that the coming of the Messiah would inaugurate an era of peace and prosperity for Israel. In this passage, Jesus recognizes that His coming to earth and inaugurating the kingdom will not produce this hoped-for result. Instead, it will produce division and strife. In particular, it will produce conflict within families as some members of the family accept Christ as the Messiah while others reject Him. The mention of specific family relationships in verses 52-53 indicates the severity of the division the coming of Christ will produce. There is certainly no conflict more painful than a father against his son or a mother against her daughter.

Jesus does not indicate specifically when He expects this conflict to begin, but the verbs used in the passage are in the future tense. The implication is that it is already beginning and will become more severe after His crucifixion. In Acts, this passage will find its fulfillment. The Holy Spirit will come, and the preaching of the gospel will produce radical changes in the Roman Empire. The gospel will be divisive in the sense that some will strongly accept it while others just as strongly reject it. Jesus uses the teachings of this passage to warn His disciples that the road ahead will not be easy. There will be much division and conflict, and they will be in the middle of it. Luke includes these verses in his Gospel to teach the same lessons to later generations of believers. The inauguration of the kingdom through Christ introduces peace with God, but it does not introduce earthly peace. The followers of Christ, of every generation, must be prepared to demonstrate their loyalty in times of difficulty.

Summary (12:1-53)

In the Travel Narrative, Luke develops two major themes, discipleship and the growing conflict between Jesus and the Jewish leaders. This passage focuses on discipleship as Jesus instructs the disciples in what it means to be a disciple. He gives special attention to the trials and difficulties the disciples will face in the future.

Luke also continues to develop the Kingdom of God. It is clear that Jesus is now attracting larger crowds, and more people are becoming interested in the unusual and challenging message He is presenting. In these circumstances, the opposition also increases. His teaching begins to attract the attention of the Jewish authorities, and they are not pleased with what they are hearing. The crowds also become increasingly divided as His message becomes sharper and more focused.

Jesus begins to devote more attention to the future. He begins to speak of the trials He will be called upon to endure. He also warns His disciples their future will be challenging and difficult. They should expect to encounter greater opposition and even persecution. It is important that they remain faithful even in times of persecution; their priority must be on serving God even in the midst of difficulties. Jesus promises His followers that the Lord will be with them and strengthen them in their hour of need.

Jesus also begins to speak of the future in a more positive sense. He presents His Second Coming in terms of a master who returns from a journey. His servants do not know the hour of their master's return, but if they are faithful, they will be properly rewarded. As this Gospel develops, Luke will give more attention to the implications of Christ's Second Coming.

Luke also emphasizes that God provides for His disciples. If God provides for the most useless of birds and causes the flowers to grow in the field, He can and will provide for the followers of His Son. There is no promise that the disciples will be exempt from persecution, but when they are called upon to suffer they will not suffer alone. God will be with them.

This passage emphasizes the need for faithfulness. The disciples must seek first the Kingdom of God; their relationship with Him must be more important than any earthly considerations of wealth, position, or luxury. They must not be overly concerned with material things; their relationship with God must always take first place in their lives. They must live lives of honesty and integrity as the Lord's representatives before the world.

The disciples must be ready at all times for the return of Christ; when He comes again there will be no time to make preparation. They must be like the servants who are expectant and prepared whenever their master returns from his journey. In this chapter, Luke also stresses the accountability of the disciples. God has given them much, and He has the right to expect much from them. They must not deny Him in times of trial and persecution.

Application: Teaching and Preaching the Passage

Luke 12:1-53 emphasizes discipleship, and the lessons are extremely important for the church of every generation. In the world today, there are far too many casual followers of Christ who have never developed into sincere disciples. The lessons found in this chapter can help all of the followers of Christ become more effective disciples. This chapter would serve well as texts for a series of lessons or sermons on what it means to be a follower of Christ.

Lesson one is that nothing can be hidden from God. He is fully aware of all His disciples think, will, and do. For this reason, the disciple needs to be sure his or her motives are pure. In reality, we have only one reason to be disciples and that is to bring glory to God. We have not become disciples in order to promote ourselves or advance our sectarian interests. Our goal must be to advance the Kingdom of God.

Lesson two is that all disciples must understand correctly the nature of the God whom they serve. He is a God who is willing and able and can be trusted to provide for the needs of His disciples. For this reason, the disciples must not be dominated by worry or anxiety. They must always remember that the future is in God's hands and not in theirs. God does not promise His disciples lives of ease and luxury, but He promises to supply those things that are necessary for effective service. The disciples, then, must learn to be content with what God provides. They must not be carried away with the desire to obtain material possessions because things are of limited value and brief duration.

The view of God presented in this chapter is a complex one. On one hand, God is presented as a caring father who provides for his children. On the other hand, God is also presented as a judge who holds His followers accountable. For some people, these two different aspects of God's nature may be difficult to reconcile, but both of them are taught here. The true disciple must have an accurate and realistic picture of who God is and what He demands.

The third important lesson is that disciples must be prepared for the future. They must be like the servants who are awake and prepared for the arrival of the master even when he returns in the middle of the night. Being a disciple of Christ is not an eight to five job; it calls for faithful service at all times. There are many things in the world that can distract the disciple and lead him away from those things that are truly important. The faithful disciple must learn to resist those forces and concentrate on following Christ.

The fourth important lesson from this chapter is that the disciple must have spiritual discernment. He must have the spiritual maturity necessary to understand what God is doing in the world and the willingness to participate fully in it. His understanding of what it means to be a disciple of Christ must be based on reality. Jesus warns His disciples that difficult days lie ahead, both for Him and for them. Christ will be called upon to suffer, and His disciples will share in that suffering. They must not view their ministry through rose-colored glasses; they must be willing to pay the price involved in becoming true disciples.

Being a disciple of Christ is not easy. It demands the very best that is within us, but it cannot be accomplished in our strength alone. There must be a daily dependence on God for leadership, direction, and strength.

E. Understanding the Times (12:54—13:9)

54 And he said also to the people, When ye see a cloud rise out of the west, straightway ye say, There cometh a shower; and so it is.
55 And when *ye see* the south wind blow, ye say, There will be heat; and it cometh to pass.
56 *Ye* hypocrites, ye can discern the face of the sky and of the earth; but how is it that ye do not discern this time?
57 Yea, and why even of yourselves judge ye not what is right?
58 When thou goest with thine adversary to the magistrate, *as thou art* in the way, give diligence that thou mayest be delivered from him; lest he hale thee to the judge, and the judge deliver thee to the officer, and the officer cast thee into prison.
59 I tell thee, thou shalt not depart thence, till thou hast paid the very last mite.

In the previous verses, Jesus has been speaking primarily to His disciples, warning them of the difficult days that lie ahead for His followers. Now Jesus speaks to a wider audience. Luke does not define the "people," probably a crowd composed of different types.

They probably include at least some of His disciples; they may also include his enemies as well as those who have some interest in His teachings. In these verses, Jesus rebukes them for not being aware of what the Lord is doing in their midst. They are wise in the ways of the world, but they cannot or will not discern what is going on around them in a spiritual sense. They need to wake up and see what God is doing in their midst.

Most people in ancient Palestine made their living in agriculture, and they understood well the role of weather in the production of crops. They knew that the rains generally came from the west, from the Mediterranean Sea. They also understood that when the wind blew from the desert areas in the south, they could expect hot, dry weather.

In verse 56, Jesus labels the people to whom He is speaking as "hypocrites" (Greek *hupocritēs*), a word originally used to describe an actor playing a role on a stage. Here the term describes people who are outwardly religious, but who reject what God is really doing in the world (Ellis 183-184). As Lieu (106) notes, the use of this term indicates their spiritual blindness is deliberate and willful. Jesus has come to earth as the Son of God, but they refuse to hear the message He has for them. "Time" (Greek *kairos*) conveys the idea that they refuse to understand and accept what God is doing in the present time. They have a good knowledge of the physical world; they understand the winds and the rain. But they are ignorant of the things of God; He is doing a great work in their midst, but they pay no heed to it.

Beginning in verse 57, Jesus gives a second illustration of the spiritual blindness of the crowd to whom He is speaking. Two men have a legal dispute; the courts are often corrupt, with the judge's decision going to the party that pays the larger bribe. A wise man, especially if his case is weak, will settle with his adversary before it ends up in front of a judge. If the case goes to court, he will probably lose the case and be forced to pay a fine or go to prison.

The last words of verse 58 describe something of the procedure that will be followed if the case actually goes to trial. The adversary will make a complaint to the magistrate, who will arrest the alleged perpetrator and take him before a judge. The judge will then decide the case. If the person is found guilty, he will be turned over to an officer who will actually imprison or fine the person. "Officer" (Greek *praktōr*) is a rather rare word that describes an officer who deals with debts and is in charge of the debtor's prison (Marshall, *Gospel* 551). Verse 59 explains that the person found responsible will not be released from the debtor's prison until he has paid every cent of his debt. The "mite" (Greek *lepton*) was the smallest coin in common use in Palestine in the first century. Barclay (171-172) presents a good analysis of the coins in common use at this time.

The point of both of these illustrations is the same. The people understand correctly the things of this world. They know the weather patterns; they also understand how to settle a case before going to court. They are, however, lacking in spiritual discernment. They have no appreciation for the great things God is doing in their midst. They need to pay proper attention to the things of God before they have to stand before Him in judgment (Creed 179). The teaching of this passage is that they should apply the same level of understanding to spiritual things that they apply to worldly things.

Jesus continues to develop for His disciples the true nature of His kingdom. He calls attention to the fact that His kingdom is spiritual in nature and quite different from the earthly kingdoms with which people in the first century were familiar.

This chapter begins with a new conception of the relationship between sin and suffering in the world. In the O. T., sickness and suffering were regarded as the direct result of sin. While Jesus would have agreed that sin and suffering in general are the result of sin, He refused to accept the commonly-held idea that suffering in the life of an individual was a direct result of some sin he or she had committed (R. Brown, NTE 172-173). Sickness or suffering in the life of an individual may be the result of actual sin, or it may be a result of living in a fallen world. In these verses, Jesus' goal is to establish that the Jewish leaders are sinners like everyone else; their privileged position in Judaism does not guarantee a right relationship with God.

13:1 There were present at that season some that told him of the Galilaeans, whose blood Pilate had mingled with their sacrifices.
2 And Jesus answering said unto them, Suppose ye that these Galilaeans were sinners above all Galilaeans, because they suffered such things?
3 I tell you, Nay: but, except ye repent, ye shall all likewise perish.
4 Or those eighteen, upon whom the tower in Siloam fell, and slew them, think ye that they were sinners above all men that dwelt in Jerusalem?
5 I tell you, Nay: but, except ye repent, ye shall all likewise perish.

Jesus uses as illustrations two incidents about which nothing is known other than the information given here (Fitzmyer II:1006). The first tells the story of a group of pilgrims from Galilee who were killed on orders of Pilate while they were in the very act of offering sacrifices at the Temple in Jerusalem. The Galileans did not like being ruled by Pilate (EGT 1:564), but there is nothing in the passage to indicate they were trying to provoke some type of rebellion. This incident serves as an example of the kind of extreme cruelty that was typical of Pilate. The traditional theology would teach to receive such a punishment they must have committed some terrible sin (Marshall, *Gospel* 553).

The second incident relates the story of eighteen workers who suffered a tragic accident while working on an old tower located near the pool of Siloam (Fitzmyer II:1005). Plummer (339) and Creed (180) conjecture that they might have been killed while working on aqueducts Pilate had ordered in order to improve Jerusalem's water system. Summers (*Luke* 166) posits that this tower was likely a part of the city wall located near the pool of Siloam. Again, the traditional theology would teach that these eighteen men must have committed some terrible sin to merit such a punishment.

Jesus responds by telling His hearers that unless they repent of their sins they will all perish in a similar fashion. This response has two implications. First, Jesus rejects the traditional view that one's outward circumstances are an indication of one's spiritual condition (Geldenhuys 370). The fact that these individuals suffered terrible deaths does not indicate they were worse sinners than others. This passage is not designed to teach that all sin is equal in God's eyes; the idea is that before God all men are guilty and all sin merits punishment. Position and prosperity do not indicate that a person enjoys a proper relationship with God.

Second, these words of Jesus emphasize that all are sinners and in need of repentance. If the crowd listening to Him, including the Jewish leaders, wishes to be part of the kingdom, they must repent of their sins. They cannot trust in their goodness, their privileged position, or their prosperity to guarantee acceptance by God. God has given them the opportunity to repent, and they should take advantage of it.

6 He spake also this parable; A certain *man* had a fig tree planted in his vineyard; and he came and sought fruit thereon, and found none.
7 Then said he unto the dresser of his vineyard, Behold, these three years I come seeking fruit on this fig tree, and find none: cut it down; why cumbereth it the ground?
8 And he answering said unto him, Lord, let it alone this year also, till I shall dig about it, and dung it:
9 And if it bear fruit, *well*: and if not, *then* after that thou shalt cut it down.

It is no accident that this brief parable follows the teaching on the need for repentance. It points out that just as a fig tree is expected to bear fruit, true repentance will also bring about changes in one's life and conduct. Repentance is more than just a change in opinion or way of thinking; it will produce radical changes in the person's manner of life.

The fact that the owner of the vineyard allows additional time for the tree to bear fruit is an indication of the patience of God. Just as the farmer is patient with his fruitless fig tree, God is patient with his rebellious children and gives them ample opportunity to repent. Still, sooner or later, that opportunity ceases and God demands real repentance.

While the fig tree is not commonly used as a symbol for the nation of Israel in the O. T., it is sometimes used that way (Hos. 9:10; Jer. 8:13, 24:1-8; and Jl. 1:7). It is likely that in this passage the fig tree symbolizes those within the nation of Israel who were unwilling to accept the message that Jesus was the Messiah (Geldenhuys 372). It was not unusual to plant various kinds of fruit trees in vineyards, especially in the corners (EGT 1:565; Marshall, *Gospel* 555). This particular tree has borne no fruit for three years. Perhaps the tree is only three years old. Even so, it has had ample opportunity to bear fruit. Three years would be enough to determine whether a particular tree is likely to be fruitful.

The owner arrives to inspect his vineyard. He understands that if the tree has born no fruit in three years it is unlikely to do so, and he is ready to cut it down. The "dresser of the vineyard" is a slave or employee who has the responsibility for the daily care of the vineyard. He understands that some trees take longer than others, and he is not ready to give up on this one. He wants to give it one more year and proposes to dig around the tree and apply dung as a fertilizer. If it does not bear fruit after this additional year, the servant agrees to cut it down. In verse 8, the servant uses the term "Lord" to address his master. This word is a title of respect used in the N. T. both as a title for God and as a title for an important person. In this context, the meaning is "master" or "sir."

Although God is patient and long-suffering, His patience is not, however, unlimited. The Day of Judgment will inevitably come when those who are rebellious will be held accountable. They need to pay heed to Jesus' message while they have the opportunity to do so. As Summers (*Luke* 167) explains, the traditional interpretation of this parable relates to Israel's failure to carry out God's purposes for it. F. Bruce (*Hard Sayings* 209) suggests that the barren fig tree is a symbol for the city of Jerusalem.

Summary
(12:54—13:9)

Jesus is addressing a larger group of people, mostly those who are outside the circle of Jesus' followers. They are not yet ready for membership in the Kingdom of God. If they wish to enter the kingdom, they must repent.

God is patient, but His patience is not unlimited. He is like the dresser of the vineyard who wants to give the fig tree one more year, but who agrees to cut it down if it does not bear fruit by then. The meaning of the passage is obvious. God wants to see people redeemed from sin, and He gives them ample opportunity to repent. But His patience does not last forever. People must repent while they have the opportunity to do so.

This passage focuses on the need for spiritual discernment. Those who lived in Israel in the first century were close to the land because most of them made their living in agriculture. They understood the seasons of the year; they knew the weather conditions that were likely to produce rain. They also understood when they were likely to be hit with a devastating east wind. The fact that they had an understanding of how God determined the weather did not mean they understood how God works in other areas. The people Jesus was addressing were spiritually blind in the sense they had no understanding of what God was doing in their world and what He wanted to do in their lives.

They also understood something of how to function within their society. They knew judges could often be bribed, and it was usually to a defendant's benefit to agree to a settlement before going to court. They had a good understanding of the things of this world, but they were lacking in spiritual perception.

Luke 13:1-9 also deals with the subject of spiritual blindness, but it approaches that subject from a different perspective. These verses show that the traditional beliefs of a society can sometimes hinder people from understanding how God works. The traditional theology of the ancient Near East, including Israel, held that one was blessed in proportion to his goodness and punished in proportion to his wickedness. Such a theology prevented the people from understanding the goodness and mercy of God. The traditional theology taught that those who suffered great tragedies must have been guilty of terrible sin. Jesus responds to this traditional theology by saying that all are sinners. Those who are the most righteous in society (like the Jewish leaders) are all guilty before God. They must repent just as others.

Luke concludes this section with the parable of the fig tree. This tree had produced no fruit in three years, and the owner was ready to cut it down and make room for a more fruitful tree. The keeper of the vineyard had mercy on the tree. He offered to give it special care and attention for one more year. It would have one last opportunity to produce fruit. The lesson is that God is long-suffering and merciful. He gives His people opportunity to repent and enter the kingdom. God's patience is not unlimited. Ultimately, He will demand that those who wish to be His followers repent of their sins.

Application: Teaching and Preaching the Passage

This passage is useful in helping people understand who God is and how He operates the world He has created. Many times our traditional concepts of God may keep us from understanding and appreciating Him. As mentioned, the traditional theology of the ancient Near East held that the righteous prosper in proportion to their righteousness, while the wicked suffer in proportion to their wickedness. In this passage, Jesus corrects that mistaken way of thinking.

It is true that all evil in the world is connected to sin in the sense that it is a result of the fall. It is not true, however, that specific, personal suffering is the direct result of some sin the person has committed. There is such a thing as innocent suffering, and Jesus is the prime example of it. The important lesson is that one's spiritual condition cannot be determined by outward circumstances. As far as God is concerned, none are innocent; all are guilty and need to repent. Unfortunately, there are still many Christians today who try to determine spirituality by such things as position, education, wealth, or other human factors. As preachers and teachers of the Word, we need to help them move to a more mature understanding of God and of our relationship with Him.

The Parable of the Fig Tree also makes a significant contribution to our understanding of God. In some ways, God is like the vine dresser; in other ways, He is like the owner of the vineyard. God is patient and merciful. Since God is patient and merciful with people, His representatives should also be. We should not be quick to give up on people because God's desire is to see repentance and reformation. At the same time, we should understand that God's patience is not unlimited. Sooner or later the day of reckoning will come; the door of opportunity may not be open forever. Today is, after all, the day of salvation.

F. The Power of the Kingdom (13:10-30)

10 And he was teaching in one of the synagogues on the sabbath.
11 And, behold, there was a woman which had a spirit of infirmity eighteen years, and was bowed together, and could in no wise lift up *herself*.
12 And when Jesus saw her, he called *her to him*, and said unto her, Woman, thou art loosed from thine infirmity.
13 And he laid *his* hands on her: and immediately she was made straight, and glorified God.

14 And the ruler of the synagogue answered with indignation, because that Jesus had healed on the sabbath day, and said unto the people, There are six days in which men ought to work: in them therefore come and be healed, and not on the sabbath day.
15 The Lord then answered him, and said, *Thou* hypocrite, doth not each one of you on the sabbath loose his ox or *his* ass from the stall, and lead *him* away to watering?
16 And ought not this woman, being a daughter of Abraham, whom Satan hath bound, lo, these eighteen years, be loosed from this bond on the sabbath day?
17 And when he had said these things, all his adversaries were ashamed: and all the people rejoiced for all the glorious things that were done by him.

During the years of Jesus' earthly ministry, He often faced challenges to His power, authority, and honor. Such is the case in this passage where He is accused of violating the Jewish law by healing on the Sabbath. For an insightful analysis of how Jesus defended His honor on this occasion see Malina and Neyrey (49-50). As usual, Luke does not identify when or where this incident took place; the event itself is the important thing. As Stein (*Luke* 375) notes, Jesus' concern for the poor and outcasts of society is an important theme in Luke's Gospel.

Apparently, this woman regularly attended the synagogue services and was known to the leaders and to the congregation. As He was teaching, Jesus immediately noticed that she suffered from an infirmity; her spine was curved, and she could not stand up straight. She had "a spirit of infirmity" from which she had suffered for eighteen years. Jesus called her to come forward and healed her immediately, in full view of the congregation. "Immediately she was made straight, and glorified God." Since this miracle was performed in the presence of both the leaders and the congregation, they could not deny the reality of what had occurred.

The ruler of the synagogue then attacked Jesus not for healing the woman, but for healing her on the Sabbath. The law made the practice of medicine or healing illegal on the Sabbath (Summers, *Luke* 168). The Jewish law made provision for emergencies on the Sabbath, but this was no emergency. She had suffered with this infirmity for eighteen years; Jesus could have healed her on another day.

The ruler of the synagogue rebuked Jesus, apparently in front of the congregation. He said that men ought to complete their work in six days as the Lord provided in the O. T. His words were not a direct quotation from the O. T., but they accurately reflected the teachings of such passages as Exodus 20:9-10 and Deuteronomy 5:13-14.

Jesus responds by calling the ruler of the synagogue a hypocrite; some manuscripts have this plural. Jesus accused the ruler and others of pretending to be faithful in their observance of the Sabbath, when in reality they were not. Jesus points out that even the most faithful Jews will take their animals to water on the Sabbath (Marshall, *Gospel* 558-559). If it is acceptable to take a domestic animal to water on the Sabbath, it must be pleasing to God to heal a human being who has suffered for many years. Jesus describes her in verse 16 as a "daughter of Abraham." She is an Israelite woman who occupies a higher status than the Gentiles. She should be entitled to at least the same consideration given to an ox or a donkey.

Verse 17 outlines the responses of two different groups to this notable miracle. The first group is described as "his adversaries." Obviously, this term refers to the Jewish leaders who have become Jesus' enemies and are determined to destroy Him. Both Jesus' action in healing the woman and His response to the attack by the ruler of the synagogue, silenced His enemies. They were ashamed in the sense that they had no response to His words and actions.

The second group is described as "all the people." Apparently, this phrase describes the common people, perhaps even including the members of the congregation who had witnessed the miracle. As Jesus' earthly ministry develops there is an increasing division between the leaders who are strongly opposed to His ministry and the common people who are much more supportive.

18 Then said he, Unto what is the kingdom of God like? and whereunto shall I resemble it?
19 It is like a grain of mustard seed, which a man took, and cast into his garden; and it grew, and waxed a great tree; and the fowls of the air lodged in the branches of it.

Jesus uses an earthly analogy to describe the Kingdom of God. Plummer (344) adopts a traditional interpretation of this parable, suggesting that it describes "the small beginning, the gradual spread, and the immense development of the Kingdom of God." C. Smith takes a different approach, holding that the emphasis of the story falls less on the process of growth and development than on the final result that is produced (76). B. Smith (120) suggests the kingdom that Jesus preached, "does not grow—it comes." The point is that the Kingdom of God emerges, often suddenly, from the smallest and most humble of beginnings (Marshall, *Gospel* 561).

The precise meaning of "mustard" in this context is debated. The question is whether it refers to the *salvadora persica*, which could grow to a height of 25 feet, or to the *sinapis nigra*, which could grow to a height of 10 feet. According to Marshall (*Gospel* 561), the mustard mentioned here is likely *sinapis nigra*, or black mustard, which produced a plant that normally reached a height of from four to nine feet.

The mustard seed was the smallest seed that was commonly planted in Palestine. According to the rabbis, it was normally grown in a field rather than in a home garden. It grew to a sufficient size that the birds could find shade in its branches. The idea is that the Kingdom of God Jesus was in the process of establishing would have a very small and rather insignificant beginning, but it would not remain small forever. Through the power of God, it would come to be a spiritual entity that would not only affect the lives of individuals, but would also touch the entire world.

20 And again he said, Whereunto shall I liken the kingdom of God?

21 It is like leaven, which a woman took and hid in three measures of meal, till the whole was leavened.

This brief parable is also found in Matthew 13. It is often interpreted to predict the future growth of the church, both in numbers and in influence (C. Smith 70). The main difficulty with this interpretation is that leaven (or yeast) is not generally used in Scripture to describe a positive process; it is generally used to describe something negative. According to Exodus 12:17-19, all leaven had to be removed from the Israelite house during the Feast of Unleavened Bread. Mark 8:15 warns the disciples to "beware of the leaven of the Pharisees, and *of* the leaven of Herod." In 1 Corinthians 5:7, Paul instructs the believers in Corinth to "purge out therefore the old leaven... ." While it is possible that Jesus is using the idea of leaven in a more positive sense than is normally found in the Bible, such use is not likely.

Several commentators have noted that this parable makes no direct comparison between the leaven and the growth of the Kingdom of God. The comparison is between the results that are produced (C. Smith 70-71). Even a small amount of leaven is enough to produce radical changes in a large amount of flour; the same thing is true in the Kingdom of God. When the Kingdom of God enters into the world, dramatic changes take place. Nothing remains the same; all people will be affected in some way. These dramatic changes may not be immediately apparent, but they will come to pass according to God's timetable. Jesus' goal in this passage is not to give a detailed picture of future events; He is reminding the disciples that the power of Almighty God will be made manifest in His kingdom. As Ellis (187) explains, "The parables do not teach a gradual growth of an earthly kingdom in the Church. The point is that insignificant 'seeds' will produce a very great effect."

22 And he went through the cities and villages, teaching, and journeying toward Jerusalem.
23 Then said one unto him, Lord, are there few that be saved? And he said unto them,
24 Strive to enter in at the strait gate: for many, I say unto you, will seek to enter in, and shall not be able.
25 When once the master of the house is risen up, and hath shut to the door, and ye begin to stand without, and to knock at the door, saying, Lord, Lord, open unto us; and he shall answer and say unto you, I know not whence ye are:
26 Then shall ye begin to say, We have eaten and drunk in thy presence, and thou hast taught in our streets.
27 But he shall say, I tell you, I know not whence ye are; depart from me, all *ye* workers of iniquity.
28 There shall be weeping and gnashing of teeth, when ye shall see Abraham, and Isaac, and Jacob, and all the prophets, in the kingdom of God, and you *yourselves* thrust out.
29 And they shall come from the east, and *from* the west, and from the north, and *from* the south, and shall sit down in the kingdom of God.

30 And, behold, there are last which shall be first, and there are first which shall be last.

Jesus continues His instructions to the disciples concerning the nature of the kingdom. This is the first in a series of episodes designed to answer the question, "Who will have the privilege of entering the Kingdom of God?" The surprising answer is "Not those you think." The Kingdom of God will not be given to those who qualify by inheritance or by religious observance. It will rather be given to those who humble themselves before God, repent of their sins, and open their hearts to Jesus as the Son of God. Those that should, on human terms, be allowed to enter will be excluded. Those whom the world would reject are welcomed into it.

Verse 22 is a transition verse; it reminds the reader that in Luke 9:51, Jesus has begun a spiritual journey that will end with His execution in Jerusalem. This verse also marks the transition between the parables that have characterized the earlier verses and the straightforward doctrinal teaching Jesus presents in the following verses. These verses continue the discussion of the significance of the Kingdom of God, but they examine the kingdom from a different perspective.

In verse 23, an unnamed person asks Jesus an important question, "Lord, are there few that be saved?" "Be saved" is used here in a future sense (Marshall, *Gospel* 564). The verb (Greek *sōzō*) expresses the idea of deliverance from some physical or spiritual danger. It is often used in the N. T. to describe deliverance from God's judgment, entrance into the Kingdom of God, or obtaining eternal life. Here the idea seems to be, "Lord, will only a few be permitted to enter the kingdom?"

In verse 24, Jesus does not directly answer the question, but He explains to His followers what they must do to obtain entrance into His kingdom. Geldenhuys (380) posits that Jesus answers the question in this manner because He doesn't want His disciples to waste their time in useless speculation about how many will be saved. They should, instead, focus their attention on what they must do to enter the kingdom.

"Strive" (Greek *agonizomai*) is the source of our English word "agonize." It is used in several different ways in the N. T., especially for participating in a race or other contest, or for labor or striving. Here the idea is that the disciples must put forth their best efforts on a continuing basis if they wish to enter the kingdom. Jesus is not teaching some form of salvation by works. The idea is the disciples cannot expect that they will automatically be granted entrance into the kingdom. Elsewhere in the N. T., conditions of salvation are repentance and faith, and those same conditions apply here. Their genuine repentance and faithful adherence to Jesus, even in difficult circumstances, is the necessary prerequisite for gaining acceptance into God's eternal kingdom.

They are to put forth their best efforts to enter the kingdom by the "strait" or narrow gate. This is similar to Matthew 7:13-14, and the two passages should probably be interpreted together. In Jesus' illustration, the contrast is between two roads and two gates leading into an ancient city. One road is broad with a wide gate that allows many people to enter at the same time. The other road is narrow and leads to a gate that is also narrow; this gate will permit the entrance of a much smaller number of people. The idea is that the kingdom gate will not be open to any and all who desire to enter. It will be open only to those who are truly repentant and faithful to Jesus and His teachings. Many will desire to enter by this narrow gate, but they will not be able to do so.

In verse 25, Jesus presents a second illustration explaining how people must enter the kingdom. The master of the house wishes to have a great feast, and, apparently, he has invited a number of people to attend. When the time to begin the feast arrives, he orders that the door to the house be closed and no one else be admitted. The guests who arrive late pound on the door, asking to be admitted, but the master refuses to permit them to enter. The last words of verse 25 could be translated, "I do not know you, from where you are." In other words, the master does not recognize them. He does not know them or from where they have come; in the ancient world people were often identified by their place of origin. Their late arrival has rendered them ineligible to share in his feast.

In verses 26-27, there is another exchange, but this one is between Jesus and those denied entrance into His kingdom. The people affirm they have listened to Jesus as He taught in their streets; they have even shared meals with Him. His response (v. 27) is similar to that given in verse 25. It could also be translated, "I do not know you, from where you are." The idea is that a casual acquaintance with Jesus and His teachings is not sufficient to gain entrance into the kingdom. It takes more than simply sharing a meal together. As Morgan (*Luke* 167) writes, "A man's salvation does not result from familiarity. It must be based on personal relationship." A much higher level of commitment than they have demonstrated is necessary. Summers (*Luke* 171) points out that many of the Pharisees and Sadducees heard Jesus teach, but they were unwilling to accept His teachings (Fitzmyer II:1023). Marshall (*Gospel* 566) opines that these words refer to Jews who had followed Jesus during His earthly ministry but who had not fully accepted His teachings.

In the last part of verse 27, Jesus orders the faithless to depart from His presence and even labels them "workers of iniquity," a phrase drawn from the Greek text of Psalm 6:8. That is a strong expression, indicating they are more committed to following the world of vice and iniquity than to following Jesus. The word translated "iniquity" could also be translated "unrighteousness" (Lenski 747; Summers, *Luke* 171). They are not excluded because God is cruel and arbitrary; their exclusion is the result of their own actions.

Jesus is not teaching that only a small number of people will be saved; He is not introducing a doctrine of election that limits the number who can be saved. The idea is that those who wish to enter the kingdom must do so in the correct manner and at the proper time. They must seek to enter while the door is open to them; the opportunity to receive salvation will not always be. To delay is to invite disaster.

In verse 28, the subject shifts from the manner of entering the kingdom to the final destiny of those who choose not to enter it. Jesus does not establish a precise chronology of events, but these verses will likely be fulfilled at the end of time when all will stand before the Lord in judgment. The picture He paints is a sad one; the consequences of being excluded from the kingdom are grievous.

The Jewish concept of a great messianic banquet lies behind verses 28-30. The Jews expected that in the future the Messiah would come and would hold a great banquet at which His people would be rewarded for their faithfulness. For a description of these Jewish beliefs see Behm (TDNT II:691). This passage emphasizes that those who have refused to enter the kingdom will be excluded. "Weeping" is also mentioned in Acts 20:37, where it describes the great sorrow experienced by the Ephesian elders as Paul was about to leave them. The idea here is that those who are excluded from the kingdom will experience great sorrow and loss. "Gnashing of teeth" also appears in Acts 7:54 to express great rage and anger. In the Greek version of Job 16:9, the same expression is used to express the anger of Job's enemies. Here it reflects the anger and rage of those excluded from the kingdom. As they look through the door into the great banquet, they see all the heroes of the O. T. enjoying the blessings, while they themselves are excluded.

In verse 29, those who have chosen not to enter the kingdom see another sight, which makes them even more angry. In the banquet hall, they also see a great multitude—probably including Gentiles!—from all parts of the earth. Verse 30 may reflect a popular proverb, also found in Matthew 19:30, 20:16, and Mark 10:31. The ones "first" probably are the Jews who were the first to receive the invitation to enter the kingdom. Those "last" probably are Gentiles who were the last to receive Jesus' invitation. Since the Gentiles received the message, the door is open to them. Since the Jews, at least many of them, refused the invitation, they will be excluded. A key theme throughout this passage is that the final outcome of the Kingdom of God will contain many surprises.

Summary (13:10-30)

Every section of this important passage relates in some way to the new kingdom Jesus is establishing. Each section also reveals something of the power and authority Jesus possesses because He is the Son of God.

Verses 10-17 deal specifically with the authority of Jesus to heal on the Sabbath. While participating in a service in the synagogue, He frees an unfortunate woman from the illness that has enslaved her for many years. The leaders of the synagogue object to what He has done because, under their law, works of healing cannot be done on the Sabbath. By His words and His actions, Jesus establishes both His power over illness and His authority over the Sabbath. The healing of this woman produces a divided reaction. The leaders of the synagogue are angry, but they remain silent because they cannot denigrate this miracle without presenting themselves as cruel and uncaring. The people, however, rejoice because of what Jesus has done in their midst.

In verses 18-21, Jesus gives two illustrations that describe the nature of the Kingdom of God. Both illustrations emphasize the kingdom starts out in a small and rather insignificant way, but it doesn't stay that way. In the beginning, it is little more than Jesus and a small band of followers preaching, teaching, and healing as they walk through the villages of Galilee. This kingdom is like the grain of mustard that a farmer plants in his field or like the small amount of leaven a women places in a significant amount of flour. It does not, however, remain small and insignificant; big results grow out of small beginnings. Through the power of God, the kingdom will ultimately touch the entire world.

Verses 22-30 include instruction given primarily to the disciples. In these verses, Jesus answers one of the important questions His disciples have already raised or will raise in the future. The question is, "Will those who are saved be few?" In other words, the disciples are asking if many people will be permitted to enter the kingdom. They probably anticipate that Jesus will answer them with a simple "No," but He does not respond in the manner His disciples expect. Instead, He tells them a story about a man who shuts the door while many guests are still outside seeking admission. Those outside plead that they have eaten and drunk with the Master; they have even heard Him teach in their streets. This type of casual acquaintance does not, however, qualify them for admission. They will be cast out and excluded from the messianic banquet. The point of the story is not that God has determined to save only so many and no more, but that those who are left out have chosen to exclude themselves through their own lack of commitment and dedication. They had the opportunity to enter, but did not meet the qualifications set by the Master.

Application: Teaching and Preaching the Passage

In this passage, Jesus reveals something of His ability as the master-teacher. He teaches both by words and by demonstration; He gives to His disciples and to all those who follow Him the kind of practical instruction that will change their lives. Jesus not only imparts information to His hearers; He shares His own life with them. As He is teaching in the synagogue, He is interrupted by a woman who has suffered from an illness for eighteen years. Jesus immediately understands that people are more important than lectures. His teaching method changes from oral communication to demonstration. He cures the woman; she is immediately made whole on the Sabbath day. The leaders of the synagogue do not like what He has done because He has broken their rules for the Sabbath. Jesus does not simply ignore their complaints; He responds in a forceful but intelligent way.

There are powerful lessons in this passage for those who have the privilege of preaching and teaching the Word of God. We must teach both by our words and by our actions. Both were important to Jesus, and both are important to us. We should be flexible. Jesus does not view the entrance of this crippled woman as an interruption of His program. We should expect opposition when we proclaim the truths of God's Word because that truth is contrary to the teachings of the world. We must also be prepared to defend the truth we proclaim.

The Kingdom of God is one of the major themes of Luke's Gospel, and it figures prominently in this passage. The kingdom is like a mustard seed or like leaven in the sense that it is an important and powerful force that begins in a small way. There is another important idea here. In the ancient world, there was no scientific explanation for the growth of a seed or for the effect of yeast upon the flour. It was simply God at work, and there was no explanation for it. Today, we cannot control the work of God; we cannot predict how and where the Kingdom of God will grow and develop. Neither can we determine whom God will choose to use in His service or where and how He will choose to use them.

This passage addresses the subject of salvation in a powerful way. Salvation is described in terms of entering into the kingdom. Jesus responds to the question, "Are there few that be saved?" This is a question that is still being asked today. Some Christians think of election to salvation in terms of numbers; they believe that God has chosen to save only a relatively few people. All others will be excluded. That is not, however, the teaching of this passage. Jesus does not focus on numbers; He focuses on those who have made the necessary preparation to enter. A casual acquaintance with Jesus and His teachings is not sufficient to obtain entrance. Those who are saved must enter by the narrow door.

Jesus also points out that in the end time, there will be many surprises. Those who are the most outwardly religious and pious may not be accepted. The determining factor will be the condition of the heart and not outward circumstances or religiosity. Preaching and teaching from this passage will not be easy, but it will be very rewarding.

G. Continued Conflict (13:31—14:35)

31 The same day there came certain of the Pharisees, saying unto him, Get thee out, and depart hence: for Herod will kill thee.
32 And he said unto them, Go ye, and tell that fox, Behold, I cast out devils, and I do cures to day and to morrow, and the third *day* I shall be perfected.
33 Nevertheless I must walk to day, and to morrow, and the *day* following: for it cannot be that a prophet perish out of Jerusalem.
34 O Jerusalem, Jerusalem, which killest the prophets, and stonest them that are sent unto thee; how often would I have gathered thy children together, as a hen *doth gather* her brood under *her* wings, and ye would not!
35 Behold, your house is left unto you desolate: and verily I say unto you, Ye shall not see me, until *the time* come when ye shall say, Blessed *is* he that cometh in the name of the Lord.

These verses describe a separate incident, and again Luke makes no attempt to establish a chronological relationship between this event and what has preceded. As always, the event itself is the important thing (Hoehner, *Antipas* 216). Jesus' conflicts with the Jewish leaders become more pronounced as the thought of Luke's Gospel develops. That is certainly the case in this passage.

Some of the Pharisees came to Jesus and warned Him to leave the territory ruled by Herod Antipas. It is impossible to determine with certainty where Jesus was when this incident occurred.

Geldenhuys (382) and Childers (544) suggest He was in the area east of the Jordan River known as Trans-Jordan or Perea. This was an area where the Jewish leaders in Jerusalem had comparatively little influence. In the time of Jesus' ministry the northern part of this territory was ruled by Herod Philip, while the southern part was ruled by Herod Antipas.

Hoehner (*Antipas* 217) offers a different opinion. He suggests the Pharisees would be much more likely to be active in Galilee or Judaea than in Perea. He argues that this event took place in Galilee shortly before Jesus and His followers left the area.

It is possible, perhaps, that these particular Pharisees were genuinely concerned for Jesus' welfare and wanted to protect Him from Herod. One difficulty with this interpretation is that there is no evidence Herod Antipas was actively seeking to kill Jesus (Summers, *Luke* 172). Another difficulty is that by this time in His public ministry, the Pharisees had become very hostile to Jesus and His message. It is difficult to see how they would be supportive in any way.

The other possibility is these Pharisees gave this warning because they were seeking to influence Jesus to leave Perea and go into other areas where the Jewish leaders had more power and influence (Morgan, *Luke* 168). If this interpretation is correct, their goal was not to protect Jesus, but to put Him within the grasp of the Jewish authorities. Hoehner (*Antipas* 219) explains that although Herod Antipas and the Pharisees were normally enemies, they could have been cooperating in an effort to put an end to Jesus. Hoehner also notes that if Herod was really planning to kill Jesus, he would not have announced his intention publicly. He would have simply moved forward with the deed. After considering the evidence, Hoehner concludes this threat was simply designed to influence Jesus to leave the territory Herod Antipas ruled.

Jesus is not at all intimidated by the threatening suggestion. He does not fear Herod; He refers to him as "that fox." In Jewish literature, the fox became a symbol for an animal that was weak but cunning (Marshall, *Gospel* 571; Hoehner, *Antipas* 220-221). Jesus views Herod Antipas as a weak but cunning ruler who poses no serious threat to His ministry. Morgan (*Luke* 168) points out this term implies a degree of sarcasm and contempt that is difficult to translate. The fact that the word "fox" (Greek *alōpēx*) is feminine only adds to the insult. Jesus' response in verse 32 indicates He does not take the Pharisee's instructions to leave the area seriously.

Verses 32-33 reflect Jesus' determination to continue with His journey to Jerusalem and the ministry that will ultimately take Him to the cross. He will not be intimidated by Herod Antipas, the Pharisees, or others. The second half of verse 32 and all of verse 33 are obscure in meaning (Creed 187) and have been interpreted in different ways by the commentators. Verse 32 speaks of "to day, and to morrow, and the third *day*." Verse 33 speaks of "to day, and to morrow, and the *day* following." Creed (187) and Hoehner (*Antipas* 221) interpret these words to mean a relatively short period within which Jesus will continue His ministry of healing and casting out demons. Summers (*Luke* 173) suggests two possible meanings for these words, either the length of time it will take Jesus to arrive in

Jerusalem, or the time needed to complete His course. (While it may be tempting to see these verses as a reference to the interval of time between Christ's death and resurrection, that interpretation does not fit the context.)

The affirmation "I shall be perfected" (Greek *teleomai*) expresses the idea of completeness. Jesus is determined to continue until His mission is brought to completion (Marshall, *Gospel* 572). Summers (*Luke* 173) suggests that, in this context, the mission may refer specifically to the journey to Jerusalem or it may refer to the larger ministry that will terminate in His death and resurrection.

The last words of verse 33 suggest that Herod's threats are meaningless because Jesus, as God's prophet, cannot die in Galilee or in Perea; He must be killed in Jerusalem. As Summers (*Luke* 173) explains, there are few actual examples of prophets being killed in Jerusalem, but, in the popular mind, Jerusalem was the site where the prophets had been murdered. Since He is a prophet, God will not allow the end of Jesus' earthly ministry to occur in any other place.

Verses 34-35 are closely related to the Jewish tradition that connected the city of Jerusalem with the martyrdom of the prophets. See Marshall (*Gospel* 574) for a good discussion of the various possible origins of this tradition. Jerusalem was also the location filled with sadness because Jesus knew His earthly ministry would come to its end there. In Jerusalem, they have killed God's prophets and stoned the ones He had sent to them. As Green (*Luke* 538) points out, stoning was the punishment inflicted in the O. T. on those who were guilty of blasphemy or apostasy. The great irony is that those whom God sent as His spokesmen were treated as if they were blasphemers or apostates.

There is also a note of sadness because Jesus knew things could have been different for the city. Jerusalem was not compelled to reject God's prophets, but that is what she had often chosen to do in the past. In the future, she will repeat that sad story and she will suffer for it.

In the latter part of verse 34, Jesus uses a common agricultural metaphor of a hen, covering her chicks with her wings to protect them from danger, to describe His aspirations for the city of Jerusalem. In this context, the city of Jerusalem, the capitol, becomes a symbol for all the inhabitants of Palestine. During His entire ministry, Jesus has tried repeatedly to bring them into His fold, but they were not willing to accept Him as their Messiah. He has not rejected them, but they have rejected Him.

Verse 35 outlines the punishment the city will suffer for its rejection of Christ as the Messiah. "Your house" is probably a direct reference to the Temple in Jerusalem (Geldenhuys 383), but many interpreters understand it to have a broader meaning. Nolland (II:742) sees it as a reference to the destruction of the city of Jerusalem. Green (*Luke* 539) understands it to refer to Jerusalem as the center of those practices and institutions that are contrary to the will of God. In this context, it refers to the Jewish system of worship, especially its leadership, which was so opposed to Jesus and His ministry.

"Desolate" means "empty." The idea is the Temple, the center of worship, will become empty in the sense that no longer will the daily sacrifices and other activities be carried on. In other words, it will be abandoned by God. Whatever may be done there, He will not accept.

The last words of verse 35 are enigmatic, and it is doubtful the disciples understood their full significance. "Blessed *is* he that cometh in the name of the Lord" is from Psalm 118:26 and was chanted on feast days by pilgrims coming into the city of Jerusalem (Stein, *Luke* 384). Many commentators see these words as a reference to the Second Coming of Christ (Stein, *Luke* 384; Geldenhuys 383). Two interpretations of this difficult phrase are possible. The first is that those who have rejected Jesus will see Him as He returns, but it will be too late for them to be saved. Their judgment is certain. The other interpretation is that Israel will be converted and ready to receive their Messiah at His coming. For good discussions of this difficult passage see Stein (*Luke* 384); Ellis (192); Marshall (*Gospel* 576-577); and Geldenhuys (383, 385).

Summers (*Luke* 175) suggests a different interpretation. In his view, this verse refers to Jesus' arrival in Jerusalem at the end of this journey and not to the Second Coming. In Jerusalem, He will make a final offer of Himself as the Messiah.

14:1 And it came to pass, as he went into the house of one of the chief Pharisees to eat bread on the Sabbath day, that they watched him.
2 And, behold, there was a certain man before him which had the dropsy.
3 And Jesus answering spake unto the lawyers and Pharisees, saying, Is it lawful to heal on the Sabbath day?
4 And they held their peace. And he took *him*, and healed him, and let him go;
5 And answered them, saying, Which of you shall have an ass or an ox fallen into a pit, and will not straightway pull him out on the Sabbath day?
6 And they could not answer him again to these things.

At this point in the Gospel, a new section begins. According to Morgan (*Luke* 170), this new section, which includes a variety of events and teachings, begins at 14:1 and continues through 17:10. In his view, all of these events probably took place on the last Sabbath prior to Jesus' entrance into the city of Jerusalem.

One interesting facet of the Gospels is Jesus often accepts the hospitality of those who are determined to destroy Him and His ministry. Apparently, His goal is to show that His ministry is for all, even for those who refuse to accept it. It is also possible that all of the Pharisees were not equally hostile to Jesus; some of them might have been somewhat open to His message. In this passage, Jesus goes to the home of one of the most important Pharisees, one who would normally be hostile to Him.

The Pharisees were committed to a multitude of laws, both written and oral, about what could be done on the Sabbath. These laws did not, however, forbid hospitality (Creed 188-189). Food could not be cooked on the Sabbath, but it could be prepared the day before and kept warm to be served on the Sabbath. Barclay (187) summarizes the complex rules on how the food was to be kept warm.

During the feast (which probably lasted several hours), a man with dropsy appears. Luke never explains how the man got into such a banquet. Lenski (767) explains that outsiders could enter and observe at a banquet like this. Plummer (354) notes the man could have been placed at the banquet as a trap for Jesus, he could have been there by accident, or he could have come hoping to be healed. Plummer thinks the third reason is the most likely. Caird (175) opines that the man is not sent there to trap Jesus; he is, rather, an intruder the host and his guests must tolerate. Barclay (188), to the contrary, suggests the man might have been planted there specifically to see how Jesus would respond to the situation.

The Gospels describe seven miracles of mercy performed on the Sabbath; five of them are found in Luke (4:35; 4:38; 6:10; 13:14; and here). The other two are found in John 5:10 and 9:14. Mark 1:26 relates the healing of a man with an unclean spirit, which is probably the miracle described in Luke 4:35. By these miracles, Jesus demonstrates He is Lord of all, including the Sabbath. He also wishes to prove that deeds of mercy can be done on any day, including the Sabbath. As Caird (175) notes, if the law of mercy outweighs the law of the Sabbath in the case of an animal, it should much more apply in the case of a person.

In verse 5, some of the early manuscripts of Luke have the word "son" where most of the manuscripts have the word "ass." The word "ass" fits the context better, but even if "son" is the correct reading, the basic meaning of the parable does not change (Caird 176; Creed 189).

"Dropsy" often refers to the accumulation of excess fluids in the tissue of the body; it was often thought to be a punishment for sin (Liefeld 976). By healing this man, Jesus directly confronts the teachings of the Rabbis. The law made provision for emergencies; if one's animal fell into an open well on the Sabbath, it was lawful to pull it out. The healing of this unfortunate man was no emergency. He had apparently suffered from this condition for some time, and Jesus could have healed him on another day. In Jesus' view, it is always appropriate to bring healing to a suffering human being, even on the Sabbath.

Verse 6 says the Pharisees who were present on that occasion could not respond to what Jesus had said and done. They could not deny His power to heal because it was obvious for all to see. If He had the power to heal a man suffering from dropsy, who had the authority to challenge Him for healing on the Sabbath? Their inability to respond to Jesus' miracles probably served only to infuriate further the Jewish leaders. This healing, no doubt, provoked many of the common people to bring their sick and suffering friends and relatives to Jesus in hope of experiencing a similar miracle.

7 And he put forth a parable to those which were bidden, when he marked how they chose out the chief rooms; saying unto them,
8 When thou art bidden of any *man* to a wedding, sit not down in the highest room; lest a more honourable man than thou be bidden of him;
9 And he that bade thee and him come and say to thee, Give this

man place; and thou begin with shame to take the lowest room.
10 But when thou art bidden, go and sit down in the lowest room; that when he that bade thee cometh, he may say unto thee, Friend, go up higher: then shalt thou have worship in the presence of them that sit at meat with thee.
11 For whosoever exalteth himself shall be abased; and he that humbleth himself shall be exalted.

Jesus presents what is commonly known as the Parable of the Wedding Feast or the Parable of the Banquet. A somewhat similar parable is found in Matthew 22. Since this parable immediately follows the story of the Pharisee who invited Jesus and others to his house for a Sabbath meal, it may relate to the same incident. Luke does not indicate, however, whether this parable was told on that occasion or on another occasion. The fact this parable speaks of a wedding feast rather than a Sabbath dinner in a home, may indicate this parable was told on a different occasion. Fitzmyer (II:1049) and Morgan (*Luke* 170) argue that all of Jesus' teaching through verse 24 took place during the Sabbath dinner in the Pharisee's home.

B. Smith (207) classifies this parable and several others in a category he labels, "Parables for Pharisee and Sinner." These parables are designed to rebuke the Pharisees for their legalism and self-righteousness. If they are to have any hope of entering the Kingdom of God, they must adopt a radically different way of thinking and acting. Humility and service must become more important than position and prestige. It is important to note that Jesus does not display contempt for the Pharisees; He seeks to bring them face-to-face with their prejudices.

Jesus sets up the hypothetical situation of a man who is invited to attend a wedding feast, probably in the home of a person who is wealthy and influential. In the honor and shame culture of that time, it was extremely important that the guests be seated in the proper order. Those places nearest to the host were reserved for the most distinguished guests. Morgan (*Luke* 172) notes that the most common seating arrangement for a banquet in an eastern home was the triclinium. In the triclinium, the guests would be seated in groups of three at small tables; the most important guests would occupy the middle position at the center table.

In the parable, Jesus gives advice which is similar to that given in Proverbs 25:6-7. Those who may arrive early should not to take the spaces nearest the host. If they do, they are likely to be embarrassed when a more distinguished guest arrives and they are told to take a lower place. It would be far better to take a place farther away from the host and then be invited to come closer. This humble action would not only avoid embarrassment, it would raise the person's esteem in the eyes of the other guests.

Jesus' purpose, in this brief and somewhat humorous parable, is not to teach proper conduct at a wedding feast. As verse 11 explains, it is designed to teach that those who seek to enter the Kingdom of God must do so with an attitude of humility. Those who exalt themselves cannot enter the kingdom; they must be brought to a position of humility before God. Those who humble themselves before God will be rewarded; they will be permitted to experience all the joys that are available to the members of God's family.

12 Then said he also to him that bade him, When thou makest a dinner or a supper, call not thy friends, nor thy brethren, neither thy kinsmen, nor *thy* rich neighbours; lest they also bid thee again, and a recompense be made thee.
13 But when thou makest a feast, call the poor, the maimed, the lame, the blind:
14 And thou shalt be blessed; for they cannot recompense thee: for thou shalt be recompensed at the resurrection of the just.

These verses are peculiar to Luke. Jesus gives advice, which would have been regarded as revolutionary in the first century. The concept of reciprocity was important in the ancient world; one would normally invite only those of one's social and economic class to share in a meal in his or her home. As Childers (549) notes, this passage does not prohibit showing hospitality to friends and neighbors; the idea is that such entertaining carries no heavenly reward. Jesus' counsel to invite the poor and the outcasts to a feast is not new. In the O. T. such passages as Deuteronomy 14:28-29, 16:11, and 26:11-13 stress the importance of including outcasts and even foreigners in communal meals and celebrations.

As Moxnes (256) explains, the wealthy Pharisees of the first century practiced a strict system of reciprocity in their social relationships. While they would have been willing to give alms to the poor, it would have been difficult for them to have invited such people into their homes for a meal. Such conduct would have resulted in a loss of face.

"Dinner" (Greek *ariston*) is generally the first meal of the day, a light meal served at mid-morning (Marshall, *Gospel* 493; Geldenhuys 390-391). "Supper" (Greek *deipnon*) is the main meal, served in the late afternoon. It was considered appropriate to invite guests to share in either of these meals (Marshall, *Gospel* 583). "Call" (Greek present imperative) should be understood as continuous or repeated action. One should not have the habit of inviting only these specific groups of people (Geldenhuys 391).

Four categories of people are not to be habitually invited. They are friends; brothers, probably meaning close relatives; kinsmen, other relatives or family members; and wealthy neighbors. These are the types of guests that would normally be invited to a special feast in the home of a wealthy individual. They would reflect the same social class as the host, and they would be in a position to repay the hospitality.

Instead of inviting such as these, Jesus lists four other groups that the rich man should invite to his feast. They are the poor, the maimed or crippled, the lame, and the blind. These groups represent the outcasts of society, the very people that a wealthy Pharisee would not want to have in his home. Many in the ancient world would have considered such people to be cursed by God. Some of them would have needed help getting to the banquet because of physical disabilities. All of them would be poor with no way to repay the rich man's hospitality. Jesus explains that a host to such guests will not receive his reward in this life but in the life to come. He often speaks of the contrast between the temporal and the eternal (Summers, *Luke* 178).

In the time of Jesus, Jewish beliefs about the end times were still developing. The Sadducees did not believe in a future bodily resurrection, while the Pharisees did. Some believed only Jews would be resurrected while others believed all would be. Jesus held the view that all would be resurrected. This passage mentions only the resurrection of the just, while John 5:29 speaks of the resurrection of both the righteous and the wicked. Jesus is not saying the wealthy host should show generosity only to obtain a heavenly reward (Summers, *Luke* 178). The idea is that a heavenly reward naturally follows the showing of mercy and generosity while on earth. Those who wish to participate in the Kingdom of God must look beyond their own selfish interests and demonstrate a genuine care and concern for others. Membership in the family of God requires a radical reorientation of one's beliefs and actions.

15 And when one of them that sat at meat with him heard these things, he said unto him, Blessed *is* he that shall eat bread in the kingdom of God.
16 Then said he unto him, A certain man made a great supper, and bade many:
17 And sent his servant at supper time to say to them that were bidden, Come; for all things are now ready.
18 And they all with one *consent* began to make excuse. The first said unto him, I have bought a piece of ground, and I must needs go and see it: I pray thee have me excused.
19 And another said, I have bought five yoke of oxen, and I go to prove them: I pray thee have me excused.
20 And another said, I have married a wife, and therefore I cannot come.
21 So that servant came, and shewed his lord these things. Then the master of the house being angry said to his servant, Go out quickly into the streets and lanes of the city, and bring in hither the poor, and the maimed, and the halt, and the blind.
22 And the servant said, Lord, it is done as thou hast commanded, and yet there is room.
23 And the lord said unto the servant, Go out into the highways and hedges, and compel *them* to come in, that my house may be filled.
24 For I say unto you, That none of those men which were bidden shall taste of my supper.

This is one of the most famous of Jesus' parables, often called the Parable of the Great Supper (Kistemaker 193). For good summaries of its history and interpretation see Kistemaker (193-201) and Stein (*Parables* 82-91). A somewhat similar parable is found in Matthew 22:1-10; Stein (*Parables* 83-84) presents a helpful analysis of the similarities and differences between the two parables.

According to many interpreters, the setting is still the home of the wealthy Pharisee where Jesus and others have been invited to a feast (Kistemaker 197). An unnamed guest makes the statement "Blessed *is* he that shall eat bread in the kingdom of God." This refers to the commonly-accepted belief that in the end times, when the Messiah comes, He will host a great banquet for all Jews (Summers, *Luke* 178). Maddox (49) explains the underlying assumption behind this statement is that the Pharisees will be invited to this great feast.

Ellis (194) posits that the declaration refers to the great feast that will officially inaugurate the Kingdom of God. While Jesus does not deny there will be a great messianic banquet in the future, the emphasis of His response is upon the present invitation He is extending to men to enter the kingdom. The Kingdom of God has already come to earth in the person of the Son of God. Although the kingdom has not yet been fully realized, Jesus is already inviting men and women to enter. They must understand, however, they cannot enter God's kingdom as they are; they must first experience a radical transformation. According to Maddox (49) the emphasis of this passage is on the reversal of expectations. Those who have expected to be included because of their righteousness will be excluded. Those who have faith in Jesus as the Son of God will be permitted to enter.

Jesus begins to tell the story of a wealthy man who made a great feast and invited a large number of people. The latter part of verse 16 implies the invitations had already been extended and the invited guests had accepted them. When time came for the banquet to begin, the host sent a servant to advise the guests that everything was ready and the banquet was about to begin. Stein (*Parables* 84) explains it was customary to extend two invitations, the first some days in advance and the second on the day of the banquet.

As the servant goes to the homes of the invited guests, there is a totally unexpected development. They all begin to make a variety of excuses and ask—at the last minute—to be excused. In the ancient world, such treatment of a host would have been regarded as extremely rude and insulting. As Kistemaker (199) points out, excuses should have been made at the time of the first invitation. To decline the second invitation, after the food had already been prepared, was considered a major insult.

In verse 18, Jesus explains that this refusal was universal; all the guests asked to be excused. Jesus then gives three excuses that illustrate the types of excuses used. The first said he had purchased some land and he must go inspect it. Marshall (*Gospel* 589) notes that a land sale might be conditioned upon a future inspection.

The second invited guest says he has purchased five yoke of oxen. Jeremias (*Parables* 177) explains that a typical farmer in Israel owned as much land as one or two yoke of oxen could plow (about 10-20 hectares). The fact that this character in the story had purchased five yoke of oxen indicates he was a wealthy landowner.

The third excuse is the most interesting. The man asks to be excused because he is newly married. Since women were not normally invited to banquets, she could not go with him. Rather than leave her at home alone, he asks to be excused from the banquet.

All three excuses reflect a lack of commitment, proper planning, and foresight. All three could have declined the invitation when it was first made. Summers (*Luke* 179) points out that banquets like this were often held at night. One would not inspect land or oxen at night; that makes the first two excuses seem even more ridiculous. All three of these characters could have made arrangements to attend the banquet if they had really wanted to go. When he hears the excuses, the host is justifiably angry (Summers, *Luke* 179). He understands their excuses are trivial and his guests simply do not consider his banquet important.

Since the food is already prepared, and the host does not want it to go to waste, he gives the servant additional instructions. He is to go quickly into the streets and lanes of the city and invite the poor, the maimed, the halt, and the blind; interestingly, these are the same four categories of people mentioned in verse 13. The phrase "streets and lanes" describes the broad avenues and narrow alleys of the city (EGT 1:574). The servant is to go into the areas of the city where the poorer people live and invite them to come.

As the parable continues, the servant fulfills his responsibility and reports to the master that there is yet room in the banquet hall for more people. The host then orders him to "go into the highways and hedges and compel them to come in." A "highway" (Greek *hodos*) means "a road" or "a way." A "hedge" (Greek *gragmos*) is a hedge or a fence, beside which there would be a path. The servant is to go outside the city to the suburbs and rural areas nearby (Nolland II:757). "Compel" (Greek *anakaz*) means "urge" or "constrain." The host has no legal authority to force them to come; the idea is that the servant is to implore them to come.

This is a parable and not a description of an actual event. In reality, the invited guests would not refuse to attend a banquet in the home of a rich man and then offer such paltry excuses. Also, it is doubtful that a rich man would have had difficulty filling his banquet hall with the poor people of the city. They would have been glad to share in such an elegant meal.

In verse 24, the parable ends and Jesus speaks directly to those who have been listening. As Ellis (194) explains, it is not unusual to end a parable with an application, but in a sense Jesus puts Himself into the parable when He says, "None of those men which were bidden shall taste of my supper." In doing this, He speaks of the great messianic banquet He will have for all of His followers in the end time. "Those men which were bidden" refers to the Jews who have been invited to enter into the kingdom but have declined the invitation. To reject Jesus' invitation to enter into the kingdom and thereby become a part of God's new family is serious business. Those who do so will be excluded from the presence of God.

This is a parable about the Kingdom of God. Many people were refusing Jesus' invitation to enter His kingdom because they were more concerned with maintaining their traditional beliefs and practices than they were with hearing and obeying His teachings. For the most trivial of reasons, they were missing out on God's open invitation. As Marshall (*Gospel* 591) explains, they will not be able to attend the messianic banquet unless they accept the invitation to do so.

Caird (177) offers an interesting and somewhat allegorical interpretation of the last section of the parable. The original guests who offered excuses are the self-righteous Jews who pay no heed to the preaching of Jesus. The second group, the poor people of the city, are "the spiritual waifs of the Jewish people, the tax gatherers and sinners whom the

Pharisees regarded with contempt." The third group, those outside the city, are the Gentiles. While his interpretation is overdrawn, Caird does raise an important point. The kingdom was first offered to the Jews, but they have been unwilling to accept Jesus as their Messiah. Their refusal will open the door for others, including Gentiles, to be accepted into the kingdom. Caird also notes that God has not determined to exclude anyone from His kingdom; their exclusion is a result of their own choice.

As Kistemaker (200) points out, the basic message of this parable is the Kingdom of God has come to earth in the person of Jesus, and all are invited to enter. They must, however, make the decision to enter while the opportunity is there; to delay is to invite disaster.

25 And there went great multitudes with him: and he turned, and said unto them,
26 If any *man* come to me, and hate not his father, and mother, and wife, and children, and brethren, and sisters, yea, and his own life also, he cannot be my disciple.
27 And whosoever doth not bear his cross, and come after me, cannot be my disciple.
28 For which of you, intending to build a tower, sitteth not down first, and counteth the cost, whether he have *sufficient* to finish it?
29 Lest haply, after he hath laid the foundation, and is not able to finish *it*, all that behold *it* begin to mock him,
30 Saying, This man began to build, and was not able to finish.
31 Or what king, going to make war against another king, sitteth not down first, and consulteth whether he be able with ten thousand to meet him that cometh against him with twenty thousand?
32 Or else, while the other is yet a great way off, he sendeth an ambassage, and desireth conditions of peace.
33 So likewise, whosoever he be of you that forsaketh not all that he hath, he cannot be my disciple.

The series of parables told in the home of the Pharisee ends at verse 24. Verse 25 begins a new section wherein Jesus instructs His followers concerning the demands that membership in the kingdom will make upon them. These verses contain some of Jesus' most important and hardest sayings. Luke notes a large number of people were following Him as He continued His journey to Jerusalem. He does not explain the makeup of this multitude, but it probably contained a mixture of genuine disciples, those who were considering becoming disciples, and more casual followers. One of Jesus' major goals in this section is to separate those who were serious about following Him from those who were not.

Beginning in verse 26, Jesus outlines three important conditions the disciples must meet if they are truly sincere and committed (Fitzmyer II:1062). First, they must be willing to subordinate family and even their own lives to the cause of discipleship. Second, they must be willing to take up "the cross," which is a symbol of self-denial. Third, they must renounce material possessions.

"Hate" (v. 26) reflects a construction (in Hebrew grammar known as a relative negative) that means "to love less" (Liefeld 978; F. Bruce, *Hard Sayings* 120). Morgan (*Luke* 175) explains that the oriental mind was accustomed to sharp contrasts. Jesus was not teaching that the disciple should develop a malicious attitude toward his loved ones; instead, the true disciple must give the highest priority to being a follower of Jesus. As Barclay (196) notes, it is possible to be a follower of Jesus without being a disciple, even as one can be a camp-follower without being a soldier. This does not mean the disciple should have no love for family members and no regard for his own life. The meaning is that all of these earthly ties must take second place to one's commitment to follow Jesus. Jesus did not intend, for example, to abrogate the commandment to honor one's parents.

Verse 27 explains the role of the disciple, using the image of cross-bearing, an image Luke has previously used (9:23-27). The disciple must not only be willing to suffer martyrdom along with Jesus; he or she must also be willing to suffer opposition and hostility in his ministry on a daily basis (Fitzmyer I:787). The disciple must be willing to identify publicly with Jesus even though that may entail suffering and death.

Jesus then gives two illustrations of the level of commitment required to be a disciple. Both of these illustrations involve some degree of advance planning and preparation for service. The first involves a man who desires to build a tower; Jesus may have in mind the kind of towers farmers built to help protect their vineyards from theft (EGT 1:575). Before he begins construction, the man must first sit down, calculate the cost, and determine whether he has sufficient resources to finish the project. He will look foolish if he begins construction and is unable to finish it.

The second illustration involves a king who is preparing for battle. If he is wise, the king will carefully examine the size of his army before taking the field. He will also obtain the best intelligence available about his enemy. If he finds that his army is badly outnumbered, he will send a delegation and make peace with his rival while the opposing army is still a distance away. If he foolishly goes into battle with a smaller army, he will probably be defeated.

Jesus comes to His conclusion in verse 33. Being a follower of Jesus requires a high degree of commitment. His followers must count the cost of being a disciple and decide if they are willing to pay the price. The tower builder must first determine he has sufficient resources to finish and then commit his resources to this project. The wise king must decide whether to send his army into battle. Both illustrations involve some degree of advance planning and preparation. The idea is that the person must determine from the outset whether he or she is willing to pay the price necessary to be a disciple. Decisions about following Jesus should not be made in haste because they require the highest level of commitment.

"Forsaketh" means to "give up." When used in the context of persons, it means to leave or to say goodbye. When referring to material things, it means "to renounce" (Liefeld 980). It is doubtful that Jesus meant His disciples had to sell or give up the use of all property, because some resources were necessary in order to render effective service as a disciple. The meaning is that the disciple must develop a proper attitude toward material things. He must no longer regard them as his own possessions; he must regard them as things on loan from God. They are to be used not in a selfish way, but in a way that advances the Kingdom of God. "Forsaketh" (Greek present tense) means a continual forsaking of those things that stand in the way of service to Christ. For Luke, a preoccupation with material wealth renders discipleship virtually impossible (Nolland II:764).

34 Salt *is* good: but if the salt have lost his savour, wherewith shall it be seasoned?
35 It is neither fit for the land, nor yet for the dunghill; *but* men cast it out. He that hath ears to hear, let him hear.

This is probably a common teaching Jesus used on different occasions (EGT 1:577). A similar saying is found in Matthew 5:13. Here the idea is that the disciple must present a consistent life of commitment to Christ. Salt was an important commodity in the ancient world; it was used in a variety of different ways, one of the most important being the preservation of meat. Much of the salt used in Israel came from evaporating the water of the Dead Sea, which included different minerals (Jeremias, *Parables* 169). For that reason, the salt that was sold in Palestine was not pure sodium chloride; it was a mixture of different minerals.

Sometimes, this mixture was used as fertilizer because it added needed minerals to the soil. Nolland (II:765) explains that if the kind of salt used in ancient Palestine were exposed to moisture, the sodium chloride would leach out and leave only the other minerals. Since there was a high tax on salt, there was also the temptation to adulterate the salt with sand (Liefeld 980; Summers, *Luke* 81). Such adulterated salt was of no value as a seasoning or as a food preservative. It was even useless as fertilizer; it was cast into the road as rubbish.

The point is the true disciple must demonstrate a sincere commitment to the kingdom. He must be like the unadulterated salt that is valuable and useful. If he does not live like a disciple, he will be of no value in the kingdom. In fact, his poor testimony may be an obstacle to the furtherance of the gospel. Black (166) explains that to speak of salt as having "lost his savour" was sometimes used to signify a person lacking good sense.

Summary (13:31—14:35)

This section begins with the story of a group of Pharisees who come to Jesus and advise Him to leave their territory because Herod (probably Herod Antipas) was threatening to kill Him. Jesus did not take their counsel seriously. In fact, He referred to Herod using the derogatory term, "that fox." Rather than flee in an effort to protect His life, Jesus determined to continue His journey to Jerusalem and complete the ministry His Father had given Him. Jesus also expresses His deep love and concern for the inhabitants of Jerusalem. In the popular mind, Jerusalem was the place where the prophets of God had been slain. Jesus did not allow this way of thinking to dissuade Him; it was in Jerusalem that His earthly ministry would be completed. He was determined to finish the ministry He had begun.

Chapter 14 begins with the healing of a man suffering from dropsy. The remainder of the chapter consists of instruction Jesus gave to His disciples and to others who were willing to hear and heed His message. Sometimes He taught by means of parables; at other times, He taught by direct instruction.

Much of the content of chapter 14 revolves around eating together and accepting or not accepting invitations to participate in a meal in someone's home. Jesus uses the example of an important person inviting guests into his home for a meal as an illustration of how God invites people into His kingdom and how individuals should respond to that invitation. This chapter illustrates several important principles about how the Kingdom of God functions and how people should respond to it. How should a person respond to an invitation to enter the Kingdom of God? According to verses 7-11, he or she should respond with humility. Whom does God invite into His kingdom? He invites those who can't repay Him (vv. 12-14). What does God do when individuals spurn His invitation? He invites those who will respond to His grace (vv. 15-24).

Jesus is invited to the home of a Pharisee to share a meal on the Sabbath. An unidentified man suffering from dropsy was present, and Jesus heals him. The legal experts and the Pharisees who were present challenged Jesus for healing the man on the Sabbath because that was a violation of the laws of the Sabbath. Jesus responded by saying that if an ox or an ass (some of the early manuscripts say a son) fell into a hole on the Sabbath day, it could be rescued. If it was acceptable to rescue an animal on the Sabbath, it should certainly be legal to heal a suffering human being.

Jesus then gave the other guests at the banquet a lesson in humility. He told them they should not seek the best places when invited to a wedding feast. Instead, they should take a lower place. If the host invited them to a place of greater honor, that would exalt them in the eyes of the other guests. Verse 11 gives the application. Those who try to exalt themselves in the Kingdom of God will be abased, while those who humble themselves will be exalted.

Beginning in verse 12, Jesus gives additional instruction to the other guests at the feast. He tells them that when they give a big supper they should not invite their neighbors in the expectation of being invited back. Instead, they should invite the poor, the maimed, the lame, and the blind who do not have the resources to repay them. They will receive their reward in Heaven; that is the way the Kingdom of God operates.

This teaching is followed by the Parable of the Great Supper. In this parable, a rich man hosts a large banquet in his home, but all of the guests, at the last minute, ask to be excused. They offer lame excuses. When he receives this news, the host is understandably angry. He sends a servant to go into the areas of the city where the poorer people live and gather them up. The servant does this, and there is yet space in the banquet room. The host sends the servant out a second time, to go to the edges of the city and implore people to come to the feast. The story closes with the host saying, "None of those men which were bidden shall taste of my supper." The idea is that those who spurn Jesus' invitation to enter into the Kingdom of God will not have additional opportunities to do so. If they are not willing to listen now, in the future it will be too late. Instead, God will open the door to His kingdom to those who are willing to enter.

Beginning in verse 25, Jesus gives some of the most direct and specific teachings of His entire ministry. He tells His disciples and those who are considering becoming disciples, very frankly and openly, that discipleship will not be easy. The idea of counting the cost is introduced in verse 28. The idea is not that they should consider the cost and then decide whether or not to become a follower of Jesus because the cost of *not* following Jesus is eternal damnation. The idea is that when they become disciples they should expect to pay a high price for being His followers. Jesus uses several different analogies to indicate just how high that price will be. The first deals with one's family relationships. The term "hate" is a strong word indicating that for the disciple, his relationship with God even outweighs his relationship with his family.

The second analogy deals with cross-bearing. The disciple must be willing to publicly identify with Christ and share in His suffering. The third analogy is the story of a man who builds a tower to protect his home or his crop. The fourth is the analogy of a king who goes to war with a smaller army than his enemy has. All of these analogies indicate that the disciple must decide in advance to follow Jesus wherever He leads and be willing to pay the price discipleship demands.

Verses 34-35 reflect a teaching of Jesus that was likely repeated in different ways and at different times in His public ministry. The follower of Jesus is compared to salt. If he or she is to reflect real discipleship, there must be genuine commitment. They cannot simply have the outward appearance of a disciple; they must also reflect the realities of discipleship.

Application: Teaching and Preaching the Passage

There are many important lessons that should be learned from this important passage. In the closing verses of chapter 13, Jesus refuses to be intimidated by the threat that Herod will kill Him. He will not allow either the Pharisees or Herod to determine the course of His life and ministry. He is headed toward Jerusalem to fulfill God's will, and He must continue on that journey. In a similar fashion, Christians today cannot allow the fears inspired by the world to determine the direction of their lives. They must be directed by God and not by their own selfish desires or by the influences of the world.

Another important theme from these verses is Jesus' love for the people of Jerusalem and His desire to see them introduced into the kingdom. In the same way, the followers of Christ must have a great love for those around them and a desire to see them become a part of God's family.

This passage would be an excellent text for a series of lessons or sermons on the difficulties of discipleship. We should never allow people to develop the false idea that following Christ is the easy way out of earthly problems; it calls for a high level of commitment and sacrifice. These verses speak eloquently of the attitudes the disciple should display. The disciple must love people and be determined to minister to them in effective ways. This love for people must include men and women from all levels of society. It is no accident that Jesus instructs those attending the banquet to invite the poor, the halt, the maimed, and the blind.

Disciples are often faced with difficult choices. Morgan (*Luke* 175-176) discusses the interpretation of the phrase "If any man come to me, and hate not," found 14:26. The idea is not that the disciple should develop a "malicious attitude of heart" toward family or friends. The idea is that there will often be conflict between human desires, such as the desire to be with one's family, and the call of Christ. In such cases, the call of Christ must take first place.

As this passage points out, religious laws and traditions are important, but they are never the priority. Christ came not to preserve existing traditions but to save people. For the sincere follower of Christ, the redemption of lost and fallen mankind must receive the priority.

The disciple must manifest an attitude of self-sacrifice; a "selfish disciple" is a contradiction in terms. The things of this world, including family, must take second place. In summary, the attitudes of this world must be replaced by attitudes inspired by Christ. In a world that viewed arrogance as a virtue and humility as weakness, Jesus instructed His disciples to sit at the lowest places at the table. In a world where family was given a high priority, Jesus told His followers that family must take second place behind the kingdom.

These verses would also be an appropriate text for a series of sermons or lessons on the true nature of God's kingdom. Many people have an incorrect view of who God is and what He is doing in the world. The Kingdom of God's is not built with great fanfare or worldly power; it is like a small seed planted in the field or the yeast that is placed in the dough. It begins with small things, but by the power of God, it becomes a meaningful force in the world. It is a kingdom that men and women must enter voluntarily. They must take advantage of the open door God has set before them. The kind of excuses people make every day are of no value. If people fail to enter while the opportunity is available, they will be excluded. We cannot take for granted that the door into the kingdom will always be open.

Finally, this passage speaks not only of the attitudes a disciple should reflect, it also outlines what the disciple must do. The disciple must be like the host who sends his servant into the streets and lanes of the city to invite people to his banquet. The disciple looks for opportunities to serve Christ in practical ways that improve the lives of people. In another sense, the disciple must be like the servant who goes out into the rural areas at the edge of the city and implores people to come to the banquet. We have the good news; we have a responsibility to share it. We must be like the salt that has maintained its saltiness.

H. The Grace of the Kingdom (15:1-32)

This chapter contains three of Jesus' best-known and most familiar parables. The parable was one of Jesus' favorite and most effective teaching devices. For a good introduction to His use of parables see Robertson (*Historian* 142-152). As A. Bruce (*Parabolic Teaching* 260-261) explains, Christ did not ordinarily group together three parables teaching basically the same lesson, but that seems to be the case here. The multiplication of parables is likely an indication of the importance Jesus attached to these teachings. These parables are designed to show His love and compassion for those whom polite society often brands as outcasts.

The Pharisees and scribes (v. 2) represent the traditional religious approach of first-century Judaism. They are very committed to observe carefully the details of both the oral law and the written law. They are especially dedicated to avoiding contact with Gentiles because such contact would render them ceremonially unclean.

These three parables suggest that not only does Jesus love those whom society rejects; He also recognizes their worth. He desires to save them and incorporate them into His kingdom. The primary lesson is that God actively seeks the salvation of lost men and women. His goal is not to condemn or chastise them, but to redeem them and bring them into His family.

A. Bruce (*Parabolic Teaching* 263) notes these three parables also have a secondary purpose. Christ not only defends His own actions in accepting society's outcasts, He also rebukes the Pharisees for their lack of love and concern for others. These parables illustrate what the Jewish leaders should have thought and how they should have acted. Plummer (367) takes a similar approach. He argues that in the first two parables, Jesus defends His own conduct in receiving sinners. In the third parable, He rebukes the Pharisees for their attacks upon Him.

It is also important to note that when Luke's Gospel was being written, the makeup of the early church was changing. Jews were no longer being saved in large numbers, and the church was becoming an increasingly Gentile movement. It is likely these Gentile believers were the first recipients of this Gospel, and they would have understood and appreciated the teachings of this chapter.

Luke 15 divides itself into four natural divisions: (1) 1-3, the setting; (2) 4-7, the Parable of the Lost Sheep; (3) 8-10, the Parable of the Lost Coin: (4) 11-32, the Parable of the Lost Son.

Hunter (*Then and Now* 51-63) classifies these three parables in Luke 15, along with the parable of the Generous Employer in Matthew 20, the parable of the Two Sons in Matthew 21, the parable of the Two Debtors in Luke 7, and the parables of the Great Supper and the Places at the Table in Luke 14, as the Parables of Grace. According to him, these parables lie at the very heart of the gospel because they stress that God consistently demonstrates kindness to unworthy men and women. These parables teach that the ministry of Christ is, first and foremost, a ministry of reconciliation. Hunter also explains that Jesus originally used these parables as a response to the criticisms leveled against Him because of His fellowship with sinners.

Hunter (*Then and Now* 52) notes that the term "sinner" used in the context of these parables may refer to two classes of people. First, it may describe people who lead immoral lives, such as adulterers and thieves. Second, it may describe people who follow dishonorable occupations, such as tax-collectors, donkey-drivers, peddlers, and shepherds.

Buttrick (177) does not use the term "Parables of Grace," but he takes a similar approach. He regards these three parables as teaching that God is the God of lost people and notes that Jesus seldom called people "sinners" but usually spoke of them as "lost" (180).

His ministry was to seek and find those lost people because they were precious to Him. The Pharisees, on the other hand, were quick to label people as sinners. In their eyes, the fact that these people did not observe the ceremonial law was sufficient justification for this condemnation. Jesus' habit of eating with them brought the same condemnation down upon Him.

1 Then drew near unto him all the publicans and sinners for to hear him.
2 And the Pharisees and scribes murmured, saying, This man receiveth sinners, and eateth with them.
3 And he spake this parable unto them saying,

These three verses serve as the introduction to this group of parables. The "publicans" were Jews who accepted employment from the Roman provincial administration as tax-collectors. They often used their power to extort money from their fellow Jews; it is little wonder they were hated. As already noted, "sinner" was used in different ways. Verse 1 indicates that the developing ministry of Jesus was provoking much discussion among the various segments within Jewish society. The Pharisees and scribes clearly represent those who were in leadership positions and who viewed the ministry of Jesus as a threat to their power and authority. In their view, Jesus should send away the publicans and sinners who wished to hear Him (Plummer 367).

The publicans and sinners are regarded as outcasts; they live on the fringes of society. While they are more open than the Pharisees to the teachings of Jesus, we should not assume they will all become followers of Jesus. It is likely they have many questions about Jesus and His ministry. The word "all" is frequently used in the sense of "many" or "a large number." That seems to be the meaning here (Plummer 367).

There is also a third group, not specifically mentioned, who probably formed part of the audience for these parables. These are the law-abiding members of the society who were neither leaders nor outcasts. They were, however, influenced by the leadership of the Pharisees. It should not be assumed the leaders were a small minority who were opposed to Jesus while the majority of the people supported Him. That is an oversimplification of the situation (C. Smith 99-100). There were, in fact, a variety of different ideas and opinions.

Verse 2 gives the primary accusation the scribes and Pharisees have against Jesus. He is receiving these outcasts and even enjoying table fellowship with them. The fact that Jesus eats with such people in violation of the food laws laid down by the rabbis is a very serious charge. As Bailey (*Poet* 143) explains, the phrase "eating with sinners" may imply Jesus was actually hosting these meals. In the minds of the Pharisees, if He does such things, there is no way Jesus can be the Messiah. As Hunter (*Then and Now* 56) explains, "These respectable churchmen were shocked to see how Jesus—who, some were whispering, was the long-expected Messiah—kept open house and table for reprobates and bad characters." As C. Smith (100-101) points out, it was acceptable to call sinners to repentance; to share table fellowship with them clearly was not.

In verse 3, Luke explains that Jesus does not respond to these attacks with a counter-attack or with harsh invective. Instead, He tells a simple story designed to encourage all of His hearers to think about the true nature of the God they wish to serve. For a detailed analysis of these three important verses see Bailey (*Poet* 142-144).

4 What man of you, having an hundred sheep, if he lose one of them, doth not leave the ninety and nine in the wilderness, and go after that which is lost, until he find it?
5 And when he hath found *it*, he layeth *it* on his shoulders, rejoicing.
6 And when he cometh home, he calleth together *his* friends and neighbours, saying unto them, Rejoice with me; for I have found my sheep which was lost.
7 I say unto you, that likewise joy shall be in heaven over one sinner that repenteth, more than over ninety and nine just persons, which need no repentance.

The first parable deals with the raising of sheep, a common agricultural pursuit in ancient Palestine. According to Jeremias (*Parables* 133), a flock of 100 sheep would have been a medium-sized flock. In this case, the owner and his family care for them because the flock is too small to afford hiring a shepherd. At the end of the day, the shepherd counts the sheep as they enter the corral where they will spend the night. One sheep is missing. Although he is hot, tired, and hungry after a long day of caring for the sheep, the shepherd leaves the ninety-nine with the other shepherds with whom he is sharing the corral and goes in search of his one lost lamb.

He finds it, and returns home with the sheep on his shoulders. He then invites the other shepherds to rejoice with him because he has found his one lost sheep. As Jeremias (*Parables* 134) notes, "It was not the high value of the animal that caused the shepherd to set out on his search, but simply the fact that it belonged to him, and without his help it could not find its way back to the fold."

Bailey (*Poet* 147) points out that the Pharisees, who considered shepherding sheep to be an unclean occupation, would have found this parable shocking. Jesus makes the hero of the story a man who follows such an occupation. Bailey (*Poet* 148) also shares a somewhat different interpretation of the parable, arguing that only a wealthy individual would own a hundred sheep. The typical family in ancient Palestine would own between five and fifteen sheep. Bailey also notes that different members of an extended family would combine their smaller flocks to form one larger flock. That is probably the situation Jesus envisions here. The shepherd is responsible for the entire flock, but that doesn't mean he is the owner of all of them. The loss of even one sheep may reflect negatively on his work as a shepherd.

Bailey (*Poet* 148) also focuses on the fact the shepherd leaves the ninety-nine sheep in the wilderness, goes in search of the one lost sheep, finds it, and then returns home (vv. 4-6). He explains that wandering shepherds would spend the night with their sheep in the wilderness while peasants who lived on the edge of the pasture lands would return home with their flocks at the end of the day.

During the night, the sheep would be kept in the courtyard of the family home. That is, apparently, the situation that Jesus has in mind.

According to verse 4, the flock is still in the pasture when one sheep is found to be missing. The shepherd probably leaves the ninety-nine with a second shepherd who will guide the flock home while he searches for the one lost animal.

Upon returning to his home in the village, the shepherd calls his friends and neighbors to rejoice with him because his one lost sheep has been found and restored to the flock. In a small peasant village, this would have been the occasion for rejoicing and congratulations. Not only has an economic loss been avoided, but the man's stature in the community as a good and faithful shepherd has been preserved.

8 Either what woman having ten pieces of silver, if she lose one piece, doth not light a candle, and sweep the house, and seek diligently till she find *it*?
9 And when she hath found *it*, she calleth *her* friends and *her* neighbours together, saying, Rejoice with me; for I have found the piece which I had lost.
10 Likewise, I say unto you, there is joy in the presence of the angels of God over one sinner that repenteth.

Jesus then tells a similar parable about a woman who has lost one of her ten silver coins. Hunter (*Then and Now* 60) posits that this parable was designed to appeal to women just as the parable of the lost sheep was designed to appeal to men. He also mentions the possibility that this lost coin might have been part of her headdress or part of her dowry, but there is no evidence to confirm this. Once again, Jesus omits many details to focus on the essential elements of the parable.

According to B. Smith (191), the silver coin is probably a silver drachma, approximately equal to a Roman denarius in value. This coin would be the typical payment for a skilled workman for one day of labor. Jesus apparently has in mind a poor family where the loss of even one silver coin would have been a serious matter; there is also the possibility that these coins had some special sentimental value.

The home of a poor peasant family would have been small and dark, with a dirt floor. In such an environment, a small silver coin could easily be lost. As the text explains, the woman lights a lamp, sweeps every part of the house, and searches diligently. After a thorough search, she finds the lost coin. She then calls her friends and neighbors to rejoice with her because the lost coin has been found.

In both parables, the point Jesus wishes to make does not become clear until the end of the parable (a feature sometimes called "end-stress"). The key element in both of these parables is the application Jesus makes. At the conclusion of the first parable, Jesus says to the crowd, "I say unto you, that likewise joy shall be in heaven over one sinner that repenteth, more than over ninety and nine just persons, which need no repentance." At the conclusion of the second parable He says, "Likewise I say unto you, there is joy in the presence of the angels of God over one sinner that repenteth."

The basic teaching is that God is merciful; He wants to see the salvation of sinners, not their condemnation. To God, every individual soul is important (Plummer 368). As B. Smith (190) explains, there is nothing new in the idea that God rejoices when sinners repent. That message is found in the O. T. What is new in these parables is that God takes the initiative and seeks the salvation of sinners. If a man will search for a lost sheep, and a woman for a lost coin, will not a merciful heavenly Father seek the salvation of lost men and women? As these parables emphasize, God seeks the salvation of the lost, and when even one sinner repents, there is joy in the presence of God. This message stands in sharp contrast to the Jewish leaders of Jesus' day who focused on God's justice in condemning sinners.

Both parables emphasize repentance, an idea with deep roots in the O. T. where it comes from a Hebrew verb that means "to turn" or "to return." In contexts such as this, it describes the decision of a human being to turn from sin to God. It involves a total reorientation in one's way of thinking and one's way of acting. In the Bible, repentance is more something one does than something one says. Neither a sheep nor a coin can repent, but these are not parables about sheep or coins; they deal with God's desire to actively seek the salvation of lost men and women. He wants to see them repent and turn to Him. As Bailey (*Poet* 154) notes, in first-century Judaism repentance was regarded as one way in which the Kingdom of God might be introduced. In the preaching and teaching of Jesus, repentance is man's response to the fact the kingdom has already been introduced.

Both of these parables also stress the joy that exists in Heaven when a single sinner repents. This rejoicing indicates the importance God attaches to the repentance of sinners. The angels of God do not rejoice over the common, ordinary things of life, but the repentance of even one sinner brings joy both to the angels and to God.

The words "more than over ninety and nine just persons, which need no repentance" (v. 7) call for special comment. Interpreters take these words in different ways. Bailey (*Poet* 154) explains there was among the rabbis a debate concerning the necessity of repentance. Some of the rabbis of Jesus' day argued there were certain persons they described as "completely righteous." They were people who were guilty of no grievous sin, and God had a special love for them. Some rabbis believed God's greatest love was extended to sinners who repented, while others believed God's greatest love was reserved for the "completely righteous."

It is doubtful Jesus was endorsing the teaching that the "completely righteous" had no need for repentance. That would contradict what He taught on other occasions. It is possible Jesus refers to this on-going debate among the rabbis in order to emphasize that God loves the repentant sinner in the strongest possible way.

Other interpreters understand the term "just" in verse 7 to refer to those who are self-righteous. They regard themselves as being so "just" they do not need to repent. It is certainly true that Jesus reserves some of His most serious condemnation for those who refuse to see their own sin and believe they do not need to repent. Plummer (369) opines that Jesus is using the term in an ironic way to refer to those who have such a strong commitment to their legal observances they can see no need for repentance in their own lives.

Liefeld (982) suggests the term "just" in this context refers to devout people who have no open sin of which they need to repent. Summers (*Luke* 182-83) offers a different interpretation. In his view, Jesus has no desire to debate whether they are truly righteous. They claim to be righteous, and, for purposes of this parable, Jesus does not contradict them. Jesus does not wish to detract from the main point of the parable, which is that God receives repentant sinners. Liefeld (983) presents a similar interpretation.

11 And he said, A certain man had two sons:
12 And the younger of them said to *his* father, Father, give me the portion of goods that falleth *to me.* And he divided unto them *his* living.
13 And not many days after the younger son gathered all together, and took his journey into a far country, and there wasted his substance with riotous living.
14 And when he had spent all, there arose a mighty famine in that land; and he began to be in want.
15 And he went and joined himself to a citizen of that country; and he sent him into his fields to feed swine.
16 And he would fain have filled his belly with the husks that the swine did eat: and no man gave unto him.
17 And when he came to himself, he said, How many hired servants of my father's have bread enough and to spare, and I perish with hunger!
18 I will arise and go to my father, and will say unto him, Father, I have sinned against heaven, and before thee,
19 And am no more worthy to be called thy son: make me as one of thy hired servants.
20 And he arose, and came to his father. But when he was yet a great way off, his father saw him, and had compassion, and ran, and fell on his neck, and kissed him.

This parable is commonly known as the Parable of the Prodigal Son, but a better title would be The Parable of the Gracious Father (Stein, *Parables* 115, 122). Hunter (*Then and Now* 60) labels it "the paragon of all parables." According to most authorities (Bornkamm, *Jesus* 126), the principal character in the story is not the younger son who requests his portion of the inheritance, squanders it, and then returns to the father's house with an attitude of humility and penitence. The main character is the father who welcomes the younger son and immediately restores him to full fellowship in the family in spite of the disgrace he has brought upon himself, his family, and his community. The father warmly receives his wayward son; he doesn't place him on some type of probation as many earthly fathers would be tempted to do. He doesn't allow his younger son to work in his fields as a hired man. The son is immediately restored to full membership in the family; he is treated not as a prodigal who has returned but as an honored and respected son. It is clear the treatment he receives is far better than he deserves. The feature called "end-stress" (above) clearly applies in the interpretation of this parable. The message of the parable is not clear until the end; it is found in the kind of reception the wayward son receives when he returns home.

Via (164) presents a contrary opinion. He argues that the younger son is indeed the principal character in the parable; he initiates the action and gives the plot its structure. It is the younger son who suffers a downfall and is then redeemed; this sequence of events is the very heart of the parable.

As Schweizer (11) explains, both this parable and other similar parables have an important future aspect to them. They do not speak of the present reality as much as they speak of the surprising and extraordinary fulfillment that becomes true in the words and actions of Jesus. As he asks, "What father would wait as patiently and welcome his prodigal son as cordially as the father in Lk. 15:11-32?"

The parables of the Lost Sheep and the Lost Coin have illustrated the fact that God not only receives repentant sinners, He actively seeks them. The third parable illustrates how God receives the sinner who comes to Him in repentance and faith. He is not placed on some type of probation and given the opportunity to earn his way into the Kingdom of God. He is immediately pardoned and received as a full member of God's family.

According to C. Smith (110), the real point of emphasis in this parable is not the contrast between the father and the prodigal son but the contrast between the father and the elder brother. The attitudes and actions of the father illustrate how God receives sinners, while the elder brother indicates how they would be regarded by the religious leaders.

The parable naturally divides itself into two parts, verses 11-24, which focus on the father and the prodigal, and verses 25-32, which deal with the conflict between the father and the elder brother. This division has led some commentators to speculate we may have two different parables that Luke has combined. Stein (*Parables* 116-117) analyzes this debate and concludes that this is one parable in two parts. C. Smith (110) comes to a similar conclusion.

The younger brother goes to his father and asks to receive his portion of the family inheritance. In the real world of the first century, no father would have granted such a request. Bailey (*Poet* 161-162), who lived and worked in the Middle East for many years, interviewed people from different countries and from different social classes concerning this issue. Without exception, they all indicated that such a request would be totally unacceptable and that any younger son making such a request would be punished. He would have been, in effect, wishing that his father were dead. Under the provisions of Deuteronomy 21:17, the first-born son would be entitled to a double portion of the father's estate. In the case of two sons, that would mean that the younger would receive one-third. The division of the estate would take place when the father died.

In Derrett's view (107), in these circumstances, the younger son would not receive a full one-third of the estate. Amounts would first be deducted for the care and maintenance of the family, including unmarried females as well as the mother and father. He estimates the younger son would actually receive about two-ninths of the estate.

Bailey (*Poet* 162-168) explains that under special circumstances the father might choose to make the division while he was alive to avoid future conflict between his sons. In such cases, each son would receive ownership of his portion of the estate, but he would not be able to sell it while the father lived. In addition, the father would be entitled to use what the land produced during his lifetime. Such an arrangement would always be at the initiative of the father; it would never be requested by the son.

In verse 13, the account of the prodigal's downfall begins. The younger son converts his portion of the estate into cash. In real life, such an action would have provoked considerable controversy both within the family and within the community (Bailey, *Poet* 169). To sell a portion of the family inheritance could do great harm to the remaining members of the family.

He then takes his fortune and goes into a far country where he wastes his money in "riotous living." "Riotous" (Greek *asōtōs*) describes one who does not save, one who is a spendthrift. The term itself does not necessarily imply sinful conduct. Later in the parable, the older brother will say the younger brother spent it all with harlots.

After some time in the far country, the young man's funds are gone, and a severe famine strikes the land. Such a famine would produce both a scarcity of food and a shortage of employment opportunities. Since he does not wish to starve, he takes the only job available, which is feeding the pigs. A. Bruce (*Parabolic Teaching* 284) notes that "joined himself" (Greek passive voice of *kollaō*) may suggest the citizen of the far country is, at first, unwilling to receive him. Only after persistent entreaty is the younger son hired. Such employment as feeding pigs would be totally abhorrent to any self-respecting Jewish man. The situation becomes so desperate he would have filled his stomach with the pods he was feeding to the pigs, but no one gives him anything to eat. Bailey (*Poet* 173) understands this phrase to mean no one is regularly giving him food.

"Husks that the swine did eat" are thought by most interpreters to refer to pods produced by the carob tree (*ceratonia silique)*, which were used as fodder for animals in ancient Palestine. They were, on occasion, eaten by poor people when no other food was available. Bailey (*Poet* 171-173) offers a contrary opinion. He suggests the common carob tree produced a fruit containing natural sugar, which was quite edible. It was, in fact, a favorite food of children. He suggests Jesus has in mind the fruit of the wild carob, which was bitter and with little food value. Although the prodigal could have eaten them, they would have provided him with little nourishment.

Verse 17 marks a sudden shift in the thought of the parable; the young man "came to himself." He realizes he has made a tragic mistake in leaving home as he did. He knows very well that even the hired servants of his father are better off than he is; they have more food than they need while he is suffering from hunger. Bailey (*Poet* 173-74) explains that "he came to himself" is sometimes used in the rabbinic literature to express the idea of repentance. After a careful examination, Bailey concludes there is not sufficient evidence in this passage to determine that full repentance has taken place, but it is clear there has been a significant change in the prodigal's attitude.

In verse 18, the young man thinks about what he will say to his father when he arrives at home; he will openly confess his sin and his unworthiness. The phrase "against heaven and before thee" indicates that the son realizes he has sinned both against God and against his earthly father. He has received and squandered his portion of the family inheritance; he has also brought disrepute upon the entire family. Because of his conduct, he knows he is no longer worthy to be considered a son. He will ask only to be hired as a servant; that is, at least, better than starving in a foreign land. Summers (*Luke* 185-187) analyzes the three words used in this passage to describe different types of servants. The word in verses 17 and 19 (Greek *misthios*) means a day laborer or one who works for wages. The word in verse 22 (Greek *doulos*) is for a slave. The word in verse 26 (Greek *paidos*) refers to a child who serves within the household.

Verse 20 describes the reception the prodigal son receives when he arrives at home. His father runs to meet him, something no father in real life would have done. In the ancient world, a mature man walked at a dignified pace; he never ran anywhere. For a man of his age and position to run in sight of the entire village would have been most undignified. The father in the parable is not concerned about the reaction of his neighbors; his focus is entirely upon his son who has returned. He has compassion on his wayward son, hugs him, and kisses him. The prodigal had done nothing to deserve this generous reception; after what he has done, he deserves no reception at all.

21 And the son said unto him, Father, I have sinned against heaven, and in thy sight, and am no more worthy to be called thy son.
22 But the father said to his servants, Bring forth the best robe, and put *it* on him; and put a ring on his hand, and shoes on *his* feet:
23 And bring hither the fatted calf, and kill *it*; and let us eat, and be merry:
24 For this my son was dead, and is alive again; he was lost, and is found. And they began to be merry.

The son begins to make the speech he has so carefully prepared, but the father never allows him to complete it. In verse 22, the reception continues. The prodigal is not received like the wayward son he is; he is received as an honored son. The father orders that he be dressed in the best robe, that shoes be placed on his feet, and that a ring be placed on his finger. The fact that shoes are placed on his feet may indicate he came home bare-footed, or it may refer to the custom of taking off one's dirty sandals when entering the house (Summers, *Luke* 187). These actions indicate that his father has restored him to full son-ship in the family (Geldenhuys 409). Jeremias (*Parables* 130) suggests the ring and the robe indicate more than the restoration to son-ship; they indicate the returning son is being treated as the guest of honor.

The crowning event is that the father orders the fattened calf be killed and a great banquet prepared; that the calf has been "fattened" means it has been fed on grain to prepare it for slaughter. Such a feast would be reserved for special occasions in the life of the family. In verse 24, the father explains the reason for this joyful reception in these words, "For this my son was dead, and is alive again; he was lost, and is found." The idea is that his son was thought to be dead but has returned to the family. "And they began to be merry" sets the stage for the arrival of the elder brother in the following verses.

25 Now his elder son was in the field: and as he came and drew nigh to the house, he heard musick and dancing.
26 And he called one of the servants, and asked what these things meant.
27 And he said unto him, Thy brother is come; and thy father hath killed the fatted calf, because he received him safe and sound.

The elder brother has apparently been working diligently in his father's fields and arrives with no knowledge of what has transpired. He hears the sound of the celebration and asks a servant to explain the cause of the merriment. Summers (*Luke* 187-188) explains the meanings of the "musick" and "dancing." The first refers to music played by instruments. The second is more difficult; it probably describes a type of folk dancing in which a scene or story is acted out. The servant explains that his younger brother has returned home and the father is giving him a welcome-home celebration.

28 And he was angry, and would not go in: therefore came his father out, and intreated him.
29 And he answering said to *his* father, Lo, these many years do I serve thee, neither transgressed I at any time thy commandment: and yet thou never gavest me a kid, that I might make merry with my friends:
30 But as soon as this thy son was come, which hath devoured thy living with harlots, thou hast killed for him the fatted calf.
31 And he said unto him, Son, thou art ever with me, and all that I have is thine.
32 It was meet that we should make merry, and be glad: for this thy brother was dead, and is alive again; and was lost, and is found.

The elder brother shares none of the father's generous spirit; he is offended by what he has heard and refuses to enter and join in the festivities. He can think only of the dishonor his younger brother has brought upon the family. Perhaps he fears that his overly-generous father will give his younger brother even more of the family inheritance. Once again, the father responds in a very uncharacteristic manner; he goes out and begs the elder brother to celebrate with them. The elder brother responds to his father's entreaty in a rude and unacceptable manner; he accuses the father of gross partiality. He asserts that his father has never given him such a party, even though he has served faithfully for many years. He is so resentful that he refuses to say the words, "my brother" and contemptuously refers to him as "this son of yours."

In the real world, a father would have strongly rebuked his elder son for making such accusations and for being so disrespectful. In the parable, the father responds with the same loving and caring attitude with which he had received the prodigal. He says, "Son, thou art ever with me, and all that I have is thine." These words may indicate that at the time of the division of the property, the elder son had also received his portion of the inheritance. In these verses, the father affirms his undying love for both of his sons.

The story ends in verse 32 where the father explains that it was most appropriate for them to rejoice because "thy brother was dead, and is alive again; and was lost, and is found." The family is together again; reconciliation is once again possible; a son and brother has been regained.

Plummer (379) notes that this parable really has no conclusion; Luke leaves it open-ended. He does not explain, for example, whether or not the elder brother went in to share in the festivities. Neither does he deal with how the prodigal conducted himself in the future. The main purpose of the parable is to illustrate how God receives sinners who come to Him in repentance and faith. Luke will allow nothing (not even a good conclusion) to detract from that important point.

Summary (15:1-32)

The three parables in this chapter make significant contributions to four of the major themes Luke is developing in this Gospel. First, they present the nature of the Kingdom of God as one of grace and mercy. While Jesus never encourages sinful conduct, these parables emphasize that membership in the Kingdom of God is not based on the legal observance of a multitude of rules and regulations. It is a much more personal relationship between a God who actively seeks the salvation of sinners and receives them joyfully and a person who comes before Him with repentance and faith.

The Jews of the first century held to differing conceptions of the Kingdom of God. Most of those conceptions focused on the observance of the requirements given in the written law in the O. T. and in the oral law, which had been developed by the rabbis over the centuries. For an insightful analysis of the development of the Kingdom of God in the O. T. see Bright.

In this passage and others, Luke changes the focus of the discussion of the Kingdom of God. No longer are the traditional ideas of power, control, and dominance over surrounding nations at the forefront. No longer is the ritualistic observance of law codes at the center of the concept. The focus is now on the personal relationship that exists between God and His people. These parables also amplify the understanding of the God who is establishing His kingdom. According to the O. T. documents, God willingly receives sinners who come to Him in humility and repentance. In the parables of the Lost Sheep and the Lost Coin, God not only receives sinners, He takes the initiative and seeks them out. He goes to extraordinary lengths to bring lost men and women to Himself.

In the Parable of the Prodigal Son, the father does not go into the foreign country and actively seek his younger son. He understands very well that his son is a human being with a mind of his own; he must come to his own decision. When the son returns, however, he receives far more than he deserves. He is received with joy and immediately restored to full membership in the family.

These parables illustrate the true nature of the Kingdom of God. God takes the initiative and seeks the salvation of lost men and women. When they accept His gracious invitation, there is great rejoicing in the presence of God. Membership in the Kingdom of God cannot be earned or merited; it must be received from the hand of a gracious and merciful God.

The second Lucan theme to which this chapter contributes is salvation. In the O. T., God is gracious in that He has given deliverance and the law to His people. He has made it possible for them to occupy the land of Canaan. He has repeatedly blessed them even in times of rebellion. One of God's greatest gifts to His people was the law, which they had the responsibility to observe. Those who were considered faithful were those who observed carefully the various commandments God had given. Those who were the most zealous—like the Pharisees—even went beyond the strict requirements of the law. In their zeal, they were determined to minimize their contacts with sinners and others who were not so careful in their observance. The Pharisees were sharply critical of Jesus because He shared table fellowship with sinners.

The Parables of the Lost Sheep and the Lost Coin provide a direct response to this kind of attitude. Rather than rejecting sinners and refusing to have table fellowship with them, these beautiful parables point out the value of even one sinner and the need to seek for them. In that sense, these two parables both defend Jesus and His ministry to outcasts and condemn the separatist attitude of the Pharisees. It is God's desire that salvation be extended to those who lie outside the bounds of acceptable society.

The third Lucan theme to which this chapter contributes is discipleship. While we should be careful not to allegorize the details of these parables, it is clear the shepherd, the woman, and the waiting father illustrate the kind of attitudes and actions the follower of Christ should exhibit. The shepherd actively seeks for the one lost sheep; the woman searches every corner of the house for one lost coin. The father waits anxiously for the return of his wayward son. When each is found, there is great rejoicing because every single person is important to God. An important part of the responsibility of every disciple is to take the initiative to go out and make other disciples.

The fourth important Lucan theme to which this chapter contributes is repentance. This is evident only in the third parable because repentance is not possible for a sheep or a coin. Luke stresses that the younger son, before he can return home, must first "come to himself." He has to realize what he has done and how his actions have affected the other members of his family. He prepares in advance a speech in which he confesses his sin and asks only to be received as a hired servant. As Bock (II:1313) explains, he comes to the father "with nothing but his need." Luke never promises that those with hard hearts and sinful ways will be received into the kingdom. That privilege is reserved for those who demonstrate repentance and faith.

The elder brother in the third parable makes an interesting contribution to the story. On one hand, he is everything a son should be: loyal, faithful, and hard working. Yet, he has one serious drawback. Because of his anger and jealousy, he cannot share in the rejoicing when his younger brother returns home. All he can think about is what he considers to be unjust treatment. His wayward brother has received a great celebration, while he has received not even a goat to share with his friends. Some interpreters, though not all, see in the elder brother the kind of self-righteous attitudes that the Pharisees reflected (Bock II:1317-1318).

Application: Teaching and Preaching the Passage

This chapter contains many resources for preaching and teaching. The first thing to keep in mind is that these narratives are parables, not historical narratives. Jesus is not describing actual events—although the parables may have some similarity to actual events; He is using the parable as a powerful and effective teaching device. The preacher or teacher should seek to discover and present clearly the meaning Jesus intended to convey when He first told these parables. Rather than allegorizing the details, modern preachers should focus on the important lessons that can be learned from them (Liefeld 983).

The first two parables clearly illustrate the nature of God and the kingdom He is establishing. God does not just receive sinners; He actively seeks their salvation. He is like a shepherd who searches for a lost sheep or a woman who seeks for a lost coin. He takes the initiative. If God takes the initiative to seek the salvation of sinners, should His followers do less? Preaching and teaching from these parables should emphasize that our God is a God who seeks and saves. The preacher should seek for ways to involve the church in this ministry of sharing the goodness of God with a lost world.

All three parables stress the idea of rejoicing. The conclusions to the first two parables note that there is "joy in the presence of the angels of God over one sinner that repenteth." In the third parable, when he returns home, the prodigal younger son receives a warm and totally undeserved welcome. As the father explains, "it was meet that we should make merry, and be glad: for this thy brother was dead, and is alive again; and was lost, and is found." What kind of reception do those who need Christ receive in our churches? What kind of reception does a sinner receive when he becomes a child of God and ceases to be a sinner?

The key character in the third parable is neither of the two sons, but the father. Even so, this is not a parable about how to be a good father; it is a parable about the grace of God. A wise father would never place the future of the family in jeopardy by giving a portion of the estate to an immature younger son. The custom of the day provided that the inheritance be distributed at the death of the father; no father would have given his younger son his portion of the estate while the father was still alive. Under no circumstances would he have permitted a younger son to sell the property and take the money and leave. Jesus' hearers would, no doubt, have been very surprised by the direction taken in this parable.

The key element in the parable is what happens when the younger son returns home and confesses his sin. He deserves nothing, but he receives everything. He is immediately restored to sonship within the family.

This parable explains how God receives sinners who come to Him in humility, repentance, and faith. He does not put them on some type of probation and allow them to earn their way back into the family. He does not criticize them for what they have done in the past; He simply forgives and restores. That is the way His followers should be today. We are not in the business of condemnation; our goal should be restoration. What are we doing in our churches and in our own individual lives to restore those who have gone astray?

There are many people today, both young and old, who are following in the footsteps of the prodigal. A. Bruce (*Parabolic Teaching* 282) suggests that the prodigal's life went through four stages: self-will, folly, misery, and repentance. These four stages can clearly be seen in the lives of men and women of every generation. As we deal with them, let us be more like the father and less like the elder brother.

Unfortunately, there are also many in our world who resemble the elder brother. They are often lacking in compassion and forgiveness; they cannot share the joy when a sinner comes home. They seem more concerned to justify their own actions and attitudes than to assist those in need. May we as preachers and teachers help the elder brothers of our world to take a different view of life.

I. Putting Possessions in Their Place (16:1-31)

This chapter begins with the parable commonly known as the Parable of the Unjust Steward; it is one of the most difficult of Jesus' parables and has been interpreted in many different ways (Caird 185; Beasley-Murray, *Kingdom* 201; Derrett 48-49). Marshall (*Gospel* 614) entitles it the Parable of the Prudent Steward; Kistemaker (227) calls it the Parable of the Shrewd Manager. Manson (*Sayings* 290-91) labels it "the clever rascal" and suggests that many interpreters have great difficulty with this parable because they try to press the details rather than searching for the main idea.

Luke does not use the term "parable" for this story, but that is the correct word for it. The interpreter must seek to answer at least three questions: (1) What has the steward done that makes him unjust? (2) What point was Jesus making when He told this parable? (3) How does Luke use this parable?

1 And he said also unto his dis-
ciples, There was a certain rich
man, which had a steward; and the
same was accused unto him that
he had wasted his goods.
2 And he called him, and said
unto him, How is it that I hear this
of thee? give an account of thy
stewardship; for thou mayest be
no longer steward.
3 Then the steward said within
himself, What shall I do? for my
lord taketh away from me the
stewardship: I cannot dig; to beg I
am ashamed.
4 I am resolved what to do, that,
when I am put out of the steward-
ship, they may receive me into
their houses.
5 So he called every one of his
lord's debtors *unto him*, and said
unto the first, How much owest
thou unto my lord?
6 And he said, An hundred mea-
sures of oil. And he said unto him,

Take thy bill, and sit down quickly, and write fifty.
7 Then said he to another, And how much owest thou? And he said, An hundred measures of wheat. And he said unto him, Take thy bill, and write fourscore.
8 And the lord commended the unjust steward, because he had done wisely: for the children of this world are in their generation wiser than the children of light.
9 And I say unto you, Make to yourselves friends of the mammon of unrighteousness; that, when ye fail, they may receive you into everlasting habitations.
10 He that is faithful in that which is least is faithful also in much: and he that is unjust in the least is unjust also in much.
11 If therefore ye have not been faithful in the unrighteous mammon, who will commit to your trust the true *riches*?
12 And if ye have not been faithful in that which is another man's, who shall give you that which is your own?
13 No servant can serve two masters: for either he will hate the one, and love the other; or else he will hold to the one, and despise the other. Ye cannot serve God and mammon.

Luke notes that Jesus is speaking to His disciples. This indicates that this teaching was designed for those who were His closest followers and upon whom the responsibility to continue the ministry would soon fall. This does not mean that others might not have heard this teaching.

"Steward" is used in different ways in the N. T. As Bailey (*Poet* 91-92) explains, the term is used to describe an agent or representative who might arrange a marriage or perform some other type of personal or family service. The term is also used to describe an estate manager who would control all the affairs, including financial matters, for a wealthy individual or family. The term could, on occasion, be used to describe an attorney who represents an individual or a family in some type of litigation. The authority given to a steward might vary widely, depending on the specific situation. In this passage, the steward is most likely an estate manager who has authority to control the finances. As Kistemaker (229-230) notes, the manager could be given total control of the master's business affairs and assets.

Derrett (52-55) provides a detailed description of the laws and traditions concerning agents in ancient Israel. He notes that a steward must function within the limits stipulated by the master. Within those limits, the steward has the same authority to act as the master. He can sign contracts, contract debts, and accept payments on behalf of his master.

There is some disagreement concerning the identity of the debtors in this parable; the most common view is they are tenant farmers who rent land from the master (Bailey, *Poet* 94). Such rental agreements might take various forms. The tenant might pay a percentage of the crop to the landowner, or he might pay a fixed amount. He might even pay a cash rent. In the case of a fixed amount of the crop, that amount could be reduced by the landowner in the event of a crop failure or other disaster. If the debtors are tenant farmers, the most likely interpretation is they have agreed to pay a fixed portion of the crop as rent.

The other possibility is that the debtors are not tenant farmers but merchants who have borrowed commodities from the master in order to engage in trade and commerce. They are business associates rather than tenants (Marshall, *Gospel* 618; Manson, *Sayings* 291).

Jeremias (*Parables* 181) calls attention to the large amount of goods mentioned in the parable. A hundred measures of olive oil would be approximately 800 gallons, or the produce of approximately 146 olive trees. A hundred measures of wheat would be the approximate yield of 100 acres. In both cases, the amount of oil and wheat forgiven by the steward would each be worth about 500 Roman denarii, a considerable sum (Bock II:1331-1332). The large amounts used in the parable have led some interpreters to conclude that the debtors are not tenant farmers but merchants who have borrowed from the landowner (Jeremias, *Parables* 181; Bock II:1330). Another possibility is that the large numbers are used for dramatic effect, to underscore the importance of the message being conveyed by the parable.

It is possible that part of the price mentioned in the parable should be regarded as interest, which the merchant is required to pay. The reduction from 100 to 50 measures of olive oil would imply an interest rate of 100% (Marshall, *Gospel* 618). The reduction from 100 measures of wheat to 80 would imply an interest rate of about 20%. As Marshall explains, these interest rates are high but not impossible under oriental conditions.

The parable begins with the simple statement that a rich man had a steward who had been accused of wasting his master's goods. Jesus' hearers could readily identify with the parable because such accusations were not surprising in the ancient Near East due to the lack of good bookkeeping and precise accounting. As Lenski (823-824) notes, "was accused" is often used to describe a secret accusation that is false. That does not seem to be the case here because the steward makes no attempt to deny the charges. That he "wasted his goods" implies the steward had squandered or misused his master's property over a period of time. How he had misused his master's property is never explained (Buttrick 119); such details are often omitted in the parables because they interfere with the progress of the story. As Kistemaker (230) explains, the assumption behind the parable is that these charges are true. The steward makes no attempt to refute this accusation (Manson, *Sayings* 291).

In verse 2, the master orders the steward to give an account of his management of the estate. This would often include an examination of whatever written records had been made. The latter part of verse 2 states that if the master is not satisfied with this accounting, the steward will be removed from his position. The implication is that the steward has some amount of time to prepare for this audit of his accounts.

The shrewdness of the steward comes out in verses 3-7 (Lenski 825; Kistemaker 230-231); he begins to think about what he will do if his service as steward is terminated. He quickly eliminates two possibilities. He is not strong enough to perform manual labor such as digging. It would be too humiliating for a man of his social standing to go out into the streets and beg. He settles on a course of action that will open doors for him in the future. While he still has the authority to act as steward, he will call in his master's creditors and reduce the amount of goods they owe to the master. Either the existing documents will be amended, or new documents will be prepared—all in the debtor's own handwriting, of course.

In verse 4, the steward's goal is to improve his standing with his master's debtors. If he does them a favor now, according to ideas of reciprocity common in the ancient world, they will be obligated to repay him in the future. Perhaps they will provide him with accommodations or help him to obtain other employment.

Verses 5-7 explain that the steward sits down with each of his master's debtors; Jesus cites two examples. The first owes 100 measures of olive oil; the second owes 100 measures of wheat. The steward instructs each of them to take his promissory note and reduce the amounts due to the master. Since the promissory note is the only evidence, and it is written in the handwriting of the debtor rather than in the hand of the steward, it will be difficult to prove that a fraud has taken place. According to the traditional interpretation, this alteration was another example of the steward's dishonesty; this continued the kind of activity that had gotten him in trouble with his master.

Kistemaker (231) suggests another interpretation. In his view, the steward reduced the amount by the usurious interest that was being charged on the various transactions. Other commentators (Fitzmyer, *Background* 175) suggest the steward reduced the amount by the commission he was permitted to charge for his services. As Fitzmyer (*Background* 174) notes, there is nothing in the parable that indicates this action was regarded as dishonest. The steward has performed dishonest acts in the past, but he is not condemned by the master for this action.

The first words of verse 8 have provoked considerable discussion (Marshall, *Gospel* 619-620; Stein, *Parables* 107; Fitzmyer, *Background* 165-166). "Lord" (Greek *kurios*) is used in the N. T. both to describe God and to describe an important person. Sometimes it is used as a title of respect, similar to "sir." Some scholars are of the opinion that in this passage the term refers to the master in the parable, who is in the process of dismissing his steward; others think it refers to Jesus. Beasley-Murray (*Kingdom* 201-202) gives a useful summary of the arguments for each position. He notes that this title is often used in Luke to describe Jesus; it is used three times in this parable to describe the master of the steward. While it is possible that "Lord," here, may refer to Jesus, it is more likely it refers to the master of the steward (B. Smith 109; Childers 563).

"Wisely" (v. 8) indicates the steward acted wisely or prudently in that he was mindful of his own self-interest and prepared for the future (Childers 563).

Another question asks where the parable itself ends and the application begins. Fitzmyer (*Background* 165-166) examines the various possibilities. He is of the opinion that the parable ends at verse 8a and the application begins at verse 8b and continues through verse 13. This seems the most likely interpretation, and that the master commends the steward not for his dishonesty but for his astuteness (Buttrick 118; Bock II:1332; Manson, *Sayings* 292).

Marshall (*Gospel* 614-617), Caird (185-188), and Fitzmyer (*Background* 161-184) provide useful summaries of the most commonly-held interpretations of this parable. The traditional interpretation is that the steward had acted corruptly throughout his employment. In the past, he had wasted his master's goods. When the end of his employment arrives, he continued his past practices by destroying the existing agreements between his master and his creditors and preparing false ones, thereby reducing the amounts owed to his master. Since all the original documents had been destroyed, the master had no evidence he could use to accuse his unfaithful steward of theft.

The parable assumes the master is left with little or no recourse. His only option is to dismiss the dishonest steward from further service. At the end of the parable, the steward is commended not for his dishonesty but for his shrewdness and foresight in preparing for the future. Geldenhuys (414-416), Morgan (*Luke* 185-186), and Nolland (II:796-803) present able defenses of this traditional interpretation.

In recent years, several expositors have suggested a different interpretation, which views the final actions of the steward in a more favorable light (Marshall, *Gospel* 615-616; Fitzmyer, *Background* 161-184; Bailey, *Poet* 86-118). According to the O. T., Jews were forbidden to charge interest to other Jews. In order to avoid this prohibition, an additional amount of the produce owed was often added to the bill (Kistemaker 229). For example, if a debt was for 50 bushels of wheat, they would write 60 on the bill with the other 10 serving as the interest due to the lender. According to this interpretation, the steward reduced the bill by the amount of interest owed to his master. While this type of transaction would seem very strange today, it becomes more understandable in light of the economic situation that existed in ancient Palestine (Fitzmyer, *Background* 173-177).

A variant form of this interpretation posits that the additional amount is the steward's commission on the transaction. If this interpretation is correct, the steward does not reduce the amount due to the master but foregoes his commission in order to gain the good will of his master's debtors. This interpretation does not excuse the conduct of the steward, but it does make his actions less culpable.

If the parable ends at verse 8a, as many commentators suggest (A. Bruce, *Parabolic Teaching* 367), then the interpretation or application begins at verse 8b with a series of statements that deal more with the application of the parable than with its interpretation (Bock II:1332). These verses reflect the lessons the disciples (and also future generations of believers) can draw from this difficult parable. In verse 8a, the master commends the steward for his prudence; in verse 8b, Jesus endorses the master's commendation, noting the master has spoken "wisely."

In verse 8b, Jesus makes the statement, "the children of this world are in their generation wiser than the children of light." "Children of this world" can also be translated "children of this age" (Nolland II:801). It describes those who lie outside the family of God; their frame of reference does not extend beyond this world. "Children of light" describes those who are God's children and was often used this way in Judaism (Bock II:1332).

The point of the verse is that those who are followers of God often fail to demonstrate the same degree of planning and foresight the children of this world demonstrate. The followers of God have a future in Heaven, and they should be just as diligent in planning for that future as the children of this world are in preparing for their earthly future. Believers should carefully consider what the long-term consequences of their actions will be (Bock II:1333).

Verses 9-13 outline three different applications or implications. According to A. Bruce (*Parabolic Teaching* 374), these applications do not give much help in interpreting the parable itself, but they do give the reader a good idea of how Jesus viewed wealth. The first application is found in verse 9; Christians should be generous in their use of material possessions because they can be used in the service of God. The word *mammon* is an Aramaic word that describes money or property. For an analysis of the meaning and derivation of this word see Nolland (II:805-806).

The phrase "mammon of unrighteousness" has several possible meanings. A. Bruce (*Parabolic Teaching* 373-374) suggests that it may refer to money or property that has been obtained by unrighteous conduct. Caird (189) understands the term to mean wealth that is legally acquired but contaminated in the sight of God. Childers (563) suggests it means simply "worldly wealth." Marshall (*Gospel* 621) understands it to mean worldly wealth as opposed to heavenly treasures. Ellis (200) suggests it does not describe money that has been obtained illegally but to worldly possessions. It is money or property that belongs to this unrighteous age. While this phrase may refer to money or property that is obtained illegally or unethically, there is nothing in this passage that suggests ill-gotten gain. The more likely meaning is that wealth is part of the world system that has great seductive force. As Buttrick (124) notes, "no human wealth is without blemish." This material wealth may, however, be used for good, which is what Jesus advocates in this verse. According to Marshall (*Gospel* 622), this is the first and primary application of the parable.

Verses 10-13 present two additional applications considered by Marshall (*Gospel* 622) to be secondary applications. Manson (*Sayings* 293-294) posits that these applications have no direct connection with the parable; they are included here because they reflect Jesus' teaching on the proper use of material possessions. The first of these applications concerns the importance of faithfulness in stewardship. The words "He that is faithful in that which is least is faithful also in much: and he that is unjust in the least is unjust also in much" reflect an idea that is not new. It has deep roots in Judaism (Manson, *Sayings* 293-294). The steward in the parable is not a faithful servant; he abuses his position and wastes his master's goods. He becomes a negative example for the disciples. The true disciple of Jesus must be faithful both in the small things, such as material possessions, and in the things of greater importance, such as spiritual ministry.

In verses 11-12, Jesus offers two rhetorical questions designed to cause the disciples to think seriously about their own stewardship. If they are not faithful in their use of material possessions, how can they be faithful with the true wealth, which is spiritual (Summers, *Luke* 191)? The obvious answer is that if they are not faithful in their use of material possessions, God will not entrust to them the spiritual values (such as the preaching of the gospel).

The second rhetorical question is closely related to the first. If the disciples are not faithful in their use of material possessions that belong to others, will God put in their hands material possessions of their own? The obvious answer is negative. The basic assumption here is the disciples do not own material possessions; they are a sacred trust from God and must be so regarded and so used.

The last application is found in verse 13. This is the familiar statement that no servant can serve two masters, which can be literally translated "no servant can be a slave owned by two masters." The lesson is that a disciple cannot give faithful service to God while at the same time giving his loyalty to the things of this world. The verb "hate" expresses the idea of "to despise" or "to hold in low regard." The term "love" in this context means to value highly and to give priority to (Summers, *Luke* 191).

While it might be possible for a slave to serve two earthly masters (provided that those masters are in agreement), it is not possible to serve God and this world. God demands the exclusive loyalty of His followers; He will accept nothing less (Marshall, *Gospel* 624). This verse is very similar to Matthew 6:24 and may reflect a teaching Jesus delivered on several occasions.

14 And the Pharisees also, who were covetous, heard all these things: and they derided him.

15 And he said unto them, Ye are they which justify yourselves before men; but God knoweth your hearts: for that which is highly esteemed among men is abomination in the sight of God.
16 The law and the prophets *were* until John: since that time the kingdom of God is preached, and every man presseth into it.
17 And it is easier for heaven and earth to pass, than one tittle of the law to fail.
18 Whosoever putteth away his wife, and marrieth another, committeth adultery: and whosoever marrieth her that is put away from *her* husband committeth adultery.

Luke returns to the familiar theme of Jesus' conflicts with the Jewish leaders. Jesus is probably responding to criticisms the Pharisees had made of His ministry (Derrett 79). The conflict centers on the issues of covetousness, material possessions, and the proper role of the law. The reference to those "who were covetous" connects these verses with what Jesus has spoken previously (Manson, *Sayings* 295). Jesus has been giving instruction primarily to His disciples, but others were able to hear. The Pharisees took offense at Jesus' statement concerning material possessions. The Pharisees were known for their covetousness (Plummer 387-388) because they considered wealth to be a sign of God's favor, and poverty as a sign of God's disfavor. In particular, they considered their wealth to be God's reward for their careful observance of the law. That "they derided him" means literally they turned their noses up at Him (Plummer 388). In other words, they ridiculed Jesus for His teachings concerning the proper use of wealth.

Manson (*Sayings* 295-296) argues these words were originally directed against the Sadducees rather than against the Pharisees. He suggests the Sadducees and the publicans were the real lovers of money in ancient Israel. While the Pharisees did not despise material possessions, they were not as obsessed with worldly gain as the Sadducees. Since the Sadducees had no well-developed concept of the afterlife, they focused all their attention on this world. While this theory is interesting, there is little evidence to support it. All of the early manuscripts contain the word "Pharisees." As Marshall (*Gospel* 625) explains, there was little difference between the Pharisees' view of earthly wealth and that held by the Sadducees.

Verse 15 should be interpreted in light of the context. The Pharisees used wealth as a spiritual indicator, which made them appear to be just in the eyes of other men. God, however, needs no spiritual indicators because He knows what is in people's hearts. Their wealth may make them righteous in the sight of men, but it does not make them righteous before God. Their wealth may not be an indication of their close relationship with God because He may regard it as an abomination. Summers (*Luke* 193) explains that "abomination" (Greek *bdelugma*) literally means something that is "displeasing or nauseating because of its stink."

In verses 16-18, Jesus widens the discussion to include not only His teachings concerning wealth but the entire body of laws on which the Pharisees relied for their relationship with God. Jesus asserts that they are guilty of abusing or misusing other areas of the law as well. The phrase "the law and the prophets" was used to describe the O. T.; it was also used to describe the old order that was based on obedience to the law (Caird 189; Lenski 839). Here it is used in contrast to the new order that is coming to pass in the life and ministry of Christ. The "kingdom of God" is this new order in which membership in God's family is not based on observance of a law code but on one's relationship with Christ. The preaching and teaching of Jesus occupy the central place in this new kingdom.

Verse 16 mentions John the Baptist as the last of the prophets; he is also the forerunner of Jesus who introduces the Messiah. It is doubtful Jesus means that the transition to the new kingdom has been completed, but that it has begun. The Kingdom of God has come to earth in the person of Jesus and it is being inaugurated.

The words "and every man presseth into it" have provoked considerable discussion. According to Lenski (840) the verb "presseth" (Greek *biazomai*) does not necessarily imply violence, but it does imply energy and decisiveness. Liefeld (989-990) offers a similar interpretation. In this context, the term "every man" includes only those who hear the teachings of Jesus and seek to follow Him. The Pharisees were certainly not pressing hard to enter into the new kingdom Jesus was proclaiming. The last words of verse 16 should be seen both as a commendation of the disciples and as a condemnation of the Pharisees. The disciples and others recognized the value of membership in the Kingdom of God, and they put forth every effort to become a part of it. The Pharisees, on the other hand, scoffed at the teachings of Jesus and spurned His invitation to the kingdom (F. Bruce, *Hard Sayings* 115-118).

Jesus always demonstrates the highest respect for the O. T. (Mt. 5:17-19). In verse 17, Jesus says it is easier for heaven and earth to pass away than for one tittle of the law to fail. Heaven and earth are not under man's control; only God can cause them to pass away. Here they are regarded as being enduring and permanent. The "tittle" is literally the "little horn;" it is interpreted in different ways. Most authorities understand it as describing a small pen stroke that was added to certain Hebrew letters in order to prevent them from being confused with other Hebrew letters. Another possibility is that the term describes the Hebrew letter *yod*, which is the smallest letter in the Hebrew alphabet. It may even describe the accents and breathing marks that were later added to the Hebrew words. For brief discussions see Nolland, (II:821) and Plummer (389). The idea is that none of the law, not even the smallest part, will be abrogated or annulled.

"Fail" (Greek *piptō*, v. 17) can have several different meanings. It may mean "fall," "fall down," or "fall to one's knees." In this context, the meaning is "to be done away with" or "to come to an end." Matthew 5:18 contains a similar statement, but that verse uses a verb (Greek *ginomai*) that means "happen," "come to pass," or "be fulfilled." The point of both of these verses is that the O. T. law is not simply canceled or brought to an end without accomplishing its purpose. The law is accomplishing its purpose. It was designed to point to the coming Messiah, and He has indeed come. For a careful discussion of the most common interpretations of verse 17, see Bock (II:1354-1356).

The fact that Jesus recognizes the eternal validity of the O. T. law does not mean He accepts how the Pharisees have interpreted, applied, and added to those laws. As is well known, the Jewish rabbis had developed a multitude of interpretations and applications of the laws laid down in the O. T. documents. This collection is known as the "oral law" or as "the tradition of the elders." The Pharisees of Jesus' day regarded this "oral law" as being as binding as the written law in the O. T.

The coming of Jesus has altered the situation. No longer are the interpretations and applications of the rabbis to be considered binding. Under the new covenant, Jesus has come to earth as the Son of God, and He has become the final authority for interpreting and applying God's laws. Jesus has not come to destroy the law but to fulfill or complete it. One aspect of that completion is to restore it to what God originally intended it to be.

Verse 18 is essentially a condemnation of the Pharisees; it illustrates how they have misused and misapplied the laws concerning divorce. As Lenski (843) and Summers (*Luke* 193-194) point out, this verse does not present a full exposition of Jesus' attitude toward marriage and divorce. It is, rather, an illustration of how the law has been abused and how it needs to be returned to its original intent. Barclay (211-12) provides a useful summary of the Jewish practices concerning divorce. One of the most important O. T. passages dealing with this subject is Deuteronomy 24:1-4, which provided that a man had the right to divorce his wife if he found "some uncleanness in her." "Uncleanness" can also mean "indecency." A woman's right to divorce her husband was limited to certain special circumstances.

The Jews of Jesus' day were divided on the interpretation of the words "some uncleanness." There were two rabbinical schools in Judea. The school of Shammai interpreted the phrase narrowly; they limited it to adultery. The school of Hillel interpreted the term more broadly; a man might divorce his wife for virtually any reason. Jesus defends the permanence of the marriage relationship in verse 18; those who violate this sacred bond are guilty of adultery. The point is that the Pharisees, with their emphasis on divorce, were undercutting the original intent of the law. While the passage in Deuteronomy permitted divorce in certain circumstances, it certainly did not encourage it. God's will is that families remain intact if at all possible.

The issue of divorce and remarriage in the N. T. is difficult and complicated, beyond the scope of this commentary. For an insightful analysis of the issues involved see Derrett (363-388).

Verses 14-18 are difficult and only loosely connected with what has gone before. As Derrett (84) notes, in this passage and in others, Jesus has questioned the traditional interpretations of the law the Pharisees defended. The key idea is that the Pharisees, in spite of their professed faithfulness to the O. T., have violated its basic moral teachings. The legalism of the Pharisees has prevented them from understanding and applying the basic moral precepts of the law. They have also failed to recognize the position of Jesus as the Son of God. He has come to earth as the Messiah, and He has the authority to define the correct interpretation and application of the law.

19 There was a certain rich man, which was clothed in purple and fine linen, and fared sumptuously every day:
20 And there was a certain beggar named Lazarus, which was laid at his gate, full of sores,
21 And desiring to be fed with the crumbs which fell from the rich man's table: moreover the dogs came and licked his sores.
22 And it came to pass, that the beggar died, and was carried by the angels into Abraham's bosom: the rich man also died, and was buried;
23 And in hell he lift up his eyes, being in torments, and seeth Abraham afar off, and Lazarus in his bosom.
24 And he cried and said, Father Abraham, have mercy on me, and send Lazarus, that he may dip the tip of his finger in water, and cool my tongue; for I am tormented in this flame.
25 But Abraham said, Son, remember that thou in thy lifetime receivedst thy good things, and likewise Lazarus evil things: but now he is comforted, and thou art tormented.
26 And beside all this, between us and you there is a great gulf fixed: so that they which would pass from hence to you cannot; neither can they pass to us, that *would come* from thence.
27 Then he said, I pray thee therefore, father, that thou wouldest send him to my father's house:
28 For I have five brethren; that he may testify unto them, lest they also come into this place of torment.

29 Abraham saith unto him, They have Moses and the prophets; let them hear them.
30 And he said, Nay, father Abraham: but if one went unto them from the dead, they will repent.
31 And he said unto him, If they hear not Moses and the prophets, neither will they be persuaded, though one rose from the dead.

This section is commonly known as the Parable of Lazarus and Dives or as the Parable of the Rich Man and the Beggar (Buttrick 137; Lenski 845). Buttrick (137) notes that the early church fathers Ambrose and Tertullian did not consider this to be a parable but a description of a historical event. He also notes there was a late tradition that the rich man's name was Nineus.

Most writers consider this passage to be a parable (Hunter, *Then and Now* 112; A. Bruce, *Parabolic Teaching* 376-377), but Summers (*Luke* 194) does not. He points out that it is not called a parable in the N. T.; it also lacks the form and structure of a parable. According to Summers, Jesus has included this as an example story that serves as an illustration (Stein, *Luke* 422). A. Bruce (*Parabolic Teaching* 384) uses the term "parable" to describe this passage although he recognizes that it is not, strictly speaking, a parable. In reality, it makes little difference in the interpretation of this passage whether it is labeled a parable or an example story. In one sense of the word, an example story from real life can be used as a parable.

Many interpreters (Lenski 845; Summers, *Luke* 196; Derrett 79) view this passage as a continuation of Jesus' earlier conflict with the Pharisees. This story challenges the commonly-accepted idea of the Pharisees that material wealth is an indication of one's righteousness and favor with God. In these verses, it is the poor man who is accepted by God while the rich man is rejected. Derrett (86) suggests this passage repeats in pictorial form the same lessons that have been presented earlier in this chapter. Stein (*Luke* 421-22) takes a similar approach.

This passage should not be viewed as a description of Jesus' views of eschatology or of the eschatological ideas of first-century Jews (C. Smith 234; Hunter, *Then and Now* 112). As Buttrick (139) explains, Jesus takes for granted there is a hereafter, but He does not attempt to make a detailed description of it. The goal of the story is not to give a detailed prediction of future events but to illustrate the fallacy of the Pharisaic teaching.

The name *Lazarus* is taken from the Hebrew name *Eleazar*, which means "he whom God helps" (Buttrick 137; Marshall, *Gospel* 635). This was an important name with a long history among the Hebrews. Jesus might have chosen this name to illustrate that the man is desperately poor and must depend on God for his help (C. Smith 236). It is doubtful that this Lazarus is the same as the Lazarus whom Jesus raised from the dead in John 11. The rich man remains unnamed; he is often called *Dives*, the word for "rich man" in the Latin version (Buttrick 137; Summers, *Luke* 195). In the writings of the early church the rich man was given several different names, including Finaeus, Finees, and Neues (Marshall, *Gospel* 634).

There are two main characters in the story, and there is a sharp contrast between them. The rich man has lived a life of luxury. "Purple" (v. 19) refers to an expensive dye; to be clothed in purple implied that one was rich, and perhaps of royal blood. "Fine linen" refers to clothing made from an expensive cloth that was available only to the wealthy. "Fared" (or "feasted") (Greek *euphrainomai*) means "make merry" or "rejoice" (Lenski 846; A. Bruce, *Parabolic Teaching* 377). "Sumptuously" means "splendidly." The idea is that his life was one of constant pleasure and enjoyment.

Lazarus, on the other hand, has lived a life of absolute poverty. He is a "beggar" (Greek *ptōchos*), meaning "one who is poor." He is desperately poor; he has no way to earn a living and is reduced to begging. That he "was laid" (Greek pluperfect) means he had been laid there by his friends or he was lying there. The implication is that he was ill or crippled and unable to walk there on his own (Marshall, *Gospel* 635; A. Bruce, *Parabolic Teaching* 377). Lenski (847) offers a slightly different interpretation, suggesting that Lazarus was thrown down or dumped at the rich man's gate; but the verb in the original does not necessarily imply this.

Lazarus became so hungry he desired to eat the pieces of bread that fell from the master's table. In those days there were no napkins; people would wipe the grease from their hands with pieces of bread and then throw the bread on the floor where it would be eaten by the dogs. Derrett (89) posits that the dogs in the story were not the wild dogs that scavenged in the cities but guard dogs belonging to the rich man. Since Lazarus was outside the gate, he did not even have access to these scraps of bread, and no one in the rich man's household cared enough to bring him anything to eat.

The last words of verse 21 explain that the dogs came and licked the sores on Lazarus' body. This expression has been interpreted in different ways; A. Bruce (*Parabolic Teaching* 388) provides a useful summary of the most common interpretations. Some understand it to mean the dogs, by licking his wounds with their soft tongues, showed more mercy to Lazarus than the rich man. Others see this as an "aggravation of the poor man's misery." Bruce understands it to present neither alleviation nor aggravation of his suffering; it simply adds vividness to the description of Lazarus' pitiful condition.

The fact the dogs can come close enough to lick his wounds may indicate he was too weak even to defend himself. It may also indicate the dogs had mercy on him even if the people did not (Plummer 392). Being licked by dogs may also indicate that Lazarus has been reduced to the lowest possible level of human existence.

Verse 22 marks a sudden shift in the scene. The focus becomes the reversal of fortunes that both of the major characters experience. Lazarus dies; there is no mention of his burial. After death he goes to Abraham's bosom where he receives all the blessings that were denied to him while he was on earth. The rich man also dies, but he receives an appropriate funeral. He then enters into a state of terrible punishment. The words "I am tormented in this flame" describe his condition well. As noted previously, this story does not present a complete explanation of future events. There is, for example, no description of the Day of Judgment or of the interval between death and the resurrection of the body. The focus of the story is on the final outcomes of the two principal characters.

Lazarus enters into a state of blessing described as being in "Abraham's bosom." Plummer (393) argues that this expression was not common in first-century Judaism, but Abraham was sometimes portrayed as welcoming a repentant sinner into paradise. A. Bruce (*Parabolic Teaching* 394) argues that it was a common expression used to describe "the abode of the blessed." The term describes Lazarus as reclining upon Abraham in a state of happiness just as a small child would rest in his father's lap or as a guest at a banquet would recline near the host (Marshall, *Gospel* 636). Although God is not specifically mentioned in this verse, Lazarus has clearly been welcomed into His presence.

The rich man is in hell, in a state of torment. "Hell" (Greek *hadēs*) is often used to translate the Hebrew word *sheol*. In the O. T., this word was used for the state into which people enter after death. Originally, there was no distinction made between the destiny of the righteous and that of the wicked (B. Smith 137). As the use of the term developed, there came to be a separation between the destiny of the wicked and that of the righteous.

The word for Hell used here occurs 11 times in the N. T., where it is used in several different ways (Summers, *Life Beyond* 27-28). Marshall (*Gospel* 636-637) suggests it describes the intermediate state, the period between death and the resurrection of the body. Summers (*Luke* 131) notes that the term most often refers to "the unseen place to which the dead go." It is not the term (Greek *gehenna*) commonly used to describe the final destiny of the wicked, but it is occasionally used that way. In this passage, it seems to describe the final destiny of the rich man; he is separated from God and in a state of constant punishment. For helpful discussions of the term see Summers (*Life Beyond* 27-30) and Plummer (397-398). The fact that he can see Lazarus enjoying a state of blessing with the patriarch Abraham only serves to intensify the rich man's suffering.

Verse 24 reflects the depth of the rich man's suffering. He is so desperate he asks Abraham to have mercy on him by sending Lazarus to dip the tip of his finger in water and cool his tongue. The irony of this verse is not lost on the reader. The rich man had no use for Lazarus while they were both on earth, but in the afterlife he has become very important. In the story, the flame causes intense suffering, but it does not destroy the body of the rich man.

Verses 25-26 present Abraham's response to this most unusual request. There are two reasons the rich man's request cannot be granted. First, while they were both on the earth the rich man received all the good things while Lazarus received all the suffering. Now the time has come for the rich man to receive his share of suffering; that is only fair (A. Bruce, *Parabolic Teaching* 392-393). The second reason is found in verse 26. These two men are now separated by a great gulf or chasm; no one can pass from one state to the other.

In verses 27-28, the rich man manifests a concern for others that he never demonstrated while he was on earth. He thinks of his five brothers at home, and he is afraid they will make the same tragic mistakes he has made. He asks that Abraham send Lazarus to his home to warn his five brothers lest they end up in the same state of torment he is in.

In verses 29-31, Abraham gives his answer to this request and explains why Lazarus cannot go. There is no need for Lazarus to go to the rich man's home and testify to his brothers because God has already spoken to them. They have "Moses and the prophets," a phrase used to describe both the books of the O. T. and the Hebrew religious system (Summers, *Luke* 193). In other words, God has already spoken to his brothers through the written word; they should heed the warning He has already given them. In verse 30, the rich man asserts that his brothers, who have not heeded God's Word, would listen if someone came to them from the realm of the dead. Jesus concludes the story in verse 31 by saying that if his brothers will not heed the words God has already spoken; they will not pay attention even if one should come back from the dead. A. Bruce (*Parabolic Teaching* 397) points out that to men who are thinking correctly, a messenger from the dead would be unnecessary; and to men who are not thinking correctly, a messenger from the dead would be "utterly useless." Barrett (*Holy Spirit* 91) takes the same approach, writing, "If the Jews do not attend to Moses a resurrection will not convince them. The direct and plain testimony of Scripture is more potent than the witness of a miracle which may very easily be misunderstood."

F. Bruce (*Hard Sayings* 190) offers a similar interpretation. He compares this incident to times when people asked Jesus to perform some miraculous sign. The rich man asks that his brothers be given some great miracle that will compel them to repent. Jesus refuses their request. If the words Jesus has spoken and the works He has done are not sufficient, then no miraculous sign will bring about their repentance.

This story has been interpreted in various ways. A. Bruce (*Parabolic Teaching* 378-400) presents a useful summary of the most important ideas presented in the story and its most common interpretations. This is a difficult story to analyze and interpret. In particular, it is difficult to determine the key teaching or the central idea Jesus wishes to present. The story certainly deals with the subject of future rewards and punishments; men will be judged for what they have done in this life.

Another important idea is the future reversal of human judgments. The rich man seems to be blessed and favored by God, but his final destiny indicates the error of such an evaluation. Lazarus seems to be cursed by God, but he is ultimately vindicated. Material wealth is no indicator of one's relationship to God.

According to A. Bruce (*Parabolic Teaching* 384) the primary teaching of this story concerns the sin of inhumanity. The rich man and Lazarus are both Jews; they share a common heritage. The rich man should provide assistance to the fellow Jew who lies at his gate, hungry and broken, but he chooses not to do so. Inhumanity is a sin without excuse.

Summary (16:1-31)

This chapter makes a significant contribution to the preparation of the disciples for future service, particularly in their proper use of material possessions. Chapter 16 divides itself into three natural divisions. Verses 1-13 present the Parable of the Unjust Steward with its applications. Verses 14-18 examine the proper use of the law in a Christian context. The final section, verses 19-31, is the story of Lazarus and Dives. These three sections are rather loosely connected; it is likely each of them grows out of Jesus' ongoing conflict with the Pharisees.

The Pharisees used material wealth as an indication of one's relationship with God. Those who possessed wealth were considered to be righteous and blessed by God. Those who were poor were often regarded as being unrighteous and out of fellowship with God. This chapter demonstrates the error of this kind of thinking. Wealth should not be used as an indicator of one's relationship with God, but it should be used in the service of God.

The first section is the Parable of the Unjust Steward, the story of a hired servant caught in a difficult predicament. He has abused his position of trust and wasted his master's goods. When he is called to account for his actions, he comes up with a clever way to extricate himself from this awkward situation. He calls in those who owe money to his master and reduces the amount of money they owe. This will place his master's debtors under obligation to him; they will be obliged to assist him when he is fired from his position as steward. In the end of the story, he is commended not for his dishonesty but for his shrewdness in handling a difficult situation.

How does Luke use this parable? The steward is unjust because he has not been faithful to his master. In the past, he has misused his master's property. Depending on how the parable is interpreted, he may also have abused his master's trust by reducing the amounts due to him.

It is not easy to determine the exact point that Jesus was making when He told the parable. The disciples must learn to use material possessions in the service of the kingdom. They must also learn to function in a secular world; they need to develop the same level of shrewdness in the work of the kingdom that the steward showed in resolving his difficult situation.

Luke was writing to a later generation of Christians. The recipients of this Gospel, the Christians of the second half of the first century, were serving the Lord in a difficult time. They needed to understand both the place of material possessions in the work of God and the ability to function and minister effectively in a pagan world.

According to Barclay (208-210) four lessons can be learned from this passage; these lessons come primarily from the applications found in verses 9-13. The first lesson is that the children of this world are often wiser than the children of light. This means the followers of Christ should demonstrate the same level of commitment in obtaining the spiritual values of life as the children of this world demonstrate in gaining material possessions.

The second lesson is that the true value of life is found in relationships; material possessions should be used to cement those relationships and not to destroy them. The third lesson is that a person's faithfulness in fulfilling smaller tasks is the best measure of his or her ability to manage larger and more important tasks.

The last lesson is that serving Christ must be the most important thing in the Christian's life. A slave had no time of his own; all of his time belonged to the master. The same principle applies in the Christian life; there is no room for part-time believers.

The middle section of this chapter (vv. 14-18) comes directly from Jesus' growing conflict with the Jewish religious leaders, the Pharisees in particular. The Pharisees were covetous in the sense they regarded material possessions as a sign of God's favor and as a reward for one's righteousness. They based this belief on their interpretation of the law (Caird 188). In these verses, Jesus corrects their erroneous understanding. He stresses two important points. First, they boasted about their faithfulness to the law, but, in fact, they were not as faithful as they claimed. Their easy acceptance of divorce was contrary to God's original intent that the family unit be preserved whenever possible.

Second, they failed to understand how the coming of Christ to earth had affected the law. They condemned Jesus for breaking the law, when in fact He was fulfilling it. The coming of Christ did not invalidate the law, but it did change how the law should be interpreted and applied. As Jesus said, "The law and the prophets were until John: since that time the kingdom of God is preached."

The final section of this chapter (vv. 19-31) is the story of Lazarus and Dives. As was noted previously, most authorities consider this story to be a parable, but some understand it as an example story.

It is a straightforward story of two sharply different men. One is rich; he lives a life of luxury and pleasure. He lacks nothing, while the other lacks everything. Lazarus is laid at the gate of the rich man, but the rich man takes no interest in him and does nothing to relieve his suffering. At death, their fortunes are reversed. Lazarus is welcomed into Abraham's bosom and receives all of the blessings he had never received on earth. The rich man is buried and then enters into a state of terrible suffering. He first asks that Lazarus relieve his suffering with a drop of water, but this request is denied. The rich man has already received his reward; he is not entitled to more. Then the rich man asks that Lazarus go and warn his five brothers. This request is also denied. If the brothers will not heed the message God has already sent them in the written word, neither will they heed a message presented by one coming from the realm of the dead.

This story develops at least three important themes. First, it establishes that material possessions are no indication of one's righteousness or relationship to God. Dives had everything, but he was condemned. Lazarus had nothing, but he was exalted. Second, the wrongs of this life will be made right in the future. Stories about the future reversal of the human situation were quite common in the ancient world (Caird 191). That certainly occurs here. There is a sharp contrast between the earthly situations of Lazarus and Dives and their eternal situations.

Third, this passage illustrates the sin of inhumanity. As Barclay (214) notes, the rich man was not cruel to Lazarus; he did not beat him or drive him from the gate. The tragedy is that the rich man did nothing; he was totally unconcerned about Lazarus' tragic circumstances.

Application: Teaching and Preaching the Passage

This chapter is difficult and should be approached with caution. In such passages, it is easy to allegorize the details and come to conclusions the writer never intended. For example, the unjust steward in the parable is apparently guilty of mishandling his master's assets. Although his conduct at the end of his employment might have been acceptable, his history was one of selfishness and abuse. We should not interpret or apply the parable in such a way that it condones that type of conduct. He is commended either for his "forward-looking use of resources" or for his "creative use of foresight" (Bock, *Luke* NIV 418). He is not commended for his unrighteous conduct.

Neither should the story of the Rich Man and Lazarus be viewed as a comprehensive statement on the eschatology of the N. T. The story, as such, illustrates the sharp reversal of fortunes that both characters experience after death. There is, however, no discussion of key themes such as the intermediate state, the Second Coming of Christ, or the resurrection of the dead. The doctrine of eschatology should be based on a careful analysis of the entire teaching of the N. T. It should not be drawn from one isolated passage.

Bock (*Luke* NIV 418) explains there is one theme that binds together the three divisions of this chapter. It is the wise use of resources. If they are to be effective servants of God, the disciples must learn to use the material possessions that have been entrusted to them in a wise and judicious manner. They must regard material things as a sacred trust from God. The wise use of resources brings glory to God and advances His kingdom. The preacher or teacher should look for ways to help the children of God use their material goods wisely and in the service of God.

While the wise use of resources is the primary application here, there are secondary applications that can and should be used in preaching and teaching. For example, the parable of the Unjust Steward discusses the issue of faithfulness. Jesus said, "He that is faithful in that which is least is faithful also in much: and he that is unjust in the least is unjust also in much." Things that may seem to be insignificant on earth are important. God wants His children to be faithful to Him in all areas of life. Only by being faithful in small things can we develop the skills necessary to be faithful in larger things.

This parable also points out the importance of planning and preparation. When the steward learns he will lose his position, he begins to prepare for the future. There is nothing unspiritual in planning ahead and preparing for the future as long as it is done under the leadership of God.

The statement "no servant can serve two masters" is theologically significant. The disciple cannot serve God and the world at the same time; he will inevitably favor one over the other. The preacher or teacher should not only emphasize the need to put God first, he should also help other believers apply that important principle in their lives.

Verses 14-18 of this chapter present several themes that can be used for preaching and teaching. The Pharisees used material wealth as one measure of a person's spirituality. Unfortunately, there are too many Christians today who reflect that same kind of attitude. It was wrong then, and it is wrong today. The amount of wealth a person has says nothing about his or her level of spirituality.

These verses also examine the role of the law in the new covenant. Jesus did not come to annul the laws given in the O. T.; in His view they are eternally valid. This does not mean, however, Jesus accepted the ways the Pharisees understood and applied the laws. The problem was not the law; it was their improper use of the law. Jesus came to earth as the Son of God; the authority to explain and apply the meaning of God's laws no longer rests with the Jewish rabbis. It now rests with Him.

The last portion of the chapter is the story of the Rich Man and Lazarus. As noted previously, some interpreters consider this to be a parable while others do not. Whether it is a parable or an example story makes little real difference in its interpretation and application. The basic teaching of these verses is that the disciple must demonstrate kindness and humanity in dealings with others. Dives does not treat Lazarus in a cruel manner; he simply ignores him. He pays no attention to the plight of the fellow Jew who lies suffering just outside his gate. Disciples can do better than that.

There is another most interesting theme for preaching and teaching in this passage. Death comes both to Lazarus and to Dives, for that is the fate of all human beings. The things that are never made right in this life will be made right after death. Lazarus knows nothing but suffering, poverty, and disgrace during his earthly life. After death he enters into the presence of God where he enjoys all the blessings of heaven. The rich man lives a life of pleasure and luxury, but after death he enters into a state where he suffers terribly. The God of the Bible is a God of perfect justice. He makes all things right, but He does so in His own time and in His own way.

J. Preparation of the Disciples (17:1—18:17)

1 Then said he unto the disciples, It is impossible but that offences will come: but woe *unto him*, through whom they come!
2 It were better for him that a millstone were hanged about his neck, and he cast into the sea, than that he should offend one of these little ones.

Some of the verses in this section grow out of Jesus' debates with the Jewish leaders, especially the Pharisees, while others deal with His training and instruction of His disciples. One of Jesus' primary concerns in the Travel Narrative is to prepare His disciples for what they will experience after they arrive in Jerusalem. It is also possible that Jesus is looking further into the future and preparing His disciples for the kind of situations they will face while serving in the church after the crucifixion. Geldenhuys (433) and Bonnet and Schroeder (635) suggest this teaching was given both to the twelve and to a wider circle of Jesus' disciples.

"Offenses" (Greek *skandalon*) is used in different ways. It may express the idea of a bait or a trap (Creed 214; Barclay 215-216). The idea here is something that leads a person into sin or causes him or her to be entrapped by sin (Stein, *Luke* 429). The warning to the disciples is that their words or actions must not cause another person to fall into sin.

Verse 2 indicates the seriousness with which Jesus regards this instruction. A "millstone" was a large circular stone that served as the upper part of a mill used to grind grain; it would be of sufficient weight to be turned by a donkey. A person thrown into the sea with such a large, heavy object tied to his neck would soon die by drowning. The implication of the verse is that a brother who causes another to fall into sin will suffer an even worse punishment than death by drowning (Geldenhuys 433). Not all interpreters agree about the meaning of "little ones" (v. 2). Geldenhuys (433) suggests that it refers to the weaker disciples. Creed (214) understands it to refer to the least and most humble. Manson (*Sayings* 138) understands it to refer to the disciples. Stein (*Luke* 428) understands it to describe believers.

3 Take heed to yourselves: If thy brother trespass against thee, rebuke him; and if he repent, forgive him.
4 And if he trespass against thee seven times in a day, and seven times in a day turn again to thee, saying, I repent; thou shalt forgive him.

"Take heed to yourselves" may serve as a conclusion to verses 1-2 or to introduce verses 3-4, more likely the latter. The idea is that the disciples should pay close attention to what they say and do because they do not want to lead others in the wrong direction.

In verse 3, Jesus begins a new teaching on forgiveness. He understands that conflicts between His followers will happen. He knows that believers will sometimes offend other believers. In order that the work of the kingdom not be hindered, it is important that the disciples learn how to resolve these conflicts. "Trespass" means "sin." A serious sin against a brother has occurred; Jesus is not thinking of a person who looks to be insulted. As He explains, the best way to handle this difficult situation is to talk directly with the offending brother. That is far better than talking with everyone else (Mt. 18:15-17). To "rebuke" can mean to "censure," "speak seriously," or "warn" (Marshall, *Gospel* 642). Summers (*Luke* 198) argues that in the N. T. it means "stop." It does not imply rude or insulting behavior, but it does imply frankness and openness.

Luke's emphasis on repentance comes out clearly here. The offending brother needs to obtain forgiveness for what he has done, and he should be given the opportunity to do that. If he repents, he is to be forgiven. That sin is in the past, and it should be left there. According to Barclay (216), the Jewish rabbis had a saying that if one forgave another person three times, he was a perfect man. In verse 4, Jesus tells His disciples that if one sins seven times in a day, and then repents seven times, he is to be forgiven. In Jewish number symbolism, seven indicated completeness. The idea is that there should be no limits on the disciple's willingness to forgive (Summers, *Luke* 198; Stein, *Luke* 430) because the goal is the brother's restoration, not his condemnation.

5 And the apostles said unto the Lord, Increase our faith.
6 And the Lord said, If ye had faith as a grain of mustard seed, ye might say unto this sycamine tree, Be thou plucked up by the root,

and be thou planted in the sea; and it should obey you.

Verses 5-6 should be understood in the light of Jesus' teaching in the previous verses (Summers, *Luke* 198). Bonnet and Schroeder (636) opine that "apostles" is used here to distinguish the twelve from the larger group of disciples mentioned in verse 1. The kind of attitude and conduct that Jesus has taught will not be easy to put into practice. He has instructed them to guard their words and their actions so they will not lead others into sin. He has challenged them to demonstrate unlimited forgiveness in their personal relationships with other believers. In order to obey Jesus' instructions, the apostles will need a greater amount of faith than they have been previously called upon to demonstrate. According to Geldenhuys (432) they are asking Jesus to give them a stronger faith, one that will enable them to fulfill the demands He has just laid upon them. Bonnet and Schroeder (636) connect this verse specifically with the instruction to forgive the sins of other believers. The apostles will need a stronger, more developed faith to forgive as Jesus has instructed them.

Jesus' reply in verse 6 is somewhat enigmatic. The idea is that the disciples already have some level of faith, but it is not really adequate to meet the need. The mustard seed is very small, but it produces a large and beneficial plant. According to Geldenhuys (432), Jesus' reply does not mean the disciples need a greater degree of the faith they already have. What they need is a new kind of faith, one that is living and dynamic. They need a faith adequate to enable them to live in the way Jesus calls them to live. The illustration of the mustard seed teaches that the faith they currently have can grow and develop into the kind of faith they will need to face the challenges of the future.

A "sycamine" tree, according Marshall (*Gospel* 644) and Summers (*Luke* 198) is a type of mulberry tree that has a very deep root system. Jesus uses the tree only as an illustration; there would be no reason to literally transplant a large tree from the ground to the ocean. The idea is that if the disciples have the right kind of faith, they will be able to do great and mighty deeds in the service of God. With this new and dynamic faith, they will be able to overcome the serious obstacles they will face in the future. Manson (*Sayings* 141) sounds a note of warning concerning the proper interpretation of this passage. It does not encourage the disciples to become "conjurers and magicians." Instead, it encourages them to imitate heroes of the faith, like those described in Hebrews 11 who persevered in the face of great obstacles.

7 But which of you, having a servant plowing or feeding cattle, will say unto him by and by, when he is come from the field, Go and sit down to meat?
8 And will not rather say unto him, Make ready wherewith I may sup, and gird thyself, and serve me, till I have eaten and drunken; and afterward thou shalt eat and drink?
9 Doth he thank that servant because he did the things that were commanded him? I trow not.
10 So likewise ye, when ye shall have done all those things which are commanded you, say, We are unprofitable servants: we have

done that which was our duty to do.

These verses address the kind of attitude the disciples must maintain if they are to render effective service in the Kingdom of God. They must always maintain an attitude of humility and service; they must never think God owes them a blessing because of who they are or what they have done.

The "servant" here (v. 7) is a slave, not a hired servant. This passage reflects one aspect of life for a slave in the ancient world. When he has completed a day of work in the fields, a slave does not come in and eat a meal that has been prepared for him by his master. Instead, the slave will prepare supper and serve while his master eats. Only after the master has eaten will the slave do so. In the ancient world, this would not have been regarded as cruel; it was simply the reality of life for a slave.

Verse 9 asks a rhetorical question with an obvious, expected answer of "No": Will the master thank the slave for his service? This could correctly be translated, "He does not thank the slave for doing what he was commanded to do, does he?" The point is that a slave does not expect his master's thanks; he has done only what he was required to do.

In verse 10, Jesus applies this lesson to the apostles. In the preceding verses, He has set a high standard for His apostles. His expectations concerning forgiveness are unprecedented. Now Jesus reminds them that even if they meet these expectations, they have done nothing about which they can boast. They have simply done what Jesus has told them to do. The underlying thought is that God has done far more for them than they can ever do for Him. There is nothing the disciples can do that will place God under obligation to them. They have no right to say, "We have done this for God, and He is now obligated to bless us." They must always maintain the proper attitude of humility and service (Summers, *Luke* 199).

"Unprofitable" (Greek *achreios*) is only used twice in the N. T.; the other is Matthew 25:30. It may express the idea of a servant who is useless; it may also express the idea of "poor" or "unworthy." In this passage, "unworthy" catches the right idea. The disciples should recognize their unworthiness even when they have followed Jesus' instructions; they have done nothing that entitles them to the status of disciple.

11 And it came to pass, as he went to Jerusalem, that he passed through the midst of Samaria and Galilee.
12 And as he entered into a certain village, there met him ten men that were lepers, which stood afar off:
13 And they lifted up *their* voices, and said, Jesus, Master, have mercy on us.
14 And when he saw *them*, he said unto them, Go shew yourselves unto the priests. And it came to pass, that, as they went, they were cleansed.
15 And one of them, when he saw that he was healed, turned back, and with a loud voice glorified God,
16 And fell down on *his* face at his feet, giving him thanks: and he was a Samaritan.

17 And Jesus answering said, Were there not ten cleansed? But where *are* the nine?
18 There are not found that returned to give glory to God, save this stranger.
19 And he said unto him, Arise, go thy way: thy faith hath made thee whole.

Verse 11 reminds the reader these events happened as Jesus and His disciples were traveling to Jerusalem. "Through the midst of Samaria and Galilee" probably means Jesus was on a road that roughly paralleled the border between Samaria and Galilee (Marshall, *Gospel* 650; Stein, *Luke* 433). There are also some differences in the readings found in the early manuscripts of this verse (Bock II:1406). The mention of Samaria helps explain the presence of a leper who is a Samaritan.

As He is entering an unnamed village, Jesus is hailed by a group of ten lepers who stand some distance away from Him—as the law required them to do. In ancient Israel, leprosy was regarded both as a disease and as a curse from God. Leviticus 13 describes the symptoms of leprosy as it was understood in ancient times; a number of different skin diseases can produce the symptoms described there. For that reason, we cannot always equate the biblical term "leprosy" with the illness known as leprosy (Hanson's Disease) today. Leviticus 13 also provides that those diagnosed with leprosy must live outside the camp and cry out they are unclean because leprosy was thought to be a highly contagious disease. Leviticus 14 explains that before a leper can be readmitted to society he has to be examined by a priest in order to verify that he has been cured.

These ten lepers cry out for Jesus to have mercy on them. They have heard of His power to heal and they beg Him to do for them what He has done for others. In verse 14, Jesus instructs them to go and show themselves to the priest as the O. T. required. The command of Jesus is a test of the lepers' faith. He tells them to go to the priest even though the healing has not yet occurred. The lepers believe the words that Jesus has spoken to them; they go to the priest and are healed on the way.

Verses 15-16 explain the reaction of those who had been healed. Only one returns to express his thanks to Jesus and to glorify God, who has made their healing possible, and that one is a hated Samaritan. The passage does not explain the actions of the other nine. Apparently they are Jews who simply go their way without returning to express thanks. Neither does the passage explain how this Samaritan comes to be in the company of Jews. Perhaps the plight they shared overcame the barriers that existed between Jews and Samaritans.

The passage describes the extravagant thanks and praise given by the Samaritan. He glorifies God in a loud voice; he even falls down at the feet of Jesus and gives Him thanks for the miracle of healing he has experienced. Since he was a Samaritan, it is doubtful he had gone to a Jewish priest to verify his healing. He had probably returned to Jesus as soon as he noticed that his body had been healed.

Verses 17-19 concludes the story with Jesus' question: "Where are the nine?" The answer is obvious; they have not taken the time to return to Him and express gratitude. The only one who has returned is this Samaritan whom Jesus describes as a "stranger" (Greek *allogenēs*), a word that occurs only here in the N. T. (Nolland II:847). It means a foreigner, one who is not a Jew. Jesus tells the Samaritan to rise up and go his way because his faith has made him whole. Some interpreters understand "whole" to describe only the physical body, in that it has been made whole. Others see it as a reference to both physical and spiritual healing. Because of his faith in Christ, it is possible this Samaritan has also experienced the forgiveness of his sins (Nolland II:847; Bock II:1405).

Childers (572) notes that all nine were healed; the implication is that the Samaritan received something more than physical healing. He also received, at least, "an inner blessing and enlargement of soul." According to Childers, this passage also implies the Samaritan demonstrated a higher quality of faith than the other nine.

A. Richardson (*Stories* 67-68) describes something of the importance of the miracles of healing in the ministry of Jesus. He suggests the healing ministry of Jesus plays a significant role in the development of the entire Christian mission. He also explains (*Stories* 65) that to the Jew of the first-century the power to heal meant the breaking of the power of sin. Only God could break the power of sin; the priests were merely witnesses to what God had done. That is probably the reason Jesus instructed the lepers to go and show themselves to the priests.

The disciples need to hear these lessons. They should understand that genuine faith is possible for anyone, even a Samaritan. They also need to understand the importance of gratitude in the work of the Kingdom of God. The children of God should always express their gratitude to God for all He has done for them. In this passage, the disciples are also brought face to face with the reality of ingratitude. In their future ministries, they will encounter many people like the nine, who see no need to express their thanks to God for the blessings they have received.

20 And when he was demanded of the Pharisees, when the kingdom of God should come, he answered them and said, The kingdom of God cometh not with observation:
21 Neither shall they say, Lo here! or, lo there! for, behold, the kingdom of God is within you.

Jesus responds to a demand of the Pharisees. His response will also give the disciples a better understanding of what they may expect in the future. The Pharisees had an understanding of the Kingdom of God that was quite common among the Jews of the first century. They anticipated the coming of the Messiah and expected Him to free the land from Roman domination and return Israel to a position of independence and self-determination (Childers 573). According to Stein (*Luke* 437), the popular conceptions of the advent of the Kingdom of God included such things as the resurrection of the dead, the destruction of the enemies of Israel, and the arrival of the Messianic king. Jesus spoke often of the Kingdom of God, but He did not accept the assumptions of the Pharisees. His understanding of the kingdom differed sharply from theirs. It was more spiritual, less political, and less nationalistic. Beasley-Murray (*Kingdom* 313-322) analyzes the key themes developed in this passage. He argues there are three themes that dominate: the coming of the Son of Man to all, the judgment of the Son of Man upon all, and the unpredictability of the event.

The Pharisees and other Jewish groups reflected a high degree of interest in the coming kingdom. They were particularly concerned with the time when the Messiah would come and inaugurate His kingdom. They believed the coming of the kingdom would be preceded by great signs in the heavens (Marshall, *Gospel* 654; Bock II:1409-1412). In these verses, Jesus is concerned to correct the understanding of the Pharisees that the establishment of the kingdom will be preceded by certain visible signs.

Barrett (*Luke* 66) offers an interesting comparison between this passage and Luke 21:25-28, where Jesus does speak of signs that will precede the end. He asserts that in Luke 17, Jesus is speaking about the end itself. In Luke 21, on the other hand, Jesus is speaking about the interval of time between the destruction of Jerusalem and the Second Coming.

In the Gospels, there are both present and future aspects to the Kingdom of God. Both the teachings of Christ and His miracles bear eloquent testimony to the fact that His coming has inaugurated a new era. The Kingdom of God has come to earth in the person and work of Christ. This does not mean the kingdom has come in all of its fullness. The understanding of the N. T. writers is that the Kingdom of God is in the process of being realized, and that process will be completed in the future at the Second Coming.

In verse 20, Jesus explains that the Kingdom of God will not come "by observation." Beasley-Murray (*Kingdom* 97-100) provides a summary of the most common interpretations of "by observation" (Greek *meta parateresis*). The phrase could be used to describe a physician observing the condition of a patient, for example, or to describe "observing" rules and regulations. It was also used to describe observing the heavens, which seems to be the idea here. Beasley-Murray notes that the Jews used observations of the heavens to determine the dates of the New Moon and of the Passover, for example. The Pharisees wanted Jesus to explain to them how, by observing the heavens, they could determine when the Messiah would come and inaugurate His kingdom. Jesus responds by explaining that there are no visible signs that can be used to determine the time.

"Neither shall they say, Lo here! Or, lo there!" serves to reinforce this idea. Since no one can determine the time of the coming of the kingdom, there is no possible way for anyone to sound a warning. No warning cries should be expected or accepted.

That "the kingdom of God is within you" has provoked much discussion. "Within" (Greek *entos*) occurs only twice in the Greek N. T. The other time is in Matthew 23:26, of the inside of a cup. Beasley-Murray (100-103) and Bock (II:1415-1417) outline the most common interpretations in both ancient and modern times. Many in the early church understood it to mean "inside you," while others understood it to mean "among you."

If it is understood to mean "inside you," the idea is that the coming of the kingdom is not an outwardly-observable event, but something that happens inside a person (Caird 197). This interpretation is strongly defended by Hendriksen (*Luke* 805). Both Beasley-Murray and Bock note the difficulty in understanding the term to mean "inside you." Nowhere else in the N. T. is the Kingdom of God spoken of as residing within a person. The term normally describes what God does in the world; it comes upon a person rather than residing within him.

Beasley-Murray notes that the early Syriac translation of this passage uses "among," which is the interpretation preferred by most modern interpreters. The idea is that the Kingdom of God is now living in the midst of the disciples in the person of the Lord Jesus. Beasley-Murray (*Kingdom* 103) understands it to mean "The Kingdom of God has entered the present in and through Jesus, and the possibility of experiencing its saving power lies within the range of all who hear the good news." A similar view is presented by Pentecost (452) and Hoekema (48). See Manson (*Sayings* 303-304).

Verse 21 raises another question: Is the statement "Lo, the kingdom of God is among you" to be understood as a description of the existing state of affairs or is it a prophecy of a future event? Manson (*Sayings* 304) notes that either interpretation is possible, and there are biblical passages that support both positions. After examining the issue, Manson concludes it is likely a prediction of a future event. The point is that the Kingdom of God will come suddenly and unexpectedly; there are no outward signs that enable one to determine when it will come. Manson goes on to explain that this passage does not contradict those passages that speak of the kingdom as being present because the Kingdom of God has both present and future aspects.

Kümmel (*Promise* 32-36) takes a somewhat different approach. After noting the difficulty he concurs that the correct interpretation phrase is "among you." He does not recognize any future aspect of this saying. He argues that the Kingdom of God is already present in the life and ministry of Jesus. He notes that his interpretation is only a hypothesis, but he suggests it is the most likely understanding.

22 And he said unto the disciples, The days will come, when ye shall desire to see one of the days of the Son of man, and ye shall not see *it*.
23 And they shall say to you, See here; or, see there: go not after them, nor follow *them*.
24 For as the lightning, that lighteneth out of the one *part* under heaven, shineth unto the other *part* under heaven; so shall also the Son of man be in his day.
25 But first must he suffer many things, and be rejected of this generation.
26 And as it was in the days of Noe, so shall it be also in the days of the Son of man.
27 They did eat, they drank, they married wives, they were given in marriage, until the day that Noe entered into the ark, and the flood came, and destroyed them all.
28 Likewise also as it was in the days of Lot; they did eat, they drank, they bought, they sold, they planted, they builded;
29 But the same day that Lot went out of Sodom it rained fire and brimstone from heaven, and destroyed *them* all.

30 Even thus shall it be in the day when the Son of man is revealed.
31 In that day, he which shall be upon the housetop, and his stuff in the house, let him not come down to take it away: and he that is in the field, let him likewise not return back.
32 Remember Lot's wife.
33 Whosoever shall seek to save his life shall lose it; and whosoever shall lose his life shall preserve it.
34 I tell you, in that night there shall be two *men* in one bed; the one shall be taken, and the other shall be left.
35 Two *women* shall be grinding together; the one shall be taken, and the other left.
36 Two *men* shall be in the field; the one shall be taken, and the other left.
37 And they answered and said unto him, Where, Lord? And he said unto them, Wheresoever the body *is*, thither will the eagles be gathered together.

These verses form the first of two important passages where Luke confronts the subject of eschatology; the other is Luke 21:7-28. This is a difficult passage and there is no general agreement on how it should be interpreted (Summers, *Luke* 202). Maddox (127) suggests its primary purpose is not to promise salvation to Jesus' followers but to warn the unrepentant of the judgment that awaits them.

Beasley-Murray (*Kingdom* 313-322) views this entire passage, with the exception of verse 25, an obvious reference to the crucifixion, as referring to the Second Coming. Bonnet and Schroeder (638-641) offer a somewhat similar interpretation. They recognize that Matthew 24 deals in part with the destruction of Jerusalem, but Luke 17 deals entirely with the Second Coming. A. Bruce (EGT I:595) argues that Luke 17:31 is connected to the crisis in Jerusalem in Matthew and Mark, but there is no reference to that crisis in Luke. Summers (*Luke* 202) notes that similar phrases are used in Luke 21 and Matthew 24 to describe the destruction of Jerusalem.

While it is obvious that most of this passage deals with the Second Coming, it is possible that some parts (especially v. 31) may relate to the coming destruction of Jerusalem. Verse 25 refers to the crucifixion.

In this passage, Jesus is not giving His disciples a detailed account of what will happen in the end times. His goal is to prepare them for the difficult days that lie ahead and to assure them that the Kingdom of God will ultimately triumph. There will be suffering and persecution, but Christ will return to judge the world. The fact that there is no mention in this passage of the resurrection of Christ, or of believers, indicates it is not intended to be a complete explanation of the end times. Jesus is preparing His disciples for what they will encounter in the future; He is not concerned to spell out all the details. While this passage certainly gives hope to the followers of Jesus, the focus is more on the coming judgment of those who refuse to accept Jesus' offer of salvation.

Verse 22 is generally seen as a reference to the Second Coming, but other interpretations are possible (Bock II:1427-1428). Hendriksen (*Luke* 806) suggests the phrase "the days of the Son of man" describes the messianic age that will occur at the end of world history. Jesus tells His disciples that in the future they will desire to see His return, but they will not see it.

Jesus does not explain why the disciples will have such a strong desire for His return. It may be due to the suffering they will endure; it may also grow out of their desire to see Jesus return and complete the establishment of His kingdom. It is clear from this verse that Luke envisions some interval of time between Jesus' earthly ministry and His Second Coming, but he makes no attempt to define how long that interval will last. While they await Christ's return, the disciples must be content with the spiritual fellowship they have with Him (Bonnet and Schroeder 639-640).

Verses 23-24 warn the disciples not to be carried away by false prophets and their reports of Christ's return. They must not allow their strong desire to see the return of Christ cloud their judgment (Fitzmyer II:1167). The return of Christ will be like a bolt of lightning that goes from one end of the heavens to the other; it will be self-evident. No one will have to go and search for it.

Verse 25 is a reference to the sufferings Christ will soon endure after His arrival in Jerusalem. While Luke does not explain the term "many things," later chapters in the Gospel will reveal that Jesus will endure rejection, unjust trials, beatings, and crucifixion. He will also suffer the indignity of being rejected by His own people, the Jews.

Verses 26-27 refer to the story of Noah and his family which is found in Genesis 7-10. Luke uses this familiar story to emphasize the need for preparedness (Hendriksen, *Luke* 806). When the flood came, only Noah and his family were prepared for it; the rest of humanity perished. In the same way, most people will be unprepared when Christ returns. The disciples need to pay heed to the example of Noah; they need to be prepared when Christ comes to consummate His kingdom. As for the observation, "They did eat, they drank, they married wives, they were given in marriage," such activities are not sinful; they are part of the normal order of events. But in the time of Noah, most people were concerned *only* about their everyday affairs; they had no interest in what God was doing in their midst. Thus Jesus warns His disciples not to fall into that trap. They must be prepared for the return of Christ, and they must not be distracted by the things of this life.

Verses 28-29 make the same point, using the example of Lot, another O. T. character, whose story is found in Genesis 13-14 and 19. Lot had chosen to live in Sodom, which was a city known for its great wickedness. When Lot warned his sons-in-law to escape the city, they mocked him. Lot and his family were forced to flee this wicked city at the last minute; they should have left much sooner than they did. It is likely they had allowed themselves to become too attached to the luxuries the city could give them.

Verse 32 is a reference to Genesis 19:26; Lot's wife looked back toward the city of Sodom and was turned into a pillar of salt. The implication is that she looked back on the city with longing and desire; she would have liked to continue enjoying the pleasures it offered. The warning is that the disciples must not become too attached to the things of this world. They must not become so caught up in the things of the world that they are unprepared when Christ returns.

Verses 30-31 are summary verses. Jesus uses Noah and Lot as examples, but His use of them doesn't mean they were completely obedient to God. They were not perfect, but they did heed God's warning (Hendriksen, *Luke* 807). The people around them, however, were not prepared when the time of crisis came; they were too preoccupied with the ordinary events of life. Jesus' goal is that the disciples will not make the same mistake, but will make the proper preparation in advance for the return of Christ. Some interpreters understand verse 31 to describe events that will happen at the time of the Second Coming. Others see it as a reference to events that would transpire in the summer of A.D. 70, when Jerusalem would be captured and destroyed by the Roman army under Titus. Hendriksen (*Luke* 807-808) suggests in the parallel passages in Matthew and Mark, these words apply to the days immediately prior to the fall of Jerusalem. Manson (*Sayings* 145) argues that verses 31 and following have nothing to do with the Second Coming and relate entirely to the fall of Jerusalem.

Verse 33 is a familiar teaching of Jesus also found, with only minor variations, in Matthew 10:39, 16:25; Mark 8:35; and Luke 9:24. Jesus cites it here because it fits the context; it is also a teaching with which His disciples are already familiar. In this context, the saying serves to reinforce the teaching given in verse 31. When the Kingdom of God comes, there will be no time to worry about material possessions. "This life" refers to the things of this life, the material and physical things that human beings find so attractive. Those who seek to maintain and protect the things of this life will lose the spiritual values. Those who willingly forfeit the things of this life in order to maintain their relationship with God will enjoy the true spiritual life.

Most interpreters (Marshall, *Gospel* 667; Geldenhuys 442; Summers, *Luke* 204-205) understand verses 34-35 to describe the final and total separation between the righteous and the wicked that will occur at the return of Christ. Barclay (220-221) understands it in a different way. He suggests the meaning is that an intimate relationship with a good person cannot guarantee salvation. One's relationship with God is an individual matter; the judgment of God is also an individual matter.

Geldenhuys (442) suggests that believers will be taken to meet Jesus while unbelievers are left to suffer judgment. Hendriksen (809) presents a similar interpretation. While such an interpretation is certainly possible, the text does not specify that the righteous are taken while the wicked are left. It is better to take the passage as an indication of eternal separation rather than as a prophecy of a future resurrection or rapture.

Verse 36 is omitted from many translations because it is not found in the earliest manuscripts of Luke, which the textual scholars tend to trust as original. Many commentators argue that it is not a part of the original text of Luke but was borrowed from Matthew 24:40 (Marshall, *Gospel* 668). Manson (*Sayings* 146) differs, suggesting that this verse reflects a Lucan writing style and was probably a part of the original text of Luke. He argues that the verse is necessary to complete the picture of the agricultural activities developed in verses 34-35. There is no doubt that verse 36 fits the context; it makes a contribution to the story even if it was not in the earliest manuscripts.

Verse 37 concludes the discussion of the coming of the kingdom. Marshall (*Gospel* 668) correctly notes that this verse is somewhat enigmatic. Luke does not explain who "they" are; probably the disciples indicated in the previous verses. The question introduced by "Where" is not the question one would expect; instead, one would expect the disciples to ask, "When." Summers (*Luke* 205) understands it to mean "where will the separation take place?" Geldenhuys (442) explains the meaning as "where will the wicked be left?" Creed (221) implies that the idea is "Where will the judgment take place?"

Jesus responds by citing a familiar proverb, "Where the body is, there the eagles will be gathered together." "Eagle" (Greek *aetos*) applies to a family of flesh-eating birds (Summers, *Luke* 205), perhaps a "vulture" (Hendriksen, *Luke* 809).

Jesus gives no direct answer to the disciples' question as to where the judgment will take place. The idea seems to be the judgment will take place wherever necessary (Creed 221). Green (*Luke* 636) views this verse as a reference to the return of Christ, which will be self-evident. Just as the presence of vultures indicate the presence of a dead body to everyone in the area, so the return of Christ will be public and known to all. Hendriksen (*Luke* 809) understands Jesus' response to mean those who are spiritually dead will be overtaken by God's judgment wherever they may be. Barclay (221) interprets this enigmatic verse to refer, not to the judgment but to the coming of Christ.

Jesus' goal is not to answer all of the disciples' questions; neither does He give them a detailed outline of future events. He has shared with them the information necessary to enable them to carry out their ministries in spite of the difficulties they will confront. He is on His way to Jerusalem where His earthly ministry will come to a bloody end. His death, resurrection, and ascension will place new responsibilities on the shoulders of the disciples; they need to have some idea what to expect. It is also possible that Jesus is anticipating some of the issues with which the disciples will have to deal in their future ministries in the church.

Luke 18:1-17 is a continuation of the instruction Jesus has been giving to His disciples throughout the Travel Narrative. The journey to Jerusalem is almost completed; the time of Jesus' suffering and death is drawing near. In these two parables, the Widow and the Judge and the Pharisee and the Publican, Jesus imparts to His disciples some important lessons they will need as the situation grows even darker. If they are to be successful during these difficult days, they must learn to persevere in prayer. They must also learn to maintain a spirit of humility and dependence upon God (Hendriksen, *Luke* 541).

Bonnet and Schroeder (641) connect this passage with the return of Christ. The disciples must learn to pray with perseverance and without discouragement in light of the tribulations they will face before the Second Coming. Lieu (139) presents a somewhat similar position. She argues that Luke may have had the early church in mind when he wrote this passage. It is possible the members of those early churches had become discouraged because their total vindication had not yet arrived.

18:1 And he spake a parable unto them *to this end*, that men ought always to pray, and not to faint;
2 Saying, There was in a city a judge, which feared not God, neither regarded man:
3 And there was a widow in that city; and she came unto him, saying, Avenge me of mine adversary.
4 And he would not for a while: but afterward he said within himself, Though I fear not God, nor regard man;
5 Yet because this widow troubleth me, I will avenge her, lest by her continual coming she weary me.
6 And the Lord said, Hear what the unjust judge saith.
7 And shall not God avenge his own elect, which cry day and night unto him, though he bear long with them?
8 I tell you that he will avenge them speedily. Nevertheless when the Son of man cometh, shall he find faith on the earth?

Tristram (228-229) relates a story similar to this parable; it took place in the Mesopotamian city of Nisibis late in the nineteenth century. There was a large judgment hall; at one end the judge sat on a raised dais surrounded by many cushions. A number of secretaries and other functionaries sat around him. The room was full of people, and they were constantly crying out for the judge to hear and decide their cases. The more prudent and knowledgeable of the litigants did not join in all this clamor; they met quietly with the secretaries and unobtrusively passed bribes to them. Word was quietly sent to the judge that the bribe had been paid, and the case was quickly called and decided.

In the midst of this crowd was a poor widow who kept crying out to the judge. Her case was a sad one indeed. She was a widow, and her only son had been drafted into the army. She was alone and unable to till her field, but she was still required to pay the tax. As a widow, she should have been exempt from the payment of this tax. The judge finally heard her case and ordered that she be exempted from the payment of the tax.

While the passage in Luke is a parable Jesus told and not a description of an actual incident, it is likely that similar events occurred in the ancient world. This was a parable with which the people of the first century could identify.

As noted previously, a "parable" is a comparison. Jesus draws a comparison between the need of the disciples to pray faithfully and the need of a poor widow woman to obtain justice from a hard-hearted judge. Not every detail of a parable must be compared to something else. In this parable, the unjust judge should not be compared to God; that is not Jesus' intention.

Verse 1 might have been spoken by Jesus or simply written by Luke; it serves as the introduction to this parable. Caird (201) notes that prayer is one of Luke's favorite themes, and he devotes more attention to it than in the other Synoptic Gospels. The disciples will face difficult and trying times in the future, and it is important they develop habits of persistent prayer.

This parable grows out of the legal practices of ancient Palestine. As B. Smith (149) explains, many of the details concerning the daily administration of justice at that time are unknown to us today. There is evidence, however, to indicate that judges were appointed in the various towns to hear and resolve local disputes. Smith posits that the judge in this parable was a local magistrate, perhaps a judge appointed by King Herod. Bock (II:1447) explains that, in the time of Jesus, the Roman overlords generally remained aloof from such local disputes; they were left to the Jews to resolve among themselves. Barclay (221) opines that the judge was clearly not Jewish, because in Jewish communities such disputes would have been resolved by a committee of elders. He suggests the parable envisions a man who was an unpaid judge appointed either by Herod or by the Roman overlords.

Marshall (*Gospel* 673) offers a slightly different opinion. He argues that the unjust judge could be either a Jewish judge or a secular judge because both could be corrupt. A. Bruce (*Parabolic Teaching* 159) notes that the judge in this parable is not just corrupt, he is totally corrupt. Most wicked men try to hide their wickedness, but this judge makes no effort to conceal his reprobate nature.

The plight of widows and orphans is often presented in both the O. T. and the N. T. (Bock II:1448). In the ancient world, they were largely defenseless. Jeremias (*Rediscovering* 122) notes that since women often married at thirteen or fourteen years of age, a woman might become a widow at a relatively young age. The fact that the woman appears alone before the judge may indicate she has no son, brother, or other male relative to defend her. She has no money with which to bribe the judge and no political power to persuade him to decide her case (A. Bruce, *Parabolic Teaching* 159). She makes use of the only resource she has, persistence.

It was probably some type of economic issue that brought her before the judge. She might have been deprived of some property to which she was entitled; or she might have been mistreated by the executors of her late husband's estate (Jeremias, *Rediscovering* 122; Buttrick 169; Hendriksen, *Luke* 816). The precise nature of the dispute is not important to the story. The adversary in the parable was probably a man of wealth and position.

In verse 3, the widow makes her petition to the judge. "Avenge" (Greek *ekdikeō*) may mean "obtain justice," "avenge," "punish," or "take revenge." Moulton and Milligan (192-193) cite several examples in the papyri where the term is used in the sense of "to vindicate" or "to do right to." In this context, the poor widow is asking for justice; she asks that what is rightfully hers be given to her (Childers 576).

Verses 4-5 explain that the judge at first refused to decide her case; he had neither fear of God nor respect for man. He turned a deaf ear to the O. T. teachings demanding that justice be done for the widow (Is. 1:17; Zech. 7:9-10). He had no compassion in his heart for a widow who had suffered an injustice. In verse 5, "weary" (Greek *hupōpiazō*) is an athletic term coming from the boxing ring. It literally means "strike under the eye" or "to give a black eye to" (Marshall, *Gospel* 673; Lenski 894; Fitzmyer II:1179). Fitzmyer suggests that in this context it serves as an idiomatic expression meaning "to wear me out completely." In the end, the judge decides to hear her case, not because her cause is just but because he has grown tired of listening to her pleas.

This is a parable of comparison and contrast. The point is not that God is like the unjust judge; He is, in fact, the opposite of the unjust judge. He is not vain and temperamental; He is the perfect blend of justice and mercy. The teaching of the parable is something like this, "If persistence can persuade an unjust judge, how much more will the God of Heaven answer the persistent prayers of his saints" (Childers 576).

The application of the parable begins in verse 6. Jesus tells His disciples to listen carefully to the message it has for them. The words "the unjust judge" probably point to the entire parable rather than just to the judge himself. In verses 7-8, Jesus applies the parable to the future and thus connects the parable with what He has told His disciples in the previous chapter. The disciples will be called upon to suffer many things because of their allegiance to Jesus. The question asked at the beginning of verse 7 is rhetorical. It is clear that God will avenge His disciples who pray to Him day and night. "Avenge" is the same as in verse 5; God will, in the end, do justice for those who are His. The term "his own elect" describes those who are His faithful followers. Marshall (*Gospel* 675) explains that this term is often used in eschatological contexts to describe the followers of Christ.

In verse 7, "bear long with them" implies the possibility of some delay. The overall message seems to be something like this: "Will not God avenge His elect, who cry to Him day and night, even though He may delay the answer?" God will certainly answer the prayers of His disciples for justice, but there is no guarantee that He will answer them immediately. He will answer their prayers at the appropriate time and in the appropriate manner. Creed (223) suggests these words express the idea "Is God patient at the misdoings of those who ill-treat the elect?"

In verse 8, Jesus tells the disciples He will avenge them "speedily (Greek *en taxei*), a phrase that sometimes means "soon" and sometimes "suddenly" or "unexpectedly." In this context, the idea seems to be that when God's vindication comes, it will come swiftly and unexpectedly (Caird 201; Childers 576). The people will be unprepared for it (Stein, *Luke* 442).

A. Bruce (*Parabolic Teaching* 164-165) suggests these verses imply that in the future the disciples will encounter difficult times when it will not be easy for them to maintain their faith in Christ. There is no guarantee that God will immediately respond to their prayers; the delay will inevitably be a trial of their faith. God's judgment may be delayed, but when it comes it will come suddenly, like the appearance of a thief in the night.

Stein (*Luke* 447) notes that "faith" (v. 7) has a definite article ("the") before it in the original. Marshall (*Gospel* 676) notes that the use of the article before the word "faith" does not occur often in the Greek N. T. In this context, it does not refer to Christian faith in general, but indicates *faithfulness* as expressed in regular and consistent prayer. Geldenhuys (449) proposes the "faith" in this context refers to the disciples' faith in Jesus Christ as the Messiah and the Son of Man.

Summers (*Luke* 207) suggests these words might have been spoken by Jesus or by Luke. If they are Luke's own observation, they reflect the fact that when this Gospel was written some Christians were beginning to lose hope because Christ had not yet returned. Geldenhuys (447) considers these words to be the words of Jesus. They are designed to encourage the disciples to remain faithful as they await the return of Christ.

A. Bruce (*Parabolic Teaching* 166) has a somewhat different perspective. He understands the "faith," here, to refer specifically to one's faith in God's actions as a deliverer. He notes that in the O. T., God's people have often ceased to hope for deliverance before the deliverance actually arrives.

Luke clearly anticipated some interval of time between Christ's first coming and His Second Coming, during which the disciples will suffer rejection and persecution. These last words of verse 8 are a poignant reminder that the followers of Jesus must remain faithful even in difficult circumstances.

Manson (*Sayings* 305) insightfully submits that the primary purpose of the parable is not so much to encourage prayer as to teach that God will answer the prayers of His saints. In his view, the real purpose of the parable is to produce the kind of faith in God that is necessary for prayer to be truly effective.

9 And he spake this parable unto certain which trusted in themselves that they were righteous, and despised others:
10 Two men went up into the temple to pray; the one a Pharisee, and the other a publican.
11 The Pharisee stood and prayed thus with himself, God, I thank thee, that I am not as other men *are*, extortioners, unjust, adulterers, or even as this publican.
12 I fast twice in the week, I give tithes of all that I possess.
13 And the publican, standing afar off, would not lift up so much as *his* eyes unto heaven, but smote upon his breast, saying, God be merciful to me a sinner.
14 I tell you, this man went down to his house justified *rather* than the other: for every one that exalteth himself shall be abased; and he that humbleth himself shall be exalted.

This parable does not fit the traditional definition because it does not present a comparison between some aspect of the natural world and some aspect of the spiritual world. It does, however, use a story to teach a lesson: in this case, a story that could easily have been taken from real life. It contrasts two markedly different actions and attitudes in the spiritual realm (A. Bruce, *Parabolic Teaching* 312). Many commentators understand the parable as being directed against the Pharisees (Creed 224; Geldenhuys 450). They considered themselves to be righteous before God because of their strict obedience to the law and looked down upon those who were less strict.

In the parable, two men, one a Pharisee and the other a publican, went up to the Temple to pray. Barclay (223) explains that official prayers were made at the Temple three times each day, at 9:00 a.m., noon, and 3:00 p.m., when the devout might come for that purpose. Stein (*Luke* 449) notes that individuals could pray privately at the Temple at any hour. The Pharisees made up one of the leading parties in Judaism, known for their observance of both the written law found in the O. T. and the oral law developed by the rabbis over a period of several centuries. They considered both to be equally binding. In this passage, the Pharisee stands and prays to God with his arms and hands extended—which was the normal posture for prayer at that time.

B. Smith (177) understands "prayed thus with himself" to mean that the Pharisee prayed silently rather than audibly. Hendriksen (*Luke* 824) and Bonnet and Schroeder (644) understand it to mean he was praying to himself rather than to God; he was congratulating himself for all the good things he had done.

The Pharisee's prayer is certainly self-congratulatory; he thanks God he is not like other men. He is not a wicked man; he does not treat others unjustly. He is not guilty of immoral conduct (Marshall, *Gospel* 679). He is not like the publican who is praying at the same time. He does not accuse the publican of any specific sins, but since the publicans served the hated Roman government and robbed their own people, they were generally despised (Childers 577).

In verse 12, the Pharisee continues the list of things for which he is thankful. He fasts twice in the week, which is more than the O. T. law required (Geldenhuys 451). The law only required Jews to fast on the Day of Atonement, but pious Jews would fast on Mondays and Thursdays (Barclay 223). Creed (224) notes that this parable is the earliest reference we have to this practice.

He also pays more tithes than the law requires. The law (Num. 18:21 and Dt. 14:22-29) required the payment of tithes on their field crops and herds. The Pharisees extended this requirement to include even garden herbs (Creed 224).

Although he is a fellow Jew, the publican is regarded by the Pharisee much like a heathen man (A. Bruce, *Parabolic Teaching* 313). In the parable, the publican prays a totally different prayer with a totally different attitude. His prayer reflects none of the pride and arrogance found in the Pharisee's prayer. He recognizes his own unworthiness; the fact that he stands far away indicates he feels unworthy to stand close to the sanctuary (Stein, *Luke* 450). He feels unworthy even to assume the normal posture when praying; he does not even lift his eyes toward Heaven. He simply beats upon his breast and cries out, "God, be merciful to me a sinner."

In verse 14, Jesus passes judgment on the efficacy of the prayers of the two men. The words "I tell you" are theologically significant, asserting that Jesus knows the mind of God and can speak with full authority (Stein, *Luke* 450). "This man," the publican, returned to his house justified rather than the other. That he was "justified," in this context, means he has been accepted by God (Creed 224). The humble prayer of the publican has brought him into a right relationship with God while the self-righteous prayer of the Pharisee has excluded him from fellowship with God. The proud Pharisee acknowledged no sin and sought no forgiveness (Childers 578). A. Bruce (*Parabolic Teaching* 314) argues that the teachings of this verse are very similar to Paul's conception of justification by grace through faith.

The last words of verse 14 provide an application of the teachings of this parable that the disciples may use in many different circumstances. Those who exalt themselves, as the proud Pharisee did, will be humbled by God. Those who adopt an attitude of humility, as did the publican, will be exalted by God. This is a favorite teaching of Jesus, also found in Luke 14:11 and Matthew 23:12. Since pride and arrogance were often regarded as virtues in the ancient world, this teaching of Jesus would have been considered revolutionary. In reality, God alone has the right to be exalted. Every human being, no matter how great, is humbled when in the presence of God.

Marshall (*Historian* 143) concludes that Luke does not view poverty as intrinsically good or wealth as automatically evil. In his view, "It is the attitude toward God that really matters." Although the Pharisee is very religious, he reflects no dependence upon God. The publican, on the other hand, humbly places his life in the hands of God.

15 And they brought unto him also infants, that he would touch them: but when *his* disciples saw *it*, they rebuked them.
16 But Jesus called them *unto him*, and said, Suffer little children to come unto me, and forbid them not: for of such is the kingdom of God.
17 Verily I say unto you, Whosoever shall not receive the kingdom of God as a little child shall in no wise enter therein.

Jesus continues to develop the theme of humility. In the previous verses, the prayer of the publican has demonstrated the kind of humble attitude with which a person must enter into the Kingdom of God. These verses continue the development of that theme. Luke does not explain when or where this incident takes place; such details are not important to the story.

In verse 15, "brought" (Greek imperfect tense) indicates the mothers continued to bring their babies to Jesus; this was not just a one-time activity. Barclay (225) notes it was the custom for mothers to bring their babies on their first birthday to a rabbi to receive a blessing. Marshall (*Gospel* 682) suggests it was customary to bring children to a rabbi for a blessing on the Day of Atonement; it is likely these customs provide the background for this passage. In verse 15, "infants" (Greek *brephē*) are babies that must be carried. In verses 16-17, "child" (Greek *paidion*), whether singular or plural, is a small child, but not necessarily a babe in arms. The "touch" in verse 15 reflects the manner in which the blessing was conveyed to the child.

When verse 15 says the disciples "rebuked" (Greek imperfect tense) the mothers, it can be interpreted in two different ways, either they began to rebuke them (inceptive) or they tried to rebuke them (conative). Stein (*Luke* 453) argues for the latter. The disciples did not attempt this rebuke because they were cruel or uncaring; they recognized that bringing babies to a rabbi to be blessed was a normal practice. They responded in this way because they were concerned about Jesus. He was in a stressful situation on the way to Jerusalem, and they did not want Him to be bothered. Jesus ignored the attempted rebuke and took advantage of the occasion both to express His love for children and to teach the disciples an important lesson in humility.

"Suffer" is an old English word that means "allow" or "permit." Jesus wants to see and touch the children because they are important to Him. In verse 17, Jesus says that those who receive the Kingdom of God must do so as a little child. This statement is somewhat unusual because Luke normally speaks of *entering* the Kingdom of God (13:24;

18:17b, 24-25). This statement emphasizes that the Kingdom of God is a divine gift that must be *received* in a humble manner. At the end of verse 17, Luke returns to the normal expression of entering the kingdom.

Stein (*Luke* 453) and Marshall (*Gospel* 683) offer helpful suggestions about the meaning of the phrase, "as a little child." The idea of humility is certainly central; a small child has not yet learned to demonstrate the arrogance or pride often found in adults. Children also demonstrate a simple faith and a trusting spirit; they also reflect a high level of helplessness and dependence. In this context, the phrase does not mean the followers of Jesus should demonstrate a child-like level of maturity or understanding. Probably the idea is that a small child can offer no good deeds or merit; he can make no claim upon God. He simply accepts the good things God offers (Lieu 142). That is the kind of attitude Jesus' disciples need to reflect.

Summary (17:1—18:17)

Jesus' goal in this section of the Gospel is to prepare His disciples for the trials and difficulties they will face in the future. As Green (*Luke* 611) explains, in this section Jesus often seems to be speaking to one audience in the presence of another audience. His primary audience is the apostolic band, the twelve disciples that constitute His closest followers. It is clear, however, that Jesus has a larger audience in mind. He understands that future generations of disciples will need the advice and counsel He is sharing. While many of the teachings are directly applicable to those in positions of leadership, they are also relevant to the lives of all of Jesus' followers. Jesus understood that life would never be easy for the dedicated follower of God. For that reason, He not only addresses the immediate needs of His disciples as they journeyed to Jerusalem with Him; He also addresses the needs of future generations of believers.

Luke 17:1-10 serves as something of an introduction to this section. It presents several important themes, including influence, faith, sin, and forgiveness. Each of these themes will be further developed in the remaining chapters of Luke. Jesus knew His disciples would serve under great stress and tension. In those circumstances, it is inevitable the disciples may do or say things that will hinder other believers. The "offences" in verse 1 are more than mere irritants; they refer to something serious that may cause a disciple to lose his or her faith (see Bock, *Luke* NIV 439). The disciples must learn to guard their words and actions.

Jesus follows this discussion of influence with a discussion of sin. He recognizes that believers may sin against God; they may also sin against other believers. In this passage, He has in mind a sin committed against a fellow believer. The context implies that it is a sin of sufficient seriousness to hinder the fellowship that must exist between believers; it is not something trivial. This serious sin must be confronted; Jesus said, "if thy brother trespass against thee, rebuke him." Then, after reconciliation is accomplished, the offending brother must be forgiven. There must be no limit on forgiveness, for any limitation will hinder the progress of the gospel.

These verses also introduce the subject of faith. If they are to have a meaningful witness in the midst of a hostile world, the disciples will need faith. They will need the special kind of faith that makes it possible for them to fulfill their ministries in the midst of great trials and difficulties.

This section concludes with a discussion of the kind of attitude a disciple needs to manifest in his or her daily life and ministry. The follower of Christ should be like the slave who goes about his duties without expecting any type of reward or special treatment. After the slave has worked in the field all day, he must then go home and prepare the master's supper. Many of the tasks a disciple performs are mundane and ordinary, but that does not make them unimportant.

The story of the ten lepers illustrates both the goodness of God and the need to demonstrate a thankful spirit. Jesus performed a notable miracle; He healed ten lepers outside an unnamed village. Yet only one of them, and that one a foreigner, returned to thank Him for what He had done. The story of this miracle illustrates how God works in the world to better the lives of human beings. It also reflects the sad fact that many people do not appreciate how good God is to them. The disciples must not allow the world's lack of thankfulness to hinder their witness; God is good whether men are willing to admit it or not.

Beginning in verse 20, Jesus responds to a demand the Pharisees had made for the benefit of His disciples. The Pharisees wanted to know when the Kingdom of God would come to earth; their concept of the kingdom was closely tied to the nation of Israel. They wanted to know when the Messiah would come and set up His earthly kingdom. In these verses, Jesus corrects their mistaken understanding of the nature of the kingdom. The kingdom will come suddenly and unexpectedly, but there are no outward signs that enable men to determine when it will come. The idea seems to be that Jesus wants His disciples to concentrate on the preaching of the gospel rather than on useless speculation about the time when the kingdom will come.

Beginning with verse 22, there is an important section of material that deals primarily, but not exclusively, with the Second Coming. There is no doubt Christ will return, but verse 25 implies there will be an interval of time between the end of Christ's earthly ministry and the Second Coming. Jesus makes no effort to indicate how long that interval will last, but it will be a difficult and trying time for the disciples. When Christ does return, His coming will be self-evident; there will be no need to search for the coming Messiah. His coming will be a time of separation between those who have chosen to follow Him and those who have not.

It is likely that Jesus spoke these words in response to the false teachings and idle speculation that surrounded the coming of the Messiah and the establishment of His kingdom. Jesus understood that this kind of false teaching would not only affect His contemporaries; it would continue to be a problem for future generations of believers.

Chapter 18 continues the instructions Jesus gave to His followers. Luke has preserved them because he knew they would also be important to future generations of believers. The next subject Jesus takes up is prayer; He begins with the Parable of the Unjust Judge, which is designed to teach the disciples the importance of persistence in prayer.

The judge in the parable is a wicked man who cares nothing for the poor widow who presents her case before him. Although he has no interest in doing justice, he is persuaded to decide her case because of her persistence. He is simply tired of putting up with her. If an unjust judge can be persuaded by the persistent appeals of a widow, how much more will a loving God be moved by the persistent prayers of His saints?

The next section offers a parable in which two men go up to the Temple to pray. The first man reflects a proud and arrogant attitude; he boasts of who he is and all he has accomplished. The second man is ashamed to lift his eyes toward God; he can only beat upon his breast and cry out, "God be merciful to me a sinner." The parable concludes by saying that the second man returned to his home in a right relationship with God, while the first man, though outwardly religious, returned to his home far removed from the love of God. Jesus then makes a universal application; the one who exalts himself will be abased while the one who humbles himself will be exalted. This is a powerful lesson in humility that Jesus' disciples of every age will need to learn, sometimes over and over again. A proud disciple is a contradiction in terms.

The final three verses also deal with the subject of humility. The people began to bring their infants and small children to Jesus so He might bless them; it was a common practice to bring small children to be blessed by a rabbi. The disciples tried to prevent these people from bothering Jesus in this way. There is no evidence to indicate the disciples were hostile to children. They knew Jesus was tired, and they wanted to allow Him to rest undisturbed. Jesus called to His disciples and told them to allow the small children to be brought before Him. Then He gave another universal application. He said those who enter into the Kingdom of God must enter into it with the humility, trustfulness, and simplicity of a small child. The Kingdom of God has no room for the pride and arrogance that is often found in the lives of adults.

Application: Teaching and Preaching the Passage

Jesus' major concern in this section of Luke is the preparation of His disciples for their future ministries. One of the most remarkable things about this portion of Luke is that the Lord reflects no concern for His own welfare; the focus of His attention is entirely on the disciples and their future ministries. The Travel Narrative is drawing to a close; the end of His earthly life in Jerusalem is drawing near. As the Son of God, Jesus understands very well the trials, suffering, and death that will soon be His fate. Yet, He never complains about the future or focuses attention upon Himself and His needs.

There are several important themes here that should be developed in preaching and teaching. One of these is the lifestyle of a disciple. In 17:1-10, Jesus outlines several important aspects of the life and character of a genuine follower. The disciple is to be a positive influence within the Christian community; his or her life and conduct must not be a hindrance to others. The believer's actions and attitudes should bring others to the faith; they should not drive them away.

Jesus also addresses the communal life that exists within the Christian community. Sin must not be allowed to disrupt the Christian fellowship, but it must be treated in the proper manner. The goal is not to exclude the believer who falls into sin; the goal is to restore him to the fold and lead him away from the devastating effects of sin. The sad reality today is that many churches do little to restore believers who have fallen into sin.

One key element in the lives of believers, both individually and collectively, is faith. Faith is absolutely essential; modern preachers and teachers need to devote time and attention to helping their congregations develop a correct understanding of it. As this passage emphasizes, faith implies more than intellectual assent. It is, first and foremost, a personal trust in Christ. There is no limit to what genuine faith in Christ can accomplish. Jesus' reference to a large tree being removed from the land to the sea is figurative and should not be taken literally. The idea is that faith in Christ is powerful; it can accomplish things which are, from a human standpoint, impossible.

Another key element in the life of a believer is service. Jesus compares the life of a believer to that of a slave. After the slave has worked in the fields all day, he does not simply come home and rest. He must prepare supper for the master before he can sit down and enjoy his own repast. The lesson for the disciples is that their lives are to be characterized by service and sacrifice. They are like slaves in the sense they have no right to bargain with God and make demands upon Him. Jesus sets a very high standard for His disciples; they must develop an attitude of humility and service. Preachers and teachers today must do the same thing; too many believers today think only of what God can do for them.

The experience of the ten lepers teaches a powerful lesson about thanksgiving. Ten lepers were healed, but only one of them—and that one a Samaritan—returned to thank Jesus for what He had done. Too many times Christians simply take for granted the blessings God bestows on them. Those who preach and teach the Word need to help followers of Christ develop a thankful spirit. This passage also stresses that God can use people of any race, nationality, or social condition in His kingdom.

A considerable portion of the teaching of this passage concerns the future. In particular, Jesus' goal is to prepare the disciples for the difficult days they will face in the future. They need to be watchful; there is always the danger that they may be carried away by false teachers. Jesus warns them there are no earthly signs that enable them to predict when the Kingdom of God will come on earth in all its fullness. According to most interpreters, at least some of the material in this section relates to the Second Coming. It is clear that Jesus anticipates some interval of time between His first coming and His second, but He gives no indication of how long that interval will last. At the time of the Second Coming, men and women will be going about the ordinary affairs of life without giving any thought to Christ's return.

Contemporary believers live in a time when there is a great deal of interest in eschatology, but much of that interest focuses on efforts to predict the time of Christ's return or to determine the precise sequence of future events. Such interest, while often well-meaning, is misguided. Christians should certainly study carefully what the Bible says about the end times, but they must always remember why they study that subject. It is not to satisfy their curiosity about the future; it is to stimulate them to lives of holiness and faithful service.

Prayer is another key element in the life of a disciple. This portion of Luke's Gospel does not give detailed instructions on how Christians ought to pray, but it does present the kind of attitude a Christian should reflect in prayer. Prayer should be persistent. The widow had no money with which to bribe the judge or political power to influence him to decide her case. She was, however, able to accomplish her goal by her persistence. Finally, the unjust judge decided her case just to get rid of her. If persistence can affect the actions of an unjust judge, how much more will the persistent prayers of His children affect a loving heavenly Father?

Jesus also tells the story of two men who went up to the Temple to pray. One of them prayed with an arrogant attitude, thanking God that he was not like the poor publican. The other reflected an attitude of humility and penance. He said only, "God be merciful to me a sinner." The second man returned to his home in a right relationship with God. The lessons to be proclaimed from this parable are obvious. No one has the right to approach God with an attitude of arrogance and self-righteousness; no one deserves to stand in His presence and make demands upon Him. Prayer is an important part of the life of a disciple, but it must be approached with humility and reverence. Modern preachers and teachers need to help their people learn what it means to pray in faith and humility.

The last three verses of this section confront the disciples with the necessity of humility. Jesus compares the life of a disciple with that of a small child. A small child has not had time to learn arrogance and pride, which are often characteristic of adults. A child does not make demands; a child trusts in his or her parents. Jesus is not saying in these verses that His disciples should be childlike in their understanding of the faith; neither is He saying they should think or act like children. They should reflect, however, the trustful spirit and the simple faith a child manifests. They should not be afraid to place their faith in Christ even during the dark days that lie in the future for them. Preachers and teachers need to develop this kind of faith in their own lives and then pass it on to those to whom they minister.

K. Sacrificing for Christ (18:18-34)

18 And a certain ruler asked him saying, Good Master, what shall I do to inherit eternal life?
19 And Jesus said unto him, Why callest thou me good? none *is* good, save one, *that is*, God.
20 Thou knowest the commandments, Do not commit adultery, Do not kill, Do not steal, Do not bear false witness, Honour thy father and thy mother.
21 And he said, All these have I kept from my youth up.
22 Now when Jesus heard these things, he said unto him, Yet lackest thou one thing: sell all that thou hast, and distribute unto the poor, and thou shalt have treasure in heaven: and come, follow me.

23 And when he heard this, he was very sorrowful: for he was very rich.
24 And when Jesus saw that he was very sorrowful, he said, How hardly shall they that have riches enter into the kingdom of God!
25 For it is easier for a camel to go through a needle's eye, than for a rich man to enter into the kingdom of God.
26 And they that heard *it* said, Who then can be saved?
27 And he said, The things which are impossible with men are possible with God.

The account of this ruler who comes to Jesus is found in all three of the Synoptic Gospels (Mt. 19:16-30; Mk. 10:17-31), with only minor variations. All three portray him as a wealthy man, but only Matthew 19:20 describes him as young. Luke establishes no connection between this passage and that which precedes or follows it; again, what is significant is the story itself.

"Ruler" (Greek *archon*) is a general term for anyone who occupies a position of authority. According to Marshall (*Gospel* 684), it likely means he is the ruler of a synagogue or a member of the Sanhedrin. This ruler addresses Jesus in a most polite and respectful manner. "Master" (Greek *didaskalos*) was generally used to describe a teacher, and teachers were held in high esteem in the ancient world. The ruler follows this polite greeting with an important question, "What shall I do to inherit eternal life?" The fact that the ruler asks Jesus' opinion on such an important issue indicates one of two things. He may be asking in an attempt to trick Jesus into saying something in conflict with the teachings of the rabbis. Or he may be sincere and has developed some degree of respect for Jesus and His teachings. Jesus responds to his question in a serious manner, and there is nothing in the passage to indicate the ruler has an ulterior motive.

"Eternal life" is important in this passage and in the N. T. as a whole. Stein (*Luke* 456) suggests that to inherit eternal life is equivalent to entering the Kingdom of God. In other words, the ruler is asking what he must do to be accepted into the coming messianic kingdom. This was a commonly-asked and much-debated question among Jews of the first century. The common answer was that one could obtain entrance into the Kingdom of God by obeying the law.

In verse 19, instead of answering the ruler's question, Jesus responds with an unexpected question of his own: "Why callest thou me good? none *is* good, save one, *that is*, God." "Good" (Greek *agathos*) generally means "morally good," commonly used to describe a person of upright character. It is difficult to determine precisely what Jesus meant by this question and statement. His question certainly does not imply He has sinned or He is not as good as the Father (Marshall, *Gospel* 684; Caird 205). Such an interpretation would contradict the entire teaching of the N. T.

Stein (*Luke* 455) presents a useful analysis of the most common interpretations of this difficult verse. The most likely interpretation is that Jesus is making no comparison between His existence and that of His heavenly Father. Rather, He wants to focus the ruler's attention on God and what God expects of His children (Lieu 142). True goodness resides in God, and it is from God that righteousness must come into the life of the ruler.

Jesus' response to the ruler's question (v. 20) does not differ greatly from the response a Jewish rabbi would have given. Jesus tells him to obey the law. It is significant to note that Jesus does not quote from the first table of the law, which deals with a man's relationship with God. He quotes from the second table, which deals with one's relationship with other human beings (Ex. 20:12-16; Dt. 5:16-20). Jesus assumes the ruler is already familiar with the first table of the law, which deals with the individual's relationship with God. Summers (*Luke* 214) gives a useful analysis of the ways Matthew, Mark, and Luke present this information.

Verse 21 gives the ruler's response to the laws Jesus has cited. He tells Jesus he has observed these commandments from his youth. "Youth" (Greek *neotātos*), in this context, probably refers to the time in a young man's life when he becomes responsible for his own actions. Bock (*Luke* NIV 467) notes that a young man would have become responsible at about thirteen years of age.

There is a sense of disappointment in the ruler's response; he expected Jesus would give him some new and different information. What he received is basically the same instructions he had received all his life (Plummer 423). There is no doubt this ruler was an outstanding man, but it is unlikely he had fully observed the law. Doing that is beyond human capability. Although Jesus could have challenged the ruler's claim, He did not do so. He did not wish to enter into a debate about the extent of this ruler's observance of the law; He had a more important issue in mind.

In verse 22, Jesus presents him with a challenge unlike any he has ever received. Jesus instructs him to sell his possessions, give the money to the poor, and become one of His disciples. This was, no doubt, shocking. Luke does not mention any particular O. T. passage that forms the basis for Jesus' requirement of the young ruler. Bock (*Luke* NIV 467) suggests the O. T. basis for His response is found in Deuteronomy 30:15-20, which calls on the people to choose whether they wish to serve God or the world.

The ruler had always been taught that riches were a sign of God's favor, and now he is being told he must dispose of them in order to become a disciple of Jesus. Since he possessed a considerable amount of wealth, this would have been a great sacrifice for him. It should be noted that Jesus did not make this demand of other disciples. It is, however, unlikely the other disciples possessed the amount of riches this ruler had.

Jesus does not explain why He makes such a stringent demand, but the words "thou shalt have treasure in heaven" give the reader a hint of what is in His mind. Apparently, the ruler has come to trust in his riches to such a great extent they have become an impediment to him. He has come to trust in them rather than in God. If he wishes to become a dedicated follower of Jesus, he must replace his confidence in earthly treasure with confidence in heavenly treasure. Barclay (228) notes there was something lacking in this ruler's life that material possessions could not fill. In order to find true happiness, he must abandon those things and concentrate on following Jesus. Plummer (424) notes the command to dispose of his property and the call to follow Jesus are two separate commands. They are connected, however, in that the first command is preparatory to the second. He must dispose of his property so he can follow Christ without being hindered.

Verse 23 is one of the saddest verses in the N. T. Instead of doing what Jesus has challenged him to do, he becomes sorrowful. Matthew 19:22 and Mark 10:22 both state he went away with sorrow. Luke does not specifically mention the ruler went away, but that is probably to be understood. This man could have accomplished so much as a disciple, but he was simply not willing to pay the price. Ellis (218) notes that the ruler has not, in fact, obeyed all the commandments. He is covetous, and his refusal to part with his possessions is proof of that covetousness.

At the end of verse 24, Jesus teaches again. "They that have riches" implies more than just having wealth or material possessions; the idea is that the person *trusts* in those riches to guarantee his future. Since Jews of the first century saw riches as a sign of God's favor (Geldenhuys 461), it is to be expected the ruler would hold this view. He thinks that because he has wealth, he already has God in his life; he needs nothing more. Such thinking is entirely fallacious. No amount of wealth can take a person into Heaven; only a personal relationship with God can do that. Jesus often views wealth as an obstacle standing in the way of a proper relationship with God.

Verse 25 continues to develop Jesus' teaching concerning the futility of trusting in riches. He explains that it is easier for a camel to go through the eye of a needle than it is for a rich man to enter Heaven. The camel was the largest animal commonly seen in first-century Palestine, and the eye of a sewing needle was the smallest opening. Summers (*Luke* 216) notes that about the fifteenth century a popular view developed that this passage refers to a small gate in the wall around Jerusalem called the Needle's Eye Gate. In order to enter this small gate, the camel had to kneel down and be unloaded. This popular interpretation is still heard today, but it has no basis in fact. There is no reference to such a gate in ancient literature; neither is there archaeological evidence for such a small gate in the city wall (F. Bruce, *Hard Sayings* 180-183). According to Fee and Stuart (25), the idea that this passage refers to a small gate in the city wall is first found in the writings of Theophylact in the eleventh century.

A more likely interpretation is that Jesus is making His point through the use of a literary device known as hyperbole, which is a deliberate exaggeration for the sake of emphasis. There is no possible way for a huge animal like a camel to pass through a small opening like the eye of a needle. The lesson is that it is equally impossible for those who trust in riches to be saved by those riches. The only way one can enter into the Kingdom of God is by trusting in Jesus. Morris (*Luke* 268) suggests Jesus uses this phrase as a humorous illustration.

Verse 26 outlines the response of the disciples, and possibly others, who witnessed Jesus' encounter with the ruler. They ask a logical question, "Who then can be saved?" The idea is "How, then, can anyone be saved?" Plummer (426) notes that the desire to acquire wealth is a universal desire; if wealth stands in the way of salvation, then no one will be saved. The fact that first-century Jews regarded wealth both as a reward for one's righteousness and as a sign of God's favor makes this question understandable.

Verse 27 reveals an important truth about salvation. Salvation is impossible for men in the sense that no person can earn it, merit it, or accomplish it on his or her own. It is, however, possible with God because it is God's gift to mankind. Salvation can no more be earned or merited than a camel can go through the eye of a needle. It can, however, be received as a free gift from God. Even a rich man can be saved, provided he can put God ahead of his material wealth.

28 Then Peter said, Lo, we have left all, and followed thee.
29 And he said unto them, Verily I say unto you, There is no man that hath left house, or parents, or brethren, or wife, or children, for the kingdom of God's sake,
30 Who shall not receive manifold more in this present time, and in the world to come life everlasting.

Peter, serving as the spokesman for the apostles, compares their situation with the situation of the ruler who has just declined to follow Jesus. The apostles have made the commitment the ruler failed to make; they have left houses and lands to follow the Master. Jesus does not disagree with Peter; He understands well the price His disciples have paid to follow Him. Jesus goes on to remind Peter and the other apostles that their sacrifice will not go unrecognized or unrewarded. They may not receive an immediate reward for following Jesus, but they will be amply rewarded both in this life and in the life to come.

Verse 29 indicates both the depth of commitment His disciples have already made and the commitment required of future generations of disciples. It is not easy to give up houses, lands, home, and family for the cause of Christ, but that has been the price countless followers of Christ have paid through the centuries. Bock (II:1489) explains that the words "or wife" should not be understood to encourage the breakup of families. He suggests the disciple may choose to forego marriage, or travel without his wife, in order to serve Christ more effectively.

Those who leave friends and family to serve Christ will find God gives them a new and even larger spiritual family. Service to Christ brings people together in ways the closest of human families cannot duplicate. The final result will be even greater; when this earthly life is over they will inherit eternal life. They will be able to share eternal fellowship with God (Bock II:1490-1491).

31 Then he took *unto him* the twelve, and said unto them, Behold we go up to Jerusalem, and all things that are written by the prophets concerning the Son of man shall be accomplished.
32 For he shall be delivered unto the Gentiles, and shall be mocked, and spitefully entreated, and spitted on:
33 And they shall scourge *him*, and put him to death: and the third day he shall rise again.
34 And they understood none of these things: and this saying was hid from them, neither knew they the things which were spoken.

Jesus now begins the final leg of His journey to Jerusalem. Creed (227) notes that this is Luke's third and final prediction of the passion; the first two are found in 9:22, 43-45. As this final section of the Travel Narrative develops, Jesus will give His disciples more detailed information about what He will experience upon arrival in the city (Nolland II:894). In previous passages (9:22, 44; 13:33-35), Jesus has given His followers some general information concerning His future suffering. In these verses, the prediction becomes more detailed and specific. In Luke 13:33-34, Jesus reminds His followers that Jerusalem is traditionally regarded as the place where the prophets of God have been slain. Jesus understands His own upcoming death to be another chapter in that sad story. In these verses, Jesus does not mention any specific O. T. passages, but He clearly views His death in Jerusalem as the fulfillment of O. T. prophecies. In this passage, "the prophets" probably refers to the entire O. T. (Stein, *Luke* 461). Summers (*Luke* 218) suggests Jesus might have had in mind the Suffering Servant passages found in Isaiah (42:1-9; 49:1-13; 50:4-9; 52:13—53:12), because He often described His ministry using terms and concepts found in those famous passages.

"Gentiles" (v. 32) clearly refers to the Roman authorities; they alone had the power to order Jesus' execution. Jesus also foretells He will suffer a severe beating as well as other acts of humiliation and cruelty. Most important, Jesus does not stop with the prediction of His execution; He also assures the disciples that His death will not be the end of the story. He will rise again on the third day.

Verse 34 indicates that the disciples do not fully understand what Jesus is saying. Jesus has spoken of His coming death in previous passages, but the disciples have trouble grasping His teaching. Their problem is not intellectual; they understand the meanings of the words Jesus has spoken. Their problem is emotional and spiritual; they find this teaching difficult to accept. They do not want to see their Teacher abused, murdered, and taken from them. Furthermore, in the Jewish tradition they are familiar with, the coming Messiah will be victorious. Since the disciples consider Jesus to be the Messiah, they find it difficult to understand and accept this announcement of such a cruel death (Geldenhuys 463-464; Stein, *Luke* 461-62). Verse 34 also says "this saying was hidden from them." Luke does not explain who has prevented the disciples from understanding the full meaning or why that understanding has been kept from them. Apparently, God has prevented them from comprehending the significance of Jesus' words because they were not yet ready to accept or fully understand them. In later years, after the resurrection, the disciples will look back on these difficult days with a much greater degree of understanding and acceptance.

Summary (18:18-34)

These verses bring Jesus' teaching on the demands of discipleship to a new level. The rich young ruler turns sadly away and refuses to accept the message of Jesus; he is blinded by his commitment to material possessions. He simply cannot break away from the traditional thinking that material possessions are a

sign of God's favor and a reward for righteousness. Jesus then uses the story of this young ruler as a basis for His discussion of how one enters the Kingdom of God. He notes that wealth can be a serious obstacle to entering the kingdom. The idea is not that the wealth itself is the obstacle; the obstacle is trusting in or relying on those material possessions.

This passage illustrates one of the great ironies of the Christian faith. Those who are unrighteous become righteous through the grace and mercy of Christ, while those who depend on their own righteousness become unrighteous in the eyes of God.

Jesus recognizes the cost of discipleship is high. When Peter makes the statement, "Lo, we have left all, and followed thee," Jesus does not contradict him. He knows His disciples have already paid a high price for following Him, and they will pay an even higher price in the future. The disciples must focus their attention on the future reward that will be theirs once they have entered fully into the kingdom.

In verses 31-34, Luke's Travel Narrative is nearing its conclusion. These verses emphasize what Jesus and His followers will face when they arrive in Jerusalem. Jesus will not be warmly received; He will be delivered into the hands of Gentile rulers where He will be severely mistreated and ultimately executed. His death will not, however, be the end of the story because He will rise again on the third day. It is important to note that Jesus views these sad events as the fulfillment of O. T. prophecies. While He does not cite any specific O. T. passages, Jesus clearly understands these events to be part of God's plan. He says, "and all things that are written by the prophets concerning the Son of man shall be accomplished."

Verse 34 indicates the disciples did not fully understand what Jesus was saying to them. They considered Him to be the Messiah, and they simply could not understand how the Messiah could suffer all of these things. In the future, the disciples would have a much better understanding of these difficult days.

Application: Teaching and Preaching the Passage

This passage is very important because of its position in Luke's Gospel; the journey to Jerusalem is nearing its end. Jesus will have few additional opportunities to give instructions to His disciples. The instructions He gives in these verses are relevant, not only to the Twelve but to those who will serve Jesus in the future. Those who preach and teach on this passage must give significant attention to the cost of following Jesus. Jesus never told His disciples that following Him would be easy and without sacrifice. In fact, Jesus often warned His disciples they would be called upon to give their lives in His service.

Many things can stand in the way of the high level of commitment Jesus demands. One of the most important of these is wealth or material possessions. The rich young ruler realized the value of following Jesus, but he was not willing to pay the price necessary to become a disciple. Unfortunately, there are still many Christians who allow the desire to accumulate things to hinder their service to Christ.

Instead of focusing their attention on the things of this world, the followers of Christ must look to the future. They must understand that those who follow

Christ will receive many rewards in this life; and, when earthly life is over, they will receive life everlasting. Contemporary Christians need to get their eyes off of the world and on the future they have with Christ.

While it does not present a comprehensive analysis of the doctrine of salvation, this passage does speak to that important subject. When the disciples asked the legitimate question, "Who then can be saved?" Jesus answered them by saying those things that are impossible for man are possible with God. The idea is that no amount of human effort can bring one into the Kingdom of God; entrance can only be obtained through the grace and mercy of God.

In the final verses of this passage, Jesus warns His disciples He will suffer greatly upon their arrival in Jerusalem. He views this suffering as a part of God's plan, and He makes no effort to avoid it. He is determined to fulfill the words the prophets have spoken in the O. T. Preachers and teachers should stress the fact that Jesus never deceived His disciples. He never led them to believe, by His words or by His actions, the way of discipleship would be easy. He often stressed the depth of commitment that would be necessary and the high price His followers would be called upon to pay. The tendency of many preachers and teachers is to stress the many blessings we receive when we follow Christ—and those blessings are many; but we should also stress the level of commitment that will be necessary. The Christian life is, by definition, a life of service and sacrifice.

L. Blessings and Mercy (18:35—19:27)

35 And it came to pass, that as he was come nigh unto Jericho, a certain blind man sat by the way side begging:
36 And hearing the multitude pass by, he asked what it meant.
37 And they told him, that Jesus of Nazareth passeth by.
38 And he cried, saying, Jesus, *thou* Son of David, have mercy on me.
39 And they which went before rebuked him, that he should hold his peace: but he cried so much the more, *Thou* Son of David, have mercy on me.
40 And Jesus stood, and commanded him to be brought unto him: and when he was come near, he asked him,
41 Saying, What wilt thou that I shall do unto thee? And he said, Lord, that I may receive my sight.
42 And Jesus said unto him, Receive thy sight: thy faith hath saved thee.
43 And immediately he received his sight, and followed him, glorifying God: and all the people, when they saw *it*, gave praise unto God.

As Jesus and His disciples traveled toward Jerusalem, they would have passed through the ancient city of Jericho. Stein (*Luke* 317) notes that Jericho was approximately seventeen miles east of Jerusalem. Luke includes two important events that took place in Jericho; these important incidents further developed Jesus' concept of Messiahship. Jesus is, indeed, the Messiah, but He is not the kind of

Messiah the Jews of His day expected. He is determined to define His Messiahship on His own terms. His kingdom is not based on military conquest or freeing Palestine from Roman rule, but on the power of God to transform lives.

As they draw near to Jericho, Jesus and His disciples encounter a blind man sitting beside the road. "Way side" describes a pathway or a road, probably a dirt path, wide enough for carts or other animal-drawn vehicles. There would not have been a great deal of distance between the blind man and Jesus, probably only a few feet. Summers (*Luke* 220) explains this is the main road leading into Jerusalem for the Passover and large numbers of people would have been traveling on it.

Luke does not indicate the cause of the man's blindness; many people in the ancient world became blind because of eye diseases the primitive medical knowledge of the day could not cure. Since blind people had few opportunities for employment, they were frequently reduced to begging.

Childers (579-580) indicates there are some differences between Luke's account of this healing and those found in Matthew and Mark. Matthew refers to two blind men while Mark and Luke refer to only one. According to Luke, the miracle takes place as Jesus enters the city of Jericho while Matthew and Mark place the event as Jesus leaves the city. Childers (579-800) and Geldenhuys (467-468) offer possible explanations of these differences.

As he was sitting beside the road, the blind man heard the noise that Jesus, His followers, and the crowd were making as they passed by. Those who were nearby explained to the blind man that the commotion was being made by Jesus and His disciples. The blind man had probably heard something about Jesus and the miracles He had performed in various places. Immediately he began to cry out, "Jesus, *thou* Son of David, have mercy on me." He wanted desperately to have his sight restored, and he hoped Jesus might perform a miracle for him. In reality, he had no other hope of regaining his sight. "Son of David" likely indicates that the blind man recognizes Jesus is the Messiah predicted in the O. T. (Creed 229).

According to verse 39, "they which went before" rebuked the blind man for crying out. Probably these were some of Jesus' followers or members of the group traveling to Jerusalem with Him. Their rebuke did not accomplish its desired goal; the more they rebuked the blind man, the more he cried out.

Jesus' heard and heeded the man's cries for help. He stopped in the road and ordered that the blind man be brought before Him. Jesus asked him (v. 41): "What wilt thou that I shall do unto thee?" There is no doubt Jesus already knew the answer to His question, but He wanted the blind man to express it for himself. The man immediately responded, "that I may receive my sight." Jesus uttered the words the man longed to hear: "Receive thy sight." His sight was immediately restored. Jesus also made the significant statement, "Thy faith hath saved thee." "Faith" expresses the idea of trust and commitment. The blind man trusted in Jesus to restore his sight. "Saved" expresses the idea of deliverance; it is used in the Bible both to describe physical deliverance and spiritual deliverance. While it is possible Jesus intended His words to say the man was saved from his sins, the more common explanation is that he was delivered from physical darkness (Geldenhuys 467). Stein (*Luke* 464) notes this physical healing symbolizes the spiritual healing that is also possible through Jesus. Summers (*Luke* 221) argues he was delivered both physically and spiritually.

Verse 43 concludes the story. Luke explains that his sight was immediately restored and the man followed Jesus as He traveled to Jerusalem for the Passover. "Followed" (Greek imperfect) and "glorifying" (Greek present) both indicate continuing action. As they journeyed to Jerusalem, the man continued to give glory to God. Luke does not explain how he glorified God; probably through public testimony of the miraculous healing he had experienced.

Verse 43 states the reaction of the crowd to the healing. All of the people praised God because of what they had seen. The crowd recognized Jesus had healed this blind man through the power of God and God should receive the glory and praise.

The healing of this blind man is a good example of how Luke deals with illness and misfortune. These are common themes both in the Gospel and in Acts. Illness was viewed very differently in the ancient world than in the modern world. In ancient times, people had no understanding of the scientific causes of disease. Such illnesses or physical problems like blindness or deafness were sometimes regarded as punishment for one's sins. For a good analysis of how illness was viewed in ancient Palestine see Pilch (181-209).

19:1 And *Jesus* entered and passed through Jericho.

2 And, behold, *there was* a man named Zacchaeus, which was the chief among the publicans, and he was rich.

3 And he sought to see Jesus who he was; and could not for the press, because he was little of stature.

4 And he ran before, and climbed up into a sycomore tree to see him: for he was to pass that *way*.

5 And when Jesus came to the place, he looked up, and saw him, and said unto him, Zacchaeus, make haste, and come down; for to day I must abide at thy house.

6 And he made haste, and came down, and received him joyfully.

7 And when they saw *it*, they all murmured, saying, That he was gone to be guest with a man that is a sinner.

8 And Zacchaeus stood, and said unto the Lord; Behold, Lord, the half of my goods I give to the poor; and if I have taken any thing from any man by false accusation, I restore *him* fourfold.

9 And Jesus said unto him, This day is salvation come to this house, forsomuch as he also is a son of Abraham.

10 For the Son of man is come to seek and to save that which was lost.

The chapter and verse divisions in the Bible were added centuries after it was written. There is no real break between chapters 18 and 19. In the last verses of chapter 18, a blind beggar is forgiven and welcomed into Jesus' family. In the opening verses of chapter 19, a wealthy tax-collector comes to faith in Jesus. These events illustrate one of Luke's principal themes, the universality of the gospel. He emphasizes that the message of salvation is for all. Bock (*Luke* IVP 305) points out that Luke often shows how much Jesus cares for the outcasts of society. A blind beggar and a rich tax-collector serve as good examples of those who would have been rejected by their culture.

Jericho was about seventeen miles from Jerusalem (Ellis 161). Lenski (936) notes that the Jericho of Jesus' day was probably not the same location as the modern town of Jericho. Hendriksen (*Luke* 853) explains that in the time of Jesus, it was a most pleasing and attractive place. The climate was mild; there were many palm trees and flowers of various kinds. It was such an agreeable place the Herod family maintained a winter palace there. It was also a center of trade and commerce. According to Lenski (936), it was known for its palm groves and balsam gardens, which produced items that were heavily taxed. As Michel (TDNT VIII:98) explains, Jericho was located on the main trade route for goods being brought into Judea from Perea. In the time of Jesus, this would have been a center for the collection of excise taxes (Hendriksen, *Luke* 208).

Luke does not pinpoint the exact location; he mentions only that Jesus had entered the city and was passing through it and proceeds to introduce Zacchaeus. Marshall (*Gospel* 696) notes that his name is of Hebrew origin, an abbreviation of the name *Zachariah*, which means "the righteous one." Luke gives him the title "chief among the publicans" (Greek *architelōnēs*), a word that occurs only here in the N. T. In other words, he was "chief tax collector," which implies he supervised those who actually collected the taxes; he, no doubt, received a portion of the tax that was collected. The next phrase indicates he was rich, implying he obtained his wealth through the collection of taxes. Michel (TDNT VIII:89-98) notes that tax collection was often farmed out to private contractors who received a cut of the taxes collected. Those Jews who accepted these positions were hated. They were regarded as turncoats or traitors because they collected additional amounts above what was required. For that reason, the people viewed them as extortionists who robbed their own people (Hendriksen, *Luke* 208). Morgan (*Teaching* 145-146) calls him a "rogue," not because he was rich but because of how he had obtained his wealth. As Morgan explains, if a tax-collector "exacted no more than his due, he never became a rich man."

The traditional interpretation of verses 3-4 is that Zacchaeus had a desire to see Jesus; he had, no doubt, heard about the teachings Jesus had given and the miracles He had performed (see Bock, *Luke* IVP 306; Green, *Luke* 667; and Bonnet and Schroeder 648). Morgan (*Teaching* 145) suggests a different interpretation, involving the words "who he was" (v. 3). In his view, these words indicate Zacchaeus was not specifically interested in learning more about Jesus. He was curious because a crowd had gathered, and he wanted to see who they were so excited about.

Zacchaeus was small of stature and unable to see Jesus because of the large crowd of people in front of him. For that reason, he ran ahead and climbed up into the branches of a nearby "sycomore tree." This tree is not what is known as a sycamore in the United States; that type of tree did not grow in ancient Palestine. Many commentators suggest it was a fig-mulberry tree (*Ficus sycomorus*) with low-hanging branches that would have been relatively easy to climb (Marshall, *Gospel* 696).

Stein (*Luke* 467) explains that climbing into a tree would have been undignified conduct for a man of Zacchaeus' wealth and position. He might have desired to hide himself in the foliage of the tree. Indeed, it might have been dangerous for a man in his position to appear in public. Many loyal Jews would have relished the idea of assassinating him.

When Jesus passed by the tree, a most unusual thing happened. He looked up into the branches of the tree and saw Zacchaeus. He called Zacchaeus by name and instructed him to come down out of the tree. Then Jesus told him in the presence of the crowd, "To day I must abide at thy house." As Shepard (470) explains, Jesus takes the initiative and invites Himself to go into the home of a leading publican. Zacchaeus hears the words of Jesus with gladness and promptly climbs down. The last words of verse 6 should probably be understood to mean Zacchaeus greeted Jesus in a joyful manner (Stein, *Luke* 468). He was both glad and honored to receive Jesus into his home (Summers, *Luke* 222). The assumption is Zacchaeus accompanies Jesus to his home.

Verse 7 describes the reaction of the crowd. They are not pleased to hear Jesus say He plans to be a guest in the home of a person who is such a notorious sinner. The common refrain among the crowd is that Jesus has gone "to be guest with a man that is a sinner." Childers (581) suggests two possible reasons the crowd is so hostile to Jesus' desire to visit in Zacchaeus' home. First, they refuse to see any good qualities in a publican. Second, they cannot see how Jesus can spend time with sinners without defiling Himself.

Luke does not give the context in which the words of verse 8 are spoken, probably, in the home of Zacchaeus after Jesus has explained to him how he can become a disciple. These words come at the end of this conversation between them (Hendriksen, *Luke* 856). "I give" and "I restore" are generally understood as futuristic (one use of the Greek present tense) referring to Zacchaeus' determination to make things right with the people he has defrauded (Marshall, *Gospel* 697-698). Shepard (471) sees in these words both a confession of his past sins and a pledge to make full restitution for all he has taken unjustly.

Zacchaeus would have understood what the law demanded, and he was determined to exceed its minimum requirements. He determines he will give one-half of his goods to the poor when the rabbis taught that 20-percent should be given to the poor (Marshall, *Gospel* 697). According to Leviticus 6:1-5 and Numbers 5:7, in some cases, an additional one-fifth had to be added to the amount that had been over charged. In other cases (Ex. 22:4, 7, 9), double the amount taken had to be repaid. In this passage, Zacchaeus commits himself to repay four times the amount he has unjustly collected.

Jesus accepts these sincere commitments as evidence of a change in the direction of this man's life; they are evidence of a true repentance (Childers 581-582). Jesus says, "This day is salvation come to this house." "Salvation" literally means "deliverance." The idea is that Zacchaeus has been delivered from the domination of material possessions. He is no longer willing to take advantage of his fellow Jews in order to obtain wealth for himself. The last words of verse 9 are significant; Zacchaeus has always been a son of Abraham by birth, but he has been living as a Gentile oppressor. As a result of the commitment he has made, he is now a true son of Abraham (Stein, *Luke* 469). He has been restored to the family. Summers (*Luke* 224) understands it to mean Zacchaeus has become a spiritual son of Abraham because he has exercised the same type of faith Abraham exercised.

Verse 10 is a summary statement, probably spoken both to Zacchaeus and to the crowd. Jesus gives a reason He came to earth: namely, to search for and redeem lost men and women. While many of the Jews of Jesus' day understood the coming of the Messiah in political terms, Jesus defined it in terms of the redemption of lost men and women. Jesus came for lost people, but He did not come in order to leave them in a lost condition. His goal was to transform them and bring them into the family of God. Barclay (235) takes "lost," as it is used here, to refer not to one who is damned or doomed but to one who has wandered away from God's family; he says, "A man is lost when he has wandered away from God; and he is found when once again he takes his rightful place as an obedient child in the household and family of his Father."

Marshall (*Historian* 138-139) provides a useful interpretation and analysis of the passage. Jesus teaches that Zacchaeus is as much a Jew as those Jews who were engaged in more respectable occupations. It was commonly believed Jews who lived in sin were beyond the reach of God's mercy and forgiveness. Jesus challenges this assumption; He asserts this tax-collector is as much eligible to be saved as are other Jews. He has come to seek and to save the lost, and that includes men and women like Zacchaeus.

11 And as they heard these things, he added and spake a parable, because he was nigh to Jerusalem, and because they thought that the Kingdom of God should immediately appear.
12 He said therefore, A certain nobleman went into a far country to receive for himself a kingdom, and to return.
13 And he called his ten servants, and delivered them ten pounds, and said unto them, Occupy till I come.
14 But his citizens hated him, and sent a message after him, saying, We will not have this *man* to reign over us.
15 And it came to pass, that when he was returned, having received the kingdom, then he commanded these servants to be called unto him, to whom he had given the money, that he might know how much every man had gained by trading.
16 Then came the first, saying, Lord, thy pound hath gained ten pounds.
17 And he said unto him, Well, thou good servant: because thou hast been faithful in a very little, have thou authority over ten cities.
18 And the second came, saying, Lord, thy pound hath gained five pounds.
19 And he said likewise to him, Be thou also over five cities.

20 And another came, saying,
Lord, behold, *here* is thy pound,
which I have kept laid up in a nap-
kin:
21 For I feared thee, because thou
art an austere man: thou takest up
that thou layedst not down, and
reapest that thou didst not sow.
22 And he said unto him, Out of
thine own mouth will I judge thee,
***thou* wicked servant. Thou knew-**
est that I was an austere man, tak-
ing up that I laid not down, and
reaping that I did not sow:
23 Wherefore then gavest not thou
my money into the bank, that at
my coming I might have required
mine own with usury?
24 And he said unto them that
stood by, Take from him the pound,
and give *it* to him that hath ten
pounds.
25 (And they said unto him, Lord,
he hath ten pounds.)
26 For I say unto you, That unto
every one which hath shall be
given; and from him that hath
not, even that he hath shall be
taken away from him.
27 But those mine enemies, which
would not that I should reign over
them, bring hither, and slay *them*
before me.

Jesus told this parable shortly before entering the city of Jerusalem for the final week of His earthly ministry. This is probably His final opportunity to instruct His disciples prior to entering the city for the events of the final week. Many scholars consider this parable to be a variant form of the Parable of the Talents given in Matthew 25:14-30 (Geldenhuys 476; Summers, *Luke* 225). Summers correctly notes these two parables are similar in some ways but differ considerably in detail and setting. Luke's Parable of the Pounds is set in the house of Zacchaeus in Jericho, while Matthew's is set on the Mount of Olives on Tuesday of Passion Week. Geldenhuys (476-477) argues that Luke's Parable of the Pounds and Matthew's Parable of the Talents are two distinct parables and not two variant forms of one parable. Stein (*Luke* 471) takes the opposite view; he argues they are two variant forms of one original parable. Luke does not indicate the place where this parable was told, but Summers is probably correct in assuming it was given in the house of Zacchaeus.

This is the only one of Jesus' parables that can be connected to a specific historical incident. Herod the Great died in 4 B.C.; he had given instructions that his kingdom should be divided among his three sons, Herod Antipas, Herod Philip, and Herod Archelaus. Since the land of Palestine was under Roman control, this division had to be approved by the Emperor in Rome. According to Josephus, Herod Archelaus, to whom his father had left Judea, went to Rome to seek the Emperor's approval to take control of the land. The Jewish leaders sent a delegation of fifty men to Rome to ask the Emperor not to give Archelaus control of the land. This Jewish delegation had some success, for Archelaus was only given control of approximately one-half of his father's kingdom with the title of Ethnarch rather than King. After he returned to Palestine, Archelaus punished severely those who had opposed his kingship (Barclay 236-237; Marshall, *Gospel* 703-704; Stein, *Luke* 473; Manson, *Sayings* 313).

Verse 11 explains why Jesus told this parable at this particular time in His ministry. His goal was to dampen the enthusiasm concerning the establishment of His kingdom. At that time, many different ideas about the nature of the Kingdom of God were being advanced, and those ideas often took on political and military overtones. It is likely that some (perhaps many) of Jesus' followers expected Him to go to Jerusalem and immediately set up His kingdom (Childers 583; Stein, *Luke* 472; Creed 232). Jesus told this parable to correct that false assumption. The kingdom would not be finally set up until the time of His future return; there will be an interval of time before the end in which the disciples will be responsible to carry on the ministry. This insight would have been particularly meaningful to Luke's readers because they were living and ministering in that interim.

The parable itself begins in verse 12. The "nobleman" is a person of noble birth or high social standing. He goes away to a far country "to receive for himself a kingdom": that is, he makes the journey to have his position as king confirmed. After confirmation, he plans to return to rule the territory that has been given to him. Since he will be gone for an extended period of time, he wants to be sure his estates are well-managed and his assets continue to grow. He calls in ten of his most-trusted servants and gives each of them an amount of money to invest. It is difficult to translate amounts of money in ancient times into their modern equivalents, but many authorities conclude that a "pound" was about 100 denarii, or three months' salary for a skilled workman (Stein, *Luke* 473). Summers (*Luke* 227) suggests this would have been a large amount of money in the ancient world, sufficient to require the services of a full-time manager. Summers also suggests that "occupy till I come" carries the implication of being involved in some type of business while the master is away. Each servant is to use the master's money to earn additional money by engaging in some type of business or profession.

That "his citizens hated him" (v. 14) refers back to the incident concerning Herod Archelaus which had occurred some years previously. The citizens disliked their new king so much they sent word to Rome that they did not want him to be king. Verse 15 explains these objections did not prevent the nobleman from receiving the kingship. Upon his return, the nobleman did two things. First, he summoned his servants so they might give account of their stewardship. Second, he punished those who had objected to his appointment as king.

The first servant reports he has used the pound to gain ten pounds. The master commends this servant and tells him he will be given control over ten cities. He has demonstrated his faithfulness in a relatively small matter and is now ready for larger responsibilities. The second servant arrives with another positive report; he has gained five pounds. The nobleman commends this servant and gives him responsibility over five cities. Bonnet and Schroeder (652) note that each servant is rewarded according to his faithfulness.

The third servant is described as "the other" servant; "other" (Greek *heteros*) means different. This servant is different from the first two. They have given positive reports, but the third servant does not. He has not traded with his master's money; instead, he has kept the coins bound up in a "napkin" (Greek *soudarion*), a piece of cloth used to protect the back of the neck from the sun (Marshall, *Gospel* 706; Manson, *Sayings* 316). This was not regarded as a safe way to store money in the ancient world; the safest place for money was to bury it in the ground (Jeremias, *Parables* 61).

This servant explains that he did not use the money in trade or business because he was afraid. That would have involved a certain amount of risk, which he was unwilling to take. He had simply held on to his master's money. He describes his master as "austere" (Greek *austēros*, only here in the N. T.), which means strict or exacting. In the papyri, it is used to describe one who expects to get blood out of a stone (Moulton and Milligan 93).

The servant means, by this characterization, the master takes advantage of other people (v. 21). Creed (234-35) notes that "taking up that which you have not laid down" is a proverbial expression meaning to unfairly take advantage of the labor of another. "Reaping that I did not sow" have essentially the same meaning. Childers (584) writes that these descriptions imply the nobleman is not only harsh and demanding, but also dishonest. He demands that to which he is not rightfully entitled. Bonnet and Schroeder (653) suggest two possible interpretations for this verse. It may mean the master takes all the benefits that result from his servant's labors and does not allow them to receive any. Another possible meaning is that the master is excessively demanding; he demands more of his workers than he should.

Verse 23 is the master's response to the third servant. In effect, he says, "If you were afraid to trade with my money, you could, at least, have put it in the bank where I could have earned some interest." In verse 24, the master orders that the money the servant has carefully guarded be taken from him and given to the one who has ten pounds. The implication is that the other man will use the money as his master intended. Luke makes no mention of what happened to the other seven servants who had received money with which to trade; they are not important to the story.

Verse 25 is found in most of the early manuscripts but not in all of them. Hendriksen (*Luke* 862) understands it as an interjection meaning, "Sir, he already has ten pounds!" Verse 26 is a general principle of discipleship Jesus specifically applies to those who are following Him into the city of Jerusalem. Those who labor in the Kingdom of God are expected to be faithful in their use of the gifts God has given them. If they will not use them as God intended, the gifts will be taken from them and given to others who will use them properly.

In the context of the parable, the "enemies" are those who opposed the nobleman's kingship. They are condemned to death. Creed (235) points out that in the ancient world those who were defeated would often be killed in the presence of those who had defeated them.

This parable should be interpreted in light of the circumstances in which it was spoken. Jesus is nearing the end of His journey to Jerusalem; He understands His earthly life will soon come to an end. He also understands that many of His followers define the kingdom in political and military terms, and they expect Him to set up His kingdom upon His arrival in Jerusalem. Jesus' goal is to continue preparing the disciples for the future and put to rest the false ideas that are being circulated. Just as the nobleman would be away from his kingdom for some time, so Jesus will be away from His disciples. They should not expect that the kingdom will be fully inaugurated during Jesus' time in Jerusalem. During the interval between Jesus' resurrection and His return, the disciples will be expected to be faithful and to fulfill the responsibilities He has entrusted to them (F. Bruce, *Hard Sayings* 193). They must not be like the third servant who is too afraid to obey his master's instructions. There is no doubt Luke's readers would have understood the importance of this parable. They were living in the interval between Christ's resurrection and His Second Coming; they were facing all the difficulties involved in being servants of Christ in a pagan world.

It is difficult to know exactly what Jesus meant by verse 27. Manson (*Sayings* 317) explains that Josephus makes no mention of Archelaus' taking vengeance on those who had opposed his kingship, but in the ancient world defeated enemies were often severely punished (Creed 235). There is no doubt that such cruelties were practiced in the ancient world, but Jesus never involved Himself in them. Bonnet and Schroeder (653) point out that political rulers often executed their opponents. They also note thousands of Jews would lose their lives in the rebellion against Roman rule that would soon occur. Perhaps the idea here is God will ultimately judge the Jews and others who actively opposed the ministry of Jesus (Childers 586; Geldenhuys 475-476; Hendriksen, *Luke* 863). Marshall (*Gospel* 709) points out that such language may sound strange to modern ears, but it was language Jesus' followers would have understood well.

Summary (18:35—19:27)

As this section begins, Jesus' journey to Jerusalem is nearing its end. The difficult days Jesus has spoken of to His disciples on several occasions are about to begin. It is important to note that, even in His most trying hours, Jesus never focuses attention on Himself and His sufferings. The emphasis is always on accomplishing the will of His heavenly Father. Jesus never loses His interest in people and their welfare. As He passes through Jericho, Jesus encounters two men in two totally different situations. The first is a blind man who continues to cry out to Jesus even as those around him urge him to be quiet. Jesus brings the man out of the shadows, asks him what he would like to receive, and then heals his blinded eyes. As a result of this notable miracle, all the people give glory and praise to God. Thus Jesus not only performs an act of mercy and kindness; He also illustrates something of the nature of the Kingdom of God. The kingdom Jesus has come to establish is characterized by kindness, love, and mercy rather than by military might and dominion. The success of this kingdom is not measured in terms of power and control but in terms of the healing of human beings, both physically and spiritually.

Jesus' second encounter in Jericho is with a tax-collector named Zacchaeus. He was an outcast, hated because of his collaboration with the Roman oppressors. He was regarded by his fellow Jews as a turncoat and a robber because he used his position to extort money from them. It is little wonder the members of the crowd murmured when Jesus called him down from the tree and expressed a desire to share in the hospitality of his home. This conduct was typical of Jesus; He frequently associated with those who were regarded as outcasts in society. Jesus went to his house, enjoyed his hospitality, and led him to totally change the direction of his life. After their time together, Zacchaeus promised to make things right with all of those whom he had defrauded.

The healing of the blind beggar and the transformation of Zacchaeus illustrate several important truths about the nature of the Kingdom of God. It is open to all; there is room for a blind beggar and a rich publican. This passage also illustrates the kind of changes the Kingdom of God introduces into the lives of individuals. Both the blind beggar and the tax-collector were transformed by their experience with Christ; they would never be the same again. These events also illustrate the great concern Jesus has for people; His kingdom is vitally concerned with the well-being, both physical and spiritual, of human beings.

This section of Luke concludes with the Parable of the Pounds, which illustrates other aspects of the Kingdom of God. The main character in the story is a man of considerable wealth who goes away to obtain the king's permission to rule over a certain territory. He entrusts ten of his most trusted servants with one pound (or one mina) each. The master's intent is that his servants invest the money entrusted to them so when he returns, he may receive both the money he left with each servant and whatever it has earned.

In the parable, the master deals with only three of the ten; the other seven are not important to the story. The first servant has gained another ten pounds. The master is very pleased, and the servant is amply rewarded. The second servant has likewise obeyed his master's instruction and gained five pounds. Once again, the master is pleased, and the servant is rewarded. The third servant makes his report. Because of his fear of the master, he has not invested the money; he has hidden it in a piece of cloth and returns it safely to his master, who is certainly not pleased. He tells the servant he could at least have taken the money to the local bankers and earned some interest. The master orders the money taken from the third servant and given to the first, who had faithfully obeyed the instructions he had received.

In verse 26, Jesus draws an important conclusion: namely, that those who faithfully use what they have been given in the service of God will be rewarded. Those who refuse to use what has been entrusted to them will not be blessed. They will, in fact, lose what had been placed in their care. The meaning is obvious. The kingdom belongs to God, but men and women have an important role in it. God expects them to be faithful in their service; those who refuse will lose their opportunity. Time, talents, and abilities will be given to those who will use them as God wishes them to be used.

Application: Teaching and Preaching the Passage

In this section of Luke's Gospel, Jesus continues to develop the theme of the Kingdom of God, but the focus is somewhat different. In earlier sections,

Luke has concentrated his discussion on Jesus' conflicts with the Jewish leaders and on His instruction of the disciples. In these verses, Jesus continues to instruct His disciples, but He does so by means of a miracle that presents the kingdom in a different light. In 18:35-43 Luke relates the story of Jesus' healing of a blind beggar. The disciples probably expected Jesus to inaugurate His kingdom with some notable demonstration of His power and authority. Instead, He performs the fourth and final miracle described in the Travel Narrative (Bock, *Luke* IVP 474). In the eyes of the disciples, this blind man is too insignificant to merit Jesus' care and attention. He should be quiet and leave the Teacher alone. Jesus surprises the crowd by calling this poor man to the forefront, talking with him, and then healing him. The implications for preaching and teaching are obvious.

Jesus has certain goals He wants to accomplish, and those goals may not coincide with the expectations of His followers. As followers of Jesus, believers must be prepared to accept the leadership and direction of God. They must not allow their prior expectations to stand in the way of God's accomplishing His will through them. The blind man's response to Jesus' invitation is also theologically significant. After years of hiding in the shadows, he steps forward and willingly accepts what Jesus wants to do in his life. Contemporary followers of Christ must have that same type of attitude.

Jesus demonstrates, once again, His care and concern for the outcasts of society. In the eyes of those around him, this poor blind man is of little importance. Jesus alone recognizes his great value and bestows on him the gift of healing. Jesus could see his potential in the Kingdom of God. The followers of Jesus today must also learn to look beyond the present and see the future contributions men and women can make to the work of God.

In chapter 19, Luke introduces the reader to another outcast who is brought face to face with the Master. Zacchaeus is a man of power and authority; he collects taxes for the Roman rulers and lines his pockets at the same time. He is hated for the manner in which he abuses his own people. The people—probably including Jesus' own disciples—murmur among themselves because He has gone to be a guest in the home of a man who is such a notable sinner. No self-respecting rabbi would have anything to do with a man like Zacchaeus. Where other men can see only an oppressor, Jesus sees a potential disciple. Jesus' ministry to Zacchaeus involves no physical miracle, but it involves a spiritual one. The heart that was formerly cold and indifferent to the sufferings of others becomes the soft heart of a disciple.

Both the story of the blind beggar and the story of Zacchaeus illustrate Jesus' redeeming love for all mankind. Modern preachers and teachers can use these stories to develop the hearts of modern believers in the right direction. The gospel is for all; all can be saved. There is no one the power of Jesus Christ cannot transform from being a sinner to being a follower of Christ. The people of God always need to be both seekers and savers.

Beginning in 19:11, Jesus relates what is commonly known as the Parable of the Pounds, probably based on the story of Herod Archelaus, who went to Rome to ask the emperor for authority to rule the territory that had been willed to him by his father. A delegation of fifty men went to Rome and asked the emperor not to give Archelaus this territory. They had some success in that he was only given about half the territory his father had ruled. Upon his return to Palestine, Archelaus severely punished those who had opposed his appointment.

In the Parable of the Pounds, a rich man leaves his estate for a time. Prior to his departure, he entrusts ten of his servants with one pound (or one mina) each. They are to invest the money and, when the master returns, return it, together with whatever has been earned with it. The first servant has gained ten pounds; he is duly commended. The second has earned five pounds; he is also commended for his faithfulness. The third servant did not obey the instructions his master had given him. He was afraid because the master was a hard and demanding man. Therefore, he did not invest the money; he hid it. The master, upon his return, did not even receive interest. This unfaithful servant was condemned; his pound was taken from him and given to the first servant who had been faithful.

This parable is a part of Jesus' training program for His disciples. They must learn that God expects His disciples to be faithful in using the resources they have received. God has blessed His people with a variety of talents, abilities, and financial resources. He expects us to be good stewards of what He has entrusted to us. Modern preachers and teachers can use this passage to challenge believers and help them become better stewards. Those who preach and teach need to move beyond general exhortations; they need to help their people develop specific strategies to make better use of the time, talents, and resources God has given them.

M. Preparations for the End (19:28-44)

At this point, Luke's Travel Narrative ends and a new section of the Gospel begins. Jesus has given instruction to His disciples through a series of teachings and acts of mercy. He has labored to prepare them both for the events that will transpire in Jerusalem during the final week of His earthly life and for the continuing ministry they will have after Jesus' death, burial, and resurrection. Now the time has come for Jesus to manifest Himself publicly in the capital city of the Jewish nation. Larson (281) notes that from the beginning of His public ministry Jesus has maintained a somewhat low profile. He has not sought out the attention of the multitudes; He has even cautioned people not to tell what He has done for them. That period in the ministry of Jesus has now ended; it is time for Him to manifest Himself publicly as the promised Messiah.

The teachings Jesus will give during the final week of His earthly life will also be of great value to future generations of disciples. They will help the followers of Christ understand better the depth of commitment required of them. It is likely the full impact of these teachings did not become apparent to His disciples at the time until after Jesus' resurrection.

28 And when he had thus spoken, he went before, ascending up to Jerusalem.

29 And it came to pass, when he was come nigh to Bethphage and Bethany, at the mount called *the*

***mount* of Olives, he sent two of his disciples,**
30 Saying, Go ye into the village over against *you*; in the which at your entering ye shall find a colt tied, whereon yet never man sat: lose him, and bring *him hither*.
31 And if any man ask you, Why do ye loose *him*? thus shall ye say unto him, Because the Lord hath need of him.
32 And they that were sent went their way, and found even as he had said unto them.
33 And as they were loosing the colt, the owners thereof said unto them, Why loose ye the colt?
34 And they said, The Lord hath need of him.

As Hendriksen (*Luke* 871) explains, Jesus' ministry in Perea has now ended, and the time has arrived for His final ministry in Jerusalem. The precise order of events during this final week cannot be reconstructed with certainty, but Hendriksen (*Luke* 872) offers a plausible chronology of the events Luke chooses to describe. He suggests Jesus and His disciples arrive in Bethany shortly before sunset on Friday and spend the night there. Jesus' entry into Jerusalem (Lk. 19:28-44) takes place on Palm Sunday. The events described in Luke 19:45-48 take place on Monday. Luke 20:1—22:6 takes place on Tuesday and Wednesday. Luke 22:7-71 occurs on Thursday night and early on Friday morning. The events of chapter 23, including the crucifixion, happen on Friday. Luke records no events that take place on either Saturday.

Luke 24:1-49 describes the resurrection, which takes place early on Sunday morning. The ascension described in Luke 24:50-53, takes place forty days later. Shepard (477-607) gives a helpful analysis of the events of the last week of Jesus' earthly life. He bases his discussion not just on Luke, but on all of the Gospels. Creed (236-239), Summers (*Luke* 232-315), Hoehner (*Life* 90-93; DJG 118-122), and Plummer (444-445) also offer chronological outlines of the events of Jesus' final week.

While Friday is regarded as the traditional day for the crucifixion, there are some scholars who argue it took place on Wednesday or Thursday. That issue will be examined in the commentary on chapter 23.

Verses 28-34 serve as the preparation for Jesus' entrance into the city of Jerusalem. The setting is the road between Jericho and Jerusalem, which passes by the Mount of Olives looking down over the city. The village of Bethany is located on the eastern slope of the Mount of Olives. Ellis (225) notes that Bethany is approximately two miles east of the city and was the home of Mary, Martha, and Lazarus. The meaning of the term "Bethany" is uncertain, but it is thought to mean "house of figs" (Plummer 445).

The location of Bethphage is unknown. According to the traditional interpretation, it is thought to have been located northwest of Bethany (Hendriksen, *Luke* 873). Some authorities assert that Bethphage is not the name of a village, but the name of the district in which Bethany is located (Plummer 445). The term "Bethphage" likely means "house of unripe figs."

Jesus and His disciples probably spend the night at the home of Mary, Martha, and Lazarus in Bethany. Early the next morning, He sends two of His disciples to a nearby village (probably

Bethphage) where they will find a colt tied near the entrance to the village. Ellis (225) suggests that a "colt" is a male donkey. Matthew, who writes to a primarily Jewish audience, understands this complex of events as the fulfillment of the O. T. and, in Matthew 21:5, cites a composite quotation from Zechariah 9:9, Isaiah 62:11, and perhaps other passages. Luke, writing for a Gentile audience, does not mention any specific O. T. passages, but it is likely he has in mind the same passages Matthew quotes. The Hebrew text of Zechariah 9:9 prophesies a future king of Israel will come to Jerusalem in a humble manner, riding upon a colt, the foal of an ass. Ellis (224) explains that the Jewish rabbis regularly understood Zechariah 9:9 to be messianic. There is little doubt Jesus views His upcoming entrance into the city as the fulfillment of the O. T.

Matthew 21:5 states that the king will come "sitting upon the foal of an ass, and a colt the foal of an ass"—quoting Zechariah 9:9. Crabtree (345) explains that both Matthew 21:5 and Zechariah 9:9 make use of a Hebrew literary device known as parallelism. The last phrase "and a colt the foal of an ass" repeats the idea expressed in the previous phrase. Neither Zechariah nor Matthew is saying Jesus rode upon two animals. Matthew 21:7 may indicate the disciples brought both the ass and the colt, but Jesus would only have ridden the colt.

According to Blomberg (*Matthew* 312) and Broadus (426), "them" at the end of verse 7 refers not to the animals but to the cloaks. Luke 19:30-35 and Mark 11:2-7 mention only one animal, the colt. D. Guthrie (*Jesus* 267) suggests Mark and Luke chose to concentrate their attention on the animal Jesus actually rode.

Jesus tells His disciples what they are to expect when they arrive in the village. The colt they are to bring is unbroken, meaning it has never been ridden. Hendriksen (*Luke* 873) and Lieu (154) understand this to mean God has reserved this colt for sacred use. The fact that Jesus is able to ride an unbroken colt in the midst of these large and noisy crowds provides another illustration of His divine power.

Jesus also tells His disciples they will probably be asked why they are taking a colt that does not belong to them. He tells them to respond, "The Lord hath need of him." Hendriksen (*Luke* 874) suggests the owners of the colt are friends, perhaps followers, of Jesus and would immediately recognize this request from His disciples. Summers (*Luke* 233) posits that Jesus had arranged the use of the colt with friends in Bethany in advance. While it is possible there was some prior arrangement for Jesus' disciples to take the colt, Luke makes no mention of any such arrangement (Marshall, *Gospel* 713). It is also possible that animals were kept there to lend or rent to travelers. Marshall also posits Jesus was well enough known in the area that such a request from His disciples would have been honored. Lieu (154) suggests the taking of animals for use by the king was a common practice, and riding into the city on a donkey was a royal act.

According to verses 32-34, these two disciples follow Jesus' instructions, and they find everything just as He said. The owners ask why they are taking the colt. The disciples respond, "The Lord hath need of him." Apparently, the owners accepted this response; Luke mentions no further discussion concerning the colt.

This passage introduces a theme that will be important throughout the final chapters of Luke. In these final days of Jesus' earthly life, it is important to understand He is in control of the events. He is not a victim of Jewish hostility or of Roman cruelty. He is the one in control of the process; His goal is always to do the will of His heavenly Father.

35 And they brought him to Jesus: and they cast their garments upon the colt, and they set Jesus thereon.
36 And as he went, they spread their clothes in the way.
37 And when he was come nigh, even now at the descent of the mount of Olives, the whole multitude of the disciples began to rejoice and praise God with a loud voice for all the mighty works that they had seen;
38 Saying, Blessed *be* the King that cometh in the name of the Lord: peace in heaven, and glory in the highest.

These verses describe what is commonly known as the "Triumphal Entry" and related in all of the Gospels (Mt. 21:1-11; Mk. 11:1-11; Jn. 12:12-16). Plummer (445) suggests it took place on Nisan 8 in the year A.D. 30. That would be a Friday, about March 31 on a modern calendar. While there are some differences in detail in the various Gospel accounts, the essential elements of the story are the same. The fact that all the Gospel writers include descriptions of the triumphal entry indicates they regard it as important. This passage not only affirms that Jesus is the long-expected Messiah, it also describes the kind of Messiah He will be. For a useful discussion of the triumphal entry see Geldenhuys (486-487).

The Messiah, Jesus of Nazareth, approaches the city in a humble manner, riding on a donkey colt. Marshall (*Gospel* 710) notes it was normal for a Jewish rabbi to ride while His disciples followed behind Him on foot. Lenski (961) notes since the time of Solomon no king of Israel had entered the city of Jerusalem mounted on a donkey. Summers (*Luke* 234) points out when Solomon was anointed king he entered the city of Jerusalem riding upon his father David's favorite mule (1 Kgs. 1:32-40). The donkey was known as an animal of peace; it served as a beast of burden. Jesus chose to ride into the city on the back of a donkey for a specific reason. He wanted to demonstrate for all to see His kingdom was one of peace; He had no desire to raise an army and begin a war with Rome.

Verse 35 notes the followers of Jesus took off their garments—their outer cloaks, no doubt—and placed them upon the bare back of the donkey where they served as a kind of saddle. Broadus (426) notes that an animal ridden by a king would be covered with elegant cloths. The disciples had no such cloths. Luke, alone among the Gospels, notes the disciples assisted Jesus in mounting the donkey. These actions were signs of honor and respect, similar to the treatment accorded to King Solomon in 1 Kings 1:33. Verse 36 explains they not only put their garments on the back of the donkey, they also spread them on the path in front of the donkey. This would have indicated the great respect the disciples had for Jesus; this is treatment appropriate for the Messiah. Luke makes no reference to palm branches, mentioned elsewhere (Jn. 12:13).

In verses 37-38, the followers of Jesus begin to sing praises to Jesus, using words drawn from the O. T. In verse 37, they give praise to God for all the good things Jesus has done. Luke does not define "the mighty works that they had seen," but he probably refers to the miracles of healing and other acts of mercy Jesus had performed during His ministry in Galilee. The words of praise found in verse 38 are drawn in part from Psalm 118:26.

"Blessed *be* the King" probably indicates the crowd rejoices because they know Jesus is from the line of David. They hope their nation will be restored with a descendant of David on the throne. The words "that cometh in the name of the Lord" indicate the crowd regards Jesus as the Messiah who comes with full authority given to Him by God. Stein (*Luke* 479) indicates the words in verse 38 were used in greeting pilgrims who came to the city to celebrate the Passover. "Peace in heaven" refers to the peace the Messiah will institute. The people looked back on the time of David as a time of war, but they regarded the time of Solomon as a time of peace. The reign of the Messiah will be a time of peace like that of Solomon (Summers, *Luke* 235). The words "the highest" are clearly a reference to Heaven. The idea is that glory should be given to God who dwells in Heaven for what He has done in sending Jesus as the Messiah.

Stein (*Luke* 477) raises the interesting question why the Roman and Jewish authorities tolerated such a public demonstration on behalf of Jesus. It is doubtful this question can be answered with certainty. Plummer (448-449) suggests the Pharisees feared the level of popular support Jesus enjoyed. The Sanhedrin had previously issued a decree that anyone might arrest Jesus if He came into the city, but the Pharisees saw no way to enforce that decree. With the large number of visitors who had arrived in the city for the Passover and the large amount of celebration going on, it is doubtful the Roman authorities took notice of Jesus and His followers. They were not yet considered to be a threat to Roman rule.

39 And some of the Pharisees from among the multitude said unto him, Master, rebuke thy disciples.
40 And he answered and said unto them, I tell you that, if these should hold their peace, the stones would immediately cry out.
41 And when he was come near, he beheld the city, and wept over it,
42 Saying, If thou hadst known, even thou, at least in this thy day, the things *which belong* unto thy peace! but now they are hid from thine eyes.
43 For the days shall come upon thee, that thine enemies shall cast a trench about thee, and compass thee round, and keep thee in on every side,
44 And shall lay thee even with the ground, and thy children within thee; and they shall not leave in thee one stone upon another; because thou knewest not the time of thy visitation.

Verse 39 may indicate the Pharisees felt powerless to quell the enthusiasm of Jesus and His followers. They were afraid their efforts to quiet the people might inflame the situation and attract the attention of the Roman rulers. Therefore, they asked Jesus to restrain His disciples. The Pharisees addressed Jesus as "master" or "teacher" (Greek *didaskalos*), the term His enemies normally used to address Him (Plummer 449).

In verse 40, Jesus refuses their request in the strongest of terms. He tells the Pharisees that if His people ceased their rejoicing, the stones would immediately take it up. His response is a sharp and open rebuke to the Pharisees, whom He considers to be even more insensitive than the rocks. Jesus' response to them may be based on Habakkuk 2:11, which reads, "For the stone shall cry out of the wall, and the beam out of the timber shall answer it." In the earlier years of His public ministry, Jesus often downplayed His messianic claims to avoid the political and military overtones often associated with the Messiah. That approach is now in the past; the time has come for Jesus and His followers to publicly declare Him to be the coming Messiah.

Verses 41-44 reflect a sudden shift in the direction of the narrative. The spirit of rejoicing suddenly gives way to sadness and sorrow as Jesus looks down over the city and weeps because of the future He knows is in store for it. Plummer (449) argues that the place where Jesus stopped to weep cannot be determined with certainty; Childers (588) and Summers (*Luke* 235) reflect the traditional view, it took place on the Mount of Olives. If this view is correct, Jesus would have looked down on a large and beautiful city with palaces, gardens, and the beautiful Temple. He would have seen the wall and the large gates with many people going through them to celebrate the Passover. Jesus begins to weep when He thinks of the sad future that lies ahead for the city He loves.

Verse 42 is poignant. There was no nation in the world that prayed more earnestly for peace and freedom than Israel. Yet Israel had known little peace and even less freedom. For much of her history, Israel had lived under the domination of foreign powers. She had the opportunity to experience real peace for the first time through the Messiah whom God had sent, but the leaders of Israel refused to accept it. The great irony is that the people of the city turned their backs on the very one who could have brought them the peace they desired. Jeremias (*Theology* 12) explains in the ancient world it was common to describe divine activity using the passive voice and without mentioning specifically the name of God. The phrase, "but now they are hid from thine eyes," may mean God has hidden from them the things that can bring peace to Jerusalem.

In verse 43, Jesus employs a series of military terms describing how a city was besieged in the ancient world (Plummer 451-452). All war is cruel, and war in the ancient world was especially cruel. A city could be under siege for months or even years. All food supplies would be cut off, and the people would literally be starved into submission. This had happened to Jerusalem in the past, and Jesus predicts it will happen again.

Verse 44 describes the brutality that will take place when the city finally falls. The words, "shall lay thee even with the ground, and thy children with thee," probably indicate the capturing army will kill the people and literally trample them under their feet. Or "lay even with the ground" may mean "dash to the ground" (Plummer 452). The phrase "not leave one stone upon another" is a proverbial way of saying the city will be totally destroyed (Stein, *Luke* 485). As Stein explains, the language used in these verses is the typical way of describing the conquest of a city by siege.

Most commentators find the fulfillment of this passage in the Jewish War of A.D. 66-70 (Geldenhuys 485; Childers 588; Stein, *Luke* 485), when the Jews sought to obtain their independence from Rome. According to the descriptions that have survived (primarily in the writings of Josephus), the Romans finally entered the city after a siege of five months, killed many Jews, and totally destroyed the city.

In the closing words of verse 44, Jesus lays the responsibility for this coming disaster on the backs of the Jewish leaders. God has chosen to visit His city in a special way by sending His Son, the Messiah, to minister to it. But these leaders have refused to accept what God was doing for them. In the future, their rejection will produce tragic consequences, for which they must accept the responsibility (Stein, *Luke* 485).

Summary (19:28-44)

Prior to this time, Jesus has made no public claim to be the Messiah, probably because of the political overtones the term had in Judaism of the first century. He has no desire to be a military leader and establish an earthly kingdom over which He will rule. At this point in the account, His approach changes; during the final week of His earthly life Jesus will affirm publicly, He is the Messiah. He is not, however, the type of Messiah the people have come to expect. He will not enter the city of Jerusalem as a military leader mounted on a white horse and followed by a large and powerful army. He will enter on a donkey, an animal of peace. He will be followed not by legions of soldiers but by a handful of disciples. He will spend His time teaching the people in the outer courts of the Temple.

Verses 28-34 set the stage for Jesus' entrance into the city of Jerusalem. Jesus sends two of His disciples, unnamed, into a nearby village to bring a colt for Jesus to ride into Jerusalem. Jesus gives His disciples instructions about where they are to find the colt and how they are to respond to those who will ask them why they are taking it. They arrive at the village and everything transpires just as Jesus said it would. They return to Jesus with the colt.

Jesus' entrance into the city is described beginning in verse 35. The disciples honor Jesus as best they can with the limited resources available to them. They take off their outer garments and place some of them on the back of the colt for Jesus to sit on, and some in the path of the donkey. The fact that Jesus is able to ride upon an untrained animal is another example of His divine power.

As they pass the Mount of Olives, Jesus' disciples begin to rejoice and praise God in a loud voice. At that point in the story, a group of Pharisees who have been a part of the multitude following Jesus began to complain and ask Jesus to rebuke His disciples. Jesus frankly and quickly refuses their request. He tells these Pharisees if the disciples did not cry out in praise to God, the stones would begin to do so.

In verse 41, the tone shifts from rejoicing to sadness and sorrow. Jesus looks down over the city of Jerusalem and begins to weep. He begins to speak of the tragic days His beloved city will experience. Jerusalem will be besieged and ultimately destroyed, and the people within its walls will perish. Many scholars are of the opinion this prophecy was fulfilled in the Jewish war for independence that lasted from A.D. 66-70.

The account concludes with verse 44: "because thou knewest not the time of thy visitation." The idea is Jesus had come to the city as its Savior; He had come with a message of salvation from the Father. But the people of the city had largely rejected Him and the message He came to bring. There is a great deal of sadness in Jesus' voice because He knows the outcome could have been different if they had been willing to heed His message.

Application: Teaching and Preaching the Passage

Luke presents several important themes that should be developed in preaching and teaching. One of these concerns the reason Jesus came to this earth; He came on a mission. He came to bring a message of hope and redemption to the world; He also came to give His life as a ransom for the sin of mankind. Jesus is the Son of God; He understood very well the suffering and death that awaited Him in Jerusalem. He determined to go to Jerusalem, and He never wavered from that commitment. His faithfulness in difficult and trying circumstances serves as an example all of His followers need to imitate. All believers need a sense of mission and purpose in life.

In the earlier sections of Luke, Jesus has been reluctant to claim openly to be the Messiah. This reluctance was probably because of the military and political overtones that often accompanied the concept of messiahship in first-century Judaism. In this passage, Jesus openly reveals Himself as the Messiah, but He insists on defining His messiahship in His own way. He does not enter the city as a conquering hero mounted on a great white horse and followed by an army. He enters riding on a donkey, an animal of peace, leading only a small group of disciples. Modern preachers and teachers should never be afraid to present Jesus as the Messiah, but they should also insist on presenting Him correctly. His goal is to conquer the sinful hearts of mankind.

Another important theme developed in this passage is Jesus' deep love and concern for all human beings. Jesus wept over the city of Jerusalem because of His love and concern for the men, women, and children that inhabited that city. As the Son of God, He could foresee the future suffering and destruction of the city, and that broke His heart. This passage reflects clearly the depth of Jesus' love and concern for human beings. In a world that is often afflicted with division, strife, and suffering, the followers of Jesus Christ need to preach and teach openly about His love.

VI. MINISTRY IN JERUSALEM (19:45—24:53)

A. Teaching in the Temple (19:45—21:4)

The final section of Luke's Gospel begins here; these verses describe some of the important events that led up to Jesus' crucifixion. One of the key themes in this section is the innocence of Jesus.

He has done nothing to deserve the sentence of death He receives; even the Roman governor realizes this. Even so, because of the sinfulness of men, He is condemned to the cruelest method of execution the ancient world could devise.

Another key theme in this final section of Luke is the growing hostility between Jesus and the Jewish leaders. This conflict is not new; it has been building since the earliest days of His earthly ministry. The cleansing of the Temple indicates just how far apart Jesus and the Jewish leaders are. His concept of how to worship God and theirs simply cannot be reconciled; the differences are too deep and too wide.

The Jewish leaders are determined to bring about His death, and Jesus does nothing to stop them. Although He is the Son of God, He makes no effort to use His divine power to prevent His execution. He accepts His suffering and death as a part of God's plan for Him and for the world. He is confident that redemption will come as a result of His sacrifice.

45 And he went into the temple, and began to cast out them that sold therein, and them that bought;
46 Saying unto them, It is written, My house is the house of prayer: but ye have made it a den of thieves.
47 And he taught daily in the temple. But the chief priests and the scribes and the chief of the people sought to destroy him,
48 And could not find what they might do: for all the people were very attentive to hear him.

At this point, Luke begins his narrative of the events that took place in Jerusalem during Passion Week. While the precise order of events cannot be determined with certainty, scholars have outlined what likely took place on each day of this final week of Jesus' earthly life. For good summaries of the events of these important days see Shepard (491-592), D. Guthrie (*Jesus* 267-346), Edersheim (*Life* II:363-581), and Walvoord (127-29).

The closing verses of this chapter are devoted to Luke's description of the cleansing of the Temple. This event is also described (with some differences in detail) in Matthew 21:12-13 and Mark 11:15-19. John 2:13-17 also describes a cleansing of the Temple. The Synoptic Gospels all locate the cleansing during the final week of Jesus' ministry on earth, while John places one at the beginning of Jesus' ministry.

Commentators have long debated whether John and the Synoptic Gospels are describing one cleansing of the Temple or two. Bock (II:1576) offers an excellent summary of the views commonly held. There are three possible understandings. First, it is possible that Jesus cleansed the Temple just once, during the early part of His earthly ministry. If that view is correct, the Synoptic writers placed the event in the last week of Jesus' life for theological reasons. Since they narrate only one visit to Jerusalem, which took place near the end of Jesus' ministry, that is the logical place to include it. This view is ably defended by Fitzmyer (II:1260-1268).

The second possibility is that Jesus cleansed the temple just once, but during the final week of His earthly ministry. If this view is correct, the Gospel of John places it near the beginning of Jesus' earthly ministry for theological reasons. This view is well defended by

R. Brown (*John I-XII* 117-118). His primary argument is that such a dramatic event was more likely to happen near the end of Jesus' ministry when the cleansing of the Temple led directly to His crucifixion. A similar view is presented by Beasley-Murray (*John* 38-39).

The third possibility is that Jesus cleansed the Temple on two occasions, once near the beginning of His ministry and the other during the final week. This view is quickly dismissed by some scholars (R. Brown, *John I-XII* 117; Beasley-Murray, *John* 38), who suggest the Jewish and Roman authorities would never have permitted such an event to happen on two different occasions. Others (Plummer 453; Geldenhuys 490; Morris, *Luke* 308) argue for two cleansings. Plummer argues that the Synoptic writers omit the first cleansing because they omit the entire early Judean ministry. John omits the second because he has already discussed the first and does not feel the necessity to include the second. Plummer concludes that there are too many differences in detail for John and the Synoptic Gospels to be describing the same event. Hendriksen (*Luke* 879) takes a similar approach.

It is difficult to determine whether there was one cleansing or two, and each view raises difficult questions. Those who argue for one cleansing, whether at the beginning or at the end of Jesus' ministry, are faced with the difficulty of explaining the differences between the accounts. Those who argue for two cleansings have to explain why the Synoptic Gospels omit the first cleansing and John omits the second. Those who argue for two cleansings are also confronted with the issue of whether the authorities would have permitted such a cleansing to happen twice. Another complicating factor in this debate is that ancient writers were less concerned than modern writers with issues of chronology. It was not unusual for ancient writers to place a given event in different places in their narratives.

While scholars of all persuasions recognize the difficulty of this issue, more conservative scholars will generally argue that the evidence for two cleansings outweighs the arguments for one. When all the evidence is considered, two cleansings are more likely than one.

Luke offers no indication of the day on which the cleansing of the Temple occurred; he writes only "and he went into the temple." As often, Luke is more concerned with what happened than when. According to Mark (11:1-19), Jesus entered the city on the day of the Triumphal Entry (probably Sunday) and looked around the Temple. He returned the next day, Monday, and performed the actual cleansing (Summers, *Luke* 237; Geldenhuys 488-489).

Verses 45-46 briefly summarize Jesus' activity. He went into the temple area and drove out those who bought and sold. Matthew and Mark give additional details. This probably occurred in the outer part of the Temple known as the Court of the Gentiles, which was open to all; the Temple proper was open only to Jews (Marshall, *Gospel* 719). Sacrificial animals were sold in this area; foreign coins were exchanged for Judean coins that could be accepted in payment of the Temple Tax (Summers, *Luke* 237; Stein, *Luke* 485).

Martin (254) suggests a Jewish pilgrim might come to Jerusalem from a distance, purchase a sacrificial animal, and have it sacrificed without ever having contact with it. This makes possible a very formalistic and ritualistic system.

Edersheim (*Life* I:365-376) gives a good summary of the activities going on in the Temple and why a cleansing was necessary.

Jesus quotes from two O. T. passages as justification for His action. The first comes from the closing words of Isaiah 56:7, written (or spoken) by Isaiah shortly before the fall of Jerusalem and the destruction of the First Temple by the Babylonians in 586 B.C. That passage reads, "for mine house shall be called an house of prayer for all people." Interestingly, Luke omits the last phrase "for all people." This omission is understandable if the Temple had already been destroyed when the Gospel was written, since it could no longer serve as a house of prayer.

The second quotation, "but ye have made it a den of thieves," comes from Jeremiah 7:11, a part of his famous Temple Sermon where the prophet condemned the abuse of the Temple that was going on shortly before the Babylonian Exile. As used by Jesus, this passage clearly reflects His disgust with what was going on in the Temple. He was not so much angry with *what* was being done as He was with *where* and *how*. The Jewish leaders began the practice of changing money and selling sacrificial animals as a service to Jewish pilgrims coming to Jerusalem from other areas of the Roman Empire. It was difficult to bring sacrificial animals with them, and the Temple authorities would not accept any coins that bore the image of the Emperor (or other persons) as payment of the Temple tax.

What had originally begun as a service to the pilgrims became a racket. The priests and other leading members of the Jewish establishment in Jerusalem obtained control over this trade, and it became a lucrative business venture for them. One reason for Jesus' objection was the fact they were charging the people high prices for sacrificial animals and for changing money. They were taking advantage of the people to enrich themselves. For good descriptions of this commercial enterprise see Edersheim (*Life* I:364-376) and Barclay (241-242). It is likely Jesus viewed these activities as a desecration of the House of God.

It is also likely Jesus was displeased with the place where this buying and selling was going on. It was going on in the Court of the Gentiles, which was the only area of the Temple where Gentiles could go and learn more about the true God. This important area was so occupied by this buying, selling, and money changing it was impossible for Gentiles to go there and worship.

Verses 47-48 provide a summary of Jesus' activities during Passion Week until the time of His arrest. That "he taught" (Greek imperfect tense) implies continuing or on-going action. Verse 47 goes on to explain that Jesus continued teaching daily within the Temple precincts. Luke does not explain where in the Temple complex this teaching was carried on, but it probably took place in one of the outer courtyards where the lay people were permitted. Summers (*Luke* 239) speculates that Jesus possibly taught in the very area from which He had chased those who bought and sold the sacrificial animals.

As Jesus continued teaching the people, and more of them learned about Him and His ministry, support for Him increased. As these verses explain, opposition to Jesus was also growing. The chief priests, scribes, and other leaders within the power structure in

Jerusalem were looking for ways to destroy Him. Luke mentions one thing prevented them from ending the ministry of Jesus early in the week, His popularity among the people. The common people appreciated Jesus and His ministry. They saw Him as their leader; He gave them hope (Plummer 455).

Morris (*Luke* 308-309) calls attention to the fact that, while we have previously encountered the chief priests and the scribes, the expression "chief of the people" is new. It indicates that opposition to Jesus was increasing among the ruling classes of the city. These leaders were afraid to openly attack Jesus because they knew it would produce a strong reaction from the common people. During the week, the leaders will continue to look for ways to defeat the ministry of Jesus, and they will finally induce one of His own followers to betray Him. Summers (*Luke* 239) notes when they finally find a way to end Jesus' ministry, they do so in secret and away from any protection of Jesus the people might have afforded.

At this point, Jesus begins to teach the people in the outer courts of the Temple; this teaching will continue through 21:4, as Jesus' conflict with the Jewish leaders in Jerusalem becomes even more pronounced. On three occasions (20:1-8, 20-26, and 27-40) deputations sent by the Sanhedrin challenge Jesus' authority to teach the people in such a public manner. They also question His relationship to the Torah, the O. T. law. Jesus responds to these challenges by warning the people their current leaders are not leading them toward the Kingdom of God but away from it. For good summaries of the teachings of these passages see Hendriksen (*Luke* 887-888) and Marshall (*Gospel* 722-723).

20:1 And it came to pass, *that* on one of those days, as he taught the people in the temple, and preached the gospel, the chief priests and the scribes came upon *him* with the elders,
2 And spake unto him, saying, Tell us, by what authority doest thou these things? or who is he that gave thee this authority?
3 And he answered and said unto them, I will also ask you one thing; and answer me:
4 The baptism of John, was it from heaven, or of men?
5 And they reasoned with themselves, saying, If we shall say, From heaven; he will say, Why then believed ye him not?
6 But and if we say, Of men; all the people will stone us: for they be persuaded that John was a prophet.
7 And they answered, that they could not tell whence *it was.*
8 and Jesus said unto them, Neither tell I you by what authority I do these things.

As to when this occasion was, Luke says only that it happened "on one of those days" apparently meaning the days of Passion Week. Summers (*Luke* 239) suggests it took place on Tuesday. Hendriksen (*Luke* 887) posits that Luke 20:1—22:7 describes events that take place on Tuesday and Wednesday of Passion Week. It is his view that there is not sufficient evidence to determine where Tuesday's events end and Wednesday's begin.

"Taught" (Greek present tense) implies ongoing action. The idea is that Jesus was teaching the people in the Temple. He was also preaching "the gospel," which literally means "good news." Luke does not explain the precise content of the gospel Jesus was preaching, but it likely centered upon the good news that He had come to earth as the Messiah.

The "chief priests," "scribes," and "elders" collectively describe the leadership of the Jewish community; these were the groups that would have been included in the Sanhedrin (Stein, *Luke* 487; Summers, *Luke* 239). The Sanhedrin had control over the religious affairs of the Jews, and this is probably an official delegation sent to question Jesus.

This official delegation questions Jesus about the things He has done. Luke does not define "these things," but they are probably what He has done since arriving in the city: namely, the teachings, the miracles, and the cleansing of the Temple. It seems likely the cleansing of the Temple was the event that had most caught the attention of the Jewish leaders. They ask Jesus to explain by what authority He has done these things, or who has given Him that authority. Jesus understands they are trying to trick Him into saying something they can later use against Him; so He responds to their question with a question of His own, asking by whose authority John the Baptist went into the wilderness and baptized many people. Did John baptize on human authority or on God's authority?

The Jewish leaders understood the implications of this question and considered their response carefully. They even discussed the issue among themselves. They correctly recognized that Jesus had placed them on the horns of a dilemma. If they should reply that John's authority came from God, Jesus would then ask them why they did not obey his preaching. If they should respond that John's authority was of human origin, they knew the people of the city would become enraged. The leaders clearly understood the people regarded John as a prophet sent by God.

These leaders then give to Jesus the only response they have; they say they do not know the source of John's authority. This answer is evasive; the truth is they are not willing to commit themselves on what was, apparently, a controversial issue. Jesus then tells them if they will not answer His question, neither will He answer theirs. Once again, Jesus demonstrates His understanding and wisdom as the Son of God. He defeats the efforts of the Jewish leaders to embarrass Him and cause Him to say something they can use against Him.

9 Then began he to speak to the people this parable; A certain man planted a vineyard, and let it forth to husbandmen, and went into a far country for a long time.
10 And at the season he sent a servant to the husbandmen, that they should give him the fruit of the vineyard: but the husbandmen beat him, and sent *him* away empty.
11 And again he sent another servant: and they beat him also, and entreated *him* shamefully, and sent *him* away empty.
12 And again he sent a third: and they wounded him also, and cast *him* out.

13 Then said the lord of the vineyard, What shall I do? I will send my beloved son: it may be they will reverence *him* when they see him.
14 But when the husbandmen saw him, they reasoned among themselves, saying, This is the heir: come, let us kill him, that the inheritance may be ours.
15 So they cast him out of the vineyard, and killed *him*. What therefore shall the lord of the vineyard do unto them?
16 He shall come and destroy these husbandmen, and shall give the vineyard to others. And when they heard *it*, they said, God forbid.
17 And he beheld them, and said, What is this then that is written, The stone which the builders rejected, the same is become the head of the corner?
18 Whosoever shall fall upon that stone shall be broken; but on whomsoever it shall fall, it will grind him to powder.

Hendriksen (*Luke* 891) notes that in order to interpret the meaning of this parable correctly one must understand something of the economic situation existing in Galilee at that time. Much of the best farmland was owned by wealthy foreigners who did not live on their land. They leased the land to local farmers who actually cultivated it. The fact the owner lived away had both advantages and disadvantages for the tenants. On one hand, they did not have to worry about the owner interfering in their work. On the other hand, the distant owners were often not understanding about problems such as drought, insects, and crop failures. There was a widespread feeling these wealthy landowners took advantage of the tenants who actually worked their land.

This parable is part of the teaching Jesus gave during His last week; it may even be considered a part of the gospel message He shared. In the O. T., the nation of Israel is often compared to a vineyard. The classic passage is Isaiah 5:1-7; see also Deuteronomy 32:32, Psalm 80:8-16, Isaiah 27:2-7, Jeremiah 2:21, and Hosea 10:1. Buttrick (213-221) points out the allegorical nature of this parable. The vineyard is clearly Israel. The husbandmen represent the leaders who have refused to heed God's prophets. The servants are the prophets God has sent to His people at different times. The lord of the vineyard represents God. The owner's son corresponds to Jesus, who comes to earth as God's personal representative to redeem His people.

As B. Smith explains (222-224), a landowner in Israel would frequently lease his land to tenants who would do the actual work in return for a percentage of the harvest. He also points out there were times when the tenants refused to pay the rent when it was due and would even assault those who were sent to collect it. Dodd (*Parables* 96-97) makes a similar point, adding there was much unrest in Palestine at this time. The land had never been completely pacified after the revolt of Judas the Gaulonite in A.D. 6. There was a great deal of resentment against absentee landlords. This parable presents a message Jesus' hearers would have readily understood.

In an effort to collect the portion of the crop due him, the landowner sends three servants. All three are mistreated by the tenants and sent away without the owner's portion. The owner then decides to send his beloved son, thinking the tenants will show more respect for a son than they have shown for the servants. Instead of respecting the son, they take him outside the vineyard and kill him. Summers (*Luke* 241) explains that, according to the oriental custom, the fact the son arrives indicates the father has died and the son has come to claim his inheritance. The tenants, by killing the heir, may be able to retain possession of the land.

After telling the parable, Jesus asks a hypothetical question, "What therefore shall the lord of the vineyard do unto them." The answer is, "He shall come and destroy these husbandmen, and shall give the vineyard to others." The application of the parable is obvious. Throughout history, God has sent His prophets to the nation of Israel, and the leaders have always rejected them. God has now sent His beloved son, the Lord Jesus Christ, to them, and they are repeating the same cycle of disobedience they have long demonstrated. The final outcome will be God's judgment upon them.

The last words of verse 16 present the response. Luke does not identify those referred to as "they," who could be either the delegation sent by the Sanhedrin or the people who had heard the parable. At any rate, their response is one of horror; they understand the parable has been spoken against them. The phrase "God forbid" can be literally translated "May it never be!" For a brief analysis of this expression see Hendriksen (*Luke* 898).

In verses 17-18, Jesus interprets His rejection by the Jewish leaders by using two quotations from the O. T. The first—"The stone which the builders rejected, the same is become the head of the corner"—is from the Greek version of Psalm 118:22 (117:22 in the Septuagint). The "head of the corner" refers to a large stone that joins two walls together. It could be either a foundation stone at the bottom of the wall or a capstone at the top (Plummer 462). This passage is often quoted by the N. T. writers, in a somewhat ironic fashion, to emphasize the importance of Christ and His ministry (Acts 4:11; 1 Pet. 2:7). The idea is that the Lord Jesus, the One the world foolishly rejected and crucified, has become the key person in God's plan of salvation for the world.

The first words of verse 18 are from Isaiah 8:14-15; the second part of the verse seems to be based on Daniel 2: 34-35, 44. The idea of the first part is that those who stumble over the message of Jesus, in the sense they refuse to accept it, will suffer a terrible judgment. The latter part of the verse repeats the same lesson but employs a different imagery. Those who reject the mission and message of Jesus will face the most severe judgment (Plummer 462-463; Stein, *Luke* 493-494).

19 And the chief priests and the scribes the same hour sought to lay hands on him; and they feared the people: for they perceived that he had spoken this parable against them.
20 And they watched *him*, and sent forth spies, which should feign themselves just men, that they might take hold of his words, that so they might deliver him unto the power and authority of the governor.
21 And they asked him, saying, Master, we know that thou sayest

and teachest rightly, neither acceptest thou the person *of any*, but teachest the way of God truly:
22 Is it lawful for us to give tribute unto Caesar, or no?
23 But he perceived their craftiness, and said unto them, Why tempt ye me?
24 Show me a penny. Whose image and superscription hath it? They answered and said, Caesar's.
25 And he said unto them, Render therefore unto Caesar the things which be Caesar's, and unto God the things which be God's.
26 And they could not take hold of his words before the people: and they marvelled at his answer, and held their peace.

The Jewish leaders correctly interpreted the teaching Jesus had just given; they understood they were the builders who had rejected the chief cornerstone. As a result of His rebuke, they were determined to arrest Jesus and get rid of him once and for all. There was one thing standing in their way; they feared how the people would respond. The common people had a high regard for Jesus, and the Jewish leaders did not want to run the risk of a riot or other disturbance. Hendriksen (*Luke* 895-896) notes it would have been difficult for the Jewish leaders to control the large crowds that had come to Jerusalem for the Passover. The recent raising of Lazarus from the dead served to increase the people's enthusiasm for Jesus.

Since the chief priests and scribes were afraid to confront Jesus openly, they devised a more subtle plan. They sent some men into the crowd who pretended to be followers of Jesus or to be interested in becoming His followers. These men would take note of Jesus' teachings. If He said anything that could be construed as treasonous by the Roman authorities, they would have the evidence to bring Him before the governor for trial and punishment.

Verse 21 notes these spies did more than listen to Jesus' teaching, they participated in the discussion with Him. They begin the discussion by calling Jesus "teacher," a title of respect, and by giving Him extravagant praise. They stated Jesus always taught correctly and He showed no partiality: that is, He did not accept anyone's person.

They then asked Him whether a faithful Jew should pay taxes to the pagan Roman government. This was an issue that was much debated at that time; it probably refers to the payment of a poll tax that was required of every adult male in the province of Judaea. The funds collected went directly into the imperial treasury (Hendriksen, *Luke* 900). Since this kind of tax helped support Roman rule in Palestine, it was particularly hated by the Jews. If Jesus answered in the affirmative, He could lose the support of Jewish patriots. If He answered in the negative, He could be in trouble with the Roman authorities (Marshall, *Gospel* 735).

The Jewish leaders expected Jesus to say that no faithful Jew should pay such a tax to a pagan government, but He surprised them. In response to their question, He asked for a coin. "Penny," in verse 24 (Greek *dānarion*, Latin *denarius*) was a small Roman silver coin that bore the image of Caesar. Jesus asks, "Whose image and superscription hath it?" The obvious answer was that it bore Caesar's image and had been issued on his authority. Jesus then gave a most memorable response, "Render therefore unto Caesar the things which be Caesar's, and unto God the things which be God's." This response would have pleased neither the Jewish leaders nor the patriotic Jews. The Jewish patriots in the crowd would have wanted Him to make a statement against Roman rule, which He declined to do. The Jewish leaders wanted Him to make some type of statement they could use against Him before Roman authorities, but He refused to fall into their trap. Once again Jesus, by the power and wisdom of God, defeated those who tried to entrap Him.

This important statement is also significant for what it says about the Kingdom of God Jesus has come to establish. He does not equate the establishment of His kingdom with the end of Roman rule. His kingdom is spiritual, not material; the presence or absence of Roman rule will not affect the establishment of His kingdom.

27 Then came to *him* certain of the Sadducees, which deny that there is any resurrection: and they asked him,
28 Saying, Master, Moses wrote unto us, If any man's brother die, having a wife, and he die without children, that his brother should take his wife, and raise up seed unto his brother.
29 There were therefore seven brethren: and the first took a wife, and died without children.
30 And the second took her to wife, and he died childless.
31 And the third took her; and in like manner the seven also: and they left no children, and died.
32 Last of all the woman died also.
33 Therefore in the resurrection whose wife of them is she? for seven had her to wife.
34 And Jesus answering said unto them, The children of this world marry, and are given in marriage:
35 But they which shall be accounted worthy to obtain that world, and the resurrection from the dead, neither marry, nor are given in marriage.
36 Neither can they die any more: for they are equal unto the angels; and are the children of God, being the children of the resurrection.
37 Now that the dead are raised, even Moses shewed at the bush, when he calleth the Lord the God of Abraham, and the God of Isaac, and the God of Jacob.
38 For he is not a God of the dead, but of the living: for all live unto him.

Now the Jewish leaders make an attempt to involve Jesus in one of their internal disputes; their goal is to trick Him into saying something they can use to discredit Him in the eyes of the people. Summers (*Luke* 245) notes that previous unsuccessful attempts to trick Jesus had been led by the Pharisees, while this one was directed by the Sadducees. The Pharisees and Sadducees were two of the major groups that dominated the religious and political life of the land of Palestine. The Sadducees dominated the Sanhedrin while the Pharisees had more influence in the local Jewish synagogues. The Pharisees believed in a future resurrection of the body; they took this belief so literally they expected to bear children in the resurrected state (Summers, *Luke* 245). The Sadducees denied the existence of a future resurrection; they believed this life is the only life that exists. This important doctrinal difference produced sharp conflicts between these two groups.

The Sadducees, here, set up a hypothetical situation based on the law of levirate marriage found in the O. T. According to Deuteronomy 25:5-10, if a man died without having fathered a child, his widow was to marry his brother and have children. The first child born to this union would be regarded as the child of the deceased brother. Barclay (249-250) posits this commandment was little used in the time of Jesus, but since it was still in the O. T. law, the Sadducees regarded it as binding. Marshall (*Gospel* 737) suggests this incident was intended to ridicule Jesus' belief in a future resurrection.

The hypothetical situation set up by the Sadducees is rather ridiculous. A woman is married to seven brothers; all of them die, and she has no children by any of them. The Sadducees then ask Jesus, "In the resurrection whose wife of them is she?" In other words, "To which of the brothers will she be married in the resurrection?"

Jesus responds to this challenge from the Sadducees by giving a lesson on marriage. He explains that marriage is an institution that exists only during one's earthly life. As Childers (589-590) notes, the purpose of marriage is to populate the earth, to replace those who die. Since there will be no death in the post-resurrection state, marriage will no longer be necessary. People will be like the angels in the sense they will never die.

In verses 37-38, Jesus defends His belief in the resurrection of the body by citing an incident found in Exodus 3:6. Since the Sadducees accepted only the Pentateuch as inspired Scripture (Stein, *Luke* 500, 503), Jesus chooses from that portion of the O. T. The Sadducees found no evidence of a future resurrection in those five books (Summers, *Luke* 247). Jesus, however, finds evidence for the resurrection in the famous passage concerning the burning bush. In that passage, God speaks of Himself as being the God of Abraham, Isaac, and Jacob. When God spoke these words to Moses, all three of these patriarchs had been dead for many years. The promise that the Lord will be their God implies God will raise them in the future so He can fulfill His promise to be their God (Marshall, *Gospel* 742-743; Stein, *Luke* 500-501). Jesus goes on to explain that God is the God of the living and not of the dead; therefore, these three ancient worthies must have the possibility of future life.

Luke gives no indication of how the Sadducees responded to Jesus' argument. Their silence indicates they were powerless to contradict what He had said. Once again, the Jewish leaders had tried to trick Jesus into saying something that could be used against Him, but they had failed miserably.

39 Then certain of the scribes answering said, Master, thou hast well said.
40 And after that they durst not ask him any *question at all.*

The scribes mentioned in verse 39 are the official interpreters of the law. In these verses, they should probably be regarded as spokesmen for all the Jewish leadership, both the Pharisees and the Sadducees. Both groups have tried to trick Jesus, but they are forced to recognize they have been defeated by Jesus' arguments. He has responded effectively to all of the points they have raised. There is no reason to continue this discussion further, but there will be additional encounters before the earthly ministry of Jesus comes to an end.

41 And he said unto them, How say they that Christ is David's son?
42 And David himself saith in the book of Psalms, The LORD said unto my Lord, Sit thou on my right hand.
43 Till I make thine enemies thy footstool.
44 David therefore calleth him Lord, how is he then his son.

Luke establishes no connection between these four verses and the previous discourse. It is difficult to determine when or where these words were spoken. Another complicating factor is that these words are but one part of a larger discussion. The most likely possibility is they form part of the teaching Jesus gave during the final week of His earthly ministry. Stein (*Luke* 505) speculates "they" refers to Jesus' enemies who regularly challenged Him to prove that He is, in fact, the long-anticipated Messiah. The question, "How say they that Christ is David's son?" probably reflects a question Jesus was often asked. "Christ" is a translation of the O. T. word "Messiah." "Son" is often used in the sense of "descendant." The meaning of their question is, "How can it be demonstrated that Jesus is really the Messiah, the Son of David?"

Jesus then answers this frequently-asked question with a quotation from Psalm 110. It is possible, but not certain, that Psalm 110 was regarded as messianic by the Jews of Jesus' day. It was clearly regarded as a messianic psalm both by Jesus and by the early church (Stein, *Luke* 505). In the Hebrew text of Psalm 110, two different names for God are used; both are translated "Lord" (Greek *kurios*) in verse 42. The first is the word *Yahweh*, often translated "LORD" in the King James Version. The second is *Adonai*, often translated "Lord" (Summers, *Luke* 249). The first refers to God the Father, while the second to Jesus as the Messiah. Among Jews of the first century, it was widely assumed the Messiah would come from the line of David. The point here is that Jesus is not only David's descendant; He is also David's Lord. He is David's son in the sense that He is a descendant of Israel's greatest king. He is also David's Lord because He is God. If He is David's Lord, He is also the Messiah.

"Sit thou on my right hand, Till I make thine enemies thy footstool" also comes from Psalm 110. In this context, it describes the exalted position Jesus occupies at the right hand of God the Father. That His enemies will become His footstool indicates the complete victory the Messiah will win over all those who oppose Him.

Verse 44 refers back to the question asked in verse 41. How can the Messiah be both David's son and David's lord? The answer is that Jesus Christ, the Messiah, is both human and divine. He is both a physical descendant of David and the Son of God. For insightful discussions of this passage see Summers (*Luke* 249-250) and Hendriksen (*Luke* 908).

45 Then in the audience of all the people he said unto his disciples,

46 Beware of the scribes, which desire to walk in long robes, and love greetings in the markets, and the highest seats in the synagogues, and the chief rooms at feasts;
47 Which devour widows' houses, and for a shew make long prayers: the same shall receive greater damnation.

Jesus continues to instruct His disciples in the kind of attitudes and actions they should demonstrate in their dealings with people. He does this by giving a negative example taken from the Judaism of His day. The "scribes" are the official teachers of the law; they occupy positions of respect and authority in the Jewish society of the first century. In this passage, Jesus accuses them of hypocrisy. They wear long robes, make long prayers, and seek the prominent seats in the synagogues. They seek to be recognized by the people and respectfully greeted in the marketplaces. They are, at the same time, devouring widow's houses.

Verse 45 indicates Jesus is still teaching a group of people (probably still in the outer courts of the Temple), but this particular instruction is designed primarily for the disciples. They will occupy positions of leadership in the church, and He does not want them to imitate the Jewish leaders.

In verse 46, Jesus makes several accusations against the scribes, and all of them revolve around the issue of arrogance and pride. They walk in the marketplace wearing long flowing robes, which indicate they are men of leisure since workingmen would never wear such attire (Morris, *Luke* 294). Bock (II:1642) notes that these robes were ostentatious and part of a fancy and expensive wardrobe. They enjoy being greeted by the people in the public squares and occupying the chief seats in the synagogue nearest to the ark, which contained the sacred scrolls. When invited to a dinner, they want to be invited to occupy the seats of honor nearest to the host.

Verse 47 presents two other condemnations. The first is that the scribes "devour widow's houses." Scholars have suggested possible interpretations of this fault. See Nolland (III:976), Marshall (*Gospel* 750), and Jeremias (*Jerusalem* 114) for summaries of the most commonly-held views. Jeremias suggests it refers to the habit of the scribes of sponging on the hospitality of people of limited means. Marshall *(Gospel* 750) suggests the lawyers who were appointed to take care of the estates of widows, who were entitled to fair compensation, took advantage of their positions by charging excessive fees.

Morris (*Luke* 294) points out that scribes were not to charge for their teaching, but they could accept offerings. It is possible the scribes were using their influence to persuade widows to make gifts beyond their means to give. While the precise meaning of the passage is difficult to determine, the idea is clear; the scribes, who were supposed to be servants of the people, were abusing and taking advantage of them.

Jesus was not saying all the teachers of the law conducted themselves in such an arrogant manner, but it was enough of a problem that Jesus was justified in condemning it. Instead of reflecting an attitude of humility and service, these teachers manifested an attitude of pride and arrogance. They demanded the people recognize them for the exalted position they held.

This is not the first time Jesus has condemned the Jewish leaders. Luke 11:39-53 provides an earlier example. Lieu (165) posits that Luke 11 deals with the situation in Galilee while this passage indicates Jesus has confronted a similar situation in Jerusalem. As Stein (*Luke* 507) correctly notes, it is difficult to determine whether Jesus gives this instruction in order to address a current issue or to encourage future leaders in the church not to adopt such attitudes. Ellis (238-39) argues that Luke has included this instruction for the benefit of future church leaders; the purpose is to encourage them not to fall into the same patterns as the Jewish leaders.

The last condemnation is they make long prayers that are not sincere; the prayers are designed to impress men rather than to present the needs of the people before God. All of these condemnations revolve around one central theme. These activities are done in order to impress men and improve the position of the scribes rather than to serve God and their fellow Jews. Leaders who do these things are not serving the people; in fact, they are abusing them.

In the words "greater damnation" (v. 47), "damnation" (Greek *krima*) often means "judgment." God will not overlook these abuses. Those leaders who abuse the people will be held to account by God for what they have done. Those who choose to lead God's people must lead them in the right way and with the right motivation.

21:1 And he looked up, and saw the rich men casting their gifts into the treasury.

2 And he saw also a certain poor widow casting in thither two mites.

3 And he said, Of a truth I say unto you, that this poor widow hath cast in more than they all:

4 For all these have of their abundance cast in unto the offerings of God: but she of her penury hath cast in all the living that she had.

Again, this teaching was probably a part of Jesus' teaching in the outer courts of the Temple during the final week of His earthly ministry. The main character in this teaching is a poor widow. As Morris (*Luke* 294) explains, life was difficult for a widow in first-century Palestine; there were few ways they could earn money.

Edersheim (*Life* V:387) explains that in the area near the Court of Women there were a series of thirteen trumpet-shaped boxes for receiving different offerings. On each box was an inscription that explained how the money placed in that box was to be used. Jesus and His disciples observed that rich people were coming by and depositing large offerings into these boxes. Some of them probably did so in a very public manner, so they might be seen and recognized for their large gifts.

Jesus and His disciples also observed that a poor widow came forward and dropped in a very small offering, only two mites. The word for "widow" (Greek *penichros*) occurs only here in the N. T. It was used in classical Greek to describe a needy widow. Bock (II:1645) suggests that in this context it may describe one who is very poor. "Mite" (Greek *lepta*) is one-hundredth of a denarius. Since a denarius represented a day's wage for a skilled workman, a *lepta* would have been a very small offering indeed. It was the smallest coin commonly used in Palestine (Morris, *Luke* 294-295; Stein, *Luke* 509).

Jesus then makes a most unusual statement. He points out that this widow had contributed more than all of those rich people who had made their large offerings. In verse 4, Jesus explains that the rich people who had made large offerings had done so out of their abundance, while she, in her poverty, "hath cast in all the living that she had." Edersheim (*Life* II:388) gives two possible interpretations for this statement. It may describe all she had been able to save from her scanty budget, or it may describe all she had to live on for that day. The point is clear; her small gift represented a much greater sacrifice than the much larger gifts of her rich neighbors.

Most commentators consider the words of Jesus to be a commendation of her generosity. Stein (*Luke* 508-509) argues that Luke's readers would have viewed her action in a positive manner. They would have understood His words to describe one who was rich toward God and not overly concerned with the things of this life. Some interpreters, however, interpret Jesus' statement not as a commendation but as a rebuke for the scribes (who "devour widows' houses," as in 20:47). In their view, she has been overly-influenced by the scribes who have persuaded her to give money that should have been used to buy food or other necessities (A. Wright, 256-265).

Summary (19:45—21:4)

This section of Luke focuses the reader's attention on a series of conflicts that illustrate just how much Jesus' teaching differs from that given by the leaders of the Jewish establishment in Jerusalem. The cleansing of the Temple, which begins this section, illustrates the sharply differing conceptions of the nature of worship (Bock *Luke* NIV 499). The Jewish leaders were content to allow the outer courtyard of the Temple to be used for the changing of money and the buying and selling of sacrificial animals. That enabled pilgrims to comply with the legal requirements they had established; it also enabled them to make a tidy profit.

Jesus looked at the issue in an entirely different way; He considered what was going on to be nothing short of blasphemy. That part of the Temple was the only area where Gentiles could pray and express their devotion to God. To Jesus, that was far more important than the trade in sacrificial animals.

Verses 47-48 provide an excellent summary of the last week of Jesus' earthly life. He is busy teaching the people, probably in and around the Temple, and they are eager to receive His instruction. The Jewish leaders are much opposed to what Jesus is doing. By His words and His actions, He is threatening their power and control. Since He is popular among the people, the Jewish leaders look for a way to destroy Him without engendering the wrath of the people. Before the week is over, they will be able to develop a strategy (with the help of Judas Iscariot) whereby they can arrest Jesus by night and bring Him before the Roman governor.

Luke 20:1—21:4 apparently presents a summary of the teachings Jesus gave during this important week. Luke makes no attempt to explain precisely when or where each teaching is given. For him, the teaching itself is the most important thing.

Luke 20:1-8 describes one of Jesus' encounters with the chief priests, scribes, and elders. They are clearly looking for some type of evidence they can use against Him; they demand to know by what authority He is preaching and teaching. Since Jesus understands their evil motive, He responds to their question with another question, asking about the authority of John the Baptist—who was regarded by the people as a prophet. With this question, Jesus places these leaders on the horns of a dilemma. They cannot admit that John's teaching was from God. If they say it was from men, the people will rise up against them. They decline to answer. If they refuse to answer Jesus' question, then He will not answer theirs. During Jesus' earthly ministry, the Jewish leaders tried to trick Him on several occasions, but Jesus never fell into their trap. He always turned the tables on them and made them look foolish.

Verses 9-16 present the Parable of the Vineyard, the story of a wealthy man who leases out a vineyard. He sends his servants to collect the portion of the crop that is due him, but the tenants beat them and send them away empty handed. The owner then sends his son, with the expectation the tenants will honor him. They do not honor him; they kill him. The owner of the vineyard will respond by punishing those tenants severely and leasing his vineyard to others.

The meaning of this parable is obvious. God has sent His Son, Jesus, into the world on a mission of mercy and redemption. The Jewish leaders have refused to recognize Jesus; at this time, they are seeking some way to destroy Him. The implication is that God will judge them severely because they have rejected His Son.

Verses 17-18 might have been spoken at the same time as the Parable of the Vineyard or at a different time. Regardless, Jesus explains why the Jewish leaders have rejected Him. He sees that rejection as the fulfillment of two O. T. passages. The first is from the Greek version of Psalm 118:22. The first words of verse 18 are drawn from Isaiah 8:14-15. The latter part of verse 18 is based on Daniel 2:34-35, 44. It was not unusual for Jesus to combine O. T. passages in this fashion. The meaning is that Jesus, whom they foolishly rejected, will become the key to God's plan of salvation for the world. These verses also emphasize that those who reject Jesus as the Messiah will suffer the most severe judgment for their rejection.

Verses 19-26 describe an incident that occurred between Jesus and the Jewish leaders at some point during this crucial week. They correctly understood that Jesus' teachings were directed against them, and they were determined to eliminate Him. The one thing that kept them from moving actively against Him was His popular support; they feared how the people would respond to Jesus' arrest. They sent spies who pretended to be His disciples in an effort to trick Him into saying something they could use to accuse Him.

The spies asked Him if it was lawful to pay tribute to Caesar, the Roman Emperor. Jesus knew what they were trying to do; He also knew the question of paying tribute to the Roman government was a hot-button issue among the Jews. He asked for a coin; the coin that was given to Him was a Roman coin because it bore the image of Caesar. Jesus then responded, "Render therefore unto Caesar the things which be Caesar's, and unto God the things which be God's." The people marveled at the astuteness of Jesus' answer, and the Jewish leaders were left in silence.

Verses 27-38 reflect another attempt by the Jewish leaders to entrap Jesus, this time by the Sadducees. They ask Jesus a hypothetical question, which seems rather ridiculous to modern readers. At that time, however, the question reflected a serious issue being debated among the Jewish religious leaders. Since the Sadducees did not believe in a future resurrection, some scholars have suggested this situation was designed to ridicule Jesus' belief that people would be resurrected in the future.

In the scenario set up by the Sadducees, a woman is successively married to seven brothers and widowed seven times. Finally, the woman also dies. The question the Sadducees asked Jesus was, "In the resurrection whose wife of them is she?" Jesus did not give them a direct answer. Instead, He corrected both their view of marriage and their view of the resurrection. He affirmed there will be a future resurrection; He also pointed out that marriage is an earthly institution. There will be no more marriage after the resurrection. Once again, the Jewish leaders have tried to trick Jesus into saying something that could be used against Him, but He has foiled their plot.

Verses 41-44 probably reflect a teaching given on a different occasion, one that probably was part of a larger discussion Luke has chosen not to include. Probably the term "they" (v. 41) refers to Jesus' enemies who challenge Him to prove He is the Christ, the long-anticipated Messiah. The term "Christ" is a translation of the Hebrew term for the Messiah. Jesus responds to this challenge by referring to Psalm 110. Jesus is David's son in the sense that He is a descendant of the great Israelite king. He is David's Lord in the sense that He is the Son of God, the divinely-appointed king.

In verses 45-47, Jesus warns His disciples not to imitate the actions and attitudes of the Jewish leaders. Jesus accuses them of hypocrisy; they wear long robes, pray long prayers, and seek the recognition of men. They do not seek to glorify God, serve His people, or advance His kingdom on earth.

This section of Luke concludes with the story of the poor widow who casts her two mites into the Temple treasury. Life was very difficult for a widow in the ancient world, and it is likely her resources were few. In contrast to the wealthy people who give out of their abundance, she gives all that she has. The traditional interpretation is that Jesus commends her for her generosity, but the problem with this approach is there are no specific words of commendation in the passage. It is also possible Jesus makes an implied criticism, not of the poor widow, but of the religious system that encourages her to give money better spent on food or other necessities.

Application: Teaching and Preaching the Passage

This section of Luke makes a significant contribution to the Christology of the N. T. This passage would provide excellent texts for a series of sermons or lessons on the authority of Christ. By His words and by His actions, Jesus gives a more comprehensive picture of His authority and position than He has done previously. Malachi 3:3 describes the coming Messiah as a purifier and a refiner. That idea is clearly evident in Jesus' cleansing of the Temple described in the closing verses of chapter 19.

These verses emphasize the authority of Christ in various ways. His authority is evident, for example, in His responses to the attacks of the Jewish leaders. They make every effort to trick Him into saying something they can later use against Him. They come to Jesus and ask Him if it is lawful to give tribute to Caesar. He responds by asking for a Roman coin that bears the image of the Emperor. He then says, "Render therefore unto Caesar the things that be Caesar's, and unto God the things which be God's."

On another occasion, the Sadducees ask Him a hypothetical question about a woman who is successively married to seven brothers and widowed each time. They ask, "In the resurrection whose wife of them is she?" Jesus understands full well the Sadducees do not believe in the resurrection; their question is not sincere. They are only trying to trick Him, and He refuses to fall into their trap. Throughout this passage, Jesus reflects the divine wisdom that enables Him to say and do the right thing at the right time. The divine wisdom Jesus possesses is another evidence of His divine authority.

Verses 41-44 are the most difficult verses in this passage to interpret because we do not know the context in which they were spoken. In these verses, Jesus claims to have greater authority than King David, who was much revered by the Jewish people of that day. The fact that Jesus is Lord over the greatest of the Jewish kings is a point that needs to be stressed in preaching and teaching.

The teachings Jesus gives in this passage also reflect His authority. He has authority to teach the Father's will even when it contradicts the traditional teachings of the Jewish leaders. He has the authority to condemn those who use the outer court of the Temple for the buying and selling of sacrificial animals. As the Son of God, He has the authority to determine what is in accord with the Father's will and what is not. He has the authority to determine that the small gift made by a widow is of greater value than the large offerings of those who are wealthy. Jesus also has the authority to warn His disciples not to be carried away by the false teachers who say one thing and do another.

There is another theme that is important: namely, Jesus' relationship with the common people of the land. The Jewish leaders wanted to destroy Jesus, but they had to be careful not to offend the masses of people who had come to Jerusalem for the feast. Jesus had established a special relationship with the common people; they could identify with Him. He taught them about how to be truly right with God. He reflected none of the selfishness, legalism, and hypocrisy they found in their own leaders.

The person and work of Christ must always be at the center of Christian preaching and teaching. Christ may not do in the modern world exactly the same kinds of things He did in Jerusalem during the last week of His earthly life, but He is always the Son of God. As the Son of God, He deserves to be at the center of our lives, our homes, and our churches.

B. Fall of Jerusalem and the End of the Age (21:5-38)

The training and preparation of the disciples was a major focus of Jesus' attention; that is especially true during His final days on earth. In this part of the Gospel, Jesus seeks to prepare His followers for the difficult days they will encounter. While this passage deals with two future events, the fall of Jerusalem and the end of the world, Jesus' goal is not to give a detailed prediction of the future. His goal is to prepare His disciples for the trials and sufferings they will have to endure. He does not want them to be taken by surprise. As Summers (*Luke* 253) notes, the time of Christ's coming is not the focus of Luke's attention. His focus is on the events that will transpire while the disciples await the return of Christ. When this Gospel was written, the Christians were already facing the reality that Christ's return would be delayed.

Green (*Luke* 731-733) provides a useful summary of the major ideas presented in Luke 21:5-38. He notes that in this passage Jesus deals both with the coming destruction of the city of Jerusalem and with the coming of the end. Jesus does not provide a precise timetable for these important events, but He does provide a rough chronology. He anticipates that the disciples will first face a time of suffering and persecution through which they will continue to bear witness. This difficult time will be followed by the destruction of the city and the "times of the Gentiles." After the "times of the Gentiles," there will be a time of signs and wonders that will cause distress upon the earth. These events will open the door for the coming of Christ. Green (*Luke* 732) emphasizes that this passage underscores the faithfulness of God and calls for faithfulness on the part of Christ's disciples.

As Green (*Luke* 731) and Bock (II:1676) explain, this passage anticipates some interval of time between the destruction of Jerusalem and the Second Coming. It gives no indication of how long this interval may last. At the same time, the passage maintains an emphasis on the imminence of the Eschaton (Lk. 21:32).

This passage and the parallel passages in Matthew 24—25 and Mark 13 are commonly known as the "Synoptic Apocalypse," but other titles are also used such as "The Prophetic Discourse" (Geldenhuys 522), "The Apocalyptic Discourse" (A. Bruce, EGT I:618), or "The Olivet Discourse (Chafer 114; Bock, *Jesus* 338). Morris (*Luke* 295) entitles it "The Eschatological Discourse" while Bonnet and Schroeder (662) call it "The Prophetic Discourse."

The Synoptic Apocalypse is one of the most difficult and controversial passages in the Gospels (Summers, *Luke* 253; Bock, *Jesus* 338), and scholars interpret it in different ways. The accounts given in the three Synoptic Gospels agree on the essential elements of the story, but they differ on the details. Each of the Gospel writers presents the story to meet the needs of the particular audience for which he is writing.

Here are some of the points all of the Synoptics have in common. Jesus and His twelve disciples leave the Temple after a day of teaching. As they are walking away, some of the disciples call attention to the great beauty of the Temple. Jesus responds with the prediction that in the future the Temple will be totally destroyed. That response takes the disciples by surprise, and, for a time, they ask no more questions. They cross the Kidron Valley and make the steep climb up to the Mount of Olives where they stop to rest. While they are resting, some of the disciples ask Jesus when this destruction will take place and what will be the signs of the Temple's destruction. Jesus responds by dividing their question into two parts. Jesus first explains the events that will take place surrounding the destruction of the Temple and the city of Jerusalem. Jesus then explains the events that will take place when He returns. It is sometimes difficult to determine which verses pertain to the destruction of Jerusalem and which pertain to the Second Coming. Luke more clearly distinguishes between these two events than do Matthew and Mark (Morris, *Luke* 295).

The wide variety of different interpretations of the Synoptic Apocalypse bears testimony to its difficulty. To begin with, Bock (II:1651-1652) explains that since the nineteenth century it has been popular to assert the Synoptic Apocalypse does not go back to Jesus Himself. Ellis (240) summarizes what is called the "little apocalypse" theory. This theory holds that the portion of the discourse that deals with the end of the world first circulated as a handbill sometime in the first century. This material was later included in the Synoptic Gospels and wrongly attributed to Jesus. Another theory popular in the nineteen century is that most of the content was the product of the Jewish-Christian church. It was not spoken by Jesus but was written by the early church and attributed to Him.

Briggs (133-135) presents a somewhat different view. He argues that these passages are very similar to Jewish apocalyptic literature. He asserts these passages may contain genuine words of Jesus, but the core behind them is a Jewish-Christian apocalyptic writing that was first used by Mark and then by Mathew and Luke. Briggs also gives a useful summary of how several nineteenth-century interpreters understood these important passages. Ellis (239-243) also presents a useful history of the interpretation of this passage.

Creed (252-254) offers a view somewhat similar to that held by Briggs. He suggests Luke's version of the Synoptic Apocalypse is largely drawn from Mark, but Mark's account has undergone significant modifications. Little or none of the material can be traced back to Jesus.

Such views are still common in certain scholarly circles. Liberal scholars often assert that little or none of the content of these passages may be traced back to Jesus. In their view, virtually the entirety of the Synoptic Apocalypse is a creation of the early church. For example, the scholars of The Jesus Seminar have printed almost the entirety of Luke 21 in black ink, which indicates that, in their opinion, Jesus spoke none of the actual words attributed to Him here (Funk and Hoover 382-383). In their view, the author of Luke has borrowed them from Mark 13. Gilmour ("Exegesis" 361) presents a similar view.

While such views are commonly held by scholars of a more liberal orientation, evangelical scholars consider these passages to reflect genuine words spoken by Jesus. A. Bruce (EGT I:49) argues that the author of this Gospel did not create new material but remained faithful to the information he had received. It is true that Luke chose what content to include and what to omit. As Bruce explains, the author strove to "combine accuracy, fidelity to fact, with practical utility."

Ellis (241-242) presents an interpretation that would be accepted by many conservative scholars today. He suggests the Eschatological Discourse reflects the teachings of Jesus and was not an invention of the early church. Jesus preached and taught about the end of the world; He also spoke about an interval of time that would transpire before the end comes. Ellis regards this passage as a collection of the Lord's sayings and not as a single sermon.

The fact that most conservative commentators accept the Synoptic Apocalypse as presenting genuine words of Jesus does not mean they agree on its interpretation. Evangelical scholarship presents a variety of different interpretations. Some scholars take most if not all of the passage as relating to the end of time while others understand most of the content as describing the destruction of Jerusalem.

Martin (257) presents an interpretation that is commonly held by those of a dispensational persuasion. Martin suggests that Jesus, in His response to the disciples' questions, spoke of two things that would begin to occur before the destruction of the temple and the city in A.D. 70. First, He warned the disciples that others would come claiming to be the Messiah. Second, Jesus spoke to them about coming wars. Jesus also warned the disciples about coming earthquakes, which would cause famines and pestilences. According to Martin (257), these events do not fit into the time period between the end of Jesus' earthly life and the destruction of Jerusalem. They belong to the period of the Great Tribulation, which will precede the return of the Lord. This author also discusses the issue of persecution. In his view, Jesus' words concerning tribulation apply both to the period before the destruction of Jerusalem and to the time of the Great Tribulation.

Chafer (118-119) offers another interpretation that is popular. He assumes the Olivet Discourse reflects true teaching of Jesus that was delivered shortly before His crucifixion. He considers most of Luke 21 to be a description of events that will take place during a future Tribulation Period. In his view, only Luke 21:20-24 describes the fall of the city of Jerusalem to the Romans in the summer of A.D. 70. He considers the rest of the passage to refer to the end times.

Matthew 24:16-20 is very similar in content to Luke 21:20-24, but Chafer finds enough difference between the two passages to distinguish between them. He considers the passage in Matthew to be a description of events that will take place during a future Tribulation Period rather than a description of the destruction of the city of Jerusalem by the Romans in A.D. 70. Pentecost (232-235) presents a similar position. In summary, the position taken by Chafer and Pentecost is that Luke 21:20-24 describes the destruction and fall of Jerusalem while the rest of the Olivet Discourse describes events that will take place at the end of time during the Tribulation Period.

N. T. Wright, an important but controversial N. T. scholar, takes a very different approach. He considers all of Luke 21 to be a description of the destruction and fall of Jerusalem in A.D. 70; none of it pertains to the end of time. Wright (348-360) also argues that the language of Luke 21 is largely drawn from O. T. prophecies of the destruction of Babylon. According to Wright, Luke has borrowed a considerable portion of the language of chapter 21 from Mark 13. He (359) explains, "Luke's reading of Mark is quite clear: all this language refers to the fall of Jerusalem."

Geldenhuys (523) presents a mediating position; he offers an interpretation widely held by conservative scholars. He posits that some portions of this chapter refer primarily to the destruction of Jerusalem while other portions refer to the end time. He suggests that verses 5-24 (with the exception of verses 8-9) deal primarily with the destruction of Jerusalem, while they may in a secondary sense deal with the end time. Geldenhuys opines that verses 25-28 refer to the final judgment that will accompany the Second Coming. He considers verses 29-33 to be a description of the signs the disciples should look for in anticipation of the destruction of Jerusalem. He views verses 34-36 as a series of warnings to the disciples and to all the church concerning events "which are to take place at a day and hour known to none save God the Father." Similar positions are found in the writings of Summers (*Luke* 252-267), Barclay (256-261), Ellis (243-247), and Jeffrey (242-251).

5 And as some spake of the temple, how it was adorned with goodly stones and gifts, he said,
6 *As for* these things which ye behold, the days will come, in the which there shall not be left one stone upon another, that shall not be thrown down.

Luke does not identify those who spoke to Jesus concerning the Temple. During the final days of Jesus' earthly ministry, it was a large and impressive edifice. For the Jewish people, it was a symbol of their relationship with God. Nolland (III:987) explains that the grandeur of this building could easily lull the people into thinking all was well between God and His world. Jesus, however, understood the impressiveness of the Temple was no guarantee that God was pleased with the way His people were serving Him. There were serious problems, which Jesus had repeatedly addressed during His earthly ministry, but the Jewish leadership always turned a deaf ear to His warnings. Jesus told His disciples the Temple would be totally destroyed. The phrase "there shall not be left one stone upon another" is a traditional way of describing such a total destruction. This destruction will symbolize the old system of worship based on the sacrifice of animals in the Temple precincts will have become obsolete. Christ has come as the Messiah to inaugurate a new system of worship, but the leaders of the Jewish community have consistently refused to heed Him.

The Temple was first constructed by Solomon on the Temple Mount about 965 B.C. (Geldenhuys 524). The first Temple was destroyed by the Babylonians about 586 B.C. The Temple was rebuilt after the Babylonian

Exile but on a much more modest scale. In the hope of gaining favor with the Jews over whom he ruled, King Herod began a large building program to expand and beautify the Temple. For this reason, the Temple that was standing in Jesus' day is often called "Herod's Temple" or the "Second Temple." Herod's renovation was still under way during the lifetime of Jesus and was not completed until several years after His crucifixion. In fact, the Temple was only completed a few years before it was destroyed by the Roman army in A.D. 70. There has been no Temple in Jerusalem since that time.

During the life of Jesus, the Temple was a large and impressive structure. For a description of the grandeur and elegance of the Temple see Josephus (*Antiquities of the Jews* book 15, chapter 11; *Wars of the Jews* book 5, chapter 5). This impressive structure was one of the seven wonders of the ancient world. Jeffrey (242-243) provides a good description of the opulence of the temple, drawn from the writings of ancient historians. Hendriksen (*Luke* 922-927) provides an excellent overview of the appearance of the temple as it existed in Jesus' day. Ellis (243) gives a good, brief summary of the design and construction of the temple.

The "gifts" (v. 5) probably refers to the elaborate decorations that had been donated by wealthy individuals or families. Lenski (1009-1010) and Jeffrey (242-243) both suggest Luke was probably referring to an elaborate vine made of gold that adorned the entrance to the temple. The branches of this vine were as tall as a man.

Most conservative commentators find the fulfillment of these verses in the destruction of Jerusalem by the Romans in A.D. 70. For a description of the terrible events that accompanied the siege and destruction, see Josephus (*Wars of the Jews*, Book 5, chapters 1-13). Hendriksen (*Luke* 927) explains the city was captured by a Roman army under the leadership of Titus, the son of Emperor Vespasian. It is possible as many as one million people perished. According to Josephus, conditions became so desperate during the siege parents even cooked and ate their own children (Jeffrey 244).

As Summers (*Luke* 255) points out, the fact that Jesus describes the fall of Jerusalem has led some interpreters to conclude these words were not spoken by Jesus, but were written after the fall of the city. Summers argues that such an interpretation is unnecessary. As the Son of God, Jesus had foresight into the future. Also, the city of Jerusalem had been besieged on previous occasions. The description given by Jesus was little different from what had happened to Jerusalem and other cities besieged in the ancient world. Summers concludes there is no reason to reject Jesus' teachings concerning the fall of the city.

7 And they asked him, saying, Master, but when shall these things be? and what sign *will there be* when these things shall come to pass?
8 And he said, Take heed that ye be not deceived: for many shall come in my name, saying, I am *Christ*; and the time draweth near: go ye not therefore after them.
9 But when ye shall hear of wars and commotions, be not terrified: for these things must first come to pass; but the end *is* not by and by.

The disciples are no doubt taken aback by the words Jesus has spoken to them. They respond by asking Him when these stupendous events will take place. Geldenhuys (525) suggests they might have thought the destruction of their Temple would lead to the construction of an even more glorious messianic Temple. It is likely the disciples thought the construction of this messianic temple would occur when the Messiah came to establish His kingdom.

Interestingly, Jesus makes no attempt to answer the first question. He does not offer the disciples any timetable of future events (Bock, *Jesus* 339). He does, however, respond to the second question by warning the disciples that difficult days lie ahead for them.

In verse 8, Jesus warns His disciples not to be led astray by those who falsely claim to be the Messiah. "Christ" (Greek *christos*) means anointed one, a translation of the Hebrew word for the Messiah. As mentioned previously, the Jews of the first century held different concepts of the Messiah, but many of these concepts were quite militaristic. They expected the Messiah to raise an army, free the Jews from Roman rule, and restore Israel's independence. Hendriksen (*Luke* 929) explains that when Jesus spoke these words the Roman Empire had enjoyed an extended period of peace and prosperity. About four decades after the earthly ministry of Jesus came to an end, the empire experienced a series of violent revolts and insurrections. The situation would become so difficult the people would look for messiahs who would come and resolve this difficult situation. Hendriksen also explains that such difficult days did not end with the fall of Jerusalem. The words of verse 10, "nation shall rise against nation, and kingdom against kingdom" have been fulfilled many times in history.

Ellis (242) notes that within twenty years after the death, burial, and resurrection of Jesus, the church was facing the problem of false teachings concerning the end times. The false teachers taught that Jesus had already returned secretly and the end of the world was imminent. When Jesus warned His disciples not to be carried away by those claiming to be the Messiah, He anticipated such false teachings.

In verse 9, "by and by" (Greek *euthus*) usually means "immediately." The idea is that the wars and insurrections do not indicate the end is about to occur. As Ellis (242) explains, these events do not mean the end of the world is about to happen. They are more a sign of the persecution of the church than of the end of the world. Luke anticipates there will be some interval of time between the fall of Jerusalem and the Second Coming, but he makes no effort to define the length of this interval. Barrett (*Luke* 66) notes it must be long enough to allow the church to complete the program outlined in Acts 1:7-8. The disciples and their followers must be prepared to endure times of suffering and persecution in the service of Christ.

According to many interpreters, the destruction of Jerusalem and the Second Coming are intertwined in this chapter. Moo (192) explains the nature of the relationship between these two key events: "Probably, then, Jesus 'telescopes' A. D. 70 and the end of the age in a manner reminiscent of the prophets, who frequently looked at the end of the age through more immediate historical events." Bock (*Jesus* 339) offers a somewhat similar explanation. In his view, these verses contain a considerable amount of typology in the sense that the destruction of Jerusalem in A. D. 70 becomes something of a type or pattern of the events that will come later. He notes the early churches did not view the destruction of the Temple as the end. They viewed it as God's judgment upon Israel, but not as the end. For an insightful analysis of the Olivet Discourse see Hoekema (148-149).

Many commentators understand verses 8-9 to refer primarily to the return of Christ but perhaps secondarily to the destruction of Jerusalem. Stein (*Luke* 511) suggests that in this context the term "the end" refers to the fall of Jerusalem. Other commentators (like Green, *Luke* 735) do not define "the end" but assume that it refers to the end of the world.

10 Then said he unto them, Nation shall rise against nation, and kingdom against kingdom:
11 And great earthquakes shall be in divers places, and famines, and pestilences; and fearful sights and great signs shall there be from heaven.
12 But before all these, they shall lay hands on you, and persecute *you*, delivering *you* up to the synagogues, and into prisons, being brought before kings and rulers for my name's sake.
13 And it shall turn to you for a testimony.

Jesus continues to develop the theme of persecution and suffering He has previously introduced; His goal is to prepare His disciples for the difficult days that lie ahead. He mentions both suffering that results from wars and suffering that results from natural disasters such as famines, earthquakes, and pestilences. The clause "signs shall there be from heaven" indicates these events are not simply natural occurrences. They reflect the hand of God as He brings judgment upon a rebellious world. Summers (*Worthy* 190) points out three major forces contributed to the downfall of the Roman Empire: natural disasters, internal decay, and external invasion. These forces are clearly reflected in this passage. According to Bock (*Jesus* 340), the signs described in these verses indicate God's divine plan is unfolding, but they do not indicate the end is about to occur.

The followers of Christ will not only suffer from these natural and political forces that affect many peoples and nations. They will also suffer persecution because of their identification with Him. They will be brought before kings and other rulers and synagogues; they will be imprisoned for their faith. This persecution will not, however, mean the end of the Christian faith. Instead, these times of persecution will give the disciples an opportunity to testify to their faith in Christ (Summers, *Luke* 257). Hendriksen (*Luke* 931) notes that the words of this passage will be fulfilled on many occasions as the disciples bear witness to Christ before kings, rulers, and others.

14 Settle *it* therefore in your hearts, not to meditate before what ye shall answer:
15 For I will give you a mouth and wisdom, which all your adversaries shall not be able to gainsay nor resist.

16 And ye shall be betrayed both by parents, and brethren, and kinsfolks, and friends; and *some* of you shall they cause to be put to death.
17 And ye shall be hated of all *men* for my name's sake.
18 But there shall not an hair of your head perish.
19 In your patience possess ye your souls.

Jesus gives the disciples additional warning about the severity of the persecution they will endure. He also gives them assurance that God will be with them in those difficult times. Verses 14-15 are designed to remind the disciples they will not be alone when the times of persecution come. They may not have the time or opportunity to prepare an adequate defense before they are called before kings or magistrates. Jesus tells them not to worry because He will be with them and will give them a defense, which their opponents will not be able to defeat. Creed (255-56) notes that "meditate before" (Greek *promeleta*) is the proper term to describe preparing a speech. The idea is that God will give them the ability to respond to the charges brought against them without elaborate preparation. It should be noted that Jesus is not discussing sermons, lectures, and other oral or written presentations that require advance preparation (Morris, *Luke* 297). He envisions the situation of disciples who are called before kings and judges in times of persecution when there is little or no opportunity for advance preparation (Bock II:1671).

In verses 16-17, Jesus returns to the theme of persecution. He warns the disciples they will not only suffer persecution from governmental authorities or from religious leaders. The situation will become so dire they will be persecuted even by their own friends and family members. Such treatment will be extremely personal and painful. Green (*Luke* 736) points out that such family relationships would ordinarily call for mutual respect and reciprocity, but the coming of the Kingdom of God renders such normal relationships obsolete. In Luke 12:53, Jesus warned His disciples that family members would be divided against each other. Here He returns to the same theme. In a world that gave much emphasis to family solidarity and cooperation, these words must have been very painful for the disciples. Jesus is confronting the sad reality that the demands of the Kingdom of God are so exclusive families are often divided. This division may grow so severe some members of the family will support the execution of other members. Jesus is again confronting His disciples with the reality of what it means to be a disciple.

Verses 18-19 sound a note of encouragement in an otherwise difficult passage. In verse 15, Jesus promised His disciples God would be with them in times of persecution and would give them the words to speak when challenged by their adversaries. Now He makes additional promises to His disciples, but, as Martin (257) explains, these verses are subject to different interpretations. Bonnet and Schroeder (664) note, "There shall not a hair of your head perish" is a popular proverb that normally means nothing bad will happen to a person. Green (*Luke* 737) takes it to mean that nothing will happen to the disciple outside the will of God and notes the promise is similar to "Even the very hairs of your head are all numbered" (Lk. 12:7). The idea is that nothing will happen to them without God's knowledge. No matter what happens to them, God will be with them. Lenski (1017) also defends this view.

A second common interpretation is that no persecution on the earth can affect the believer's eternal salvation. Bonnet and Schroeder (664) prefer this interpretation. Barclay (260) endorses it in these moving words: "The man who walks with Christ may lose his life but he can never lose his soul." Creed (256) and Bock (*Jesus* 342) agree.

In verse 19, the exhortation is "patience" (Greek *hupomonē*), which means perseverance or endurance, and holding out bravely under adverse circumstances (Lenski 1018). As Hendriksen (*Luke* 933) notes, the idea is the disciples should hold firm in their faith no matter how severe the persecution may become. "Souls" (Greek *psychē*) sometimes identifies the immaterial part of a human being, the "soul" or "spirit," and sometimes the entire person or self. Here the idea seems to be the disciples, by their faithful endurance in times of trial, will preserve their souls in the sense their relationship with God will remain secure even if they suffer physical death. Martin (257) explains by doing this they will show themselves to be members of the believing community in contrast to those who deny the faith in times of trial. Lenski (1018) takes a similar position.

There is a textual variant of some significance in verse 19, involving the word "possess." Most of the early manuscripts have the verb (Greek *ketaomai*) that means "to gain" while a few have the verb (Greek *sōzō*) that means "to save." There is little theological difference between "gaining" ones' soul and "saving" it.

20 And when ye shall see Jerusalem compassed with armies, then know that the desolation thereof is nigh.
21 Then let them which are in Judaea flee to the mountains; and let them which are in the midst of it depart out; and let not them that are in the countries enter thereinto.
22 For these be the days of vengeance, that all things which are written may be fulfilled.
23 But woe unto them that are with child, and to them that give suck, in those days! for there shall be great distress in the land, and wrath upon this people.

"When ye shall see Jerusalem compassed with armies" is clearly a reference to the siege prior to the future fall of the city in the summer of A.D. 70, which would result in the destruction of the Temple. Geldenhuys (527-535) explains that a long history of conflict between the Jews in Palestine and the Romans preceded the fall of the city. The actual war for Jewish independence began in A.D. 66 and ended with the destruction of the city in A.D. 70. As the Roman armies marched across the country, thousands fled into the city of Jerusalem as a place of refuge. The city simply did not have the resources to sustain this large population during the siege. After a siege of about five months, the Roman army under Titus captured and destroyed the city; thousands of Jews were killed or taken prisoner. The early church historian Eusebius (111) notes there were "thousands and thousands of men of every age who together with women and children perished by the sword, by starvation, and by countless other forms of death." For a good explanation of these events see Geldenhuys (535). No Jews were allowed to live in the city for many years after its fall.

The Christians took seriously Jesus' instructions to flee from the city. Eusebius (111-112) notes that the Christians inside the city, heeding the words of Jesus, left before it was fully encircled and fled to the city of Pella.

In verse 20, Luke says, "when ye shall see Jerusalem compassed with armies," while the parallel passage in Mark 13:14 uses the phrase "when ye shall see the abomination of desolation, spoken of by Daniel the prophet." The phrase "abomination of desolation" is also found in Matthew 24:15. Scholars have offered different explanations for this significant difference between Luke and the other two Synoptic Gospels. Geldenhuys (532) notes the term "abomination of desolation" is a Jewish term found in Daniel 9:27 and 12:11. Bock (*Jesus* 342) asserts that the phrase "abomination of desolation" refers to the type of desolation of the Temple that was performed by Antiochus Epiphanes during the inter-biblical period. Hoekema (155) notes that Antiochus profaned the Temple in Jerusalem by dedicating it to the Greek god Zeus and by using it to offer pagan sacrifices, including swine.

A number of scholars have examined this significant difference between Luke's wording and that found in Matthew and Mark, and they have come to differing conclusions. Marshall (*Gospel* 771) offers a useful summary of the major positions. Some scholars argue the difference is due to the fact that Luke has made use of a source different from that used by Matthew and Mark. Another popular theory is Luke has used the wording "when ye shall see Jerusalem compassed with armies" in order to make the passage more understandable to Gentile readers. According to this interpretation, it is doubtful the Gentile Christians who were the original recipients of this Gospel would have understood the reference to Jewish history during the inter-biblical period. The view that Luke's wording is designed to meet the needs of Gentile readers is defended by Geldenhuys (532) and Ellis (244). While it is certainly possible Luke used a source different from that used by Matthew and Mark, the more likely explanation is Luke is using this expression so his Gentile readers will correctly understand the message. Marshall (*Gospel* 771) notes the language used in this passage by all of the Synoptic writers is heavily influenced by the O. T. Luke's description of these events is not sufficiently detailed to prove his account was written after the fall of the city.

Marshall (*Gospel* 772) and Lenski (1018-1019) discuss the meaning of the word translated "armies" (Greek *stratopedon*), which was originally used to describe an encampment; it later came to be used to describe a legion or a body of soldiers. The idea here is the Roman army was preparing for a long siege by establishing a series of camps around the city of Jerusalem.

Pikaza (593), in his analysis of the parallel passage in Mark, offers an insightful analysis of the theological significance of the destruction of the Temple. He argues it is, first, a judgment on the nation of Israel for its refusal to accept Jesus as its Messiah. Second, it is also an important step in

God's plan to save all who will come to Him. The destruction of the old Temple indicates Christ has come to offer a salvation banquet to the poor of the world. This dramatic change must have come as a great shock to those Jewish nationalists who saw the Temple as the epitome of God's work in the world.

Verse 23 gives a brief summary of the terrible conditions that will exist in the land of Palestine during these difficult days. While it is possible this verse describes the plight of the Christians who are fleeing from the city, it is more likely it refers to the situation of those Jews who are fleeing to, or are inside, the city during the siege. They will suffer terribly. The worst suffering will fall on the mothers who are nursing infants or caring for small children. The term "this people" probably describes the Jews who are greatly affected by the Roman invasion.

24 And they shall fall by the edge of the sword, and shall be led away captive into all nations: and Jerusalem shall be trodden down of the Gentiles, until the times of the Gentiles be fulfilled.

Jeffrey (245) presents a historical analysis of the words "until the times of the Gentiles be fulfilled," which occurs only in Luke. He explains that most Christian interpreters, in both ancient and modern times, have understood the "times of the Gentiles" to refer to the time period between the destruction of Jerusalem in A.D. 70 and the miraculous signs that will accompany the Second Coming. Lenski (1021) and Hendriksen (*Luke* 939) both accept this traditional interpretation. Ellis (245) suggests the term refers to the time when the Gentiles are in control of the city of Jerusalem, which may extend to the Second Coming.

Hendriksen (*Luke* 939) points out that some commentators believe "the times of the Gentiles" ended on May 14, 1948, when Israel became an independent state. According to Scofield (1106), the "times of the Gentiles" began with the captivity of Judah under Nebuchadnezzar described in 2 Chronicles 36:1-21 and continues down to the present day. Summers (*Luke* 259) takes a very different approach. He understands this phrase to refer to the brief period of time when the Roman army was actually destroying the city.

25 And there shall be signs in the sun, and in the moon, and in the stars; and upon the earth distress of nations, with perplexity; the sea and the waves roaring;
26 Men's hearts failing them for fear, and for looking after those things which are coming on the earth: for the powers of heaven shall be shaken.
27 And then shall they see the Son of man coming in a cloud with power and great glory.
28 And when these things begin to come to pass, then look up, and lift up your heads; for your redemption draweth nigh.

These verses are normally understood to refer to the Second Coming rather than to the destruction of Jerusalem (Marshall, *Gospel* 774). Plummer (483) observes that the terms and expressions used in these verses are similar to those found in several O. T. passages such as Isaiah 13:10, Ezekiel 32:7, and Joel 2:10. As Bock (*Jesus*

345) explains, this passage moves far beyond a conflict between the Jewish people and a pagan Roman Empire. The exact nature of the "signs" mentioned in this passage is not explained. Barrett (*Luke* 66) opines these signs are not designed to predict when the end will come to pass. They will occur during the interval between the destruction of Jerusalem and the Second Coming.

The idea is that when these signs occur all the world will be affected; they will be self-evident. No human interpretation or explanation will be necessary. When these dramatic changes take place in the physical universe, the return of Christ will not be far behind. Although Luke is not interested in precise chronology, the impression left by these verses is that these cosmic events will occur shortly before the Second Coming.

Such dramatic events will produce an immediate effect upon the people. They will be terrified, but their terror will not last for long. As Jesus explains, "Then shall they see the Son of man coming in a cloud with power and great glory." This promise must have been a great encouragement to Jesus' disciples. Jesus has warned them they will suffer greatly because of their allegiance to Him, but that suffering will not last forever. At the proper time, Christ will return in all His power and glory. In this context, the phrase "your redemption" refers to the final salvation of the followers of Jesus, which occurs at the time of His return to earth.

29 And he spake to them a parable; Behold the fig tree, and all the trees;
30 When they now shoot forth, ye see and know of your own selves that summer is now nigh at hand.
31 So likewise ye, when ye see these things come to pass, know ye that the kingdom of God is nigh at hand.
32 Verily I say unto you, This generation shall not pass away, till all be fulfilled.
33 Heaven and earth shall pass away: but my words shall not pass away.

Luke narrates the Parable of the Fig Tree that Jesus told His disciples during the final week of His life. As noted previously in this commentary, it is difficult to determine if all of these teachings were delivered on one occasion or if Luke has brought together teachings delivered on different days. This parable presents basically the same lesson taught in verses 25-28 (Marshall, *Gospel* 778). There are signs that will occur immediately before the return of Christ. When the disciples see these signs coming to pass, they can take heart because they will know the return of Christ is near.

Fig trees and other fruit trees were commonly grown in Palestine, and all the disciples would have been familiar with their cultivation. When the trees begin to bring forth their leaves and buds, it is apparent to all that the winter weather is over (Martin 257). Spring has arrived and summer is just around the corner. "These things" (v. 31) probably refer to the signs Jesus has mentioned in the immediately preceding verses. When these events begin to happen, the disciples can rest assured the Kingdom of God "is nigh at hand." The Kingdom of God is described by Luke both as a present reality and as a coming event. Here the idea is that the kingdom will reach its consummation in the Second Coming of Christ.

Verse 32 is one of the most difficult and controversial verses in this Gospel. Most of the controversy revolves around the interpretation of the words "this generation." Marshall (*Gospel* 780) explains that the word "generation" (Greek *genea*) is used in several ways. It may refer to people sharing a common ancestor. It may also refer to a group of people—even a particular group or set of people—living at the same time.

Ellis (246), Maddox (111-115), and Marshall (*Gospel* 780) provide summaries of the most common interpretations. This term may refer to Jesus' generation. Another view is that it refers to the generation living at the end time when the signs described in verses 25-26 actually come to pass. Another possibility is the term refers to Jews, either all believing Jews or all unbelieving Jews. Other interpreters understand it to mean all believers. Conzelmann (131) understands it to refer to humanity in general.

Lenski (1026) argues that "this generation" refers to unbelieving Jews. He suggests there have always been Jews like the Pharisees and Sadducees who rejected Jesus when He was here on earth. Jews, generally speaking, will continue to reject Jesus as the Messiah. Marshall (*Gospel* 780) notes the goal of the passage is not to limit or determine the time of the end, but to assure the disciples "the last events have begun and will be brought to a consummation."

Martin (257-258) argues that "this generation" refers to the generation living when the cosmological events described in verse 25 begin to take place. Plummer (485) presents an interpretation that is still held by some interpreters: namely, the term can refer only to the generation living at the time Jesus spoke these words. Plummer understands the prophecy to refer directly to the fall of Jerusalem, which he regards as a type of the end (see also Marshall, *Gospel* 780). Maddox (115) defends strongly the view that the term refers to those who were living at the time of Jesus. He argues that any other meaning is forced and unnatural.

Ellis (246-247) offers the interesting interpretation that in the Qumran literature the phrase "last generation" was used to describe several lifetimes, and "this generation" describes the generation living during the end times. In his view, this term includes all those who are living between the earthly ministry of Jesus and the Second Coming.

The view of Ellis has much to commend it. In His discussions of the end times, Jesus has consistently refused to establish a timetable for His return. The signs He has given are general in nature and point to the certainty of His return rather than to a specific time. Jesus understood there would be some interval of time between the teachings He gave in Jerusalem during the final week of His earthly life and the Second Coming. In this context, the term "this generation" seems to describe this interval, however long or short it may be.

If the term "this generation" is given its normal meaning of those who were living at the time of Jesus, the idea seems to be all of the signs that will precede Jesus' return will be fulfilled within that generation. The passage does not say Christ will return within the lifetime of that generation; it says only the signs will all be fulfilled.

34 And take heed to yourselves, lest at any time your hearts be overcharged with surfeiting, and

drunkenness, and cares of this life, and *so* that day come upon you unawares.
35 For as a snare shall it come on all them that dwell on the face of the whole earth.
36 Watch ye therefore, and pray always, that ye may be accounted worthy to escape all these things that shall come to pass, and to stand before the Son of man.

In these verses, Jesus offers some practical advice to help His disciples face the difficult days that lie ahead for them. "Heart" (Greek *kardia*) is used in different ways in the N. T., generally as a psychological term. It often describes the center of one's thought and intention, and that seems to be the use here. The point is the disciples should not be distracted from their mission by the temptations the world may offer them. Jesus then enumerates three specific temptations, which should not be understood as the only temptations the disciples may face. They are representative of the kind of temptations the disciples will face in coming days. As Plummer (486) points out, the disciples must always be vigilant.

The first temptation mentioned is "surfeiting" (Greek *kraipalē*), which may describe drunkenness but generally refers to the effects of intoxication or a hangover (Marshall *Gospel* 782). The second temptation is "drunkenness" (Greek *methē*). The third is the "cares of this life" (Greek *merimnais biōtikais*). This is a rather rare expression; another form of this expression occurs in 1 Corinthians 6:3-4. Plummer (486) discusses the history and derivation of these words. The point is that the disciples must not allow the concerns of daily life to distract them from their spiritual mission.

"That day" is obviously a reference to the return of Christ (Plummer 486). Jesus' followers must not become so involved in the affairs of this life they fail to make adequate preparation for Christ's return.

The "it" in verse 35 probably refers to "the cares of this life" mentioned in the previous verse. If disciples do not make adequate preparation, the return of Christ will take them by surprise in the same way an animal is suddenly caught in a snare (Martin 258). The last words of verse 35, significantly, explain that Jesus' instructions in this passage do not apply only to the disciples. The return of Christ will affect the entire world. All mankind will be required to stand before the Son of man in judgment, and they all need to make the proper provision while they have the opportunity to do so.

37 And in the day time he was teaching in the temple; and at night he went out, and abode in the mount that is called *the mount* of Olives.
38 And all the people came early in the morning to him in the temple, for to hear him.

These two verses provide Luke's summary of Jesus' activities during the last week. Plummer (488) suggests these verses, more narrowly, summarize Jesus' ministry on the day of the triumphal entry and the next two days. Jesus spent the daylight hours teaching in the Temple, probably in the outer courts. Luke does not describe those who came to hear His teaching, but they probably included a mixture of His followers and other interested people. During the nighttime hours, Jesus retired to the Mount of Olives where He rested and talked with His disciples. Verse 37 does not necessarily imply Jesus and His disciples slept out in the open, but that was a common practice during the Passover (Marshall, *Gospel* 784).

Verse 38 indicates Jesus' teaching had a considerable amount of popular appeal. "All the people" does not mean every single person in Jerusalem; the idea is His teachings were so popular that significant numbers of people from different groups and social classes came to hear Him teach. That they "came early in the morning" may imply the people were diligently seeking Jesus (Marshall, *Gospel* 784; Lenski 1032). It was, however, a common practice to teach and transact business during the morning hours to take advantage of the cooler temperatures.

In verse 36, Jesus offers instructions on how to avoid the temptations mentioned in verse 34. He tells His disciples to "watch" and "pray." The first exhorts the disciples to maintain an attitude of spiritual wakefulness at all times (Marshall, *Gospel* 783). They must not allow themselves to be lulled into an attitude of spiritual complacency. The second instruction, to pray, is a common theme in Luke. All of the Gospel writers stress the importance of prayer, but Luke gives more emphasis to it than the others do. If the disciples are to be prepared to stand before Christ on the Day of Judgment, they must make the proper preparation in advance. Watchfulness and prayer are important aspects of that preparation.

Summary (21:5-38)

This chapter outlines the teaching Jesus gave to His disciples during the final week of His earthly life. It is likely some of these teachings were given to the disciples in private, while others were given in a more public setting. It is possible all of these teachings were given in one setting, but it is more likely Luke has given a summary of Jesus' teachings during the week. While this passage does deal with the future, Jesus' primary purpose is not to give a detailed account of upcoming events. His goal is to prepare the disciples for the difficult days that lie ahead. After His death, burial, and resurrection, the disciples will almost immediately be called upon to assume leadership positions in the Christian movement. If they are to be successful in this endeavor, they need to have an understanding of what they can expect.

The passage begins with a casual remark made by some of Jesus' disciples. They admired the beauty of the Temple and remarked about the precious stones and beautiful decorations that adorned the building. These remarks clearly reflect the pride the Jews of Jesus' day took in their Temple. It was one of the wonders of the world.

Jesus responds to their innocent remarks in a most surprising fashion. Rather than endorsing the favorable comments of His disciples, Jesus tells them frankly that this beautiful Temple will be destroyed at some time in the future. After some contemplation, the disciples—probably in a more private setting—asked Jesus for more explanation.

In particular, they ask two questions. They ask when this destruction will occur and what signs would precede this coming destruction. In light of the circumstances, these are reasonable questions; they indicate the disciples are taking Jesus' teaching seriously.

In Luke's account, Jesus makes no response to the first question; He offers them no timetable. Jesus does respond to the second question by describing a series of signs that do not predict the precise time of the coming destruction. However, what He tells them does instruct the disciples concerning the difficult days that lie ahead for them. While the theme of suffering is important in this passage, the focus is clearly on the return of Christ rather than on the suffering of the disciples.

The first sign is the arrival of false christs. These false teachers will claim to be the true fulfillment of the O. T. messianic prophecies, but they will not speak the truth. The fact is Jesus is the Messiah, the fulfillment of the O. T. promises. The disciples are not to be carried away by such false teachings.

The second sign deals with wars and conflicts. Jesus tells His disciples these events must come to pass, but they do not indicate the time of destruction has yet arrived. At this point in the story, it becomes evident Jesus is moving beyond the destruction of the Temple in Jerusalem. He talks about nation rising against nation and kingdom against kingdom. As Hoekema (149) notes, this passage does not deal exclusively with the destruction of Jerusalem by the Romans. It also deals with the end of the world, and these two themes are intertwined.

The third sign concerns natural disasters. Jesus predicts the world will have to endure earthquakes, famines, and plagues. There will be "fearful sights and great signs" from Heaven.

The fourth sign is persecution. The disciples will be brought before kings and judges; they will have to suffer severe trials. They will even be betrayed by friends and relatives; some will be put to death. These severe trials, however, will give them opportunities to give testimony to the love of Jesus. Jesus assures His followers they will not go through these hours of trial alone; God will be with them and give them the words to say. These severe trials may bring about the death of the body, but the persecutors cannot kill the soul that belongs to God.

Beginning in verse 20, Jesus continues to develop the theme of suffering, but from a different perspective. The focus is no longer on the disciples but on those who will endure the war with Rome that will last from A.D. 66-70. Based on the available evidence from church history, it is likely the followers of Jesus fled from Jerusalem as the siege was beginning. The suffering described in these verses relates to the thousands of Jews who fled *into* the city for refuge and suffered terribly during the siege and the fall of the city. Thousands were killed; others were sold into slavery.

Verses 25-28 deal more with the Second Coming and the end of the world than with the fall of Jerusalem. Signs in the heavens will cause great fear to fall upon all mankind; then they will see the Son of man coming in power and great glory. When these events begin to occur, the followers of Jesus are told to "look up and lift up your heads" because they know the return of Christ is near and they will dwell with Him forever.

Verses 29-38 form the conclusion to the Olivet Discourse as it is given in Luke. The Parable of the Fig Tree is designed to remind the disciples they must be eternally vigilant. The signs listed in verse 25 and elsewhere in this chapter do not enable the disciples to predict the time of Christ's return, but they point to the certainty of it. Just as the budding of the trees is a sign that spring has arrived and summer is on its way, the signs given in this chapter emphasize the certainty of Christ's return. The fact that they are Christ's disciples does not mean they are automatically prepared for the Second Coming. They must prepare themselves by spiritual vigilance and prayer; they must also avoid the temptation to be caught up in worldly affairs and pleasures.

The last two verses indicate the message of Jesus was well received by the people of Jerusalem and by those who had come to celebrate the Passover. Luke does not specifically identify those who came to hear Jesus' teaching, but they probably included His followers as well as many of the common people of the land. It is doubtful that many of the leaders came to hear Jesus; their hostility toward Him was undiminished. Perhaps some of the leaders came in search of information they could use against Him.

Application: Teaching and Preaching the Passage

There are many important themes in this chapter that preachers and teachers should address. It is obvious the future is one of these important themes. Jesus gives a broad outline of what His disciples may expect in the future. These verses predict two upcoming events, the fall of Jerusalem and the return of Christ. Luke distinguishes between these two events more clearly than Matthew or Mark, but they are still intertwined. Sometimes, it is difficult to determine the event with which a particular verse is dealing. The fall of Jerusalem becomes something of a sign of the Second Coming. Luke anticipates some interval of time between these two events, but he makes no effort to define the length of that interval.

Suffering is another major theme of this passage. One of Jesus' major goals in the Olivet Discourse is to prepare His followers for the difficult days that lie ahead. They will be persecuted and betrayed even by their own families and friends. Jesus does not want His disciples to be taken by surprise. Preparation will not alleviate the suffering, but it will help the disciples remain faithful in the difficult times.

Perseverance is closely related to suffering; it is also one of the main themes of this passage. In verses 10-28, Luke outlines some of the trials and sufferings Jesus' disciples will be forced to endure. Jesus always warned His disciples about the difficulties they would face as they devoted their lives to service in the Kingdom of God, but in this passage those warnings become especially poignant. Jesus' goal is to prepare them and inform them about some of the dangers they will face. They must be ready to persevere in the face of terrible trials.

In particular, Jesus outlines four specific areas in which they must be prepared to persevere. First, they must persevere in the face of false teachings (v. 8). The most likely explanation of this warning is that these false prophets would claim Jesus was not the true Messiah because He had not defeated the Romans and established His kingdom on earth. Jesus warns His followers not to be carried away by such false teachings. Jesus was the true Messiah and the fulfillment of the O. T. expectations.

Second, they must persevere in the face of war and conflict (v. 9). The ancient world was a world that was often filled with wars and armed conflicts; this was especially true of the Roman Empire in the first century. Serious conflicts may often lead people to forget about the goodness and mercy of God. They may even cause people to turn their backs on God entirely. The disciples must understand the significance of what is going on around them and maintain their faith in God, even in the most adverse of circumstances.

Third, Jesus' disciples must persevere in the face of natural disasters (v. 11). This verse describes events that are totally beyond human control; they must be considered acts of God. Earthquakes, famines, and plagues were frequent occurrences in the ancient world, and they caused untold suffering. Such events could easily cause men and women to lose their faith in God. The disciples must resist such temptations; they must persevere in spite of events they cannot understand or explain.

Fourth, they must persevere in the face of persecution (v. 12). This persecution would be a direct consequence of the disciples' commitment to Christ, and it would tempt them to deny their allegiance to Him. This is a temptation they must resist; they must remain faithful to Jesus in spite of active persecution from both Jewish and Roman authorities.

The difficulties modern believers encounter are not the same as those faced by the early followers of Jesus, but they are just as real. It is never easy to be a sincere follower of Christ. There will always be opposition of some kind, and this opposition may even develop into active persecution. Believers will always face tragedies and natural disasters they cannot explain.

Every generation of believers must learn the lessons of perseverance. Pastors and other Christian leaders not only need to teach perseverance, they need to demonstrate it in their daily lives. Verse 36 mentions two specific activities that can help believers persevere through difficult times; they are spiritual awareness and prayer. These two resources are just as important today as they were when Jesus spoke these words many centuries ago.

C. Betrayal and the Last Supper (22:1-53)

The last natural division of Luke's Gospel begins here; it moves rapidly to the end of Jesus' earthly ministry. This final division includes chapters 22—24, which deal with the passion, the resurrection, and the ascension. These chapters have much in common with the other Gospels, especially Mark, but Luke has added material from other sources in several places. For an analysis of the passages unique to Luke, see Stein (*Luke* 533-534).

Luke 22:1-53 may be divided into four sections: (1) verses 1-6, the plot to betray Jesus; (2) verses 7-23, the last supper; (3) verses 24-38, various teachings; and (4) verses 39-53, Jesus' agony in the garden and arrest. In this chapter, Jesus confronts the greatest crisis of His earthly ministry. He must deal with His own emotions, the final preparation of the disciples for their future ministry, His arrest, the hostility of the Jewish leaders, and the denials of Peter. This is certainly a crucial chapter in Luke's account of the life and ministry of Christ.

1 Now the feast of unleavened bread drew nigh, which is called the Passover.
2 And the chief priests and scribes sought how they might kill him; for they feared the people.
3 Then entered Satan into Judas surnamed Iscariot, being of the number of the twelve.
4 And he went his way, and communed with the chief priests and captains, how he might betray him unto them.
5 And they were glad, and covenanted to give him money.
6 And he promised, and sought opportunity to betray him unto them in the absence of the multitude.

Verse 1 mentions two events, the Feast of Unleavened Bread and the Passover, which were closely connected in Judaism. The Feast of Unleavened Bread was celebrated during a seven-day period from the fifteenth through the twenty-first days in the month of Nisan. Nisan was the first month of the Hebrew calendar; it began about the middle of our March. By the first century, it was closely connected with the Passover, which was celebrated on Nisan 14-15 (Marshall, *Gospel* 786-787; Stein, *Luke* 119, 535; Barclay, 262-263). It is likely Luke uses "Passover" (v. 1) to include both feasts (Plummer 490; Geldenhuys 548; Summers, *Luke* 267; Jeremias, TDNT V:897). For a summary of the feasts and fasts that were observed by the Jews both before and after the Exile see Isaacs (ISBE 11:1103-1104).

The "chief priests and scribes" were the members of the Sanhedrin, the leaders of the Jewish community. Matthew 26:3-5 notes the Jewish leaders had a secret meeting in the palace of Caiaphas, the high priest, to develop a plan to kill Jesus. The word "how" is the key term in verse 2. By this time, the Jewish leaders had already decided to assassinate Jesus; the difficulty was finding a way to do it without arousing the anger of the crowds, who had great respect for Him (Summers, *Luke* 267). There were numerous pilgrims in Jerusalem to celebrate the Passover, and many of them, especially those from Galilee, would have been sympathetic to Jesus.

The verb "sought" (Greek imperfect tense) indicates an action in past time that was continuous, habitual, or repeated. They kept searching for some way to eliminate Jesus without arousing the anger of the people. Mark 14:2 explains they had decided not to take Him on a feast day; apparently they planned to wait until the Passover was over, and the crowds had gone home, to arrest Jesus.

In verses 3-6, the Jewish leaders receive a most pleasant surprise. One of Jesus' own disciples, Judas Iscariot, offers to betray Him and help arrest Him in secret. Since Judas knows Jesus well, he can identify Him even in the dark or in the midst of a group of people. The leaders certainly do not want to run the risk of allowing Jesus to escape while they are arresting the wrong man. In verse 4, "betray" (Greek *paradidōmi*) means "hand over." In this context, the idea is Judas will identify Jesus so the officers can arrest Him. "Covenanted" (v. 5) indicates the Jewish leaders had reached an agreement with Judas. In return for a sum of money, Judas would facilitate Jesus' arrest at a place and time when it could be done quietly. Luke does not mention the amount of money, but Matthew 26:15 notes Judas agreed to betray Jesus in return for thirty pieces of silver.

The only explanation Luke offers for Judas' willingness to betray Jesus is that Satan has entered into him. Lenski (1034) explains that, in this context, "Satan" refers, specifically, to the one who is the head of the "infernal kingdom." He is the archenemy of God. Summers (*Luke* 268) notes Satan's entering Judas does not indicate a case of demon possession. Rather, Judas allowed Satan to take control of him and use him as his instrument in betraying Jesus. Plummer (490) notes Judas did not flee from Satan; he opened his heart and allowed Satan to enter his life. Hendriksen (*Luke* 955) explaines Satan's influence does not absolve Judas of guilt. He could have resisted Satan's temptation, but he did not do so. Lenski (1034) suggests Satan's entrance into Judas' life was made gradually or in stages. Little by little, Satan planted thoughts in his mind about betraying Jesus.

It is impossible to determine all the factors that might have contributed to Judas' betrayal of Jesus (Geldenhuys 548-549). Probably greed was a contributing factor. Another possible factor is that Judas was disappointed because Jesus made no attempt to become a political Messiah. Like many Jews of his day, Judas looked forward to the coming of the Messiah who would liberate the Jewish people from Roman rule. For an insightful analysis of the various factors that might have motivated Judas to betray Jesus see Caird (235).

In verse 4, Luke explains that Judas met with the "chief priests" and "captains." The "chief priests" were the leaders of the Sanhedrin. The "captains" (Greek *stratēgoi*) were a corps of Levites who stood guard around the Temple (Plummer 491); Bonnet and Schroeder (670) and Lenski (1034) suggest these were the commanders of the Temple guards. It is likely the members of the Temple guard were the soldiers who would actually arrest Jesus. According to verse 4, Judas meets with them, probably to work out the details of the arrest and advise them of Jesus' movements. Verse 6 continues the thought developed in verse 4. Judas agrees to work with them, and he promises to look for an opportunity to betray Jesus in private and away from the multitudes.

7 Then came the day of unleavened bread, when the passover must be killed.

8 And he sent Peter and John, saying, Go and prepare us the passover, that we may eat.

9 And they said unto him, Where wilt thou that we prepare?

10 And he said unto them, Behold, when ye are entered into the city, there shall a man meet you, bearing a pitcher of water; follow him into the house where he entereth in.

11 And ye shall say unto the goodman of the house, The Master saith unto thee, Where is the guestchamber, where I shall eat the passover with my disciples?

12 And he shall shew you a large upper room furnished: there make ready.
13 And they went, and found as he had said unto them: and they made ready the passover.
14 And when the hour was come, he sat down, and the twelve apostles with him.

Technically, the Passover was celebrated on the day before the beginning of the Feast of Unleavened Bread. The time had come for the Passover lamb to be sacrificed, probably on Thursday, the fourteenth of Nisan, (Hendriksen, *Luke* 953, 956). In verse 7, the "Passover" refers to the Passover lamb.

Geldenhuys (551) describes the procedures that would have been followed. All leaven would first be removed from the house. On the afternoon of the fourteenth of Nisan, probably between 2:30 and 6:00 p.m., the lambs would have been taken to the Temple to be ritually slain in the presence of the priests and made ready for the Passover. The people would then go to the place where they intended to celebrate the Passover, to cook the lamb.

The Jewish custom required the Passover be celebrated within the walls of the city of Jerusalem (Stein, *Luke* 538), and Jesus had no place inside the city where He and His disciples could celebrate together. Jesus sent two of His most trusted disciples, Peter and John, into the city to find a suitable location. He told them as they were entering the city, they would encounter a man carrying a pitcher of water. They were to follow him to the house where Jesus and His disciples would celebrate the Passover. Most commentators are of the opinion Jesus had previously worked out these arrangements with the owner of the house (Geldenhuys 552; Stein, *Luke* 538). Hendriksen (*Luke* 957) suggests the owner was possibly a disciple of Jesus.

Stein (*Luke* 538) explains that at that time it would have been most unusual to see a man carrying a jar of water since that task was normally done by women. Hendriksen (*Luke* 957) posits that men usually carried water in a skin while women carried it in a jar or pitcher. Either way, it would have been easy for Peter and John to identify the man. Luke does not identify the man carrying the pitcher of water. It is possible he is the owner of the house, but it is more likely he is a servant (Bock II:1711; D. Guthrie, *Jesus* 304). Jesus tells His disciples to follow the man to the house where they are to celebrate the Passover. The man carrying the water will guide them to the correct house (Nolland III:1034).

Upon arriving, they are to ask the master of the house where the room they are to use is located. He will show them to a large upper room where preparations have been made for the Passover. This is possibly a large room on the roof of the house with an outside stairway leading up to it. It is more likely, however, it is an upstairs room (Nolland III:1034). The fact the room is furnished probably means the cushions and the table to be used during the Passover are already in place. The owner has provided the necessary furnishings; the disciples must make the other preparations—the lamb, the bitter herbs, the unleavened bread, the wine, etc. Geldenhuys (556) notes it was common for inhabitants of the city of Jerusalem to lend or rent rooms to pilgrims for the celebration of the Passover.

The normal rent was the skin of the Paschal lamb.

Church tradition suggests this was a room in the house of Mary, the mother of John Mark (Bock II:1713). There is, however, no biblical evidence to support this tradition. Shepard (534) assumes the supper took place in the home of John Mark's parents.

The disciples found everything just as Jesus had told them. They followed the man to the house and were led to the upper room. They obeyed the Lord and began to complete the necessary preparations for the Passover meal. Geldenhuys (560) and Hendriksen (*Luke* 959-960) give brief summaries of how a Passover meal was conducted in the first century. A more detailed account may be found in Edersheim (*Temple* 208-228).

Jesus probably arrived about sunset. The meal itself would have begun when the sun had fully set, approximately 6:00 p.m., (Edersheim, *Life* II:490). Hendriksen (*Luke* 958) points out the Jews often counted sunset as the beginning of a new day. If this is correct, they would have eaten the Passover meal at the beginning of Friday, the fifteenth of Nisan. They would not have eaten the meal sitting in chairs around a table as in modern times. The table would have been low, only a few inches above the floor; the men would have reclined on cushions on their left sides and eaten with their right hands (Edersheim, *Life* II:492).

15 And he said unto them, With desire I have desired to eat this passover with you before I suffer:
16 For I say unto you, I will not any more eat thereof, until it be fulfilled in the kingdom of God.
17 And he took the cup, and gave thanks, and said, Take this, and divide *it* among yourselves.
18 For I say unto you, I will not drink of the fruit of the vine, until the kingdom of God shall come.
19 And he took bread, and gave thanks, and brake *it*, and gave unto them saying, This is my body which is given for you: this do in remembrance of me.
20 Likewise also the cup after supper, saying, This cup *is* the new testament in my blood, which is shed for you.

The institution of the Lord's Supper is an important part of the gospel story. It is told four times in the N. T. (Mt. 26; Mk. 14; Luke 22; and 1 Cor. 11). There are also references and allusions to it in other passages (DJG 444). The oldest of these accounts is found in 1 Corinthians. The story of the Lord's Supper was an important part of the early Christian tradition. In 1 Corinthians 11:23, Paul writes, "For I have received of the Lord that which also I delivered unto you." "Received" and "delivered" are technical terms used to describe the passing down of oral tradition (DJG 444-445).

Luke's account is the most unique of the Gospel accounts. It alone has the cup before the bread (Lk. 22:17); the other accounts have the bread first. It is also the only account to mention the Kingdom of God (Lk. 22:16). The uniqueness of his account is probably because of Luke's desire to meet the needs of his Gentile readers who may not have been familiar with the Jewish customs.

All three of the Synoptic Gospels connect the Lord's Supper with a Passover meal (Mk. 14:12-16; Mt.

26:17-19; Lk. 22:14-16). According to the Synoptic Gospels, the Passover meal would have begun shortly after sunset; this sunset would have begun the fifteenth of Nisan. Jesus would have been tried and crucified the next morning, which would still have been the fifteenth of Nisan, (R. Brown, *John XIII-XXI* 555). Marshall (*Gospel* 801-810) offers a detailed comparison of the accounts of the Lord's Supper found in the Synoptic Gospels and in the writings of Paul. For an overview of recent scholarship on this issue see Nolland (III:1042-1049).

John presents a somewhat different picture from that presented in the Synoptics. It does not describe Jesus and His disciples' participation in a Passover meal; neither does it describe the institution of the Lord's Supper. According to some interpreters, John 13:1, 13:29, 18:28, and 19:31, imply that the institution of the Lords' supper took place before the Passover. John 13:1 begins with "Now before the feast of the Passover." John 13:2 begins with "And supper being ended," but the verse does not specify it was a Passover supper. Many scholars assume it was a supper that took place the day before the official beginning of Passover. John 18:28 and 19:31 both seem to imply Jesus was crucified before the Passover and not after it.

This seeming contradiction between John and the Synoptic Gospels has attracted much attention from scholars. R. Brown (*John XIII-XXI* 555-556) gives a summary of the conclusions drawn by several scholars who have studied this issue. Derrett (412-417) carefully examines the various issues involved. He concludes there are several possibilities concerning the institution of the Lord's Supper: (1) it was instituted during a Passover meal; (2) it was instituted during a ceremony after the Passover meal; (3) it was instituted during a ceremony in lieu of a Passover meal; and (4) it was instituted during a ceremony the evening before the Passover meal.

Jeremias (*Eucharistic* 1-60) carefully examines the issues involved, including the arguments both for and against connecting the institution of the Lord's Supper with the Passover meal. He concludes there is no doubt the Lord's Supper was instituted during the Passover meal. In his view, both the Gospel of John and the Synoptics identify Jesus' final meal with His disciples as the Passover meal.

Hendriksen (*John* 220-227) takes a similar approach. He explains that some scholars understand the Synoptics to teach that Jesus was crucified after the Passover while John teaches He was crucified before the Passover. Some scholars argue that the Synoptic Gospels are correct and John is wrong; others argue that John is right and the Synoptic Gospels are wrong. Hendriksen argues these are not the only possible interpretations. In his view, it is possible to reconcile the statements found in the Synoptics with those found in John.

While the relationship between John and the Synoptics is not easy to define, Jeremias and Hendriksen are correct in arguing that the Lord's Supper was instituted during the Jewish Passover meal on Thursday evening. Nolland (III:1055) concludes the Lord's Supper was likely instituted during a Passover meal. He suggests some of the differences in detail are due to the fact the Gospel writers are not simply relating history; they are also explaining the significance of the life and ministry of Jesus. If the institution of the Lord's Supper took place late on Thursday night, the crucifixion would then have taken place on Friday.

The words "with desire I have desired" have been interpreted in various ways. Stein (*Luke* 541) summarizes the most common interpretations. He concludes Jesus looked forward to this last Passover meal with His disciples so He might instruct them concerning the new covenant and bring His work on earth to a close. Geldenhuys (553) suggests they indicate the intensity with which Jesus had anticipated this last Passover meal with His disciples. Jesus was well aware His time on the earth was rapidly drawing to a close. He wanted to do everything He could to help prepare His disciples for the difficult days that lay ahead. The phrase "before I suffer" is clearly a reference to the type of death He was to experience and all the suffering that would be part of that death.

Geldenhuys (553) points out that in these final chapters of the Gospel, Luke tells the story in as few words as possible. The Gospel is a long one, and it is nearing the maximum length for a single scroll. Another possible reason for Luke's brevity in this part of his Gospel is that the story was already well known among Christians when he wrote.

In Luke 22:16, Jesus tells His disciples He will not eat the Passover with them again on earth. The words "until it be fulfilled in the kingdom of God" probably refer to the messianic banquet He will share with His disciples in Heaven (Geldenhuys 553-554; Stein, *Luke* 541-542; Nolland III:1050). This great banquet will be much greater than the Passover meal and will render the Passover no longer necessary because it will have accomplished its purpose.

"I will not any more eat thereof" reflect the strongest way to make a negative statement (Greek subjunctive of emphatic negation). Jesus emphasizes the fact that He will never again eat the Passover meal with His disciples. The implication is He will not eat it with them again because in Heaven it will no longer be necessary to eat the Passover (Nolland III:1050).

The story of the institution of the Lord's Supper begins in verse 17, but it is difficult to determine the precise order of events. Luke mentions that Jesus took the cup, blessed it, and gave it to His disciples (v. 8). Ellis (254) explains that "fruit of the vine" was an expression for wine, specifically used in the context of a Passover meal. Then in verse 19, Jesus took the bread, blessed it, and distributed it to His disciples. In verse 20, the discussion returns to the cup; Jesus explained its spiritual significance to His disciples. In Matthew 26:26, Mark 14:22, and 1 Corinthians 11:24, Jesus took the bread first and then the cup. In this passage, as in other passages, Luke seems more concerned with what happened than with the chronology (Hendriksen, *Luke* 960).

Luke does not indicate at what point, in the Passover meal, Jesus institutes the Lord's Supper, but Edersheim (*Life* II:511), suggests it began with the third cup of wine, which was called the Cup of Blessing. Stein (DJG 447) explains that four cups of wine were used during the Passover meal, each mixed with three parts water to one part wine. Stein agrees with Edersheim that the institution of the Lord's Supper probably took place after the third cup. Marshall (*Gospel* 797-798) notes that not all scholars agree with this majority opinion.

In verses 17-18, Jesus takes a cup of wine from the table, blesses it, and tells His disciples, "Take this, and divide it among yourselves." Edersheim (*Life* II:511) explains that a portion of the unleavened bread was broken off at the beginning of the meal and set aside. That portion was eaten at the end of the meal after the Paschal lamb had been consumed. In verse 19, Jesus took some of this unleavened bread from the table, blessed it, and gave it to the disciples. Jesus then explained, "This is my body which is given for you." Most interpreters have interpreted the verb "is" in a metaphorical way meaning "to represent" or "to symbolize" (Stein, *Luke* 543; Geldenhuys 555). Morris (*Luke* 306) explains that the verb "is" need not imply a physical transformation. He cites other statements such as "I am the door" and "I am the bread of life," where Jesus does not imply a physical transformation. The idea here seems to be the bread "signifies" or "represents" the body of Christ.

Nothing in the passage indicates Jesus actually transformed the bread into His flesh. Neither does the passage indicate that Jesus partook of the bread and wine; it says only He gave the elements to His disciples.

In verse 20, Luke writes that Jesus did something similar concerning the cup. He took the cup and said, "This cup *is* the new testament in my blood, which is shed for you." "The cup" obviously refers to the wine and water mixture in the cup, not the cup itself. A "testament" implies "a covenant" or "an agreement." Nolland (III:1057) notes that during the Passover meal each person would usually have his own cup. Apparently, what happens here is that Jesus takes His own cup and shares it with His disciples. Luke does not state whether Jesus drinks from the cup; the point is that the cup is an expression of Jesus' fellowship with His disciples.

"New" (Greek *kainos*) means something new in kind. "Blood" refers to the suffering and death Jesus will experience in just a few hours. The lesson is that through His suffering and death, Jesus will open the door for the world to enjoy a new relationship with God. It will be a new kind of relationship based on faith in Christ rather than on the blood of animal sacrifices and obedience to the law. The fact that Jesus ordered the contents of the cup be divided among all His disciples is, however, an indication of the unity that existed among His disciples (Hendriksen, *Luke* 961).

Marshall (*Gospel* 799-800) and Tolbert (167) note that verses 19b-20 are not found in some of the early manuscripts (the "Western Text"); they are present in the majority of them and are considered authentic by most of the textual scholars.

21 But, behold, the hand of him that betrayeth me *is* with me on the table.
22 And truly the Son of man goeth, as it was determined: but woe unto that man by whom he is betrayed!
23 And they began to inquire among themselves, which of them it was that should do this thing.
24 And there was also a strife among them, which of them should be accounted the greatest.
25 And he said unto them, The kings of the Gentiles exercise lordship over them; and they that exercise authority upon them are called benefactors.

26 But ye *shall* not *be* so: but he that is greatest among you, let him be as the younger; and he that is chief, as he that doth serve.
27 For whether *is* greater, he that sitteth at meat, or he that serveth? *is* not he that sitteth at meat? but I am among you as he that serveth.

Verse 21 refers to Judas Iscariot, who betrayed the Lord to the Temple authorities. Judas was physically present at the meal. He was there not as a faithful disciple, but as a traitor (S. Brown 83). Jesus did not exclude him from the disciple band; it was Judas who chose to separate himself from Jesus by his apostasy. As S. Brown (83) notes, Luke has a poignant warning for his Gentile readers, "Mere presence at the eucharist is no assurance of perseverance." Luke does not say when Judas left the supper and went to betray Jesus to the Jewish authorities, but it probably occurred at the end of the institution of the Lord's Supper.

Verse 23 indicates that at this time the disciples did not yet know which of them would betray Jesus. Luke's account is very brief; Mark 14:19 notes the disciples began to ask Jesus, "Is it I?" Jesus does not specifically identify Judas Iscariot as the betrayer, but He said, "but woe to that man by whom the Son of man is betrayed! good were it for that man if he had never been born" (Mk. 14:21). Matthew 26:23-24 are very similar to Mark. Matthew 26:25 gives additional information; in that verse, Judas himself asks, "Master, is it I?" Jesus answered him, "Thou hast said." Most interpreters understand this to be a positive response (Crabtree 437; Broadus 527; Blomberg, *Matthew* 389). Broadus (527) equates it to "Thou hast said what is true." He writes that this was a common form of an affirmative reply.

Verse 24 takes the discussion in a different direction, noting that conflict and rivalry exist within the apostolic band. Luke does not specifically state this conflict rises to the surface during the Lord's Supper, but that seems to be his implication (Hendriksen, *Luke* 970). Summers (*Luke* 278) explains that other passages, such as Mark 10:42-45 and Matthew 20:25-28, present very similar words, but they are set in other contexts. Hendriksen explains that several passages in the Gospels contain parts of this teaching. It seems likely this conflict is another example of the spiritual immaturity of the disciples. No doubt Jesus gave this kind of instruction on more than one occasion and in different contexts.

The disciples were arguing over which of them would occupy the leading position. Luke does not explain what provoked this exchange. It is possible it was brought about by the apostasy of Judas. His fellow disciples might have been arguing over who would take his place as treasurer. Bonnet and Schroeder (673-674) offer another possibility, noting also this was not the first time the disciples had argued over which of them was the most important. They suggest the disciples are arguing over which of them will occupy the seats of honor closest to the Master. It is also possible none of the disciples wished to occupy the lowest places where they might be called on to help with the required washings that preceded the Passover meal.

Bock (II:1735-1736) offers a different view: namely, they are arguing about which of them will occupy the positions of greatest prominence in the new kingdom Jesus is establishing. It is difficult to determine which of these possibilities is most likely. The idea they were arguing over the seating around the table is the explanation that seems to best fit the context. Jesus had previously rebuked them for this kind of attitude, and He rebukes them again here.

In verses 25-27, Jesus draws a sharp contrast between the way worldly leaders operate and the way He expects His disciples to serve in His kingdom. In the ancient world, rulers did not generally think of themselves as guardians and protectors of the people over whom they ruled. They were dictators who often ruled in an arbitrary manner and for their own benefit (Lenski 1058). Such leaders often boasted of their accomplishments and took such titles as "benefactor" (Greek *euergetēs*), which literally means "one who does good." Bertram (TDNT 654) explains this word was used as a title for gods, kings, statesmen, philosophers, and others. Keener (250) explains this term was used in the ancient world to describe people in positions of power who bestowed favors on their subordinates. It is possible Jesus is using the term with a sense of irony because the Gentile rulers claim to be doers of good when, in reality, they are tyrants.

Jesus then explains to His disciples they are to be servants, servants of God and also servants of the people of God. In a society that venerated age, those who were younger served those who were older (Morris, *Luke* 336). The disciples are to view themselves as younger; they are to serve rather than be served. Jesus reinforces that thought in verse 27, comparing His kingdom to the home of a rich man who has servants. The master sits at the table and enjoys his meal while the servants wait on him; the one who is served is greater than the one who serves. Jesus concludes these verses with these powerful words, "I am among you as he that serveth." A different standard applies in the Kingdom of God; Jesus has come to earth not to be served but to serve. Jesus serves as their example. The disciples should seek to imitate Him and not imitate those who follow the ways of the world. Morris (*Luke* 336) explains that "serve" (Greek *diakoneō*) was originally used to describe one who waited tables in an inn or tavern. It later came to imply any type of lowly service.

28 Ye are they which have continued with me in my temptations.
29 And I appoint unto you a kingdom, as my Father hath appointed unto me;
30 That ye may eat and drink at my table in my kingdom, and sit on thrones judging the twelve tribes of Israel.

Jesus addresses His disciples, sharing with them an important lesson they will need in the difficult days and hours that lie ahead. In verse 28, Jesus recognizes that the disciples have paid a price to be His followers. They have not suffered as much as He has, but they have suffered. They have continued with Him during the difficult days of His earthly ministry. "Temptations" (Greek *peirasmoi*) means both "trials" or "testings" and "temptations" (Bonnet and Schroeder 674). The implication is that His disciples will continue to suffer with Him during the remaining hours of His earthly life.

In verses 29-30, Jesus tells His disciples their sacrifice will not go unrewarded. They will not only be with Jesus in the future; they will have the privilege of sharing with Him in the new kingdom His Father will give Him. The future will involve a great messianic banquet in which the disciples will share. They will also have the privilege of sharing with Jesus in His reign. They will sit on thrones judging the twelve tribes of Israel. Morris (*Luke* 337) points out that "judging" in this passage means "ruling." (The word is used in much the same way in the Book of Judges in the O. T.) Jesus does not explain all the ramifications of this statement, but the idea is the disciples will be amply rewarded for their faithfulness to Jesus in His hours of trial. A similar statement may be found in Matthew 19:28.

Bock (II:1741) explains the reference to the thrones has its roots in the O. T. He also explains the circumstances surrounding the end of Jesus' earthly life may seem to indicate God's plan for Israel has gone astray, but it has not. It will continue. Some commentators see the term "Israel" as a reference to physical Israel that persecutes Jesus and His disciples. Others see it as a reference to the new Israel that Jesus is in the process of forming (Marshall, *Gospel* 818).

Nolland (III:1068) points out the promises made in this passage are designed to encourage the disciples. They will be faced with the difficult task of spreading the gospel in the midst of an often hostile world; they will be abased and humiliated. This passage assures them they will be rewarded in Heaven for their humble service on earth.

31 And the Lord said, Simon, Simon, behold, Satan hath desired *to have* you, that he may sift *you* as wheat:
32 But I have prayed for thee, that thy faith fail not: and when thou art converted, strengthen thy brethren.
33 And he said unto him, Lord, I am ready to go with thee, both into prison, and to death.
34 And he said, I tell thee, Peter, the cock shall not crow this day, before thou shalt thrice deny that thou knowest me.

Now Jesus specifically addresses Peter, the spokesman for the apostolic band. All four of the Gospels tell the story of Jesus' foretelling of Peter's denial, but each of them tells it in his own way (Mt. 26; Mk. 14; Jn. 13). Luke alone mentions the involvement of Satan (Morris, *Luke* 337). While it is possible Jesus spoke these words to Peter in private, it is more likely this conversation took place in the presence of the other disciples. Luke does not explain when or where the words were spoken. It is very likely they were spoken the evening before the crucifixion. Geldenhuys (566) suggests they were spoken after Jesus and Peter had left the house where the Passover was celebrated. Green (*Luke* 774) proposes the conversation took place in the presence of the other disciples while they were still reclining around the table. Bock (II:1745) points out these verses teach that Jesus has a full understanding of what lies ahead for Him and for His disciples.

Verse 31 begins with the words "Simon, Simon." The repetition of the name probably indicates the deep concern Jesus has for Simon Peter (Hendriksen, *Luke* 973; Lenski 1062).

Jesus will not again address him as "Peter" until verse 34. It is difficult to determine whether the use of the name "Simon" is theologically significant here. Since "Peter" means "rock," the use of "Simon" may imply that Simon Peter is a weak human being and not yet the spiritual rock he may claim to be.

"You" in verse 31 is plural. The idea is that Satan has desired to bring all of the disciples under his control. The metaphor "that he may sift you as wheat" is not often found in the Bible; Hendriksen (*Luke* 973) suggests it is an agricultural metaphor. He notes that in the ancient world, women would place the newly-harvested wheat in a sieve and shake it vigorously. The shaking would cause the grains of wheat to separate from the chaff. Both Geldenhuys (566) and Morris (*Luke* 337) opine that, in this context, the phrase implies severe trials. The idea is Satan wishes to place the disciples under such a severe temptation they will abandon Christ (Hendriksen, *Luke* 973-974).

In verse 32, the singular "thee" and "thou" indicate Jesus has prayed specifically for Peter, that his faith will not fail when the hour of trial comes. "Converted" (Greek *epistrephō*) means literally "to turn" or "to return." Bonnet and Schroeder (675) understand this statement to mean the disciples, including Peter, did not understand all the implications of salvation until after the Day of Pentecost. After Peter has come to a more complete understanding of salvation, he will then be in a position to strengthen his fellow disciples.

Green (*Luke* 772-773) offers a somewhat different explanation. He considers Peter's denial to be a "temporary failure." After this time of denial, he will need to "turn back" to the Lord. Green also notes the word translated "converted" is often used to describe repentance. The idea of this verse is Peter will deny the Lord, but his failure will not be permanent. He will turn back to Christ in repentance and faith; he will then be in a position to strengthen the other disciples.

In verse 33, Peter boasts he is ready to accompany the Lord to prison or even unto death. While Peter's words are sincere and well-meaning, he does not understand the gravity of the trials that lie ahead. Neither does he understand the weakness of human beings. This verse points out the overconfidence of Peter; he has no idea of the seriousness of the temptation he will face (Lenski 1066).

The words of verse 34 must have come as a terrible shock to Peter. He probably expected Jesus to commend him for his dedication and commitment. Instead, Jesus points out the reality of the situation. He declares Peter will not go with Him to prison or death. Jesus knows that when the hour of severe trial comes, Peter will fail Him. Jesus says, "Peter, the cock shall not crow this day, before thou shalt thrice deny that thou knowest me." "This day" indicates the betrayal will not take place at some future date; it will happen within the next few hours. A rooster crows during the night; Mark 13:35 refers to the early morning hours as the time of "cock-crowing." Keener (250) points out that in ancient literature, the crowing of the cock often indicated the advent of dawn was near. He also points out in Palestine roosters might begin to crow as early as 12:30 a.m. Lenski (1066) suggests roosters would crow once about midnight and again just before dawn. The words "that thou knowest me" are telling; Peter will deny even having a casual acquaintance with Jesus. His rejection of Christ will be total and complete.

35 And he said unto them, When I sent you without purse, and scrip, and shoes, lacked ye anything? And they said, Nothing.
36 Then said he unto them, But now, he that hath a purse, let him take *it*, and likewise *his* scrip: and he that hath no sword, let him sell his garment, and buy one.
37 For I say unto you, that this that is written must yet be accomplished in me, And he was reckoned among the transgressors: for the things concerning me have an end.
38 And they said, Lord, behold, here *are* two swords. And he said unto them, It is enough.

Jesus gives important instructions to all the apostles. His goal is to prepare them for the trials they would soon face. Luke does not specify whether this discussion takes place in the upper room; *what* is said is more important than *where*. Jesus reminds them of how they have obeyed His instructions in the past, and God has always provided for them. They have gone out to preach and heal without taking any of the provisions a traveler would ordinarily take, but God has always provided for them. They have lacked nothing. But now the situation is different; God will still provide for them but in a different way (Lenski 1067). They must now make proper preparations for serving Jesus. "Purse" (Greek *ballantion*) ordinarily describes a small bag for carrying money (Arndt and Gingrich 130). "Scrip" (Greek *pēran*) means a knapsack or a traveler's bag (Arndt and Gingrich 662). The disciples will no longer be able to depend on those who are sympathetic to Jesus for their support. They will be largely on their own, and they must make adequate provision for the journey.

In the latter part of verse 36, Jesus advises them to take a sword also. He regards this as so important that if they do not already have one, they should sell part of their clothing in order to buy one. The idea is they can no longer count on God to protect them in the same way He has in the past. During their missionary journeys in Galilee, they were largely working among people who were favorably disposed to Jesus and His ministry. That will not be the case in the future. They will be working among those who are hostile to the gospel, and they must be prepared to defend themselves.

Jesus' instruction to purchase a sword is interpreted by the scholars in different ways. Some take it literally. Lenski (1068), for example, understands Jesus to mean the disciples should purchase a short, Roman sword to be used for defensive purposes. Ellis (256) makes similar comments. Summers (*Luke* 282), however, suggests Jesus is speaking ironically, exposing the fact that in the past the disciples have found the way of Jesus to be adequate but now believe they must use worldly methods and depend on the sword. Bonnet and Schroeder (676) interpret the phrase figuratively, arguing that Jesus is not condoning violence; instead, He uses the sword as a figure of speech to drive home the point that conflicts lie ahead and the disciples must prepare for them. Hendriksen (*Luke* 976) also interprets the term "sword" in a figurative manner.

He suggests it stands for the courage the disciples will need in the future.

In verse 37, Jesus continues to warn His disciples about the dangers they will soon face. He turns to the O. T. to explain the challenges. The world has already decided to reject Jesus and His message; the disciples must be prepared to share that rejection (Bock II:1747). Jesus' reference to "this that is written" (Greek perfect tense for past action with continuing results) implies the words of the O. T. were written down long ago, and they still possess binding authority. Jesus then quotes the clause "He was reckoned among the transgressors" from Isaiah 53:12 (Bock II:1747). "Must" reflects that the words of Isaiah will necessarily be fulfilled. Isaiah's prophecy has come to full realization in Jesus Christ.

The first words of verse 38 constitute a rather thoughtless response on the part of the disciples. Apparently, they thought Jesus wanted them to prepare for an immediate confrontation with the Jewish officers. They went looking for swords and found two. Plummer (506) suggests the disciples might have brought these swords for protection against robbers as they traveled to Jerusalem. Lenski (1070-1071) surmises the swords had not been brought by the disciples but were hanging in the room when Jesus and His disciples arrived.

Jesus' response, "It is enough," probably does not mean two swords would be sufficient to defend Him and His disciples in the event of conflict. More likely, what He says reflects a Hebrew idiom used to dismiss a subject from further discussion (Plummer 507). Ellis (257) and Lieu (184) offer similar interpretations; both understand the phrase to mean "enough of that." Caird (241) understands the expression to mean Jesus is dismissing the subject with sadness. Jesus wants no more discussion of a physical confrontation with the soldiers. He is disappointed with the lack of spiritual understanding His closest disciples have demonstrated (Hendriksen, *Luke* 977).

Bonnet and Schroeder (676) offer a different explanation, suggesting the two swords will, ironically, be more than sufficient for the establishment of the Kingdom of God. Jesus' reign cannot be established by the power of the sword because it is a spiritual kingdom.

39 And he came out, and went, as he was wont, to the mount of Olives; and his disciples also followed him.
40 And when he was at the place, he said unto them, Pray that ye enter not into temptation.
41 And he was withdrawn from them about a stone's cast, and kneeled down, and prayed,
42 Saying, Father, if thou be willing, remove this cup from me: nevertheless not my will, but thine, be done.
43 And there appeared an angel unto him from heaven, strengthening him.
44 And being in an agony he prayed more earnestly: and his sweat was as it were great drops of blood falling down to the ground.
45 And when he rose up from prayer, and was come to his disciples, he found them sleeping for sorrow,
46 And said unto them, Why sleep ye? rise and pray, lest ye enter into temptation.

47 And while he yet spake, behold a multitude, and he that was called Judas, one of the twelve, went before them, and drew near unto Jesus to kiss him.
48 But Jesus said unto him, Judas, betrayest thou the Son of man with a kiss?
49 When they which were about him saw what would follow, they said unto him, Lord, shall we smite with the sword?
50 And one of them smote the servant of the high priest, and cut off his right ear.
51 And Jesus answered and said, Suffer ye thus far. And he touched his ear, and healed him.
52 Then Jesus said unto the chief priests, and captains of the temple, and the elders, which were come to him, Be ye come out, as against a thief, with swords and staves?
53 When I was daily with you in the temple, ye stretched forth no hands against me: but this is your hour, and the power of darkness.

Luke's account of Jesus' agony in the Garden of Gethsemane is briefer than the accounts found in the other Synoptic Gospels (Mt. 26:36-46; Mk. 14:32-42) and differs in some details; but it is, essentially, the same story (Summers, *Luke* 283). Jesus and His disciples came out of the house where they had celebrated the Passover. They walked across the Kidron Valley and came to the Mount of Olives (Summers, *Luke* 284). Luke does not mention the specific place where they stopped, but Matthew and Mark call it "Gethsemane," which means "oil-press" (Plummer 508). It was probably a garden located on the lower slopes of the mountain. Shepard (567) posits the garden was located on the side of the Mount of Olives but a little higher up the mountain than the traditional site. He also speculates this was private property, probably belonging to John Mark's mother or to some other friend or relative of Jesus.

Luke alone notes it was Jesus' custom to retire to this place to escape the crowds. In 21:37, Luke indicates that during Passion Week, Jesus spent the nights in this garden (Lenski 1071-1072). It is significant to note that Jesus, although He knew what was in store for Him, made no effort to avoid Judas and those coming to arrest Him (Bonnet and Schroeder 677). John 18:2 indicates Judas was familiar with this garden and knew exactly where to find Jesus. Morris (*Luke* 311) calls attention to the importance of what took place here on the Mount of Olives. Jesus did not drink of the cup of suffering there, but He consented to drink it.

When Jesus and His disciples arrived at the garden, He asked eight of the disciples to remain near the entrance to the garden (Mt. 26:36-37). Perhaps He wanted them to serve as guards to avoid being surprised (Shepard 567). He asked His disciples "to pray that ye enter not into temptation." "Temptation" (Greek *peirasmos*) also means "a testing." Jesus knew that in the upcoming hours the faith of His disciples would be severely tested. They would see Him arrested, beaten, and finally crucified. The Jewish leaders might also try to destroy all those associated with Him. Jesus also understood very well the spiritual weakness of His disciples. Ellis (257) suggests that "enter into temptation" implies to be overtaken or destroyed by it. The idea seems to be that Jesus instructs His disciples to pray they will not be tempted or tested above their ability to bear it.

Morris (*Luke* 311) offers a somewhat different interpretation, positing that "temptation" may refer either to a temptation to sin or to a time of trial and suffering. It is possible Jesus is asking His disciples to pray they may be preserved from either one.

Jesus then left His disciples and withdrew a short distance—about a stone's throw—from them. Bock (II:1758) suggests "a stone's throw" was a figurative expression for a distance of several yards. Jesus wanted to have some privacy while still being close enough He could respond to the disciples if needed. Jesus then knelt down and begin to pray. Luke notes He knelt to pray, while Matthew and Mark state He fell on His face. Lenski (1073) suggests Jesus first knelt and then fell prostrate. When they prayed, the Jews normally stood with their hands outstretched. According to Bock (II:1758), the fact that Jesus prayed lying prostrate on the ground is an indication of His humility. Plummer (508) notes Jews normally prayed while standing but were known to pray while kneeling in times of humiliation or great emotion. Jesus' kneeling position probably indicates something of the agony and deep emotion He was experiencing (Morris, *Luke* 311).

Luke's wording of the prayer is somewhat different from that found in Matthew and Mark, but the content is basically the same (Summers, *Luke* 284). It is doubtful any of the accounts of the prayer should be considered as word-for-word transcriptions. Jesus probably prayed for a considerable amount of time, and the three Synoptic Gospels present summaries of His prayer.

According to verse 42, Jesus makes a difficult but understandable request of His heavenly Father. He asks that the "cup" be removed from Him. In this context, the "cup" obviously refers to the suffering and death He will face within just a few hours; Morris (*Luke* 311) notes in the O. T. the word "cup" is often associated either with suffering or with the wrath of God.

Bonnet and Schroeder (677) understand the cup to refer to "the unspeakable sufferings of the Savior." Plummer (509) points out that a "cup" was a common metaphor used to describe a person's fortune, whether good or bad. He also notes that in the N. T. it often refers to Jesus' suffering. Summers (*Luke* 285) correctly notes that Jesus not only shrank from the physical pain that accompanied death, He also shrank from the kind of death He would be called on to suffer and the conditions under which He would die. He would die the most painful and humiliating death Roman cruelty could devise. He would also be rejected by the very people He came to save. Finally, He would die while bearing upon Himself all the weight of human sin (Caird 242-243).

This cry of Jesus reveals much about His humanity. The traditional teaching of the Christian faith is that, while He was here on earth, Jesus was fully divine and (with the exception of sin) fully human. This prayer helps us see something of Jesus' human feelings and emotions. No person would have wanted to endure what lay before Him (Hendriksen, *Luke* 982; Morris, *Luke* 311).

The prayer begins with the word "Father," which indicates the loving relationship that exists between God the Father and Jesus the Son. In reference to the words "if thou be willing,"

Summers (*Luke* 284) explains there are two words in the N. T. Greek that can mean to will or wish. The first (Greek *thelō*) implies a wish or desire; the second (Greek *boulomai*) implies a plan or a counsel. The second is used here; the idea is "If it is a part of your plan, remove this cup from me."

At the heart of His prayer, Jesus' humanity becomes evident. Asking the cup be removed from Him does not express a lack of faith but simply reflects the terrible reality that exists. It is important to note Jesus' prayer does not end with these words but with the words, "Nevertheless not my will, but thine, be done." As Lenski (1074) expresses, this expression reflects absolute surrender to the will of God. As much as He may dread what lies ahead, Jesus is fully prepared to fulfill the mission for which He came to earth. For Him, the single most important thing is doing the will of the Father. Barclay (272) correctly notes that, in these words, Jesus does not portray a tone of helplessness or that He has been beaten into submission. Instead, He affirms complete and total trust in His Father. His desire is the Father's will may prevail (Morris, *Luke* 311).

Creed (273) and Plummer (509) explain that verses 43-44 are not found in all the early manuscripts, but they are found in most of them and should be regarded as part of the text; see also the comments of Ellis (258). Stein (*Luke* 559) takes the contrary view. He argues they are not found in the earliest and best manuscripts and they interrupt the flow of the narrative. In the opinion of most authorities, however, these verses should be regarded as part of the original text of the Gospel.

The angel sent from Heaven was clearly God's messenger; his ministry was to strengthen the Lord Jesus in this difficult hour. Luke does not explain why the strengthening was necessary. Marshall (*Gospel* 832) suggests this strengthening enabled Jesus to pray even more earnestly in verse 44. Hendriksen (*Luke* 983) posits that the angel strengthened both His body and His soul. God knew Jesus' most difficult hours were still ahead, and He was determined to strengthen His Son for the coming trials.

"Agony" (Greek *agōnia*) occurs only here (v. 44) in the N. T. It often expresses agony, anxiety, or fear. Once again, the humanity of Jesus comes to the forefront. It is not surprising Jesus would feel a great deal of anxiety in these circumstances. It is possible Jesus was afraid He might not be able to fully complete His mission. It is important to note that in this hour of maximum peril, Jesus turned to His heavenly Father, not away from Him. He did not cease to pray; in fact, He prayed even "more earnestly."

This prayer was so intense it produced a physical reaction. His sweat was "as it were great drops of blood falling down to the ground." "Great drops" (Greek *thromboi*) was often used in classical Greek to describe drops of blood. Marshall (*Gospel* 832) gives a list of the most common interpretations of the statement. He notes that it may mean the sweat was falling to the ground like drops of blood. Or it may mean the sweat was the color of blood. Another possible interpretation is the sweat was mixed with blood. Plummer (510-511) cites examples of blood being exuded from the pores of the body. Hendriksen (*Luke* 983), suggesting this was a case of what is called *hermatidrosis*, offers that Jesus' sweat was mixed with drops of blood. The most likely interpretation is that Jesus' mental anguish was so intense His sweat fell to the ground like great drops of blood.

In verse 45, Jesus rises from His prayer; Luke, who does not share our modern interest in precise chronology, gives no indication of the amount of time Jesus had devoted to prayer. Jesus comes to His disciples and finds them asleep. Interestingly, they are sleeping "for sorrow" (Greek *lupē*), which can mean "grief." Geldenhuys (575) explains the disciples had been through a lot in the last few days. It was now late at night after a long day. It is not surprising they were simply too worn out to stay awake any longer. Caird (243) suggests the disciples had fallen asleep as a result of nervous exhaustion.

S. Brown (66-74) offers an insightful analysis of Jesus' relationship with His disciples during this difficult time. He understands the temptation not as a test of the genuineness of the disciples' faith but as a danger the disciples must struggle to escape through persevering prayer. Brown regards the apostles' sleeping not so much as disobedience to Jesus' instructions as a psychological event. As Luke points out, they sleep "for sorrow." Jesus' command to "rise and pray" in verse 46 need not be understood as a rebuke for their past disobedience but, instead, as a necessary element in the developing story. They must wake up in order to participate in the events surrounding Jesus' arrest. Mark 14:50 says, "They all forsook him, and fled." Luke makes no mention of such a desertion.

In verse 49, the disciples offer to defend Jesus with the sword, and one of them cuts off the right ear of the servant of the high priest. Shepard (571) speculates that he used one of the two short swords that were used in preparing the Passover lamb. Luke does not identify the disciple who severs the ear, but John 18:10 identifies him as Peter. John also notes the servant's name was Malchus. Jesus immediately restored the severed ear; apparently, He also forbade any further resistance by force.

Verse 47 notes that a crowd of people, including Judas Iscariot, arrived. According to John 13:30, Judas left the Passover meal before it was over. Luke does not explain where Judas went after he left the Passover meal. He probably went to the authorities and developed the plan to arrest Jesus later that night (Hendriksen, *Luke* 984). In verse 52, Luke notes that this crowd included the chief priests, the captains of the temple, and the elders. It is likely the group included a contingent of Temple police. Hendriksen (*Luke* 984-985) and Shepard (570) suggest that since the Temple police were not always reliable, a company of Roman soldiers accompanied them. John 18:12 may indicate that some of the soldiers were not Jews; if that is true, they would likely have been some of the Roman soldiers stationed in Jerusalem.

Judas drew near to Jesus for a kiss of greeting (v. 47). Walker (ISBE III:1813D-1814) gives an overview of the customs related to kissing in the ancient Near East. It was customary to kiss on the cheek, the forehead, or the beard as a form of greeting. As a general rule, men only kissed other men, and women only kissed other women. This type of kissing was not done on the lips, and it did not have the romantic connotations that accompany the act of kissing in the modern world. Günther (NIDNTT 549) explains that kissing was a normal way a rabbi greeted other rabbis. In later years, the "holy kiss" (Rom. 16:16, etc.) became a standard way for Christians to greet other believers.

Verse 47 does not state that Judas actually kissed Jesus, but that is probably the implication (Bock II:1768). According to Summers (*Luke* 287), "to kiss" (Greek present tense) indicates the kissing was prolonged. Hendriksen (*Luke* 986) asserts that Judas did kiss Jesus, perhaps fervently or repeatedly. He correctly observes that, in this context, the kiss serves to identify Jesus so the authorities may be sure to arrest the correct person.

As Judas drew near, Jesus asked him a question, "Judas, betrayest thou the Son of man with a kiss?" Those words are more a rebuke than a question. In the ancient Near East, the greeting kiss was a sign of friendship and respect. Judas, however, was using this sign of friendship as a way to betray Jesus into the hands of the Jewish authorities. Morris (*Luke* 313) points out that the use of a kiss to betray a person was especially heinous. Bonnet and Schroeder (679) note the importance of the order of words for emphasis in the original, which could literally be translated, "Judas, *with a kiss* do you betray the Son of man?"

"Son of man" is used twenty-five times in Luke (Hendriksen, *Luke* 298), most often by Jesus to designate Himself. Hendriksen suggests Jesus used this title both to emphasize His uniqueness and to distinguish Himself from the nationalistic conceptions of the Messiah, which were current in first-century Judaism. For a useful analysis of the usage see Marshall (DJG 775-781).

Hendriksen (*Luke* 985) offers an analysis of the makeup of the crowd that came to arrest Jesus. Keener (251) notes the "captains of the temple" were probably the temple guards. Their task was to arrest Jesus and take Him back to the city of Jerusalem.

Verses 49-50 present the response of the disciples to the arrival of the crowd that has come to arrest Jesus. "They which were about him" seems to refer to the disciples. Geldenhuys (580) suggests it may refer to the two disciples who are armed with swords. One of these two armed disciples asks, "Lord, shall we smite with the sword?" Before Jesus has time to respond to this question, one of the disciples takes a sword and cuts off the right ear of the high priest's servant (Stein, *Luke* 560-561).

Green (*Luke* 784) suggests the high priest's servant—literally, "slave"—is there as his personal representative. As such, he functions as the leader of the group that has come to arrest Jesus. He is probably in front of the group and standing close to Jesus and His disciples.

Jesus responds immediately to Peter's impetuous act by saying, "Suffer ye thus far." "Suffer" (Greek *eaō*) has several meanings: "allow," "permit," "leave," "let go," or "leave alone" (Arndt and Gingrich 211-212). What Jesus means is debated (Morris, *Luke* 313) The most common interpretation is Jesus is saying to His disciples that He doesn't want any more of this type of conduct. Some take it to mean, "Let them have their way." For an analysis of possible meanings see Morris (*Luke* 313) and Stein (*Luke* 561). By this rebuke, Jesus clearly indicates He is determined to offer no armed resistance to the crowd that has come to arrest Him. He is fully convinced these events are a part of God's plan for Him; He also understands that His kingdom will never be established by force of arms.

Jesus is not content to simply rebuke the disciples for their spiritual immaturity and Peter's impulsive attack upon the servant of the high priest. He exercises His divine power by immediately healing the ear Peter had cut off. This healing is an important statement about the nature of the kingdom Jesus has come to establish. It will not be built on force and violence but on love. Healing, both physical and spiritual, are key elements in His earthly ministry. There is little doubt this instantaneous healing of the servant's ear affected both the disciples and the crowd, but Luke makes no mention of their reaction. Luke's immediate goal is to move the story forward to Christ's trial and crucifixion.

In verses 52-53, Jesus delivers a short sermon to those who have come to arrest Him. Since the disciples were also present, this message is also designed for their benefit. Jesus points out that the authorities did not have to come after Him during the night, in an isolated location, with arms. They did not have to come after Him with force and violence as they would pursue a common thief (Summers, *Luke* 288). He has been teaching daily in the Temple, and there have been many opportunities to arrest Him during daylight hours. He would have submitted peacefully to them.

Jesus does not mention that the Jewish authorities were afraid to arrest Him in public because they knew He had widespread support among the people. He represents the reason they have come to arrest Him this way by saying, "This is your hour, and the power of darkness." They have come to arrest Him at night because that is when evil men do their evil deeds. Darkness is often used in the Bible as a symbol of evil (Summers, *Luke* 288). Geldenhuys (581) points out that these men are not acting out of a commitment to right and justice but are acting in an underhanded manner and for evil motives.

"The power of darkness" is an obvious reference to Satan. Satan is the motivating force behind all of the evil deeds that have been done and will be done to Jesus during the next few terrible hours. Stein (*Luke* 562) explains these events imply more than a conflict between Jesus and the Jewish leaders; they make up one part of the larger cosmic struggle between God and Satan.

The Jewish leaders and others have rejected the true light Jesus came to bring to the earth. For the moment, evil has triumphed, and evil will continue to triumph for several more hours. But Satan's victory will not last forever; Sunday is coming.

Summary (22:1-53)

This chapter begins the final portion of Luke's account of the life and ministry of Jesus Christ and will cover the passion, the resurrection, and the ascension. Chapter 22 deals specifically with the plot to betray Jesus, the last supper, and Jesus' agony and arrest in the garden. It also includes several of Jesus' teachings that are designed to prepare the disciples for the difficult days they face.

The chapter opens with Judas' plot to betray Jesus into the hands of the Jewish leaders. The Temple authorities had long harbored resentment against Jesus. He challenged their teachings and their leadership; in their mind, He was trying to turn the people against them.

They were looking for a way to eliminate Jesus without arousing the ire of the crowds. During the week of the Passover when large numbers of pilgrims were in Jerusalem, one of His own disciples, Judas Iscariot, offered to betray Judas to them. They gladly accepted this offer and agreed to give Judas a sum of money in return for his help. Luke does not explain why Judas decided to betray Jesus; the money was, no doubt, an attraction. He might also have been disappointed because Jesus had not instituted the kind of physical and material kingdom Judas wanted to see.

Luke then narrates the story of Jesus' final meal with His disciples and the institution of the Lord's Supper. Since the Passover had to be celebrated within the city of Jerusalem, Jesus sent two of His most faithful disciples, Peter and John, to prepare a suitable place. Jesus told them to look for a man carrying a pitcher of water and follow him. They obeyed Jesus' instructions and were led to a large upper room where everything was ready for Jesus and His disciples to eat the Passover together.

While they were eating the Passover, Jesus instituted the Lord's Supper. There are four accounts of the institution of the Lord's Supper in the N. T., and Luke's is the most unique. He alone mentions the cup before the bread; his is also the only account to mention the Kingdom of God. As for the differences in the four accounts, the most common view is that the Lord's Supper was instituted during a Passover meal, probably on Thursday evening. Luke's account is brief, probably because when the Gospel was written it was already well known within the Christian community.

During the meal, Jesus announced that "the hand of him that betrayeth me is with me on the table," clearly referring to Judas Iscariot. Luke does not explain when Judas left the meal, but he probably left after the institution of the Lord's Supper.

After instituting the Lord's Supper, Jesus gave the disciples a series of teachings designed to help prepare them for the trials they would soon face, teachings He has probably given them on several occasions. There was an issue of rivalry within among the disciples; they were arguing over which of them should be considered the greatest. Jesus responded by saying such conflicts were common in the secular world but have no place in Christian leadership. Jesus said, "He that is greatest among you, let him be as the younger; and he that is chief, as he that doth serve."

Jesus also shares important information about the future with His disciples. He assures them their service and sacrifice will not go unrewarded. They will eat and drink at Jesus' table in His coming kingdom; they will also sit on thrones judging the twelve tribes of Israel.

Jesus prays for Simon Peter by name. He then announces that before the cock crows to mark the beginning of a new day, Peter will deny knowing Jesus three times.

The closing verses of this section are especially poignant; they describe Jesus' arrest and the agony He experienced before the arrival of the soldiers and the Jewish leaders. He went to the Mount of Olives with His disciples, where He prayed earnestly to His heavenly Father. His prayer was so intense the sweat dripped from His brow like great drops of blood.

In this account, Jesus' humanity comes out clearly, especially in His prayer, "Father, if thou be willing, remove this cup from me." It was certainly not Jesus' desire to suffer the kind of death He knew He would have to endure. But that was not the end of His prayer; Jesus concluded, "Nevertheless not my will, but thine, be done." Jesus was willing to endure a horrible death to accomplish God's plan for Him.

While Jesus was speaking with His disciples, a group of men arrived, led by Judas Iscariot. Luke explains that Judas drew near to Jesus in order to greet Him with a kiss. That served to identify Jesus for the group of Jewish leaders and temple guards who had come to arrest Jesus. The disciples responded instantly to this situation; one of them struck the servant of the high priest and cut off his right ear. Because Jesus had no intention of establishing His kingdom by force and violence, He touched the servant's ear and immediately healed him.

Jesus concludes this sad story of His arrest with a question and assertion, "When I was daily with you in the temple, ye stretched forth no hands against me: but this is your hour, and the power of darkness." It looked as if sin and Satan had won a great victory, and, for the moment, they had. When all is said and done, however, it is Jesus who will emerge victorious.

Application: Teaching and Preaching the Passage

This passage begins the final series of events in the earthly life and ministry of Jesus Christ. It includes the institution of the Lord's Supper, the prediction of Peter's denials, and the apostasy of Judas Iscariot. It also includes the final teachings Jesus was able to give to His disciples before His trial and crucifixion. The preacher and teacher should keep in mind this passage does not stand alone; it should be interpreted in light of the overall message of Luke's Gospel. It should also be understood as preparatory for the final events of Jesus' earthly life, to be told in chapters 23 and 24.

The tragedy of sin is one of the key themes in this passage. It was sin that led the chief priests and scribes to seek the death of Jesus. Sin blinded these Jewish leaders to all the good things Jesus had done and the wise words He had spoken. They saw Him as a threat that had to be eliminated by whatever means necessary. They understood His popularity among the common people; for that reason, they looked for some way to take Jesus into custody without arousing the ire of the crowds. Sin is deceitful and often operates in secret. They rejoiced when Judas Iscariot came to them and offered to betray Jesus to them. That helped them avoid the responsibility for their evil deed because they could blame it on Judas.

It was sin that moved Judas Iscariot to betray the One who had loved him and accepted him into the apostolic band. Sin led Peter, the spokesman of the apostles, to deny three times that he even knew who Jesus was. Sin produced the spirit of rivalry Jesus had to deal with within the apostolic band. Ultimately, it was sin that brought the Jewish leaders and the Temple guards to the Mount of Olives to arrest Jesus.

This passage would be an excellent text for a series of sermons or lessons on the tragedy of sin. This passage illustrates the various ways in which sin can destroy an individual's life. It can also destroy the cohesiveness of a group dedicated to serving the Lord. A spirit of contention and rivalry will always do great harm to the work of the Lord.

This would also be an excellent text for a series on the Lord's Supper. As mentioned, this passage contains one of four accounts of the institution of the Lord's Supper in the N. T. The Lord's Supper illustrates the fellowship that exists between Jesus and His followers. It also illustrates the spiritual bond that ties believers together. "This cup is the new testament in my blood" does not mean the contents of the cup are magically transformed into the blood of Christ; the cup symbolizes the blood of Christ. The word "testament" means a covenant or an agreement. The idea is that the shedding of Christ's blood on the Cross has instituted a new relationship between God and His children. This relationship is no longer based on the observance of the law and the practice of animal sacrifices; instead, it is based on the life, death, and resurrection of Christ. His blood has made it possible for believers to enjoy a relationship with God that was previously unavailable to them.

This passage also contains some profound statements about the nature of Christian leadership. In the ancient world, leadership meant power and control; kings and other rulers ruled with an iron hand. As a general rule, they were little concerned with the welfare of the people over whom they ruled. They used their positions for their own benefit. They could be, and often were, arbitrary and dictatorial. Jesus explains that Christian leaders do not follow this worldly model but are to lead by setting an example of service. He is not teaching that Christian leaders should be unwilling to make decisions, even difficult ones, when necessary. But Christian leaders do not serve for their own benefit; they serve for the benefit of the people. Their goal is not to advance their own position, power, or authority. Their goal is to advance the work of God. They are to lead God's people in the right direction; they are not to abuse them or take advantage of them. Christian leaders need to consider carefully the teachings of this passage both for their own ministries and for the benefit of the congregations they serve.

While eschatology is not a major theme of this passage, the future of the children of God does receive some emphasis. In 21:29-30, Jesus promises His disciples if they faithfully serve Him, they will be rewarded in eternity. While they are on earth, the faithful followers of Christ will often receive little or no recognition for their labors. That will not be true in Heaven. There they will not only be received by God; they will also be honored for the faithful service they have rendered. This would be a good text for a lesson or devotion dealing with the future blessings God has for His people.

The outstanding person of this passage is Jesus. This passage illustrates several of Christ's attributes that should be stressed in preaching and teaching. Verse 42 is one of the key verses in understanding the life and ministry of Jesus. The fact He prays to His heavenly Father indicates the nature of the relationship that exists between them. Jesus is not afraid to make known to God His most profound desires. His humanity comes out clearly in the words "If thou be willing remove this cup from me." Throughout history, the Christian faith has taught that Jesus was (with the exception of sin) fully human. As a human being, He had no desire to suffer the kind of death He knew was in store for Him. No one would want to experience that suffering, pain, and degradation. The words "Nevertheless not my will, but thine, be done" reveal another important aspect of Jesus character. He was willing to accept the Father's will for His life even if it meant suffering and death. While this passage contains no well-developed doctrine of the atonement, it is clear Jesus is freely giving His life for the benefit of His followers. Salvation is one of the major themes of Luke's Gospel (Marshall, *Historian* 116). Whatever Jesus has to suffer, to obtain salvation for lost and fallen mankind, He is willing to do. His most important goal is the will of God be done on earth. Those who preach and teach from this passage should certainly give attention to what it says about the person and work of Christ.

D. Trials (22:54—23:23)

Following Jesus' arrest He was subjected to several hearings before different people. None of the Gospels gives a complete list of these hearings; each author includes those most relevant to his purpose. Shepard (573-589) presents the traditional outline of these various hearings:

1. A preliminary hearing before Annas, the Ex-High Priest. (Jn. 18:12-14, 19-23.)
2. First hearing before Caiaphas and the Sanhedrin. (Mk. 14:53, 55-65; Mt. 26:57, 59-68; Lk. 22:54, 63-65; Jn. 18:24.)
3. Formal condemnation by the Sanhedrin. (Mk. 15:1; Mt. 27:1; Lk. 22:66-71.)
4. First hearing before Pilate. (Mk. 15:1-5; Mt. 27:2, 11-14; Lk. 23:1-5; Jn. 18:28-38.)
5. Hearing before Herod Antipas. (Lk. 26:6-12.)
6. Second hearing before Pilate. (Mk. 15:6-15; Mt. 27:15-26; Lk. 23:13-25; Jn. 18:39–19:16.)

As this list demonstrates, the traditional view is that there were six different trials or hearings; Luke discusses four of them. The one that receives his greatest attention is the second hearing before Pilate, where Jesus is officially condemned to crucifixion. For an analysis of these hearing see D. Guthrie (*Jesus* 326-342).

54 Then took they him, and led *him*, and brought him into the high priest's house. And Peter followed afar off.

After Jesus' arrest, He is taken to the home of the High Priest where He is questioned by members of the Sanhedrin. At that time, Caiaphas was actually the high priest, but his father-in-law, Annas, continued to have great power and influence. Plummer (515) suggests that Caiaphas and Annas might have shared the same palace, with each living in separate quarters. Luke makes no mention of the outcome of this hearing. Since it was conducted during the nighttime hours, it was not an official trial and no verdict could be given (Plummer 514). Peter follows at a distance. When he arrives at the home of the high priest, he goes into the courtyard with others whom Luke does not identify.

55 And when they had kindled a fire in the midst of the hall, and were set down together, Peter sat down among them.

Peter warms himself with several others around a fire built in the open courtyard. At that time, houses of wealthy individuals were often built around such a courtyard. Gilmour ("Exegesis" 392-393) explains that the rooms of the house surrounded the open courtyard, which was entered through a vestibule. Lenski (1086) suggests the fire was made of charcoal, which made no smoke. The men would sit around the fire warming themselves. Luke does not indicate when this event occurred, but it probably took place during the middle of the night following Jesus' arrest.

56 But a certain maid beheld him as he sat by the fire, and earnestly looked upon him and said, This man was also with him.
57 And he denied him, saying, Woman, I know him not.
58 And after a little while another saw him, and said, Thou art also of them. And Peter said, Man, I am not.
59 And about the space of one hour after another confidently affirmed, saying, Of a truth this *fellow* also was with him: for he is a Galilaean.
60 And Peter said, Man, I know not what thou sayest. And immediately, while he yet spake, the cock crew.

Three times Peter denies even knowing Jesus, thus fulfilling the prophecy Jesus had made in 22:34. The denials are regarded as so important they are included in all four of the Gospel accounts. Plummer (514) discusses the similarities and the differences found in these accounts. The servant girl is not identified; she is probably a slave of Caiaphas. Luke does not explain whether or when she had seen Peter with Jesus. Since Jesus had been teaching that week in the outer courts of the Temple, she might have noticed him then. It is somewhat surprising that she recognized Peter in the darkness; the robe he was wearing would have covered both his body and his head.

The maid tells the men present that she has seen Peter with Jesus. This recognition puts Peter at risk of being examined and tried along with Jesus. By saying "Woman, I know him not," Peter denies having any acquaintance with Jesus. In effect, he is saying, "I do not even know who he is."

Sometime later, one of the men present makes a similar statement: "Thou art also of them," by which he means Peter has been one of the group of Jesus' disciples. For the second time, Peter strongly denies any association with Jesus and His disciples: "Man, I am not."

Approximately an hour later, a second man sees Peter and says, "Of a truth this fellow also was with him: for he is a Galilaean." This man probably recognizes Peter is a Galilean by his accent. He may know Peter is a disciple of Jesus, or he may simply assume this from Peter's Galilean accent.

For the third time, Peter denies any association with Jesus. His response might be paraphrased, "Man, I don't know what you are talking about." As Peter was speaking, a nearby rooster began to crow; the prophecy of Jesus was fulfilled. For good analyses of these three denials see D. Guthrie (*Jesus* 330-332) and Lieu (187-188).

61 And the Lord turned, and looked upon Peter. And Peter remembered the word of the Lord, how he had said unto him, Before the cock crow, thou shalt deny me thrice.
62 And Peter went out, and wept bitterly.

It is impossible to determine with certainty where Jesus was when He looked at Peter. Probably this occurred as Jesus was being led across the courtyard from the room where the hearing had taken place to His prison cell. Wherever it occurred, Jesus' eyes met Peter's. Apparently no words were spoken, but as he looked into the eyes of Jesus, Peter remembered how the Lord had predicted his denials. He was so affected by this he went out into the street and wept bitterly. His heart was filled with genuine sorrow for the terrible deed he had committed (Hendriksen, *Luke* 995).

S. Brown (71), commenting on Peter's denial, argues that Peter's faith has not failed. Peter has denied knowing Jesus, but he has not denied that Jesus is the Messiah. His sin is cowardice, and he is able to return very quickly to his position in the apostolic band.

63 And the men that held Jesus mocked him, and smote *him*.
64 And when they had blindfolded him, they struck him on the face, and asked him, saying, Prophesy, who is it that smote thee?
65 And many other things blasphemously spake they against him.

Luke does not explain precisely when this abuse occurred; it probably took place after the night-time hearing was completed. It is likely Jesus was left in the care of the guards until the next hearing would take place (Morris, *Luke* 316). These guards took advantage of their position to mock and humiliate Jesus. They had, no doubt, heard something of His prophetic powers. They blindfolded Him, struck Him on the face, and asked Him to prophesy who had hit Him. If Jesus responded to these insults, Luke does not include His response. Luke's goal is to illustrate the unjust and inhuman treatment Jesus received; He deserved none of this. D. Guthrie (*Jesus* 332) suggests this mistreatment by the soldiers was less painful to Jesus than the betrayals of His friends. Verse 65 is Luke's summary of the kind of treatment Jesus received during this entire process.

66 And as soon as it was day, the elders of the people and the chief priests and the scribes came together, and led him into their council, saying,
67 Art thou the Christ? tell us. And he said unto them, If I tell you, ye will not believe:
68 And if I also ask *you*, ye will not answer me, nor let *me* go.
69 Hereafter shall the Son of man sit on the right hand of the power of God.
70 Then said they all, Art thou then the Son of God? And he said unto them, Ye say that I am.
71 And they said, What need we any further witnesses? for we ourselves have heard of his own mouth.

Morris (*Luke* 317) notes it is difficult to determine all the details concerning the different trials and hearings to which Jesus was subjected. There were two main stages. The first was a Jewish hearing before the Sanhedrin. Since capital cases could not be heard at night, the Sanhedrin had to meet in an official session after daybreak to ratify the decisions that had been made during the night. They also had to finalize the charges they would present to Pilate. The second stage was the Roman trial before the governor. Many commentators assume only the Roman governor had the authority to order the death penalty. Caird (245) is not so sure; he notes that scholars are divided on this issue. He suggests the Sanhedrin might have had the authority to order Jesus' execution, but it did not do so. They sent the issue to Pilate. Morgan (258) asserts the Jewish Sanhedrin previously had the power to order execution, but they had lost that power.

It is important that in the formal trial after daylight the Sanhedrin presented no witnesses to testify against Jesus. They attempted to get Jesus to incriminate Himself. As noted previously, "Christ" (Greek *christos*) is the same as the Hebrew word for the Messiah. The members of the Sanhedrin are asking Him, "Are you the Messiah?" Jesus refuses to give them a direct answer. In effect, He says to them, "If I tell you that I am the Christ, you will not believe me." Verse 68 is difficult. Probably the idea is, "If I try to discuss this issue with you, you will refuse to do so" (Plummer 518). The idea is that they will not release Him no matter what answer He gives. He knows the deck is stacked against Him; He also understands that all of these events are part of God's plan for Him.

Since "Messiah" was used with many different connotations among Jews of the first century, Jesus reverts to the title "Son of man," which He often uses to describe Himself. In verse 69, Jesus asserts that His power to rule has come from God. The members of the Sanhedrin think they are in control of the situation, but they are not. They are not judging Jesus; He is judging them (Caird 245-246).

In verse 70, the members of the Sanhedrin ask Jesus directly, "Are you the Son of God." Jesus answers, "Ye say that I am." As Marshall (*Gospel* 851) notes, this is neither an affirmative response nor a denial. Since Jesus did not deny He was the Son of God, the members of the Sanhedrin take it to be a positive response. For them this is sufficient evidence to convict Jesus of blasphemy. Morgan (257) takes a different approach, concluding this is a positive response. In effect, Jesus is saying, "What you are saying is true. I am the Son of God."

Verse 71 is the conclusion to this hearing before the Sanhedrin. Jesus has not denied He is the Son of God, and the members of the court consider that to be a positive response. They have heard enough; they do not need to hear any more witnesses.

This may have been enough to convict Jesus of blasphemy before a Jewish court, but it was not enough to convict Him before a Roman court. The Roman governor would not consider blasphemy to be a legitimate charge deserving execution at the order of a Roman court.

Bock (*Luke* NIV 577) explains this trial violates several rules of procedure set out in the Jewish Mishnah, which was written about A.D. 170. While it is not certain all of these rules applied in the first century, it is probable many of them did. As Bock points out, the statements of Jesus do not meet the technical definition of blasphemy. Also, the Mishnah required an interval of two days between the hearing and the sentencing in a capital case. There was no such interval in the trial of Jesus.

23:1 And the whole multitude of them arose, and led him unto Pilate.
2 And they began to accuse him, saying, We found this *fellow* perverting the nation, and forbidding to give tribute to Caesar, saying that he himself is Christ a King.
3 And Pilate asked him, saying, Art thou the King of the Jews? And he answered him and said, Thou sayest *it*.
4 Then said Pilate to the chief priests and *to* the people, I find no fault in this man.
5 And they were the more fierce, saying, He stirreth up the people, teaching throughout all Jewry, beginning from Galilee to this place.

These verses describe the first of two hearings before Pilate (Shepard 583). During this hearing, the Jewish leaders do not bring up the charge of blasphemy because such a charge would have made no impact in a Roman court. Pilate was the Procurator from A.D. 26 to 36 (Shephard 582). During most of the year he resided in his palace in Caesarea, but he went to Jerusalem during the feasts so he would be present to suppress any riots or disturbances the Jews might stir up. Hendriksen (*Luke* 1007-1008) suggests he possessed little common sense and liked annoying the Jews.

"The whole multitude" (v. 1) may indicate the entire membership of the Sanhedrin appeared to make the charges against Jesus. It may also indicate the entire membership of the Sanhedrin supported the charges. Verse 2 outlines the charges the leaders of the Sanhedrin presented before Pilate. They brought basically three charges: (1) they accused Him of perverting or misleading the nation; (2) they accused Him of forbidding people to pay taxes to Caesar; (3) they accused Him of claiming to be Christ, a King. All three of these charges are general and have political overtones.

"Accuse," in verse 2 (Greek *katēgoreō*) is a technical term meaning to bring charges against someone in a court (Nolland III:1117). The first of these charges is deliberately vague (Hendriksen, *Luke* 1009). "Perverting" (Greek *diastreph*) is often used in the sense of "to lead astray." Here the idea seems to be that Jesus is accused of leading the Jewish nation away from its faithfulness to Caesar (Nolland III:1117). This sounds like a serious charge, but the members of the Sanhedrin cite no actual incidents where Jesus has tried to turn the people away from their loyalty to Caesar.

The second charge is more specific; they accuse Jesus of teaching the people not to pay taxes to Caesar. This is more serious, but once again the Jewish leaders provide no supporting evidence. Luke 20:21-26 affirms this charge was blatantly false.

The third charge is that Christ has claimed to be the Messiah or king. As noted previously, many of the Jews in the first century interpreted the term

"Messiah" in militaristic terms. They looked for a political Messiah who would put an end to Roman rule and restore the nation to a position of independence. The leaders of the Sanhedrin thought this charge might be accepted before Pilate. Pilate knew the Jews did not like being ruled by Rome; riots and rebellions occurred frequently. The Roman procurator would be expected to respond quickly to anything he saw as a threat to Roman rule in Palestine.

Pilate virtually ignores the first two charges. He asks Jesus, "Art thou the King of the Jews?"—obviously in reference to the third charge. Hendriksen (*Luke* 1009) suggests Pilate asked this for his own protection; he did not ask it because he took the charge seriously. Jesus' response could be translated, "It is as you say." As Matthew 26:25 and John 18:36-37 confirm, Jesus' response is in the affirmative. He does not deny being the King of the Jews. According to John 18:33-38, Jesus explains He means this claim to be the King of Israel in a spiritual sense and not in a political sense. He has no plan or desire to overthrow Roman rule in Palestine.

Apparently, Pilate understood the situation correctly; he saw that Jesus was no political threat to Rome. Therefore he said, "I find no fault in this man." Under normal circumstances, the trial would have ended then and there. Jesus would have been acquitted and released.

According to verse 5, the Jewish leaders were so determined to get a conviction they continued to press the issue. They levy no new charges against Jesus, but they continue to insist He is stirring up the people over the entire country. The term "Jewry" might also be translated "Judea," but in this context, it probably refers to the entire territory occupied by the Jews (Hendriksen, *Luke* 1010). They accuse Jesus of stirring up trouble from Galilee in the north to the city of Jerusalem.

6 When Pilate heard of Galilee, he asked whether the man were a Galilaean.

7 And as soon as he knew that he belonged to Herod's jurisdiction, he sent him to Herod, who himself was at Jerusalem at that time.

8 And when Herod saw Jesus, he was exceeding glad: for he was desirous to see him of a long *season*, because he had heard many things of him; and he hoped to have seen some miracle done by him.

9 Then he questioned with him in many words; but he answered him nothing.

10 And the chief priests and scribes stood and vehemently accused him.

11 And Herod with his men of war set him at nought, and mocked *him*, and arrayed him in a gorgeous robe, and sent him again to Pilate.

12 And the same day Pilate and Herod were made friends together: for before they were at enmity between themselves.

When Pilate heard the word "Galilee," he thought he had found a way out of this awkward situation. According to Roman law, an accused person might be tried for a crime either in the territory where the alleged crime had been committed, or in his home territory (Hendriksen, *Luke* 1011; Nolland III:1123). It is also true the crimes of which Jesus was accused could have been committed both in Judaea and in Galilee. Since Jesus could be considered a Galilean, Pilate could wash his hands of the whole matter by sending Jesus to be tried in Galilee. Fortunately for Pilate, the ruler of Galilee was also in Jerusalem for the feast.

This Herod is Herod Antipas. Upon the death of his father, Herod the Great, in 4 B.C., Herod Antipas was made the ruler of Galilee and Perea. This was the same Herod who was strongly rebuked by John the Baptist for taking his brother's wife; he then had John the Baptist executed.

Luke does not tell where in Jerusalem Herod Antipas was staying; Hendriksen (*Luke* 1012) suggests it was probably the Hasmonean Palace. Pilate arranged to have Jesus sent there. It is clear Pilate's goal was to transfer jurisdiction to Herod Antipas. Since Jesus had spent much of His public ministry in Galilee, there is no doubt Herod had heard at least some things about Him.

In verse 8, Luke explains that Herod was pleased to see Jesus. He had heard of Jesus' miracles, and he hoped Jesus would perform some miracle in his presence. Nolland (III:1122) points out that neither Pilate nor Herod Antipas had any real interest in this case. They viewed it as a power struggle within the Jewish community, and they had no desire to become involved.

Verse 9 gives a summary of the interview between Herod and Jesus; it did not go well. Herod asked Jesus a series of questions Jesus refused to answer. While this was going on, the Jewish leaders had followed Jesus to this interview and continued to make accusations against Him. Herod was a king, and he was not accustomed to being treated with such disrespect. In order to punish Jesus for His insolence, he turned Jesus over to his soldiers.

Verses 11-12 explain how Jesus' interview with Herod Antipas finally turned out. That Herod and his men "set him at nought" means they treated him as nothing (Lenski 1111). Jesus had refused to answer Herod's questions, and now He was to be punished. The soldiers mocked Jesus; they put a fancy garment on Him and sent Him back to Pilate. The phrase translated "gorgeous robe" (Greek *esthēta lampran*) literally means "a shining garment" (Lenski 1112). This was a mockery of the claim Jesus was the king of the Jews. After this humiliation and ridicule, Jesus was returned to Pilate. Herod Antipas had no interest in resolving this matter. Lenski (1112-1113) makes an interesting observation. He notes that neither Pilate nor Herod Antipas found Jesus to be dangerous. They considered Him a harmless fanatic.

In verse 12, Luke presents one rather unexpected result of the trial of Jesus. Pilate and Herod Antipas, who had formerly been enemies, now became friends. Nolland (III:1124) and Shepard (587) offer no reason for the earlier estrangement between Pilate and Herod Antipas. It is possible their common belief that Jesus was innocent brought them together.

13 And Pilate, when he had called together the chief priests and the rulers and the people,
14 Said unto them, Ye have brought this man unto me, as one that perverteth the people: and, behold, I, having examined *him* before you, have found no fault in

this man touching those things whereof ye accuse him:
15 No, nor yet Herod: for I sent you to him; and, lo, nothing worthy of death is done unto him.
16 I will therefore chastise him, and release *him*.
17 (For of necessity he must release one unto them at the feast.)
18 And they cried out all at once, saying, Away with this *man*, and release unto us Barabbas:
19 (Who for a certain sedition made in the city, and for murder, was cast into prison.)
20 Pilate therefore, willing to release Jesus, spake again to them.
21 But they cried, saying, Crucify *him*, crucify him.
22 And he said unto them the third time, Why, what evil hath he done? I have found no cause of death in him: I will therefore chastise him, and let *him* go.
23 And they were instant with loud voices, requiring that he might be crucified. And the voices of them and of the chief priests prevailed.

This second hearing before Pilate ultimately results in a sentence of death. Luke's account provides a great deal of information both about the character of Pilate and about the political situation existing in Palestine at that time. Luke does not indicate when this hearing took place; Shepard (587) believes it happened near sunrise on Friday morning. Pilate is convinced Jesus has done nothing worthy of death, but he calls for another hearing, probably at the request of the Jewish leaders.

In verses 14-15, Pilate gives a summary of what has happened so far in this case. The Sanhedrin has brought charges against Jesus, and He has appeared before Pilate and before Herod Antipas. Pilate notes that neither he nor Herod Antipas have found any reason to condemn Jesus. In verse 16, Pilate gives his verdict; he will order that Jesus be punished and then released. "Chastise" (Greek *paideuō*) is used with a wide variety of different meanings. It can mean "train up," "educate," "correct," or "discipline." It is sometimes used with the meaning "to beat" or "to whip," (Arndt and Gingrich 608-609), no doubt as a form of "discipline." The idea here seems to be that Pilate ordered Jesus whipped and then released.

Jesus was declared to be innocent of these crimes; Pilate should have ordered His immediate release with no punishment whatsoever. If Jesus had been a Roman citizen, that would no doubt have occurred. Since He was not a Roman citizen, Pilate had more discretion. He probably ordered the beating as a concession to the Sanhedrin. He thought this severe punishment would satisfy them, and the case would be closed (Lenski 1116-1117). Luke does not indicate the severity of the beating Pilate has in mind. Individuals were known to die as a result of a Roman flogging. It is also possible Pilate had a lighter flogging in mind (Morris, *Luke* 322-323).

This sentence illustrates the uneasy relationship that existed between the Jewish leaders and their Roman overlords. Pilate knew very well the Jewish leaders could stir up riots and cause problems for him if they chose to do so. He decided to punish an innocent man rather than run that risk.

Verse 17 is found in some of the early manuscripts but is absent in others.

Some translations of the Bible include this verse; others do not. The idea that the governor would release a prisoner is also found in Matthew 27:15, Mark 15:6, and John 18:39. These passages indicate that as a goodwill gesture, the Roman governor would release one prisoner at the time of the Passover (Hendriksen, *Luke* 1017).

It is clear from verse 18, the members of the Sanhedrin were unwilling to accept the compromise that would allow Jesus to be scourged and released. They were determined that He be executed. In the face of their continued opposition, Pilate tries another compromise to avoid condemning a man he believes to be innocent. He proposes to use his custom of releasing a prisoner during the feast as a way to release Jesus. The Jewish leaders refuse to accept this compromise. Instead, they demand the release of Barabbas, who was probably a terrorist who had been condemned to death for the crime of murder. Nothing is known about Barabbas other than what is written in the Gospels. Spence (236) suggests he was the leader of a group that rebelled against Roman rule; such groups were common at this time.

Verses 20-23 indicate Pilate made one last attempt to persuade those present to accept something other than crucifixion of Jesus. He asked, "What evil hath he done? I have found no cause of death in him." This did not persuade the Jewish leaders; they continued to cry out loudly for Jesus' crucifixion. After this, Pilate finally caved in to the pressure. He concluded that maintaining the uneasy peace with the Jewish leaders was more important than protecting the life of an innocent man.

Summary (22:54—23:23)

This section begins with the sad story of Peter's three-fold denial of any relationship with the Lord Jesus. Within the space of a few hours in the courtyard of the high priest, Peter denies three times that he even knows the Lord Jesus. As Morgan (253) notes, these denials did not indicate Peter's faith had failed. He still loved Jesus and believed in Him. His courage failed him; Peter's hope for the future was gone. Peter had probably been affected to some degree by the common thinking that the Messiah would be victorious. But now the Lord whom he loves seems anything but victorious; He is treated as a common criminal. Under these circumstances, it is not surprising Peter experienced a lack of courage. Peter was deeply troubled by his denials. According to verse 62, he "went out and wept bitterly."

This failure of courage was not, however, the end of Peter's service as a disciple. He would soon resume his leadership of the apostolic band. God used this sad experience as a way to prepare Peter for even greater service in the future.

Verses 63-65 describe the cruel treatment Jesus received, probably at the hands of the guards in the palace of Caiaphas. Perhaps the guards had been treated cruelly by their masters. At any rate, they inflict such treatment on Jesus. They mock Him and strike Him. They blindfold Him and demand He identify the one who hit Him. If Jesus responded to this cruel treatment, Luke makes no record of it. One of Luke's purposes is to show that Jesus is an innocent man who suffers unjustly. This passage helps develop that theme.

Verses 66-71 describe Jesus' official hearing before the Sanhedrin. The earlier meeting had been held during the night and did not constitute an official meeting. The rules required they have another meeting in the daytime to confirm the decision reached at the earlier, informal meeting. Jesus refused to cooperate with the Sanhedrin. In response to their questions, He said, "If I tell you, ye will not believe." Near the end of the interview, Jesus does not deny He is the Son of God. His response should probably be understood to mean, "You are correct to say that I am" (Bock, *Luke* NIV 574). The members of the Sanhedrin took this to be a positive response, and they considered it to be blasphemy; how could any human being claim to be the Son of God?

Luke 23:1-23 describes a series of three hearings; two of them are before Pilate and one is before Herod Antipas, the ruler of Galilee. In the first hearing, the leaders of the Sanhedrin present their charges against Jesus before Pilate. They do not bring up the charge of blasphemy because it is a religious charge that will carry no weight in a Roman tribunal. They accuse Jesus of misleading the people, forbidding people to pay taxes to Caesar, and claiming to be a king. Pilate ignores the first two of the charges, but he responds to the third. He asks Jesus, "Art thou the King of the Jews?" Jesus does not deny being the King of the Jews. In John, Jesus explains He understands the term "king" in a religious sense and not in a political sense. At the end of the hearing, Pilate says, "I find no fault in this man." He finds Jesus is not a threat to the political stability of Palestine. Jesus has made no effort to foment rebellion or overthrow Roman rule. Pilate probably thought of Him as nothing more than a religious fanatic in a land where religious fanatics were common.

Herod Antipas, the ruler of Galilee, was in Jerusalem to celebrate the feast. Since Jesus was a Galilean, Pilate saw an easy way to remove himself from this situation. He tried to turn the case over to Herod, but his attempt was not successful. Herod Antipas interviewed Jesus, but Jesus refused to respond to his questions. After his soldiers had abused Jesus, Herod Antipas ordered that He be returned to Pilate.

After a second hearing, Pilate can find no evidence that would justify a sentence of death as the Jewish leaders demanded. In an effort to conciliate them, Pilate offers them two compromises. First, he offers to have Jesus beaten and then released. Second, he offers to release Jesus following the custom the Roman governor release a prisoner in honor of the Passover. The members of the Sanhedrin refused both compromises. They continued to demand that Jesus be condemned to death by crucifixion. At the end of the hearing, Pilate agreed to their request. He ordered that Barabbas be released and Jesus be crucified.

Luke has carefully structured this entire scene to illustrate the injustice of the entire process. Jesus is an innocent man; He has done nothing worthy of death. From the standpoint of justice, He should have been released with no penalty whatever. Luke's goal in this passage is to show just how much Jesus suffered, not as a result of His own sins but in order to bring salvation to the world.

Application: Teaching and Preaching the Passage

This passage focuses on the trials Jesus suffers before being sentenced to death by crucifixion. There are few passages in the Bible that demonstrate as clearly as these verses the tragic consequences of sin. This passage illustrates the depths to which mankind will sink when sin is allowed to become the controlling force in people's lives. There are many lessons that can be learned from this important passage.

One approach is to examine how the various characters interacted with each other and how they viewed these tragic events. Pilate and Herod Antipas are tragic figures. They both have an incorrect view of Jesus; they simply cannot accept that He is, in fact, the Son of God. They view Him as a religious fanatic unworthy of receiving serious attention. They are weak in the sense they know Jesus is innocent of the charges that have been brought against Him, but they are unwilling to defend Him in the face of the hostility of the Jewish leaders. They are also opportunistic because they want to use this situation to advance their own position and power. They have no real sense of justice; they are only interested in protecting themselves and their privileged positions. Religious faith is, in reality, unimportant to them.

Unfortunately, there are many individuals in the modern world who possess these same characteristics. They are concerned, first and foremost, with their own ease and comfort. They have little or no sense of justice. They look upon religion as nothing more than a superstition. In our preaching and teaching, we need to emphasize the importance of having true religious faith and point out the difference it makes in our lives.

The guards and soldiers also make a significant contribution to this story. They reflect no concern for the suffering they inflict on Jesus; they have little or no respect for the value of human life. To them, Jesus is little more than an object to be used for their own amusement. Unfortunately, there are many people in the modern world who still reflect this kind of attitude. Christians must teach and preach that human life is valuable because it is a gift of God. All human beings deserve to be treated with dignity and respect.

Peter is the only disciple who contributes to this passage in a significant way, and there are several lessons modern believers can learn from him. We are all weak and subject to failure. Peter's faith did not fail; he never lost his assurance that Christ was the Messiah. What failed was Peter's courage. He simply could not defend his relationship with Christ in the midst of strong trials. Modern believers should not be hasty in standing in judgment on Peter; they have not been called upon to walk in his shoes.

Peter's failure in the garden did not lead to a permanent rejection of Christ as the Messiah. Peter recognized his sin, confessed it, and then went forward in the service of Christ. Within a short time, he would become one of the leading defenders of the Christian faith. Modern believers should learn to accept their weaknesses; we may all fail in times of great trial. We should also learn another important lesson from Peter. We should never allow past failures to prevent us from serving Christ today.

The greatest lessons found in this passage can be learned from Jesus' example. He was unjustly accused. As the Son of God, He possessed divine power. He could have liberated Himself from these situations of grief and suffering, but He chose not to do so. In one sense, Jesus was on trial before Jewish and Roman authorities, but in a larger sense, they were on trial before Him. How would they respond to what God was doing in their midst? Would they even recognize that God was working in a special way in their lives?

Jesus' suffering is vicarious. He has done nothing to deserve the abuse heaped upon Him. He suffers all of these things because they are necessary to God's plan for the salvation of mankind. However high the price may be to accomplish that goal, Jesus is willing to pay it. This passage, along with many others, demonstrates the depth of Jesus' love and commitment both to those whom He came to save and to the plan of God for redeeming mankind.

For modern believers, Jesus is both our Savior and our example. He is the Savior in the sense that He gave His life to redeem our lives. He is our example in that He demonstrates before us what it means to be a faithful follower of God. Modern preachers and teachers should emphasize both the price Christ paid for our redemption and the great changes in our lives that redemption brings about.

E. Crucifixion and Burial (23:24-56)

The crucifixion of Christ has produced considerable debate and discussion among students of the life of Christ. The day of His crucifixion and the year it took place have been at the forefront of this discussion. Hoehner (*Life* 65-114) provides a useful analysis of the positions most commonly held. While a detailed discussion of these issues is beyond the scope of this commentary, some attention to them seems warranted.

Determining the chronology of Christ's life and death is not easy. The Gospel writers (especially Luke) were more concerned with what happened than when it happened. Indeed, writers in the ancient world were less concerned than modern writers about chronology. For that reason, chronological references in the Gospels are few and subject to different interpretations. Another complicating factor is that in the ancient world there was no standard calendar; events were often dated in relationship to the reign of a king or emperor. Hoehner (*Life* 85-86) points out that there was no uniform way of defining when a day began. Sometimes days were counted from sunup to sunup; at other times, they were counted from sundown to sundown.

The first issue is to determine the day of the week when Christ was crucified. There are basically three views: Wednesday, Thursday, or Friday. The traditional view is He was crucified on Friday (Shepard 595). This view was universally accepted in the early church and is still the most widely-held view today (Hoehner, *Life* 72, 74). According to this, He was put on the cross at approximately 9:00 a.m. on Friday. He died and was entombed before 6:00 p.m. His body was in the tomb all day on Saturday; the resurrection occurred early on Sunday morning.

The arguments in favor of the crucifixion occurring on Wednesday revolve around a literal interpretation of Matthew 12:40, where Jesus says, "For as Jonas was three days and three nights in the whale's belly; so shall the Son of man be three days and nights in the heart of the earth." Scroggie (569-575), for example, takes this very literally, which requires the crucifixion on Wednesday. He adds to this the verses that speak of Jesus' resurrection occurring "after" three days (Mk. 8:31, 9:31, 10:34; Mt. 27:63; Jn. 2:19). He also includes a list of passages that speak of Jesus being raised "on the third day" (Mt. 16:21, 17:23, 20:19, 27:64; Lk. 9:22, 13:32, 24:7, 21, 46; Acts 10:40; 1 Cor. 15:4). Scroggie recognizes the Jews considered any part of a day to be a day, but he doesn't see this fact as sufficient to reconcile Matthew 12:40 with the traditional view.

Scroggie's second argument in favor of a Wednesday crucifixion is that the traditional chronology allows only a three hour window between Jesus' death and His burial; He died about 3:00 p.m. and was buried by 6:00 p.m. Scroggie (572-573) gives a list of twenty events which, according to the Gospels, took place between Jesus' death and His burial. He concludes the three hours allowed by the traditional chronology were simply not enough time for all of these events to occur. In his view, the crucifixion took place on the morning of Wednesday, the fourteenth day of Nisan. The body was buried shortly before sundown on that day and was in the tomb from Wednesday night until early Sunday morning when the resurrection took place (574-575). This timeframe allows ample time for the events described in the Gospels.

The main arguments against a Wednesday crucifixion are presented by Hoehner (*Life* 66-67). If Scroggie's reconstruction is correct, then Jesus arose on the morning of the fourth day, not on the morning of the third day. There are several passages in the N. T. that speak of the resurrection as occurring on the third day (Mt. 16:21, 17:23, 20:19, 27:64; Lk. 9:22, 18:33, 24:7, 21, 46; Jn. 2:19-22). The statement that Christ arose on the third day is also found in many of the early Christian statements of faith (Schaff II:17-71). Hoehner (*Life* 66) explains it is common knowledge the Jews of the first century considered any part of a day to be a day. For that reason, most interpreters have not insisted on a literal interpretation of Matthew 12:40; they consider it to be an expression Jesus' audience would have understood.

Another possibility is that Jesus was crucified on Thursday; this view is defended by Roger Rust (4-5). Rust suggests Jesus ate the Last Supper with His disciples on Wednesday afternoon. After that, He was arrested and tried. The crucifixion took place on Thursday morning and He died about 3:00 p.m. He was in the tomb from Thursday evening until early on Sunday morning. Rust also argues there were two Sabbath days that week. The fifteenth day of Nisan was a high day (Jn. 19:31) and was observed as a Sabbath, although it took place on Friday. The regular Sabbath was then observed on Saturday. Similar positions are taken by Shari Abbott and James D. Tabor.

Hoehner (*Life* 66-74) defends the traditional view that the crucifixion took place on Friday. He notes that arguments for the crucifixion taking place on Wednesday or Thursday are largely based on a literal interpretation of Matthew 12:40. He concludes a number of different events took place between Christ's death and His burial, but his view is they could have been done, within the limited time available, with the help of several different people. He also notes these views (particularly the Thursday view) require that the Triumphal Entry take place on the Sabbath, which Hoehner considers unlikely. The strongest argument in favor of the traditional chronology is the many references (Mt. 16:21; Mk. 8:31; and Lk. 9:22, for examples) to the resurrection occurring on the third day. If Jesus was crucified on Wednesday and resurrected early on Sunday morning, He was resurrected on the fifth day. If He was crucified on Thursday and resurrected early on Sunday, He was resurrected on the morning of the fourth day. There are also several passages that speak of the burial as occurring on the day of preparation (Mt. 27:62, 28:1; Mk. 15:42; Lk. 23:54; Jn. 19:31), which would have been Friday.

There is also evidence to indicate the traditional Friday-Sunday chronology was accepted in the early church. In paragraph 67 of the *First Apology of Justin Martyr*, we find these words, "For they crucified him on the day before Saturday, and on the day after Saturday, he appeared to His apostles and disciples and taught them these things which I have passed on to you also for your serious consideration" (C. Richardson 287-288).

While Matthew 12:40 is important for its comparison to Jonah, the preponderance of the evidence points toward the traditional view that the crucifixion took place on Friday. The burial then occurred late on Friday afternoon and the resurrection during the predawn hours on Sunday.

The second important issue is determining the year of Christ's crucifixion. This matter has attracted less attention from scholars, but it is important. Hoehner (*Life* 95) notes the suggested dates range from A.D. 21 to A.D. 36. In an effort to determine which year is the most likely, he considers evidence both from the N. T. and from astronomy. If Christ was crucified on Friday, the fourteenth day of Nisan, Hoehner (*Life* 100) concludes the crucifixion might possibly have taken place in 27, but more likely in 30, 33, or 36. Hoehner notes that many scholars favor A.D. 30, but he considers A.D. 33 most likely. Hiebert ("Chronology" 164) has also carefully examined the evidence, and he concludes the crucifixion occurred at the Passover of A.D. 30. While this Passover is not the only possibility, that seems the most likely date for the crucifixion.

24 And Pilate gave sentence that it should be as they required.
25 And he released unto them him that for sedition and murder was cast into prison, whom they had desired; but he delivered Jesus to their will.
26 And as they led him away, they laid hold on one Simon, a Cyrenian, coming out of the country, and on him they laid the cross, that he might bear *it* after Jesus.
27 And there followed him a great company of people, and of women, which also bewailed and lamented him.
28 But Jesus turning unto them said, Daughters of Jerusalem, weep not for me, but weep for yourselves, and for your children.
29 For, behold, the days are coming, in the which they shall say, Blessed *are* the barren, and the

wombs that never bare, and the paps which never gave suck.
30 Then shall they begin to say to the mountains, Fall on us; and to the hills, Cover us.
31 For if they do these things in a green tree, what shall be done in the dry?

Although he was convinced of Jesus' innocence, Pilate succumbed to pressure from the Jewish leaders and from the crowd they had stirred up. Geldenhuys (600) provides a brief overview of Pilate's service as Roman governor of Syria and Palestine. He served from A.D. 26-36. He was widely known for his cruelty; he often mistreated and executed people without even the pretense of a trial. He was a tyrant who had little regard for the people he ruled. He understood, however, that Rome expected him to maintain peace in the difficult province of Palestine. He knew the authorities in Rome would not look favorably upon riots and other civil disturbances fomented by the Jews. Rather than risk the wrath of his superiors in Rome, he consented to the execution of an innocent man.

In order to satisfy the mob, Pilate ordered the release of Barabbas, who was guilty of terrorism and murder. He also ordered the execution of Jesus. The "they" in verse 26 probably refers to the detachment of Roman soldiers who were appointed to carry out the crucifixion.

The custom was that the condemned man had to carry his cross to the place of execution. Some scholars argue that the condemned man carried only the large and heavy cross-piece while the upright post was left in the ground at the place of execution. Others suggest the condemned man was required to carry the entire cross. Stein (*Luke* 585) understands it to refer to the crossbeam.

As they were on their way to the place of execution, the Roman soldiers exercised their power to compel the assistance of civilians when necessary (Barclay 282). They compelled a man named Simon, a Cyrenian, to carry the cross, probably walking behind Jesus. Luke does not explain why it became necessary for someone else to carry the cross. Geldenhuys (602-603) suggests Jesus was in such a weakened physical state that He simply was not able to do so. He had been severely beaten and abused by the soldiers; there is no doubt He was exhausted and weakened from loss of blood.

Simon is identified as a man from Cyrene in North Africa, which was known for its large and influential Jewish community (Summers, *Luke* 300). Barclay (282) notes this is the modern city of Tripoli. Simon was a common Jewish name; he was probably a Jew who had come to celebrate the Passover in Jerusalem and was picked at random from the crowd. There is no evidence to indicate he was black or that he was chosen because of his racial background. It is more likely he was a rather prominent Jew who was compelled to carry the cross as another way of insulting the Jewish community. The fact that he was "coming out of the country" indicates nothing more than he had spent the night outside the city. It provides no information concerning his background or occupation.

It is possible Simon later became a believer. Mark 15:21 identifies him as the father of Alexander and Rufus, who would probably have been believers known to Mark's readers. There is no doubt that participating in the crucifixion deeply impacted Simon, but Luke provides no details.

In verse 27, Luke explains that a company of people followed Jesus as He made His way to the crucifixion; apparently, they were favorably disposed toward Him. Luke does not specifically identify this group, but it probably included some of the disciples and women who had followed Him from Galilee. It might also have included those from Jerusalem who were sorry to see an innocent man treated in such a horrible manner (Hendriksen, *Luke* 1024). The women mourned and wailed as they followed Jesus. Summers (*Luke* 301) explains that such outward demonstrations of grief were common in ancient Palestine. Stein (*Luke* 585) suggests these women might have been part of a group that gave a drink composed of wine and frankincense to condemned men as an act of mercy.

In the midst of His suffering and facing His upcoming death, Jesus turns His attention to these women. He tells them not to cry for Him but for themselves and for their children. The days are coming, He says, when people will say women unable to bear children are blessed. This is totally contrary to the common attitude toward motherhood. It was the goal of every woman to bear children; the inability to bear children was regarded as a disgrace (Stein, *Luke* 586). Jesus is warning that a day of terrible destruction is in store, and women who have children will have to watch their children suffer. Hendriksen (*Luke* 1024) suggests Jesus gives this warning to the women because they are unregenerate and need the gospel Jesus offers to them. He is suffering intensely now, but they will suffer even more intensely in the future. Geldenhuys (604) understands Jesus to be looking ahead to the intense suffering the people will endure during the war of A.D. 66-70. Hendriksen (*Luke* 1024) suggests the suffering the people will endure at the hands of the Romans serves as a prelude to the even greater suffering they will endure at the Judgment.

Verse 30 is based on Hosea 10:8, where the prophet speaks of the destruction of Samaria at the hands of the Assyrians. Summers (*Luke* 302) suggests two possible interpretations for this rather enigmatic verse. It may be a poetic way of asking the mountains and valleys of Judea to protect them from the Roman onslaught. The other interpretation, which Summers prefers, is that a quick death from falling mountains would be better than a slow, agonizing death at the hands of the Romans (Hendriksen, *Luke* 1024-1025; Marshall, *Gospel* 864-865).

Verse 31 is difficult and is interpreted in various ways. All interpreters recognize this is a proverbial expression containing symbolic language, but they interpret the symbols differently. Childers (607) understands the verse to be a comparison between what the Romans are doing to Jesus and what they will do to Jerusalem in the future. The green tree represents Jesus who has done nothing to overthrow Roman rule. The dry tree represents the Jews who have always been disloyal to Rome. If the Romans will treat Jesus, who has been loyal to them, in such a cruel manner, how much more cruel will they be to the rebellious Jews?

Summers (*Luke* 302) takes the green tree to represent the presence of Jesus and the offer of forgiveness He has extended to the Jewish people. The dry tree refers to the time when the city will be destroyed and there will be no opportunity for deliverance. The general idea of this verse is that if Jesus, who is entirely innocent, is now called upon to suffer, how much more will those who reject Him be forced to suffer in the future (Barclay 284)?

32 And there were also two other, malefactors, led with him to be put to death.
33 And when they were come to the place, which is called Calvary, there they crucified him, and the malefactors, one on the right hand, and the other on the left.
34 Then said Jesus, Father, forgive them; for they know not what they do. And they parted his raiment, and cast lots.
35 And the people stood beholding. And the rulers also with them derided *him*, saying, He saved others; let him save himself, if he be Christ, the chosen of God.
36 And the soldiers also mocked him, coming to him, and offering him vinegar,
37 And saying, If thou be the king of the Jews, save thyself.
38 And a superscription also was written over him in letters of Greek, and Latin, and Hebrew, THIS IS THE KING OF THE JEWS.

Jesus was not crucified alone; He was executed along with two other men, one on His right and the other on His left. "Malefactor" is a general term for a criminal (Lenski 1129-1130). Matthew and Mark describe them as thieves or robbers. Luke does not explain why these two men were crucified; Lenski (1130) speculates that Jesus was crucified between two common criminals to embarrass the Jews. The act of crucifying one who claimed to be their king in the midst of two common criminals was another attempt at ridicule (Crabtree 464). Mark 15:27-28 notes this fulfilled the prophecy of Isaiah 53:12, that He would be "numbered with the transgressors." Green (*Luke* 819) explains these two men must have been dangerous and violent or they would not have been sentenced to die by crucifixion.

Matthew and Mark use the Aramaic word "Golgotha," which means "the place of a skull," for the place where Jesus is crucified. Luke calls the place "skull" (Greek *kranion*), since "Golgotha" would have had no meaning for his Gentile readers (Plummer 530). The English word "Calvary," which has the same meaning, is from the Latin Vulgate (Lenski 1130).

The precise location of Golgotha has been much debated. R. Brown (*Death* 937-938) relates how the architects employed by Constantine selected the place where it was believed that the crucifixion had taken place for the construction of a sacred enclave. That structure was later rebuilt in the time of the Crusaders; the Church of the Holy Sepulchre stands today on that traditional site. Unger (104) suggests the crucifixion took place on a hill outside the city wall as it existed at that time, to the northwest of the city of Jerusalem.

It the nineteenth century, another site, adjoining what is commonly known as the "Garden tomb," was proposed. It lies about 820 ft. north of the existing wall, which was built in the time of the Turks, near what is known as the Damascus Gate. The knoll near this tomb looks something like a skull. While this site does give the modern person some idea of what the tomb and crucifixion site might have looked like, there is no historical evidence indicating this is the actual place (R. Brown, *Death* 938-939).

In verse 33, Luke describes the crucifixion of Jesus in the briefest of terms: "They crucified him." He provides no description of how the crucifixion was done because no explanation was necessary; his readers understood well what it meant to be crucified—the slowest, most painful, most humiliating, and most cruel method of execution known in the ancient world. It was designed not only to punish wrongdoers, but also to intimidate people and deter them from further rebellion. Victims were normally crucified naked, but there is an early tradition that Jesus wore a loincloth. Crucifixion was so detested by the Jews they would not practice it; they ordinarily executed by stoning a condemned person to death. Dosker (ISBE II:760-762) provides a brief summary of how crucifixion was done in the Roman Empire. Given the nature of crucifixion, the Jews naturally questioned how anyone crucified could be the Messiah.

Dosker also explains that different types of crosses were used by the Romans, and Luke does not say which form was used in Jesus' crucifixion. Probably, Jesus was crucified on a *crux immissa*, which had a shorter crosspiece nailed to an upright post, with part of the post sticking out above the crosspiece. The victim was severely beaten and forced to carry his cross—either the crosspiece or the entire cross—to weaken him and hasten his death. The victim was then nailed or tied to the cross and left to die. Death by crucifixion was slow and painful, and the suffering was intense, especially in hot climates. Rarely did a young and relatively healthy victim die before enduring at least thirty-six hours of agony; death could be hastened by breaking the victim's legs. The fact Jesus died after only six hours was viewed with astonishment.

Victims were first affixed to the crosspiece by being nailed or tied. Then the crosspiece, with the body attached, was lifted up, using forked poles, and placed into a notch cut into the upright. The Gospels do not indicate whether Jesus was nailed or tied to the cross. Luke 24:39 and John 20:25, 27 may indicate Jesus was nailed. It is likely at times both nails and ropes were used to secure the body to the cross. Edersheim (*Life* II:589) notes that the bodies of those being crucified were not lifted high into the air; the feet were generally only one or two feet off the ground.

Crucifixion was widely practiced in the Roman Empire and in several other ancient cultures. According to Josephus, Alexander Jannaeus (one of the Maccabean rulers of Judea before Christ) executed 800 prisoners by this method in the first century B.C. During the Roman domination of Palestine, it became a regular practice. Josephus also notes that the governor of Syria executed 2,000 Jews by crucifixion in 4 B.C. (R. Brown, *Death* 946). Crucifixion was not abolished until the time of Constantine when Christianity became a legal religion in the Roman Empire. There are references in ancient literature to large numbers of people being executed by this method. It was normally meted out for such crimes as treason, desertion in the face of the enemy, piracy, and other things equally serious. Roman citizens were protected from this form of punishment; it was normally reserved for prisoners, such as terrorists, and slaves.

There are many references to crucifixion in the literature of the period, but archaeology has discovered the physical remains of only one individual who was executed in this way. McRay (204-206) explains the bones of a man who had been crucified were discovered in Israel in 1968. He was a male between twenty-four and twenty-eight years of age and was crucified about the middle of the first century. There is some disagreement among the scholars concerning how he was positioned on the cross and whether his arms and feet were tied or nailed to the cross. Yamauchi (657) notes that the ossuary (a box in which bones were placed after the body's decomposition) contained a heel bone with a four-and-a-half-inch iron nail still attached. The bones also revealed that nails had penetrated his forearms and not his hands. His leg bones had been shattered to hasten his death. For an analysis of the crucifixion of Jesus see Green (DJG 146-163).

The Gospels record seven sayings spoken by Jesus on the cross, although none include all seven. Luke includes three, with the first in verse 34. Walvoord (129-130) and Hendriksen (*Luke* 1027-1028) give lists of these seven sayings. While the precise order of these sayings cannot be determined, it is likely Luke has included the first, second, and seventh. Perhaps Luke included these three because he considered them to be the most meaningful for his Gentile readers.

As Jesus was suffering the agonies of crucifixion, He prayed for those who were crucifying Him, saying, "Father, forgive them; for they know not what they do." Summers (*Luke* 304) and R. Brown (*Death* 975) explain these words are found in many but not all of the early manuscripts of Luke. For a good analysis of the textual evidence concerning this verse see Marshall (*Gospel* 867-868). Jesus begins His prayer with the word "Father." Even as He is dying on the cross, He does not lose sight of the special relationship He has with His heavenly Father. The word "forgive" is the normal word used to describe the pardoning or sending away of sin.

By "them" Jesus could be referring to the Roman soldiers who cause His suffering, but He probably also includes His Jewish persecutors who are responsible for His execution (R. Brown, *Death* 973-974). He prays for the forgiveness of all of those who have rejected Him and refused to heed the message of hope He came to bring.

The last part of verse 34 points out that the Roman soldiers divided up His clothing. Barclay (285) notes Jews normally wore five articles of clothing—an inner tunic, the outer robe, a girdle, sandals, and a turban. The four soldiers divided these articles of clothing among themselves; they probably cast lots for the outer robe, which would have been the most valuable of Jesus' garments. Because of the strong feelings the Jews had about nudity, it is possible Jesus and other Jews were crucified wearing a loincloth (R. Brown, *Death* 953).

Verse 35 discusses two groups present at the crucifixion, the people and the rulers. The "people" probably included some of Jesus followers who had come with Him from Galilee and people from Jerusalem who were sympathetic to Jesus. It is also possible some were there simply to view the spectacle. The "rulers" were probably leaders of the Jews in Jerusalem; Stein (*Luke* 589) posits they were probably members of the

Sanhedrin. These Jewish rulers ridiculed Him by saying the one who claimed to be the Messiah could not even deliver Himself from the Cross. Luke's Gentile readers would have immediately seen the irony in this statement. Little did the Jewish rulers realize He could have saved Himself from the crucifixion, but He chose not to do so. He was dying for their redemption.

In verse 36, the Roman soldiers who were doing the crucifixion joined in the ridicule. They drew near Him, mocked Him, and offered Him vinegar to drink. "Vinegar" (Greek *oksos*) was the sour wine the soldiers and the common people drank (Marshall, *Gospel* 869-870). It seems likely the soldiers were drinking it as they waited for the condemned men to die. The offer of this sour wine can be interpreted in two different ways. It may be viewed as an act of mercy; those being crucified suffered from acute thirst. It may, however, be another act of ridicule and mockery. The small amount of alcohol the cheap wine contained would not have significantly reduced the pain. Luke does not indicate whether Jesus accepted or refused this offer. Matthew 27:34 and Mark 15:23 note Jesus refused the wine that was offered to Him. The word for the wine is likely drawn from the Greek version of Psalm 69:21, which indicates offering the vinegar was an act of scorn and contempt.

The soldiers continue the mockery by taking up the idea earlier expressed by the Jewish leaders: "If thou be the king of the Jews, save thyself" (v. 37). The soldiers had no better understanding of the true mission and message of Jesus than the Jewish leaders.

In verse 38, Luke calls attention to another act of ridicule. Pilate had ordered a sign be placed over His head indicating His crime, written in Greek, Latin, and Hebrew so all might read it (Jn.19:19-22). The "Hebrew" may refer to the language spoken by the Jews in the first century, which would have been Aramaic. Picirilli (417-418) suggests that it was a board or tablet of some kind that indicated the crime of which the person being crucified had been convicted. Bock (II:1853-1854) notes such an inscription was known as a *titulus*; it generally contained the name of the person being executed and the crime of which he had been convicted. Shepard (596) explains this placard was normally carried before the person as he walked to the place of execution; sometimes it was hung around the man's neck.

Critics have pointed out the words written on this sign are found in all four of the Gospels, but the wording does not always agree. Conservative interpreters explain these differences in various ways. Probably each Gospel writer is giving a summary, or the gist, of the words on the sign. It is also possible some Gospel writers depended on the Greek text, while others depended on the Hebrew or Latin text. Marshall (*Gospel* 870) suggests Luke's quotation is based on Mark. The best explanation is that each writer is giving a summary he knows will be meaningful to his readers.

This superscription above Jesus' head was not only designed to ridicule Him; it was also designed to ridicule the Jews. Luke does not indicate who determined the wording to be placed on the placard, but the Gospel of John attributes it to Pilate, who probably intended it to convey some of the contempt he had for the people he ruled. How could this poor man who is dying by crucifixion be considered a king? Kings are victorious; they do not die in such a fashion. Given the low esteem in which the Romans held the Jews, this man is, in their eyes, a proper king for the Jewish people.

39 And one of the malefactors which were hanged railed on him, saying, If thou be Christ, save thyself and us.
40 But the other answering rebuked him, saying, Dost not thou fear God, seeing thou art in the same condemnation?
41 And we indeed justly; for we receive the due reward of our deeds: but this man hath done nothing amiss.
42 And he said unto Jesus, Lord, remember me when thou comest into thy kingdom.
43 And Jesus said unto him, Verily I say unto thee, To day shalt thou be with me in paradise.

In verse 39, one of the criminals being crucified with Jesus begins to mock Him with words similar to those spoken by the soldiers in verse 37. The malefactor tells Jesus that if He is indeed the Messiah, He can save Himself and them from the horrible suffering all three are enduring.

Only Luke includes the story of the one malefactor who confessed Jesus' innocence and asked His forgiveness. R. Brown (*Death* 999-1000) explains this passage is more than just an expression of Jesus' mercy and generosity. It continues the theme of God's mercy toward sinners, which has been a part of Luke's message from the beginning of the Gospel.

In verse 40, this criminal rebukes the other by saying, "Dost not thou fear God?" This question implies that the speaker probably is a Jew who fears God. It is clear this man understands that Jesus has some relationship with God, but it is doubtful he fully understands who Jesus is and why He has come to earth. In verses 40b-41, he contrasts their situation with that of Jesus. The two criminals are suffering justly in the sense they are guilty of the crimes for which they have been tried. Jesus, on the other hand, has done nothing to deserve crucifixion; He is suffering innocently. Luke is careful to point out there are those involved in the crucifixion—including Pilate—who recognize Jesus' innocence.

This condemned man not only recognizes Jesus' innocence, he also makes a very special request of Jesus: "Lord, remember me when thou comest into thy kingdom" (v. 42). By "thy kingdom," he probably means the future kingdom the Messiah was expected to establish. To be in that kingdom means to be blessed and to be in the presence of God. Jesus responds with a great promise. "Verily" (Greek *amēn*) can also be translated "truly." By these words, Jesus is not verifying the truthfulness of the statement He is about to make; He is emphasizing its importance.

Some interpreters understand the word "today" to refer to the day on which these words were spoken. If that interpretation is correct, the meaning would be, "I say to you today, that you will be with me in Paradise." Most interpreters, however, understand the term to indicate before the day is over, this criminal will be with Jesus in Paradise (R. Brown, *Death* 1009). Ellis (268) explains that "today" is often used as a technical term describing the day of salvation. Ellis understands it to refer to the day of Christ's resurrection and exaltation. It is interesting to note Jesus has not responded to the accusations that had been made against Him, but He takes time to respond to this man's petition.

The word "paradise" (Greek *paradaisos)* is of Persian origin; its original meaning is "park" or "garden." This word was gradually adopted into the Greek and Hebrew languages (Caird 252), where it was used in several different ways. In the Septuagint, it was used for the Garden of Eden. It was later incorporated into the Jewish understanding of eschatology. Jewish beliefs about eschatology were not uniform; some Jews used this term to describe the interval of time between death and the resurrection. Others used this term to describe the idea that the souls of the righteous went immediately into Heaven upon death. That seems to be the idea here. For a rather detailed discussion see R. Brown (*Death* 1010-1013). Jesus tells the repentant malefactor that, upon death, he will go with Him, and they will be ushered into the presence of God. It is not Jesus' purpose in this brief statement to give a detailed chronology of future events; His goal is to assure this man his repentance gives him great hope for the future.

44 And it was about the sixth hour, and there was a darkness over all the earth until the ninth hour.
45 And the sun was darkened, and the vail of the temple was rent in the midst.

In these two verses, Luke describes two supernatural events that indicate God the Father is actively involved in this terrible scene. Since the Jews counted time from sunrise, the sixth hour would be about noon; the ninth hour would be about 3:00 p.m. During the hours when the sun would normally shine its brightest, there is darkness. The word translated "earth" can also mean "land." Some interpreters understand this word to describe the entire earth; others see it as describing the land of Judea. Either interpretation is possible.

There is a textual variant in the first part of verse 45. Some manuscripts say the sun was eclipsed or failed, while others say it was darkened or obscured. In this context, the difference between these two words is not great. The idea is that during this three-hour period the sun did not shine as it normally would. Various natural phenomena have been offered to explain this darkness, including an eclipse, sunspots, solar storm, thunderstorm, etc. (R. Brown, *Death* 1040). An eclipse is the least likely explanation. The Passover occurred at the time of the full moon, and eclipses do not occur during a full moon. Also, there is no record of any eclipse in Palestine that lasted for three hours. Edersheim (*Life* II:604) mentions that an earthquake is another possibility, but he does not consider it likely. It is clear this event is a miracle sent by God, and it is possible there is no natural explanation for it.

Verse 45b states the veil in the Temple was "rent in the midst" or "torn in the middle." According to Jeremias (*Jerusalem* 38), this curtain was made from expensive materials imported from Babylon. Ellis (269) notes there were thirteen curtains used in the Temple. R. Brown (*Death* 1109-1113) explains the various veils used in Herod's Temple. As

Bock (*Luke* NIV 596) points out, this may refer to the veil that separated the Holy of Holies from the Holy Place or to the outer veil that provided entrance to the Holy Place (R. Brown, *Death* 1101). Ellis (269) suggests it was likely the curtain that separated the Holy of Holies from the Holy Place.

Bock (*Luke* NIV 596) writes the Temple was the center of the Jewish religion; for that reason, the rending of the veil was of special significance. In his view, this rending might indicate the time of God's judgment had arrived, and the Temple would be included in that judgment. He notes the tearing of this veil might signify the way had been opened for direct access to God. According to R. Brown (*Death* 1067), the darkness and the rending of the veil symbolized God's judgment on those who had mocked Jesus.

46 And when Jesus had cried with a loud voice, he said, Father, into thy hands I commend my spirit: and having said thus, he gave up the ghost.

With these brief words, Luke describes the death of Jesus. "Father, into thy hands I commend my spirit" are drawn from the Septuagint version of Psalm 31:5. In that Psalm, the writer is affirming his trust in God, praying for his deliverance from enemies. The final words of Psalm 31:5 are "Thou hast redeemed me, O LORD God of truth." Jesus has now completed the ministry the Father sent Him to accomplish. The time for His deliverance has come.

That Jesus "gave up the ghost" is Luke's way of saying Jesus' earthly life came to an end. "Ghost" (Greek *pneuma*) can also mean "breath," "wind," or "spirit." Since the Hebrews thought of life as being found in the breath or in the blood, the idea is that Jesus died. The time of Jesus' death is not mentioned; it probably occurred at the ninth hour, about 3:00 p.m. (v. 43).

Nothing is said about the deaths of the two malefactors who were crucified with Jesus. They were probably still alive when Jesus was taken down from the cross.

47 Now when the centurion saw what was done, he glorified God, saying, Certainly this was a righteous man.
48 And all the people that came together to that sight, beholding the things which were done, smote their breasts, and returned.
49 And all his acquaintance, and the women that followed him from Galilee, stood afar off, beholding these things.

One of Luke's consistent themes in the story of Jesus' death has been the contrast between those who cried out for His crucifixion and those who knew He was innocent. That theme is continued here. The centurion, who was in charge of the detail of Roman soldiers who crucified Jesus, recognized He was a "righteous man." R. Brown (*Death* 1162-1163) discusses the possible meanings of the term "righteous." This Roman military officer had done his duty, but he understood the crucifixion of Jesus was an unjust act.

Verses 48-49 mention other groups and individuals who were supportive of Jesus in His final hours. When the crucifixion was over, they beat on their breasts as a sign of mourning and returned to their homes. Some of His acquaintances, including the women who had come with Him from Galilee, stood some distance away in sorrow. There was nothing they could do, but they cared too much for Jesus to leave Him even in death.

50 And, behold, *there was* a man named Joseph, a counsellor; *and he was* a good man, and a just:
51 (The same had not consented to the counsel and deed of them;) *he was* of Arimathaea, a city of the Jews: who also himself waited for the kingdom of God.
52 This *man* went unto Pilate, and begged the body of Jesus.
53 And he took it down, and wrapped it in linen, and laid it in a sepulchre that was hewn in stone, wherein never man before was laid.
54 And that day was the preparation, and the sabbath drew on.
55 And the women also, which came with him from Galilee, followed after, and beheld the sepulchre, and how his body was laid.
56 And they returned, and prepared spices and ointments; and rested the sabbath day according to the commandment.

Jews and Romans had sharply differing attitudes concerning the treatment of the bodies of those who had been executed. R. Brown (*Death* 1207-1211) notes that Roman law provided the bodies of those executed should be given over to be buried by their families or by others. There is, however, ample evidence to indicate this was not always observed. The bodies of Christian martyrs of the second century were left exposed for six days, as an example to others, and then burned. Sometimes bodies were left on a cross to rot or be eaten by the birds. In the provinces, the disposal of bodies of those who were not Roman citizens was left to the discretion of local governors. There is little doubt Pilate had the authority to release the body of Jesus, but it is somewhat surprising he chose to do so. One would expect Pilate to be afraid that Jesus' followers would use His body in an effort to make Him a martyr.

Jewish attitudes concerning the bodies of those who had been executed would have been governed by Deuteronomy 21:22-23. That passage provides that the body of a condemned criminal should not be left hanging overnight; it should be removed and buried before nightfall.

Joseph of Arimathea went to Pilate and asked for the body of Jesus in order to give it a proper burial. He is described as a counselor, a good and just man, one who waited for the Kingdom of God, and one who had not consented to the crucifixion of Jesus. "Counselor" means he was a member of the Jewish high council, the Sanhedrin. "Good" and "just" are descriptions of character; he was faithful in his obligations in support of the Jewish religion. That he "waited for the kingdom of God" indicates he looked forward to the day when the Messiah would come and establish His righteous reign on earth. The fact he had not supported the Sanhedrin's decision to seek the execution of Jesus is significant. While it does not necessarily indicate Joseph was a follower of Jesus, it does indicate he saw the injustice of what they were doing. It also indicates he was a man of strong character who was not afraid to stand up for what he believed.

Matthew 27:58 states Pilate ordered the body of Jesus be given to Joseph. In Luke, the fact he was allowed to take the body down from the cross indicates the same thing. Luke does not specifically state why Pilate gave the body of Jesus to him; it is possible Pilate was troubled by the knowledge he had condemned an innocent man to death. According to verse 53, Joseph took the body down, probably with the help of others, and wrapped it in a linen cloth. It was then laid in a sepulcher, or tomb, which had been hewn from the rock where no body had previously been placed. Matthew 27:60 mentions this tomb had been prepared for Joseph himself.

According to verse 54, these events took place on Friday, which was the day of preparation before the Sabbath. As the verse explains, the beginning of the Sabbath was drawing near, at sundown, and they did what they could to prepare the body for burial. After they had done what they could, the women returned to Jerusalem and obtained the necessary spices. After the Sabbath, they planned to return to complete the anointing of the body for burial according to the Jewish custom. Green (DJG 88-91) and Edersheim (*Life* II:617-619) describe the sequence of events that took place during the brief time available to prepare the body for burial.

The fact they returned early on Sunday morning to complete the anointing indicates they did not have sufficient time to complete the process before the Sabbath began. The last words of verse 56 indicate these women were faithful Jews; they rested on the Sabbath day as the Jewish law provided.

Summary (23:24-56)

This passage deals with the crucifixion and death of Jesus; it raises several important issues. Two of the most important and most debated are the day of the week when He was crucified and the year in which the crucifixion took place. The crucifixion might have taken place on Wednesday, Thursday, or Friday, and each of those days has its defenders. The traditional view is Christ was crucified on Friday, placed in the tomb before 6:00 p.m., and arose from the dead early on Sunday morning. This traditional view was universally accepted in the early church and is still the most widely-held view. One of the strongest arguments in favor of the traditional view is that several N. T. passages (Mt. 16:21, 17:23, 20:19, 27:64; Lk. 9:22, 18:33, 24:7, 21; and Jn. 2:19-22) state Jesus rose on the third day.

The arguments for a Wednesday crucifixion are based primarily on a literal interpretation of Matthew 12:40, "For as Jonah was three days and three nights in the whale's belly; so shall the Son of man be three days and three nights in the heart of the earth." Scroggie is one of the principal defenders of a Wednesday crucifixion. He presents two arguments. First, he interprets Matthew 12:40 literally. In his view, the crucifixion took place on Wednesday morning, the fourteenth day of Nisan. The resurrection occurred early on Sunday morning. He argues this timeline allows ample time for the completion of all the events mentioned in the Gospels. Second, Scroggie argues the traditional chronology allows only a three-hour window between Jesus' death and His burial. In his opinion, that was not sufficient time for the twenty events that took place between Jesus' death and burial.

The main difficulty with Scroggie's proposal is that a Wednesday crucifixion demands Christ be resurrected on the fourth day. That runs contrary to the clear statements of several N. T. passages. For this reason, the majority of conservative scholars maintain the traditional chronology that Christ was crucified on Friday and resurrected early on Sunday morning.

The year of Christ's crucifixion has attracted less attention from scholars but is still an important issue. Hoehner has extensively analyzed this issue, using information both from the Bible and from astronomy. If the crucifixion took place on Friday, the fourteenth day of Nisan, it could conceivably have happened in A.D. 27, 30, 33, or 36. Hoehner notes that many scholars prefer A.D. 30, but he feels that A.D. 33 is most likely. While the year cannot be determined with absolute certainty, the most likely possibility is that Jesus was born about 4 or 5 B.C. and crucified about A.D. 30.

In this passage, Luke explains Pilate gave in to the demands of the crowd and ordered that Jesus be executed by crucifixion. Barabbas, who was probably a terrorist, was released. According to the Roman custom, the condemned man was required to carry his cross—probably the large crossbeam—to the place of execution. Because His body had been so weakened by the abuse He had suffered, Jesus was not physically able to carry the cross. The soldiers then ordered a man named Simon, from Cyrene in North Africa, to carry His cross. Simon was probably a Jew who had come to Jerusalem to attend the Passover; he was probably chosen at random.

Beginning in verse 27, Luke explains that a crowd of people follow Jesus as He makes His way to the place of crucifixion; at least some of them seem to be favorably disposed toward Him. Along the way Jesus speaks to some of the women who follow. He tells them not to weep for Him but for themselves and their children. He speaks briefly to them of the difficult days that lie ahead; He predicts that conditions will become so terrible people will wish to die rather than continue in suffering.

Jesus and two other men were led to a place called Calvary, where they were crucified with Jesus in the middle. The Gospels record that Jesus spoke several times during His hours on the cross. Luke records three of them. In verse 34, Jesus prays, "Father, forgive them; for they know not what they do." In verse 43, Jesus says to the penitent thief, "Verily I say unto thee, To day shalt thou be with me in paradise." The last of the three sayings is found in verse 46; Jesus cries with a loud voice, "Father, into thy hands I commend my spirit." These three sayings reveal a great deal about the life and ministry of Jesus. Even while He was suffering all the tortures Rome could produce, He never lost sight of His mission. He never lost His love for lost and fallen mankind; He even prayed God's forgiveness on the soldiers who were crucifying Him.

According to Luke, the cruel treatment Jesus had received in the hours before the crucifixion continued while He was on the cross. The soldiers cast lots for His clothing. The Jewish leaders who were present mocked Him saying, "He saved others; let him save himself, if he be Christ, the chosen of God." The soldiers also mocked Him by offering Him some of the cheap wine they were drinking.

The normal practice was to place a placard over the head of the man being crucified, listing the crimes he had committed. Above Jesus' head was placed a sign reading, "This is the King of the Jews." This saying was designed to make a mockery not only of Jesus but also of the Jewish community.

In Luke's account, one character stands out. One of the thieves being crucified with Him recognizes Jesus is an innocent man who has done nothing worthy of death. This unnamed thief says to Jesus, "Remember me when thou comest into thy kingdom." Jesus responds by saying, "Verily I say unto thee, To day shalt thou be with me in paradise."

Application: Teaching and Preaching the Passage

Luke presents the story of Jesus' crucifixion from two perspectives, and these perspectives should be carefully considered in preaching and teaching from this passage. First, Luke focuses the readers' attention on the different groups and individuals that participate in one way or another in this gruesome event. Second, Luke focuses on Jesus' own contribution to these tragic events. There are many lessons modern believers can learn both from Jesus and from those around Him.

First, there is the reaction of the Jewish leaders and their followers. This group views Jesus as an enemy of the Jewish religion; they consider Him to be a blasphemer. They cannot accept the fact Jesus might truly be the Son of God. They view Him as a threat to their power and control, and also to their very way of life. They understand, correctly, that if they accept Jesus' claims to be the Messiah they will have to change radically their conception of what it means to be a follower of God. It is clear the Jewish leaders were under the control of sin and Satan. They give us a good example of what happens in the lives of people when sin is on the throne.

Second, there are the followers of Jesus who are present during and after the crucifixion. They are totally broken by this series of events, but they do not lose their faith in Jesus as the Messiah. They are not part of the power structure, and they can do nothing to stop the crucifixion. When it is finally over, they care enough to retrieve the body of Jesus and give it a proper burial. They remain loyal to Jesus even in death. One of the heroes of the story is Joseph of Arimathaea, who goes to Pilate and asks for the body of Jesus so it may receive a proper burial. It is somewhat surprising that Pilate grants his request. Joseph and the women do what they can to prepare the body for burial in the limited amount of time they have.

The penitent thief should probably be included in this group. The thief comes to faith in Christ while hanging with Him on a cross. It is difficult to imagine a conversion taking place in more unlikely circumstances, but God's power to forgive sin is available under all circumstances.

These individuals remain faithful to Jesus even in the most difficult of circumstances. They are willing to publicly identify with Him even in the face of public hostility and official condemnation. That is real faith; the members of this group serve as an excellent example for believers today.

Third, there are those who recognize the injustice of the crucifixion, but they are unwilling or unable to do anything about it. Pilate is the most notable member of this group. He knows that Jesus has done nothing worthy of death, but he surrenders to the threats of the Jewish leaders. This is exactly the kind of weakness and indecision that characterizes many people in the world today. They may realize Jesus is the Son of God and the Savior of the world, but for political or social reasons they are unwilling to make a commitment to Him. Preachers and teachers can use the members of this group as illustrations of what can happen to us if we give too much power and control to Satan.

The centurion also belongs in this group. He was in charge of the detail of soldiers who actually carried out the crucifixion. In one sense, we have to feel sorry for him. He realized he was doing something wrong, but he was a soldier under orders. He had no choice but to obey Pilate's orders.

The members of this third group point out clearly the vicarious nature of Christ's death. Jesus dies as an innocent man; He has done nothing to deserve the cruel death He suffers. He dies for others. He dies so they may have the opportunity to hear the good news and receive Christ into their lives.

The most important lessons in this passage can be learned from Jesus. In the midst of great suffering, He never loses His composure. He remains focused on the ministry God has given Him. He never becomes bitter or vengeful. Even in His hour of great suffering, He always remains more interested in others than in Himself. He prays for those who are abusing Him; He accepts the confession of the penitent thief.

In verse 46, when the hour of death has finally arrived, Jesus gives public testimony to His faith in His heavenly Father: "Father, into thy hands I commend my spirit." The words and actions of Jesus serve as an inspiration to believers of every age. We are not the Son of God; we cannot do all the things Jesus did. We are, however, His disciples. We can take Him as our example and follow in His footsteps; we can place our trust in Him.

F. Resurrection and Ascension (24:1-53)

The resurrection is clearly the key event in Jesus' earthly ministry. As Shepard (608) explains, "The resurrection of Jesus is the keystone to the arch of Christianity." Henry (147) echoes a similar sentiment. The theological significance of the resurrection is underscored by Paul who wrote, "And if Christ be not raised, your faith *is* vain; ye are yet in your sins. Then they also which are fallen asleep in Christ are perished" (1 Cor. 15:17-18).

No one actually witnessed the resurrection (Morris, *Luke* 332), but the fact that all four of the Gospels include discussions of the resurrection serves to underscore its importance in the preaching and teaching of the early church (Mt. 28:1-16; Mk. 16:1-8; Jn. 20:1-17). All four of the Gospels agree on the essential elements of the story. They all point out that when the earliest witnesses arrived at the tomb, they found it to be empty (Summers, *Luke* 318; Morris, *Luke* 332). Later witnesses also found the tomb to be empty. No one was present at the time the resurrection took place, but the empty tomb clearly implied that the body of Jesus had been resurrected prior to the arrival of the women. The Gospels all agree that Jesus appeared to different individuals and groups of believers after His resurrection. Wilckens (33) notes there is one basic fact that binds all of the accounts together; it is the fact that the One who was crucified by the hands of men has been raised by the power of God.

While all the Gospels agree on the essentials, there are some differences in detail. For example, according to Matthew 28:2-5, the women were greeted by one angel who had rolled the stone away and then talked with them. In Mark 16:5, the women were greeted by a young man. According to Luke 24:4, they were greeted by two men who are later identified as angels. According to John 20:12, when Mary Magdalene arrived at the tomb for the second time, she was greeted by two angels. For good discussions of the similarities and differences in the Gospel accounts, see Summers (*Luke* 315-322); Marshall (*Gospel* 882); and Hendriksen (*Luke* 1051-1060).

Caird (256) notes that the accounts of the resurrection found in Luke and Mark have much in common, but there are at least four significant differences. Mark mentions one young man at the tomb; Luke mentions two. In Mark, the women are told to go and inform the disciples that Jesus is going before them into Galilee. Luke does not include this information; in its place, he makes reference to teachings formerly given in Galilee. According to Mark, the women fail to deliver the message because of their fear. In Luke, they make a full report to the disciples. The final difference concerns the names of the women. Mark includes Salome while Luke includes Joanna.

Shepard (609) notes that it is difficult to harmonize all the details of the resurrection accounts. He asserts there are no contradictions in the Gospel accounts, but none of them give a complete description of the post-resurrection appearances. Edersheim (*Life* II:621-622) suggests that various factors may have contributed to the differences in detail. The narratives are compressed; none of the writers had the space to give all the details. It is also probable the Gospel writers depended on different sources that contained different information. Each writer also composes his narrative with a certain audience in mind, and he includes the information that will be most relevant for that audience (Morris, *Luke* 332). In addition, each writer has certain goals and objectives he wishes to accomplish, and these goals and objectives influence the selection and presentation of the material. Under the leadership of the Holy Spirit, the Gospel writers present the information that will be most useful to their recipients.

According to S. Brown (74), Luke's account of the resurrection is designed to accomplish three specific objectives: (1) to restore the unity of the apostolic band by the restoration of two disciples whose faith has been hindered by the events of the passion; (2) to assure His followers of the bodily nature of Christ's resurrection; and (3) to demonstrate through the Scriptures that the Messiah must be a suffering Messiah.

It is important that Luke's Gentile readers understand the resurrection was not simply some type of vision or spiritual resurrection. The post-resurrection body of the Lord was capable of eating, talking, and interacting in different ways. Finally, Luke wants his readers to have a correct understanding of the Messiah. This means they must reject the political and often military ideas generally connected with the Messiah. They need to understand that a suffering Messiah is the fulfillment of the O. T. Scriptures.

1 Now upon the first *day* of the week, very early in the morning, they came unto the sepulchre, bringing the spices which they had prepared, and certain *others* with them.
2 And they found the stone rolled away from the sepulchre.
3 And they entered in, and found not the body of the Lord Jesus.
4 And it came to pass, as they were much perplexed thereabout, behold, two men stood by them in shining garments:
5 And as they were afraid, and bowed down *their* faces to the earth, they said unto them, Why seek ye the living among the dead?
6 He is not here, but is risen: remember how he spake unto you when he was in Galilee,
7 Saying, The Son of man must be delivered into the hands of sinful men, and be crucified, and the third day rise again.
8 And they remembered his words,
9 And returned from the sepulchre, and told all these things unto the eleven, and to the rest.
10 It was Mary Magdalene, and Joanna, and Mary *the mother* of James, and other *women that were* with them, which told these things unto the apostles.
11 And their words seemed to them as idle tales, and they believed them not.
12 Then arose Peter, and ran unto the sepulchre; and stooping down, he beheld the linen clothes laid by themselves, and departed, wondering in himself at that which was come to pass.

The Jewish Sabbath would have ended at 6:00 p.m. on Saturday. After the Sabbath ended, the women completed the preparation of the spices they would need to finish anointing the body of Jesus (Geldenhuys 623). Early the next morning, they went to the tomb for this purpose. The "first day of the week" is the typical way of describing Sunday. The phrase "and certain others with them" is found in many of the early manuscripts of Luke, but not in all of them (Marshall, *Gospel* 884). This phrase should be interpreted in light of verse 10. The idea is that Mary Magdalene, Joanna, and Mary took other women along as they went to the tomb.

"Very early in the morning" (Greek *orthrou batheōs*) means "at first dawn" (Marshall, *Gospel* 883). Probably the idea is the women began their journey to the tomb just as dawn was beginning to break. Edersheim (*Life* II:631) explains it was not unusual for friends and relatives to go to the grave during the first three days to verify the person was, in fact, dead. He also suggests there may have been two groups of women who had agreed to meet at the tomb (*Life* II:630-631).

When the women arrived at the tomb, they immediately noticed a most remarkable thing. The large stone, which had sealed the tomb, had been moved away from the entrance. Fitzmyer (II:1544) explains that first-century tombs in the area around Jerusalem were generally sealed with large circular stones that could be rolled in a track cut in the rock. This large circular stone concealed the rectangular door that led into the tomb. Hooke (115) compares the various Gospel writers' explanation of the rolling away of the stone.

Luke offers no explanation how the stone was rolled out of the way. The implication is this was, in some way, an act of God. It should be noted the stone was not removed so Jesus could exit the tomb but so the women and the disciples could enter. The women entered the tomb and found the body of Jesus was gone. Luke makes no mention of the earthquake or the position of the grave clothes, discussed in other Gospels (Mt. 28:2; Jn. 20:6-7). As usual, Luke focuses on the most important element in the story, the absence of the body. For useful discussions of textual variants that occur in this section of Luke see Robertson (*Textual Criticism* 225-237), and Creed (293).

The women are perplexed; they do not know what to think or how to interpret what they have found. "Much perplexed" (Greek *aporeō*) means "to be at a loss" or "to be uncertain" about something. The absence of the body has caught them unprepared; they do not know what to make of it. Luke then notes that two men stand beside them in shining garments, but he does not indicate whether this is while the women were still in the tomb or after they had stepped outside. The two men are dressed in "shining garments." Marshall (*Gospel* 885) asserts this manner of dress distinguishes them from ordinary men. Marshall also notes this description is reminiscent of the Transfiguration experience narrated in Luke 9. In Luke 24:23, these two men are specifically identified as angels. Keener (256) explains that in the O. T. angels often appear as human beings; they also appear in radiant apparel.

The women are so frightened by the appearance of these men in dazzling apparel they bow their faces to the earth. "Were afraid" (Greek *emphobos*) literally means "to be full of fear" or "to be terrified." When the two men spoke to the women, they asked a very telling question, "Why seek ye the living among the dead?" Creed (293) sees a slight rebuke in these words. In verse 6, the men go on to explain that Jesus is no longer among the dead; He has been resurrected. The women need to look for Him among the living and not among the dead. The men then remind the women that Jesus had spoken of His resurrection when He was with His followers in Galilee. Hendriksen (*Luke* 1053) provides a list of these passages, including Luke 9:22, 44 and 18:31-34. Luke concludes this portion of the narrative by noting the women then remembered this teaching Jesus had given.

Summers (*Luke* 319) and Stein (*Luke* 605) point out that the words "He is not here but is risen" are not found in all of the manuscripts of Luke, but they are present in most. These words are omitted in some modern translations but Summers observes they are definitely part of the original text.

According to Luke, both the women and the disciples are surprised by the resurrection. How is it that Jesus disciples failed to understand the teaching He had given concerning His death and resurrection? Summers (*Luke* 320) posits that the explanation can be found in the unwillingness of His disciples to accept the idea that He would die. They wanted Him to continue with them. They had developed a mental block, which made it difficult for them to understand or accept Jesus' teachings in this regard. Keener (256) offers a somewhat different explanation. He notes one reason for the unbelief of the disciples is that a resurrection of this nature was contrary to the commonly-accepted ideas of the coming of the Messiah.

Plummer (550) suggests the disciples understood Jesus' references to rising again as referring to His returning in glory, either in a new body or as an incorporeal being. It seems none of them understood it to refer to a bodily resurrection.

In verse 7, the two men share with the women a brief summary of what Jesus had taught in Galilee at an earlier stage of His public ministry. These words from verse 7 are not a quotation drawn from a specific passage but a summary of what Jesus had taught (Geldenhuys 625). This verse emphasizes three elements of Jesus' teaching: His betrayal, His crucifixion, and His resurrection. Summers (*Luke* 319) explains that before He began the journey to Jerusalem, Jesus taught His disciples concerning these events (Lk. 9:21-22, 43-45). Luke 9:45 had already indicated that the disciples "understood not this saying, and it was hid from them." The implication is that God prevented them from understanding this aspect of Jesus' teaching. This helps explain why the women and the disciples had a difficult time understanding and accepting Jesus' resurrection.

Verse 8 points out that after the two men had spoken these words, the women then remembered the teachings Jesus had given. Verses 9-12 continue the story. The women hurried back to Jerusalem to tell the disciples what they had seen and heard. Verse 10 mentions three women by name, Mary Magdalene, Joanna, and Mary the mother of James; it also mentions that other unnamed women also participated. Creed (294) notes these women were the first to receive and pass on to others the information about Jesus' resurrection, and it was important their names be preserved. For Luke, it was important that a significant number of credible witnesses had found the tomb to be empty.

The women recounted these events to the eleven disciples who remained after the apostasy of Judas Iscariot, but the disciples were unwilling to accept their testimony. Summers (*Luke* 320-321) asserts that the disciples found the story so incredible they simply could not accept it. "Idle tales" (Greek *lēros*) has the idea of "nonsense," a word sometimes used for what those who were delirious said (Plummer 550). Liefeld (1049) and Keener (256) explain that in ancient Israel the testimony of women was not held in high regard. Even so, the disciples' unbelief was involved. They simply were not yet ready to accept the fact of Jesus' resurrection; they had to go and see for themselves.

In verse 12, Peter, who continues to function as the leader of the apostolic band in spite of his denials of Christ, runs to the tomb to see for himself whether the words spoken by the women are indeed true. Luke gives only a brief description of Peter's visit to the tomb, noting only that Peter also found the tomb empty and the grave clothes still in their place. The fact the grave clothes—probably the strips of cloth wrapped around the body—are still there is significant. If the body had been stolen, the thieves would have taken the body, grave clothes, and all. The fact the grave clothes are left in the tomb is an evidence the body was not stolen but resurrected (Summers, *Luke* 321). For a description of the grave clothes see Hooke (131-132).

The last words of verse 12 are significant. They explain that even Peter, the leader of the apostles, did not understand what was happening. As he left the tomb and returned to Jerusalem, he continued to ponder the significance of what he had seen and heard. These words are also significant because they lay the groundwork for the next episode, Jesus' encounter with the two disciples on the road to Emmaus. That encounter will help both the disciples and the readers of Luke's Gospel to understand these important events better.

13 And, behold, two of them went that same day to a village called Emmaus, which was from Jerusalem *about* threescore furlongs.
14 And they talked together of all these things which had happened.
15 And it came to pass, that, while they communed *together* and reasoned, Jesus himself drew near, and went with them.
16 But their eyes were holden that they should not know him.
17 And he said unto them, What manner of communications *are* these that ye have one to another, as ye walk, and are sad?
18 And the one of them, whose name was Cleopas, answering said unto him, Art thou only a stranger in Jerusalem, and hast not known the things which are come to pass there in these days?
19 And he said unto them, What things? And they said unto him, Concerning Jesus of Nazareth, which was a prophet mighty in deed and word before God and all the people:
20 And how the chief priests and our rulers delivered him to be condemned to death, and have crucified him.
21 But we trusted that it had been he which should have redeemed Israel: and beside all this, to day is the third day since these things were done.
22 Yea, and certain women also of our company made us astonished, which were early at the sepulchre;
23 And when they found not his body, they came, saying, that they had also seen a vision of angels, which said that he was alive.
24 And certain of them which were with us went to the sepulchre, and found *it* even so as the women had said: but him they saw not.
25 Then he said unto them, O fools, and slow of heart to believe all that the prophets have spoken:
26 Ought not Christ to have suffered these things, and to enter into his glory?
27 And beginning at Moses and all the prophets, he expounded unto them in all the scriptures the things concerning himself.
28 And they drew nigh unto the village, whither they went: and he made as though he would have gone further.
29 But they constrained him, saying, Abide with us: for it is toward

evening, and the day is far spent. And he went in to tarry with them.
30 And it came to pass, as he sat at meat with them, he took bread, and blessed *it*, and brake, and gave to them.
31 And their eyes were opened, and they knew him; and he vanished out of their sight.
32 And they said one to another, Did not our heart burn within us, while he talked with us by the way, and while he opened to us the scriptures?
33 And they rose up the same hour, and returned to Jerusalem, and found the eleven gathered together, and them that were with them.
34 Saying, The Lord is risen indeed, and hath appeared to Simon.
35 And they told what things *were done* in the way, and how he was known of them in breaking of bread.

The beautiful story of Jesus' encounter with Cleopas and another unnamed disciple is found only in Luke (Mk. 16:12-13 may refer to it). Luke does not identify the source of the information, but Plummer (551) asserts it most likely came from one of these two disciples. "That same day" indicates the same day the women went to the tomb and found it empty. This incident probably took place sometime during the afternoon. These two are committed followers of Jesus, but not part of His inner circle. They are apparently walking from Jerusalem to their home in Emmaus.

Luke never identifies the second person. Wilcock (208) suggests the unidentified disciple may be the wife of Cleopas. He notes that "them" (Greek masculine plural) would be used for a group that included both men and women. The traditional interpretation is this second disciple is an otherwise unidentified male (Childers 611).

Emmaus was located about sixty "furlongs" (Greek *stadia*), approximately 6.8 miles, from Jerusalem. The exact location of this village is unknown (Summers, *Luke* 322; Morris, *Luke* 337). In the early church, it was often identified with the town later known as Nicopolis (Creed 294), but this can hardly be the correct location because it was located about 176 stadia from Jerusalem. According to Geldenhuys (636), the most likely location is the village of Kubeibeh, located about seven miles northwest of Jerusalem. See Fitzmyer (II:1561-1562) for an extensive analysis of the possible locations of Emmaus.

As they were walking along, these two disciples were discussing the events that had transpired during the last few days. Apparently, it was an animated discussion. "Reasoned" (Greek *suzēteō*) is used to describe both a discussion and a dispute (TDNT VII:747-748). Luke does not describe the content of their conversation, but they probably shared the same fears and frustrations Peter and the other disciples reflected (Keener 256-257).

The resurrected Jesus joined them on the journey, but they did not recognize Him. Keener (256) points out there were many pilgrims in Jerusalem at this time, and it would not have been unusual for someone to join them on the road. Cleopas and his fellow disciple probably assumed the stranger was a pilgrim on his way home. H. Wright (39) explains that Jesus dealt with these two disciples in a most effective manner. He first built rapport with them as they walked along. He then asked some non-directive questions to give them an opportunity to vent their fears and frustrations. Only after He had built rapport with them and given them an opportunity to share their feelings did Jesus confront them with their misunderstandings both of His teachings and of the O. T. As Wright observes, Jesus' rebuke to them was "gentle but firm."

Verse 16 explains that "their eyes were holden that they should not know him." Luke does not explain what prevented them from recognizing Jesus, but the implication is that divine initiative stood in the way. If they had immediately recognized Jesus, the conversation would have gone in a totally different direction.

In verse 17, Jesus asks an open-ended question designed to engage the two disciples in conversation. In essence, He asks, "Why are you so sad?" Cleopas is somewhat surprised by Jesus' question. "Stranger" (Greek *paroikos*) could include anyone from another place, thus a visitor. Cleopas, then, asks if He is the only such person in Jerusalem who is not familiar with the events that have transpired. In verses 19-24, Cleopas gives a brief summary of what he has seen and heard. These events focus on Jesus of Nazareth, whom they considered to be "a prophet mighty in deed and word before God and all the people." The O. T. prophets were important people in the work of God. They served as His spokesmen; on occasion they performed miracles. Jesus' followers considered Him to be a prophet because He had performed miracles and had given teachings, which impressed them as being from God.

Cleopas recognizes the responsibility for Jesus' crucifixion rested not on the people but on the Jewish leaders. Pilate would not have ordered His execution if the Jewish leaders had not demanded it.

Verse 21 reveals what sort of Messiah many of the people of Israel expected. That they "trusted that it had been he which should have redeemed Israel" reflects something of their hopes and dreams (Morris, *Luke* 338). Geldenhuys (633) explains they hoped Jesus would reveal His power as the Messiah and would deliver the nation of Israel from all her enemies, both material and spiritual. The crucifixion had shattered these hopes. The people expected the Messiah to be victorious, but Jesus had suffered a horrible and humiliating execution.

Cleopas also notes that "to day is the third day since these things were done." In Jewish thought, there was some hope the dead might come back to life during the first three days. That time is past, and from their perspective, there is no longer any hope that Jesus can be the Messiah.

Verses 22-24 show that Cleopas and the other disciple had heard about the women who had visited the tomb and found it to be empty. They were also aware that some of the disciples had visited the tomb and also had found it empty. It seems these two disciples understood that certain events had transpired earlier in the day, but they did not know what to make of them.

In verses 25-27, Jesus speaks openly with these two disciples. He begins to explain to them the kind of Messiah the O. T. documents anticipated. "O fools, and slow of heart to believe" may not be as severe a rebuke as they sound, but Jesus does chide them for their failure to comprehend and accept the understanding of the O. T. Scriptures He had shared with them. Jesus does not cite any specific passages at this point, but the idea is that the O. T. writings speak of a suffering Messiah. These two disciples, and other disciples also, had failed to understand that part of the message. They had considered only those O. T. passages that spoke of the Messiah as being victorious. They did not pay sufficient attention to passages that taught the Messiah's victory would be obtained through suffering.

Verse 27 is a summary of what Jesus told these two committed but uninformed disciples. The name "Moses" was often used to describe the first division of the Hebrew O. T., known today as the Pentateuch. "The prophets" referred to the second division of the Hebrew O. T., which included the historical and prophetic books. In this context, the expression "Moses and all the prophets" probably meant the entire O. T. revelation (Geldenhuys 634; Summers, *Luke* 326). Summers (*Luke* 326) suggests Jesus might have used Isaiah 53 and other passages that described His suffering and death.

In verses 28-30, Jesus and the two disciples are drawing near the village of Emmaus, and Jesus' manner is as though He plans to continue past Emmaus. Keener (257) notes that unless Jesus had been invited to spend the night with them, this was the polite way for Him to act. How Jesus communicated He was going to continue, Luke does not say. The disciples then invite Jesus to spend the night with them, saying "It is toward evening, and the day is far spent." The disciples have had a long day, and they are looking forward to some rest. Keener (257) points out that travel at night, especially away from Jerusalem, was dangerous. It was the custom of Jews to offer hospitality to fellow Jews. It is also possible they wished to continue their conversation with Jesus; He consented to remain with them in the village.

The disciples are, no doubt, hungry after their trip from Jerusalem, and food has been prepared for them. At this point, Jesus becomes the host rather than the guest. He blesses the bread and divides it among those present. Creed (297) notes that blessing and breaking bread was something Jesus characteristically did during His earthly ministry. Geldenhuys (634-635, 637) notes that Jesus' action is somewhat similar to what He did when He instituted the Lord's Supper, but the meal in Emmaus is not a celebration of the Lord's Supper. It is an ordinary meal blessed by the presence of the resurrected Jesus.

These disciples then realized the man with whom they had been speaking was Jesus. Luke explains, "their eyes were opened, and they knew him." The implication is that their eyes were opened by the power of God. The word "knew" in this context means they understood for the first time that they had been talking with the resurrected Christ. Jesus has now accomplished His mission to enlighten these two disciples. He then miraculously disappears from their sight. By this time, Jesus has taken on His resurrection body, which is not subject to the physical limitations of an earthly body. He can appear and disappear as necessary.

Verses 32-35 describe how these disciples responded to their incredible meeting with the risen Christ. "Did not our heart burn within us?" indicates both the emotional nature and the transformative nature of their experience with

Christ. In ancient times, the "heart" meant the center of thought and intention. This was no superficial experience; these two disciples were affected deeply, down to the very depths of their souls. This was also a transformative experience, in that now they had a correct understanding of who Jesus was and why He had suffered. His suffering did not indicate He was not the Messiah. Quite the contrary, His suffering was now seen as a strong evidence of His messiahship. The result of this encounter with Jesus was their thinking and actions were significantly altered. They could now be effective witnesses for Jesus Christ.

In verse 33, Luke notes at that very hour they began the return journey to Jerusalem to share what they had seen and heard with the eleven apostles and other followers of Christ gathered with them. Apparently, the lateness of the hour was no longer important. The urgency of the matter demanded an immediate return to the city. Lenski (1194) speculates they arrived in Jerusalem about 9:00 p.m.

The words of verse 34 provide a summary of news the two disciples from Emmaus received when they arrived back in Jerusalem. They learned Jesus not only appeared to them, but He also appeared to Simon Peter. Verse 35 notes the disciples who had arrived from Emmaus also shared with the followers of Jesus in Jerusalem what they had experienced. The last words of verse 35 indicate that as Jesus was breaking bread with them their spiritual eyes were opened and they realized who He was. They understood He was truly the long-anticipated Messiah.

36 And as they thus spake, Jesus himself stood in the midst of them, and saith unto them, Peace *be* unto you.
37 But they were terrified and affrighted, and supposed that they had seen a spirit.
38 And he said unto them, Why are ye troubled? and why do thoughts arise in your hearts?
39 Behold my hands and my feet, that it is I myself: handle me, and see; for a spirit hath not flesh and bones, as ye see me have.
40 And when he had thus spoken, he shewed them *his* hands and *his* feet.
41 And while they yet believed not for joy, and wondered, he said unto them, Have ye here any meat?
42 And they gave him a piece of a broiled fish, and of an honeycomb.
43 And he took *it*, and did eat before them.

Verses 36-43 form a unit of material designed to demonstrate the reality of the resurrection. As Marshall (*Gospel* 900) points out, Luke has two purposes in mind. First, he wants to emphasize that the resurrected Jesus is the same person as the Jesus who lived and taught in the land of Israel. Second, he is seeking to establish the physical reality of Jesus' resurrection body. He is not simply a ghost or spirit. The resurrected body is different from Jesus' earthly body, but it is a real body.

In verse 36, Jesus suddenly and miraculously appeared in the midst of His disciples. Since He had, by this time, received His glorified or resurrected body, Jesus was no longer subject to the limitations of a human body. John 20:19 describes what is likely the same incident, noting the doors were shut "for fear of the Jews." Lenski (1196) explains the doors or walls of a building would no longer hinder Jesus' movements. He could appear and disappear wherever and whenever necessary.

The resurrection of Jesus is clearly different from what had happened to Lazarus and others who had been restored to life. Lazarus and others were resuscitated; their human life was restored to them. They returned to the earthly life they had enjoyed before death. Jesus was resurrected; He was not simply restored to the human plane of existence. He received a glorified body that possessed supernatural qualities. For useful comparisons between the resurrection of Jesus and the resuscitations of other individuals see Hooke (109-112) and R. Brown (*Christology* 162).

Jesus suddenly appeared as the two disciples from Emmaus were talking with a group of Jesus' disciples in Jerusalem. Luke does not outline the subject of their discussion, but they were no doubt talking about the events that had transpired earlier in the day. The words "peace be unto you" are a common Hebrew greeting (Lenski 1197), but in this context they are clearly designed to comfort His troubled disciples. By His appearance, Jesus brings to fulfillment the promise He has often made to bring them into a state of peace with God.

The disciples are terrified by the appearance of Jesus. The last words of verse 37 explain they thought they had seen a "spirit"—perhaps meaning a ghost. It is clear the disciples are not expecting an appearance by the risen Lord; they are taken completely by surprise.

Jesus responds to their fear and concern by asking two questions. The first is, "Why are you troubled?" This question implies the disciples should have recognized their Lord. It also implies they should have anticipated His return from the dead. He had, on occasion, spoken to them about His resurrection. The second question is, "Why do thoughts arise in your hearts?" In Hebrew thinking, the heart is the center of thought and intention. Jesus does not expose the "thoughts" but probably refers to the fear and lack of understanding that dominate the thinking of the disciples. They are skeptical and do not know what to believe. Jesus' question implies they should have had a higher level of understanding than they had.

In verse 39, Jesus offers evidence to His disciples that He is really appearing to them; they are not seeing some spirit or ghost. He invites them to examine His hands and feet. Luke does not say whether the prints of the nails were visible in Jesus' resurrected body. Hendriksen (*Luke* 1074) and Plummer (559) explain the marks from the crucifixion on Jesus' hands and feet are not mentioned here, but they are implied. The basic idea is Jesus is asking them to note that He has real flesh and bones, which are things no ghost or spirit possesses (Geldenhuys 640; Ellis 279). As Hooke (132) notes, there is no mention in the Gospels of how Jesus was dressed after the resurrection. He was probably wearing a long robe like those worn by men in first-century Palestine. In verse 40, Jesus pulls up the long robe He was wearing so the disciples might see His hands and feet with their own eyes. The disciples are invited to look at Jesus' hands and feet so they may have visible evidence of the resurrection. A ghost or spirit would not possess physical hands and feet.

Verse 41 gives the initial reaction of the disciples. They are still not convinced Jesus has really appeared to them; they continue in unbelief. The word "joy" expresses the idea of happiness or joyfulness. The idea is the disciples are not manifesting the spirit of joy and happiness Jesus' appearance should have produced.

Then Jesus asks them a third question, whether they have any "meat," an old English word describing any type of food. Literally this is "anything (or something) edible" (Greek *ti brōsimon*). They gave Him a piece of broiled fish. The words "and of a honeycomb" are not found in the earliest manuscripts of the Gospel. There is no mention that the disciples ate with Him; the idea is that Jesus ate before them as a way to demonstrate the reality of His resurrection body (Bock II:1934). Keener (258) supports this interpretation when he notes that in the Jewish traditions, angels did not ordinarily eat human food.

44 And he said unto them, These *are* the words which I spake unto you, while I was yet with you, that all things must be fulfilled, which were written in the law of Moses, and *in* the prophets, and *in* the psalms, concerning me.
45 Then opened he their understanding, that they might understand the scriptures,
46 And said unto them, Thus it is written, and thus it behoved Christ to suffer, and to rise from the dead the third day:
47 And that repentance and remission of sins should be preached in his name among all nations, beginning at Jerusalem.
48 And ye are witnesses of these things.
49 And, behold, I send the promise of my Father upon you: but tarry ye in the city of Jerusalem, until ye be endued with power from on high.

In the minds of many scholars, this section of chapter 24 raises questions of chronology. Luke gives no clear statement about when these events took place. It is possible all the events narrated in verses 36-49 took place on the same day, the Sunday on which He was resurrected. Another possibility is Luke has given a condensed version of events that took place over several days. Geldenhuys (641) argues that Luke has already determined to write a second volume in which he will give more detail. Probably, in verses 44-49, Luke gives a brief summary of events that took place during the 40 days between His resurrection and the ascension (see Acts 1:3). Marshall (*Gospel* 904) and Plummer (561) present somewhat similar positions. They suggest Luke is summarizing the teachings Jesus gave His disciples in a series of resurrection appearances. Lenski (1203) takes a different view. He suggests there is no evidence that verses 44-49 is a summary and argues these verses were spoken on the evening of the day of His resurrection and they continue the narrative given in verse 43.

One way or another, verses 44-49 contain a set of final instructions Jesus gave to His disciples. Marshall (*Gospel* 903) notes that all the Gospels include a final commission Jesus gives His disciples. He also notes this passage in Luke is somewhat similar to John 20:21-23 and Matthew 28:16-20. These words would have been of great value both to the disciples who received them and to later generations of Christians who read this Gospel. Verses 44-48 are instructions designed to prepare the disciples for the important mission that lies before them. Verse 49 is the actual commission; it gives the disciples specific instructions as to how they are to begin their discipleship ministry.

Verse 44 is a review of what Jesus has been teaching them. The key idea is that Jesus interprets His life and ministry as the fulfillment of the O. T. Scriptures. This verse reflects the three-fold division of the O. T. books that was used by the Jews. The "law of Moses" is the first division of the OT, what we call the Pentateuch. The "prophets" is the second division of the O. T., the historical books and the prophets. The "psalms" represent the third division of the O. T., since the Psalms came first, along with all the poetic books and other writings not included in the first two divisions. This third division of the Hebrew O. T. is known today as the "Writings" (or the *Kethubim*). The fact that the messianic ministry of Jesus is a fulfillment of the O. T. will become a key aspect of the preaching and teaching of the disciples. The inclusion of all three divisions of the Hebrew O. T. indicates that Jesus is the fulfillment of the entire O. T. and not just the fulfillment of its messianic passages (Morris, *Luke* 343).

Verses 45-46 continue the thought presented in verse 44. They relate to what Jesus has taught them about the nature of the Messiah's ministry. Morgan (283) explains that "he opened" (Greek *dianoigō*) means to thoroughly open up. The idea is Jesus removed from their minds all the prejudice and pride that prevented them from understanding the nature of His messianic ministry.

Prior to this time, it seems the disciples shared with the whole Jewish community the idea that the Messiah would be victorious and defeat all the enemies of Israel. As Jesus explains in these verses, this understanding was not entirely wrong, but it was incomplete. Jesus wanted them to understand that the Messiah's victory would be won not through military might but through suffering (verses 25-26). By His actions and by His teachings, Jesus had opened their eyes to understand His ministry was indeed the fulfillment of the O. T. messianic prophecies (Marshall, *Gospel* 905). In verse 46, Jesus emphasizes that both His suffering and His resurrection on the third day came about as the fulfillment of the O. T. Scriptures. Without this understanding, it would have been impossible for the disciples to fulfill their missionary commission. Green (*Luke* 857) points out that Jesus does not mention any specific O. T. passages and it would be difficult to locate any specific passages that emphasize His suffering and resurrection on the third day. The idea is, rather, that all of the O. T. Scriptures point to these important events. The O. T. promise has now been fulfilled in Jesus.

In verse 47, the thought begins to move in a somewhat different direction. Now that the disciples have a clearer understanding of *His* messianic ministry, Jesus begins to talk with them about the future direction of *their* ministry. Their ministry will be one of proclamation; they have a specific message they are to share with all nations. Marshall (*Gospel* 903) calls attention to the fact that this passage in Luke shares with Matthew and John the commission to go to the nations and the promise of the power of the Spirit.

"Repentance" (Greek *metanoia*) was used in classical Greek to describe changing one's opinion or manner of thinking. In the N. T., it acquires a moral connotation. It basically means to turn from serving self and sin to serving God. It implies a transformation of life and character, which can only be accomplished through the power of the Holy Spirit. For a comprehensive analysis of this important term see Goetzmann (NIDNTT 357-359). The disciples are commissioned to preach the total transformation of human character that can be accomplished only through the power of the risen Christ.

Repentance leads to the remission or forgiveness of sins. As Plummer (563) explains, it is the messiahship of Jesus that makes repentance effectual. The goal of the disciples' preaching ministry is more than the building of an institution or the development of an organization. It is the restoration to wholeness for people whose lives have been tragically affected by sin.

The phrase "in his name" implies that Jesus has given them the authority to share this message with all the world (Bonnet and Schroeder 701). It also connects the preaching mission of the disciples with the ministry of Christ in the sense that they will continue to proclaim the same themes Jesus preached during His earthly ministry. It is the death, burial, and resurrection of Christ that makes repentance and forgiveness possible. By His death, He has paid the price for their sins. This phrase also expresses the idea of authority. The disciples are not to preach the message of repentance on their own authority; only through the power of the risen Christ can lives be transformed.

This ministry of reconciliation is not to be limited to any one place or to any one people. It is to be carried to "all nations beginning at Jerusalem." A "nation" in the ancient world did not imply a specific territory or region, or a political entity with defined boundaries. It described a group of people sharing a common language and culture, similar to the modern term "people group." This ministry was to begin in Jerusalem. Plummer (563) notes that the nation of Israel, in spite of its rejection of the Messiah, still has the right to hear the gospel. All peoples need the gospel message, and none are to be excluded, no matter what they have done.

Interestingly, in such O. T. passages as Isaiah 2:1-3 the Bible speaks of Gentile nations coming to Jerusalem in the future to learn the ways of the Lord. In this passage, however, the nations do not come to Jerusalem. Rather, the disciples go forth from Jerusalem to carry the good news the Messiah has come and salvation is available through Him.

In verse 48, Jesus tells the disciples they are witnesses of "these things." Luke does not name "these things," and the phrase is explained in different ways by the interpreters. Bonnet and Schroeder (701) suggest it refers to the great events such as the suffering and resurrection of Christ mentioned in verses 46-47. Green (*Luke* 858) expresses a similar viewpoint. What is important is that Christ is not sending them out simply to share information they have received from others. The disciples are witnesses in the sense they have had the opportunity to participate in these events and to receive first-hand instruction from the risen Christ Himself. The passion and resurrection of Christ will be key elements in their teaching and preaching (Plummer 563). They will be able to testify to what they have seen and heard.

In verse 49, Jesus states He will bestow upon the disciples what the Father has promised. Green (*Luke* 859) suggests this is the Holy Spirit, which the Father has promised to send to empower the disciples for the difficult task of sharing the good news. Fitzmyer (II:1585) also believes the Holy Spirit is the gift the Father has promised. This promise will be fulfilled in Luke's second volume, the Book of Acts.

50 And he led them out as far as Bethany, and he lifted up his hands, and blessed them.
51 And it came to pass, while he blessed them, he was parted from them, and carried up into heaven.
52 And they worshipped him, and returned to Jerusalem with great joy:
53 And were continually in the temple, praising and blessing God. Amen.

According to the traditional interpretation, these verses describe the ascension of Jesus (Marshall, *Gospel* 907; Lenski 1209). As Hooke (145) notes, Luke is the only Gospel writer who explains the disciples witnessed the ascension. Wilcock (205) suggests a different interpretation. He argues these verses do not describe the ascension of Christ but a disappearance similar to the one described in verse 31. Ellis (279-280) advocates a similar position.

The relationship between this passage and Acts 1:3 has provoked some discussion among scholars. Acts 1:3 states specifically the ascension took place 40 days after the resurrection. Luke does not state when the ascension occurred, but he gives no indication here of a significant interval of time between the resurrection and the ascension. If one had nothing but Luke 24, the natural interpretation would be the ascension took place on the evening of the resurrection day.

Scholars have offered various explanations of this difference between Luke 24 and Acts 1. Lenski (1209) suggests the Gospel offers only a very brief account of the events, since Luke's intention was to give a fuller account in the opening chapter of Acts. Marshall (*Gospel* 907-908) advocates a similar explanation. He points out that Luke's account is brief and does not contain the amount of detail found in Acts. Marshall admits it is possible Luke obtained additional information between the writing of the Gospel and the writing of Acts, but he discounts that possibility. A more likely explanation is Luke reserved the more complete account for the opening chapter of Acts and gave only a brief summary in the Gospel. Summers (*Luke* 336) offers a similar interpretation.

According to verse 50, Jesus led His disciples to the village of Bethany, which was located on the lower slopes of the Mount of Olives, the side away from the city of Jerusalem eastward (Summers, *Luke* 337). Acts 1:12 indicates the ascension took place on the Mount of Olives. After they arrived in Bethany, Jesus lifted up His hands and blessed His disciples in the same way the High Priest would bless the people after completing a sacrifice (Summers, *Luke* 337). As He was pronouncing this blessing, Jesus parted from them and was taken up into Heaven. Marshall (*Gospel* 908) notes some manuscripts omit the words "and carried up into heaven," but these words are found in the vast majority of the manuscripts and most of the textual scholars conclude they were original.

Verses 52-53 are Luke's summary of how the disciples reacted to Jesus' departure. Verse 52, literally, says, "And they, worshipping Him, returned to Jerusalem with great joy." "Returned" is the main verb; the disciples did not remain in Bethany, where Jesus had ascended into Heaven, but returned to Jerusalem so they could share the good news with the other disciples. That they were "worshipping" describes the manner of their return: not with sadness and sorrow because Jesus had been taken from them, but worshiping Him with joyful hearts because they had come to understand He was indeed the Messiah. And then they were continually in the Temple praising and worshiping God for all He had done in and through His son, Jesus Christ. It is clear from the Book of Acts that the disciples continued to worship in the Temple after the resurrection (Stein, *Luke* 625). How long they were able to continue this practice is difficult to determine.

Summary (24:1-53)

This chapter serves several purposes. For one, it provides a fitting conclusion to Luke's account of the life and ministry of Christ. His death is not the end; He is resurrected by the power of God. The chapter also presents the key doctrine of the Christian faith, the resurrection of Christ, to Luke's Gentile readers. It demonstrates how the initial reluctance of the disciples is overcome by the empty tomb and by the appearances of the risen Christ. It also presents for Luke's Gentile readers a correct understanding of the messiahship of Jesus. He is indeed the Messiah predicted by the O. T., but He is not the type of Messiah many Jews expected. His victory over the forces of evil is not gained by military might or political power but by His suffering. The resurrection demonstrates in a powerful way that Jesus is truly the Son of God and worthy of the devotion and worship of all mankind.

This chapter naturally falls into four divisions: (1) verses 1-12, women disciples bearing witness to the resurrection; (2) verses 13-35, Jesus' appearance to Peter and other disciples; (3) verses 36-49, additional appearances to Jesus' disciples and His final instructions; and (4) verses 50-53, Jesus' ascension and its immediate results.

According to Luke, the first of Jesus' disciples to become aware of His resurrection are the women who come to the tomb early on Sunday morning to complete the anointing of the body. They arrive and are surprised to find the stone has been rolled away. They enter into the tomb and find the body of Jesus is no longer there, and they do not know what has happened to it. The women are confronted by two men—subsequently identified as angels. These men inform them, "He is not here but is risen." For that reason, the women should be seeking Him among the living rather than among the dead. The two men also remind the women Jesus had taught that He must be delivered into the hands of evil men, crucified, and be raised again on the third day. The women hurry back to Jerusalem where they tell the apostles what they have seen and heard. The apostles do not accept the statement of the women; they consider it to be an "idle tale."

This visit to the tomb by a group of female disciples raises some interesting issues. Given the subordinate role women occupied in the ancient world, it is not surprising the male disciples find it difficult to accept their testimony. It should also be noted the account of the empty tomb is so surprising and dramatic the disciples would have difficulty accepting it even if the testimony had come from a group of men. The fact the first witnesses to the resurrection are women is, somewhat ironically, an evidence for the historicity of the resurrection. If the story of the resurrection had been created by the early church (as some modern scholars assert), they would never have made a group of women the first witnesses (Bock, *Luke* NIV 607).

Another interesting issue is the surprise demonstrated first by the women and later by the male disciples. In Luke's account, both the men and the women are totally unprepared for the resurrection. Jesus had clearly taught He would be crucified, buried, and raised on the third day, but His followers did not grasp His teaching. It is difficult to determine how much emphasis Jesus had given to this teaching, but the disciples should have had some inkling He would be resurrected. They seem, however, to be totally unprepared for these dramatic events. After they have the opportunity to interact with the resurrected Jesus, their doubts are removed and replaced by faith. As Benware (145) notes, this transformation in the lives of the disciples becomes yet another evidence for the historicity of the resurrection.

Beginning in verse 13, the circle of Jesus' followers who are aware of the resurrection widens. Luke relates the beautiful story of Jesus' encounter with two of His disciples who are walking to their home in the village of Emmaus. One was named Cleopas; the other, unnamed, might have been the wife of Cleopas but was probably another male disciple. They knew about Jesus' crucifixion; they had even heard the report about the visit of the women to the tomb early that morning. They did not know what to make of these reports; they also found it difficult to accept that Jesus had been resurrected.

As these two disciples were walking toward Emmaus, they were talking about the events that had transpired. Jesus joined them on the journey, but they did not recognize Him. Luke explains they were prevented from recognizing Him—probably by divine intervention. Jesus gave these two disciples the opportunity to share their fears and frustrations. They had hoped Jesus would be the coming Messiah who would deliver Israel from all her enemies. They were extremely sad because none of their hopes had been realized.

Then Jesus reveals Himself to them and begins to explain from the O. T. Scriptures that the Messiah would accomplish His ministry not through military or political power but through suffering. His crucifixion and death do not prove Jesus is not the Messiah. To the contrary, His suffering is a powerful proof He is the Messiah predicted in the O. T.

These two disciples persuaded Jesus to spend the night with them in Emmaus, but He suddenly disappeared from their sight. The time they had spent with Jesus deeply affected these disciples. In spite of the lateness of the hour, they felt compelled to return to Jerusalem and share their experience with the other disciples. After arriving in the city, they related how Jesus had appeared to them as they were eating a meal. They learned that the Lord had also appeared to Peter.

Then a most surprising event happened; Jesus suddenly appeared in their midst and said to them, "Peace be unto you." They were taken completely by surprise; they were afraid. They thought they had seen a ghost or a spirit.

Jesus immediately begins to assure them He is really in their midst. They have not seen a spirit; they have seen the resurrected Christ. He offers His disciples two proofs that He has truly risen from the dead. He first shows them His hands and feet; He even invites them to touch Him so they can be assured of the reality of His resurrected body. Second, He asks for food. They give Him a piece of broiled fish, which He eats in their presence.

As noted previously, verses 44-49 are interpreted in two different ways by students of Luke. Some understand them to present words Jesus spoke to His disciples on the evening after His resurrection. Others see these verses as a summary of the teachings Jesus gave during the forty days between the resurrection and the ascension. In light of Acts 1:3, it is probably better to interpret them as a summary of Jesus' teachings during the interval between His resurrection and His ascension.

In these verses, Jesus focuses on two main themes. First, He wants His disciples to have a correct understanding of the teachings of the O. T. The O. T. documents, when correctly interpreted, prophesied of a suffering Messiah. Jesus, in His death on the Cross, has fulfilled these prophecies. The words of verse 46 do not represent a quotation from a specific O. T. passage; they are Jesus' summary of the teachings of the O. T. Rather than serving as an evidence against His messiahship, as most Jews would have thought, Jesus' sufferings serve as a powerful evidence for it. Once they have a correct understanding of the message of the O. T., the disciples can undertake the missionary ministry Jesus has for them.

The second theme concerns the future ministry of the disciples. They are not to be idle. They are to wait in Jerusalem until they have been "endued with power from on high." This probably means they are to wait until they have received the filling of the Holy Spirit before beginning their ministry. Their ministry will be one of proclamation; they are to go out among all peoples in the power and by the authority of Jesus. Their message will focus on two key themes, repentance and the remission of sins.

When Jesus promises the disciples will be witness of "these things" (v. 48), He is probably referring both to the events that have transpired and to the understanding of those events He has shared with them. They have observed the life, death, and burial of Jesus. They did not witness the resurrection, but they have had the opportunity to learn from the resurrected Christ. All of this information is now a part of the message the disciples are to share with the world.

The two phrases "promise of my Father" and "power from on high" (v. 49) should probably be taken together. The disciples now have the content of the message they are to proclaim, but they must await the power to proclaim it. God has promised to bestow His Holy

Spirit upon them, but they are not ready to begin their new ministry until God has actually empowered them.

Verses 50-53 are generally understood to describe the ascension and the events related to it. In the Gospel, Luke gives no indication when the ascension takes place. As noted, this has led a few commentators to conclude these verses do not describe the ascension but a disappearance of Jesus similar to the one described in verse 13 when he was suddenly away from the two disciples in Emmaus.

Most interpreters, however, view verse 51 as a description of the ascension. They suggest there is no conflict between what Luke writes here and what he writes in Acts 1:3. In the Gospel, Luke gives only a brief summary because he plans to offer more detail at the appropriate place in Acts.

It is important to note the new attitude of the disciples. Jesus has just been taken from them, but they do not return to Jerusalem filled with sadness and sorrow. They now have a much better understanding of the messiahship of Jesus; they understand that His death, burial, and resurrection has not brought them defeat but victory. They can return to Jerusalem filled with joy as they continue worshiping their risen Master. Keener (258) explains that ancient writers often began and ended their stories at the same point. That is true for Luke's Gospel; it begins and ends with people worshiping God in the Temple.

Application: Teaching and Preaching the Passage

The resurrection is clearly the key doctrine of the Christian faith; if Christ is not risen from the dead the Christian message is robbed of its strength and validity. The writers of the N. T. clearly understood the importance of this doctrine, and they did not expect people to believe it simply on their word alone. They understood very well that skeptics would deny the reality of the resurrection, and they offer three lines of evidence in support of the resurrection. The first is the empty tomb. No one actually witnessed Jesus' coming back to life, but all the Gospels affirm that when the earliest witnesses arrived at the tomb, Jesus' body was no longer there. He had already been resurrected. Luke emphasizes they "found not the body of the Lord Jesus." There was no evidence to indicate the body had been stolen or the women had gone to the wrong tomb. The only possible explanation was the body had been resurrected by the power of God.

The second line of evidence is the series of appearances the Lord made to different individuals and groups. It is interesting to note all of these appearances were to His followers; there is no record Jesus ever appeared to unbelievers after His resurrection. This line of evidence is presented both by the Gospels and by the Apostle Paul. The longest and most comprehensive list of these appearances is found in 1 Corinthians 15. None of the N. T. books include all of the appearances. Luke focuses his attention on the appearances in and around the city of Jerusalem.

The third line of evidence is the dramatic change the resurrection produced in the hearts and minds of the disciples. Prior to the resurrection, Jesus' disciples were defeated and discouraged. They viewed His crucifixion as a defeat. During His earthly ministry, Jesus had taught about His suffering, death, and resurrection, but the disciples had not grasped the importance of that teaching. The news of the resurrection changed the situation completely. Jesus not only appeared to His disciples to restore their confidence, He also explained to them the nature of His messiahship. Contrary to the popular opinion, His suffering and death did not constitute a defeat. They gave powerful proof He was truly the promised Messiah.

There is no better commentary on this passage than Hebrews 1:1-4 (Bock, *Luke* NIV 618). God has spoken to His children through His Son whom He has made heir of all things; He has made Him superior even to the angels.

Modern preachers and teachers must be prepared to defend the historicity of the resurrection of Christ. The skepticism of the present age has led many people to view the story of Jesus' resurrection as no more than a myth created by the early church. In this atmosphere, sermons and lessons defending the reality of the resurrection are absolutely necessary. Those who preach and teach the Word of God must have a good understanding of the resurrection and the arguments that can be used to defend it.

Preachers and teachers must also understand the various Gospel accounts agree on the essentials while they differ on the details. Plummer (546) gives a summary of the points all the Gospels share in common. These include the fact no one actually witnessed the resurrection itself, the witnesses were at first filled with doubts and fears, and the witnesses saw angels before they actually saw the Lord. Plummer explains that each Gospel presents the story of the resurrection to meet the needs of its particular audience. Each writer also makes use of the information available to him, and all the writers might not have had access to the same information. Hooke (137) points out these differences do not destroy the validity of the biblical teaching. They reflect the realities that "naturally arise when the same occurrence is related by different people, or by the same person on different occasions."

There are several important themes that should be developed in preaching or teaching from this important chapter. The first is the uniqueness of the resurrection of Christ. There are several accounts in both the O. T. and the N. T. where people who had died were restored to life. (Lazarus, in John 11, is a good example of this.) These were not, technically speaking, resurrections but resuscitations. Lazarus and others did not receive their glorified bodies; they were simply restored to the same plane of existence they had enjoyed before death. They were not endowed with eternal life, and it seems obvious they died again at some future time.

Jesus was resurrected; He was not simply restored to human life. He entered into a new state of existence; He received His glorified body. It was a real body, but it was very different from the human body He had previously. He was apparently no longer subject to any of the limitations of human existence. Hooke (110-113) explains several of the significant differences between the resurrection of Jesus and the resuscitations of other biblical characters.

Another important theme for preaching and teaching is the new perspective the resurrection of Christ gives to the believer. As a result of their encounters with the risen Lord, the disciples had an entirely new understanding of the significance of Jesus' life and ministry. His suffering and death were no longer signs of defeat; instead, they provided powerful evidence He was indeed the promised Messiah. For the believer today, the Christian faith is a resurrection faith. As Paul explained many years ago, "If in this life only we have hope in Christ, we are of all men most miserable." It is the resurrection that gives meaning and purpose to the Christian life. As Paul also explained, "And if Christ be not raised, your faith is vain; ye are yet in your sins." As Hooke (148) notes, the effects of the resurrection "shape and sustain the life of the Christian in the world."

A third important theme for preaching and teaching on the resurrection is victory. During His earthly ministry, Jesus won many victories over the forces of sin and evil. He healed the sick, raised the dead, and multiplied food for the hungry. The greatest of His victories, however, is the resurrection. As Paul notes, the greatest enemy of mankind is death. Jesus, by His resurrection, defeated this greatest of enemies. No longer could the wiles of Satan or the machinations of evil men triumph over Him; He is, in every sense of the word, the victor. Those who are believers will one day be able to share this victory with Him.

This chapter in Luke presents several other important theological themes of which a preacher or teacher should take note. The resurrection of Christ makes an important contribution to the doctrine of salvation. Both the crucifixion and the resurrection, as presented by Luke, are essential elements in God's plan for the salvation of the world. Luke emphasizes, more than the other Gospels, that the preaching mission of the apostles includes both Jews and Gentiles. The fact the apostles are to proclaim the good news to all nations beginning at Jerusalem underscores Luke's emphasis on the evangelization of Jewish people.

The first words of verse 47 also make an important contribution to Luke's understanding of salvation. "Repentance" and "remission of sins" are two key elements in the gospel message. As Osborne notes, the word translated repentance occurs 25 times in Luke and Acts. It implies both a negative act (turning from sin) and a positive act (turning to God). It is "a change of heart which results in changed behavior" (Osborne 132). He also notes, appropriately, that the remission or forgiveness of sins is God's response to man's repentance.

The resurrection also contributes in a significant way to the doctrine of the church. The resurrection serves as the bridge between the ministry of Jesus during His time on earth and the ministry of the disciples. It serves to prepare the disciples for the ministry Luke will describe in Acts, his second volume. That this ministry will be "in his name" (v. 47) means the church must carry out this commission in the power and authority of Jesus. The apostles themselves have neither the power nor the authority to accomplish this important ministry on their own.

The fact that the earliest witnesses to the resurrection were women is significant. They saw the empty tomb and returned to tell the disciples what they had seen and heard. Luke names several of the women in verse 10, which indicates they have taken their place among those credible witnesses who can testify to the veracity of the resurrection.

Verse 52 and other passages in Luke emphasize the importance of worship. Osborne (141) concludes that "Worship also permeates the entire Gospel." The important events in Jesus' life, such as His baptism and His dedication, produced worship and adoration. His visit to the Temple at age 12 and His preaching in the synagogue in Capernaum serve to underscore the importance of worship in Luke's account. It is by design that after Jesus' ascension, the disciples worshiped Him and returned to Jerusalem filled with great joy.

These important themes, and others also, should be presented in preaching and teaching. They are important subjects that Luke develops in his own unique way. For a useful analysis of the major theological themes developed in Luke 24, see Osborne (99-146).

BIBLIOGRAPHY: WORKS CITED IN THIS COMMENTARY

Reference Works (cited by the following abbreviations)

DJG *Dictionary of Jesus and the Gospels,* eds. Joel B. Green, Scot McKnight, and I. Howard Marshall (InterVarsity, 1992).

EGT *The Expositor's Greek Testament* (5 volumes), ed. W. Robertson Nicoll (Eerdmans, 1967).

ISBE *The International Standard Bible Encyclopedia* (5 volumes), ed. James Orr (Eerdmans, 1956).

NIDNTT *The New International Dictionary of New Testament Theology* (3 volumes), ed. Colin Brown (Zondervan, 1971).

NDBT *The New Dictionary of Biblical Theology*, eds. T. Desmond Alexander and Brian S. Rosner (InterVarsity, 2000).

NTE *New Testament Essays* (Paulist, 1965).

TDNT *Theological Dictionary of the New Testament* (10 volumes), ed. Gerhard Kittel, trans. and ed. Geoffrey W. Bromiley (Eerdmans, 1964-1976).

Articles (cited by author's last name)

Alexander, Lovejoy, "Luke's Preface in the Context of Greek Preface Writing" (*Novum Testamentum* 1986, 48-74).

Augustine, Saint, "The Harmony of the Gospels," in *A Select Library of the Nicene and Post-Nicene Fathers of the Christian Church,* vol. vi:65-236; ed. Philip Schaff (Eerdmans, 1980).

Baudissin, Wolf, "Priests and Levites," in *A Dictionary of the Bible* IV:67-97; ed. James Hastings (Charles Scribner's Sons, 1909).

Beckwith, C. A., "Virgin Birth," in *The New Schaff-Herzog Encyclopedia of Religious Knowledge,* 12:201-214; ed. Samuel Macauley Jackson (Baker, 1953).

Burkitt, F. C., "The Use of Mark in the Gospel According to Luke," in *The Beginnings of Christianity,* Part 1, vol. 2:106-120; eds. F. J. Foakes Jackson and Kirsopp Lake. (Baker, 1979).

Cadbury, Henry J., "Commentary on the Preface of Luke," in *The Beginnings of Christianity,* Part 1, vol. 2:489-510; eds. F. J. Foakes Jackson and Kirsopp Lake. (Baker, 1979).

Cadbury, Henry J., "The Tradition," in *The Beginnings of Christianity,* Part 1, vol. 2:209-264; eds. F. J. Foakes Jackson and Kirsopp Lake. (1979).

Gilmour, S. MacLean, "A Critical Re-Examination of Proto-Luke" (*Journal of Biblical Literature* LXVII [1948], 143-152).

Gilmour, S. MacLean, "The Gospel According to St. Luke—Exegesis," in *The Interpreters Bible,* VIII:1-434; ed. George Arthur Buttrick (Abingdon, 1952).

Guthrie, Jr., H. H., "Fast, Fasting," in *The Interpreter's Dictionary of the Bible*, II:241-244; ed. George Arthur Buttrick (Abingdon, 1962).

Hiebert, D. Edmond, "Chronology, New Testament," in *The Zondervan Pictorial Bible Dictionary*, 164-165; ed. Merrill C. Tenney (Zondervan, 1967).

Jackson, F. J. Foakes, and Lake, Kirsopp, "The Internal Evidence of Acts," in *The Beginnings of Christianity*, Part 1, vol. 2:121-204; eds. F. J. Foakes Jackson and Kirsopp Lake (Baker, 1979).

Malina, Bruce J., and Neyrey, Jerome H., "Honor and Shame in Luke-Acts: Pivotal Values of the Mediterranean World," in *The Social World of Luke-Acts*, 25-65; ed. Jerome H. Neyrey (Hendrickson, 1991).

Marberry, Thomas L., "The Parable of the Good Samaritan in Modern Study" (*Integrity: A Journal of Christian Thought* 6 [Summer 2016] 11-32.

Minear, Paul S., "Luke's Use of the Birth Stories," in *Studies in Luke Acts*; eds. Leander E. Keck and J. Louis Martyn (Fortress, 1980).

Moo, Douglas J., "The Case for the Posttribulation Rapture Position," in *The Rapture, Pre-, Mid-, or Post-Tribulational*, 169-211; ed. Richard R. Reiter (Zondervan, 1984).

Moxnes, Halvor, "Patron-Client Relations and the New Community in Luke-Acts," in *The Social World of Luke-Acts*, 241-268; ed. Jerome H. Neyrey (Hendrickson, 1991).

Pilch, John J., "Sickness and Healing in Luke-Acts," in *The Social World of Luke-Acts*, 181-209; ed. Jerome H. Neyrey (Hendrickson, 1991).

Rust, Roger, "The Day He Died" (*Christianity Today* XVIII:13 [May 29, 1974] 4-6).

Schweizer, Eduard, "The Significance of Eschatology in the Teaching of Jesus," in *Eschatology and the New Testament*; ed. W. Hulitt Gloer (Hendrickson, 1988).

Scott, E. F., "The New Criticism of the Gospels" (*Harvard Theological Review* [April 1926] 143ff.

Stewart, R. A., "Sheep," in *New Bible Dictionary*; ed. J. D. Douglas. (Eerdmans, 1962).

Vila, Samuel, and Escuain, Santiago, "Jesucristo," in *Nuevo Diccionario Bíblico Ilustrado* (Editorial Clie, 1985).

Vine, W. E., "Fool, Foolish, Foolishly, Foolishness," in *An Expository Dictionary of New Testament Words* (Revell, 1940).

Warfield, Benjamin Breckinridge, "The Supernatural Birth of Jesus," in *Biblical and Theological Studies,* 157-168; ed. Samuel G. Craig. (Presbyterian and Reformed, 1952).

Windisch, H., "The Case Against the Tradition," in *The Beginnings of Christianity,* Part 1, vol. 2:298-348; eds. F. J. Foakes Jackson and Kirsopp Lake. (Baker, 1979).

Wright, Addison G, "The Widow's Mites: Praise or Lament?—A Matter of Context" (*Catholic Biblical Quarterly* 44 [1982] 256-265.

Yamauchi, Edwin M., "Archaeology and The New Testament," in *The Expositor's Bible Commentary*, I:647-669; ed. Frank E. Gaebelein (Zondervan, 1979).

LUKE

Books (cited by author's last name)

Alexander, Loveday, *The Preface to Luke's Gospel* (Cambridge University Press, 1993).

Arndt, William F., and Gingrich, F. Wilbur, *A Greek-English Lexicon of the New Testament and Other Early Christian Literature* (University of Chicago Press, 1971).

Bailey, Kenneth E., *Poet and Peasant* (Eerdmans, 1976).

Bailey, Kenneth E., *Through Peasant Eyes* (Eerdmans, 1980).

Barclay, William, *The Gospel of Luke*, rev. (Daily Study Bible, Westminster, 1975).

Barrett, C. K., *The Gospel According to St. John* (S.P.C.K., 1960).

Barrett, C. K., *The Holy Spirit in the Gospel Tradition* (S.P.C.K., 1970).

Barrett, C. K., *Luke the Historian in Recent Study* (Wipf & Stock, 2009).

Barth, Karl, *Church Dogmatics: The Doctrine of the Word of God,* I.2; eds. G. W. Bromiley and T. F. Torrance; trans. G. T. Thomson and Harold Knight (Charles Scribner's Sons, 1956).

Beasley-Murray, G. R., *Jesus and the Kingdom of God* (Eerdmans, 1986).

Beasley-Murray, G. R., *John,* 2nd ed. (WBC, Thomas Nelson, 1999).

Benware, Paul N., *Lucas: El Evangelio del Hijo del Hombre*; trans. Santiago Escuain (Editorial Portavoz, 1995).

Bernard, J. H., *A Critical and Exegetical Commentary on the Gospel According to St. John*, vol. 1; ed. A. H. McNeile (ICC, Charles Scribner's Sons, 1929).

Black, Matthew, *An Aramaic Approach to the Gospels and Acts*, 3rd ed. (Oxford University Press, 1967).

Blaiklock, E. M., *The Archaeology of the New Testament* (Zondervan, 1970).

Blomberg, Craig L., *The Historical Reliability of the Gospels,* 2nd ed. (IVP Academic, 2007).

Blomberg, Craig L., *Interpreting the Parables* (InterVarsity, 1990).

Blomberg, Craig L., *Matthew* (NAC, Broadman, 1992).

Bock, Darrell L., *Jesus According to Scripture* (Baker Academic, 2002).

Bock, Darrell L., *Luke* (IVP NTC, InterVarsity, 1994).

Bock, Darrell L., (I and II) *Luke Volume 1: 1:1—9:50*; *Volume 2: 9:51—24:53* (BECNT, Baker, 1994, 1996).

Bock, Darrell L., *Luke* (NIV Application Commentary, Zondervan, 1996).

Bonnet, Luis, and Schroeder, Alfredo, *Comentario Del Nuevo Testamento*, Tomo 1 (Casa Bautista de Publicaciones, 1982).

Bornkamm, Günther, *Jesus of Nazareth*; trans. Irene and Fraser McLuskey with James M. Robinson (Harper and Row, 1960).

Broadus, John A., *Commentary on the Gospel of Matthew*; ed. Alvah Hovey (ACNT, Judson, 1886).

Briggs, Charles Augustus, *The Messiah of the Gospels* (Charles Scribner's Sons, 1894).

Bright, John, *The Kingdom of God* (Abingdon, 1953) .

Brown, Raymond E., *An Introduction to New Testament Christology* (Paulist, 1994).

LUKE

Brown, Raymond E., *The Birth of the Messiah* (Doubleday, 1977).
Brown, Raymond E., *The Death of the Messiah,* vol. 2. (Doubleday, 1994).
Brown, Raymond E., *The Gospel According to John I-XII* (AB, Doubleday, 1966).
Brown, Raymond E., *The Gospel According to John XIII-XXI* (AB, Doubleday, 1970).
Brown, Schuyler, *Apostasy and Perseverance in the Theology of Luke* (Pontifical Bible Institute, 1969).
Bruce, Alexander Balmain, *The Parabolic Teaching of Christ*, 4th rev. ed. (Hodder and Stoughton, 1884).
Bruce, F. F., *Commentary on the Book of the Acts* (Eerdmans, 1954).
Bruce, F. F., *The Hard Sayings of Jesus* (InterVarsity, 1983).
Brunner, Emil., *The Mediator*; trans. Olive Wyon (Westminster, 1967).
Buttrick, George A., *The Parables of Jesus* (Harper & Brothers, 1928).
Cadbury, Henry J., *The Making of Luke-Acts* (S.P.C.K., 1968).
Caird, G. B., *The Gospel of St. Luke* (Pelican Gospel Commentaries, Seabury, 1963).
Carson, D. A., *From Sabbath to Lord's Day* (Zondervan, 1982).
Carson, D.A., Douglas J. Moo, and Leon Morris, *An Introduction To The New Testament* (Zondervan, 1992).
Chafer, Lewis Sperry, *Systematic Theology*, vol. 5 (Dallas Seminary Press, 1948).
Childers, Charles L., *Luke* (BBC, Beacon Hill, 1964).
Coleman, Robert E., *The Master Plan of Evangelism* (Revell, 1964).
Conzelmann, Hans, *The Theology of St. Luke*; trans. Geoffrey Buswell (Harper & Row, 1961).
Crabtree, Jeffrey A., *Matthew* (RHBC, Randall House, 2015).
Creed, John Martin, *The Gospel According to St. Luke* (Macmillan, 1930).
Cullmann, Oscar, *The New Testament*; trans. Dennis Pardee (SCM, 1968).
Dana, H. E., *The New Testament World*, 3rd ed. rev. (Broadman, 1937).
Deissmann, Adolf, *Light from the Ancient East*; trans. Lionel R. M. Strachan (Baker, 1978).
Denney, James, *The Death of Christ*; ed. R. V. G. Tasker (Tyndale, 1951).
Derrett, J. Duncan M., *Law in the New Testament* (Darton, Longman & Todd, 1970).
Dodd, C. H., *Historical Tradition in the Fourth Gospel* (Cambridge University Press, 1963).
Dodd, C. H., *The Parables of the Kingdom* (Charles Scribner's Sons, 1961).
Earle, Ralph, *The Gospel According to St. Luke* (WBC, Eerdmans, 1964).
Edersheim, Alfred, *The Life and Times of Jesus The Messiah* (Eerdmans, 1971).
Edersheim, Alfred, *The Temple Its Ministry and Services* (Eerdmans, 1975).
Ellis, E. Earle, *The Gospel of Luke* (Wipf and Stock, 2003).
Eusebius, *The History of the Church from Christ to Constantine*; trans. G. A. Williamson (Augsburg, 1965).
Evans, Craig, *Fabricating Jesus* (InterVarsity, 2006).
Farmer, William R. *The Synoptic Problem* (Mercer University Press, 1976).

Fee, Gordon D., and Stuart, Douglas, *How to Read the Bible for All It's Worth*, 3rd ed. (Zondervan, 2003).

Finegan, J., *Handbook of Biblical Chronology* (Princeton University Press, 1964).

Fitzmyer, Joseph A., (I and II) *The Gospel According to Luke I-IX; The Gospel According to Luke X-XXIV* (AB, Doubleday, 1981, 1985).

Fitzmyer, Joseph A., *The Semitic Background of the New Testament* (Eerdmans, 1997).

France, R. T., *Matthew Evangelist and Teacher* (Zondervan Academic, 1989).

Funk, Robert W., Roy W. Hoover, and the Jesus Seminar, *The Five Gospels* (Macmillan, 1993).

Geldenhuys, Norval, *Commentary on the Gospel of Luke* (NICNT, Eerdmans, 1951).

Grant, Frederick C., *An Introduction to New Testament Thought* (Abingdon, 1950).

Green, Joel B., *The Gospel of Luke* (Eerdmans, 1997).

Guerra, Eduardo, *La Parábola del Buen Samaritano* (Editorial CLIE, 1999).

Guthrie, Donald, *Jesus The Messiah* (Zondervan, 1972).

Guthrie, Donald, *New Testament Introduction,* 3rd ed. (InterVarsity, 1970).

Harrison, Everett F., *Introduction to the New Testament*, rev. ed. (Eerdmans, 1971).

Hendriksen, William, *Exposition of the Gospel According to Luke* (NTC, Baker, 1978).

Hendriksen, William, *Exposition of the Gospel According to John* (NTC, Baker, 1979).

Henry, Carl F. H., *God, Revelation, and Authority,* vol. 3 (Word, 1979).

Hiebert, D. Edmond, *An Introduction to the New Testament: Volume One The Gospels and Acts* (Moody, 1975).

Hoehner, Harold W., *Chronological Aspects of the Life of Christ* (Zondervan, 1978).

Hoehner, Harold W., *Herod Antipas* (Zondervan, 1972).

Hoekema, Anthony A., *The Bible and the Future* (Eerdmans, 1979).

Hooke, S.H., *The Resurrection of Christ* (Darton, Longman & Todd, 1967).

Hultgren, Arland J., *The Parables of Jesus* (Eerdmans, 2000).

Hunter, A. M., *Interpreting the Parables* (Westminster, 1960).

Hunter, A. M., *Introducing New Testament Theology* (Westminster, 1957).

Hunter, A. M., *The Parables Then and Now* (Westminster, 1971).

Hunter, A. M., *The Work and Words of Jesus* (Westminster, 1950).

Jeffrey, David Lyle, "Luke" in *Brazos Theological Commentary on the Bible* (Brazos, 2012).

Jeremias, Joachim, *Jerusalem in the Time of Jesus*; trans. F. H. and C. H. Cave (Fortress, 1969).

Jeremias, Joachim, *New Testament Theology;* trans. John Bowden (Charles Scribner's Sons, 1971).

Jeremias, Joachim, *Rediscovering the Parables;* trans. Frank Clarke (SCM, 1966).

Jeremias, Joachim, *The Parables of Jesus*, 2nd rev. ed.; trans. S. H. Hooke (Charles Scribner's Sons, 1972).
Jeremias, Joachim, *The Eucharistic Words of Jesus*; trans. Arnold Ehrhardt (Macmillan, 1955).
Josephus, Flavius, *Josephus Complete Works*; trans. William Whiston (Kregel, 1960).
Keener, Craig S., *The IVP Bible Background Commentary—New Testament* (InterVarsity, 1993).
Kelly, William, *An Exposition of the Gospel of Luke* (Klock and Klock, 1981).
Kistemaker, Simon, *The Parables of Jesus* (Baker, 1980).
Kümmel, Werner Georg, *Introduction To The New Testament*, rev. Eng. Ed.; trans. Howard C. Kee (Abingdon, 1975).
Kümmel, Werner Georg, *Promise and Fulfilment*; trans. Dorothea M. Barton (SCM, 1969).
Ladd, George Eldon, *I Believe in the Resurrection of Jesus* (Eerdmans, 1975).
Larson, Bruce, "*Luke*" The Communicator's Commentary, vol. 3; ed. Lloyd J. Ogilvie (Word, 1983).
Lenski, R. C. H., *The Interpretation of St. Luke's Gospel* (Wartburg, 1955).
Liefeld, Walter L., *Luke* (EBC, Zondervan, 1984).
Lieu, Judith, *The Gospel of Luke* (EC, Epworth, 1997).
Lightfoot, J. B., *The Epistle of St. Paul to the Galatians* (Zondervan, 1957).
Machen, J. Gresham, *The Virgin Birth of Christ* (Baker, 1965).
Mackinnon, James, *The Synoptic Tradition*, in Contemporary Thinking About Jesus; ed. Thomas S. Kepler (Abingdon-Cokesbury, 1944).
Maddox, Robert, *The Purpose of Luke-Acts* (T&T Clark, 1982).
Manson, T. W., *The Sayings of Jesus* (Eerdmans, 1957).
Manson, T. W., *The Teachings of Jesus* (Cambridge University Press, 1951).
Marshall, I. Howard, *Luke: Historian and Theologian* (Contemporary Evangelical Perspectives, Zondervan, 1971).
Marshall, I. Howard, *Luke*; eds. Donald Guthrie and J. Alec Motyer (NBC, Eerdmans, 1970).
Marshall, I. Howard, *Luke*; eds. G. J. Wenham, J. A. Motyer, D. A. Carson, and R. T. France (NBC 21st Century Edition, InterVarsity, 1994).
Marshall, I. Howard, *The Gospel of Luke* (NIGTC, Eerdmans, 1978).
Marshall, I. Howard, *Luke and His "Gospel,"* in The Gospel and the Gospels; ed. Peter Stuhlmacher (Eerdmans, 1991).
Martin, John A., *Luke*; eds. John F. Walvoord and Roy B. Zuck (LCC, Victor Books, 1989).
Matthews, Victor H., *Manners and Customs in The Bible* (Hendrickson, 1988).
McRay, John, *Archaeology and the New Testament* (Baker, 1991).
Miller, Madeliene, S. and Lane, J., *Harper's Encyclopedia of Bible Life*; rev. by Boyce M. Bennett, Jr. and David H. Scott (Harper and Row, 1978).
Morgan, G. Campbell, *The Gospel According To Luke* (Revell, 1931).
Morgan, G. Campbell, *The Teaching of Christ* (Revell, 1953).

Morris, Leon, *The Apostolic Preaching of the Cross*, 3rd rev. ed. (Eerdmans, 1965).

Morris, Leon, *The Gospel According to St. Luke*, rev. (TNTC, Eerdmans, 1974).

Moulton, James Hope, and Milligan, George, *The Vocabulary of the Greek Testament Illustrated from the Papyri and Other Non-Literary Sources* (Eerdmans, 1930).

Nolland, John, (I, II, III) *Luke 1—9:20*; *Luke 9:21—18:34*; *Luke 18:35—24:53* (WBC, Word, 1989, 1993, 1993).

Osborne, Grant R., *The Resurrection Narratives* (Baker, 1984).

Packer, J. I., Merrill C. Tenney, and William White, Jr., *The Bible Almanac* (Thomas Nelson, 1980).

Pentecost J. Dwight, *Things to Come* (Zondervan 1958).

Pikaza, Xabier, *Comentario al Evangelio de Marcos* (Editorial Clie, 2013).

Picirilli, Robert E., *Mark* (RHBC, Randall House, 2003).

Plummer, Alfred, *A Critical and Exegetical Commentary on the Gospel According to St. Luke*, 5th ed. (ICC, Charles Scribner's Sons, 1922).

Ramsay, Sir William, *The Bearing of Recent Discovery on the Trustworthiness of the New Testament* (Baker, 1979).

Ramsay, Sir William, *Luke The Physician* (James Family Publishing, n.d.).

Ramsay, Sir William, *Was Christ Born in Bethlehem?* (James Family Publishers, 1978).

Reiling, J. and Swellengrebel, J. L., *A Handbook on the Gospel of Luke* (United Bible Societies, 1971).

Richardson, Alan, *The Gospel According to Saint John* (SCM, 1959).

Richardson, Alan, *The Miracle Stories of the Gospels* (SCM, 1941).

Richardson, Alan, *An Introduction to the Theology of the New Testament* (Harper & Row, 1958).

Richardson, Cyril C., ed., *Early Christian Fathers* (Library of Christian Classics, vol. 1, Westminster, 1953).

Robertson, Archibald Thomas, *A Harmony of the Gospels for Students of the Life of Christ* (Broadman, 1922).

Robertson, Archibald Thomas, *An Introduction to the Textual Criticism of the New Testament* (Sunday School Board of the Southern Baptist Convention, 1925).

Robertson, Archibald Thomas, *The Gospel According to Luke* (Word Pictures in the New Testament, Broadman, 1930).

Robertson, Archibald Thomas, *Luke the Historian In the Light of Research* (T. & T. Clark, 1920).

Schaff, Philip, ed., *The Creeds of Christendom*, vol. II. (Baker, n.d.).

Scofield, C. I., *The Scofield Reference Bible* (Oxford University Press, 1909).

Scroggie, W. Graham, *A Guide to the Gospels* (Pickering & Inglis, 1948).

Shepard, J. W., *The Christ of the Gospels* (Eerdmans, 1939).

Schürer, Emil, *The History of the Jewish People In the Age of Jesus Christ (175 B.C. – A.D. 135)*; eds. and trans. Geza Vermes and Fegus Millar (T. & T. Clark, 1973).

Smith, B. T. D., *The Parables of the Synoptic Gospels* (Cambridge University Press, 1937).
Smith, Charles W. F., *The Jesus of the Parables* (Westminster, 1968).
Spence, H. D. M., *St. Luke* (Pulpit Commentary, vol. 16, Eerdmans, 1962).
Stauffer, Ethelbert, *Jesus and His Story*; trans. Richard and Clara Winston (Alfred A. Knopf, 1960).
Stein, Robert H., *An Introduction to the Parables of Jesus* (Westminster, 1981).
Stein, Robert H., *Jesus the Messiah* (InterVarsity, 1996).
Stein, Robert H., *The Synoptic Problem: An Introduction* (Baker, 1987).
Stein, Robert H., *Luke* (NAC, Broadman, 1992).
Stonehouse, N. B., *The Witness Of Luke to Christ* (Eerdmans, 1953).
Streeter, Burnett Hillman, *The Four Gospels* (Macmillan, 1953).
Summers, Ray, *Commentary on Luke* (Word, 1972).
Summers, Ray, *The Life Beyond* (Broadman, 1959).
Summers, Ray, *Worthy Is the Lamb* (Broadman, 1951).
Taylor, Vincent, *Behind the Third Gospel* (Clarendon, 1926).
Tenney, Merrill C., *New Testament Times* (Hendrickson, 1965).
Tolbert, Malcolm O., "Luke," in *The Broadman Bible Commentary* vol. IX; ed. Clifton J. Allen (Broadman, 1970).
Tristram, Henry Baker, *Eastern Customs in Bible Lands* (Thomas Whittaker, 1894).
Twelftree, Graham H., *Jesus the Miracle Worker* (InterVarstiy, 1999).
Unger, Merrill F., *Archaeology and The New Testament* (Zondervan, 1962).
Via, Dan Otto, Jr., *The Parables* (Fortress, 1967).
Walvoord, John F., *Jesus Christ Our Lord* (Moody, 1969).
Whitacre, Rodney A., *John*; ed. Grant R. Osborne (IVPNTC, InterVarsity, 1999).
Wilckens, Ulrich, *Resurrection*, trans. A. M. Stewart (John Knox, 1978).
Wilcock, Michael, *The Message of Luke*; ed. John R. W. Stott (The Bible Speaks Today, InterVarsity, 1979).
Wilkins, Michael J., *Matthew*; ed. Terry Muck (NIVAC, Zondervan, 2004).
Wright, H. Norman, *Marital Counseling* (Hendrickson, 1981).
Wright, N. T., *Jesus and The Victory of God* (Fortress, 1996).

Blogs (cited by author's last name)

Abbott, Shari. "Was Jesus Crucified on Wednesday, Thursday, or Friday?" *Reasons for Hope* Jesus Blog,* April 10, 2017. Accessed November 8, 2017. http://www.reasonsforhopeJesus.com.
Tabor, James D. "The Day Christ Died—Was it on a Thursday or Friday?" *James D. Taylor Blog,* June 3, 2015. Accessed November 8, 2017. https://www.huffingtonpost.com/james-d-tabor/the-day-christ-died_b_6999324.html.

LUKE

Videos (cited by author's last name)

Larson, Rick, *The Star of Bethlehem*, produced by Stephen McEveety (Mpower Distribution, 2009).

Websites (cited by author's last name)

Barton, George A., *et. al.*, "Nazarite," *The Jewish Encyclopedia*. Accessed June 27, 2017. http://www.jewishencyclopedia.com.

www.ingramcontent.com/pod-product-compliance
Lightning Source LLC
Chambersburg PA
CBHW020408100426
42812CB00001B/243